Contemporary Interpersonal Theory and Research

Contemporary Interpersonal Theory and Research

Personality, Psychopathology, and Psychotherapy

Donald J. Kiesler

John Wiley & Sons, Inc.

New York • Chichester • Brisbane • Toronto • Singapore

Copyright © 1996 by John Wiley & Sons, Inc.

Library of Congress Cataloging-in-Publication Data:

Kiesler, Donald J.
      Contemporary interpersonal theory and research : personality,
psychopathology, and psychotherapy / by Donald J. Kiesler.
          p.   cm. — (Wiley series in clinical psychology and
personality)
      Includes bibliographical references and index.
      ISBN 0-471-14847-4 (alk. paper)
      1. Social adjustment.   2. Interpersonal relations.   3. Adjustment
disorders.   4. Psychotherapy.   5. Object relations (Psychoanalysis)
6. Psychotherapist and patient.   I. Title.   II. Series.
      [DNLM: 1. Interpersonal Relations.   2. Personality.   3. Social
Behavior.   4. Personality Disorders.   5. Psychotherapy.   HM 132
K47c   1996]
      RC455.4.S67K54   1996
      155.2—dc20
      DNLM/DLC
      for Library of Congress   95-39129

To Us!

Sarah, Ben, Rachel, Allison, Don

Series Preface

This series of books is intended to provide scientists and practitioners in the mental health disciplines with up-to-date summaries and critiques of clinical theory, diagnosis, assessment, intervention, and prevention. The major common thread binding the series is its focus on the scientific basis underlying effective clinical work.

It is extremely difficult for scientific investigators to keep up with the burgeoning empirical work, even with regard to specific disorders; it is impossible for the practicing clinician, especially those who treat a range of disorders, to do so. Each book in this series attempts to distill the most pertinent information covered by that book's topic, and presents it in a scientifically valid and practitioner-friendly manner. Great strides have been made in recent years in all aspects of clinical practice and especially in developing valid diagnostic criteria, scientifically acceptable assessment processes, and effective disorder-specific treatments; less progress has been made with prevention efforts, but exciting large-scale longitudinal studies are underway. Our biggest problem is getting the current scientific information available in a utilizable form; that is the major purpose of this series.

W. Edward Craighead

University of Colorado
Boulder, Colorado

Preface

Our transactions with each other
Express automatic and stubborn reactions.
If the pattern remains intractable,
Our shared destiny is ensured.
If, however, we can shatter the cycle,
The opportunity becomes ours
To co-create our "in-between" world.

More than we humans ever care to admit, we are responsible for the world that we experience. My genes and my childhood establish the basic pattern of the person I think I am. This core pattern acts as a who-I-am template filtering what I remember, what I see and hear, what I think, what I feel, what I anticipate. In the here and now, my template highlights the part of the world that I choose to experience, the part that I notice and tune in, the world to which I respond. The human condition is such that my response to "my world" is determined as much by my who-I-am template as by the ongoing events "really" happening. To a disturbing degree, I actively create my world—the events that occur, my reactions to them, and the chains of actions and reactions that follow.

The most important objects in my world are other humans—persons who coinitiate the events to which we take turns reacting. Right now you are a person of whom I am acutely aware. We—I and my template of you, "the reader"—are in a real sense cowriting this book.

As social animals, we humans require transactions with others to satisfy our needs, attain our goals, and fulfill our potentialities. Seldom in our lives do we encounter a no-person world, rarely do we experience solitary, impersonal moments. Alone on mountaintops, our minds still project continuous streams of "people" pictures, memories, thoughts, and dialogues—internal transactions with others. In the most solitary moments of sleep, our brains continue to conjure up exciting and seductive interpersonal scenes and transactions. Ordinarily, we remain mostly unaware of these transactions, but whenever we look inward, we can spot human shadows in every nook and cranny.

Who we really are can be discovered best in the patterns of our public and private transactions with people. Apart from people, we do not exist—do not think, do not feel, do not desire, do not remember. Yet, at least in our Western world, we prefer to ignore the basic social embeddedness of our being; we opt to believe that we are self-made, self-contained, and self-sufficient individuals who pick and choose the extent to which we include others in the pursuit of our lives. In line with this myth of individuality, our thoughts draw firm boundaries between "self" and "other." We aspire to be autonomous crafters of our own destinies. We protect who-we-are (our basic personalities) inside a deeply private world of experience that we consider mostly inaccessible to others.

The part-truth of the Western myth is that we do indeed meet the world with our who-I-am templates and create our own worlds. By definition, our templates distort our experience of events in the world. Experiences filtered by our templates cannot be directly perceived nor totally understood by anyone else. The existential part-truth, then, is that we are alone and isolated beings who interact with fantasized others whose outlines we shape trhough our who-I-am templates.

The false part of the Western myth is that our who-I-am templates took form gradually, resulting from interactions of our genetic dispositions with the "significant other" persons who traveled with us over the terrain of our childhood and present adult lives. Reflected appraisals from my significant persons progressively defined what was "good," "bad," and "not" me—my who-I-am template with which I now create my world. A major paradox is that my present Western perception of self-agency and self-creation was built on the foundation of my mostly passive incorporation, when an infant and child, of what my particular significant others happened to value, devalue, and abhor in me.

Although another individual cannot validly understand my internal experience, neither can I. What is possible for us both are formulations guided by successive approximations. Although my templates distort my experience of world events with others, others' templates also simultaneously distort their experience of me. What transpires between us is a moment-by-moment interactive process in which our respective templates attempt to shape and alter each other's reactions in self-confirming directions.

Since transactional outcomes are conjointly determined, I participate with others in creating our respective worlds. I need to assume responsibility for the extent of my automatic and rigid participation in these negotiations. The more I cling to a rigid, boldly etched who-I-am template that distorts others' intents or acts and bully others into reacting as my template dictates, the more I sabotage any possibility of experiencing surprising, mutually fulfilling, and dyadically unique outcomes.

Our entire lives are embedded in interpersonal relationships. Originally, they constructed our transactional templates. In the here and now, these encounters both maintain and revise our who-I-am templates depending on our ability to transcend automatic and rigid self-presentation. In a real sense, we are isolated and autonomous beings insulated by our templates. In an equally real sense, however, the exclusive business of our templates involves others, and human fulfillment requires moments with others during which we conjointly create unexpected and reciprocally pleasurable shared outcomes.

One of the latter dyadic moments often occurs within the institutionalized human encounter we call psychotherapy. A major section of this book summarizes a therapeutic process that I will call "contemporary interpersonal psychotherapy."

An essential outcome pursued within the interpersonal psychotherapeutic encounter is an experience during which clients authentically confront, with the help of another person, the self-defeating interpersonal consequences that constitute their thematic maladjustments or problems. With therapist support, clients come to appreciate that they actively create their worlds—their interpretations of events that happen, their reactions, and the chains of actions-reactions that follow. They learn that "who-I-am" is discovered best within the repetitive patterns of public and private transactions with people. During the therapy session, clients experience live the human process in which their vulnerable and rigid who-I-am template attempts to shape and change the therapist's reactions in self-confirming directions. Through recurrent therapist metacommunicative feedback during the session, they learn that the part of the interpersonal process for which they need to assume responsibility is the manner and extent to which they participate rigidly in negotiations with the therapist and others. Finally, with innovative efforts to reduce the rigid input and to find alternative interpersonal negotiations, clients learn to stop bullying others into reactions that their own templates unilaterally dictate. Ultimately, they may be lucky enough to enjoy moments with others in which they conjointly create unexpected and reciprocally joyful outcomes.

The primary goal of this book is to provide an exhaustive coverage of contemporary interpersonal theory and research into personality, psychopathology, and psychotherapy. My usage of the term contemporary interpersonal theory is distinctive and refers to the theoretical and research tradition beginning with Sullivan (1953a, 1953b), through Leary (1957) and Carson (1969), down to present-day researchers and theoreticians. Major interpersonal works by these key authors are listed on page xiii.

There are three essential theoretical and methodological components of this tradition: (a) the core theoretical and clinical writings of Sullivan; (b) the *interpersonal circle,* beginning with the Kaiser Permanente group's original offering (Leary, 1957) down to and including subsequent interpersonal circle revisions and amplifications; and (c) the *interpersonal transaction cycle,* which originally was presented by Carson (1969) as the "unbroken causal loop" and subsequently was amplified by Safran.(1984a) as the "cognitive interpersonal cycle" and by Kiesler (1986a, 1988) as the "maladaptive transaction cycle." Although various other contemporary interpersonalists offer their own particular amplifications of these basic ingredients, the interpersonal circle and the interpersonal transaction cycle remain as defining conceptual-empirical models that differentiate contemporary interpersonal applications to personality, psychopathology, and psychotherapy.

A second goal of this book is to provide comprehensive coverage of contemporary interpersonal theory and research while simultaneously weaving in, as unifying threads, my own interpersonal communication formulations. The distinctiveness of my interpersonal communication theory and research derives from its integration of three conceptual traditions: Sullivan's interpersonal therapy and its contemporary interpersonal theory derivatives, interactional psychiatry, and research in nonverbal communication. The most recent prior summary of my interpersonal communication approach can be found in Kiesler (1988).

My overarching hope is that, despite inevitable bias from my own formulations and emphases, you will encounter within the covers of this book competent, fair, and comprehensive coverage of this contemporary interpersonal theory and research. As a scientist-professional clinical psychologist, I hope also that the excitement of your discovery will stimulate further pursuit of your own clinical, scholarly, and scientific interests.

Throughout 12 chapters, I attempt to provide a comprehensive summary of available contemporary interpersonal theory and research. The book contains two major parts. Part One surveys contemporary interpersonal notions of personality and maladjustment. Chapter 1 defines interpersonal behavior in detail and summarizes circumplex inventories that have been developed to measure individual differences in interpersonal behavior. Chapter 2 discusses potential moderating variables for interpersonal behavior (e.g., gender, situations, and time) and reviews critiques of two-dimensional interpersonal theory. Chapter 3 analyzes the covert components of interpersonal behavior including the concepts of selective attention and perception, self and self-other schemas, emotion, and significant others. Chapter 4 reviews in detail the central notions of self-fulfilling prophecy and interpersonal complementarity, defines complementarity as it is measured on the interpersonal circle, and highlights important issues underpinning the considerable empirical literature on complementarity. Chapter 5 defines my central interpersonal communication notion of "impact message" and describes in detail the rationale and development of the Impact Message Inventory as it is used in personality, psychopathology, and psychotherapy. Chapter 6 reviews general interpersonal principles of maladjusted behavior, then concentrates on definitions and applications of the Maladaptive Transaction Cycle to conceptualize Axis I and Axis II *DSM* disorders.

Part Two concentrates on applications of contemporary interpersonal theory to assessment-diagnosis of psychopathology and to psychotherapy and supervisory approaches. Chapter 7 outlines in detail interpersonal principles of diagnosis as well as applications of the Maladaptive Transaction Cycle and assessment of interpersonal problems to diagnosis of *DSM* disorders. Chapter 8 sidetracks briefly to discuss the place of nonverbal communication in interpersonal behavior and to define and illustrate the unique "meaning frames" vocabulary used in subsequent chapters. Chapter 9 analyzes various notions of psychotherapy relationship from contemporary interpersonal perspectives, including the concepts of resistance or countercontrol, transference or parataxic distortion, and countertransference. It then highlights a discussion of relationship as an essential context for effectiveness of psychotherapy interventions. Chapter 10 focuses on how the interpersonal therapist, throughout therapy, targets various components of the patient's Maladaptive Transaction Cycle, and how the interpersonal circle and principles of complementarity are used to plan essential therapeutic goals and interventions. It also summarizes available interpersonal stage models of psychotherapy, differential interpersonal treatments, and analyzes the issues of patient-therapist matching, predicting responsiveness to psychotherapy, and measuring client improvement in psychotherapy. Chapter 11 concentrates exclusively on the central process of "therapeutic metacommunication," first defining this process in detail, then presenting a two-stage model and a series of principles to guide the therapist's applications of metacommunication throughout the therapy course. Finally, Chapter 12 presents an interpersonal communication analysis of psychotherapy supervision that defines "parallel process" as a central supervisory event. It offers a series of supervisory interventions and emphasizes the metacommunicative priority in dealing both with therapeutic and supervisory impasses.

The reader needs to be forewarned that I will be using circles, transaction cycles, circumplex interpersonal inventories, and the like in attempting to explain essential aspects of ongoing interpersonal transactions, especially those occurring within psychotherapy. These models and measures often specify alternative actions that a therapist might initiate to facilitate some shift in a client's transactional themes. The therapist who becomes overly enamored of these moves and countermoves easily can lose touch with the authentic experience of the client (and of him- or herself) during their momentary encounters within the session; the therapist tends to get sidetracked into manipulating the client through preplanned, overprogrammed, and for the most part disrespectful and ineffective behavioral maneuvers.

A therapist can stay out of this undesirable cul-de-sac only by constant self-monitoring of ongoing cognitions and reactions, or by helpful monitoring from other supervisory eyes and ears. When applying any conceptualization of psychotherapy, a therapist's understandings and speculations regarding the client need to be confined to between-session periods. On entering the room with a client, the therapist needs to cast conceptualizations into the ground of his or her experience so that the client-of-the-moment can emerge in clear figure and, as much as possible, can be perceived and experienced fresh and anew.

DONALD J. KIESLER

Virginia Commonwealth University
April 1996

KEY VOLUMES IN CONTEMPORARY INTERPERSONAL PSYCHOLOGY

Anchin, J. C., & Kiesler, D. J. (1982). *Handbook of interpersonal psychotherapy.* Elmsford, NY: Pergamon.

Andrews, J. D. W. (1991). *The active self in psychotherapy: An integration of therapeutic styles.* New York: Gardner.

Benjamin, L. S. (1993). *Diagnosis and treatment of personality disorders: A structural approach.* New York: Guilford.

Carson, R. C. (1969). *Interaction concepts of personality.* Chicago: Aldine.

Kiesler, D. J. (1988). *Therapeutic metacommunication: Impact disclosure as feedback in psychotherapy.* Palo Alto, CA: Consulting Psychologist Press.

Leary, T. (1957). *Interpersonal diagnosis of personality.* New York: Ronald.

Oden, T. C. (1976). *TAG: Transactional awareness game.* New York: Harper & Row.

Plutchik, R., & Conte, H. R. (Eds.). (in press). *Circumplex models of personality and emotion.* Washington, DC: American Psychological Association.

Safran, J. D., & Segal, Z. V. (1990). *Interpersonal process in cognitive therapy.* New York: Basic Books.

Sullivan, H. S. (1953a). *Conceptions of modern psychiatry.* New York: Norton.

Sullivan, H. S. (1953b). *The interpersonal theory of psychiatry.* New York: Norton.

Wiggins, J. S. (Ed.). (in press). *The five-factor model of personality: Theoretical perspectives.* New York: Guilford.

Contents

Part One   Personality and Psychopathology

1. Overt Interpersonal Behavior and the Interpersonal Circle   **3**

Some Basic Assumptions about Human Behavior   4

Interpersonal Behavior   5

Two Basic Dimensions of Interpersonal Behavior   7

The Interpersonal Circle   11

Interpersonal Circumplex Inventories   23

Evaluating Circumplexity and Scoring of Interpersonal Inventories   30

2. Interpersonal Behavior   **35**
Moderating Factors and Other Issues

Critique of the Two Interpersonal Dimensions   35

Interpersonal Inventories: Measures of Interpersonal
Acts? or Interpersonal Styles?   38

Gender and Interpersonal Behavior   42

Situations in Interpersonal Behavior   45

The Temporal Dimension in Interpersonal Behavior   49

Implications for Behavior Theory and Social Learning   51

3. Covert Components of Interpersonal Behavior   **53**

Sullivan's Self-Dynamism   54

Cognition in Interpersonal Behavior: Contemporary Formulations   56

Interpersonal Research into Selective Attention, Expectancies, and
Cognitive Construal of Interpersonal Information   59

Self and Self-Other Schemas in Interpersonal Theory   67

Emotion in Interpersonal Behavior   71

The Nature of Significant Others   73

Conclusion   82

4. Interpersonal Behavior and Our Bids for Complementarity   **83**

    Self-Presentation and Self-Confirmation   84

    Self-Fulfilling Prophecy   87

    Interpersonal Principles of Complementarity   88

    Empirical Research in Complementarity   102

    Conclusion   109

5. Measurement of the Covert Complementary Response   **111**
The Impact Message Inventory

    Impact Messages within Psychotherapy   111

    Development of the Impact Message Inventory   112

    Unique Advantages of the Impact Message Inventory   119

    Empirical Research with the Impact Message Inventory   120

6. Maladjusted Interpersonal Behavior   **125**
General Principles and Formulations for Specific **DSM** *Disorders*

    General Interpersonal Principles of Maladjusted Behavior   127

    Interpersonal Maladjustment: Empirical Research   134

    Positive Illusion: Maladaptive? or Normal?   138

    The Maladaptive Transaction Cycle   141

    A Transactional Conceptualization of *DSM* Dsythymia   143

    Interpersonal Conceptualizations of Other *DSM* Disorders   148

    Conclusion   167

Part Two   Diagnosis, Psychotherapy, and Supervision

7. Interpersonal Assessment and Diagnosis   **171**

    The Interpersonal Circle: A Conceptual Map for
    Psychiatric Diagnosis   172

    Some Circumplex Methodological Considerations   173

    Psychiatric Symptoms and Interpersonal Problems   174

    Interpersonal Circle Diagnosis of *DSM* Personality Disorders   174

    Some Principles of Interpersonal Circle Diagnosis   176

    An Interpersonal Circle Translation of the *DSM-III*
    Personality Disorders   184

    Interpersonal Empirical Findings   186

    Assessment of the Maladaptive Transaction Cycle   194

    The Inventory of Interpersonal Problems   197

    The Interaction Record and Functional Analysis of
    Interpersonal Behavior   198

    The Process of Interpersonal Assessment and Diagnosis   199

    Issues in Interpersonal Diagnosis   201

 8. **A Vocabulary for Interpersonal Interventions**   **204**
    Interpersonal Communication, Nonverbal Behavior, and
    the Meaning Frames

    Interpersonal Communication   204

    Principles of Interpersonal Communication   206

    Nonverbal Behavior   209

    The Meaning Frames   210

 9. **The Relationship in Psychotherapy**   **217**
    An Interpersonal Communication Analysis

    Interpersonal Relationships   217

    Relationship in Psychotherapy: An Interpersonal
    Communication Analysis   218

    Distinct Relationship Events in Psychotherapy   222

    Relationship: A Context for the Effectiveness of
    Psychotherapy Interventions   232

    Other Interpersonal Research on the Psychotherapy Relationship   234

10. **Interpersonal Communication Interventions**   **236**
    Interpersonal Complementarity Principles

    An Encapsulation   236

    Prologue   237

    Targeting the Maladaptive Transaction Cycle   239

    Interpersonal Circle Principles of Intervention   242

    Other Presentations of Contemporary Interpersonal Interventions   252

    Interpersonal Stage Models of Psychotherapy   254

    Complementarity Patterns over the Stages of Psychotherapy:
    Formulations and Research   261

    Differential Interpersonal Treatments   267

    Empirical Interpersonal Research on Psychotherapy   270

11. **Interpersonal Communication Interventions**   **282**
    Therapeutic Metacommunication

    Metacommunication Defined   284

    A Two-Stage Model   287

    Principles of Metacommunication   291

    Empirical Studies of Impact Disclosure   302

    Impact Disclosure in Contemporary Psychoanalytic
    Psychotherapy   305

    Conclusion   306

12. Interpersonal Communication Supervision and the Parallel Process   **308**

    Task and Transaction Components   308

    Parallel Process: An Interpersonal Analysis   309

    Transactional Supervisory Interventions   311

    The Metacommunicative Priority   312

    Disengagement Interventions in Interpersonal
    Communication Supervision   315

    Summary   317

    Parallel Process: Empirical Research   317

13. Conclusion   **321**

References   **323**

Author Index   **373**

Subject Index   **383**

PART ONE

Personality and Psychopathology

CHAPTER 1

Overt Interpersonal Behavior and the Interpersonal Circle

Interpersonal behavior refers to recurrent patterns of reciprocal relationship present among two persons' covert and overt actions and reactions studied over the sequence of their transactions with each other.

Contemporary interpersonal personality and psychotherapy relies heavily on the seminal contributions of Harry Stack Sullivan (1953a, 1953b). As an antidote to the individualistic theoretical emphasis of his time, Sullivan insisted that human behavior can be understood only in relation to its historical and current interpersonal contexts. It follows that, within the psychotherapy arena, what needs to be studied and understood is the pattern of transactions between the client and other persons (including the therapist)—not the behavior of the client in conceptual isolation.

An interpersonal approach endorses circular (rather than linear) causality (Danziger, 1976). A person or client's behavior is not viewed as being driven solely either by situational factors or by intrapsychic motivations. Rather, the client's relationships (including that with the therapist) are framed as two-person groups in which members exert mutual influence (bidirectional causality).

Contemporary interpersonal theory was inaugurated with a series of publications emanating from the Kaiser Permanente research project (M. B. Freedman, 1985; M. B. Freedman, Leary, Ossorio, & Coffey, 1951; LaForge, 1977, 1985; LaForge, Freedman, & Wiggins, 1985; LaForge, Leary, Naboisek, Coffey, & Freedman, 1954; LaForge & Suczek, 1955; Leary, 1955, 1957; Leary & Coffey, 1954, 1955; Leary & Harvey, 1956; Leary, Lane, Apfelbaum, Croppa, & Kaufmann, 1956; Strack, 1996; Wiggins, 1985b). A significant scientific contribution, the Kaiser interpersonal circumplex made possible, for the first time, empirical tests of key propositions embedded within Sullivan's interpersonal theory. As Leary and Coffey (1955) noted, their group assumed the task of "developing a methodology of investigation which is consistent with Sullivan's theory and gives it some operational meaning" (p. 111).

Subsequent major contributions to the literature of the contemporary interpersonal tradition include those by Carson (1969), Anchin and Kiesler (1982), Kiesler (1988), Safran and Segal (1990), Andrews (1991), Benjamin (1993), Plutchik and Conte (in press), and Wiggins (in press). Recounts of the development of contemporary interpersonal theory and an articulation of its major assumptions can be found in these works.

SOME BASIC ASSUMPTIONS ABOUT HUMAN BEHAVIOR

Leary (1957) felt that "to understand a human being is to have probability evidence about his relationships with others (perceived, actual, or symbolic), about the durable interpersonal techniques by which he wards off anxiety, and about the reciprocal responses these techniques pull from others" (pp. 55–56).

Leary (1957, pp. 59–60) offered nine working principles for an interpersonal theory of personality:

1. All interpersonal behaviors are attempts by a person to avoid anxiety or to establish and maintain self-esteem.
2. Any personality measure should be able to assess, on the same continuum, the whole range of behavior from normal, adjustive to abnormal, extreme.
3. Assessment of interpersonal behavior requires a broad collection of specific behavioral measures that are systematically related to each other.
4. For valid assessment of interpersonal behavior, the same measures (at the corresponding levels) used to characterize the behavior of Person A need to be applied equivalently to the interactant, Person B.
5. To be precise, any statement about personality must indicate the level of personality to which it refers.
6. The theoretical levels of personality must be specifically listed, defined, and measured.
7. The same system of variables should be used to measure interpersonal behavior at each level of personality.
8. Measurements of interpersonal behaviors must be public and verifiable operations, which permit conclusions presented, not as absolute facts, but as probability statements.
9. A system of personality should be able to measure behavior in a specific functional context (which for Leary and his Kaiser colleagues was the interpersonal behavior to be expected in the psychiatric clinic).

In the *Handbook of Interpersonal Psychotherapy* (Kiesler, 1982b), I document six additional central interpersonal assumptions regarding human personality:

1. *Human Transactions.* Interpersonal study focuses on human transactions, not on the behavior of individuals. Activity is to be understood and explained as interpersonal, which necessitates focus on at least a dyad or two-person group.

2. *Construct of Self.* A central theoretical position is accorded to a construct of self that is interpersonal and transactional in its development and functioning throughout life. A central and pervasive feature of our transactions is self-presentation—the automatic, predominantly unaware, and recurrent manner in which we centrally view ourselves, which in turn leads to acted-out claims on others (evoking messages) regarding the kind of reactions and relationships we seek from them.

3. *Basic Dimensions of Interpersonal Behavior.* A person's recurrent pattern of interpersonal situations (Person A's covert and overt behaviors together with Person B's covert and overt reactions) represents distinct combinations or blends of two basic dimensions of interpersonal behavior: control (dominance-submission) and affiliation (friendliness-hostility).

4. *Mutual Influence.* Interpersonal transactions consist of two-person mutual influence. Causality is simultaneously bidirectional; it is circular (Danziger, 1976) rather than linear. Interpersonal behavior is embedded in a feedback network in which the effect influences or alters the cause—in which Person A both shapes and is shaped by the environment (especially by Person B).

5. *An Interactionist Position.* At a minimum, interpersonal theory incorporates an interactionist position in which Person A's behaviors are the interactive product of both A's predispositions toward transactions and situational-environmental events. Further, the environment as perceived by A (the psychological environment) is prepotent and the most important class of situations is that of other persons, especially significant others. A recent transactional alternative to interactionism, Duke's (1987) "situational stream hypothesis," is even more congruent to the interpersonal perspective.

6. *Communication.* The vehicle for human transactions is communication—the verbal and nonverbal messages exchanged between Person A and Interactant B over the course of their transactions. Since nonverbal messages predominate in emotional and relational communication, understanding of interpersonal behavior requires simultaneous study of both the report (linguistic) and, especially, the command (nonverbal) levels of human communication (Duke & Nowicki, 1982; Kiesler, 1979; Kiesler, Bernstein, & Anchin, 1976).

In line with the last assumption, a significant notion in interpersonal theory is that, in a predominantly automatic and unaware manner, we individuals communicate important self-definitional bids through our verbal and nonverbal behavior. In the process of emitting distinctive interpersonal "force fields" we attempt to influence others into reactions that confirm our definition of self and others.

INTERPERSONAL BEHAVIOR

At a minimum, interpersonal behavior refers to our actions in the presence of other humans—our social behavior. Interpersonal theorists, however, do not focus their study on what an individual does with others in one or various circumstances; they do not concentrate on *the behavior of an individual* in either social (dyads, families, groups, etc.) or impersonal situations.

Interpersonal behaviors are not simply responses to stimuli, they also tend to elicit particular reactions from other persons:

> Interpersonal study focuses on human transactions, not on the behavior of individuals. What needs to be studied is not conceptually isolated "human behavior," but rather the behavior of persons relating to and interacting in a system with other persons. That human activity to be understood and explained is interpersonal or social, which necessitates focus on at least a dyad or two-person group. (Kiesler, 1982b, p. 5)

Measurement of interpersonal behavior, then, requires, at a minimum, measurement of at least two persons' conjoint behaviors during their interactions. Assessment focuses on what Person A and Person B do reciprocally to and with each other during their transactions. Interpersonal meaning cannot be extracted by aggregating measures of what A does with B, thereby summarizing A's behavior in that particular social context. Rather, by measuring both A and B's interactional behaviors, interpersonal meaning is extracted from the lawful interrelationships of each person's unfolding behaviors to those of the other. As many others have suggested, what needs to be studied is interaction (action-reaction), rather than action.

Leary (1957) stated this emphasis as follows:

> The most functionally important aspects of human behavior seem to be interpersonal. To understand a human being is to have probability evidence about his relationships with others (perceived, actual, or symbolic), about the durable interpersonal techniques by which he wards off anxiety, and about the reciprocal responses these techniques pull from others. (pp. 55–56)

Accordingly, the basic unit of interpersonal behavior is the interaction unit (Peterson, 1989), variously referred to as the "interpersonal proceeding" (Murray, 1951), "interaction sequence" (Peterson, 1979a; Raush, 1965), "interaction episode" (Kelley et al., 1983), and "relational scenario" (Gergen, 1987). The interaction unit consists of an action by A and the accompanying reaction by B; in communications terminology, it consists of a speech turn by A and the subsequent speech turn of B. In studying interaction units over various temporal lengths of a dyad's transactions, researchers can draw conclusions regarding the probabilities of recurrent sequences of their actions-reactions. Importantly, as Murray (1951) cogently observed (Peterson, 1989; Thorne, 1986), in understanding interaction units, Person B must be given the same conceptual status as Person A; our explanation must include as much formulation of Person B's thought and action as of Person A's thought and action.

Murray's comments highlight another central emphasis. Interpersonal behavior encompasses not merely overt transactions between two individuals; it refers also to the private, unobservable, symbolic (fantasized) interactions and dialogues with the self and other conducted by either. Study of these symbolic interactions attempts to understand not only the cognitive schemas (Sullivan's "personifications"), for both the other member of the dyad and for persons more generally, but the reciprocal relationships of each person's cognitive events (both person and self-schemas) to the action-reaction sequences occurring in the arena of their conjoint overt behavior.

For Leary (1957), the basic unit of human behavior was the interpersonal "reflex." The interpersonal act occurs in a two-group or dyadic system and functions according to what Sullivan (1953b) described as the "theorem of reciprocal emotion" and what Leary (1957) named the "principle of reciprocal interpersonal relations." What either principle asserts is that any interpersonal act is designed to elicit from a respondent reactions that confirm, reinforce, or validate the actor's self-presentation and that make it more likely that the actor will continue to emit similar interpersonal acts. As Leary stated, "interpersonal reflexes tend (with a probability significantly greater than chance) to initiate or invite reciprocal interpersonal responses from the 'other' person in the interaction that lead to a repetition of the original reflex" (1957, p. 123). In Foa's (1961) words, an interpersonal act is "an attempt to establish the emotional relationship of the actor toward himself and toward the other, as well as to establish the social relationship of self and the other" (p. 350).

Interpersonal behavior, thus, refers to *recurrent patterns of reciprocal relationship present among two persons' covert and overt actions and reactions studied over some period (sequence) of their transactions with each other.* The length of period studied can range from a single interaction unit ("cycles"), to "phases," to "episodes," to "sequences," and so on (Peterson, 1989)—all the way to the entire history of transactions between two individuals. Interestingly, the concept of interpersonal behavior overlaps, to a great extent, that of interpersonal communication (Kiesler, 1979, 1988; Kiesler et al., 1976), defined as recurrent patterns of reciprocal relationship present among two persons' verbal-nonverbal message exchanges over some period of their communications with each other.

As I described elsewhere (Kiesler, 1991, p. 438), in an *individualistic sense,* interpersonal behavior refers to a person's actions in the presence of other humans—the behavior of an individual directed toward one or more interactants. In a *transactional sense,* interpersonal behavior refers to two people's conjoint behaviors during their interactions with each other—what Person A and Person B do reciprocally to and with each other during their transactions.

Many current "interpersonal" conceptualizations of human behavior (e.g., Argyle, 1972) or of psychopathology and psychotherapy (e.g., Klerman & Weissman, 1992; Klerman, Weissman, Rounsaville, & Chevron, 1984) are interpersonal primarily in the individualistic sense. None of the essential features of the approaches (conceptualization, assessments, treatments) focus predominantly on transactions; instead, they focus on important interpersonal situations and identification of individualistic solutions to those situations.

As I have emphasized (e.g., Kiesler, 1991; cf. Segrin & Abramson, 1994), if the conceptual or empirical analysis does not conceptualize the patient and other (significant other and/or therapist) as a transactional unit, the analysis is *not* interpersonal in the transactional sense. The stance adopted so forcefully by Sullivan (1953a, 1953b) and subsequently by contemporary interpersonal researchers (and the stance you will encounter throughout this volume) is that of transactional interpersonal psychology. As stated in the Preface, both the interpersonal circle and the interpersonal transaction cycle are essential themes and constructs that define contemporary interpersonal psychology. The interpersonal transaction cycle (see Chapter 6 and Figures 6–1 and 6–2 for a presentation of my own Maladaptive Transaction Cycle) defines concretely what interpersonal means in its transactional sense.

Interactants' interpersonal needs always seek conjoint expression and resolution; interpersonal behavior can be understood only from a perspective that includes interactants as a system. Each person's acts are designed to elicit reactions from respondents that confirm or validate the person's self-perceptions and self-presentations. The acts function, then, as automatic ways of attempting to fulfill his or her basic interpersonal needs.

TWO BASIC DIMENSIONS OF INTERPERSONAL BEHAVIOR

The original (M. B. Freedman et al., 1951; Leary, 1957) and all subsequent interpersonal circles reflect the assumption that *human interpersonal behavior represents blends of two basic motivations: the need for control (power, dominance), and the need for affiliation (love, friendliness).* Persons interacting with each other continually negotiate two major relationship issues: how friendly or hostile they will be with each other, and how much in charge or control each will be in their encounters. The interpersonal circle directly incorporates this assumption by placing control (dominance-submission) and affiliation (friendliness-hostility) along its vertical and horizontal axes respectively.

Interpersonal circles, or circumplexes (Guttman, 1954), designate a specific arrangement of categories (e.g., 16ths) along the circumference. As McCrae and Costa (1989) observed, circumplex models are defined in terms of a systematic increasing and decreasing pattern of correlations among the variables, and can be visually portrayed in terms of a circle in which adjacent variables are highly correlated and opposing variables are inversely correlated. Dimensional models, in contrast, describe variables in terms of their salience on one or more dimensions, illustrated most frequently through applications of factor analysis. McCrae and Costa (1989) elaborated that, for two-dimensional displays, circumplex models are most appropriate when variables are evenly distributed around the circumference of a two-dimensional plot; dimensional models are better suited to cases with a clear simple structure (all the variables cluster around one axis or the other) or with more than two substantive dimensions.

The research evidence on which circle representations of interpersonal behavior have been based has been reviewed in various places (Berzins, 1977; Bierman, 1969; R. Brown, 1965; Carson, 1969; Foa, 1961; Kiesler, 1983; Plutchik & Conte, 1986; Schaefer, 1959, 1961; Wiggins, 1980, 1982). Equivalent two-dimensional representations have been documented for *parent-child interactions* (Becker & Krug, 1964; Becker, Peterson, Luria, Shoemaker, & Hellmer, 1962; Rollins & Thomas, 1979; Schaefer, 1959, 1961; Steinmetz, 1979), *adult interpersonal behavior* (Benjamin, 1974, 1993; Birtchnell, 1987, 1990; Bochner, Kaminski, & Fitzpatrick, 1977; Conte & Plutchik, 1981; M. B. Freedman et al., 1951; Kiesler, 1983; LaForge & Suczek, 1955; Leary, 1957; Lorr & McNair, 1963, 1965, 1966; Lorr & Suziedelis, 1969; Solomon, 1981; Triandis, 1977, 1978; Wiggins, 1979a, 1979b, 1981), *biologically mandated societal needs and roles* (Birtchnell, 1987, 1990, 1993; Hogan, 1983) *the structure of phenomenal domains* (Rinn, 1965), *perception of social situations* (Forgas, 1979; Wish, Deutsch, & Kaplan, 1976); *cognitive interactionism* (Solomon, 1981), *interpersonal evaluation* (H. H. Blumberg, 1972), *interpersonal emotion* (Kemper, 1978a; Plutchik & Conte, in press; Russell, 1980; Russell, Lewicka, & Niit, 1989; Schlosberg, 1952), *personality traits and lexicons: interpersonal language* (De Raad, 1995; Goldberg, 1981; McCrae & Costa, 1989; Merenda, 1987; Trapnell & Wiggins, 1990; White, 1980; Wiggins, 1979a, 1979b), *psychological universals across cultures* (Foa, 1964; Foa & Foa, 1974; Longabaugh, 1966; Lonner, 1980; Russell et al., 1989; Triandis, 1977, 1978, 1990; White, 1980), *character depictions in literary works* (Adamopoulos, 1982a, 1982b, 1984; Adamopoulos & Bontempo, 1986), *identity development in psychobiography* (McAdams, 1985, 1993), *historical evolution of language terms* (Benjafield & Carson, 1985; Benjafield & Muckenheim, 1989), *close relationships* (Gaelick, Bodenhause, & Wyer, 1985), *mate selection and marriage* (Bermann & Miller, 1967; Winch, 1958), *psychological adjustment* (Fineberg & Lowman, 1975), *vocational choice behavior* (Holland, 1973, 1985a, 1985b; Roe, 1956, 1957), *psychopathology* (Leary & Coffey, 1955; Lorr, Bishop, & McNair, 1965; Schaefer & Plutchik, 1966), *individual psychotherapy* (Bierman, 1969), *family therapy* (Hurley, 1980; Olson, 1986; Olson, Russell, & Sprenkle, 1983; Olson, Sprenkle, & Russell, 1979; Sprenkle & Olson, 1978), and *small groups, T-groups, and group psychotherapy* (Borgatta, 1960, 1964; Borgatta, Cottrell, & Mann, 1958; L. F. Carter, 1954; Hurley, 1976, 1980; Whitaker & Lieberman, 1964).

Agency and Communion

More recently, attempts have been made to conceptualize the two basic dimensions within a broader theoretical framework (Birtchnell, 1993, 1994; Wiggins, 1991a; Wiggins & Trapnell, in press). Wiggins (1991a; Wiggins & Trapnell, in press) based his analysis on Bakan's (1966) concepts of "agency" (being a differentiated individual, manifested in strivings for mastery and power which enhance and protect that differentiation, as expressed in frequent dominant acts and infrequent submissive acts) and "communion" (being part of a larger social or spiritual entity, manifested in strivings for intimacy, union, and solidarity with that larger entity, as reflected in frequent agreeable behaviors and infrequent quarrelsome ones). Bakan (1966) argued that agency was prototypically masculine, whereas communion was prototypically feminine. Bakan's (1966) major concern was with the integration of these two opposing tendencies within interpersonal relations, especially relationships between men and women.

Wiggins (1991a; Wiggins & Trapnell, in press) conceptualized the control and affiliation dimensions of interpersonal behavior as aspects of the larger personality domains of agency and communion. He argued, "The meta-concepts of agency and communion underlie, in fundamental and complex ways, our world views, our understanding of persons, our language that describes social relations, and our view of the relations between men and women" (p. 106).

Wiggins traced the philosophical and scientific roots of the two terms down through present-day personality and interpersonal theory and research:

> From the time of the neo-Freudians to the present, the concepts of agency and communion have occupied an increasingly explicit role in theories of personality, particularly since the appearance of Bakan's (1966) essay. This increasing emphasis on the cultural matrix in which personality is embedded has suggested the possible universality of agency and communion as organizing concepts for social life. (Wiggins, 1991a, p. 97)

Wiggins' major conclusion was that agency and communion are necessary conceptual coordinates for the measurement of interpersonal behavior and "are viewed as the essential ingredients of a well-ordered and harmonious society and of a psychologically fulfilled and well-integrated individual" (Wiggins, 1991a, p. 105).

The Big Five Factors of Personality

Research has documented convincingly that five dimensions emerge universally as higher order factors within the empirical measurement of personality (Costa & McCrae, 1985, 1992; Digman, 1990; Goldberg, 1990; Norman, 1963; Tupes & Christal, 1961; Wiggins & Pincus, 1992). It also has demonstrated that *the dimensions of control and affiliation, which underlie the interpersonal circle, are two of these Big Five factors* (Hofstee, de Raad, & Goldberg, 1992; McCrae & Costa, 1989; Saucier, 1992; Trapnell & Wiggins, 1990; Wiggins & Trapnell, 1994, in press).

The first two dimensions of the model (surgency/extraversion and agreeableness) can be considered simple-structure variations of the interpersonal circle dimensions

(Goldberg, 1990, 1992; Hofstee et al., 1992; McCrae & Costa, 1989), or the interpersonal circle dimensions, in distinct circumplex form, can be used to represent the first two factors of the Big Five (Pincus & Wiggins, 1992; Trapnell & Wiggins, 1990). In his analysis of Bakan's work, Wiggins (1991a) also observed, "Clearly the concepts of agency and communion, by themselves, do not fully capture the broad spectrum of important individual differences that characterize human transactions" (p. 109); rather, such a full characterization requires use of all the Big Five factors.

Wiggins (in press) provides detailed descriptions of the major theoretical conceptualizations of the Big Five factors: his own dyadic-interactional theory as well as trait theory, socioanalytic theory, evolutionary theory, and lexical theory.

An Analysis of Human Relations

In a recent book, Birtchnell (1993; see also Birtchnell, 1994) argued for an alternative conceptualization of the two principal axes of what he calls human relating. He defined a horizontal axis that is concerned with interpersonal proximity (closeness . . . distance), and a vertical axis that is concerned with power (able to influence another, superior, relative strength . . . eagerness to be influenced, inferior, relative weakness):

> The continuity between the relating of animals and the relating of humans is emphasized. Their capacity to move enables animals to relate in the way that they do. Through movement they adjust their position in relation to one another (the proximity axis) and exert influence over one another (the power axis) . . . . Human relating can be classified with the same broad categories as those of animals. (pp. 37–38)

Birtchnell (1993) named the end points of the bipolar proximity axis "distance" and "closeness" and the end points of the bipolar power axis "upperness" and "lowerness." He then combined the axis possibilities into his "interpersonal octagon." On the octagon, the octants range (counterclockwise from the top) as follows: upper-neutral, upper-distant, neutral-distant, lower-distant, lower-neutral, lower-close, neutral-close, and upper-close. He offered his interpersonal octagon as being superior to interpersonal circles in the Leary tradition (cf. Birtchnell, 1994).

Birtchnell (1993) briefly noted two self-report questionnaires that he developed to measure the octants of his octagon. The "Persons Relating to Others Questionnaire" (PROQ) is used for an individual's self-report of his or her typical interpersonal behavior. The "Couple's Relating to Each Other Questionnaire" (CREOQ) is a set of four questionnaires by which each spouse rates self relating to the other, and other relating to the self. Birtchnell (1993) critiqued interpersonal circles in the Leary tradition from various perspectives (also see Birtchnell, 1990, 1994) and argued for the advantages of his octagon system.

Birtchnell's (1993, 1994) system is difficult to bring into theoretical or empirical focus. He offered no empirical data that might illuminate structural validation of his octagon system or the degree of empirical correlation of its scales with circumplex inventories in the Leary tradition. He also did not offer a systematic presentation of this octagonal-spatial theory, did not enumerate propositions or predictions that might be empirically tested with his PROQ and CREOQ inventories, and neither offered nor cited studies that have applied these inventories.

THE INTERPERSONAL CIRCLE

Contemporary interpersonal theory provides an empirically based model that specifies and organizes the full range of normal-to-abnormal interpersonal behavior. The model is referred to as the interpersonal circle (Carson, 1969; Kiesler, 1983; Leary, 1957; Wiggins, 1980, 1982, 1985a). As Wiggins (1982) documented in his historical review of contemporary interpersonal theory and research, the first published reference to an interpersonal system of personality diagnosis, and the premiere presentation of the interpersonal circle, was the article by M. B. Freedman et al. (1951).

The interpersonal circle representation of the domain of interpersonal behavior depicts interpersonal variables as vectors in a two-dimensional circular space formed by the coordinates of dominance and love (Wiggins, Phillips, & Trapnell, 1989). Wiggins (1982) observed, "It is a well-established empirical generalization that interpersonal variables have a circular structure. This fact can contribute to systematic assessment and prediction in the absence of any theoretical speculations about the nature of interpersonal behavior" (p. 214).

Moreover, when circumplex (Guttman, 1954; Wiggins, Steiger, & Gaelick, 1981) and other trigonometric properties are also incorporated (e.g., Gurtman, 1993, 1994; Kiesler, 1983; C. C. Wagner, Kiesler, & Schmidt, 1995), the circular representation becomes a powerful structure for generation of theoretical propositions regarding interpersonal behavior. As Wiggins and Broughton (1985) note:

> The principal advantage of the Interpersonal Circle is that it provides a theory-based definition of the universe of content of interpersonal behavior within which the expected relationship between a given vector of interpersonal behavior and all other vectors of interpersonal behavior may be specified with geometric precision with reference to the two orthogonal coordinates of *status* (power, agency, dominance) and *love* (solidarity, communion, affiliation). As a consequence, measures derived from circumplex methodology permit assessment of the full range of interpersonal behavior in a non-redundant fashion and alert the investigator to notable "gaps" in coverage of this range. (p. 2)

All interpersonal inventories, to greater or lesser degrees, can be used to measure individuals' self-report characterizations of their own behavior, interactants' characterizations of each other's behaviors, or observers' ratings of interactants' behavior. The circle is also a key conceptual map that guides both interpersonal assessment-diagnosis and interpersonal psychotherapy (Kiesler, 1983, 1986a, 1986b, 1988, 1991, 1992; Van Denburg, Schmidt, & Kiesler, 1992). Through use of one or more inventories or coding systems, the clinician can assess a maladjusted patient's interpersonal behavior and precisely locate that behavior on the surface of the interpersonal circle. This placement, in turn, permits both exact specification of the patient's predominant maladaptive pattern of living as well as precise prediction of various components of the optimal treatment plan for that patient.

Gurtman offered a circumplex-related methodology (Gurtman, 1993, 1994) and amplified guidelines (Gurtman, 1991, 1992a, 1992b) that permit researchers in personality measurement to evaluate the "interpersonalness" of scales and inventories. Gurtman (1991, 1992a) provided three reasons for establishing and applying an interpersonal taxonomy of personality constructs:

1. It is important to know what a scale measures, specifically what it shares with other broad factors of individual differences.
2. Objective data concerning interpersonal content are important in establishing construct validity.
3. Many constructs are assumed to be interpersonal simply on an a priori basis without regard to their relations with the established interpersonal dimensions of personality.

Gurtman (1991, 1992a, 1992b) illustrated these points by using the interpersonal circumplex as an objective criterion to evaluate the interpersonalness of a number of putative interpersonal scales.

Adult Two-Dimensional Interpersonal Circles

At present, four two-dimensional interpersonal circles have been offered as attempts to represent a valid taxonomy of interpersonal behavior that specifies precise trigonometric relationships among the categories of behaviors. The first, provided by M. B. Freedman et al. (1951) and by Leary (1957), was followed subsequently by Lorr and McNair (1965), Wiggins (1979a,1979b, 1981), and Kiesler (1983, 1985). Subsequent circle revisions represented attempts to clarify and validate the substantive ordering of segments to improve the psychometric and trigonometric properties of the assessment inventories. Summaries of the historical development of these circles can be found in LaForge et al. (1985) and Wiggins (1980, 1982, 1985a, 1985b).

Benjamin's (1974, 1983, 1987c, 1988a) Structural Analysis of Social Behavior (SASB) Intrex questionnaires have been applied fruitfully in many studies of psychopathology and psychotherapy. In contrast to the two-dimensional circle inventories, Benjamin's (1974, 1993) SASB constitutes what can be called a three-dimensional, or two-plane, model that adds new categories of interpersonal behavior as well as provides, on a third plane, assessment of a covert dimension of intrapersonal behavior. Benjamin redefined the dominance-submission dimension into two separate dimensions of autonomy versus dominance and autonomy versus submission. Her model uniquely defined autonomy as the opposite of control and submission as its complement. The first two diamond-shaped planes or surfaces of her model contain not only the four Leary-tradition quadrants (in Benjamin's terms: "friendly-influence," "hostile-power," "friendly-accept," "hostile-comply"), but also four additional quadrants ("encourage friendly autonomy," "invoke hostile autonomy," "enjoy friendly autonomy," "take hostile autonomy"). Her third, intrapersonal or introject, surface assesses persons' behaviors toward themselves ("manage, cultivate self," "oppress self," "accept, enjoy self," "reject self"). Since comparable circumplex and other empirical convergences of the SASB planes with the two-dimensional models being presented here have yet to be demonstrated, one has to be careful about comparisons and easy translations (Benjamin, 1994; Van Denburg, Kiesler, Wagner, & Schmidt, 1994; Wiggins, 1994). We will return to her system toward the end of the chapter.

The 1982 Interpersonal Circle

The most recent empirical-conceptual reconstruction of Leary's original circle is Kiesler's 1982 Interpersonal Circle (1983), which is shown in Figure 1–1. Figures 1–2 and 1–3 present Kiesler's (1985) corresponding Acts version.

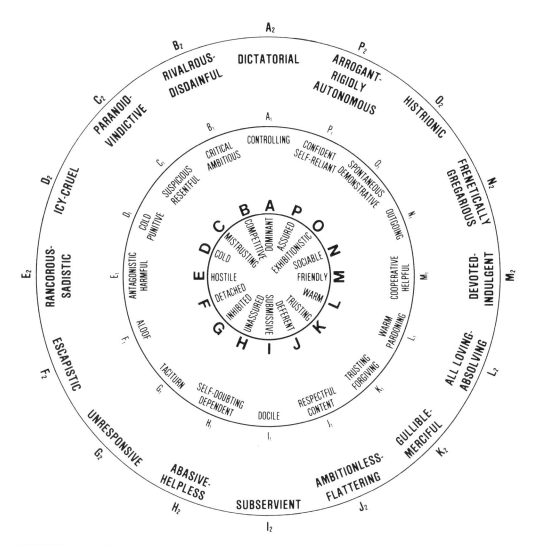

FIGURE 1–1. The 1982 Interpersonal Circle.

The 1982 Circle was introduced as a circular taxonomy that provided a conceptual-empirical integration of earlier two-dimensional circle measures. The taxonomy defined a large item sample of the universe of possible control and affiliation interpersonal behaviors. The complete classification system (Kiesler, 1982c) contains 350 bipolar interpersonal items, 3 to 9 of which define one of 64 segment-pair subclasses at the mild-moderate or extreme level of each of the 16 segments. Each of the two levels of each segment is defined by 3 to 5 subclasses, with the number of items defining each of the 32 levels ranging from 17 to 28. Each of the 16 segments (including both levels) is defined by 37 to 53 items.

Evidence supporting the validity of Kiesler's specific 1982 Circle structure has been found by Benjafield and Carson (1985), Chapman (1987), Gurtman (1991), Kiesler and Chapman (1988), and Wiggins, Trapnell, and Phillips (1988b). Benjafield and Carson (1985) presented empirical evidence that the octant categories of the 1982

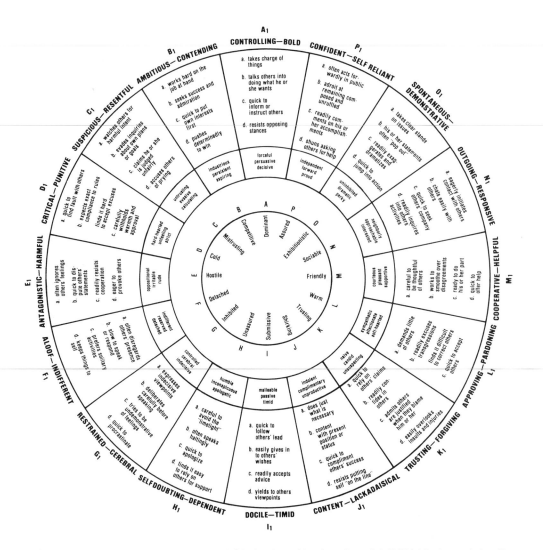

FIGURE 1-2. The 1982 Interpersonal Circle: Acts Version. Level 1 (Mild-Moderate) Act Descriptors for each of the 16 Interpersonal Categories (3 prototypical adjective descriptors for each category are listed in the middle concentric ring). Copyright © 1985 by Donald J. Kiesler.

Circle can be ordered historicodevelopmentally. Words belonging to octants closest to the circle axes of control or affiliation (LM, DE, PA, HI) have the earliest "dates of entry" into the language, as determined by *Oxford English Dictionary* counts; whereas words belonging to octants falling in the middle of the circle quadrants (NO, BC, FG, JK) had significantly later dates of entry.

Inspection of Figure 1-1 reveals that each of the 16 segments of the 1982 Circle is assigned three separate labels. One label designates the entire continuum (the circle radius) of interpersonal behaviors constituting a particular segment (e.g., A: Dominant, E: Hostile, I: Submissive, M: Friendly). A second label designates the mild-moderate (more normal) level of a particular segment continuum (e.g., A_1: Controlling, E_1: Antagonistic-Harmful, I_1: Docile, M_1: Cooperative-Helpful). A third label names

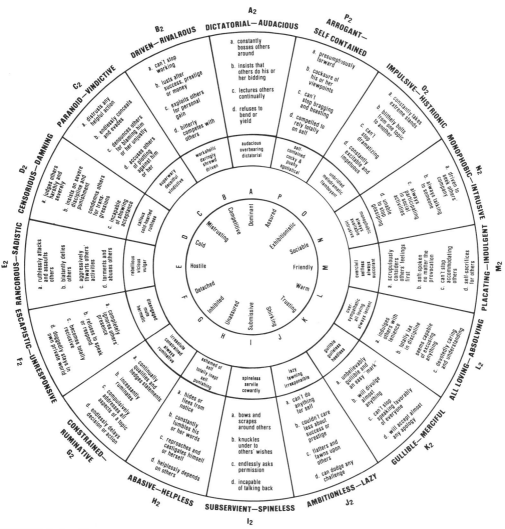

FIGURE 1–3. The 1982 Interpersonal Circle: Acts Version. Level 2 (Extreme) Act Descriptors for each of the 16 Interpersonal Categories (3 prototypical adjective descriptors for each category are listed in the middle concentric ring). Copyright © 1985 by Donald J. Kiesler.

the extreme (more abnormal) level of a particular segment (e.g., A_2: Dictatorial, E_2: Rancorous-Sadistic, I_2: Subservient, M_2: Devoted-Indulgent. Hence, the entire continuum of segment A is designated Dominant, the mild-moderate (more normal) level is called Controlling, and the extreme (more abnormal) level is named Dictatorial.

Sixteen segments (counterclockwise A to P) on the circumference of the circle define the range of possible trigonometric blends of the two underlying dimensions—so many units of control, so many units of affiliation. For example, exhibitionistic actions fall at segment O and represent approximately two units of dominance and two units of friendliness. In contrast, inhibited actions (segment G) denote the polar opposite to O and represent approximately two units of submission and two units of hostility.

Interpersonal circle categories can be defined also in terms of their trigonometric angle locations with reference to the horizontal affiliation axis. For example, interpersonal octant scales can be designated as friendly (F; 0°), friendly-dominant (FD; 45°), dominant (D; 90°), hostile-dominant (HD; 135°), hostile (H; 180°), hostile-submissive (HS; 225°), submissive (S; 270°), and friendly-submissive (FS; 315°).

Depending on the precision of analysis sought, interpersonal behaviors measured by circle inventories can be analyzed as (a) a sum vector score; (b) summary axis scores (control, affiliation); (c) hemisphere scores (friendly and hostile or dominant and submissive); (d) quadrant scores (hostile-dominant, hostile-submissive, friendly-submissive, friendly-dominant); (e) octant scores, which summarize pairs of adjacent 16ths; or (f) all 16 segments separately (counterclockwise using 1982 Circle labels: dominant, competitive, mistrusting, cold, hostile, detached, inhibited, unassured, submissive, deferent, trusting, warm, friendly, sociable, exhibitionistic, assured).

The 16 circle radii represent continua of normal (near the midpoint) to abnormal (near the circumference) versions of each segment's interpersonal acts. Component actions subsumed by each segment vary in terms of their *intensity or extremeness*. The more extreme the act, the more maladjusted it is, and the more aversive its effects on interactants.

Figures 1–2 and 1–3 (Kiesler, 1985) provide the specific $level_1$: mild-moderate and $level_2$: extreme interpersonal acts respectively—as well as prototypical adjective descriptors—that define the 16 categories of the 1982 Interpersonal Circle. Comparative examination of the figures provides concrete illustration of differences between more normal (Figure 1–2) and more maladjusted (Figure 1–3) interpersonal actions.

For example, along the full continuum of segment O: Exhibitionistic in Figure 1–1 (from the origin of the circle to the circumference) one finds O_1: Spontaneous-Demonstrative ($level_1$) and O_2: Histrionic ($level_2$) subcategories. Figure 1–2 provides a breakdown of the specific classes of mild-moderate interpersonal acts that define O_1: Spontaneous-Demonstrative (e.g., "b. his or her statements often 'pop out'"); Figure 1–3 details the specific classes of extreme interpersonal acts that define O_2: Histrionic (e.g., "b. blithely bolts from one topic to another"). Along the continuum of segment O: Exhibitionistic acts, extreme $level_2$ interpersonal actions are more maladaptive than milder segment O versions at $level_1$.

It is important to note, however, that a minority position has emerged among interpersonal researchers in regard to a circumplex definition of maladjusted behavior. Baumrind (1960) as well as Lorr and McNair (1963) proposed that the right (friendly) half of the interpersonal circle may be indicative of adjustment, whereas the left (hostile) half may denote maladjustment. In the same vein, Leary, Lane, Apfelbaum, Croppa, and Kaufmann (1956, p. 22) found that the "ideal self" descriptions of 90% of persons who had been tested fell within the top-right (friendly-dominant) quadrant. That is, the overwhelming majority of subjects strove to conform to an ideal concept that emphasizes dominant interpersonal behavior expressed in an affiliative manner. As Baumrind (1960) observed, "It is not unreasonable to conclude that the society places a premium on such behavior, and that this behavior, in turn, enhances the likelihood of successful adjustment to the demands of the society" (p. 398). This issue will be discussed further in Chapter 6.

Tables 1–1 and 1–2 provide more detailed descriptors of behaviors characteristic of mild-moderate and extreme levels respectively that are summarized in Figures 1–2 and 1–3. These descriptors were adapted from the items catalogued in the Appendix of

TABLE 1–1. **Paragraph Definitions of the Sixteen Level 1 (Mild-Moderate) Categories of the 1982 Interpersonal Circle: Male Version**

A: Controlling-Bold. This person is eager to take charge of things, often leads conversations, and tells others what to do. He pushes hard to get his own way and talks others into doing what he wants. He is quick to inform or instruct others, to persuade others to his viewpoint, and readily offers advice or opinions. He finds it easy to stand up to others, resists opposing stances, and struggles against others' taking charge. He impresses others as being decisive, forceful, and persuasive.

B: Ambitious-Contending. This person works hard on the job at hand and is persistent when first efforts fail. He takes on and initiates new projects, and energetically produces and achieves. He seeks success and admiration, and is single-minded in pursuing prestige or money. He gets others to work toward his goals, is adroit at taking credit, and downplays or ignores others' contributions. He is eager to take on challenges and pushes determinedly to win. He impresses others as being aspiring, industrious, and persistent.

C: Suspicious-Resentful. This person doubts others' good intentions and is careful to watch others for harmful intent. He often checks up on others, seeks hidden reasons, and readily distrusts helpful acts. He prefers to conceal his own intentions and frequently evades inquiries about his own plans or goals. He is quick to claim that he is being judged unfairly, tends to accuse others of prying, and finds it difficult to forgive injuries. He impresses others as being calculating, evasive, and untrusting.

D: Critical-Punitive. This person regularly expects best efforts from others and is quick to find fault with others and to judge them strictly. He insists on firm discipline, lays down prohibitions, expects exact compliance to rules, and finds it hard to accept excuses. He sets tough conditions for his acceptance of others, is careful to withhold warmth and approval, and seldom bestows praise. He impresses others as being hard-hearted, strict, and unfeeling.

E: Antagonistic-Harmful. This person frequently is discourteous, often seems to ignore others' feelings, and is quick to take what he wants. He often complains and quarrels, tends to dispute others' statements, and finds it easy to tell others off. He prefers to resist cooperation, to refuse requests from others, and readily obstructs others' activities. He seems eager to provoke others, and to annoy and insult them. He impresses others as being irritable, oppositional, and rude.

F: Aloof-Indifferent. This person can be expected to disregard others' presence and to be engrossed in his own thoughts. He seldom initiates conversation, is slow to speak or respond, and often replies tersely. He prefers to remain distant from others, is quick to turn down invitations, and seeks solitary activities. He finds it easy to keep things to himself, shuns inquiring into others' affairs, and is careful to guard his own privacy. He impresses others as being detached, indifferent, and reserved.

G: Restrained-Cerebral. This person is careful to withhold clear expressions of his views, often equivocates, and can be expected to express indecisive viewpoints. He tries to deliberate carefully before speaking, attempts to use words precisely, and often seems to preface and qualify his statements. He frequently appears reflective, easily gets "bogged down" with indecision, and is quick to procrastinate. He prefers to be serious and rational, and works hard at controlling emotional expressions. He impresses others as being cerebral, controlled, and indecisive.

(Continued)

TABLE 1–1. *(Continued)*

H: Self-Doubting-Dependent. This person prefers to stay in the background and is careful to avoid the limelight. He often speaks haltingly, readily rattles, and can be expected to embarrass easily. He finds it easy to doubt and downplay his own abilities, is quick to criticize himself, and apologizes frequently. He tends to act needy, often seems to depend on others, and is adroit at relying on others for support. He impresses others as being apologetic, humble, and inconspicuous.

I: Docile-Timid. This person is quick to take direction from others and to follow their lead. He is comfortable in letting others direct conversations and states his preferences hesitantly. He is quick to agree with others and to yield to others' viewpoints. He easily gives in to others' wishes and backs down quickly. He often seeks directives from others, eagerly adopts others' opinions, and readily accepts advice. He impresses others as being malleable, passive, and timid.

J: Content-Lackadaisical. This person seems hesitant to produce or achieve, is slow to take on responsibility, and does just what is necessary. He appears satisfied with his present position or status, is careful to avoid challenges, and resists putting himself "on the line." He is quick to give up if first efforts fail and needs frequent supervision. He admires others' achievements, finds it easy to give credit to others, and is eager to compliment others' successes. He impresses others as being complimentary, indolent, and unproductive.

K: Trusting-Forgiving. This person finds it easy to trust others, is unguarded around them, and tends to be taken advantage of by others. He is quick to rely on others' claims, and prefers to believe that others have good intentions. He is slow to accuse others of harmful intent, easily overlooks insults and injuries, and is quick to accept apologies. He readily confides in others and candidly reveals his own intentions and plans. He is comfortable in admitting that others are justified when they blame him. He impresses others as being candid, naive, and unsuspecting.

L: Approving-Pardoning. This person finds it hard to judge others, demands little of them, and treats others leniently. He prefers to impose easy discipline, readily excuses transgressions, and finds it difficult to correct others. He is quick to accept others and finds it easy to express warmth and approval. He is eager to understand others' problems, to support their good efforts, and is adroit at finding others' good qualities. He impresses others as being affectionate, soft-hearted, and sympathetic.

M: Cooperative-Helpful. This person tries hard to be thoughtful of others and is careful to respect others' rights. He cooperates easily, and is ready to do his part. He can be expected to speak softly and tactfully, finds it easy to remain patient with irritations, works to smooth over disagreements, and is difficult to rile. He seeks to comfort others, seems eager to accede to their requests, and is quick to offer help. He impresses others as being courteous, pleasant, and supportive.

N: Outgoing-Responsive. This person is quick to notice and acknowledge others, eagerly initiates contact with them, and seeks to make others feel welcome. He is comfortable at initiating conversations and chats easily with others. He is eager to seek others' company and to invite others to participate in activities. He enjoys being with others and attempts to mix widely. He is adroit at inquiring into others' activities and is ready to relate his own experiences. He impresses others as being approachable, interested, and neighborly.

TABLE 1–1. *(Continued)*

O: Spontaneous-Demonstrative.   This person finds it easy to express his viewpoints and to take clear stands on issues. He often seems to talk on and on, is adroit at embellishing stories, and can be expected to exaggerate and dramatize. His statements frequently just pop out, and his conversation regularly is emotionally charged. He readily drops in startling comments and is comfortable making loaded statements. He tends to make hasty decisions and is quick to jump into action. He impresses others as being dramatic, perky, and uninhibited.

P: Confident-Self-Reliant.   This person expresses his views confidently and is adroit at remaining composed and unruffled. He can be expected to rely on himself and shuns asking others for help. He often seems satisfied with himself and finds it easy to turn conversation to his own activities or to comment on his own accomplishments. He often acts forwardly in public, is eager to be noticed, and is quick to speak or act pretentiously. He finds it difficult to apologize to others. He impresses others as being forward, independent, and proud.

Note: Adapted from *The 1982 Interpersonal Circle: Acts Version,* by D. J. Kiesler, 1985, unpublished manuscript, Virginia Commonwealth University, Richmond.

TABLE 1–2. Paragraph Definitions of the Sixteen Level 2 (Extreme) Categories of the 1982 Interpersonal Circle: Male Version

A: Dictatorial-Audacious.   This person constantly bosses others around, barks out orders, and can't stop dominating others. He insists that others do his bidding and seems unable to stop "steamrolling" them. He abruptly interrupts others, lectures them continually, and dogmatizes his own viewpoints. He forcefully resists anyone telling him what to do, refuses to bend or yield, and fights to the finish for his views. He strikes others as being audacious, dictatorial, and overbearing.

B: Driven-Rivalrous.   This person can't seem to stop working, relentlessly pursues the job at hand, and doggedly attacks all obstacles. He continually plans and initiates new projects, and seems driven to produce and achieve at all costs. He lusts after success, prestige, or money. He bitterly competes with others and is single-minded in winning at all costs. He demeans others' contributions, seizes credit from them, and exploits others for personal gain. He strikes others as being daringly shrewd, driven, and a workaholic.

C: Paranoid-Vindictive.   This person distrusts any helpful action and sees personal danger everywhere. He seems driven to expose others' selfish motives, doubts everyone's loyalty, constantly tests others, and often spies on them. He seems compelled to conceal and evade, and seems unable to forgive even minor injuries or insult. He denounces others for unjustly blaming him, reproaches others for plotting against him, and accuses others of persecuting him. He strikes others as being deceitful, superwary, and vindictive.

(Continued)

TABLE 1–2. *(Continued)*

D: Censorious-Damning. This person judges others harshly and severely and can't seem to stop finding fault with them. He demands absolute compliance to rules, insists on severe discipline and punishment, and finds it impossible ever to bend his standards in judging others' conduct. He disdains any excuses, condemns others for transgressions, and insists that they make retribution. He seems incapable of showing acceptance or of praising anyone and spurns any show of warmth. He strikes others as being callous, cold-hearted, and ruthless.

E: Rancorous-Sadistic. This person continually violates others' rights, blatantly defies them, and ruthlessly attacks and assaults them. He rancorously disputes with others, and rudely screams at and berates them. He constantly rebels against directives and aggressively thwarts others' activities. He belligerently refuses requests for help, ridicules and scorns others, seems determined to torment and abuse them, and revels in hurting them. He strikes others as being rebellious, vicious, and vulgar.

F: Escapistic-Unresponsive. This person can be counted on to ignore others' presence and refuses to speak or respond. He remains totally unresponsive, is constantly lost in his own thoughts, and appears compulsively uncommunicative. He doggedly ignores all social overtures, and resists intrusions into his privacy. Whenever possible, he avoids others and becomes totally reclusive. When around others, he is totally disinterested and relentlessly stays in his own private world. He strikes others as being disengaged, hermetic, and mute.

G: Constrained-Ruminative. This person continually qualifies and hedges his statements, seems to express ambiguous positions on everything, and can't seem to stop vacillating. He incessantly ruminates and is regularly distracted by his own endless deliberations. He scrupulously weighs his choice of words and compulsively considers all aspects of a topic. He seems captively indecisive and endlessly delays decision or action. He seems driven to be serious and rational at all times and seems capable of snuffing out any expression of feeling. He strikes others as being always irresolute, constantly ruminative, and constrained.

H: Abasive-Helpless. This person scrupulously avoids any conspicuous statement or action and regularly hides or flees from notice. He seems continually nervous around people, constantly fumbles his words, and comes across as totally inept. He continually blames himself, can't seem to stop putting himself down, frequently reproaches and castigates himself, and seems to apologize for everything. He seems driven to depend on others and is quick to plead for help. He strikes others as being ashamed of himself, self-punishing, and totally inept.

I: Subservient-Spineless. This person is easily led around by the nose and can be talked into doing almost anything. He regularly seeks directives from others, endlessly asks their permission, and sheepishly capitulates to their views. He finds it impossible to talk back, and will agree with almost anything. He bows and scrapes around others, and constantly caters to those in charge. He seems incapable of standing up to others and spinelessly knuckles under to their wishes. He strikes others as being cowardly, servile, and spineless.

J: Ambitionless-Lazy. This person complacently lets others do the work, and seems totally disinterested in producing or achieving. He couldn't care less about success or prestige. He seems incapable of doing anything for himself, mostly doesn't even try, and requires constant supervision. He hides or flees from responsibility, avoids all new projects, and adroitly dodges any challenge. He flatters and fawns on others. He strikes others as being fawning, irresponsible, and lazy.

TABLE 1–2. *(Continued)*

K: Gullible-Merciful.   This person implicitly trusts everyone and seems oblivious to personal harm. He credits everyone with good intentions, and believes few persons harm others intentionally. He is unbelievably gullible and an easy mark, is improbably candid, and will divulge almost anything. He goes out of the way to exonerate others and can't stop speaking favorably of everyone. He can be counted on to forgive anything and regularly accepts any apology. He strikes others as being guileless, gullible, and heedless.

L: All Loving-Absolving.   This person indulges others with lenience and finds it impossible to judge others. He seems totally lax in discipline, can't bring himself to lay down prohibitions, and seems capable of excusing anything. He goes out of his way to praise any good effort, regularly finds something to like in everyone, and seems unable to disapprove of anyone. He finds it easy to accept others unconditionally, is effusively warm and accepting, and is devotedly caring and understanding. He strikes others as being all-loving, always lenient, and oversympathetic.

M: Placating-Indulgent.   This person scrupulously considers others' feelings first and goes out of his way to respect others' rights. He is soft-spoken no matter what the provocation and seems incapable of complaining or griping. He can be counted on to defuse tense situations and seems impossible to rile. He constantly does more than his part and can't seem to stop accommodating others. He compulsively spends energy doing for others, regularly self-sacrifices for them, and indulges and dotes on them. He strikes others as being overcivil, selfless, and always succorant.

N: Monophobic-Intrusive.   This person can't seem to tolerate being alone, seems driven to seek others' company, and goes out of his way to greet and chat with others. He continually initiates conversations and seems always to be talking to someone. He constantly participates in social activities, regularly invites others to share in his, and parties endlessly. He can't seem to stop broadcasting his own experiences, incessantly pries into others' business, and finds it impossible to stop gossiping. He strikes others as being always available, intrusive, and monophobic.

O: Impulsive-Histrionic.   This person seems compelled to monopolize conversations, blithely bolts from one topic to another, and can't seem to stop blurting out his viewpoints. He endlessly embellishes stories, unabashedly exaggerates, seems driven to dramatize, and constantly takes extreme stands. He wears his feelings on his sleeve and can't resist making startling statements. He seems constantly excitable and impetuous, and is impulsive to a fault. He strikes others as being flamboyant, melodramatic, and unbridled.

P: Arrogant-Self Contained.   This person is presumptuously forward, usurps the center of attention, and seems constantly to put on airs. He appears incapable of self-criticism, can't resist speaking or acting brazenly or cockily, and seems impossible to embarrass. He is inordinately enamored of himself, can't seem to stop bragging or boasting, and seems enthralled with his own words. He seems driven to rely totally on himself and can't bring himself to ask for help with anything. He strikes others as being cocky and pushy, egotistical, and self-contained.

Note: Adapted from *The 1982 Interpersonal Circle: Acts Version,* by D. J. Kiesler, 1985, unpublished manuscript, Virginia Commonwealth University, Richmond.

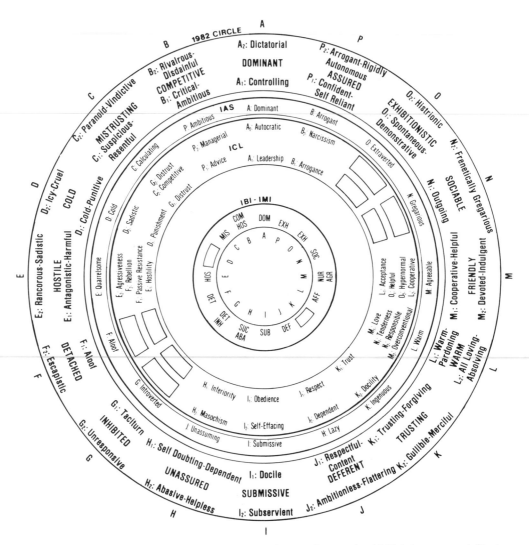

FIGURE 1–4. Location of IAS, ICL, IBI, and IMI Categories on the 1982 Interpersonal Circle.

Kiesler's (1985) Acts Version monograph. For historical and comparative purposes, Figure 1–4 provides a pictorial summary of the relative locations of the Interpersonal Adjective Scales (IAS), the Interpersonal Check List (ICL), the Interpersonal Behavior Inventory (IBI), and the Impact Message Inventory (IMI) scales on the circumference of the 1982 Interpersonal Circle.

A Suggestion and a Caution

At this point, you should take some time to study Figures 1–2 and 1–3. These operational descriptors represent the basic anchors of interpersonal assessment and interpersonal interventions. Throughout the remainder of the book, you will find these figures helpful in translating more concretely the interpersonal principles that are discussed.

You also need to keep in mind that most adult two-dimensional circle inventories were devised originally to measure the comprehensive domain of 16 categories of interpersonal behavior. In practice, however, only 8-scale (octant) versions (obtained by empirically or conceptually collapsing adjacent 16ths) have attained the trigonometric ideal of circumplex structure (e.g., Wiggins et al., 1981; Gurtman, 1993, 1994) that is needed for precise tests of many propositions of contemporary interpersonal theory. Available two-dimensional circle inventories that satisfactorily meet these criteria include the IAS-R (Wiggins, 1991b; Wiggins, Trapnell, & Phillips, 1988b), the Inventory of Interpersonal Problems-Circumplex Version (IIP-C; Alden, Wiggins, & Pincus, 1990), and the IMI octant version (Kiesler & Schmidt, 1993).

Other interpersonal circle inventories including the ICL (LaForge & Suczek, 1955), the IBI (Lorr & McNair, 1967), and the Check List of Interpersonal Transactions-Revised (CLOIT-R; Kiesler, 1987a) show certain psychometric and/or circumplicial inadequacies (although in the case of the CLOIT-R, see Tracey & Schneider, 1995) that necessitate both careful analysis of octant scores and cautious interpretation of specific results.

Whenever possible in subsequent discussions, this book will take advantage of the full 16 segments of the 1982 Interpersonal Circle defined in Figures 1–1 through 1–3 and Tables 1–1 and 1–2. Use of the more comprehensive 16 categories can demonstrate dramatically the potential heuristic power of interpersonal circle theory for psychopathology and psychotherapy. Realization of this promise, of course, will require future sophisticated psychometric measures that can reliably and validly measure the full 16 categories.

INTERPERSONAL CIRCUMPLEX INVENTORIES

The Interpersonal Check List (ICL)

The "granddaddy" of interpersonal inventories was developed as a collective product of the Kaiser Permanente Research Group during the early 1950s. It was first published by LaForge and Suczek (1955) and subsequently popularized and presented in interpersonal circle format by Leary (1957). The ICL consists of 128 items that yield 16 segment scores (counterclockwise around the circle: A through P). Each of the 16 scales is measured by 8 items, each of which is weighted according to one of four levels of intensity or extremeness of the respective category of interpersonal behavior. Manuals for research (LaForge, 1977) and clinical (Leary et al., 1956) applications are available; a recent bibliography of 140 ICL studies published from 1967 through 1979 (Clark & Taulbee, 1981; also an annotated version: Taulbee & Clark, 1982) have been published; updated college norms have become available (Lees-Halet, 1981). Evidence regarding reliability and circular properties of the ICL can be found in LaForge (1977) and in Paddock and Nowicki (1986, 1987); further psychometric data as well as extensive validity information can be found in LaForge (1977), Leary (1957), Leary et al. (1956), and in the studies listed in Clark and Taulbee (1981) and Taulbee and Clark (1982).

The ICL includes items in both adjective and verb-phrase format. Most researchers have followed Leary's procedure of combining two adjacent scales into octant scores, in contrast to LaForge's (1977) strong recommendation that users analyze all 16 segments. The ICL has been used for self-report (respondents can characterize themselves as they are or would like to be), for characterizations of interactants (respondents can characterize spouses, parents, friends, etc.), or for observer ratings of interactants (observers as respondents).

Several important critiques of the ICL have appeared. A major identified shortcoming is that the ICL contains serious measurement gaps in the top-right (segments N and O) and bottom-left (segments F and G) circle quadrants (Chartier & Conway, 1984; Kiesler, 1983; Lorr & McNair, 1965; J. Lyons, Hirschberg, & Wilkinson, 1980; Paddock & Nowicki, 1986, 1987; G. G. Stern, 1970; Wiggins, 1979a, 1982). This critique implies that the ICL cannot measure a good one fourth of the range of two-dimensional interpersonal actions. A second major shortcoming, documented by Wiggins (1979a, 1982), is the ICL's lack of polarity between variables opposite to each other on the circle. More detailed analyses of the strengths and weaknesses of the ICL can be found in Kiesler (1983), Paddock and Nowicki (1986, 1987), and Wiggins (1982).

Several act-by-act coding systems have been developed from LaForge and Suczek's (1955) ICL and the Leary (1957) circle. The earliest grew out of the Kaiser Permanente group's original codings of interpersonal behavior occurring among group psychotherapy participants. The *ICL Coding Manual* (O'Dell, 1967, 1968) was adapted by O'Dell from Freedman et al. (1951) and LaForge and Suczek (1955) for ratings of group psychotherapy interactions. The Manual provides coding rules for the 16 segments of Leary's interpersonal circle. J. F. Alexander (1970) developed a content rating system from parent-child interactions based on Leary's (1957) circle. In Alexander's system, all interpersonal behavior is coded in terms of the two circle axis dimensions: dominance-submission and hostility-affection. The two dimensions are coded by separate raters and decision rules are provided for coding both verbal and nonverbal behaviors from videotape samples. Phelps and Slater (1985) developed a modified version of Alexander's coding system that provides expanded decision rules for the dominance-submission dimension only.

Duke (1978) developed simplified interpersonal style rating scales that can be used to measure both verbal and nonverbal aspects of the interpersonal communication process, to permit an alternative to the typical assumption that a subject's verbal reports (e.g., on the ICL) reflect both the verbal and nonverbal aspects of the person's actual interpersonal style. In his approach, raters judge the intensity of interpersonal Control and Affiliation of a subject's observed behavior on two 160 mm lines, anchored by respective definitions of the two circle axis behaviors. Duke (1978) reported significant correlations with corresponding ICL axis scores ($r = .78$ for Control, $r = .82$ for Affiliation). Nowicki and Manheim (1991) applied Duke's measure to construct experimental dyads in their study of interpersonal complementarity and time of interaction in female relationships.

Strong and his colleagues have adapted the ICL into an act-by-act version, the *Interpersonal Communication Rating Scale* (ICRS) and its accompanying Manual (Strong, Hills, & Nelson, 1988). The ICRS is a manualized coding system, based on Leary's (1957) interpersonal circle, in which each of the octants is defined in paragraph form, with examples of representative behaviors listed. Raters watch videotapes and read transcripts of interactions and assign each speaking turn to the actual octant that it best fits. Strong and his students have used the ICRS in their studies of interpersonal influence theory (Strong, 1987a, 1987b, 1987c, in press; Strong & Claiborn, 1982; Strong et al., 1988).

The Interpersonal Behavior Inventory (IBI)

Lorr and McNair (1963, 1965, 1966, 1967; Lorr, Bishop, & McNair, 1965; Lorr, Suzidelis, & Kinnane, 1973; McNair & Lorr, 1965) sought to develop an acts-item interpersonal inventory as an alternative to the adjective-saturated ICL items for measurement of interpersonal behavior in psychotherapeutic and other clinical settings. They also wanted to construct additional scales that would fill in the ICL gaps in the friendly-dominant and hostile-submissive circle quadrants. The final result was their 140-item IBI (Lorr & McNair, 1967), which provides 15 segment scores (items per segment range from 7 to 11). Primary applications of the IBI have been for characterizations of interactants (e.g., therapist respondents characterize the interpersonal behaviors of their patients) or for ratings of interactants (observer respondents). Information on reliability, circular properties, and validity can be found in the preceding references as well as in Lorr and McNair (1966). Kiesler, Anchin et al. (1976, 1985; Perkins et al., 1979) used the IBI as a point of departure and source of paragraph descriptions for generating items for their Impact Message Inventory. Apparently, no other review or compilation of IBI studies has surfaced.

Lorr and his colleagues have developed a new measure called the *Interpersonal Style Inventory* (*ISI*; Lorr, 1986, 1990; Lorr & Suziedelis, 1990; Lorr & Youniss, 1986). It contains 300 true-false statements and expands measurement of interpersonal behavior patterns to include more complete coverage of personality patterns in a manner similar to Big Five inventories. The ISI provides scores on 14 bipolar scales designed to assess five primary dimensions of personality: interpersonal involvement (sociable, help-seeking, nurturant), level of socialization (conscientious, trusting, tolerant), autonomy versus dependency (directive, independent, rule-free), self-control versus impulse expression (deliberate, orderly, practical), and emotional stability (stable, approval seeking). An ISI Manual is available (Lorr, 1986) as well as a short-form version (Lorr & DeJong, 1986).

The Interpersonal Adjective Scales (IAS)

In the process of developing a taxonomy of trait-descriptive terms in the English language, Wiggins (1979a, 1979b, 1980, 1981, 1982; Wiggins et al., 1981) attempted to differentiate interpersonal traits from other categories such as temperament, moods, and cognitive traits. As discussed earlier, the ICL was used as an original marker system but was abandoned because of the top-right and bottom-left quadrant gaps and the lack of bipolarity between variables opposite to each other on the circle. The result (Wiggins, 1979a, 1981) was the 128-item (all in adjective format) IAS, which provides scores for 16 segments (8 items for each of the 16 scales).

The revised Interpersonal Adjective Scales (IAS-R; Wiggins et al., 1988b) were constructed to provide a more convenient short-form version of the IAS, with improved substantive and structural characteristics. The IAS-R comprises 64 simple adjectives to which subjects respond by indicating the degree of self-descriptive accuracy on an 8-point Likert scale ranging from *extremely inaccurate* to *extremely accurate*. Item responses are cumulated to form eight scales, each alphabetically labeled in a counterclockwise direction around the circle: Assured-Dominant (PA), Arrogant-Calculating (BC), Cold-hearted (DE), Aloof-Introverted (FG), Unassured-Submissive (HI), Unassuming-Ingenuous (JK), Warm-Agreeable (LM), and Gregarious-Extraverted (NO).

Description of psychometric and circumplex properties as well as normative data for the IAS-R can be found in Wiggins (1991b), Wiggins et al. (1988b), and Yarnold and Lyons (1987). Among interpersonal measures, Wiggins IAS-R demonstrates the best fit to circumplex structure attained to date (Lorr & Strack, 1990; Wiggins, 1991b; Wiggins et al., 1981; Wiggins et al., 1988b).

The IAS and IAS-R have been used primarily for self-reports (respondents' characterizations of themselves); however, they can also be used for characterizations of interactants (Respondent B characterizes Interactant A) or ratings of interactants (observer respondents).

The IAS and IAS-R have been related to a variety of individual difference measures within the fields of personality and social psychology (Wiggins & Broughton, 1985), including the big-five dimensions of personality research (McCrae & Costa, 1989; Trapnell & Wiggins, 1990); person perception (Gascoyne, 1985); attitudes toward need expression (Sikes-Nova, 1990); psychological androgyny (Wiggins & Holzmuller, 1978, 1981); preferences in mate selection (D. M. Buss & Barnes, 1986); the use of interpersonal manipulation tactics (D. M. Buss, Gomes, Higgins, & Lauterbach, 1987); and ratings of nonverbal social behavior (Gifford & O'Connor, 1987). The inventories have also been studied in relation to psychopathology (Pincus & Wiggins, 1990; Wiggins et al., 1989; Wiggins & Pincus, 1989, 1994), to Type A behavior patterns (Yarnold, Grimm, & Lyons, 1987), and for evaluating the effectiveness of a paradoxical intervention for hostile-dominant therapy clients (Buranyi, 1989).

Check List of Interpersonal Transactions (CLOIT) and Check List of Psychotherapy Transactions (CLOPT)

Kiesler (1984, 1987a) constructed several versions of the same inventory to measure the interpersonal behavior of target persons on dimensions corresponding to the 16 segments of the 1982 Interpersonal Circle (Kiesler, 1983, 1985). CLOIT and CLOPT, rationally derived inventories having identical item content, consist of 96 items (exclusive acts form) that are checked as present or absent either by interactant (CLOIT) or observer (CLOPT) respondents. The inventory has been used for self-reports (respondents' characterizations of themselves: CLOIT: Self-Report Form), characterizations of interactants (Respondent B characterizes Interactant A: CLOIT: Transactant Form), and for observer ratings of interactants in psychotherapy contexts (CLOPT: Client Form; CLOPT: Therapist Form).

Subsequent empirical applications and analyses of these CLOPT/CLOIT ratings revealed less than ideal psychometric and circumplex structural properties. The newly available 1985 Acts Version of the Circle was used next, together with empirical findings, to construct a new item pool that became CLOIT-R/CLOPT-R (Kiesler, 1987a). Because these revised versions still exhibited psychometric and circumplex inadequacies when scored for 16ths, a manual (Kiesler, Goldston, & Schmidt, 1991) concluded that the CLOIT-R or CLOPT-R forms should be scored as octant versions only (by combining adjacent 16th-scale scores). Several studies (Kiesler, Goldston, Paddock, & Van Denburg, 1986; Kiesler, Schmidt, & Larus, 1988, 1989; Van Denburg, 1989; Weinstock-Savoy, 1986) report adequate internal consistency, test-retest, and interrater reliabilities for the 16 CLOIT-CLOPT scales.

Tracey and Schneider (1995) examined the circular structure of the CLOIT-R and CLOPT-R in samples of college students and therapy dyads. For the undergraduates, circular structure was found to fit both the CLOIT-R and the IAS-R scales, especially for the octant scores. For the therapy dyads also, the CLOPT-R was found to fit the circular model, both for therapists and clients, again especially in the case of octant scores. Finally, intercorrelations of the client and therapist octant scores strongly confirmed interpersonal propositions of complementarity. In light of their findings, Tracey and Schneider (1995) argued for usage of the CLOIT-R and CLOPT-R in empirical tests of interpersonal theory.

Conway reported a study by one of his students (Wilkie, 1987) for which an act-by-act CLOIT-CLOPT coding system was adapted from Kiesler's (1985) Acts Version of the 1982 Interpersonal Circle. Octant scores were generated; interrater reliabilities for quadrant placement, using a weighted kappa, ranged from .50 to .92 over 24 dyads, with a mean of .74.

Several validity studies were summarized in considerable detail in Kiesler et al.'s (1991) *Manual*. The inventory scales and octants have confirmed predicted positive correlations with corresponding octants of Wiggins's IAS measure (Kiesler et al., 1989; Weinstock-Savoy, 1986) and to self-reported gender orientation and mood variation (Carson & Shapiro, 1985). Kiesler and Goldston (1988) used the CLOPT to differentiate the interpersonal behavior of three prominent therapists (Rogers, Ellis, Perls) and their complementary fit to the patient, Gloria. Kiesler and Watkins (1989) examined, on a sample of outpatient dyads, the relationship between the working alliance and client-therapist complementarity during early counseling sessions. Kiesler, Van Denburg, Sikes-Nova, Larus, and Goldston (1990) used the CLOPT to provide empirical interpersonal circle diagnoses for seven *DSM-III* (American Psychiatric Association, 1980) personality disorder patients. Van Denburg and Kiesler (1993) provided initial validation of a new interpersonal principle of "transactional escalation," according to which a normal individual's pattern of typical interpersonal behavior becomes rigid and extreme under stressful interpersonal conditions. Weinstock-Savoy's (1986) first study demonstrated that CLOPT and IAS scores differentiated four role-played therapy interactions designed to represent the four circle quadrants; her second study demonstrated that high patient-therapist complementarity during initial therapy sessions was positively associated with successful patient outcome.

Other CLOIT/CLOPT studies, including more recent CLOIT-R/CLOPT-R studies, include Bingi (1994); S. R. Campbell (1991); S. R. Campbell and Brown (1990); Chewning (1991); Golden (1989); Goldston (1990); Gonick (1987); Heffner (1988, 1993); Kerr, Patton, Lapan, and Hills (1994); Kivlighan and Angelone (1992); Kivlighan, Marsh-Angelone, and Angelone (1994); Kivlighan, McGovern, and Corazzini (1984); Kivlighan and Mullison (1988); Kivlighan, Mullison, Flohr, Proudman, and Francis (1992); Liggett (1993); Mahalik, Hill, O'Grady, and Thompson (1993); Mahalik, Hill, Thompson, and O'Grady (1989); McMullen and Conway (1994); Pollock (1990); Radecki-Bush (1989); Robbins and Dupont (1992); Schmidt (1989); Shean and Uchenwa (1990); Shuler (1994); S. Stuart, Pilkonis, Heape, Smith, and Fisher (1992); Thompson, Hill, and Mahalik (1991); Tracey and Schneider (1995); Whiffen, Dudley, and Sasseville (1990); Wilkie (1987); and Wilkie and Conway (1988).

The Impact Message Inventory (IMI)

All the previous circle inventories are designed to designate the overt interpersonal behavior of target persons by measuring the perceptions of the targets themselves (self-report), of interactants, or of external observers. In contrast, the IMI and Wiggins's (1984) Affective Reactions Questionnaire (ARQ) are designed to designate the overt behavior of target persons by measuring the covert reactions targets induce or evoke in interactants or observers.

The IMI (Kiesler, 1987c; Kiesler, Anchin, et al., 1976, 1985; Perkins et al., 1979) was constructed on the assumption that the interpersonal or evoking style of Person (A) can be validly defined and measured by assessing the covert responses or "impact messages" of Person(s) (B) during interactions with or observations of A. The IMI is a self-report instrument, since a transactant (B) reports the emotional, behavioral, and cognitive internal engagements experienced during interactions with a targeted partner (A). It is a transactional device since Respondent B's reported impacts or engagements are scored to characterize the interpersonal behavior of the targeted interacting partner (A). The IMI, thus, is a *self-report transactional* inventory used to identify the interpersonal behavior of normal and maladjusted individuals by measuring the covert consequences within other persons of the individual's interpersonal behavior patterns.

Items from the 15 scales of Lorr and McNair's (1967) IBI were used to generate paragraph descriptions of the overt interpersonal behavior typical of each of 15 pure interpersonal types (Perkins et al., 1979). These paragraphs then served as stimuli to elicit internal reactions (direct feelings, action tendencies, cognitive attributions), which formed provisional item pools, to each of the 15 types. The generalizability of these item classifications was then assessed in a group of 451 undergraduates; item-analysis procedures were employed to select the final IMI Form II. The IMI consists of 90 items and yields scores for the 15 Lorr and McNair interpersonal segments (6 items per segment: 2 direct feelings, 2 action tendencies, 2 cognitive attributions).

Reliability, circular properties, and validity information can be found in *The Research Manual for the Impact Message Inventory*, which also summarizes 40 IMI studies conducted before 1983 (Kiesler, 1987c). Reviews and critiques of the IMI can be found in Borgen (1985), Kiesler (1983), McCarthy (1985), Strong (1985), and Wiggins (1982). Wiggins (1984; Wiggins et al., 1988a) developed an *Affective Reactions Questionnaire* for purposes similar to the IMI; apparently no subsequent work with the measure has been pursued. The IMI will be presented in considerable detail in Chapter 5.

Inventory of Interpersonal Problems-Circumplex Version (IIP-C)

The Inventory of Interpersonal Problems (IIP; Horowitz, 1988; Horowitz, Rosenberg, Baer, Ureno, & Villasenor, 1988) will be reviewed comprehensively in Chapter 6. Alden et al. (1990) developed a circle version (IIP-C) of the IIP that has demonstrated excellent circumplex properties.

Alden et al. (1990) administered the IIP to two samples of university students. Principal components analyses were conducted on each sample and found to yield similar solutions. The first two components to emerge in each sample were problem versions of the two dimensions commonly found to underlie interpersonal behavior, which in this domain of interpersonal problems were labeled Domineering versus Nonassertive and Self-Compromising versus Cold. Eight scales were developed to mark each octant of the interpersonal problem circle by selecting items on the basis of angular location relative to the two primary components and on communality and thematic content. These scales assess interpersonal problems related to (moving counterclockwise from the Domineering pole) Domineering Others, Vindictiveness, Coldness (inability to feel intimate feelings), Social Avoidance, Nonassertiveness, Compliant Behavior, Self-Compromising Behavior, and Intrusiveness—which represent all combinations of

Domineering and Coldness. Both the structure and the thematic content of the eight octant scales were cross-validated on a large ($N = 970$) university sample and on two samples of psychiatric outpatients.

Alden et al. (1990) reported clear circulant relationships between IAS-R (Wiggins et al., 1988b) and the IIP-C: Circumplex analyses revealed that the first two dimensions to emerge from the IIP were problem versions of the same two dimensions of the interpersonal circle and also identified 8-item subset-scales from the 127 IIP items that were both equally spaced within the two-dimensional space and met statistical criteria for a circumplex ordering. The 64-item, 8-scale version of the IIP that correlates strongly with Wiggins's IAS-R measure is described and listed in Horowitz (1988).

Structural Analysis of Social Behavior (SASB)

All the preceding inventories (ICL, IBI, IAS-R, IMI, CLOIT-R/CLOPT-R) are constructed in the same interpersonal tradition: two-dimensional circles or circumplexes organized around the axes of control (dominance-submission) and affiliation (hostile-friendly). Since Leary (1957), these measures and their respective circle representations have reflected 16 segments or categories (the IBI and IMI have only 15). With the exception of the IMI, all these measures also assess the *overt* behavior of target persons, either from the perspective of the target persons themselves (self-report), of an interactant (interactant respondents), or of observers (observer respondents).

Benjamin's (1974, 1983, 1987c, 1988a) SASB measures, in contrast, constitute what can be called a three-dimensional or two-plane model that adds new categories of interpersonal behavior as well as provides, on a third plane, assessment of a covert dimension of intrapersonal behavior not found in the two-dimensional measures.

Benjamin (1974, 1977, 1979a, 1979b, 1982, 1983, 1984, 1986a, 1986b, 1987a, 1987b, 1987c, 1988a, 1988b, 1989, 1990, 1992, 1993, 1994; Benjamin, Foster, Giat-Roberto, & Estroff, 1986; Benjamin, Giat, & Estroff, 1981; Benjamin & Wonderlich, 1994; Humphrey & Benjamin, 1986; McLemore & Benjamin, 1979) attempted to reconcile the interpersonal circle models developed by Leary (1957) for adults and by Schaefer (1959, 1961, 1965) for parent-child interactions. Leary-tradition models view the poles of control as dominance and submission; Schaefer viewed the poles as control and autonomy. As described earlier, Benjamin incorporated both viewpoints by defining autonomy as the opposite of control and submission as its complement.

SASB assessment is based on a series of INTREX questionnaires (Benjamin, 1983, 1987c, 1988a) completed by subjects and/or interactants. Various forms of the questionnaire have identical item content: 144 items, each rated on a scale ranging from 0 *(never, not at all)* to 100 *(always, perfectly)* in intervals of tens. Items are in verb phrase and sentence format; different versions of the questionnaire are used to obtain interpersonal characterizations of self (self-report) and others (respondents' characterizations of interactants). Computer analyses of INTREX questionnaires provide analyses of self-concept and significant interpersonal relationships, "maps" of how subjects interact with important others, interpretive narratives of SASB profiles, and the like.

Information regarding reliability and validity of the INTREX questionnaires is summarized in Benjamin (1974, 1993). A recent list of 59 SASB studies, theses, and dissertations has been compiled by and is available from Benjamin (1988b). SASB studies described elsewhere in this book (other than those listed at the beginning of this section) include Alpher (1991), Alpher and France (1993), Brokaw (1983), Brokaw and McLemore (1988), Henry, Schacht, and Strupp (1986, 1990), Humphrey (1989), Johnson,

Popp, Schacht, Mellon, and Strupp (1989), Laird and Vande Kemp (1987), Pond (1985), Rudy, McLemore, and Gorsuch (1985), and Talley, Strupp, and Morey (1990).

Critiques of the SASB can be found in Alpher (1988), Van Denburg et al. (1994), and Wiggins (1994). An act-by-act SASB coding system has also been constructed for sequential analysis studies and a coding manual is available (Benjamin et al., 1981).

EVALUATING CIRCUMPLEXITY AND SCORING OF INTERPERSONAL INVENTORIES

Assessment of Circumplex Structure

The interpersonal circle defines a circular array of categories or segments for which the ordering is without beginning or end. Each circle category represents the conjoint influence of two orthogonal underlying dimensions (control and affiliation). Hence, in the case of a circle measure that demonstrates perfect, two-dimensional circumplex structure, each category should show *zero correlations* with theoretically orthogonal categories. Because the array of categories is circular, it can be described by Euclidian geometry in which sine and cosine values define the joint operation of the two axis dimensions. Categories on the circumference then should demonstrate a circumplex ordering (Guttman, 1954) wherein adjacent segments are highly *positively correlated,* and increasingly distant categories around the circumference show increasingly lower positive correlations. Each category on the circumference represents a behavioral opposite to the category found at the other end of the diameter; hence, in the case of a perfect circumplex measure, each category would be highly *negatively correlated* with its opposite. Gurtman (1994) adds two additional criterial properties: constant radius and equal spacing between adjacent categories. The joint operation of these mathematical and statistical properties defines an interpersonal circumplex. Hence, an interpersonal circumplex "may be regarded as both a taxonomy of the interpersonal domain and a structural summary of how the domain is organized" (Gurtman, 1994, p. 243).

To illustrate these circumplicial features, we can focus on one circle category or segment—A: Dominant (see Figure 1–1). A should be positively correlated with its adjacent categories (B and P), and show decreasing correlations with categories further removed on the circumference (e.g., C and O, then D and N). A should show zero correlations with categories anchoring the circle axis orthogonal to its axis; hence A should correlate zero with both E and M. Finally, A should correlate negatively with the category directly opposite it on its diameter; hence, A's intercorrelation with I should approach -1.00.

To be valid and heuristic measures, interpersonal circle inventories such as the ones reviewed in this chapter must demonstrate close fit to the circumplex characteristics just defined. Precise fit of segments of a particular circle inventory to these circumplex structural properties is necessary to take advantage of the full empirical power of an inventory (a) to assess the entire range of individual differences in interpersonal behavior among both normal and maladjusted subjects and (b) to provide precise tests of interpersonal propositions, especially those of complementarity (which will be presented in detail in Chapter 4).

The IAS-R (Wiggins et al., 1988b) has set the standard for development of interpersonal circumplex measures by demonstrating outstanding fit to circumplex criteria (Wiggins, 1979a, 1982, 1991b; Wiggins & Broughton, 1985, 1991; Wiggins et al.,

1989; Wiggins et al., 1981; Wiggins et al., 1988b). Other circle inventories demonstrating good-to-excellent fit are the IIP-C (Alden et al., 1990) and the octant scoring version of the IMI (Kiesler & Schmidt, 1993).

The original statistical test for fit of an interpersonal inventory to circumplexity (Guttman, 1954) evaluated a particular measure for presence of the above described pattern of intercorrelations among the 16 segments or 8 octants. Such an ordering exists in a correlation matrix when "the highest correlations are next to the principal diagonal which runs from the upper left to the lower right corner. Along any row (or column) the correlations decrease in size as one moves farther away from the main diagonal and then increase again" (Lorr & McNair, 1965, p. 824). Lorr and McNair (1965) also offered a curve-fitting test of circumplex ordering wherein the correlations of each interpersonal segment (or octant) were plotted as ordinates against the predicted circumplex sequence. A strong fit to circumplexity would result in a smooth curve resembling a cosine pattern.

Wiggins et al. (1981) presented a sophisticated multivariate procedure designed specifically to evaluate the extent to which a correlation matrix of inventory scores conforms to a circumplex ordering. Their procedure essentially tests the goodness of fit between an obtained and theoretically estimated circulant correlation matrix. In addition, the procedure examines the covariance structure further by extracting five different kinds of principal components:

1. *Circumplex.* The proportion of the variance accounted for by the two principal components that anchor a circulant.
2. *General.* The proportion of variance accounted for by a global, response set variable.
3. *Polarity.* The extent to which the bipolarity of variables opposite on the circle is less than perfect.
4. *Orthogonality.* The proportion of variance accounted for by deviations from orthogonality among circle categories.
5. *Specificity.* The extent of deviation from a structure in which all variables have positive and exactly equal loadings on that component.

By analyzing data using these different principal components, researchers can analyze with fine precision the extent to which a circumplex model accounts for the observed covariance among the inventory scales. Paddock and Nowicki (1987) used the Wiggins et al. (1981) procedure to demonstrate poor fit of the ICL to circumplex structure as well as significant ICL scale omissions for the top-right and bottom-left circle quadrants.

Multidimensional scaling (MDS) analysis (e.g., Davison, 1983) also has been used to assess the degree of circularity among interpersonal inventory scales or items (e.g., Kiesler & Chapman, 1988; J. Lyons, Hirschberg, & Wilkinson, 1980; Paddock & Nowicki, 1986). The analysis provides a spatial representation (similar to a map) of the relative location of the interpersonal scales to each other. Statistics can also be calculated to determine goodness of fit between the data and the obtained MDS solution.

Tracey and Schneider (1995) provide a circumplex analysis based on Hubert and Arabie's (1987) randomization test of hypothesized order relations. The method relies on an exact specification of the order relations predicted by a particular model. It provides an explicit descriptive measure of the degree to which these hypothesized order relations are satisfied by a given data set, and a significance level that is based on a specific null conjecture of how the order relations were chosen. The method presents a "correspondence index (CI)" that indexes the relative fit of the predicted order to the actual data, specifying the proportion of predictions that are confirmed by the data minus the proportion of predictions that are disconfirmed. Tracey and Schneider (1995) applied the CI index to an analysis of the circumplexity of the CLOIT-R, CLOPT-R, and IAS-R.

Wiggins and colleagues (Wiggins, 1991b; Wiggins et al., 1988b) offered a psychometrically refined alternative that is perhaps the most popular statistical analysis for evaluating circumplexity of inventory items or scales. The procedure combines principal components analysis and rotation to Procrustean structure applied either to inventory scales (16ths or octants) or to inventory items (for item analysis and/or selection). Gurtman (1994) and Schmidt (1994) discussed the relative merits of the Procrustes procedure in contrast to MDS analysis.

Wiggins and colleagues first ipsatize (Block, 1957; Cattell, 1944) all inventory scores. In factor analyses of interpersonal circle inventories, raw scores are routinely ipsatized to remove the acquiescence response set factor that emerges first. Next, Wiggins and colleagues intercorrelate all inventory scales (or items), and extract the first two principal components (usually control and affiliation). These two components are then rotated to an a priori Procrustean pattern with the target matrix designed to minimize the least squares difference between the ideal and obtained angular locations of items for all octants. The Procrustes program provides figures that visually depict the obtained circular arrangement of either the scales or the items.

What happens next depends on whether the investigator has factor analyzed scales or items. For scales, correlation coefficients are obtained between theoretically derived factor scores (where equation weights are based on a theoretically perfect circumplex) and empirically obtained factor scores (whose weights are calculated as part of the previous principal components analysis). Very high positive coefficients provide evidence of excellent circumplexity for the particular inventory scales.

In the case of item analysis or selection, rotated factor scores are computed for all subjects in the sample and the scores correlated with all available inventory items. The correlation of a given item with the affiliation factor scores provides the location of that item on the X axis; the correlation of that item with the control factor provides the location on the Y axis. The arctangent of Y/X provides the angular location and the square root of Y^2 plus X^2 provides the distance of the item from the center of the circle according to the theorem of Pythagoras. This procedure yields "communality" (distance from the center of the circle, indexing degree of interpersonalness of an item) and "angular location" (precise values between 0.0 and 360 degrees, with category M given, by convention, the location of 0.0 degrees) of each inventory item. Visual comparison of obtained item angular locations with theoretically ideal (trigonometric) locations within a particular scale sector permits selection of items in the case of original inventory construction, or evaluation of items in the case of previously constructed circumplex inventories. For other item analysis procedures for circumplex inventories, refer to McCormick and Kavanagh (1981) and Phillips (1983).

C. C. Wagner et al. (1995) have added some routine follow-up analyses to the Wiggins and colleagues' Procrustean procedure. First, a statistical analysis based on the work of Fisher (1983; Fisher, Heise, Bohrnstedt, & Lucke, 1985) and Gurtman (1991) is performed to determine the degree to which the empirical angular placements of an inventory's scales (or items) correspond to their theoretical placements. The index is termed Fisher's A° and ranges from 0 to 1, where 0 equals the greatest possible (180°) displacement between obtained and predicted scales and 1 equals perfect alignment. Fisher's (1983) chi-square formula is then used to evaluate the fit indexed by A°.

Second, C. C. Wagner et al. (1995) assess the extent to which obtained scales (or items) are equivalently saturated with interpersonal content (demonstrated by having high loadings in the factorial space). Vector length scores of the scales (or items) are calculated to determine their saturation with interpersonal content. The ratio of the standard deviation to the mean vector length provides an index of variation of vector lengths calibrated on a common scale (Fisher et al., 1985), thus allowing examination of the circularity of the scales. Least variation in scale (or item) vector length (as indexed by ratio scores approaching 0.0) indicates best circularity for the given inventory scales or items.

For more detail, consult the references cited in this section (see also Browne, 1992). For more general discussion of evaluation of circumplexity of interpersonal inventories, consult Gurtman (1991) and Wiggins (1991b).

Scoring Interpersonal Inventories

LaForge (1977), Mardia (1972), and Wiggins (1991b) provide a general discussion of the various interpersonal scores (e.g., segment, octant, quadrant, axis, sum vector) that can be calculated for use in various data analyses.

Gurtman (1994) has offered a methodological "primer" that is a significant contribution to the field and merits special emphasis here. His chapter presents "methods of analysis appropriate when individuals are assessed in reference to a circumplex model" (p. 243). The second section of his chapter presents his curve-fitting procedure for profiling and graphically representing individuals within circumplex space, based on the fact that the circular structure of measures tends to produce profile patterns having sinusoidal form.

From the empirical curve obtained from a given individual's set of interpersonal inventory scores, Gurtman assesses four summary features of the resulting interpersonal profile:

1. *Angular displacement.* The number of degrees counterclockwise from the friendly pole of the affiliation axis represents the central tendency; it indicates the predominant theme or category of interpersonal behavior within the profile.

2. *Elevation.* This is the mean level, total score, or overall general factor; it indicates the overall extremeness or intensity of interpersonal behavior within the profile.

3. *Amplitude.* This is the vector length, the degree of patterning or circular variability; it indicates the degree of distinctiveness of angular displacement versus a less distinctive spread of behaviors around the circle circumference.

4. *Goodness-of-fit* (to the best-fit cosine curve). This identifies the degree of prototypicality versus "complexity" of a profile—poor fit (complexity) can arise from measurement error, confounding any interpretation; or it may reflect true, substantive inconsistencies or conflicts within the constellation of behaviors of the individual (e.g., Leary's "oscillating" tendencies).

In Gurtman's analysis, these four indexes provide "what amounts to the *structural summary* of the key properties of an individual's circular profile" (p. 251).

Gurtman's (1994) methodology provides perhaps the most succinct yet comprehensive system to date for scoring individuals' interpersonal inventory profiles preparatory to subsequent data analysis. His amplitude measure, for example, is a simple but elegant index for studies of interpersonal rigidity as an index of interpersonal maladjustment. His system also can be adapted (Gurtman, Kiesler, Schmidt, & Wagner, 1994) to develop a standard comprehensive index of interpersonal complementarity for analysis of dyadic pairs of interpersonal inventory profiles. Chapter 4 will be devoted exclusively to discussion of interpersonal theory for complementarity in human transactions.

The Interpersonal Circle as a Nomological Net

Gurtman (1991, 1992a, in press) also has demonstrated how the interpersonal circumplex constitutes a nomological system to validate measures of interpersonal constructs, including traditional measures of personality traits. Following on the earlier analyses of Wiggins and Broughton (1985), Gurtman argues that, as an operationalization of the universe of interpersonal content, the interpersonal circle provides a way of evaluating the basic "interpersonalness" of different personality constructs and measures. Essentially, the interpersonal circumplex

> offers a powerful means of establishing the construct validity of a scale because, for scales with claimed interpersonal content, the pattern of relationships with circumplex variables should conform to the correlational structure of those variables themselves. So, for example, a measure of shyness should show an orderly (ideally, sinusoidal) pattern of correlations, with its peak at the Inhibited segment of the circumplex. (Gurtman, 1991, p. 671)

Gurtman's (1991) approach defines the interpersonalness of any given personality measure in terms of its vector in a two-dimensional interpersonal space:

> Thus, the interpersonalness of a scale can be evaluated by two criteria: the *length,* or magnitude, of its vector, which indicates *how much* interpersonal content the scale has, and the *direction* of the vector, which indicates the *kind* of content. (p. 671)

In a series of studies (Gurtman, 1991, 1992a, in press), Gurtman demonstrated the heuristic value of the circumplex as a nomological net for determining the construct validity of a variety of putative interpersonal versus noninterpersonal personality measures including loneliness, trust, self-monitoring, Machiavellianism, empathy, narcissism, dependency, the California *Q*-Set, and the like. Gurtman (e.g., 1992a) cautioned that his circumplex methodology is useful primarily for construct validation of measures that have substantial interpersonal content; such measures load mainly on the first two factors of the Big Five factors of personality.

CHAPTER 2

Interpersonal Behavior

Moderating Factors and Other Issues

A pat answer is the enemy of a fresh question.
(Kelly, 1969, p. 115)

In this chapter, we turn to a series of more esoteric but theoretically vital considerations for an interpersonal theory of personality. The first section reviews critiques of the interpersonal circle that have questioned whether it validly represents actual interpersonal behaviors during human transactions. We will find that the issue is subtle but important, and that its resolution increasingly favors the validity of the circle's behavioral representation. The next section considers a bottom-line scientific issue: Which unit of interpersonal behavior is being assessed by various inventories and other measures? Does interpersonal assessment characterize act-by-act negotiation, delimited time-sampled patterns of behavior, or long-standing interpersonal dispositions or styles? Next, the chapter addresses the influence of three important moderator variables—gender, situations, and time—on emergent interpersonal transactions. Inasmuch as, at a minimum, interpersonal theory adopts an interactionist position, interpersonal theory cannot *not* address the effects of these important variables on interpersonal enactments. The final section of the chapter details some central implications of the interpersonal circle for an expanded, more specific, and more heuristic theory of social reinforcement.

CRITIQUE OF THE TWO INTERPERSONAL DIMENSIONS

A number of observers (D'Andrade, 1974; D. N. Jackson & Helmes, 1979; Shweder, 1975, 1980, 1982; Shweder & D'Andrade, 1979) argue that interpersonal circle inventories, especially scales such as Wiggins's Interpersonal Adjective Scales (IAS), provide either (a) a taxonomy tapping little more than "response styles" or (b) an elegant statement of a near universal "implicit personality theory."

D. N. Jackson and Helmes (1979) suggested that interpersonal adjective scales confound content with "response style"; as a result, the circumplexity of, for example, the IAS-R may be artifactual. According to Jackson's theory of stylistic responding, individual differences in sensitivity to social desirability (salience) combined with differences in the threshold of socially desirable responding (threshold) would lead to a two-dimensional array of trait endorsements. Wiggins's (1979a) item-selection procedures for the original IAS might have selected trait terms particularly prone to the influence of these two stylistic parameters; accordingly, his circumplex may have no substantive basis.

D. N. Jackson and Helmes (1979) simulated the responses of 500 subjects to the interpersonal adjective scale taxonomy. Factor analysis of the simulated responses yielded two factors that accounted for almost 95% of the variance; these two factors closely resembled the salience and threshold dimensions from Jackson's theory. Jackson and Helmes also argued that the inclusion in the IAS of unusual terms such as "uncrafty," "unwily," and "warmthless" supported the view that item characteristics, rather than individual differences in traits, determined the structure. D. N. Jackson and Helmes (1979) stopped short of claiming that the new taxonomy taps "nothing but" response style, but they concluded that response style represents a plausible alternative explanation for Wiggins's (1979a) results.

According to Gifford and O'Connor (1987), D. N. Jackson and Helmes' (1979) argument is part of a larger critical tradition that denies the importance of substantive content in personality scales. In this tradition, the basic question is whether interpersonal circles "merely map the way observers think about interpersonal behaviors" or "can map or order the behaviors themselves" (Gifford & O'Connor, 1987, p. 1019). It has been suggested by Shweder (1982), D'Andrade (1965), and Shweder and D'Andrade (1979) that any measured network of personality traits (e.g., the two-dimensional interpersonal circumplex) is more a reflection of the culture's linguistic network of word-word associations than of a behavioral network of trait-trait associations. As a result, when respondents rate themselves or others on, for example, interpersonal inventories, "propositions about language are confused with propositions about the world" (D'Andrade, 1965, p. 215).

Shweder and D'Andrade (1979) offered a "systematic distortion hypothesis" according to which adjective scale circumplex models are simply reflections of the cognitive ordering (a cognitive template) of interpersonal behavior existing solely in the minds of observers or raters rather than an objective ordering of these behaviors by actors in the real world. Empirical support for the systematic distortion hypothesis was provided by Passini and Norman (1966), who instructed unacquainted undergraduates to rate each other's personalities by simply imagining what the other person was like. Resulting ratings yielded a factor structure nearly identical to that produced in other studies using the same set of personality scales. In light of this and other considerations, Shweder (1980) suggested that the personality structures in self-reports and in ratings generally reflect cognitive schemas rather than true relations among traits. Any instrument that requires use of memory and judgment in assessing personality or interpersonal style may be subject to the same set of cognitive biases.

Several lines of rebuttal and evidence have been advanced against both the Shweder and D'Andrade (1979) and the D. N. Jackson and Helmes (1979) arguments. First, Wiggins and Broughton (1985) found a wealth of external correlates for the IAS scales among a very large set of personality instruments; further, even scales from Jackson's own Personality Research Form conformed to the predicted circumplex ordering. McCrae and Costa (1989) argued that it is quite unlikely that all these other personality instruments suffered from the same alleged defects (p. 587).

Second, research (Kendrick & Funder, 1988) suggests that Shweder and D'Andrade's "systematic distortion" hypothesis is invalid. D. S. Weiss and Mendelsohn (1986) showed that the pattern of trait ratings stayed the same even under procedures to prevent subjects from relying on semantic similarities. Naturalistic and laboratory studies have demonstrated that trait attributions are indeed based on observable behavior (Gormly & Edelberg, 1974; Small, Zeldin, & Savin-Williams, 1983) and that the structure of traits found in implicit personality theory accurately reflects covariation among observed behaviors (Borkenau & Ostendorf, 1987). Several investigators (e.g., Weiss & Mendelsohn, 1986) have demonstrated that as the level of acquaintanceship increases, both interobserver and self-other agreement on personality scales increases. Paunonen, Jackson, Trzebinski, and Forsterling (1992), in a cross-cultural comparison, found that the structure of personality was remarkably robust, whether measured by traditional verbal questionnaires or by nonverbal materials. Furthermore, similar patterns of relations emerged when verbal and nonverbal formats were compared across four groups differing in language, culture, and nationality (Canada, Finland, Poland, and Germany). The authors argue that these findings imply strongly that "the measured organization of personality does not crucially depend on a common language or verbal heritage" (p. 454).

Third, in the specific case of the interpersonal circumplex, Gifford and O'Connor (1987; see also Gifford, 1991) attempted to circumvent the problem of cognitive bias by using objectively measured (nonverbal codings) social behaviors as criteria for validation of Wiggins's (1979a, 1979b) IAS. Their results demonstrated that self-reported personal space and several conversational behaviors, particularly those over which people have more control, can be mapped on the interpersonal circle. They concluded that the fact that Wiggins's "interpersonal adjective scales, which admittedly were developed from a purely lexical-statistical basis, so successfully order actual behavior lends strong support to the idea that they are not merely a mental map of dispositions, nor a fancy way to measure response bias" (Gifford & O'Connor, 1987, p. 1025). However, although their results provided strong support for the veridicality of the interpersonal circumplex, the scope of their study was limited to demonstrating (a) behavioral criteria (personal space preferences) related to the IAS Cold-Quarrelsome scale and (b) significant correlations between verbal and nonverbal involvement behaviors and the Aloof-Introverted versus Gregarious-Extraverted IAS scales.

Fourth, McCrae and Costa (1989) argued that if circumplex structure is artifactual, self-reports and ratings should define separate factors and separate circumplexes; if the structure is substantive, however, both should be represented in a single circumplex with the hypothesized circular ordering. To test their opposing hypotheses, they examined joint factors derived from self-reports on Wiggins's IAS and peer and spouse ratings made on their NEO Personality Inventory. Five factors that emerged were defined clearly from all three data domains, with the interpersonal circumplex occupying the two-dimensional plane defined by the Big Five factors of extraversion and agreeableness. McCrae and Costa (1989) concluded:

> Together with previous research using self-report instruments (Wiggins & Broughton, 1985) and observations of interpersonal behavior (Gifford & O'Connor, 1987), the ordering of interpersonal traits is a substantive finding, not an artifact of response biases, as D. N. Jackson and Helmes (1979) had suggested, or a projection of the subject's implicit personality theory. (p. 590)

Fifth, several studies bear on the convergent validity of the interpersonal dimensions of control and affiliation across modes of measurement within the same population. Hamilton (1971) found a high level of convergence between the dominance dimension of LaForge and Suczek's (1955) ICL and three other measures of dominance: self-ratings, the dominance scale of the CPI, and peer ratings of dominance. Golding and Knudson (1975) conducted a multitrait-multimethod study of sets of self-report and peer-rating instruments, including the Personality Research Form (PRF), the ICL, the Schedule of Interpersonal Response (SIR), the Rational S-R Inventory (RSR), the Marlowe-Crowne Social Desirability Scale, and peer and self-ratings of similar dimensions on 5-point Likert scales. Golding and Knudson's (1975; see also Knudson & Golding, 1974; Mungas, Trontel, & Winegardner, 1981) findings provided strong support for the cross-method convergence of the aggressive-dominance, affiliative-sociability, and autonomy dimensions.

Finally, D. N. Jackson and Paunonen (1980) cogently criticized the systematic distortion hypothesis simply by pointing out its proponents' failure to explain how such a linguistic framework could possibly arise independently of a behavioral network. In contrast, the basic assumption of lexical approaches to personality is that the most salient and socially relevant individual differences in people's lives will eventually become encoded into their language.

INTERPERSONAL INVENTORIES: MEASURES OF INTERPERSONAL ACTS? OR INTERPERSONAL STYLES?

An issue closely related to the situational band-width of interpersonal behavior (which will be discussed in a section to follow) involves conceptual and measurement distinctions between interpersonal actions versus interpersonal dispositions (traits or styles).

If our empirical analysis focuses on the interpersonal behavior of Person A, we can extend our measurement to A's behavior, not only with an interactant, Person B, but with various other persons with whom A interacts (or has interacted) in his or her life. Within interpersonal theory, personality is a complex set of interrelated intrapsychic and behavioral processes of persons that endure across time and situations. In Sullivan's (1953b) terms, personality is "the recurrent set of interpersonal situations which characterize a person's life" (pp. 110–111).

Study of A's interactions with other persons, then, ultimately involves characterizations of the environmental contexts in which these interactions occur, the defined roles of both A and the interactants in each of these contexts, the interface of the various A-B dyadic units with larger interpersonal systems (e.g., family, group, subculture) in which the dyad is embedded, and so on. Characterization of interpersonal behavior requires delineation of some duration of the A-B-A-B (etc.) interaction sequence. As we saw in Chapter 1, the period focused on can range from the "interaction unit" (A's speech turn, B's speech turn), through phases, episodes, and sequences, all the way to the entire history of transactions between A and B.

At *the most microanalytic level* of interpersonal behavior (the interaction unit), characterization of A's interpersonal behavior is in terms of acts (A's actions, B's re-actions; B's actions, A's reactions). At *the most macroanalytic level,* where A's (or B's) interpersonal behavior is measured from the viewpoint of a wide band of time- and persons-situations, characterization of A's interpersonal behavior is in terms of style or disposition. Within the circumplex model, traits are characterized by their angular position in the two-dimensional factor space. At levels between micro and macro, A's interpersonal behavior can be characterized only with newly invented terms because the available language of psychology offers no appropriate words.

Many interpersonal measures were constructed as inventories to measure interpersonal style in normative attempts to characterize and assess the comprehensive domain of interpersonal behavior; these attempts resulted in the various interpersonal circles constituting the conceptual-empirical models that guide both interpersonal theory and research. However, many of these same measures have also been adapted for ratings of acts (within interaction units) for the purpose of sequential analysis studies. Benjamin applied SASB codings (Benjamin et al., 1981) in a series of clinical applications (e.g., Benjamin, 1977, 1979a, 1979b, 1982; Benjamin et al., 1986; see also Brokaw, 1983; Brokaw & McLemore, 1988; Henry et al., 1986, 1990). Strong applied interpersonal circle codings (ICRS; Strong, Hills, & Nelson, 1988) in a series of studies summarized in Strong, Hills, Kilmartin, et al. (1988). Wilkie (1987) applied a 1982 Circle Acts Version (Kiesler, 1985) in a sequential analysis of complementarity in dyadic interaction.

Chapter 3 will detail the five levels of personality measurement conceptualized by the Kaiser research group (M. B. Freedman et al., 1951; Leary, 1957). Especially relevant to the present discussion are Levels I and II. Level I, "public communication," targets the overt interpersonal behavior of an individual as rated by another person, thereby describing what an individual does—the action level. Level II, "conscious description," targets the individual's covert experience by recording his or her self-reported perceptions of self or of others.

I (Kiesler, 1991) pointed out elsewhere that the preceding levels of analysis, in reality, are only end points on a continuum. At one end is the interaction unit describing the interpersonal behaviors of two actors in a reciprocally influential momentary transaction cycle. At the other end is the enduring pattern of interpersonal behaviors enacted by a person, which are assumed to demonstrate temporal stability and cross-situational consistency. In other words, the microanalytic level can be described more accurately as subsuming a sequential analysis describing interpersonal behaviors of two actors in a delimited (e.g., 10-minute) reciprocal transaction cycle. At the other end of the continuum (macroanalysis) is the more enduring pattern of interpersonal behaviors enacted by an individual over much longer periods, which is presumed to demonstrate considerable temporal stability and cross-situational consistency. The latter pattern is characteristic of a disposition or trait concept, especially as the trait concept has been broadened to include nonobservable behaviors such as emotions, motives, and attitudes (A. H. Buss, 1989; Funder, 1991; McCrae & Costa, 1990; McCrae & John, 1991; Tellegen, 1991).

It should be pointed out (cf. Kiesler & Goldston, 1988) that raters using checklist interpersonal inventories (e.g., ICL, CLOPT-R) do not in fact code the act-by-act behaviors of interactants by assessing the most microanalytic level, as do coders in interpersonal studies using sequential analysis (e.g., Billings, 1979; Henry et al., 1986, 1990; Shannon & Guerney, 1973). Although checklist respondents check, or do not check, the occurrence of specific overt behaviors of interactants, these judgments invariably are made after some elapsed period of focused interaction or observations (e.g., after 15 minutes of viewing a film). Even with relatively brief time lapses, checklist respondents still must base their judgments regarding the 16 circle categories on short-term memory. This short-term memory factor can add to checklist judgments unknown amounts of systematic bias resulting from the preferred interpersonal styles of the raters themselves.

The checklist rating task, thus, falls somewhere between more molecular, act-by-act codings and more molar ratings based on the entire history of the rater's previous transactions with (or observations of) a ratee. Ultimate answers to theoretical questions about interpersonal behavior, then, also require consideration of this important temporal dimension operative in developing relationships (Kiesler, 1983; Orford, 1986). I will discuss this more later in this chapter.

The adjective versus verb-phrase item format of the various inventories represents another difference among interpersonal measures that is conceptually related to the act-style continuum. *Verb-phrase items* seem designed, and necessary, for microanalytic coding or rating of interpersonal acts; *adjective items* seem designed for macroanalytic ratings of individuals' styles or dispositions. The pioneers in the empirical study of interpersonal behavior, the Kaiser Permanente research group (M. B. Freedman et al., 1951), were acutely aware of this difference:

> In rating the observed and recorded interactions [of group therapy participants], it was noticed that transitive verbs were the handiest words for describing what the subjects did to each other, e.g., *insult, challenge, answer, help.* In rating the content of the spoken or written descriptions of self-or-other, it was noted that adjectives were more often suitable . . . [e.g.] 'I am *friendly, helpful, strong;* they are *hostile, selfish, wise, helpful.*' A clear relationship seemed to exist between these two types of interpersonal description, such that the adjectives seemed to express an interpersonal attribute or potentiality for action, while the verbs described the action directly. (Leary, 1957, p. 63)

D. M. Buss and Craik (1983a) defined an act as a specific behavior in context (e.g., "When I am on a committee, I take charge of things"); a trait or disposition, in contrast, refers to a label that summarizes frequently occurring acts of a particular class. Importantly, in their view, no one-to-one correspondence exists between a single act and its signified disposition; to validly reflect a disposition, multiple constituent acts need to be sampled across situations and time.

The upshot is that interpersonal measures vary along an adjective (style, disposition) to verb-phrase (act) continuum of item format that affects, in some presently unknown manner, the results from studies of interpersonal behavior.

Interpersonal measures, further, can be used differently depending on the design focus of a particular investigation (Kiesler, 1987c, p. 17). The focus essentially can be on the actor, the inventory respondent (rater, interactant), or the actor-respondent transaction. In *"Actor-Focused"* studies, the central aim of the investigator is to characterize the overt behavior of Actor A, or the individual differences present in the overt interpersonal behaviors of selected groups of Actors. The design strategy is to eliminate any variance present in the Actor(s)'s interpersonal scores that derives from real differences in the interpersonal decoding styles of the Respondent(s). The investigator accomplishes this by using a sample of Respondents to rate the Actor's interpersonal behavior.

In *"Respondent-Focused"* studies, the aim of the investigator is to characterize the covert decoding or construal style of Respondent B, or of a group of Respondents. The design strategy is to randomize any variance present in the Respondent(s)'s item responses that derives from real differences in the overt interpersonal behavior of the Actor(s). By standardization or randomization of Actor subjects or conditions, the investigator attempts to ensure that the Respondent(s)'s item responses averaged across Actors will be good estimates of the "true" variance attributable to the Respondent(s)'s characteristic interpersonal decoding style.

Finally, *"Transaction-Focused"* studies incorporate the most complicated design strategy but the one most relevant to testing interpersonal hypotheses. In these studies, the investigator's central purpose is to characterize patterns in the conjoint, systemic, transactional behavior evident in some sample of Actor-Respondent dyads. A clearly distinguishing feature of these studies is that Actor and Respondent labels are interchangeable, in that each interactant's actions are coded in sequential analysis, or each interactant fills out an inventory on the other and dyadic scores are derived from the set. These studies, thus, always produce two sets of interpersonal measures: either one for A, one for B in act studies; or, in more microanalytic studies, alternative Respondent roles for each of two samples of subjects. The focus of analysis is on description of the system properties of various combinations of Actor-Respondent matches. As a result, neither the interpersonal behavior of the Actor nor that of the Respondent is of interest in and of itself. Instead, it is the degree and/or kind of fit, match, or "complementarity" of interpersonal actions or styles that is the crucial concern.

It seems that a comprehensive and sophisticated understanding of interpersonal behavior requires studies with all three concentrations: Actor, Respondent, and Transaction. This is especially the case for studies attempting to test the various propositions of interpersonal complementarity as articulated within the context of the interpersonal circle (Kiesler, 1983).

T. L. Wright and Ingraham (1986; Ingraham & Wright, 1987), further underlining the importance of these distinctions, have argued and demonstrated that the social relations model (Kenny & La Voie, 1984) provides a method to separate individual differences (Actor or Respondent) effects from relationship-specific (Transaction) effects in analysis of interpersonal behavior. The social relations model addresses both relationship effects and outgoing and incoming individual differences in social behavior by providing a method to partial out three separate sources of variance in a dyadic system: A's average behavior toward a sample of other persons (actor or perceiver effect); B's average behavior toward a sample of other persons (partner effect); and the dyad-specific adjustment A and B make to each other (relationship effect). Relationship effect, then, is the regular variability in an individual's behavior associated with interaction in a specific relationship, above and beyond individual differences of either member.

Using Round Robin analyses of variance (Warner, Kenny, & Stoto, 1979) of graduate students IMI ratings of each other in experiential groups, T. L. Wright and Ingraham (1986) tested for interpersonal complementarity and found clear support for correspondence of affiliative behavior but inconclusive results for reciprocity of control behavior.

Marcus and Holahan (1994), in a replication and extension of T. L. Wright and Ingraham's (1986) study, asked 27 women and 18 men from nine time-limited therapy groups to report their impressions of their fellow group members using the IMI and to respond also to self-report measures of assertiveness and self-esteem. A social relations analysis (Kenny & La Voie, 1984) of the data revealed both assimilation (i.e., a significant perceiver effect: how individual group members see people in general) and consensus (i.e., a significant partner effect: how group members as a whole see a particular group member) for the four traits (dominant, hostile, submissive, friendly) assessed by the IMI. However, the *relative* contributions of perceiver and partner effects appeared to vary depending on the trait assessed. The least consensus occurred for submissiveness, with subjects appearing to rely more on their own general ways of perceiving people when making these judgments. Findings also revealed a relationship between how subjects saw themselves before therapy and how they were seen by other group members. With regard to assertiveness and self-esteem, subjects' self-images were generally consistent with how their interpersonal behavior was perceived in group. The authors suggest:

> This finding is striking because the subjects completed the self-report questionnaires at least 2 weeks before the IMIs were completed, and the groups had only met for two 90-minute sessions at the time the IMIs were completed. Furthermore, different instruments were used for the self-report data . . . and for assessing the group's perceptions. (p. 780)

Marcus and Holahan (1994) strongly reiterated T. L. Wright and Ingraham's (1986) earlier conclusion that an integration of the social relations model and the 1982 Interpersonal Circle can provide a powerful framework for studying and understanding relationships.

GENDER AND INTERPERSONAL BEHAVIOR

A series of investigators have examined the role of gender as a moderating factor influencing interpersonal behavior: Carson and Shapiro (1985), Estroff and Nowicki (1992), J. M. Fitzgerald (1978), Goethe (1984), Gonick (1987), Kiesler, Wenzel, Chewning, and Davidson (1982), Lerner (1983), Moskowitz, Suh, and Desaulniers (1994), Pond (1985), Radecki-Bush (1989), Scheiner (1969), Wenzel (1980, 1984), Wiggins (1991a), and Wiggins and Holzmuller (1978, 1981).

As discussed in Chapter 1, Wiggins (1991a) aligned the concepts of agency and communion with the role expectations of human males and females. He noted, "Despite exceptions and potential difficulties, males have enacted agentic roles and females have enacted communal roles in most societies, up to and largely including the present era" (pp. 101–102). Reviewing research into sex roles and expectations from this two-dimensional perspective, Wiggins (1991a) cautiously concluded that precise application of Bakan's two concepts to the concepts of masculinity and femininity has yet to be realized. After reviewing the sizable literature on psychological masculinity and femininity, Helgeson (1994) concluded that the personality traits of both agency and communion are required for optimal well-being.

Research seems to establish that *sex-role stereotypes,* as measured by S. L. Bem (1974) and Spence, Helmreich, and Holahan (1979), subsume distinct and nonoverlapping patterns of interpersonal behavior. Findings suggest that masculine sex-typed persons are characterized by hostile-dominant interpersonal behaviors and feminine sex-typed persons by friendly-submissive behavior; in comparison, androgynous persons are less hostile-dominant than masculines and less friendly-submissive than feminines. In two studies, Wiggins and Holzmuller (1978, 1981) found that the masculinity and femininity scales of the BSRI are colinear with the dominance and nurturant axes measured by the IAS.

Estroff and Nowicki (1992) used subjects' ICL quadrant scores to construct complementary (hostile or friendly) or anticomplementary dyads of either same-sex or mixed-sex composition. The dyads then performed two cooperative tasks: completion of a jigsaw puzzle and generation of as many words as possible in response to a word association task. Results showed first that, whether hostile or friendly, complementary dyads performed better than anticomplementary ones on both tasks, significantly so on the jigsaw puzzle. Second, results revealed that gender had a significant impact on performance when dyads were complementary along the hostile dimensions (HD-HS pairings). Specifically, when males were dominant and females submissive in a hostile complementary dyad, the dyad performed worse on the puzzle than in any other complementary pairing; in fact, their performance was more similar to that of the anticomplementary dyads. Estroff and Nowicki (1992) speculated, in regard to the latter findings, that hostile-submissive women may evoke "oppositional aspects of the hostile-dominant men's style" and/or may have foiled the HD men "with subtle stalling or encumbering tactics" (p. 355).

Pond (1985) compared the interpersonal behavior of androgynous individuals with that of more rigid masculine and feminine sex-typed subjects. He put 72 women subjects from the three groups into pairs (M-F, M-A, F-A, A-A) and observed their behavior during a brief unstructured waiting-room interaction. In addition to coding a number of verbal and nonverbal behaviors, researchers rated the interpersonal behavior for each 15-second segment using the SASB coding system (Benjamin et al., 1981). Findings showed that dyads containing feminine women (F-A), compared with other dyads (which showed no differences), looked at each other less often and for shorter durations and engaged in fewer and briefer periods of mutual eye contact; the partners smiled less frequently; the dyads demonstrated less interpersonal complementarity and produced lower mutual attractiveness ratings. Further, the feminine women in the dyad talked significantly less than did all other women in the study; the androgynous partners of the feminine women displayed fewer directed gazes and nods and rated their feminine partners as less attractive. Pond (1985) concluded that the interpersonal impact of the feminine women was substantial; their anxiety and behavioral inhibition evoked inhibition in their partners that, in turn, reinforced their own inhibition and fulfilled their image of themselves as unattractive and inadequate. Their partners, whether masculine or androgynous, were not able to compensate for or override the feminine women's rigid self-presentations.

Moskowitz et al. (1994) examined the influence of situational variables on the appearance of gender differences in self-reported interpersonal behavior. They found that social role, but not gender role, influenced their subjects' "agentic" (control) behavior. At work, both males and females were more dominant when they were in a supervisory role with co-workers and were more submissive when they were in the role of supervisee. In regard to "communal" (affiliative) behavior, however, gender exerted a predominant influence: Independent of social role, men were more quarrelsome than women. Further, women with women were more communal than men with men. Moskowitz et al. demonstrated that gender differences were present in work situations only for communal behaviors, particularly when same-sex dyads were composed; in contrast, agentic behavior at work was primarily influenced by social roles varying in status and power.

J. M. Fitzgerald (1978) had a sample of undergraduates use the ICL to provide self-characterizations and to rate the behavior of a typical elderly person (over 65 years), and also obtained ICL self-ratings from a sample of elderly persons. Findings showed that among the college students, although differences in dominance and competitiveness were not clear-cut, females were found to be more nurturant, cooperative, and dependent. Likewise, few gender differences appeared within the elderly sample, although males appeared somewhat more power oriented than females. On the other hand, clear differences were found between the generational self-ratings and the college students' perceptions of elders in general. Elder men saw themselves as more cooperative and helpful than the college males saw themselves. Although both generations of women saw themselves as nurturant, college females saw themselves as much more dominating and hostile than did the elder women. J. M. Fitzgerald (1978) speculated, "The between generation differences indicate that the interpersonal style of older men and women may generally be more positive in affective tone and less concerned with power and control than the younger generation" (p. 400). Importantly, in contrast to the elders' self-ratings, the students' perceptions of their elders were characterized by more extreme ratings of dominance, competitiveness, and aggression. J. M. Fitzgerald (1978) concluded that descriptive differences were clearly present between the way older adults saw themselves and the way they were perceived by college students.

Radecki-Bush (1989) administered four self-report measures to a large sample of undergraduates. She performed a discriminant function analysis using the four Bem Sex Role Inventory (BSRI) types (instrumental, expressive, androgynous, undifferentiated) as groups and scores on the CLOIT-R, FIRO-B, and IIP as predictors. She identified two functions that accounted for about 82% of the variance: low instrumentality and low expressiveness, corresponding to hostile-dominant and friendly-submissive patterns of interpersonal behavior. Other analyses showed that low instrumentality predicted interpersonal problems with self-assertiveness, self-independence, and self-esteem. Low expressiveness, in contrast, predicted problems in being interpersonally supportive. Low levels of both traits (instrumentality and expressiveness) were related to interpersonal problems in being intimate, supportive, sociable, and too aggressive. Finally, consistent with the thesis that persons with more flexible interpersonal patterns are better adjusted, findings showed that subjects who displayed a wide range of both instrumental and expressive interpersonal behavior reported low levels of interpersonal problems. Radecki-Bush (1989) concluded that BSRI instrumentality and expressiveness are related to self-described interpersonal behaviors that reflect patterns of control and affiliation behaviors.

Wenzel (1980) investigated the effects of interviewer touch on androgynous versus traditional female interviewees. She hypothesized that androgynous interviewees, having found the conventional rules of touching and status to be unacceptable, would report more friendly and less dominant impacts when an interviewer did not touch them; that traditional women, having internalized the sex-role standards based on a disparity of status, would report more friendly and less dominant impacts when an interviewer did touch them.

Samples of androgynous and traditional female undergraduates were interviewed by three female androgynous graduate students who had been trained to standardize their interview behavior. During the interview, half the subjects were touched three times, half were not. At the end of the session, each interviewee filled out an IMI on the interviewer. A series of analyses of the IMI and other data showed no significant effects. As a result, none of Wenzel's (1980) hypotheses was confirmed.

In a follow-up study, Wenzel (1984) investigated the effects of interviewer touch by male and female interviewers as it interacted with affiliative versus dominant nonverbal behavior upon the impacts experience by interviewees exposed to these conditions. Female undergraduates were randomly assigned to touch versus no-touch, affiliative versus dominant nonverbal context, and male versus female interviewer conditions. Four graduate students (two female, two male) served as interviewers. Again, at the end of the interview the undergraduates filled out IMIs on their interviewers.

Wenzel's (1984) results showed that, regardless of the other two conditions, all interviewers in the dominant nonverbal context impacted subjects as being less friendly and more dominant. Experimental manipulation of the nonverbal context, thus, was highly successful and discriminating. Other results showed that the dominant nonverbal context also produced higher levels of subjects' anxiety and lower verbal productivity; whereas the affiliative context resulted in lower subject anxiety and higher productivity. Interestingly, all female subjects reported higher anxiety with male interviewers. Finally, once again, Wenzel's predictions regarding the effects of touching were not confirmed.

Goethe (1984) used the IMI to evaluate a treatment program for persons with self-reported deficits in heterosocial skills. Videotaped segments, extracted from pre- and posttreatment standardized interviews, were presented to a group of observers (two males, two females) who filled out IMIs on each subject after viewing a particular segment. Analyses showed that all low-heterosocial-skills subjects impacted opposite-sex observers, in contrast to same-sex observers, as being more detached and succorance-seeking and less nurturant and affiliative; in addition, all subjects impacted opposite-sex observers as being less friendly and more hostile. Goethe (1984) speculated that the different impacts experienced by same versus opposite-sex observers reflect a more critical, scrutinizing, or high-expectancy stance among opposite-sex observers.

Gonick (1987) found that sex of clinician was not related overall to clinical judgments of diagnostic severity and prognosis. However, male (versus female) clinicians were less severe in their diagnoses of a hostile-submissive client (as determined by CLOPT ratings); female (versus male) clinicians were less severe in their diagnoses of a friendly-submissive client.

Kiesler et al. (1982) studied the impacts of psychiatric outpatients on male and female intake interviewers in a mental health training clinic. Findings showed that patient gender had no effect on IMI engagements reported by the intake interviewers as a whole. However, gender of the *interviewer* did show an important effect: Male interviewers reported stronger submissive impacts from all patients than did female interviewers. Also, male interviewers reported stronger mistrusting engagements from female patients; female interviewers reported more mistrust of the male patients. Finally, only male patients evoked different levels of affiliation from the interviewers, with male interviewers reporting stronger affiliative impacts than did female interviewers. Within the therapy context, gender seemed to matter as follows: Male interviewers were impacted more strongly by submissive patient behaviors, regardless of patient gender; all interviewers reported more mistrust to opposite-sex patients, male therapists additionally reporting stronger friendly impacts for male patients.

SITUATIONS IN INTERPERSONAL BEHAVIOR

Several investigators have examined the function of situations as moderators of interpersonal behavior: Carson (1969), Duke and Nowicki (1982), Kiesler (1982b, 1983, 1986b, 1991), Kiesler, Bernstein, and Anchin (1976), Moskowitz (1982, 1986, 1988, 1990, 1993, 1994), Moskowitz and Cote (1995), Moskowitz et al. (1994), and Schwaninger-Morse (1979).

The extent of generalization of personality trait or interpersonal behavior across various situations or contexts has been an enduring concern for theorists and researchers. The earliest, radical trait, position was that personality characteristics generalize across situations, with minimal influence from specific situations. Mischel (1968) served as a gadfly to the entire field with his documented view that human behavior is highly specific to situations and that generalizations incorporating notions such as personality traits cannot be validly made across situations.

In the mid-1970s Mischel's argument was successfully refuted and replaced with an interactionist position (e.g., Endler & Magnusson, 1976; Magnusson & Endler, 1977; Mischel, 1973) asserting that both traits and situations contribute important and varying proportions to determination of human behavior. Most recently, the earlier notion of emphasis of traits without specific reference to situational influences has started to re-appear (e.g., Funder, 1991; McCrae & John, 1991).

Contemporary interpersonal authors have argued that *interpersonal theory adopts an interactionist position whereby a person's interpersonal acts reflect the conjoint effects of person and situation factors* (Carson, 1969; Duke & Nowicki, 1982; Kiesler, 1979, 1982b, 1983; Kiesler, Bernstein, & Anchin, 1976). The interactionist view holds that overt behavior is a function of the continuous feedback between the person and the situation; the person is an intentional and active agent in the interaction process; cognitive factors are the essential determinants of behavior; and the psychological meaning assigned to the situation is a major determinant of behavior.

I have argued further that *by far the most important class of situations consists of "other persons," or more precisely, of the presenting interpersonal style of various interactants.* Interpersonal theory asserts that interpersonal behavior is an interaction between the characterological dispositions of the individual and the situational influences of interactants' behavior. From a similar perspective, Goffman (1961) noted that the situation refers "to the full spatial environment anywhere, within which an entering person becomes a member of the gathering that is (or does then become) present. Situations begin when mutual monitoring occurs and lapse when the next to last person has left" (p. 144).

Modern trait theory (e.g., Funder, 1991; Tellegen, 1991), which can subsume contemporary interpersonal theory, conceives traits as descriptions of not only how a person behaves in certain situations; of equal importance, traits describe something about the intrapsychic functioning of the individual. Although the presence of a trait can be inferred only on the basis of overt behavior, the construct refers to both overt behavior and the psychological structures and processes that mediate the overt behavior. Modern conceptions of traits encompass both the covert and overt components of the interpersonal transaction cycle that characterizes interpersonal behavior.

M. L. Snyder and Ickes (1985), after reviewing the literature on selective interaction, concluded (as would contemporary interpersonal theory) that *persons choose situations that provide them with opportunities to express their characteristic dispositions and preferred patterns of interpersonal behavior.* Through this process, humans come to display the transsituational consistency and transtemporal stability so integral to trait conceptualizations.

An important task for interpersonal investigators is to specify classes of situational factors relevant (and irrelevant) to elicitation of interpersonal acts from the respective octants of the interpersonal circle. For example, what kinds of situations does a HD: Cold-Hostile person tend to seek out as well as to avoid? Which aspects of others' interpersonal behaviors tend to be selectively perceived (and selectively filtered out)? In which contexts is the HD person's style likely to be elicited most strongly (or not at all)? This issue will be reviewed in detail in Chapter 3. Duke and Nowicki (1982), addressing the point that most interpersonal theorists have not specified situations beyond the general category of significant others, described an initial taxonomy of situations that has guided their social-learning/interpersonal research program.

Interpersonal complementarity theory (Carson, 1969; Kiesler, 1983) itself provides one component of any valid situational taxonomy by specifying the predicted complementary, anticomplementary, and acomplementary octant pulls of a particular interactant's interpersonal behavior. "Complementary interactions evoke approach behaviors from both participants, anticomplementary ones lead to avoidance or escape actions, and acomplementary interactions evoke a mixture of approach and avoidant responses from both participants" (Kiesler, 1983, p. 209). Quite supportive of this suggestion is the work of Forgas (1979), who studied people's perceptions of everyday social situational contexts or social episodes. Application of multidimensional scaling and hierarchical clustering methods to his data produced two-dimensional representations of "situation perception" that often bear striking resemblances to the two-dimensional interpersonal domain. Nevertheless, it is crucial that investigators address the interactions of these transactional patterns with other environmental or contextual factors.

Schwaninger-Morse (1979) tested the assumption that a person's overt task behaviors would reflect primarily situational demands, whereas the person's interpersonal style (expressed through more subtle nonverbal behaviors) would be more consistent and generalizable across situations. Using the IMI, she measured the impacts of subjects on female observers over a series of four role-playing situations. Each subject enacted either a dominant or submissive role while engaging in either a positive or negative interaction with a partner. As measures of overt behavior, she used two temporal speech measures: talk-time and turn-taking frequency.

Her hypothesis that subjects' speech behavior would vary according to role conditions was supported for the talk-time measure: Subjects spoke longer when participating in the dominant role assignments. Swaninger-Morse's (1979) hypothesis that interpersonal impacts would be generalizable across conditions was partially supported: Impacts from subjects' dominant interpersonal behavior were mostly consistent across the role and interaction conditions; however, impacts from affiliative and submissive behavior were not.

In a systematic program of research, Moskowitz has examined the cross-situational generality of the control and affiliation behaviors that anchor the axes of the interpersonal circumplex (Moskowitz, 1982, 1986, 1988, 1990, 1993, 1994; Moskowitz & Cote, 1995; Moskowitz et al., 1994). Moskowitz (1994) reviewed her own and others' studies that have demonstrated clear limits on the cross-situational generality of dominance (interestingly the bipolar opposite of dominance, submissiveness, has been rarely studied). As Moskowitz (1994) speculated, dominance does not generalize across different categories of "agentic" relationships, that is, across interaction partners such as teachers versus peers for children and friends versus strangers for university students. However, when others in the situation represent "communal," or familiar, relationships dominance generalizes across many types of activities during childhood and adolescence.

In regard to behaviors on the affiliation axis, Moskowitz (1994) reviewed research indicating that *friendliness is consistent across different types of interaction partners, such as familiar and unfamiliar others; however, the evidence is inconsistent as to whether friendliness generalizes across different types of activities.* Moskowitz speculated that friendly and quarrelsome interpersonal behaviors should show moderate levels of generality across situations involving communal relationships.

In her own study, Moskowitz (1994) examined the influence of situational variables (status roles: boss, co-worker, supervisee; gender-match or not) of interactants on gender differences in interpersonal behavior sampled from the control (dominant, submissive) and affiliation (friendly, quarrelsome) axes of the interpersonal circle. Samples of subjects' interpersonal behavior were obtained in their natural (work) settings using an "experience sampling method" in which subjects recorded daily (for 20 days) their control and affiliation behaviors during significant interactions (any one lasting at least 5 minutes); they also recorded the interactant's gender, work relationship, and personal relationship vis-à-vis the subject.

Moskowitz (1994) found modest-to-low generality for control behaviors across "agentic" situations in which individuals varied in power and status (supervisor and co-worker). She observed that this finding was not surprising for dominance behaviors given the extensive literature on dominance hierarchies in the social organization of humans and other primates. On the other hand, cross-situational generality was moderately high for affiliation behaviors across communal situations (acquaintances and friends). Moskowitz (1994) commented:

> This level of generality across communal situations was particularly striking given Mischel's (1968) critique of traits. He had argued that cross-situational generality did not exceed .3, whereas the present research indicated that across communal situations, cross-situational generality typically exceeded .5. (p. 930)

When examining gender differences, Moskowitz found that both men and women adapted their agentic behaviors to fit power/status differentials ascribed by the work setting; both men and women were more dominant when they were in a supervisory role than when they were with co-workers or in the role of supervisee. However, gender differences were found for communal behaviors in work situations, particularly when same-sex dyads were compared: Women with women were more communal than men with men; in particular women with women were less quarrelsome than men with men. Moskowitz (1994) concluded:

> Whereas the demonstration of consistency across one set of situations supports the status of [interpersonal] traits as predictor variables, the demonstration of specificity across another set of situations points to the need to incorporate situational variables into the study of traits. (p. 932)

In a second study using the same experience sampling method, Moskowitz and Cote (1995) contrasted three trait models in relative ability to predict pleasant affect from interpersonal traits. The *global* trait model correlated interpersonal traits (agreeable, quarrelsome, dominant, submissive—the four axis poles of the interpersonal circumplex) with pleasant affect aggregated over occasions and situations (60 data points over 20 days). The *situational congruence* model assessed the relationship of dominant and submissive behavior with pleasant affect in specific trait-relevant situations only (interactions with boss vs. co-worker over 20 days). The *behavioral concordance* model assessed the extent to which pleasant affect was associated with occurrence of trait-relevant behaviors regardless of situation (only occasions over the 20 days when trait-relevant behaviors occurred).

Moskowitz and Cote (1995) found no support for either the global or situational congruence trait models. However, hypotheses generated from the behavioral concordance trait model were fully supported for the interpersonal traits of agreeableness and quarrelsomeness; one of the two hypotheses concerning dominance was supported; neither hypothesis for submissiveness was supported. Their study generally confirmed the behavioral concordance model's prediction that individuals will feel pleasant affect when they behave consistently with their traits (e.g., S's high on quarrelsomeness experienced pleasant affect when they engaged in quarrelsome behaviors, and unpleasant affect when they engaged in agreeable behaviors).

Moskowitz and Cote (1995) speculated that one reason they did not obtain confirmation for three of four predictions on the control axis may have stemmed from the important distinction between imposed and chosen situations. Emmons and his associates (Emmons & Diener, 1986; Emmons, Diener, & Larsen, 1986) found for a sample of undergraduates that traits and affect are more closely related in chosen situations than they are in imposed situations. Moskowitz and Cote suggested that affect may be more related to traits in situations in which individuals perceive a greater degree of control over their own behavior and perceive more influence over what happens as a consequence of their behavior.

In line with the "imposed versus chosen" situational dichotomy, Proposition 4-9, which I present in Chapter 4, will state that interpersonal complementarity applies primarily to *naturally occurring, relatively unstructured interpersonal situations;* the extent to which it applies in various structured situations or in other environmental contexts remains to be determined. Examples of natural, unstructured situations are informal conversations at parties, free-time activities and encounters, intimacy transactions, and open-ended therapy interviews. The common feature in all these situations is that minimal expectations exist regarding socially correct or desirable responses or social role definitions (e.g., boss-employee, teacher-student). "Essentially, an unstructured situation is one that can appropriately elicit from interactants the entire range of interpersonal acts. Also, typically it is in unstructured situations that most interactions with significant others occur" (Kiesler, 1983, p. 209).

Finally, when considering situational factors, we must keep another point in mind: *The "radical trait" assumptions of transituationality and transtemporality* (Mischel, 1968) *more validly apply to maladjusted persons than they do to more normal* (mild-moderate levels, more flexible behavior choices) *individuals.* The interpersonal definition of maladjusted behavior (extreme and rigid acts on the interpersonal circle), as Chapter 6 will elucidate, plainly indicates that, relative to normals, the actions of abnormal individuals tend to override differences in situational parameters, including different behavioral patterns of interactants.

THE TEMPORAL DIMENSION IN INTERPERSONAL BEHAVIOR

A number of investigators have examined the role of time in general, and stage of relationship in particular, as moderating factors influencing interpersonal behavior: Coulter (1993), Dietzel and Abeles (1975), Duke and Nowicki (1982), Kiesler and Watkins, (1989); Nowicki and Manheim (1991), Pincus (1994), Tasca (1988), Tasca and McMullen (1993), Tracey (1993), Tracey and Ray (1984), and Tracey and Sherry (1993). As C. M. Werner and Haggard (1985) observed, "Time is an integral aspect of interpersonal relationships. Relationships grow and change, continue, develop, and even disintegrate over time" (p. 59).

Study of interpersonal transactions that persist over time inevitably takes one into the realm of human "relationship." Generally, the relationship between two persons consists of the total pattern of recurrent interactions between them. Development of a relationship requires a history of transactions that typically is differentiated into five general stages (Peterson, 1989): acquaintance, buildup, continuation, deterioration, and ending.

It seems face valid that *patterns of interpersonal behavior are influenced by different constraints and perform different functions depending on which phase of a relationship a particular dyad finds itself.* Pincus (1994), for instance, cautioned, "It is unlikely that the majority of interpersonal transactions of importance in understanding [normal and] maladaptive personality take place at 'zero acquaintance' but are rather one point in an ongoing relationship" (pp. 123–124).

If, in studying interpersonal behavior, we choose to focus at the microanalytic level using interpersonal act-by-act coding systems, it is possible to describe in some detail the nature of a specific interpersonal transaction as it unfolds. In this regard, Pincus (1994) noted that investigators have yet to establish the most useful duration to measure an interaction sequence. For example, we can adopt a sequential analytic strategy, attempting to code covert and overt action-reaction units stochastically (Kiesler, 1986a, 1991; Peterson, 1977, 1979a, 1979b, 1979c, 1982). However, as Pincus observed, at this point a paradox occurs for interpersonal assessment. Although a maladaptive transaction cycle may recycle only once, the interpersonal situation of interest will more often involve a significant number of cycles of covert and overt responses. At some point in the transaction, we begin to describe not a unit of specific interpersonal acts, but a set of covert and overt interpersonal behavior patterns.

Duke and Nowicki (1982) proposed that interpersonal relationships progressed through four temporal phases: choice, beginning, deepening, and termination. From their perspective, the negotiation of relationship definition is not as essential during the earliest stages of a relationship, but becomes more important as the interaction continues over time. Thus, complementary transactions should be less important, with overlearned codes of manners more important, when the interaction is a brief one between strangers. However, as a relationship continues past its early stage, the importance of overlearned conventions fades and the basic negotiation of the relationship in terms of complementary transactions begins to take place. Complementary transactions ought to determine relationship valence only when interactions progress past the initial stage.

In line with this formulation, Nowicki and Manheim (1991) predicted that the positive effects of complementary interactions would be obtained in a longer as opposed to a shorter term relationship. Specifically, they predicted that in a longer term interaction (75 minutes vs. 5 minutes) complementary female dyads performing laboratory tasks would show a higher number of verbalizations, prefer less interpersonal distance between themselves, and report more attraction toward one another. Confirmatory findings were obtained for the longer interacting dyads only, for the two behavioral measures (verbalizations and distance); the third measure, level of self-reported attraction, failed to differentiate the complementary groups during the longer interaction. Hence, while interacting, the longer duration dyads demonstrated "the positive impact of complementary interpersonal styles" (p. 330) through their greater number of verbal exchanges and their maintenance of closer interpersonal distance—but not through their greater attraction.

Nowicki and Manheim (1991) speculated that the lack of consistent empirical support for the complementarity hypothesis reported by Orford (1986) may be due, in part, to an inability to pinpoint precisely the time at which interactants should be affected by the degree of complementarity of their interpersonal behaviors. They note further that, consistent with the results of their study, other investigators who have found support for the complementarity hypothesis went beyond a single brief interaction or studied interpersonal behavior over differing lengths of time (e.g., Dietzel & Abeles, 1975; Rausch, 1965; Shannon & Guerney, 1973).

Another arena in which the temporal relationship has been shown to exert powerful influence on the pattern of complementarity is during the stages of psychotherapy. An often confirmed interpersonal prediction has been that during successful therapy the patient and therapist will move from rigid and extreme complementary transaction early in therapy, to a noncomplementary position in the change-oriented middle phases of therapy, to a final-stage transactional pattern that exhibits mild and flexible complementarity. A series of related studies supporting this prediction (e.g., Coulter, 1993; Dietzel & Abeles, 1975; Kiesler & Watkins, 1989; Tasca, 1988; Tasca & McMullen, 1993) will be discussed in detail in Chapter 10.

IMPLICATIONS FOR BEHAVIOR THEORY AND SOCIAL LEARNING

Several theorists have drawn important implications of interpersonal principles for behavioral and social learning analyses (Brokaw & McLemore, 1983; DeVogue & Beck, 1978; Kiesler, Bernstein, & Anchin, 1976; Safran, 1984a, 1984b; Safran & Segal, 1990; Safran, Vallis, Segal, & Shaw, 1986; Turner, Foa, & Foa, 1971). DeVogue and Beck (1978) argued that "behavioral technology has become limited by the failure of behaviorists to incorporate into their viewpoint a broad theory of human relationship" (p. 204). Applying Leary's (1957) interpersonal model to their review of the social reinforcement literature, they concluded:

> Only in friendly dominant/friendly submissive dyads . . . would social "reinforcement" in the form of praise and approval have its maximum effect. In any nonreciprocal [i.e., noncomplementary] dyad . . . we could predict less frequent use of the target response by the subject in this reciprocal dyad. . . . Especially when the subject attempts to use hostile dominance vis-à-vis the reinforcer, the subject may show *a decrease* in the target response in order to avoid the aversive stimulation of praise and approval. (p. 221, italics added)

Hence, in psychotherapy and other helping relationships:

> The utility of a warm, empathic approach quite possibly is limited to those clients who present themselves initially to the therapist as friendly and submissive, since they would constitute the only clients who would find the approach nonaversive. (p. 235)

In a similar vein, Brokaw and McLemore (1983) argued that a significant portion of current social-reinforcement research utilizes friendly reinforcers assumptively, without demonstrating their reinforcement efficacy for the particular behaviors targeted. Their study contrasted the assumptive notion with the interpersonal prediction that different reinforcers are required for different behaviors. Their findings supported the *interpersonal principle* that *"reinforcers will vary according to the complements of targeted behaviors"* (p. 1018; italics added): For subjects' targeted hostile-dominant behaviors, confederates' hostile-submissive reactions produced significantly more frequent continued hostile-dominant target behaviors than did confederates' friendly-submissive reactions. Brokaw and McLemore concluded, "The interpersonal conceptualization of complementarity represents an important component of the reinforcement construct" (p. 1019).

Kiesler, Bernstein, and Anchin (1976) argued that behavior therapies had ignored, deemphasized, or had not developed constructs and operational assessments for key therapeutic factors that loom central in interpersonal communication theory. Various chapters of their book developed the assertion that *the multiple phenomena of client-therapist relationship need to be systematically incorporated into behavior therapy theory and practice.* They analyzed traditional constructs of resistance and transference from their interpersonal communication perspective, highlighting that the self-defeating interpersonal relationship messages that a patient sends the therapist may be representative of the patient's central self-defeating interactions with other significant persons. Kiesler (1979) detailed a list of operational indices of relationship in psychotherapy and elsewhere.

Safran (1984a, 1984b) has argued convincingly for a rapprochement between cognitive-behavioral and interpersonal therapies. For example, Safran (1984b) documented how Sullivan's concepts of personification, parataxic distortion, selective inattention, security operations, and dynamism predated but are compatible with contemporary theory and research in cognitive psychology and can be contributory to important amplifications of contemporary approaches to cognitive therapy. Safran (1984a; Safran et al., 1986) detailed specific ways in which incorporation of interpersonal principles can broaden and enrich cognitive therapy's theoretical and practical scope: (a) understanding and dealing with problems in both therapeutic compliance and maintenance, (b) broadening its conceptualization of the role of emotions in psychotherapy, and (c) incorporating the technique of pinpointing dysfunctional automatic thoughts of a client as part of the interpersonal intervention of metacommunication (Kiesler, 1988). Safran's interpersonal elaborations of cognitive behavioral therapy will be presented in greater detail in Chapters 3, 9, and 10.

CHAPTER 3

Covert Components of Interpersonal Behavior

The most important risk in interpersonal action is the risk of self. In every encounter people take the risk that their self might be confirmed or disconfirmed; their face might be lifted, enhanced, lost, or totally destroyed. For that matter, their character might be redeemed or lost.

(Swensen, 1973, p. 439)

Although a major focus of interpersonal research has been study of overt interpersonal behavior through applications of interpersonal circle measures, considerable emphasis has been placed also on the covert, cognitive events that are central to human transactions. As Pincus (1994) noted, interpersonal theorists have emphasized various interpersonal intrapsychic processes: personifications, selective attention, and parataxic distortions (Sullivan, 1953a, 1953b); emotions, action tendencies, and dyadic interpretations (Kiesler, 1982a, 1987c; Kiesler et al., 1985; Kiesler, Schmidt, & Wagner, in press); expectancies (Carson, 1982); fantasies and self-statements (Brokaw & McLemore, 1991; Safran, 1990a, 1990b); and cognitive interpersonal schemas (Foa & Foa, 1974; Hill & Safran, 1994; Muran, Samstag, Segal, & Winston, 1992; Muran & Segal, 1992; Safran, 1990a, 1990b; Safran & Hill, 1989; Safran & Segal, 1990; Wiggins, 1982).

Snugly within the Sullivanian tradition, Leary (1957) defined personality as "the pattern of interpersonal processes employed to reduce anxiety, ward off disapproval, and maintain self-esteem" (p. 119)—as "the multilevel pattern of interpersonal responses (overt, conscious, or private) expressed by the individual" (pp. 15–16). Carson (1969) defined personality as "nothing more (or less) than the patterned regularities that may be observed in an individual's relations with other persons, who may be real in the sense of actually being present, real but absent and hence 'personified' or 'illusory' " (p. 26).

It seems evident that an individual's characteristic cognitive or construal style, whether disordered or not, contributes significantly to both encoding and decoding processes inherent in interpersonal transactions. The closely associated term, trait, refers to both overt behavior and the psychological structures and processes that give rise to it (Funder, 1991; Tellegen, 1991). Modern trait theory conceives traits both as descriptions of how a person behaves in certain situations and, equally important, as descriptions of something about the intrapsychic functioning of the individual's mind (Funder, 1991).

SULLIVAN'S SELF-DYNAMISM

Sullivan (1953a, 1953b) felt that *humans basically strive to minimize insecurity.* We accomplish this when we are able to minimize the disapproval of significant other persons, thereby minimizing the experience of anxiety. The major function and *raison d'être* of the self-system, thus, is to avoid, evade, or eliminate anxiety. We attempt to integrate interpersonal situations in terms of affiliation and power. By satisfying people who matter to us, we are spared the experience of uncanny anxiety. By avoiding disequilibrium (disjunctive relationships) in our interpersonal situations, we retain a good feeling about who we are as well as participate reciprocally with others in dynamic interaction.

Sullivan articulated an *anxiety mechanism* by which we respond empathically to the mood of others; if that mood is hostile or disapproving, we experience the mood directly as a tension or anxiety. Anxiety is always triggered or evoked interpersonally and serves as (a) a major indicant of insecurity, (b) a signal of danger to self-respect, and (c) the major disruptive force in interpersonal relations.

In Sullivan's writings, emotional reactions or feelings reflect the pattern of needs that are at play in the interpersonal situation. If the level of emotion is too great in a situation (the range extends from euphoria to uncanny emotion), the integration will suffer as the person finds the tension impossible to direct properly.

Sullivan (1953a, 1953b) considered interpersonal anxiety to be basic in human development. The major learning involves discovery by the infant and child that some behaviors reduce or eliminate the intensity of interpersonal anxiety, while other behaviors increase or exacerbate anxiety. A gradient of anxiety becomes associated with different behaviors, potentially ranging from relatively mild anxiety-provoking behaviors to acts that elicit intense anxiety or terror. In discriminating increasing from decreasing anxiety, the child learns to alter his or her behavior in the direction of the latter. In Sullivan's words:

> People who ride on roller coasters pay money for being afraid. But no one will ever pay money for anxiety in its own right. . . . Not only does no one want anxiety, but if it is present, the lessening of it is always desirable, except under the most extraordinary circumstances. (Sullivan, 1954, p. 100)

According to Sullivan's *anxiety-transmission theory,* the tension of anxiety, when present in the mothering one, induces anxiety in the infant:

1. If the mother's momentary state while interacting with her child is relaxed, confident, loving, and at ease, the child experiences euphoria; any concurrent behaviors being enacted by the child, as a result, become personified as "Good Me."
2. If the mother's state while interacting with her child is uncertain, unloving, rejecting, and tense, the child experiences dysphoria; any concurrent actions of the child become personified as "Bad Me."
3. Finally, if the mother's state while transacting with her child is beset with terror, horror, loathing, impending doom ("uncanny" emotion), whatever the child

was doing concurrently becomes dissociated from consciousness, residing in the self-dynamism as "Not Me."

A child's self-definition is shaped by a continuum of experienced anxiety. His or her self-personification contains a set of Good Me interpersonal behaviors that have been associated with minimal anxiety, that are highly valued and frequently performed, as well as a set of Bad Me behaviors that have been associated with moderate anxiety, that are highly devalued and infrequently performed. In addition, totally outside phenomenal awareness, but operative within the self-dynamism (self-schema), resides the dissociated Not Me that targets behaviors that have been associated with maximum anxiety and are seldom, if ever, performed or even available to the person as options during interpersonal transactions.

Ingraham and Wright (1987) used Kenny and La Voie's (1984) social relations model to investigate the importance of interpersonal relationships in anxiety. Two studies examined a training group of graduate students and an outpatient psychotherapy group. In both studies, Ingraham and Wright found that relationship-specific variance was significant and accounted for a substantial proportion of the variance, thus supporting Sullivan's hypothesis of the importance of relationships in anxiety. On the other hand, they found only partial support (in the psychotherapy group only) for Sullivan's hypothesis that anxiety is exclusively a function of relationship rather than of individual difference factors; in the training groups, they found that anxiety was a function of both individual differences and relationships.

It is challenging, as well as important theoretically, to speculate as to how Good Me, Bad Me, and Not Me self-personifications might be represented on an individual's summary profile plotted from his or her scores obtained on an interpersonal circle inventory. First, it seems relatively straightforward that a subject's *peak scores* (two or three highest segments; or highest octant) would characterize the behavioral expression of his or her Good Me personification; the Peak scores, after all, express the person's preferred interpersonal style of interaction with others. To illustrate, let's say that a hypothetical subject's peak scores fall at the friendly-dominant octant. This person's self-definition, then, places a core value on interacting with others from a friendly-dominant stance.

Second, it seems plausible that subjects' *Nadir segments* (typically zero scores; Goldston, 1990) and/or subjects' *segments (or octant) directly opposite their peak scores* would define interpersonal behaviors that rarely, if ever, are available to them during transactions; these unavailable behaviors would express individuals' Not Me conceptualizations, which are mostly unconscious (in Sullivan's theory, which are part of their self-dynamisms rather than being part of their self-personifications proper). Enactment of these behaviors would be extremely threatening to an individual because they are inconsistent with the person's self-definition (self-presentation) on both axes of the circle. For our hypothetical subject, the octant opposite to friendly-dominant, hostile-submissive, would represent his or her Not Me behavioral expression. Hostile-submissive behaviors are inconsistent with friendly-dominant behaviors on both circle axes—hostile contradicts friendly, and submissive contradicts dominant.

Lastly, it seems plausible that *segments (or octant) that are anticomplementary to subjects' peak scores* would define subjects' Bad Me self-personifications. These segments represent behaviors that are inconsistent with a subject's self-definition (self-presentation) on one of the two axes only. For our hypothetical subject, the octant anticomplementary to the Peak (friendly-dominant) octant is hostile-dominant.

Hostile-dominant behaviors are inconsistent with friendly-dominant behaviors on the affiliation axis only (hostile contradicts friendly), whereas dominant is consistent with dominant.

I will summarize this discussion in the form of a theoretical assumption:

Proposition 3–1.   Based on scores obtained from an interpersonal circumplex inventory, a subject's peak segments characterize the behavioral expression of the subject's Good Me personification; scores on the nadir segments and/or segments directly opposite the peak segments represent the individual's Not Me personification; and segments that are anticomplementary to the subject's peak segments define his or her Bad Me personification.

The types of complementarity will be clarified and elaborated in Chapter 4.

Sullivan's (1953b), thus, put a heavy emphasis on the schema-equivalent construct of "self-dynamism" and the associated concepts of "self-personification" and "personification of others." The *self-dynamism* was defined as *a complex system, mainly unconscious, that was formed out of the person's experiences with the approval and disapproval of others that leads the person to behave so as to avoid the insecurity (anxiety) of disapproval;* by use of this system we satisfy the people who matter to us and therefore satisfy ourselves, and are spared the experience of anxiety. For Sullivan, the self-dynamism is mostly unconscious; controls awareness through a subception-like process ("selective inattention"); serves primarily to avoid disapproval; is primarily defensive in preservation of security; is entirely interpersonally determined through "reflected appraisals" from significant others that determine the Good Me, Bad Me, and Not Me subdivisions of the self; and controls the direction of development the personality will take.

The self-personification—phenomenological and less inclusive than the self-dynamism—combines the Good Me and the Bad Me into a single self-image. The Not Me, because it includes images and behaviors that evoke uncanny emotion, remains hidden in dissociated, unconscious regions of the self-dynamism. Andrews (1991) adds:

> Each person achieves a self-consistent feedback environment through a complex of large and small self-fulfilling prophecies that support his or her initial expectations about self and experience. People will selectively counteract, avoid, or discount feedback that suggests that they are not who they think they are. This establishes a negative feedback loop that tend to return a system to its original equilibrium after a disturbance. (p. 12)

COGNITION IN INTERPERSONAL BEHAVIOR: CONTEMPORARY FORMULATIONS

Within contemporary interpersonal theory, increasing emphasis is being placed on the covert, cognitive events that are central to human transactions. It seems evident that an individual's characteristic cognitive or construal style, whether disordered or not, contributes significantly to both encoding and decoding processes inherent in interpersonal transactions. Sullivan's (1953a, 1953b) original interpersonal statement put a heavy emphasis on the schema-equivalent constructs of "personification" of self and of others.

M. B. Freedman et al. (1951) and Leary (1957) provided a five-levels model for measurement of interpersonal behavior that included *assessment of both overt and covert behaviors* along a continuum of awareness to unconsciousness. Leary and Coffey (1955) described their task as follows:

> First, we define the important levels of behavior—this is an a priori, theoretical decision. Then we measure these levels separately. . . . We rate each level by itself. Then we fit the unilevel ratings into a pattern which reflects the dynamic interplay among the levels. (p. 115)

Leary also emphasized the importance of empirical indices that document the degree of variability or inconsistency in characterizations of a person from these multiple perspectives (see also Madison & Paddock, 1983).

The five levels Leary (1957) articulated were as follows:

- *Level I,* "public communication," targets "the overt behavior of the individual as rated by others along the 16-point circular continuum" (p. 77). It designates what a person does, the action level, the communication process. Level I data are objective or public (rather than subjective or private), a measurement of the person's social stimulus value.
- *Level II,* "conscious description," refers to "the verbal content of all the statements that the subject makes about the interpersonal behavior of himself or 'others' " (p. 78). It targets the person's phenomenological field by recording the person's reported perceptions of him- or herself and his or her interpersonal world. Level II data are subjective and private self-reports. While a single interactant's ratings of a person would constitute Level II data, the mean ratings from a group of interactants or observers would constitute Level I data.
- *Level III,* "private perception/communication," refers to "the expressions that an individual makes . . . indirectly about an imagined self in his preconscious or symbolic world" (p. 154). Measurement taps the person's fantasies, wishes, and dreams to characterize the interpersonal motives and actions attributed to the characters of the fantasy play. Level III data employs projective measures like the TAT to characterize what the person preconsciously symbolizes about self and others.

Leary (1957) added two other levels to the previous three originally advocated by the Kaiser Permanente groups (Freedman et al., 1951).

- *Level IV,* "the unexpressed," refers to "those interpersonal themes which the [person] consistently, significantly, and specifically omits in the three other levels" (p. 192)—themes that are not expressed consciously and preconsciously. It targets interpersonal themes that are systematically and compulsively avoided in the person's phenomenological field and that are "conspicuous by their inflexible absence" (p. 80). Level IV is measured by inspection of circle profiles to discover what is omitted, which can then be characterized by some "omission" or "avoidance" score.
- *Level V,* "values" or "ego ideal," refers to "the interpersonal traits and actions that the subject holds to be 'good,' 'proper,' and 'right'—his picture of how he should be and would like to be" (Leary, 1957, p. 88). It characterizes how the person wants us to see his or her ideals, which values he or she consciously stresses.

Leary recommended that researchers study the interpersonal behavior of a person at all five levels. He felt ("organismic assumption") that "any level takes on its full meaning only in relationships to all the other levels, that is, to the total personality organization" (p. 157). He believed, further, that charting the measurements for all levels of behavior "on the same circular grid provides a systematic pattern diagnosis of the structure of personality at one time" (p. 75). Finally, he offered some "variability indices" (Leary, 1957, p. 252, Table 10) "by which we can measure conflict and inter-level discrepancy . . . which relate behaviors at different levels" (p. 240). Despite Leary's differentiation of five levels, by far the majority of interpersonal research has concentrated on the Kaiser group's first two levels.

Carson (1969, 1971, 1979, 1982, 1991) provided an in-depth analysis of interpersonal behavior with particular emphasis on cognitive components. His 1969 volume provided an incisive review of Sullivanian constructs, which he translated into the cognitive language of "plans" and "strategies" in the tradition of G. A. Miller, Galanter, and Pribram (1960). Reviewing evidence for the circumplex arrangement of interpersonal behavior, Carson then analyzed interpersonal complementarity using constructs from Secord and Backman's (1961, 1965) balance theory. In the final section of his book, Carson merged the four quadrants of the interpersonal circle with rewards and costs derived from Thibaut and Kelley's (1959) exchange theory; then constructed a 4 × 4 matrix for classifying interaction sequences for the study of interpersonal transactions in personality, psychopathology, and psychotherapy.

Carson (1982) offered the fundamental cognitive hypothesis that *a person's behavior is designed to produce consequences in and reactions from others that confirm the principal hypotheses (perceptions, expectations, or construals of other persons) organizing his or her world.* In Carson's view, an "unbroken causal loop" (p. 66) exists among (a) a person's social perceptions or cognitions, (b) his or her behavioral enactments, and (c) reactions of interactants that confirm the person's cognitions or expectancies. Carson (1979) further speculated that persons who are dispositionally passive count on others to assume the dominant position with them; consequently, their world is largely populated by assertive and dominant individuals. Affiliative persons, on the other hand, do not usually bring an expectation into a relationship but instead wait to see what the other person is going to be like; if anything, affiliative persons tend to have a generalized positive attributional set toward others, thereby judging differences along the affiliation-hostility dimension to be more salient than differences in dominance-submission.

Safran (1984a), like Carson, argued that "cognitive activities, interpersonal behaviors, and repetitive interactional or *me-you patterns* are linked together and maintain one another in an unbroken causal loop" that he named the "cognitive interpersonal cycle" (p. 342). Safran concluded that "a full assessment in the context of a *cognitive-interpersonal* therapy requires that the therapist conduct a comprehensive exploration of both the specific interpersonal behaviors and me-you patterns that impair the client's interpersonal relations, and the particular cognitive activities that are linked to them" (pp. 345–346). Kiesler (1986a, 1988) developed both Carson's and Safran's notions of causal loops into a more comprehensive model for general psychopathology, the "Maladaptive Transaction Cycle," which will be presented in detail in Chapter 6 (see also Figures 6–1 and 6–2).

Meddin (1982) argued that symbolic interactionism (the dominant social psychological perspective in sociology) is complementary to cognitive therapy and that, when combined, the two present an enlarged picture of personality dynamics and thereby offer enhanced opportunities for intervention and change:

> Given the reciprocal interaction between cognition and interpersonal behavior, a good case can be made for increasing focus upon what the client is *doing in specific social interactions,* as well as continuing a focus upon what the client is thinking. More specifically, what is the client doing that *influences the thought processes* via feedback from others and the self? What are the messages or meanings *elicited by the client from others* that exacerbate perceptions of threat, inadequacy, rejection, and so on, and that also result in increased negative input to conceptions of the self? (pp. 158–159)

Meddin advocated that while continuing to concentrate on changing an individual's self-dialogue, comparatively more systematic attention needs to be directed toward the questions of (a) the origins of self-conversation and, most importantly, (b) the role of the environment in sustaining inner dialogue over time. "Symbolic interactionism directly addresses both these issues" (Meddin, 1982, p. 151).

INTERPERSONAL RESEARCH INTO SELECTIVE ATTENTION, EXPECTANCIES, AND COGNITIVE CONSTRUAL OF INTERPERSONAL INFORMATION

In Sullivan's system, through selective attention a person avoids attending to an anxiety-arousing situation by attending to other things. Because the person refuses to recognize that the situation exists, he or she does not experience anxiety about it. The paradoxical result is that the individual must pay close but unacknowledged attention to some aspects of the self or of relationships with others to make sure that he or she never becomes aware of them (Sullivan, 1953b, p. 319). Sullivan (1953b) observed, for example, that "the person who greatly respects himself for his 'generosity,' which is probably always of a very public character, finds an incredible number of people ungenerous, stingy, mean, and so on" (p. 309).

A series of investigators have examined individual differences in interpersonal expectancies and selective attention as well as in cognitive construal of interpersonal information: Alimiras (1967), Alpher and France (1993), Altrocchi (1959), Benjamin and Wonderlich (1994), Carson (1979), Chirico (1977, 1980), DeSoto and Kuethe (1959), Dodge and Somberg (1987), Dodge and Tomlin (1987), Forgas (1979), Frey (1981, 1986), Gascoyne (1985), Golding (1977, 1978), Golding and Knudson (1975), Golding, Valone, and Foster (1980), Haslam (1994), Hokanson, Hummer, and Butler (1991), Holton and Pyszczynski (1989), Hudgins (1982), Kivlighan and Angelone (1992), Kivlighan et al. (1994), Lochman (1987), McNeel and Messick (1970), Meredith (1986), Monts, Zurcher, and Nydegger (1977), Olsson (1968), Pasciuti (1982), Perlmutter (1980), Pyszczynski, Greenberg, and LaPrelle (1985), Saxby (1982), Scheiner (1969), Sikes-Nova (1990), Smelser (1961), and Taplin (1968).

In a series of studies, Forgas (1979) applied multidimensional and hierarchical clustering methods to the study of people's perceptions of everyday social situational contexts or social episodes. His two-dimensional representations of "situation perception" often bear striking resemblance to the two-dimensional interpersonal domain.

Golding (1978) argued that the field must come "to grips with the apparent fact of individually different psychological realities" (p. 85). Golding and colleagues (Golding, 1977, 1978; Golding & Knudson, 1975; Golding et al., 1980) attempted to define covert variables as *psychological organizing principles* of perception.

> If psychological experience, and hence psychological reality, can be shown to be lawfully organized within the person, and further, if such organizational principles can be assessed and related to various developmental, genetic, and experiential events, then we can be in a position to study psychological functioning at an epistemological level consistent with the phenomena themselves. (Golding, 1978, p. 82)

Golding et al. argued that construal is a dynamic process of active interpretation using selected cues that individuals repeat in a characteristic fashion. Construal, according to these authors, takes place in three stages: (a) selective attention focuses on specific salient cues; (b) decoding these cues is directed by motives or goals; and (c) cognitive representation of these cues occurs in terms of affect or linguistic cues that represent the traits, judgments, intentions, or motives observed.

After reviewing the research, Golding et al. (1980) concluded that *subjects differ in the dimensions they use to evaluate others.* However, although some research exists to relate construal style to personality correlates or motivational states, they observed that this is often difficult to replicate, possibly due to restricted population, methodology, or simplistic theories about construal.

In an earlier study, Golding (1977) demonstrated that attribution or construal style is, to some extent, consistent with interpersonal self-definition as measured by the ICL's four quadrant patterns: H-D, H-S, F-S, F-D. Golding found that during ongoing relationships in which complementary styles prevailed, friendly-submissive individuals overattributed traits of dominance and friendliness to others. Hostile-dominant persons instead attended to the control dimension far more than to the affiliation dimension, thereby overattributing both hostility and submissiveness to others. In regard to the latter finding, Golding (1977) found that Machiavellian individuals (a) exhibited a generalized tendency to attribute unfriendliness, hostility, and dishonesty to others, (b) tended to place much more weight than average individuals on the perceived dominance-submission of an interpersonal act in arriving at social judgments, and (c) tended to overattribute hostility and submissiveness to the same interpersonal acts that the average person sees as less hostile and more dominant. On the other hand, friendly-dominants and hostile-submissive individuals exhibited no clear construal sets. Thus, some persons acting on their beliefs about satisfying the needs of control and affiliation with others demonstrated an attributional style (expectancies) and behavior consistent with those beliefs.

Altrocchi (1959) hypothesized that a person chooses to interact with, and tends to perceive other people in terms of, the complement of his or her own degree of interpersonal dominance (a person who is highly dominant tends to see others as highly submissive; a moderately submissive person tends to see others as moderately dominant). Altrocchi's results, however, failed to confirm his hypothesis.

Carson (1979) conceptualized internal variables as cognitive categories of interpersonal expectancies developed in early life and out of conscious awareness. He drew on the research of Golding (1977) to support his hypotheses about expectancies. According to Carson, distinctive behavior is derived from distinctive expectancies carried by the individual. These beliefs are related to the way we satisfy our needs for love and status; we have a preferred mode designed to maximize outcome for satisfaction of these needs. In general, individuals tend to perceive the world in a manner that confirms or justifies their self-definitions. *Each of the four quadrant styles implies beliefs about others in the world and a preferred style for satisfying needs.* For example, hostile-dominant people tend to act in accordance with their view of others as winners or losers; their interpersonal behavior tends to evoke hostile-submissive behavior from others; as a result, a self-fulfilling prophecy is repetitively enacted.

Carson (1979) detailed the specific kinds of interpersonal experience persons in each interpersonal style type would be *un*likely to have in their relations with others:

> The world of people who comport themselves passively is one largely populated by dominant, assertive others. . . . The rigidly hostile-dominant personality . . . lives in a world in which love is largely unknown; it is a jungle, and in that jungle there are only winners and losers. . . . The hostile-submissive personality . . . also lives in a jungle, but one in which, besides himself, there are only winners. . . . It is only the affiliative-dominant individual who . . . has an essentially unconstrained experience with others, an experience that should enable him or her to be relatively unbiased when assessing the behaviors of others. (pp. 262–264)

Carson (1979) conceptualized that, during interpersonal transactions, a given individual, depending on his or her circle quadrant diagnosis, would rarely, if ever, perceive certain interpersonal patterns of behavior. The hostile-dominant (H-D) individual would rarely experience friendly-dominant (F-D) or friendly-submissive (F-S) interactant behaviors; the hostile-submissive (H-S) individual would rarely experience F-D, F-S, or H-S; and the friendly-submissive would rarely experience H-S or F-S; in contrast, the friendly-dominant individual has the freedom to experience interactant behavior from all four quadrants.

Olsson (1968) found that, compared with a moderately friendly (ICL) group, overly friendly subjects perceived less hostility in hostile persons; the two groups did not differ in their hostility ratings for neutral and friendly persons. Also, hostile-dominant subjects attributed more hostility to hostile interactants, whereas hostile-submissive subjects attributed more hostility to neutral (neither hostile nor friendly) and friendly interactants.

Sikes-Nova (1990) found that therapists' IAS-R ratings of their patients yielded distinct patterns among the quadrant groups regarding attitudes toward expression of needs. Overall, she found that the hostile groups (H-D and H-S) and the friendly-submissive group accounted for the most problematical motivational structure. The H-S group demonstrated the most negative attitudes toward assertive needs and other needs concerning the dominant-submissive dimension. The F-S group seemed to demonstrate a similar trend, with less extreme scores. The H-D group showed a tendency to deny or suppress the need for autonomy, suggesting infrequent and extreme expression, and also demonstrated unusual and unrealistic beliefs about how men express and satisfy the rejection need. Finally, the F-D group appeared relatively free from problematic motivation variables.

Sikes-Nova (1990) found that the relationship between selective attention measures and interpersonal quadrant style was complex. For discrepancy-angle-index scores, the H-D group was found to account for a large proportion of high scores (based on therapist ratings); the next largest proportion was accounted for by the F-S groups. Subject self-report placement did not yield any relationship to discrepancy angle scores. These results confirmed Carson's (1979) suggestions that the H-D and F-S groups tend to overattribute interpersonal characteristics. Her discrepancy-vector-index score was not found to be significantly related to any one interpersonal quadrant based on either patients' self-report or therapist ratings; however, the same trend found for the discrepancy-angle-index emerged.

Analysis of Inventory of Interpersonal Problems (IIP) revealed that F-D and H-S patients who were objectively labeled (therapist ratings) tended to endorse problems consistent with their quadrant placements. F-D patients did not report any significant level of problems while, in 11 of 12 problem categories, the H-S group reported the most problems.

Alpher and France (1993) noted the established relationship of childhood abuse to DSM disorders involving difficulties with identity development (dissociation disorder, multiple personality disorder, and borderline personality disorder). They tested the assumption that childhood psychosocial trauma (sexual, physical, and emotional abuse) influences perceptions and expectations about interpersonal relations. Perceptions of relationships with childhood abusers were examined for a clinical sample of adult DSM dissociative disorder and multiple personality disorder patients. Alpher and France (1993) hypothesized that repeated scenarios of *appeasement* ("behavior of the victim that is *less* hostile and controlling than behavior of the initiator," p. 503) for the abuser could lead to dysfunctional long-term consequences for the abused child in interpersonal behavior and self-concept. They observed that, although abuse may be perceived by the victim as hostile and controlling behavior, the victim's response of continued friendliness and toleration of such behavior may predict later involvement in dysfunctional relationships.

Results showed that, years after the occurrence of abuse, the internalized relationship with the abuser, as reflected in SASB ratings, manifested both *non*complementarity and a developmentally significant appeasement response to social provocation. Alpher and France (1993) concluded that "clarification of a noncomplementary appeasing relationship paradigm may be important in providing a context for recall and psychotherapeutic reconstruction of such experiences" (p. 508).

Benjamin and Wonderlich (1994) used SASB to compare the social perceptions of borderline, unipolar, and bipolar-depressed inpatients. As predicted, borderline patients were found to differ in their social perceptions, viewing their relationships to their mother, hospital staff, and other patients as more hostile and autonomous than did mood-disordered patients.

Gascoyne (1985) studied the effects of interpersonal self-perceptions on judgments that a sample of undergraduates made about others. After providing self-ratings on the IAS, subjects rated on the IAS two videotaped interactions in which target subjects had been trained to portray either hostile-dominant or hostile-submissive interpersonal patterns. Results showed that subjects with extreme self-ratings of interpersonal style assigned higher, more extreme ratings to both videotaped individuals than did the less extreme, more flexible subjects. Also, subjects assigned the most extreme IAS ratings to the videotaped individual whose behavior was opposite on the circle to their own (e.g., the hostile-dominant videotaped person was rated more extremely by friendly-submissive subjects). Gascoyne (1985) observed that subjects assigned the most extreme ratings to the stimulus who greatly epitomized the impression they were endeavoring to avoid. Finally, less extreme subjects rated the hostile-dominant video-taped individual as more extreme than they rated the hostile-submissive individual; more extreme subjects, in contrast, did not differ in their ratings of the two individuals. Gascoyne (1985) concluded that interpersonal self-descriptions and descriptions of others are, indeed, systematically related.

Scheiner (1969) examined differential perceptions of the average U.S. citizen obtained from samples of Buddhist Japanese and Moslem Middle Eastern students who had been in the United States less than one year. Subjects filled out ICLs on self, on their cultural ideal, and on the average American of their experience. Results showed that the Japanese students differentiated themselves from Americans on the dominance circle axis; Middle Eastern students differentiated themselves most markedly from Americans on the love axis. The students' like versus dislike of Americans had no effect on their ratings of Americans on the respective superordinate axis (dominance for the Japanese, affiliation for the Moslems). However, students who liked Americans (vs. those who did not) described Americans as very similar to themselves on the axis that was subordinate in their self-descriptions—the Japanese described Americans as more like them in affiliative behavior, the Middle Eastern students described Americans as more alike in dominant behavior. Scheiner (1969) concluded that areas of interpersonal behavior that are culturally patterned (for Japanese, higher vs. lower status; for Moslems, generosity, hospitality, and nurturance) constitute areas in which cross-cultural person perception operates independently of affective (like-dislike) reaction. In contrast, positive affective reaction highlights those subordinate characteristics that people expect in other citizens of their country whom they like.

Chirico (1977) investigated perceptual/decoding differences between psychometrically selected (nonclinical) groups of obsessive and hysteroid individuals. Obsessive and hysteroid female undergraduates recorded their reactions to a simulated interview in which the interviewer portrayed a dominant, and the interviewee a submissive, interpersonal style. The interview was presented in the form of either visual cues only (a silent videotape), vocal cues only (audiotape masked by a random splicing procedure), or verbal cues only (a typescript of the interview).

"Channel dominance" for the obsessive versus hysteroid observers was hypothesized to be reflected in the differential strength of their responses to the three interview presentation conditions, as indexed by their reactions to the interviewee on the submissive and inhibited scales of the IMI and on potency items on a semantic differential measure.

Chirico (1977) found that his obsessive (versus hysteroid) female observers, in the typescript condition, reported stronger corresponding impacts to the submissive interviewee and characterized the interviewee as being less potent. In contrast, the hysteroid observers reported stronger submissive and impotent reactions after viewing the visual-only presentation. The audio-paralanguage condition produced no differences. Chirico (1977) concluded that his results support the notion that personality groups differ in perceptual/decoding abilities and may show differential channel-input dominance in their decoding of interpersonal behavior.

Chirico (1980) sought to replicate and extend his previous study using the same videotaped interaction between a submissive interviewee and dominant interviewer. Again, psychometrically selected obsessive and hysteroid female subjects were used, but this time they were assigned to one of four communication channel groups: face-only video, body-only video, audio only, or verbal only (typescript). In addition to viewing one of the four channel conditions, each subject also subsequently viewed the unedited all-channel videotape. After each presentation, subjects completed the IMI and semantic differential measure on the submissive interviewee.

Replicating the finding of his previous (1977) study, Chirico found that obsessives (vs. hysteroids) registered stronger submissive-inhibited impacts in reaction to the linguistic (typescript) channel; moreover, obsessives were impacted as strongly from the typescript as they were from the all-channel original videotape. These findings confirmed again the importance an obsessive individual places on words in the decoding process.

Contrary to the earlier finding that hysteroids decode better than do obsessives on nonverbal channels, results showed that obsessives recorded stronger impacts to the submissive interviewee in all four channel conditions as well as for the all-channel videotape. Chirico (1980) speculated that, although the literature suggests that hysteroids seem to be better communication *encoders* than obsessives, his results suggest that obsessives have the upper hand in *decoding* a submissive interpersonal communication style. Finally, Chirico (1980) found that both personality groups showed weaker impacts from the vocal than from the linguistic presentation; both personality groups also recorded stronger submissive impacts from the body-only visual display than from the head-only presentation.

Hudgins (1982) used Chirico's videotape of a female actress portraying a submissive interviewee to examine whether differences between Whitehorn and Betz's A versus B therapist types could be linked to perceptual/decoding preferences on the same visual-only, audio (paralinguistic), and linguistic (typescript) conditions Chirico's (1977) study used. Hudgins' analyses of IMI and semantic differential scores found that, of the three conditions, the visual-only channel evoked the strongest submissive and inhibited impacts on all subjects (the audio-only condition produced the weakest impacts). A-types (versus B-types) reported stronger submissive impacts from the visual-only presentation. Finally, Hudgins (1982) found no differences between male and female subjects in decoding ability across the communication channels.

Saxby (1982) used the IMI in a study of person perception. He investigated how a subject's sex, a labeling (psychiatric versus normal) of the person being observed, and the interpersonal behavior (dominant versus submissive) of the observed target person is actually perceived as registered by subjects' impacts. Undergraduates were presented one of four written scripts in which dominant or submissive "psychiatric patients" or "normal" interactants were portrayed, after which they filled out IMIs on the target person. Results showed that the dominant and submissive portrayals were validated by the corresponding impacts recorded. Further, both male and female subjects were affected by the presence of the psychiatric label but responded to it differently. Males scored both the submissive and dominant interviewee as being less submissive when that person was labeled a mental patient; females perceived both interviewees as more submissive when the interviewee was labeled a mental patient.

Yalom (1985) proposed that *group therapy members respond differently to the same stimuli; that is, each group member may perceive and experience the group in different ways.* Kivlighan and Angelone (1992) tested this notion by examining the relationship between group members' interpersonal problems (IIP-C) and their perceptions of the group atmosphere or climate (using a group climate questionnaire). They hypothesized (a) that group members who perceived themselves as too dominant, relative to those who see themselves as too submissive, would characterize the group atmosphere as primarily promoting submissive behaviors—avoidance (relying on others for support and guidance) and anxiety (unsure in their interactions); and (b) that persons who viewed themselves as too cold, relative to those who saw themselves as too nurturant, would perceive the group atmosphere as colder (in conflict, and not engaged). Results generally supported Kivlighan and Angelone's (1992) predictions, although other specific analyses were not consistent with expectations from interpersonal theory. They concluded that their results "demonstrate that not everyone perceives the group in a similar manner . . . differences in perception of group climate depend on individual interpersonal problems" (p. 472).

Kivlighan et al. (1994) conducted a similar study to that of Kivlighan and Angelone (1992) using a large number of undergraduate growth group members. They hypothesized that a positive relationship would exist between members' problems along the control or affiliation dimension of the interpersonal circle and members' perceptions of the group leader along the same respective dimensions. Prior to participation in the growth groups, members filled out the IIP; after each group session, members filled out a scale measuring seven facets of group leader behavior. Results revealed that, over the first 10 group sessions, too-dominant group members perceived group leaders as more dominant; too-cold group members perceived the group leaders as less affiliative. Also, findings showed less relationship between member interpersonal problems (measured pretherapy) and leader ratings over time, with decreases in association being more pronounced along the control than the affiliation dimension. The authors concluded that their results, coupled with those of Kivlighan and Angelone (1992), indicate:

> Group member interpersonal problems may reflect a cognitive set through which the group members filter their experience of the group leader and group interactions. . . . By selectively perceiving others in terms of one's own interpersonal problems, the group members set up a self-fulfilling prophecy which can maintain their interpersonal problems. (Kivlighan et al., 1994, p. 102)

This conclusion is supported by other studies showing that group members' interpersonal style is related to the types of events the member perceives as most helpful (S. M. Freedman & Hurley, 1979; Kivlighan & Goldfine, 1991; Kivlighan & Mullison, 1988).

Other explorations of the cognitive components of interpersonal behavior have found additional suggestive results. Hokanson et al. (1991) found that depressed subjects overestimated hostility in their roommates while underestimating friendly roommate behavior; in contrast, normal subjects overestimated the frequency and degree of friendly responding by their roommates. Holton and Pyszczynski (1989) found that liking or disliking someone may lead a person to selectively seek information that provides an informational basis to justify his or her evaluation of that individual. The greater a person's desire to positively or negatively evaluate someone, the more he or she will selectively seek information consistent with such an evaluation. Frey (1981, 1986) and Pyszczynski et al. (1985) demonstrated that individuals selectively search for information consistent with self-serving attributions.

Several researchers have produced evidence of a *positivity bias* in the perception of interpersonal interactions. De Soto and Kuethe (1959) found that *subjects rated the occurrence of positive interpersonal relations more probable than negative interpersonal relationships.* McNeel and Messick (1970) found that subjects assumed a positive interpersonal encounter would ensue before obtaining any information about the two interacting individuals or the interaction context. Alimiras (1967) found that ratings of liked acquaintances were overwhelmingly positive, while ratings of disliked acquaintances reflected both positive and negative traits; he concluded that these results were evidence of a general reluctance to ascribe negative characteristics to interpersonal relationships. However, other research shows that individuals with competitive conceptualizations of self believe that the world is populated homogeneously by competitive others; whereas individuals with cooperative concepts of self believe that the world is populated by both competitive and cooperative people (Kelley & Stahelski, 1970).

Several studies have found that aggressive elementary school boys frequently interpret innocent actions by others as personally threatening (Dodge & Somberg, 1987; Dodge & Tomlin, 1987; Lochman, 1987). Dodge and Somberg (1987) showed aggressive and nonaggressive boys a videotape in which one boy spills paint on another boy's art project, with the result being that the first boy wins a painting contest. Although the videotape was deliberately unclear about whether the spill was malicious or accidental, the aggressive boys tended to interpret the act as intentionally harmful; further, they were more likely than the nonaggressive boys to say they would respond with anger. Lochman (1987) found that aggressive boys often fail to see their own acts as aggressive, but are quick to interpret other boys' actions against them as acts of aggression.

An important recent study suggests that the relationships between our covert construal of interpersonal behavior and actual patterns of overt interpersonal activity may be quite complex. Haslam (1994) investigated the mental representation process for social/interpersonal relationships. He noted that, although a broadly consensual circumplex model of understanding social behavior exists involving dimensions of affiliation and control, no agreed-on model of mental representation of social relationships has emerged.

Haslam felt that the categorical relational models theory proposed by Fiske (1991, 1992) offered considerable promise. The model proposes four basic relational frames or structures that are cognitive sources for generating social action, for making sense of others' social behavior, and for coordinating and evaluating social interaction. The four frames are communal sharing, equality matching, authority ranking, and market pricing.

Haslam (1994) hypothesized that categorical forms corresponding to Fiske's relational models theory would provide superior prediction of interpersonal behavior prototypicality judgments than would the Kiesler and Wiggins complementarity models (see Chapter 4). In preparation for a judgment task, subjects were instructed:

> Some possible combinations of two people's interpersonal behaviors are better examples of relationships than others. That is, some combinations seem less likely, less plausible, and less easily imagined than others; they don't seem to go together and to fit our idea of what social relationships tend to be like. (p. 579)

Results of two studies provided convergent evidence that implicit knowledge of social relationships is modeled better by a small number of logical, discontinuous representations or categories (Fiske's relational models theory) than by the dimensional complementarity laws of either Kiesler or Wiggins. Both of two Fiske categories contributed significantly and independently to the prediction of prototypicality judgments in the two studies, and both yielded stronger effects than the alternatives.

Haslam (1994) concluded:

> The apparent superiority of the categories suggest that it is necessary to question the appropriateness of theories of the organization of actual social relationships when these are used as accounts of their cognitive organization . . . [Theories that] have proven to be very fruitful for the behavioral investigation of social relationships and interpersonal interaction . . . may not be appropriate when mental representations are the focus of study. (p. 583)

Until recently, contemporary interpersonal theory has concentrated on explanations of overt behavior and has devoted little attention to the cognitive and other events that occur simultaneously under the skins of individual participants. Many questions need answers. For example, what are the specific self-definitions, cognitive assumptions, expectancies, and the like that characterize a person exhibiting a DE: Cold-Hostile pattern of interpersonal behavior? What are the specific attributes that such a person values in self and others? Or despises? Or finds frightening? What are the specific rational and irrational self-statements that propel this person's preferred self-presentations to others? What are the cognitive styles that shape and color his or her perceptual and other experience? Specification of the distinctive content and style of a person's cognitive events is necessary if we are to fully understand that person's overt interpersonal behavior and if we are to intelligently design differential therapeutic interventions.

It's important, then, to emphasize that *interpersonal behavior encompasses not merely overt, observable transactions between two individuals; it refers also to the private, unobservable, symbolic (fantasized) interactions and dialogues between self and other conducted by either.* Study of these symbolic interactions attempts to understand not only the nature of the active cognitive schemas or "personifications," for both the other member of the dyad and for persons more generally, but the reciprocal relationships of each person's cognitive events to respective action-reaction sequences occurring in the arena of their conjoint overt behavior.

Interpersonal behavior refers to recurrent patterns of reciprocal relationship present among two persons' *covert and overt actions and reactions* studied over some period (sequence) of their transactions with each other (Kiesler, 1991).

SELF AND SELF-OTHER SCHEMAS IN INTERPERSONAL THEORY

In recent years, the concept of schema has become central in cognitive theories of psychopathology and psychotherapy. The functioning of self-schemas derived from social interaction has been detailed in several reviews (e.g., Markus & Zajonc, 1985; Wyer & Gordon, 1984). The schematic structure that has received most attention from cognitive therapists is the self-schema. This working model of the self influences attention, encoding, storage, retrieval, inference, and planning and anticipation.

A common usage of the self-schema concept derives from research and theory in the social cognition domain. In this tradition, Markus (1977) defined *self-schemas* as "cognitive generalizations about the self, derived from past experience, that organize and guide the processing of self-related information contained in an individual's social experience." These self-schemas are "deeply involved in the processing, interpretation, and memory of personal information" (T. Rogers, Kuiper, & Kirker, 1977, p. 677).

Markus (1990) documented the development of self-schemas in the context of significant interpersonal experiences, consistent with the accumulation of developmental research establishing the role of parent and peer relations in self-development (e.g., Harter, 1990; Stern, 1985). In Markus's (1977) formulation, *self-schemas influence whether information is attended to, how information is structured, and how easily information can be remembered.* Markus demonstrated that people with particular self-schemas (e.g., independence) process relevant information with ease, retrieve relevant behavioral evidence, and resist evidence contrary to the self-schema. *Self-schemas also have self-confirming effects:* They are readily activated with little information; they influence what we attend to, particularly self-consistent information; and they are used to actively solicit self-confirming evidence from others and to present ourselves in ways that will elicit such evidence. Further, self-schemas are formed on the basis of how others perceive us and from our direct experiences, especially the emotionally significant experiences we have with others.

Considerable research on the self-schema construct has confirmed the existence in memory of a relatively cohesive and extensive knowledge base about oneself that individuals draw on to process emotional information in specific situations (e.g., see Segal, 1988, for a review). Later, in recognition that the traditional self-schema approach may be unduly restrictive, Markus and Nurius (1986) proposed the notion of "possible selves," which include "individuals' ideas of what they might become, what they would like to become, and what they are afraid of becoming" (p. 954).

Mead's (1934) symbolic interactionism predated the early interpersonal theory offered by Sullivan (1953a, 1953b) and served as the basis for Sullivan's developmental formulations. According to Mead, three components develop as the socialization process unfolds. The first is the "I," the initial component of personality, consisting of the impulsive, nonreflective part of the mind; the second is the "me," the human capacity to reflect on one's thoughts, feelings, and actions, to see one's self as an object. The third is the "generalized other," the synthesis of the many roles played by the members of the groups to which the person belonged over the years—the synthesis of the prescriptions and proscriptions transmitted by significant others in diverse social contexts and situations. Mead (1934) further underscored the interpersonal dynamics by which the self both originates and continues to be maintained.

Sullivan (1953a, 1953b) employed the term "security operations" to designate various psychological or interpersonal operations that function to maintain self-esteem. One of Sullivan's central theoretical propositions was that self-esteem is ultimately an interpersonal phenomenon: a person feels good about him- or herself when satisfying his or her generalized cognitive representation of others. Sullivan viewed anxiety as the inverse of self-esteem; anxiety is evoked by the anticipated disintegration of interpersonal relationships. Sullivan's theory also articulated that both our enacted behaviors and our perceptions or construals of others' behaviors toward us are substantially affected by our concept of who we are—by our mostly unaware "self-systems" and our phenomenological "self-personifications."

In its most simple statement, repression means rejecting from and keeping something out of consciousness. Erdelyi and Goldberg (1979) list, as well-established experimental facts, the following four essential elements of repression:

1. Rejection of selective information from awareness.
2. Avoidance of aversive stimuli.

3. Striving to defend the organism against pain.

4. Occurrence of many psychological processes outside of awareness.

It now seems experimentally established that different forms of information processing routinely take place outside awareness (e.g., Erdelyi, 1974; Kihlstrom, 1987, 1990; Lewicki, 1986; Shevrin & Dickman, 1980). Similarly, cognitive behavior therapists have argued for an increasing role for the concept of the unconscious in cognitive theory (e.g., Meichenbaum & Gilmore, 1984; Safran & Greenberg, 1987). Meichenbaum and Gilmore (1984), for example, developed the viewpoint that unconscious processes reflect well-established or overlearned constructs, schemas, or metacognitions (e.g., rules of memory retrieval and various biasing rules accepting information thratening to self-beliefs). Further, certain patterns of information address beliefs that are more central or self-oriented and are likely to evoke complex affective responses.

As Chapter 4 explains in detail, what we are about during our transactions with others is to define and present ourselves and negotiate the kind of interactions and relationships we seek from others. We negotiate much of this through mostly unconscious, automatic covert and overt processes.

A basic tenet of interpersonal theory, then, is that personality emerges and is maintained (is best understood) within the context of interpersonal transactions with real or eidetic (personified) interactants (Carson, 1969; Sullivan, 1953a, 1953b). *A central postulate of the interpersonal perspective is that some of the more important survival-relevant events for human beings involve interactions with other human beings.* As Safran (1990a) emphasized, such a perspective starts with the assumption that "there is a wired-in propensity for maintaining relatedness to others and that this wired-in propensity plays an important role in the survival of the species (Bowlby, 1969, 1979; Greenberg & Safran, 1987; Safran & Greenberg, 1987, 1988; Schachtel, 1959; Sullivan, 1953a, 1953b, 1956)" (p. 92). Cognitive-behavioral therapists have increasingly highlighted the relevance of interpersonal factors in the etiology of the self and human disturbances (Guidano, 1987, 1991; Mahoney, 1991; Safran, 1990a; Safran & Segal, 1990).

Safran (1984b, 1990a, 1990b) adopted the notion of an *interpersonal* schema that is abstracted from an individual's personal experiences and serves as a generic representation of self-other interactions:

> It may be useful to think of an interpersonal schema as being somewhat like a *program for maintaining relatedness* . . . The perspective . . . is that the basic goal of maintaining interpersonal-relatedness is biologically wired in. The specific information, strategies, and principles that are employed in order to obtain this goal are learned. (Safran, 1990a, p. 93)

Humans are by nature attuned perceptually to detect any clues regarding the disintegration of interpersonal relationships and are programmed to respond with anxiety. This is a restatement of Sullivan's (1953a) notion of "selective inattention" to anxiety-provoking stimuli, both external and internal; from an information-processing perspective, information that is schema inconsistent is not attended to or is discounted (Beck, 1976; Nisbett & Ross, 1980). Safran (1990a) hypothesized that people establish a subjective sense of potential interpersonal relatedness by (a) engaging in life-plan strategies to increase the probability of maintaining relatedness to others, (b) using interactional maneuvers designed to maintain relatedness, and (c) distorting the processing of information that might threaten their subjective sense of interpersonal relatedness (p. 95). In all of this, the individual's goal is to enhance his or her sense of relatedness "in an abstract, generalized sense"—not to a specific person in a specific interaction. In sum, the audience the person plays to is an internal one (Sullivan, 1953a, 1953b).

Measurement of Interpersonal Schemas

Hill and Safran (1994) described development of an instrument called the *Interpersonal Schema Questionnaire (ISQ,* Safran & Hill, 1989), which was based on the 1982 Interpersonal Circle (Kiesler, 1983). The ISQ requires individuals to imagine themselves exhibiting certain interpersonal behaviors and then to anticipate how various significant others would respond. Anticipated responses are coded on three indices: Desirability, Affiliation, and Control. Analyses revealed that the Desirability and Affiliation indices showed good internal consistency and test-retest reliability as well as significant correlations with a symptom checklist measure and depression inventory. The Control index showed lower levels of reliability. Analyses also revealed that the ISQ was a reasonable representation of the 1982 circumplex model. Hill and Safran (1994) concluded:

> From an interpersonal perspective (Safran, 1990b) patterns of interaction which have been useful in maintaining relatedness with attachment figures may be repeated inappropriately in other relationships, including the therapeutic relationship. These problematic interpersonal schemas could be assessed via responses to the ISQ and the generalizability and stability of therapeutic changes could also be monitored. (pp. 376–377)

Muran and colleagues (Muran, 1993) developed a different assessment strategy called *Interpersonal Scenarios* (Muran et al., 1992; Muran & Segal, 1992; Muran, Segal, & Samstag, 1994) in which idiographic vignettes are used to assess the self in an interpersonal context. Self-scenarios depict highly distressing events that consist of four components reflecting schematic structures: a stimulus situation and cognitive, affective, and motoric responses. They are scaled in a 9-point Likert format on multiple parameters and can be rated following each therapy session, thus providing for longitudinal tracking of self-schemas over the course of treatment. The method is adapted from that used in self-scenarios (Muran, 1991; Muran & Segal, 1992; Muran, Segal, & Samstag, 1994; Segal & Muran, in press) and is being used to measure the outcomes of psychotherapy. The scenarios represent prototypical patterns of how an individual acts toward others, how others react to the individual, and how the individual experiences self during the interpersonal transaction.

The information for interpersonal scenarios is gathered from a single semistructured interview involving a patient and an interviewer-therapist. From the interview information, a third-party observer constructs two sets of three interpersonal scenarios: one set when the patient is at his or her best, the other set when the patient is at his or her worst. Each scenario contains specific information regarding three components, in a fixed order: (a) automatic thoughts and immediate feelings regarding self, (b) interpersonal act of the self, and (c) interpersonal response of the other. An example might be the following: "When I am at my worst, I feel very self-conscious, very foolish and incompetent. I act very nervously and awkwardly in front of others, and others respond to me by ignoring and avoiding me" (Muran, 1993, pp. 71–72).

After each therapy session, the patient rates the two most clinically relevant scenarios on eight parameters: frequency of recent occurrence, degree of concern, accessibility to imagination, accuracy of self-other representation, chronicity of scenario in the patient's life, availability of alternative scenarios, confidence in ability to enact alternatives, and recent enactment of alternative scenarios. These multiple variables have been found to be relevant to cognitive activity (Muran, 1991) and have demonstrated differential predictability of short- versus long-term change in reaction to time-limited cognitive therapy (Muran, Segal, & Samstag, 1994).

EMOTION IN INTERPERSONAL BEHAVIOR

Chapter 5 will present the Impact Message Inventory (IMI; Kiesler, 1987c; Kiesler, Anchin, et al., 1976, 1985; Kiesler & Schmidt, 1993; Perkins et al., 1979), which was designed to measure Person A and Person B's distinctive *covert* behaviors as they reciprocally interact during a particular episode of interpersonal transaction. Kiesler et al. (in press) argue that these covert interpersonal engagements, in turn contributing toward mediation of Person A and Person B's overt reactions, can best be conceptualized as components of a *transactional emotion* process that is peculiarly essential to interpersonal behavior itself.

To be described in detail in Chapter 5, impact messages are the command or relationship messages registered covertly by interactants in response to a person's interpersonal actions. The person's acts impose a condition of emotional and other covert engagement on interactants as a result of which they are pulled to respond as the person desires. These emotional, cognitive, behavioral, and fantasy covert responses of an interactant are named the "impact message."

Four subclasses of impacts are differentiated (Kiesler, 1982a, 1987c, 1988):

1. *Direct feelings.* When interactant B is with person A, person A arouses distinct feelings and pulls specific emotions from him or her (e.g., bored, angry, suspicious, competitive, cautious, etc.).

2. *Action tendencies.* Interactant B also experiences definite urges or pulls to do or not do something when with Person A (e.g., I should avoid interrupting him; I should leave her alone; I should defend myself; I have to be gentle with her; I have to find some answers soon.).

3. *Perceived Evoking Messages.* When with Person A, various thoughts run through Interactant B's head about what Person A is trying to do to him or her, or what he or she thinks Person A wants Interactant B to do, thoughts about what Person A is feeling or thinking about Interactant B (e.g., this person wants me to put him on a pedestal; she thinks I can't be trusted; he would rather be left alone; she is determined to be in control of me; he wants to be the center of attention.).

4. *Fantasies.* When with Person A, Interactant B may experience more or less vivid images of him- or herself in concrete interactions with Person A (e.g., Persons A and B on separate rafts floating out to sea; Interactant B holding Person A in her

lap in a rocking chair; Persons A and B playing poker, each wearing dark glasses; Persons A and B making love on a white sand beach.).

Kiesler et al. (in press) document that the IMI measures central covert components of the complex emotional response as detailed in recent emotion theory; it also measures these important covert events within the context of specific interpersonal encounters.

A consensus has emerged among a sizable group of emotion theorists: Arnold (1960a, 1960b), Averill (1980), Frijda, (1986), Greenberg and Safran (1987), Kemper (1978a, 1978b), Lazarus and colleagues (Lazarus & Averill, 1972; Lazarus & Folkman, 1984; Lazarus, Kanner, & Folkman, 1980), Plutchik (1962, 1980, 1991), and Safran and Greenberg (1987, 1988). These theorists agree substantially that *emotion refers to a complex chain of covert responses that are triggered by an individual's intuitive appraisal of an environmental event or object as significant or important*—as desirable or undesirable, valuable or harmful. This appraisal, in turn, triggers a complex, distinctive set of covert behaviors including *(a) subjective feeling reactions, (b) urges to action* (action impulses, action tendencies), *(c) physiological-somatic reactions,* and *(d) somatic-kinesthetic feedback resulting from expressive facial reactions.* These distinctive reactions moderate the individual's subsequent actual overt response. Finally, each component of this emotional process (cognitive appraisal, subjective feeling, urge to action, physiological response, facial feedback, overt reaction) can be subjected to inhibitory and regulatory processes that serve as normal to abnormal defensive operations in protecting the self-system.

Kiesler et al.'s (in press) analysis makes it clear that *the four major classes of impact messages* (direct feelings, action tendencies, perceived evoking message, fantasies) *overlap remarkably with major components of the covert emotion process as detailed by contemporary emotion theorists.* Further, whether an interactant's covert impact responses, which result from a person's interpersonal actions, get enacted or not depends on the presence and strength of competing inhibitory-defensive processes.

Another growing consensus among recent emotion theorists is that *a central, if not ubiquitous, class of environmental objects or events that trigger the human emotion sequence is social, interpersonal, and transactional.* The strongest transactional statement to date comes from Kemper's (1978a, 1978b) social interactional theory of emotions and is based in his proposition that most human emotions result from outcomes of interaction in social relationships. Kemper's basic argument is that "events in the social environment instigate emotions. The most important events are the ongoing or changing patterns of social relations between actors" (Kemper, 1978a, p. 26). "I do not claim that all emotion is of this [interpersonal] character, nor that any given emotion results only from social relationships" (p. 347). Kemper's general hypothesis is that "*a very large class of emotions results from real, imagined, or anticipated outcomes in social relationships.* To account for emotions that have a social locus, we must be able to specify the full range of real, imagined, and anticipated relational outcomes" (Kemper, 1978a, p. 43).

It follows, as Kiesler et al. (in press) document (also see Chapter 2), that the interpersonal behavior of other individuals (within specific transactional episodes and over larger periods of transactional history) forms the major, most significant class of environmental events and objects that trigger the emotion sequence. This interpersonal behavior includes both that imposed by social roles and conventions (Averill, 1980) and that emerging from more enduring interpersonal dispositions and self-presentations (e.g., Carson, 1969; Kiesler, 1982b, 1983, 1988; Leary, 1957). Further, as considerable evidence (summarized in Chapter 1) documents, this interpersonal behavior—this major class of environmental stimuli—forms a domain organized on various interpersonal circumplexes (Kiesler, 1983; Wiggins, 1982) around the bipolar axes of control and affiliation.

Kiesler et al. (in press) conclude that researchers could profit considerably from use of the IMI as a key measure of covert events occurring during various instances of transactional emotion. In addition, the circumplex model of overt interpersonal behavior (cf. Figures 1–1 to 1–3), to which the IMI is empirically linked, provides a comprehensive model of the classes of interpersonal behavior that can define significant environmental events or objects that trigger the emotion sequence as well as the corresponding classes of complementary overt reactions that are mediated by covert components of the emotion process. In sum, a significant class of emotional phenomena is transactional-interpersonal in nature, and emotion is an essential component of the cyclical interpersonal transaction process (depicted later in Figure 6–1).

THE NATURE OF SIGNIFICANT OTHERS

Within interpersonal theory, the preeminent situational determinants of a patient's maladaptive actions are other persons, especially those whom a person considers "significant." "The seed of one's self-concept is the internalization of how significant others, beginning with parents, have communicated *to* one, *about* one, in the past" (Andrews, 1991, p. 8).

Sullivan (1953a) noted that the self-dynamism "has a tendency to focus attention on performances with the significant other person which get approbation or disfavor. And that peculiarity, closely connected with anxiety, persists thenceforth through life" (p. 21). Villard and Whipple (1976) framed the phenomenon in a contrasting positive light:

> That factor that we believe enables man to journey out into the culture, respond to all its demands, pressures, and need for conformity and still retain some semblance of his authentic self is the interpersonal life line that he constructs and maintains with the significant others in his life. (p. 177)

"Significant persons are those whose opinions about the [person] 'as a person' matter, with whom the [person] spends considerable time in either imaginary or real transactions, and who serve as potential sources of intimacy and regard in the [person's] life" (Kiesler, 1986a, p. 11). Present approaches both to brief dynamic psychotherapy (e.g., Luborsky, 1984; Strupp & Binder, 1984) and to psychodynamic interpersonal psychotherapy (Klerman et al., 1984; Klerman & Weissman, 1992) focus to a large extent on interpersonal relationships between the patient and significant others. Until recently, however, no systematic procedures have been available to the clinician or researcher to help chart the scope and nature of these past and present relationships.

C. H. Cooley (1902) was a pioneer in the quest for a clearer understanding of important other persons in one's life—those whom Sullivan (1953b) subsequently labeled "significant others"—and their relationship to an individual's development and maintenance of self-functioning and identity. Cooley's efforts were elaborated subsequently by symbolic interactionists such as Mead (1934), Denzin (1966), and M. Webster and Sobieszek (1974) as well as by interpersonal theorists such as Sullivan (1953a, 1953b) and myself (Kiesler, 1982b).

C. H. Cooley (1902) introduced the phrase, the *looking glass self,* to encapsulate the notion that humans see themselves as they imagine others see them. He felt that an individual's construal of how others assess him or her (the looking glass) is a crucial, but not exclusive, determinant of the individual's self-conception. He also postulated that not all others are equally significant, influential, or valued in this construal process. In line with Cooley's notions, it has become axiomatic that the importance of others' evaluations to a person's self-concept lies in the individual's perception of that evaluation, more than in the actual or objective evaluation itself (Kinch, 1968; Rosenberg, 1979; Shrauger & Shoeneman, 1979).

Mead (1934), elaborating on Cooley's work, offered the term *generalized other* as "the organized community or social group which gives to the individual his unity of self . . . The attitude of the generalized other is the attitude of the whole community . . ." (p. 154). Mead's conceptualization highlighted the importance of the society at large of which individuals are a part, particularly through their adoption of various societal roles. Mead and other symbolic interactionists (e.g., Stryker & Statham, 1985; Vallacher, 1980) thus emphasized that people become objects to themselves by coming to see themselves as they are seen by important others; the generalized other, then, becomes the participatory audience for self-awareness.

Sullivan (1953a, 1953b) placed heavy emphasis on the importance of significant persons, especially parents, in development of the self-dynamism and self-personification. He is given credit for the term significant other, using it specifically to refer to those persons who socialize the young child—most importantly the mother and father. Significant others are all those individuals in a person's life who mediate cultural standards through reflected appraisals. Through interactions with these important persons, the self-system emerges. These persons, thus, have made us what we are today and are carried by us throughout life as "eidetic people."

Significant others fulfill the criteria for a close relationship as specified by Kelley et al. (1983). According to these authors, "relationship" refers to the situation in which two people's behaviors, emotions, and thoughts are mutually and causally interconnected—are interdependent. In a similar vein, a "close relationship" results to the extent that it endures and involves strong, frequent, and diverse causal interconnections. The definitions of significant other found in Table 3–1 specify distinct aspects of causal interconnectedness that can easily be subsumed under this definition of close relationship.

The concept of significant other has been used to denote not only those primarily involved in early development and socialization of the child, but more generally, to designate any other individual who subsequently and presently is important and influential in an adult person's life—whose presence, actions, and speech are central in sustaining that person's self-view and worldview. Both current symbolic interactionist theory (Rosenberg, 1979) and interpersonal theory (Anchin & Kiesler, 1982; Kiesler, 1982b) emphasize that evaluations from significant others are crucial in the development and maintenance of the self-system. An agreed-on definition of significant others is conspicuously lacking, and various theorists emphasize different essential characteristics.

Larus's (1989) comprehensive review of the literature led to identification of numerous characteristics deemed by various theorists to be essential in a person who becomes a significant other. These essential characteristics are summarized in Table 3–1.

TABLE 3–1.   Essential Components of Significant Others Emphasized in the Theoretical Literature

1. One who shares Person A's values (C. H. Cooley, 1902, p. 8).
2. One whose relationship engenders personal growth in Person A—with whom Person A feels "the presence of an influence that is broadening and uplifting" (C. H. Cooley, 1902, p. 8).
3. One whose opinions and actions "matter" to Person A—whose esteem or approval is sought and whose disapproval is avoided by Person A (Mead, 1934, p. 9; Kiesler, 1986a, p. 11; M. Webster & Sobieszek, 1974, p. 13).
4. One to whom Person A is most fully, broadly, and basically committed emotionally and psychologically (Kuhn, 1964, p. 10).
5. One whose evaluations of Person A as a person are of considerable concern to Person A (Denzin, 1966, p. 187).
6. One who is judged by Person A as competent to provide evaluative feedback (M. Webster & Sobieszek, 1974, p. 63).
7. One who makes important decisions about things in Person A's life (Blyth et al., 1982, p. 430).
8. One whom Person A likes a lot and/or who likes Person A a lot (Blyth et al., 1982, p. 430).
9. One to whom Person A goes for advice (Blyth et al., 1982, p. 430).
10. One whom Person A would like to be like (Blyth et al., 1982, p. 430).
11. One who provides evaluative feedback that is a source of influence on Person A's self-concept (Shafer & Keith, 1985, p. 965).
12. One with whom Person A spends considerable time in either imaginary or real transactions (Kiesler, 1986a, p. 11); with whom Person A has frequent contact or spends time or does things (Blyth et al., 1982, p. 430).
13. One who serves as a potential source of intimacy and regard in Person A's life— whom Person A desires to include more intimately in his or her life (Kiesler, 1986a, p. 11).

Empirical Research

Until recently, no systematic procedures have been available to help the clinician or researcher chart the scope and nature of these past and present relationships; empirical research on significant others has been virtually nonexistent (Shrauger & Schoeneman, 1979).

Shrauger and Shoeneman (1979) and Larus-McShane (1993) reviewed research on Cooley's "looking glass self." Generally, findings are supportive that persons' construals of others' assessments of them are centrally involved in the persons' self-conceptions. Evidence is more conclusive when selection of others is made by the person rather than by the researcher. Also, the more the assessing-others are perceived as competent and their opinions deemed valuable by a person, the more likely it is that he or she will accept and consider the feedback received.

Research that specifically addresses significant others was comprehensively reviewed also by Larus-McShane (1993). As she emphasized, most studies have focused on significant others as delineated by researchers—what has come to be referred to as "putative others" (Rosenberg, 1979). Shrauger and Shoeneman (1979), Rosenberg (1979), and Shafer and Keith (1985) caution that these previous studies have failed to empirically identify those others who are in fact significant to a given individual in providing evaluative feedback.

The first study that attempted empirically to discover the *range* of significant others operative in individuals' lives was that of Denzin (1966). He adapted a Significant Other Test that was designed earlier by Mulford (1955) as one of the earliest attempts to generate a list of individualized, nonputative significant others. Denzin asked undergraduates to list significant others who came to mind after reading two paragraphs. The first category was "role-specific" ("those persons or groups of people whose evaluation of you as a *student* . . . concern you the most"); the second was "orientational" ("those persons or groups of people whose evaluation of you as a *person* concern you the most"). Denzin found that (a) subjects identified significant others in both categories and had a clear history of relationship with those in the orientational category, (b) both males and females listed family members and friends in both categories, and (c) males tended to list more nonfamily members generally, whereas females tended to list more family members as orientational others. Denzin's findings were replicated by Shoeneman and Olson (1984).

Woelfel (1969) developed the Wisconsin Significant Other Battery, which was designed to identify significant others who are influential in development of the educational and occupational attitudes of high school students. Woelfel found that the significant others listed by these high school students did not vary across socioeconomic status, residence, or level of occupational aspiration. However, males and females both tended to choose gender-congruent significant others. Also, males more frequently listed fathers, nonnuclear family members, and peers; females more frequently listed peers, mothers, fathers, and nonnuclear family members.

Blyth, Hill, and Thiel (1982) used their Social Relations Questionnaire to study the significant others of early adolescents. Significant others were defined as important people who met at least one of the following criteria: (a) people you spend time with or do things with; (b) people you like a lot or who like you a lot, or both; (c) people who make important decisions about things in your life; (d) people whom you go to for advice; or (e) people you'd like to be like. Their findings revealed that most early adolescents listed as significant others their parents, siblings, and at least one extended family member or nonrelated adult. Also, opposite-sex friends were listed more frequently as significant others as subjects' age increased.

Chewning (1983), as part of a study focusing on internal and external locus of control, developed a Significant Other Survey that asked general questions about those persons subjects considered "highly significant." The instrument assessed the relative importance of each listed person's opinion about the subject in regard to Denzin's (1966) role-specific and orientational categories as well as the amount of time devoted to each significant other listed. Chewning found a predicted relationship between the closeness of a significant other (stranger vs. acquaintance vs. friend) and the amount of interpersonal distance maintained in a particular relationship.

Shulman (1975) examined relationships with others across different stages of the life cycle. He found that married persons reported fewer significant others than did unmarried. Also, single adults reported fewer family members as significant others than did married adults.

Juhasz (1989) studied subjects who ranged from kindergarten children to undergraduates. She found that across different age, ethnic, and gender differences, it was most useful to approach research on significant others by probing specifically for the following sets of information: (a) who is significant from the perspective of the subject, (b) what others do or say that affects the subject's feelings about self, (c) how the subject reacts to the feedback received from others.

Two studies used an instrument developed by Furman and Buhrmester (1992), the Network of Relationships Inventory (NRI). Clark-Lempers and Lempers (1991) used the NRI to determine what relationship differences might be present for samples of early, middle, and late adolescents. Studying five "putative" significant other roles, they found a decrease from early to late adolescence in the rated importance of the relationship with mother and father, but an increase in the importance of friendships.

Furman and Buhrmester (1992) replicated and extended Clark-Lempers and Lempers's (1991) study employing adolescents from the 4th, 7th, and 10th grades as well as college undergraduates. They found also that different relationship roles vary in importance at different stages of development. Generally, subjects reported a greater dependency on friends as autonomy from the family increases. Also, during middle adolescence, a time of reported strong conflict with parents, intimacy and affection with friends were rated as most valued. Finally, the importance of romantic partners increased with age for the adolescent to late adolescent subjects.

A semistructured interview, the Interpersonal Relations Assessment (IRA; reported by S. Stuart et al., 1992) was developed at the Western Psychiatric Institute and Clinic to assess patients' patterns of attachment (Bowlby, 1979; Pilkonis, 1988) as evident in past and present relationships. Special attention is paid to attachments that are formed with parents, siblings, and significant others, and to patterns that appeared to characterize a patient's relationships. Following this interview, patients are rated on a global assessment scale and a personality assessment form to arrive at a profile of the patient's attachment style based on degree of fit to seven prototypical attachment patterns: securely attached (secure, probably secure, marginally secure, insecure), anxious-avoidant, and anxious-ambivalent. Stuart et al. (1992), using the IRA on a sample of patients and therapists, found:

1. There were highly significant differences between patients and therapists with respect to their personality styles and security of attachment.
2. The attachment styles were reflected in a predictable way in the patients' and therapists' in-therapy behavior.
3. The match between the attachment styles of the patient and therapist appeared to have an impact on the rate of early dropout from psychotherapy.

Assessment of Significant Others

Klerman et al. (1984, pp. 86–87), as part of their interpersonal treatment of depression, emphasize an assessment procedure called the *interpersonal inventory,* which is completed through the process of the therapist's questions in early therapy sessions. The questioning has as its goal a review of key persons and issues in the patient's life, past and present. The therapist has the option of pursuing this exploration further by asking the patient to write an autobiographical statement containing interpersonal information.

Either exploration seeks to gather the following information about each person who is important in the patient's life:

1. Interactions with the patient including frequency of contact and activities shared.
2. The expectations of each party in the relationship, including some assessment of whether the expectations were or are fulfilled.
3. A review of satisfactory and unsatisfactory aspects of the relationship with specific, detailed examples of both kinds of interactions.
4. The ways the patient would like to change the relationships, whether through changing his or her own behavior or bringing about changes in the other person.

Chewning (1983) constructed her Significant Other Survey (SOS) for standardized use in interpersonal research and therapy. Her survey asks the respondent to "list the names of all the persons who you consider to be highly significant in your life." For each person listed the respondent then supplies the following information:

1. A rating of the importance of the person's opinion of the respondent as a person.
2. A rating of how much imaginary and real time is devoted by the respondent to each person.
3. A list of three positive and three negative "traits, characteristics, or behavior patterns" characteristic of the respondent.
4. A list of three positive and three negative traits that characterize each significant person listed.
5. A rating of the extent to which the respondent has actually discussed each of his or her traits in actual conversation with each significant other.
6. A rating of the extent to which each significant other has actually discussed his or her traits in actual conversation with the respondent.

The Significant Other Inventory-Revised

Larus and Kiesler (1988) developed a revised inventory, *Significant Other Inventory* (SOI), to be more simple in both size and structure. Respondents are asked (a) to list 3 to 6 of the most significant persons in their lives, (b) to characterize the most prominent role each significant other (SO) occupies vis-à-vis their particular relationship, and (c) to rate each SO on a series of 21 characteristics chosen to represent different definitions of SOs and other theoretical features present in the literature. To counter the prevalence of usage in previous studies of putative significant others, the SOI was designed to permit the subject to designate his or her own list of significant others and then rate each on items designed to represent the distinctive qualities of significant others as postulated by theorists (summarized in Table 3–1).

Larus-McShane (Larus, 1989) conducted an initial validation study of SOI. Findings showed that men and women subjects chose the same top six significant others (in order of frequency): friend, mother, partner, father, sister, and brother. Also, 80% of the significant others listed by our undergraduates fell into three major categories: friends and close friends; members of their family of origin (mother, father, sister, brother, grandmother); and members of their present family (partner, son). These data confirmed patterns of significant others reported by Blyth et al. (1982), Denzin (1966), Furman and Buhrmester (1992), Shoeneman and Olson (1984), and Woelfel (1969).

Larus-McShane's study (Larus, 1989) also identified four underlying factors that accounted for the ratings obtained across the various roles of significant others named by subjects:

- *Support/Sharing*. The extent to which the other provides the subject various forms of emotional and financial support in time of need.
- *Influence*. The extent to which the other's opinions and evaluations of the subject are important to the subject's view of self.
- *Similarity*. The extent to which the other and subject find themselves to be similar in personality and values.
- *Mutuality*. The extent to which the opinions of both other and subject are important to each other.

The distinct patterns of factor loadings that emerged across the study's various analyses suggested that the role a significant other occupies directly defines which components (the four factors) are considered most relevant. The mother role seemed to exemplify this distinctive difference most vividly. Whereas the degree of Similarity was deemed most relevant by subjects in regard to friends and most other roles, in the case of mother, Similarity was minimally relevant as a defining component. Instead, the degree to which mother showed a distinct factor, Acceptance of the subject, emerged as most centrally relevant. Larus-McShane concluded that there are important differences among specific classes of significant others that can be described by different factors of the SOI items. Specificity of role seems to play an important part in determining the qualities central to a person's significance for another.

The findings of this original study as well as further study and analysis led us to revise substantially our original measure, the result being the Significant Other Inventory-Revised (SOI-R; Larus-McShane, Kiesler, & Murray, 1990). Larus-McShane's original findings (Larus, 1989) both invited and merited follow-up research. We felt it was crucial, first, to construct a larger set of items to measure systematically with the hope of cross-validating the principal components factors found for the original sample. Second, we felt it was vital to define each of our factors with items worded not only in a positive direction (as were all the SOI items), but with a matched number of items describing corresponding negative attributes. For example, although some significant others serve as facilitators of our self-esteem, others can be quite destructive. Because no negative items were found during our search of the previous work on significant others, we decided to construct and add a comparable set of negative items for each factor to study more carefully these "negative" significant others and their impact on emotional well-being. Accordingly, the 26-item SOI was expanded to the 55 items of the SOI-R (subsequently reduced to 45 factor scale items) to explore the positive and negative aspects of significant others. Larus-McShane (1993) then administered the SOI-R to 168 female and 127 male undergraduates.

Once again, results showed that the significant others most consistently selected by subjects were mother, father, friend, and mate (spouse, girlfriend, boyfriend). This time, principal components analysis generated a total of five factors. Three were positive factors:

I. *All-Inclusive Approval*. The extent to which the other approves of the subject, makes the subject feel good about self, and is fun to be with in joint activities.

    IV. *Influence/Guidance.* The extent to which the other has an important influence on how I feel about myself, provides me helpful problem-solving advice, and helps me to grow and realize my potential.

    V. *Sharing/Support.* The extent to which the other provides emotional and financial support to the subject.

Two were negative factors:

    II. *Unavoidable Contact.* The extent to which it is no fun to be with the other and the subject would avoid contact with and terminate the relationship with the other if the subject could.

    III. *Disappointing Disapproval.* The extent to which the other disapproves of me, makes me doubt my own worth, makes me feel anxious around him or her, and makes it difficult for me to know what my real feelings are.

Five factor scales were then constructed based on obtained factor loadings: I consisted of 12 items (7 positively worded, 5 negatively worded); II had 6 items (5 positive, 1 negative); III had 11 items (9 positive, 2 negative); IV consisted of 11 items (7 positive, 4 negative); and V had 5 items (4 positive, 1 negative)—a total of 45 items. For the five scales constructed from the principal components analysis, internal consistency reliability was very good, with Cronbach alphas being respectively: .85, .76, .80, .82, and .74.

Analysis of the newly constructed factor scales yielded some interesting findings. Notable differences emerged across significant other roles for three of the five factors. Mother and father generally received higher ratings on the positive factors than did others in different roles. The one exception was for All-Inclusive Approval, which scored highest for the role of friend (followed by mother, then father). On Sharing/Support mother was scored highest, followed by father and then friend. All three roles were seen as minimally disapproving on the Disappointing Disapproval factor; but within this range, father was rated more disapproving than mother and friend.

When roles were then compared across the five factors, similarly intriguing findings emerged. For both mother and father, the most important factor was Influence, followed in order by Sharing/Support, Approval, Unavoidable Contact, and Disappointing Disapproval. However, quite different findings were obtained for friend, for whom the most important factor was Approval, followed in order by Influence/Guidance, Sharing/Support, Unavoidable Contact, and Disappointing Disapproval.

Male and female subjects were equivalent in their ratings of female significant others. However, male subjects rated male significant others more harshly (less Approval, Influence, Sharing/Support; more Unavoidable Contact) than they rated their female significant others, and more harshly than female subjects rated male significant others. On the other hand, both males and females saw more positive qualities (more Approval, Influence, Sharing/Support) in significant others of the opposite sex.

In regard to psychopathology, the results showed that the more psychiatric symptoms a subject reported on a checklist, the more that subject was likely to perceive Disappointing Disapproval in significant others. Finally, Larus-McShane found limited support for her hypothesis that instances in which parents are not considered seminal or significant people (e.g., mother is not spontaneously listed by a subject as a significant other) are associated with more extreme levels of psychopathology.

Larus-McShane (1993) concluded that the SOI-R generated in her study provides both operationalization and detailed definition to the construct of significant others which permits assessment of the positive and negative range of significant relationships. The inventory, further, shows promise toward assessment of (a) the psychological functioning of individuals, including various patterns of psychopathological functioning and (b) subjects' psychological construal of individuals of varying gender, role, and intimacy of relationship:

> This information is potentially useful in clinical settings where it is very important to quickly and objectively assess and document the degree to which a person has positive or negative relationships in his/her life. This information ultimately reflects a person's general well-being, as the ability to form constructive relationships is essential to mental health. (p. 165)

Subsequently, the SOI-R has been adapted for applications to adolescent populations (SOI-R:A; Larus-McShane, Kiesler, Murray, Dowdy, & Kliewer, 1993).

As a postscript, it is helpful to point out that study of *significant others somewhat overlaps, but is mostly distinct from, the study of social support* (Albrecht & Adelman, 1987; Henderson, Duncan-Jones, Byrne, & Scott, 1980; Lein & Sussman, 1983; Powers, Champion, & Aris, 1988; Sarason, Sarason, & Pierce, 1990; Sarason, Shearin, Pierce, & Sarason, 1987). There is obvious overlap between the two constructs and their respective measures. First, the essential characteristics of significant others described by some theorists refer to clearly supportive behaviors. Second, members of a person's present social support network include individuals who are significant others to the person (family members, spouse, relatives, etc.).

On the other hand, in Larus-McShane's (1993) principal components analyses, social support did not emerge as an independent factor, but appeared only as part of Factor V (Sharing/Support). Moreover, two of the first three factors that emerged targeted *negative* behaviors on the part of significant others: II. Unavoidable Contact, III. Disappointing Disapproval. Analysis of the factor content of the SOI-R, thus, makes it abundantly clear that significant other refers to a domain of behaviors by others that is considerably larger and more complex than the domain of social support. What seems central is that identification of significant others of necessity will target not only individuals who are supportive and facilitative of Person A's physical and emotional development, but also those who have been or are obstructive and destructive of the person's development. Of necessity, significant others include persons who have had negative influences on a person and who, therefore, represent past and present significant interpersonal stressors for Person A—a class of persons anathema to either the concept or assessment of social support.

Another central difference reflects that the concept of significant other is related centrally to conceptualization of the development of Person A's personality, especially of his or her self-system, from childhood through adulthood. In contrast, the concept of social support concentrates on currently available social-environmental provisions that can serve as buffers to present physical or psychiatric stress or pathology. As a result, the interpersonal, transactional relationship between these others and the self-esteem of Person A represents only a minor focus of social support measures (Sarason et al., 1987).

In sum, the goal of studying significant others is not just to assess the support they offer; instead it is to investigate *all essential qualities* of the respective relationships.

What are the specific factors, instead of or in addition to social support, that influence the choice and maintenance of each interactant as a particular person's significant others? Our present SOI-R results suggest that there are four specific factors other than social support (in order): All-Inclusive Approval, Unavoidable Contact, Disappointing Disapproval, and Influence/Guidance. Future studies with the SOI-R and other similar measures will continue to provide stimulating answers to this and many other relevant interpersonal questions.

CONCLUSION

To understand the complex workings of interpersonal behavior, important situational factors need to be identified and their interactive effects demonstrated (Kiesler, 1982b; see also Chapter 2). It's also clear that a central source of situational influence resides in the dispositional patterns of interpersonal behavior characteristic of interactants (Kiesler, 1982b). The interpersonal propositions of complementarity are postulated to operate most straightforwardly in situations without structure and clearly defined expectations (Kiesler, 1983). Further, as Orford (1986) documented, there is considerable evidence that interpersonal contingencies are affected by factors of role and status. It is within this multivariate complex of interactive situational influence, including also various types of personal relationships (e.g., strangers, acquaintances, close friends), that the measurement and study of significant others becomes so critical. Moreover, in interpersonal therapy it is crucial that the therapist be able to identify the significant relationships in a patient's life in order to explore, define, and alter the patient's Maladaptive Transaction Cycle. Perhaps the assessment procedures of both Larus-McShane et al. (1990) and Klerman et al. (1984) may become part of an eventual standardized interpersonal assessment battery.

CHAPTER 4

Interpersonal Behavior and Our Bids for Complementarity

> *You are mainly responsible for your life situation. You have created your own world. Your own interpersonal behavior has, more than any other factor, determined the reception you get from others. Your slowly developing pattern of reflexes has trained others and yourself to accept you as this sort of person—to be treated in this sort of way. You are the manager of your own destiny.*
>
> *(Leary, 1957, p. 117)*

A basic tenet of contemporary interpersonal theory is that personality emerges and is maintained within the context of interpersonal transactions with real or eidetic (personified) interactants (Carson, 1969; Sullivan, 1953a, 1953b). In the interpersonal tradition, a person's actions can be understood only as they derive *conjoint* meaning from the historical and present interpersonal transactions in which they are embedded. A client's actions, similarly, need to be understood as communicative "force fields" that influence, and simultaneously are influenced by, other force fields from present-day interactants in important lawfully reciprocal ways.

A personality can be comprehended only as "the relatively enduring pattern of recurrent interpersonal situations which characterize a human life" (Sullivan, 1953b, pp. 110–111). To be fully cognizant of oneself or of another requires an observational stance offering a clear view of the sequence of events played out tenaciously and recurrently by a person or patient in encounters with significant others.

Since Sullivan (1953b, p. 198) articulated his revolutionary "theorem of reciprocal emotion," *a central construct of interpersonal theory has been the reciprocity or complementarity governing the exchanges of human interactants.* That is, "Our interpersonal actions are designed to invite, pull, elicit, draw, entice, or evoke 'restricted classes' of reactions from persons with whom we interact, especially from significant others" (Kiesler, 1983, p. 198). The name "impact message," which refers to these restricted classes of covert reactions, comes from one of the major constructs in my interpersonal communication theory (Kiesler, 1979, 1982a, 1982b, 1983, 1986a, 1986b, 1988, 1991, 1992; Kiesler, Bernstein, & Anchin, 1976; Kiesler et al., in press; Kiesler & Van Denburg, 1996; Van Denburg & Kiesler, 1995; Van Denburg et al., 1992).

Goffman (1959) emphasized that two people are compatible to the extent that they make complementary attributions that fit into a coherent image of the relationship . . . and that confirm each other's perception of the self. Wachtel (1977) added:

> The signals we emit to other people constitute a powerful force field. The shy person does many (sometimes almost invisible) things to make it difficult for another person to stay open to him very long. Even a well-intentioned person is likely eventually to help confirm his view that others aren't really very interested. (p. 52)

SELF-PRESENTATION AND SELF-CONFIRMATION

Sullivan (1953b) speculated that individuals use interpersonal maneuvers to achieve both satisfaction of their basic biological needs and security through avoidance of the debilitating effects of anxiety. Individuals, thus, learn to foster the growth of interactions that lead to satisfaction and security. Sullivan postulated an anxiety mechanism by which we respond empathically to the mood of others; if that mood is hostile or disapproving, we experience the mood directly as a tension or anxiety. Anxiety is always triggered or evoked interpersonally and serves as (a) a major indicant of insecurity, (b) a signal of danger to self-respect, and (c) the major disruptive force in interpersonal relations.

In Sullivan's writings, emotional reactions or feelings reflect the kinds of needs that are at play in the interpersonal situation. If the level of emotion is too great in a situation (the range extends from euphoria to uncanny emotion), the integration will suffer as the person finds the tension impossible to direct properly.

According to Sullivan's *theorem of reciprocal emotion,* integration in an interpersonal situation is "a process in which (a) complementary needs are resolved (or aggravated), (b) reciprocal patterns of activity are developed (or disintegrated), and (c) foresight of satisfaction (or rebuff) of similar needs is facilitated" (Sullivan, 1953b, p. 198). For Sullivan, complementary needs refer to the situation in which a need of one person articulates with that of another in such a way that the behavior relevant to the two basic needs (closeness, power) tends to produce satisfaction (resolution) for both persons. In the interpersonal situation, then, situations are either conjunctive (characterized by harmony and a desire to come together) or disjunctive (characterized by tension and a desire to separate).

The underlying theory is that our interpersonal behaviors establish distinctive kinds of relationships with others that are comfortable and anxiety-free, and that serve to confirm our conceptions of who we are as individuals. To establish comfortable (conjunctive, complementary) relationships and to avoid uncomfortable (disjunctive, noncomplementary) relationships, it is necessary that we, in automatic and minimally aware ways, maneuver persons who are interacting with us to adopt relationship positions that are complementary to, or reinforcing of, the positions we are proffering. The first effect of this transactional negotiation is that we begin to restrict the covert experience (feelings, images, cognitions, action tendencies) of persons interacting with us in a manner that makes it more likely they will respond overtly in the way we desire. Carson (1991) referred to this as an *interbehavioral contingency process* in which "there is a tendency for a given individual's interpersonal behavior to be constrained or controlled in more or less predictable ways by the behavior received from an interaction partner" (p. 191).

The idea of the self as the center of personal consistency or stability is a key element in many personality theories (e.g., Lecky, 1945; C. R. Rogers, 1959) including that of Sullivan (1953b). In Sullivan's framework, "the self-system is extraordinarily resistant to change by experience . . . from its nature [it] tends to escape influence by experience which is incongruous with its current organization and functional activity" (Sullivan, 1953b, p. 190).

Villard and Whipple (1976) emphasized that "behavior is ultimately predictable in terms of self-concept . . . each of us is largely who we believe ourselves to be. We behave and respond to others in a manner that has a direct relationship to our self-definition" (p. 93). According to Andrews (1991):

> Each person achieves a self-consistent feedback environment through a complex of large and small self-fulfilling prophecies that support his or her initial expectations about self and experience. People will selectively counteract, avoid, or discount feedback that suggests that they are not who they think they are. This establishes a negative feedback loop that tends to return a system to its original equilibrium after a disturbance. (p. 12)

Rosenberg (1979) and Markus and Zajonc (1985) argued that findings from research on cognitive dissonance reflect a person's attempts to minimize perceived discrepancies between the self-concept and other aspects of experience. An important extension of these views is the notion that people constantly reconfirm their self-concepts through current social interaction (Goffman, 1959; Sullivan, 1953a, 1953b). When the self-confirmation process is unsuccessful, anxiety results and individuals escalate their bids in the form of more extreme and rigid interpersonal behaviors. Over time, this anxiety-driven escalation results in the various patterns of abnormal behavior that characterize maladjusted individuals.

At an early developmental stage, a person settles on a distinctive interpersonal style, role, and/or self-definition that leads the person repeatedly to make interpersonal claims on others in terms of how close or intimate and how much in charge or dominant the person wants to be with others. In subsequent interactions, this relatively constant self-presentation is reciprocally reinforced or validated by responses the person pulls from interactants.

Interpersonal theory asserts that each of us continually exudes a force field that pushes others to respond to us with constricted classes of control and affiliation actions; thereby we pull from others complementary responses designed to affirm and validate our chosen style of living and being. As Pincus (1994) observed, "The primary dynamic principle of interpersonal theory is that behavior serves the goal of self-definition and the mechanism through which this goal is attained is via the elicitation of a limited class of interpersonal reactions from others which are perceived as congruent with how one views oneself" (p. 121).

In social and personality research, the *self-confirmation hypothesis is that people constantly reconfirm their self-concepts through current social interaction* (e.g., Secord & Backman, 1961, 1965). Because of the inherently ambiguous nature of social reality, people seem to require constant consensual validation of their self-concepts to bolster their confidence in their self-perceptions (J. R. Greenberg, Pyszczynski, & Solomon, 1986; Swann, 1983). The self-confirmation hypothesis has been substantiated by a sizable body of empirical research, as reviewed by Andrews (1988, 1991), Backman (1985), Baumeister (1982), Felker (1974), Rosenberg (1979), M. L. Snyder and Ickes (1985), and Swann (1983, 1985, 1987).

Swann (1987) asserted that individuals attempt to verify their personal system of self-schemas in their interactions with others: *A person's system of self-constructs not only may affect how he or she perceives the world or remembers past events but also influences the manner in which the person relates to others:*

> One way to stir people up is to tell them that they are not what they think they are. . . . After they recover from their surprise, people will often rush to find ways to discredit or dismiss the feedback. Furthermore, they will probably take steps to insure that they never encounter such appraisals again. In these and other ways people may strive to sustain their beliefs about themselves. (Swann, 1983, p. 33)

According to Swann (1983, 1985, 1987), people adopt various interaction strategies for self-confirmation purposes: (a) they may choose appropriate interaction partners and social settings; (b) they may acquire signs and symbols of who they are which they then display as identity cues for others to reinforce; or (c) they may adopt specific self-consistent interaction strategies; and/or (d) they may use self-confirmatory modes of encoding, retrieving, and interpreting information. Swann (1983, 1985, 1987; Swann & Hill, 1982; Swann & Read, 1981a, 1981b) has demonstrated convincingly that people adopt interaction strategies that elicit self-confirmatory feedback from others.

For example, Swann and Hill (1982) provided subjects with either self-confirming or disconfirming feedback about their level of interpersonal dominance. When the information was self-confirming, subjects accepted the feedback and passively continued to play the suggested role. When the feedback was contrary to their own beliefs about their dominance, subjects reacted strongly, resisting the feedback, and behaving so as to convince the other person that was not the kind of person they were. Self-perceived dominants who were given feedback that they were submissive, acted especially dominant; self-perceived submissives who were told they were dominant acted especially submissive.

Moskowitz and Cote (1995) found support for "behavioral concordance" in their study of the relationship of affect to interpersonal behavior. Findings supported the *behavioral concordance* prediction that *individuals will experience pleasant affect when they behave consistently with their interpersonal traits, and unpleasant affect at the time of trait-discordant behaviors.* For example, they found that highly quarrelsome subjects experienced pleasurable emotion while engaging in quarrelsome behaviors, and unpleasant affect while engaging in agreeable behavior.

J. D. Brown and McGill (1989) speculated about the maladaptive effects of instances of invalidation of one's self-presentation. In their formulation, "identity disruption" refers to an erosion of a person's identity or sense of self that occurs when the individual is exposed to events that are inconsistent with that identity. J. D. Brown and McGill (1989) hypothesized that identity disruption is a source of stress that can increase a person's vulnerability to pathogenic agents, both physical and mental. They emphasized that this disruption may also occur in the face of any change of a person's life circumstances, because change can produce a new perception of the self, thereby forcing a readjustment of the self-concept.

After his incisive review of the self-confirmation literature, Andrews (1991) concluded:

> Personality is stable and enduring, not because it is composed of fixed traits or because it is controlled by external social arrangements, but because it is sustained by the active self via an intricate set of feedback loops with the environment . . . by continuous interaction cycles, shaped partly by the individual, that provide self-confirmation. (pp. 123–124)

SELF-FULFILLING PROPHECY

Carson (1982) offered the fundamental *cognitive statement of interpersonal complementarity: A person's behavior is designed to produce consequences in and reactions from others that confirm the principal hypotheses (perceptions, expectations, or construals of other persons) organizing his or her world.* In Carson's view, an "unbroken causal loop" (p. 66) exists among (a) a person's social perceptions or cognitions, (b) his or her behavioral enactments, and (c) reactions of interactants that confirm the person's cognitions or expectancies. In interpersonal theory, this cycle is governed by the principle of complementarity.

As an illustration, Carson (1979) speculated that persons who are dispositionally passive count on others to assume the dominant position with them; consequently, their world is largely populated by assertive and dominant individuals. Affiliative persons, on the other hand, do not usually bring an expectation into a relationship; instead, they wait to see what the other person is going to be like. If anything, these persons tend to have a generalized positive attributional set toward others, thereby judging differences along the affiliation-hostility dimension to be more salient than differences in dominance-submission. The cycle will be presented in a much more elaborated general form, as the Maladaptive Transaction Cycle, in Chapter 6. Conway (1987) echoed Carson's theme by observing that within interpersonal theory "people are seen as actively constructing their social worlds so as to promote complementary interactions with others, which in turn provide the social feedback that maintains preferred interpersonal styles and views of self and others" (p. 13).

The *self-fulfilling prophecy* mechanism (Merton, 1948, 1957) that underlies the unbroken causal loop described by Carson (1969, 1982) has received considerable empirical confirmation (Darley & Fazio, 1980; Jones, 1977; Jussim, 1986; D. T. Miller & Turnbull, 1986; Rosenfeld, 1967; Rosenthal & Rubin, 1978; M. L. Snyder & Gangestad, 1981). Darley and Fazio (1980) documented how social expectancies are confirmed in a feedback loop that includes behavior, the impressions and responses of a target person, and selective interpretations of the target's reaction. In Bruner and Taguiri's (1954) "implicit personality theory," each person has his or her own personal theory of what people are like and how they operate. In a relatively consistent fashion, the perceiver selectively seeks out and evaluates those characteristics he or she deems most important in others. The notion of self-fulfilling prophecy takes this position one step further by asserting that *a person brings about the very consequences of his or her own prediction (expectation) simply by virtue of the effects of the prediction itself.* The result is that a *self-perpetuating* cycle or "general interaction sequence" (Darley & Fazio, 1980) is formed that is highly resistant to change.

If, for example, individuals with competitive orientations treat other people as if they were competitive and thereby elicit competitive responses from others, then individuals with such orientations may "not only provide behavioral confirmation of their stereotypical beliefs that all people are competitive, but also justify and maintain their own competitive dispositions" (M. L. Snyder, 1981, pp. 313–314).

Self-fulfilling prophecies can take many forms (e.g., Rosenthal, 1973; Scheff, 1966; Ward, Zanna, & Cooper, 1974). When they occur between individuals, they are known as interpersonal expectancy effects or behavioral confirmation. A review of the huge literature on interpersonal expectancy effects led to the conclusion that expectancy effects do occur and can have a magnitude of social importance (Rosenthal & Rubin, 1978).

Darley and Fazio's (1980) general interaction sequence can be translated into an interpersonal transaction cycle as follows. Person A develops a generalized expectancy about Person B. The expectancy leads A to behave in a manner consistent with the expectancy; for example, Person A may act detached and inhibited (hostile-submissive) if he or she believes that Person B is critical and mistrusting (hostile-dominant). Person B then responds to A's behavior in an expectancy-consistent manner, in this example by actually behaving coldly and warily. This, in turn, verifies and strengthens Person A's initial impression; moreover, Person B may begin to internalize cold and wary behavior and to alter his or her self-concept accordingly.

INTERPERSONAL PRINCIPLES OF COMPLEMENTARITY

Since Sullivan (1953a, 1953b), a central construct of interpersonal theory has been the reciprocity or complementarity governing the exchanges of human interactants. This reciprocity occurs within the context of what can be called a human "relationship."

In Kelley et al.'s (1983) formulation, "relationship" refers to the situation in which two people's behaviors, emotions, and thoughts are mutually and causally interconnected—are interdependent. As Peterson (1982) observed, "To describe a relationship [and therefore to understand it], one must identify the recurrent patterns of interaction that take place between the people involved in the relationship" (p. 150). Villard and Whipple (1976) expanded on the interdependence notion by defining relationship as "the negotiation process by which two people determine the focus and boundary rules of their relationship and thereby define those identities, behaviors, and activities that are to be included and excluded from that relationship" (p. 219).

The purpose of this section is to provide a systematic statement of propositions of complementarity inherent in the interpersonal circle in general, and in the 1982 Circle in particular. Before proceeding with this task, however, two other traditions that have addressed the notion of interpersonal reciprocity need to be mentioned.

Relational Control Complementarity

The first tradition is that of interactional communication or relational control theory (e.g., Bateson, 1958; Haley, 1963; D. D. Jackson, 1959; Watzlawick, Beavin, & Jackson,

1967; Watzlawick & Weakland, 1977). Relational control formulations concentrate on reciprocity as it operates on the control dimension *only*. That is, reciprocity in an interpersonal exchange represents the constant struggle by each person to control what sort of power relationship is to exist between them (Haley, 1963).

> In a *complementary* relationship the two people are of equal status in the sense that one appears to be in the superior position, meaning that he initiates action and the other person appears to follow that action; [in contrast,] a *symmetrical* relationship is one between two people who behave as if they have equal status. (Jackson, 1959, pp. 126–127)

Lederer and Jackson (1968) added a third type of reciprocity, a *parallel* relationship, wherein control not only tends to have an equal distribution among interactants but also flows easily and alternatingly from A to B to A as the situation changes and dictates.

Friedlander (1993a, 1993b) reviewed the evidence for complementarity within interpersonal personality theory (IPT) versus relational control theory (RCT). Her analysis concentrated on only observational coding or rating studies. She pointed out that "because of the conceptual differences and a wide array of research methods, the literature on complementarity is replete with confusing, contradictory results" (Friedlander, 1993a, p. 457). She concluded, "The evidence tends to support IPT in the context of individual therapy and RCT in the context of family therapy" (1993a, p. 457).

FIRO-B Complementarity

A second alternative tradition regarding complementarity comes from Schutz's (1958) three-dimensional theory of interpersonal behavior, and from research with his Fundamental Interpersonal Relations Orientation Scale (FIRO-B). In Schutz's system, three types of interpersonal reciprocity or compatibility are possible as the result of the operation of three classes of needs: inclusion, control, and affection:

1. *Reciprocal* compatibility exists when each participant's level of "expressed" behavior matches the other's level of "wanted" behavior for each of the three needs.
2. *Originator* compatibility describes reciprocity in regard to who originates and who receives behaviors for each of the three needs. If both participants prefer to originate behaviors, "competitive" incompatibility exists; if both prefer to receive, "apathetic" incompatibility occurs.
3. *Interchange* compatibility designates the degree to which both participants rank similarly the respective importance of the three need areas.

The FIRO-B (Schutz, 1958) was designed to measure each of these three types of compatibility. Interestingly, the FIRO-B scales appear to be almost completely unrelated to the two generally accepted interpersonal circle dimensions (Hurley, 1990).

Complementarity in Contemporary Interpersonal Theory

The third tradition, contemporary interpersonal theory, which is the focus of this book, offers notions of reciprocity directly derivable from the interpersonal circle itself. Derived originally from Sullivan's (1953b) "theorem of reciprocal emotion," the broadest meaning of interpersonal complementarity is that "our interpersonal actions are designed to invite, pull, elicit, draw, entice, or evoke 'restricted classes' of reactions from persons with whom we interact, especially from significant others" (Kiesler, 1983, p. 198). Leary (1957) called this the "principle of reciprocal interpersonal relations;" Carson (1991) more recently referred to this interpersonal situation as "interbehavioral contingency."

Carson (1969) was the first to define explicitly how this principle related to the interpersonal circumplex. Kiesler (1983) summarized and clarified the propositions of complementarity articulated by Carson (1969), offered expanded and new propositions for personality tied operationally to the 1982 Interpersonal Circle, and articulated other propositions that related to psychopathology and to the goals and procedures of psychotherapy. The result was 11 propositions of complementarity as they applied in personality, psychopathology, and psychotherapy. This chapter will review the 11 and add several new propositions of complementarity.

The principle of complementarity is a major feature of the self-confirmational process described earlier, where individuals attempt to influence others into confirming their familiar transactional patterns. Hence, reactions by others to our acts are not random, nor are they likely to include the entire range of possible reactions. Instead, reactions to each of us tend to be restricted to a relatively narrow range of interpersonal responses. As Wachtel (1982a) noted: "Each person may be seen rather regularly to produce a particular skewing of responses from others that defines his idiosyncratic, interpersonal world" (p. 48). In short, an interpersonal behavior and its most probable interpersonal reaction are said to be complementary.

Interpersonal complementarity designates a range of behaviors aligned on a continuum of anxiety. An individual bids for responses from others, and reacts to others, with responses that maximize feelings of security while minimizing feelings of anxiety. Interpersonal transactions that incorporate complementary behaviors reduce, eliminate, or minimize interpersonal anxiety; transactions that include noncomplementary behaviors increase, exacerbate, or maximize anxiety. Conway (1987) noted, "We learn how to 'train' others to respond to us in security-maintaining fashion by acquiring and displaying the requisite interpersonal behaviors to match our enduring self-perceptions" (p. 19). Goldston (1990) added:

> The individual's security operations, including selective inattention, seek interactions reinforcing of the Good Me while avoiding interactions which bring attention to Bad Me, and disowning interactions bringing attention to the Not Me . . . Arriving at so called rules of complementarity for selected dyads is crucially dependent upon an assessment of each individual's Good Me, Bad Me, and Not Me interpersonal anxiety continuum. (pp. 45–46)

At mostly unaware and automatic levels, then, our actions are designed to push or force others to respond in ways that are complementary to our acts, in ways that confirm our self-definitions and self-presentations. This principle can be stated as follows:

Proposition 4–1.   A person's interpersonal actions tend (with a probability significantly greater than chance) to initiate, invite, or evoke from an interactant complementary responses that lead to a repetition of the person's original actions (Kiesler, 1983, pp. 200–201).

Caspi and Bem (1990) differentiated three kinds of interaction that play particularly important roles both in controlling the trajectory of a person's life course and in promoting the continuity of personality across the life course. One of these they called "evocative" interaction, which occurs when an individual's personality evokes distinctive processes from others. As support of this concept, they cited Patterson's (1976, 1982) work with aggressive boys. The aggressive boys' coercive behaviors were found to initiate a cycle of parental anger and further aggression until the parents finally withdraw, thereby reinforcing the initial aggression. In turn, the immediate reinforcement of withdrawal both short-circuited the boys' learning more controlled and adaptive behaviors and increased the likelihood that coercive behavior will recur whenever similar interactional conditions arise later in the life course (Caspi, Bem, & Elder, 1989; Caspi, Elder, & Bem, 1987). The basic notion, then, is that in evocative interactions "the person acts, the environment reacts, and the person reacts back in mutually interlocking evocative interaction" (Caspi & Bem, 1990, p. 565).

Another way to look at complementary reactions is in terms of emotion-confirmation. Klinger (1971, 1977a, 1977b) emphasized how needs and desires, along with associated fantasies, impel interpersonal behavior and how feelings or emotions inform the behaving person about whether the needs are being met. As Klinger (1977a) stated: "People initiate interpersonal behaviors and maintain close relationships *in order to experience certain feelings and avoid experiencing others*" (p. 167). Emotion, then, is "the currency in terms of which close-relationship balance sheets are tallied" (pp. 167–168).

One also can consider complementary relationships in terms of fit of expectations of the interactants. In this sense, two people are more compatible to the extent that they make complementary attributions that fit into a coherent image of the relationship and that confirm each other's perception of self (Goffman, 1959). Andrews (1974–1975, p. 30) pointed out that the complement of any interpersonal behavior is a response that meets the expectations communicated by the behavior, which will tend to evoke further behavior of the same type; the outcome is a stable, self-perpetuating interaction or system. We can state:

Proposition 4–2.   A person's expectancies regarding the reactions of an interactant to his or her interpersonal behaviors are defined and described by the specific content of the 1982 Interpersonal Circle segments complementary on the circle to the person's preferred (peak) segment of interpersonal behavior.

Proposition 4–3.   Within interpersonal theory, complementarity is specifically defined in terms of interpersonal behavior as operationalized by the two-dimensional interpersonal circle. Complementarity occurs on the basis of (a) "reciprocity" in respect to the control dimension or axis (dominance pulls submission, submission pulls dominance) and (b) "correspondence" in regard to the affiliation dimension (hostility pulls hostility, friendliness pulls friendliness) (Kiesler, 1983, p. 201; see also Carson, 1969, p. 112).

Figure 4–1 presents the complementary quadrants and segments of the 1982 Interpersonal Circle. In that figure, it is apparent that when interacting with someone who behaves in a friendly-dominant manner (using behaviors from categories in the top-right quadrant of the circle), transactional partners will be pulled into responding in a friendly-submissive way (using behaviors from categories in the bottom-right circle

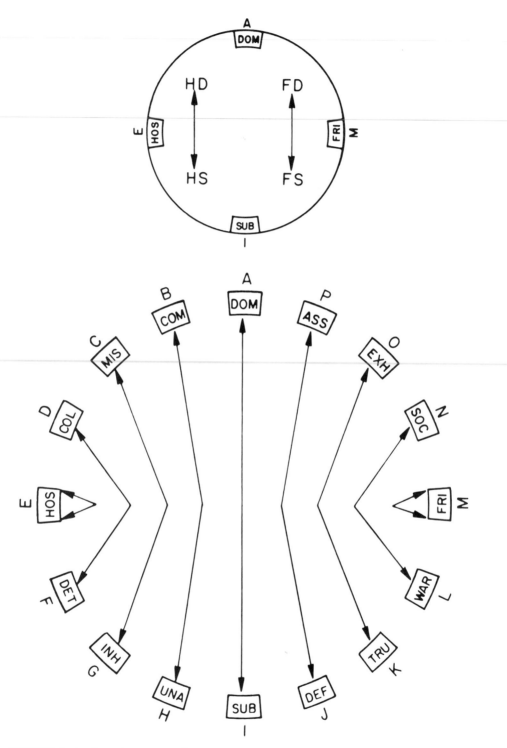

FIGURE 4–1. Complementary Quadrants and Segments of the 1982 Interpersonal Circle.

quadrant). In the case of the friendly-dominant, friendly-submissive matchup, Interactant B accepts Person A's control bid with reciprocity (submission in reaction to dominance) and accepts Person A's affiliation bid with correspondence (friendliness in reaction to friendliness). Complementarity exists among interactants when Respondent B reacts to Person A with interpersonal acts both reciprocal in terms of control and corresponding in terms of affiliation. Through complementary responses, Respondent B essentially confirms Person A's self-presentational bids on both the control and affiliation axes. It's also apparent from Figure 4–1 that the complementary response always occurs vertically within the circle and always within the right or within the left halves of the circle. For completeness, Figure 4–2 presents the complementary *octants* for the 1982 Interpersonal Circle.

Proposition 4–4.   In addition to the complementary response, there are two other broad categories of "noncomplementary" responses one interactant may emit in

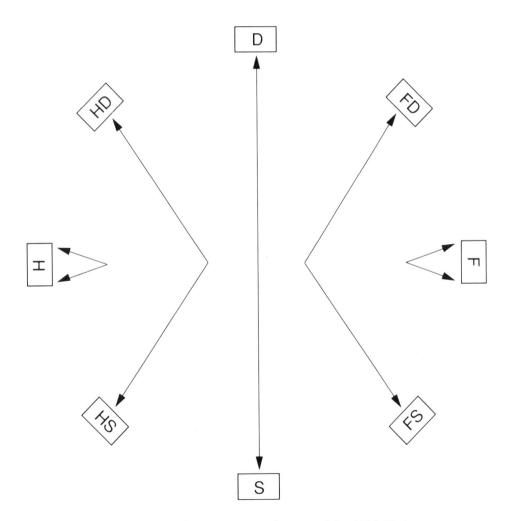

FIGURE 4–2. Complementary Octants of the 1982 Circle.

reaction to another. An *a*complementary response occurs when an individual reacts to another with actions either corresponding on affiliation or reciprocal on control, but not both (Kiesler, 1983, p. 202).

Figure 4–3 presents the *a*complementary quadrants and segments of the 1982 Interpersonal Circle. Continuing to use the friendly-dominant person as an example, an interactant's acomplementary response would be either friendly-dominant ("isomorphic acomplementarity"; Kiesler, 1983, p. 202) or hostile-submissive ("semimorphic acomplementarity"; p. 202). In the case of the friendly-dominant/friendly-dominant matchup, Respondent B accepts Person A's affiliation bid with correspondence (friendly in reaction to friendly), but rejects Person A's control bid with nonreciprocity (dominant in reaction to dominant). In the case of the friendly-dominant/hostile-submissive dyad, Respondent B accepts Person A's control bid with reciprocity (submissive in reaction to dominant), but rejects Person A's affiliation bid with noncorrespondence (hostile in reaction to friendly). In both instances, Respondent B accepts the friendly-dominant person's self-claim on one dimension, but rejects it on the second.

Proposition 4–4 (continued).   The third broad category of response is the anticomplementary reaction in which an individual reacts to Person A in a way that is both noncorresponding in terms of affiliation and nonreciprocal in terms of control.

Figure 4–4 presents the *anti*complementary quadrants and segments of the 1982 Interpersonal Circle. Continuing our example, it can be seen in Figure 4–4 that the anticomplementary response to a friendly-dominant individual is hostile-dominant. In the case of the friendly-dominant/hostile-dominant matchup, Respondent B rejects Person A's affiliation bid with noncorrespondence (hostile in reaction to friendly) and rejects Person A's control bid with nonreciprocity (dominance in reaction to dominance). In sum, Respondent B rejects Person A's self-definitional bid on both circle dimensions.

Anticomplementary personalities tend to be generally devalued more than complementary ones. Also, persons enacting anticomplementary behaviors are likely to be avoided and/or ignored by a person; in being avoided or ignored, they never become truly known or familiar. The result is that the person seldom risks trying out unfamiliar transactions that might offer new, challenging, and expanding life experiences.

Proposition 4–5.   Dyads characterized by complementary interactions tend to form stable relationships; dyads characterized by anticomplementary interactions are unstable and tend to terminate further transactions; dyads characterized by acomplementary interactions are unstable and conducive to change (either toward greater complementarity and stability, or toward greater anticomplementarity and termination).

"Complementary interactions evoke approach behaviors from both participants, anticomplementary ones lead to avoidance or escape actions, and acomplementary interactions evoke a mixture of approach and avoidant responses from both participants" (Kiesler, 1983, p. 209). C. C. Wagner (1995) noted:

What is important about complementarity is its function in the development and maintenance of relationships. Ongoing, stable relationships are expected to be

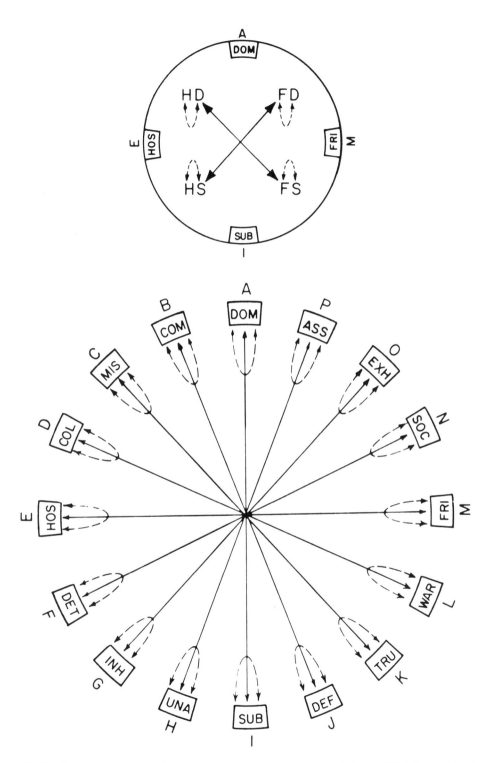

FIGURE 4–3. Acomplementary Quadrants and Segments of the 1982 Interpersonal Circle.

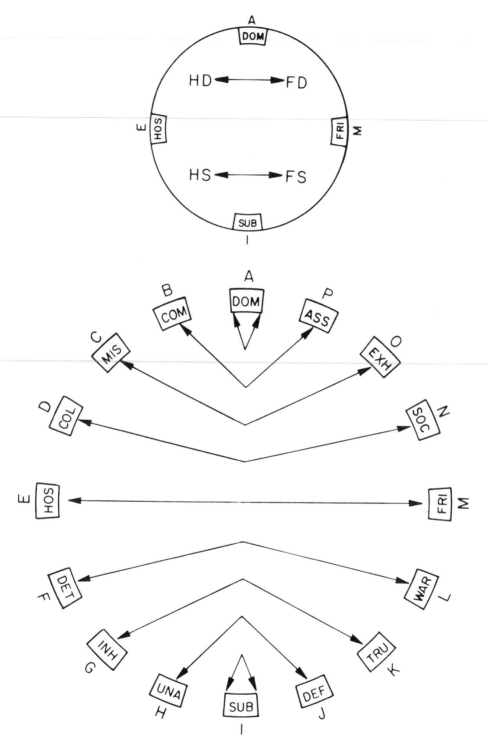

FIGURE 4–4. Anticomplementary Quadrants and Segments of the 1982 Interpersonal Circle.

characterized by complementary interactions, whereas those relationships that are characterized by frequent non-complementary interactions are expected to be less stable and enduring. (p. 6)

The amount of acceptance or rejection of individuals' self-definitional claims determines the level of comfort or anxiety present between the transactants. The most comfortable and least anxious matchup is a complementary one; the most uncomfortable and most anxiety-provoking dyad is an *anti*complementary one; the *a*complementary response produces a moderate level of discomfort or anxiety. Andrews (1974–1975) noted, "The complement of any style . . . is defined as a response which meets the expectations communicated by the style . . . , and which will tend to evoke further behavior of the same type" (p. 30). The result is a stable, self-perpetuating interaction or system. Noncomplementary relationships put interactants into a state of what might be called "relational conflict" (Villard & Whipple, 1976): "a state of system imbalance stemming from a perceived threat to the personal goals and/or interpersonal needs of either or both members of the relationship" (p. 219).

Conway (1987) summed it up this way:

> Complementary interactions are high probability ones, they are reinforcing to both participants, they maintain existing behavior patterns, and minimize anxiety and promote relatedness. Conversely, anticomplementary interactions . . . are thought to increase anxiety, are nonreinforcing, and increase the probability of the relationship terminating. (p. 19)

Goldston (1990) observed that it is important to conceptualize *anti*complementarity in a manner different from that implicit in Figure 4–4—deriving it trigonometrically relative to the peak scale in an individual's circle profile. He argued that anticomplementarity, instead, should be *defined empirically by the Nadir scale* obtained on a subject's circle profile—by the scale with a zero score, reflecting interpersonal behaviors that are extremely unlikely to occur (the "uncircle") (p. 54). If, for example, Subject A obtains a peak scale score on Segment O, his or her anticomplementary category is defined trigonometrically from Figure 4–4 as C. If, however, Subject A's empirical profile identifies his or her Nadir scale (usually zero) as D, then category D (not C) is the actual anticomplement for Subject A.

Goldston's (1990) "uncircle" is based on derivation of anticomplementarity, not from circle geometry, but directly from Sullivan's Bad Me/Not Me constructs. Bad Me behaviors for a particular individual are associated with moderate anxiety, are highly devalued, and are infrequently performed. Not Me behaviors are associated with maximum anxiety and are seldom, if ever, performed or even available as options to the person during interpersonal transactions. Anticomplementary behaviors, then, are those that constitute Bad Me and Not Me components of the self-dynamism—in both instances sets of behaviors with a very low probability of occurrence for a particular individual. As assessed with interpersonal inventories, behaviors of unlikely occurrence for a particular subject show up on a circle profile as the Nadir scale(s)—the category of interpersonal behavior *least preferred* by that person. Goldston (1990) advocated that we

> reconceptualize interpersonal complementarity as a continuum of behaviors ranging from those which are the most anxiety eliciting (Not Me or Bad Me maximum) to those which are least anxiety provoking in the individual (Good Me maximum).

Thus, the continuum ranges from response behaviors which are least complementary to those which are most complementary. (pp. 56–57)

Proposition 4–6.   Interpersonal complementarity and noncomplementarity operate precisely only within the same level or intensity of behavior. That is, interpersonal actions at a particular level of intensity tend (with a probability significantly greater than chance) to initiate, invite, or evoke from interactants complementary responses at the equivalent level of intensity (mild-moderate actions pull mild-moderate complementary responses, extreme acts pull extreme complementary responses) (Kiesler, 1983, p. 203).

This principle has implications, as we will see later, both for testing complementarity hypotheses and for the therapist's disengagement from extreme relationship impasses.

Proposition 4–7.   A given instance of the complementary response consists of a two-stage sequence occurring rapidly in an interactant: (a) a covert response, labeled the 'impact message,' and (b) the subsequent overt action, labeled the 'complementary response' (Kiesler, 1983, p. 205).

This principle also has central implications for valid tests of complementarity theory and has definitional relevance for our discussion of impact messages in Chapter 5.

Proposition 4–8.   The more extreme and rigid (maladjusted) the interpersonal style of Interactant B, the less likely he or she is to show the predicted complementary response to the interpersonal actions of Person A. An important exception occurs when the predicted complementary response to A falls at the exact segments that define B's extreme and rigid style (Kiesler, 1983, p. 206).

This proposition expresses that a maladjusted interactant tends to respond with his or her extreme and rigid style regardless of the segments and levels of interpersonal actions presented by Person A. Chapter 6 will examine this aspect of maladaptive interpersonal behavior in detail.

Unless the person interacting with maladjusted Interactant B presents a style exactly complementary to B's, B will resist strongly any other prompt or bid that would require him or her to move to other segments of the circle. To illustrate, Interactant B is defined at the extreme level of Octant KL, that is, at K_2L_2: Gullible-Merciful/All Loving-Absolving (cf. Figure 1–1). If B is interacting with a person whose style is exactly complementary (at Octant NO: Sociable-Exhibitionistic), B will respond to that person with K_2L_2 behaviors. But if B is interacting with a person with any other circle octant style, B will also respond with K_2L_2 behaviors, instead of with the predicted complementary response. In the latter instances, B uses extremity and rigidity of his or her interpersonal behavior to push A around, to impose an unyielding demand on A, or to exert maximum control on the relationship.

What this proposition also implies is that the radical trait assumptions of transsituationality and transtemporality (Mischel, 1968) "more validly apply to maladjusted persons than they do to more normal (mild-moderate level) individuals. The interpersonal definition of maladjusted behavior (extreme and rigid acts on the interpersonal circle) indicates clearly that the actions of abnormal individuals tend to override differences in situational parameters, including different styles of interactants" (Kiesler, 1983, p. 209).

> *Proposition 4–9.*   Interpersonal complementary applies primarily to transactions in naturally occurring, relatively unstructured interpersonal situations. The extent to which it applies to interactions occurring in various structured situations or in other environmental contexts remains to be determined (Kiesler, 1983, pp. 208–209).

The effect of situations as moderating factors for interpersonal transactions was discussed in Chapter 2. An important task for interpersonal investigators is to specify classes of situational factors relevant (and irrelevant) to elicitation of interpersonal acts from the respective octants of the interpersonal circle.

Until these clarifications appear, propositions of complementarity seem to apply precisely only to naturally occurring, relatively unstructured transactions such as during informal conversations at parties or other loosely structured social events, free-time activities and encounters, intimacy transactions, and open-ended psychotherapy interviews. The feature common in these situations is that minimal expectations exist regarding socially correct or desirable responses or social role definitions (e.g., boss-employee, teacher-student). Essentially, an unstructured situation is one that can appropriately elicit from interactants the entire range of interpersonal acts found on the circle. Also, typically it is within unstructured situations that most adult interactions with significant others occur.

> *Proposition 4–10.*   It is unclear how interpersonal complementarity applies over the temporal range of continuing transactions between interactants. Stages of sequential outcome for complementary and noncomplementary transactions need to be specified for all octants of the 1982 Interpersonal Circle (Kiesler, 1983, p. 209).

Interactions represent stochastic transactions of varying frequency and duration, over varying periods of lifetime. Friendly and unfriendly, close and casual, relationships are made up of various developmental stages. The temporal dimension as a moderating factor for interpersonal behavior was discussed in Chapter 2.

We have little systematic knowledge regarding the lawful redundancies that characterize the natural sequence of distinct interpersonal transactions. Proposition 4–10 underlines the necessity of charting empirically the distinctive course of different transactions and relationships. Stochastic methodologies are particularly able to accomplish this by assessing sequential codependencies between interactants, by revealing patterned redundancies occurring over time. Sequential analysis methods exclusively measure properties of a transacting dyad, in contrast to assessing individual behavior within a dyad. Stochastic methods capture all three aspects of circular causality (Danziger, 1976)—feedback, redundancy, and nonsummativity—which is a defining feature of interpersonal transactions.

We will see in later chapters that complementary, *a*complementary, and *anti*complementary responses that combine to define the principle of complementarity are basic to the definition of psychopathology (Chapter 6) as well as to specification of therapeutic goals and interpersonal interventions for a particular maladjusted client (Chapter 10).

Wiggins's Complementarity Analysis.   Wiggins (1982) offered an alternative octant formulation of complementarity based on the work of Foa (1961, 1964; Foa & Foa, 1974) and Carson (1969, 1979). It reflects the hypothesis that interpersonal behavior is structured around three facets: directionality (giving vs. taking, accepting vs. rejecting), object (self, other), and resource (status, love). Wiggins (1982) aligned the eight combinations of these three facets with respective octants of his earlier IAS circle. He derived from the facet structure of each octant the specific "kinds of dyads formed when an initial definition of an interpersonal situation is accepted by the other participant" (p. 216); that is, the specific complementary pairs of octants derived from his facet analysis. For example, Wiggins's complementary response to PA: Ambitious-Dominant behavior is LM: Warm-Agreeable, a response in which LM grants love but not status to self while granting both love and status to PA, as requested.

Wiggins's predictions for complementarity offer a clear theoretical alternative to the octant predictions of the 1982 Circle (see Figure 4–2). In no case do the corresponding octant predictions agree (for the example cited before, the 1982 PA pulls IJ, not LM; etc). These contrasting definitions of complementarity provide competing guides to future interpersonal theory and research (cf. Orford, 1986).

Benjamin's SASB Complementarity.   Benjamin (1984) defined complementarity in terms of the first two diamond surfaces of her SASB model. In SASB terminology, the highest value of complementarity represents a response of an interactant that is complementary in focus, affiliation, and interdependence. The *focus* is complementary when one participant focuses on self and the respondent focuses on other, or vice versa. *Affiliation* is complementary when both participants express the same type and intensity of affect (their affiliation responses fall in the same octant). *Interdependence* is complementary when both interactants express the same type and intensity of interdependence (their independence responses fall in the same octant).

Psychometric Indices for Analysis of Complementarity

Although a cluster of complementarity indices have been used in previous research on interpersonal complementarity, very few if any, attempts have been made to compare empirically their joint applications to a set of data. To a large degree, the available methodology has only scattered instances of application, accumulated normative data on the indices is nonexistent, and psychometric properties of the indices have not been studied systematically. The distinguishing characteristic of all indices of complementarity is that they are derived from a set of two circle inventory scores: One protocol characterizes Interactant A of a dyad, the second protocol describes Interactant B.

Ordinal Indices.   Perhaps the earliest procedure for obtaining an index of complementarity (Andrews, 1973) involved calculation of a correlation coefficient between a pair of subjects' predicted and obtained profile of inventory scores. Before one can use dyadic coefficients in further statistical analyses, however, each dyad's coefficient needs first to be transformed to its Fisher z-score equivalent.

A more recent index, which might be termed the "summed squared differences" (SSD) index, applies Andrews' logic to obtain scores that can be used in ANOVA, MANOVA, and various other multivariate analyses. Examples of its application can be found in Auerbach, Kiesler, Strentz, Schmidt, and Serio (1994), Kiesler and Goldston (1988), Kiesler and Watkins (1989), and Weinstock-Savoy (1986).

The basic procedure is as follows: In a perfectly complementary dyad, the inventory scores Person A obtains on each octant (or segment) would be equivalent to the scores Person B obtained on the respective complementary octants (see Figure 4–4). For example, A's score on the FS octant would equal the score B obtained on the FD octant; A's score on F would equal B's score on F; A's score on the FD octant would equal B's score on the FS octant; and A's score on S would equal B's score on D. Hence, to obtain a SSD index for a particular experimental dyad, each of person A's octant scores is subtracted from person B's on each of the respective complementary octants; each difference score is squared and then summed to constitute the SSD index. The closer a SSD score is to zero, the greater the complementary fit between Person A and Person B's interpersonal behavior.

A third continuous index of complementarity (Goldston, 1990) has seldom been incorporated in previous studies using circle inventories. The index is limited to inventories in checklist form that have at least two levels of item intensity (e.g., ICL, CLOIT-R). Using the Average Intensity Level (AIN) score originally described by LaForge (1977) as a measure of the overall intensity present in a given interpersonal profile, Goldston (1990) first calculated AIN scores for each member of a dyad and then calculated an AIN difference score for each dyad in his sample. The lower the AIN difference score, the closer Person A and Person B's overall intensities of interpersonal behavior match each other. The AIN difference scores for each dyad can be used as measures of intensity correspondence to test directly Proposition 4–6.

Nominal Indices.   A useful nominal index of profile complementarity can be obtained from an analysis of Person A and Person B's *peak quadrant* scores. For each person in a given dyad, the highest obtained quadrant score is determined. For each dyad, identified peak quadrants will then fall into one of three patterns: complementary (HD-HS, FD-FS), acomplementary (HD-FS, HS-FD, HD-HD, HS-HS, FS-FS, FD-FD), or anticomplementary (HD-FD, HS-FS). These patterns are apparent in Figures 4–2 and 4–3. These three groupings can be used to form independent or dependent variable groupings for subsequent analyses. Dietzel and Abeles (1975) used the peak quadrant procedure to arrive at a set of dimensional complementarity scores by assigning a dyadic score of "3" for complementary, "2" for acomplementary, or "1" for anticomplementary classifications.

Goldston (1990) argued that the peak quadrant classification is often imprecise since its determination ignores the actual location of subject's peak segment score; it forces all subjects to be characterized at the middle of the peak quadrant (e.g., Segment O), when their actual peak segment may fall anywhere within the quadrant (e.g., Segment N). Goldston's solution is to identify Person A's (also Person B's) actual highest segment score, then tailor A's precise quadrant by including adjacent segments of each side of the peak segment. Then these modified peak quadrants are used to arrive at complementary, acomplementary, or anticomplementary classifications.

More recently, two comprehensive and sophisticated procedures for analyzing complementarity have been introduced. The first is Tracey's (1994; Tracey & Schneider, 1995) confirmatory test of complementarity using Hubert and Arabie's (1987) randomization test of hypothesized order relations. This method relies on an exact specification of the order relations predicted by a particular model. It provides an explicit descriptive measure of the degree to which these hypothesized order relations are satisfied by a given data set, and a significance level that is based on a specific null conjecture of how the order relations were chosen. The method presents a "correspondence index" (CI) that indexes the relative fit of the predicted order to the actual data, specifying the proportion of predictions that are confirmed by the data minus the proportion of predictions that are disconfirmed. A CI of 1.0 indicates perfect fit; a CI of −1.0 indicates perfect mismatch (the case where each prediction is the opposite of what it should have been). The interested reader is referred to Tracey (1994) and Tracey and Schneider (1995) for more detail and illustration.

Gurtman, Kiesler, Schmidt, and Wagner (1994) derived a test of interpersonal profile complementarity based on the curve-fitting profile scoring developed by Gurtman (1994) and described earlier in Chapter 1. The authors sought to develop and demonstrate an approach to testing for interpersonal complementarity in a way that integrates interpersonal measurement with interpersonal theory. They argued that an adequate test of theory requires (a) that measures conform closely to the prescribed circumplex structure of the circle, (b) that individuals' interpersonal tendencies be represented using measurement practices that are consistent with interpersonal theory, and (c) that dyadic relations be evaluated by correlation measures that follow naturally from circle representations. They derived a measure of complementarity that met all three of these criteria, called the "cosine-difference correlation," which assesses the cosine of the angular discrepancy between the actual and predicted positions on the circle (between Person A and Person B's central tendencies or peak interpersonal categories). They also described how the curve-fitting indices of amplitude and goodness-of-fit can be used to investigate the respective variables of strength/extremity and clarity of interactants' interpersonal maneuvers, which they hypothesized may moderate the extent of complementarity present in interactions.

Gurtman et al. (1994) concluded that since the cosine-difference correlation is an index tied directly to the circle it is "an ideal measure with broad applicability to the kinds of research questions and methodologies typically found in most complementarity studies. . . . We hope that adoption of our standardized method and indices for complementarity analysis will facilitate emergence of [a] more robust set of findings" (p. 23).

EMPIRICAL RESEARCH IN COMPLEMENTARITY

A prodigious literature examining interpersonal complementarity in day-to-day and in psychotherapy transactions has accrued. To date, the best detailed review of these studies can be found in Orford (1986), although his review covered only a percentage of available studies.

It would require a separate book to review comprehensively this enormous literature. To assist that future task, and to give the reader a picture of the amount of research activity in this area, a detailed citation of studies of which I am aware will be presented at this point.

The first large group of studies examined the process of *interpersonal complementarity* as it operates *between normal interactants* in various contexts: Auerbach et al. (1994), Bluhm, Widiger, and Miele (1990), Brokaw and McLemore (1988), J. Campbell (1980),

S. R. Campbell (1991), S. R. Campbell and Brown (1990), Celani (1974), Delgado (1990), Duke and Ekstrand (1980), Duke and Mendelson (1980), Duke and Nowicki (1982), Edquist (1973), Ekstrand (1980), Estroff and Nowicki (1992), Fiore (1975), Gaelick, Bodenhause, and Wyer (1985), Gillespie (1961), Goldfarb (1980), Goldston (1990), L. M. Horowitz et al. (1991), Kerckhoff and Davis (1962), Ladd, Nowicki, and Duke (1979), Lovejoy and Busch (1993), Moos and Speisman (1962), Nowicki and Manheim (1991), O'Connell (1979), Okiyama and Vande Kemp (1991), Palmer and Byrne (1970), Patterson (1976, 1982), Raush (1965), Raush, Dittman, and Taylor (1959), Raush, Farbman, and Llewellyn (1960), Reid (1968), P. L. K. Rice (1970), Rosenfeld (1967), D. Schwartz (1980), K. M. Schwartz (1980), Shannon and Guerney (1973), Smelser (1961), Sox (1983), Strong, Hills, Kilmartin, et al. (1988), Teyber, Meese, and Stollak (1977), Thibodeau (1979), Thorne (1987), Tracey (1994), Valone (1982), C. C. Wagner (1995), Wetter (1984), Wilkie (1987), Wilkie and Conway (1988), Winch (1958), and T. L. Wright and Ingraham (1986).

The second large group of studies examines the propositions of *complementarity* as they apply for *psychopathological groups or within the psychotherapy context:* Alpher and France (1993), Andrews (1973, 1974–1975, 1990), Bandura, Lipsher, and Miller (1960), Beery (1970), Berzins (1977), Bierman (1969), S. R. Blumberg and Hokanson (1983), Bohn (1965, 1967), Brokaw (1983), Brokaw and McLemore (1983, 1988), Celani (1974), Chance (1966), Coulter (1993), Crowder (1972), Dietzel and Abeles (1975), Filak, Abeles, and Norquist (1986), Freeman (1971), Friedman and Di Matteo (1979), Gaffin (1981), Gamsky and Farwell (1966), Gonick (1987), Halpern (1965), Heller, Myers, and Kline (1963), Henry et al. (1986, 1990), Hertel (1972), L. M. Horowitz et al. (1991), Kell and Mueller (1966), Kiesler and Goldston (1988), Kiesler and Watkins (1989), Knight (1992), Laird and Vande Kemp (1987), Mueller (1969), Mueller and Dilling (1968, 1969), A. P. Nelson (1984), Pande and Gart (1968), P. L. K. Rice (1970), Rottschafer and Renzaglia (1962), Rudy et al. (1985), Salzman, Shader, Scott, and Bonstock (1970), Schopler (1959), Schuldt (1966), Shean and Uchenwa (1990), Svartberg and Stiles (1992), Swaney and Stone (1990), Swensen (1967), Tasca and McMullen (1993), Thompson et al. (1991), Tracey and Hays (1989), Tracey and Schneider (1995), Tracey and Sherry (1993), Van Denburg and Holifield (1993), B. C. Wagner (1984), Weinstock-Savoy (1986), Whiffen et al. (1990), and Wyrick (1979).

Orford's Critique

Empirical research supporting the complementarity principle (Kiesler, 1983) was challenged by Orford (1986; see also Orford, 1994). Orford critically examined the evidence for interpersonal complementarity cited by Kiesler (1983) and concluded that the only prediction finding support was on the friendly side of the circle (that friendly-dominant and friendly-submissive behaviors are mutually evoking). Disconfirming findings reported by Orford were that (a) hostile-dominant acts are frequently responded to with further hostile-dominant behavior (rather than with predicted hostile-submissive behavior), and that (b) hostile-submissive behavior is frequently met with friendly-dominance (rather than with predicted hostile-dominance). Orford (1986) discussed in detail the conceptual and methodological problems with research into complementarity and appealed for a critical reexamination of Kiesler's (1983) propositions in complementarity research. He also suggested that moderator variables significantly affected predictions of complementarity. In particular, Orford postulated that inter-personal contingencies are influenced by setting, status, and temporal factors that were discussed, but not emphasized, in Kiesler's (1983) propositions.

Orford's (1986) specification that setting, status, and temporal factors operate as moderator variables for determination of complementary and noncomplementary out-comes is quite consistent with Propositions 4–9 and 4–10. Proposition 4–9 stated that interpersonal complementarity applies primarily to naturally occurring, relatively un-structured interpersonal situations; the extent to which it applies in various structured situations or in other environmental contexts remains to be determined. Proposi-tion 4–10 added that it is unclear how interpersonal complementarity applies over the temporal range of continuing transactions between interactants; the stages of sequen-tial outcome for complementary and noncomplementary transactions need to be speci-fied for all octants of the 1982 Interpersonal Circle.

A new proposition can be added at this point that provides more specificity in re-gard to appropriate situational parameters—

Proposition 4–11. The condition of complementarity is likely to obtain and be maintained in a dyadic relationship only if the following conditions are operative: (a) the two participants are peers, (b) are of the same gender, (c) the setting is un-structured, and (d) the situation is reactive (in the sense that what one person does is able to influence what the other person does).

Counterpoint

Kiesler (1987b, 1991) suggested caution regarding Orford's conclusions and offered several clarifications to place Orford's review in a more balanced perspective. *First,* since multiple interpersonal circles exist, valid tests of complementarity for any par-ticular circle require the use of measures which fit the structure of that circle. Orford drew strong conclusions about the Kiesler and Wiggins circles from studies that exclu-sively used the ICL—a measure tied specifically to Leary's circle and one that pro-vides a poor fit to the Kiesler and Wiggins circles.

Second, as Orford noted, few available studies have analyzed "interaction units" (action-reaction sequences), in contrast to aggregated data; the most valid tests of complementarity can be discovered only by looking at the moment-by-moment sequen-tial negotiations occurring between dyadic interactants. In this regard, we have noth-ing that even resembles normative data that might provide representative percentages of complementary and noncomplementary transactions or negotiations that occur day in and day out throughout this country, or throughout the world. As Conway (1987) observed: "Certainly, other interactional patterns occur frequently, e.g. Friendly-Dominance/Friendly-Dominance, Hostile-Submission/Hostile-Submission, and are more common, I think, than Leary or Kiesler might lead one to believe" (p. 14).

Third, all available studies of complementarity have analyzed only the overt-action/overt-reaction chain of the circular transaction cycle; whereas propositions of complementarity seem most veridically applicable to the overt-action/*covert*-reaction link of the chain (Person A's overt action, Person B's covert-impact response, as stated in Proposition 4–7). None of the research in regard to which Orford drew his mostly pessimistic conclusions studied the crucial overt-to-covert link in the interpersonal transaction cycle. Interpersonal complementarity can never be precisely tested solely by matching two interactants' patterns of overt behavior. Tests at this level are one link removed in the interpersonal transaction cycle and invariably can provide only approximate confirmations. Instead, precise tests require matching of one person's pattern of *overt* behavior with an interactant's pattern of *covert* behavior. As Kiesler et al. (in press) document, whether interpersonal feelings plus action tendencies that reflect the pulled-for complementary response get enacted or not depends on the presence and strength of competing inhibitory-defensive processes. These inhibitory-defensive processes arise when inconsistencies exist between person B's characteristic style of self-definition and self-presentation and (a) behaviors inherent in the pulled-for complementary response; (b) behaviors under the control of environmental factors such as physical setting and social/interpersonal variables (role expectations, status, gender, and other interactant factors—as Orford, 1986, articulated).

Duke and Nowicki (1982) emphasized that another covert component, the *perception* of dyadic complementarity, is an important factor. They argued that the perception may be more important in relation to satisfaction than the actual overt complementarity of a couple. Further, each member of a dyad may perceive the relationship differently, which, in turn, might affect judgments of overall relationship satisfaction. In a sequential analysis study of interpersonal complementarity, Federman (1980) summarized his obtained pattern of IMI findings as follows:

> Self-report (A) is related to behavior (B), and behavior is related to the IMI (C), but self-report is, by and large, unrelated to the IMI. What exists is a chain of events (A-B-C) that are significantly but moderately correlated at each link. The relationships are not so strong, however, that the middle link can be eliminated and still allow an observer to know that the two events on the end are connected. It is like hearing a story third hand: there is probably some basis for it in the original event, but without the intervening links, it is difficult to establish the tie. (p. 112)

In the same vein, Pincus (1994) pointed out that interpersonal complementarity should not be conceived of "as some sort of stimulus-response process based solely on overt behavioral actions and reactions. He continued that most interpersonal theorists have emphasized some intrapsychic processes that color individuals' perceptions of their interpersonal world and thus their overt reactions to others: personifications, selective inattention, parataxic distortions (Sullivan, 1953a, 1953b); emotions, action tendencies, and interpretations (Kiesler, 1987a; Kiesler et al., in press); expectancies (Carson, 1982); fantasies and self-statements (Brokaw & McClemore, 1991); and cognitive interpersonal schemas (Foa & Foa, 1974; Safran, 1990a; Wiggins, 1982).

Fourth, interpersonal theory does *not* postulate that any randomly selected relationship between two interactants will show complementary patterns of behavior as defined by the interpersonal circle. What the theory does postulate is that one interactant's interpersonal behavior *tends to pull* complementary behaviors from the other interactant; whether a complementary outcome occurs for one interactant in a particular dyad depends crucially on what the other person concurrently wants, seeks, and is most comfortable with. When the self-presentation behaviors of two interactants mesh and are mutually confirming, the outcome is complementarity; when they clash, the outcome is anticomplementarity; when they only partially mesh, the outcome is acomplementarity (Kiesler, 1983). Tracey (1994) made the point succinctly: "To expect complementarity to hold equally in all situations is not reasonable. Interpersonal theorists argue that the eliciting power of behavior has a substantial effect on an individual's response, not that it will have a determining effect" (p. 876). Theoretically, then, the investigator does not expect to find complementary pairings in all (or even most) interpersonal encounters, as Orford's thesis assumes. Depending on interactant mixes and the other important contextual and intervening factors amplified by Orford, any one of the three outcomes may occur.

Horowitz et al. (1991), in their journal article on the interpersonal impact of self- and other-derogations, discussed a number of methodological and conceptual issues relevant to tests of complementarity. They emphasized that interpersonal theory does not claim that every reaction to a given behavior will be complementary; rather, it claims that when interactants' behaviors are not complementary, the interactants seek to resolve the discrepancy through further negotiation. Further, noncomplementary responses, particularly on the dominance axis, seemed to occur as opening transactional moves, especially in situations that impose an expectancy of power or status negotiation. They concluded: "Complementarity should not be expected from every sequence of action and reaction. Instead, the effects of different types of noncomplementary reactions on the subsequent interaction should be explored experimentally" (Horowitz et al., 1991, p. 77).

Fifth, it is crucial to remember that the degree of rigidity and extremity of an interactant's behavior serves as an important moderator of whether or not a complementary pattern will exist within a particular transaction. As Proposition 4–8 stated, the more extreme and rigid (maladjusted) the interpersonal style of Interactant B, the less likely he or she is to show the predicted complementary response to the interpersonal actions of Person A. The maladjusted individual, thus, is an interactant who rarely exhibits the complementary behavior to anyone—except in the relatively rare instances during which he or she is interacting with a perfectly complementary partner.

Sixth, we need to determine empirically the degree of situational constraint operative for expression of interpersonal behaviors. In their review of the literature, Duke and Nowicki (1982) reported that complementary dyads attain higher ratings of performance on tasks requiring cooperation, whereas anticomplementary dyads perform better on tasks requiring competitive behaviors (Duke & Ekstrand, 1980). Moskowitz (1994), demonstrated that the level of generality for interpersonal behaviors (dominance, submissiveness, agreeableness, quarrelsomeness) was lower in agentic (work-status) situations than for interpersonal behavior in communal (acquaintance-friend) situations. She speculated that behavior in agentic situations (e.g., with a supervisor) may be substantially influenced by role expectations. In contrast, in a communal situation that involves friends or acquaintances, individuals may have greater freedom to act in accordance with their individual behavioral tendencies (Moskowitz, 1994, p. 931). Her suggestion is consistent with Propositions 4–9 and 4–11, which state that complementarity can be expected to occur primarily in natural, relatively unstructured, and peer situations.

Seventh, Tracey (1993; Tracey & Guinee, 1990) argued that friendly and hostile behaviors are reacted to differently. Acting in a complementary manner to a friendly behavior is more in keeping with social convention than acting in a complementary manner to a hostile behavior: It cannot be assumed that friendly and hostile behaviors are equal in their eliciting power. Tracey (1993) also argued that these base-rate effects should be most prominent in relationships in the early stages or those interactions determined more by social norms (where there is limited familiarity). As familiarity grows over the course of interaction, there should be a decreased need to take account of the base-rate differences between friendly and hostile behaviors.

Tracey (1994) applied his earlier analysis by advocating that one reason for past equivocal results from empirical studies of complementarity, especially those using act-by-act sequential analyses, has been neglect of the importance of differential base rates across the circle interpersonal behaviors, especially the different base rates for friendly and hostile behaviors. Generally, depending on various social contexts, some behaviors are more likely to be enacted than others, regardless of preceding antecedent behaviors; yet, in sequential analysis studies researchers control only for the base rate of the antecedent behavior. This procedure ignores the possibility that, if base-rate differences in consequent behaviors exist, an individual is more likely to respond in some manners than others.

In an empirical analysis of complementarity, Tracey (1994) demonstrated that when base rates of the different behaviors were controlled, complementarity was more strongly supported, especially negative complementarity (given hostile antecedent behaviors). Only by taking account of the general trends of individuals to be friendly was negative complementarity demonstrated. The fact was that respondents did not match hostile behaviors with hostile behaviors; rather what was observed was an *increase* in hostility when presented with preceding hostile behavior. Tracey (1994) concluded:

> The constraining effect of behavior was moderated by the specific type of behavior (i.e., friendly or hostile) and by the different base rates in behaviors demonstrated. Once the moderating effects of behavior type and base rate are accounted for the support for the presence of complementarity in interaction is supported. (p. 877)

In a similar vein, C. C. Wagner (1995) observed:

> Whatever the baseline frequency of a particular behavior for a particular individual, that behavior will be exhibited more frequently when the person is in the presence of an interactant who frequently exhibits the complementary behavior (and less frequently around another interactant who rarely exhibits the complementary behavior. (p. 19)

He argued that it is important to differentiate *selection* versus *transactional* complementarity (C. C. Wagner, 1995, p. 17). In the case of selection complementarity, a particular relationship permits the interactants to be reinforced for engaging in their typical, baseline behavior. However, in the case of transactional complementarity, the participants are "pulled" to deviate their behavior from baseline to meet the act-by-act demands of the current interactant. C. C. Wagner (1995) concluded:

> It is yet to be determined the extent to which complementarity exerts its primary influence situationally by "pulling" act-by-act complementary behaviors from interactants or more subtly, by influencing individuals to select relationships that naturally reinforce their preferred interpersonal style. (p. 21)

An equivalent argument is made also by proponents (e.g., Marcus & Holahan, 1994; T. L. Wright & Ingraham, 1986) of the social relations model (Kenny & La Voie, 1984), as discussed in Chapter 2. This model provides a method to separate individual differences (Actor or Respondent) effects from relationship-specific (Transaction) effects in analysis of interpersonal behavior. The social relations' individual differences (individual reciprocity) effect is equivalent to C. C. Wagner's (1995) selection (dyadic baseline) complementarity; the social relations transaction (unique dyadic reciprocity) effect is equivalent to Wagner's transactional complementarity.

Eighth, Nowicki and Manheim (1991) noted that investigators have yet to determine how much time is required for complementarity to make its impression on a relationship:

> It is possible that the lack of consistent empirical support for the complementary hypothesis reported by Orford (1986) may be due, in part, to an inability to pinpoint precisely when interactants are engaged in transactions which are affected by interpersonal complementarity. Consistent with the results of the present study, investigators who have found support for the complementary hypothesis are usually those who went beyond a single brief interaction or studied interpersonal behavior over differing lengths of time (e.g., Dietzel & Abeles, 1975; Raush, 1965; Shannon & Guerney, 1973). (p. 330)

A summary of research on reciprocity using the social relations model (Kenny & La Voie, 1984) similarly concluded that only in long-term relationships is there compelling evidence for reciprocity; in short-term relationships (e.g., interactions with strangers), no evidence emerges.

Ninth, Van Denburg and Kiesler (1993) suggested that their proposition of *transactional escalation* "may help explain some of the inconsistent empirical results regarding the proposition of interpersonal complementarity in transactions" (p. 16). The principle states that among both normal and abnormal subjects, during periods of stress a person's prototypical interpersonal behaviors become more extreme and rigid—the individual relies on and escalates behaviors that are most familiar and most automatically performed. Van Denburg and Kiesler (1993) observed that another plausible explanation for the lack of consistent findings supporting complementarity is that "in some instances studied interactants may simply be maintaining or escalating their typical interpersonal behaviour pattern in reaction to their perception of threat in the particular interpersonal situation" (p. 17). Making an argument similar to Tracey's (1993, 1994), they noted:

> Unfortunately, for the most part the research on complementarity has neglected to measure the baseline interpersonal style of interactants. . . . As a result, noncomplementary behaviours to an interactant's evoking behaviour may in some cases simply represent a person's typical . . . stylistic escalation in reaction to stress. (Van Denburg & Kiesler, 1993, p. 17)

Horowitz et al. (1991) provided the only recent experimental evidence for "reciprocity" on the control axis and proposed a number of methodological and theoretical hypotheses of importance to interpersonal complementarity research. Based on their studies of semantics and on the interpersonal impact of self- and other-derogations, they arrived at a series of conclusions:

1. Judgments of nurturance are not independent of judgments of dominance—people seen as friendly or hostile are more apt to seem self-assured or assertive, whereas people who seem submissive, helpless, or passive are more apt to be seen as neutral in nurturance.

2. Previous research has often forced individuals to rate the two interpersonal dimensions independently, thus obscuring the rating dependency they discovered.

3. Interpersonal theory does not claim that *every* action to a given behavior is complementary; rather, it claims that when the interactants' behaviors are not complementary, the discrepancy needs to be resolved through further negotiation.

4. Noncomplementary responses (particularly on the dominance axis) seem to occur as opening moves under certain conditions, implying a need to negotiate power or status.

Interpersonal research has a long way to go before a heuristic body of data becomes available that can offer replicable answers to interpersonal complementarity theory. Other issues, besides the crucial ones just articulated, include (a) the necessity of using circle measures demonstrating close fit to circumplex structure (at present, only the IAS-R, the IIP-C, and the octant version of the IMI satisfy this requirement); (b) whether vector point, axis, hemisphere, quadrant, octant, or segment scores are used in calculations (segment scores represent the most conservative and powerful test); (c) whether the scores used are raw (normative) or ipsatized (Block, 1957; Cattell, 1944; Paddock, Potts, Kiesler, & Nowicki, 1986); (d) whether the complementarity index is constructed from a correlation coefficient between interactants' profiles, a summed difference score squared, a summed absolute value difference score, or from cross-product scores in regression analysis; (e) whether data are from self-reports, participant ratings, or nonparticipant observations; (f) whether nonverbal as well as verbal interactant behaviors are being rated in observational studies; (g) whether the interactional context is structured (with clear roles or rules for each participant) or unstructured (novel, or unfamiliar); (h) whether the transactants are strangers, acquaintances, friends—more generally, significant others—or not; (i) whether noticeable age or status differences exist among the interactants; (j) whether the interactants are of same or opposite gender; and (k) whether the investigator measures all the seven possibilities of covert and overt reactions to noncomplementary situations hypothesized by Secord and Backman (1961, 1965).

Finally, researchers should keep in mind that a set of *five* conceptually distinct operationalizations have been offered under the rubric of interpersonal complementarity. Investigators who use the two-dimensional adult interpersonal circles in the Leary (1957) tradition can find either (a) the Carson (1969) and Kiesler (1983) predictions or (b) the Wiggins (1982) predictions. Those who use Benjamin's (1974, 1993) three-dimensional diamond model will find the SASB predictions of complementarity. Researchers favoring the communications psychiatry tradition find relational control indices of complementarity (Friedlander, 1993a, 1993b) that focus on reciprocity on the control dimension. Finally, workers who prefer the Schutz (1958) tradition can find FIRO-B definitions of complementarity that utilize expressed and wanted levels of three basic interpersonal dimensions. *Caveat emptor!*

CONCLUSION

By now, it should be obvious that interpersonal complementarity refers to a complex process! Interpersonal complementarity "should not be conceived of as some sort of stimulus-response process based solely on overt behavioral actions and reactions"

(Pincus, 1994, p. 121). Rather, complementarity springs from the psychological meaning attributed to others' overt behavior, not simply from the behavior itself.

Although the research evidence is far from conclusive, it remains theoretically compelling that, within day-to-day encounters, complementary transactions (a) increase the probability that existing behavior patterns will be maintained, (b) are reinforcing and self-confirming to both participants, (c) minimize anxiety, (d) promote relatedness, and (e) increase the likelihood of an enduring relationship. Noncomplementary (especially anticomplementary) transactions, in contrast, (a) challenge existing behavior patterns, (b) are to varying extents aversive to both interactants, (c) increase anxiety, (d) interfere with relatedness, and (e) increase the probability of relationship disruption and termination.

CHAPTER 5

Measurement of the Covert Complementary Response

The Impact Message Inventory

The most illuminating encounters for personology are moments during which inter-actants are moved by the feeling that they are adjusting to the Other's idiosyn-cratic tendencies. It is during such moments that one is aware of being influenced by personality.

(Thorne, 1986, p. 11)

The previous chapter documented that a central construct of interpersonal theory involves the bids for complementarity governing the exchanges of human interactants. Our interpersonal behaviors serve to establish distinctive kinds of relationships with others—complementary relationships that are comfortable and anxiety-free, and that serve to confirm our conceptions of who we are as individuals. It is necessary that we, in automatic and minimally aware ways, maneuver persons who are interacting with us to adopt relationship positions that are complementary or reinforcing of the positions we are advancing. The first effect of this transactional negotiation is that we begin to restrict the covert experience (feelings, images, cognitions, action tendencies)—the impact messages—of persons interacting with us in a manner that makes it more likely they will respond overtly in the way we desire.

IMPACT MESSAGES WITHIN PSYCHOTHERAPY

In the psychotherapy situation, to the extent that the therapist represents or becomes a significant person to the client, he or she will experience complementary or impact responses similar to those experienced by other persons in the client's life. The client's evoking messages to the therapist are representative of the client's self-defeating style with other significant persons in his or her environment. The therapist's emotional and other engagements, then, represent vital cues for targeting the client's problem—for targeting the self-defeating patterns of the client's particular rigid and extreme interpersonal style.

If, for example, a therapist repeatedly and strongly feels pulled into a competitive struggle with his or her client, it is likely that other important people in the client's life (spouse, colleagues, etc.) have experienced the same interpersonal engagement. Or a therapist may notice herself continually feeling entertained or engaged sexually by a particular client. Or he may find himself pulled in early and often to take charge of, give advice to, or make decisions for a client. Or, in the case of the obsessive, the therapist may become very cautious in what she says, holding back spontaneous replies and having difficulty concentrating on what the client is saying. And so on.

During psychotherapy sessions, it is crucial that therapists be able to identify the distinctive patterns of abnormal interpersonal behavior being enacted by their patients. A major way of accomplishing this is for *therapists to monitor routinely the internal engagements* (the objective countertransference feelings; see Chapter 9) *being evoked from them during the therapy transaction.* The repetitive central patterns being enacted with the therapist and with significant others outside therapy constitute the major problems targeted by psychotherapy.

From this contemporary interpersonal perspective, the attempt to understand personality, maladjustment, and the psychotherapeutic process requires the ability to measure the "restricted classes" of reactions or impacts that persons evoke from others through their interpersonal behaviors. The Impact Message Inventory (IMI; Kiesler, 1987c; Kiesler et al., 1985; Kiesler & Schmidt, 1993) was designed to measure the distinctively different covert reactions to the full range of behaviors found around the 1982 Interpersonal Circle. *The IMI's items measure the distinctive "direct feelings," "action tendencies," and "perceived evoking messages" that characterize each of the categories of interpersonal behavior found around the circle's circumference.*

Although interactants ordinarily are not clearly aware of their internal engagements or impacts in reaction to others, these covert reactions become available and reportable as attention is concentrated on them. Response to the IMI items demands a focus on these internal events, which typically occur as ground in an individual's transactions with others. The Inventory, thus, taps the automatic, relatively unconscious sets of emotional and other covert responses we have to others. It assesses one person's pattern of interpersonal behavior by measuring the subjective, covert engagements (emotions, action tendencies, attributions) that person distinctively evokes in interactants.

DEVELOPMENT OF THE IMPACT MESSAGE INVENTORY

A research program to test interpersonal communication theory needed an empirical device that could assess the impact message. Our solution came from the literature on interpersonal behavior and specifically from the interpersonal circumplex.

Wiggins (1982) noted that, at the time, a number of empirical schemes had been proposed for classification of characteristic interpersonal behavior, including those by LaForge and Suczek (1955), Lorr and McNair (1963, 1965, 1967), Schaefer (1959, 1961), G. G. Stern (1970), and Schutz (1958). Since interpersonal communication theory was anchored specifically in the Kaiser (M. B. Freedman et al., 1951; Leary, 1957) interpersonal circumplex, the first option our research group considered was LaForge and Suczek's (1955) Interpersonal Check List (ICL).

In developing items for the ICL, the Kaiser group had been careful to differentiate between items using transitive verbs to describe interpersonal acts, in contrast to items in the form of adjectives that describe the attributes or characteristics of interactants.

However, our examination of the ICL items left us dissatisfied with the adjectival content of many of the items. This item format did not facilitate constructing standard descriptions of interactants' *overt* interpersonal behaviors (actions) as the necessary first step in deriving item responses for our planned impact message inventory. For this purpose, we needed an inventory whose items would be exclusively in transitive verb form, more suitable for behavioral ratings. We were also concerned about the measurement gaps found in the friendly-dominant and hostile-submissive quadrants of the Kaiser circle that researchers (e.g., Lorr & McNair, 1963) had reported from empirical analyses of ICL ratings.

Our search soon identified Lorr and McNair's (1963, 1965, 1967) Interpersonal Behavior Inventory (IBI) as ideal for our purposes. Studies with both the ICL and the IBI had confirmed that interpersonal behavior in the normal and psychoneurotic realms exhibited a circular ordering that expressed the joint activity of two (or perhaps three) underlying factors. For both measures, the circular ordering consisted of categories of interpersonal behavior located around the circumference of the circle; LaForge and Suczek's (1955) ICL measured 16, whereas Lorr and McNair's (1967) IBI measured 15 interpersonal categories. The ICL consisted of both adjective and verb phrase items that respondents judged as applicable or not in describing their own interpersonal behavior or the behavior of someone with whom they had interacted. Lorr and McNair (1965, 1966) had criticized the ICL in that its adjective items often elicited diverse connotations within different subjects and thus lacked informational precision. To correct this shortcoming, Lorr and McNair had designed their IBI items to assess exclusively manifest acts or overt interpersonal behaviors.

In a series of IBI investigations carried out within the context of psychotherapy with adult patients, Lorr and McNair (1963, 1965, 1967; Lorr et al., 1965) developed their own interpersonal behavior circle. The 140 items of manifest interpersonal behaviors that came to compose the IBI (Lorr & McNair, 1967) yielded 15 category scores arranged on the circumference of their circumplex. The 15 IBI categories were labeled dominant, competitive, hostile, mistrustful, detached, inhibited, submissive, succorant, abasive, deferent, agreeable, nurturant, affiliative, sociable, and exhibitionistic.

Lorr and McNair's (1967) IBI items offered our research group operational descriptions of the domain of overt interpersonal behaviors or actions. However, what was needed for our to-be-developed measure of impact messages was a representative sample of *the corresponding emotional and other covert engagements that individuals exhibiting the 15 behavioral patterns produced in interactants.*

The strategy of scale construction we arrived at for the IMI was one in which descriptions of the overt interpersonal actions of a person would be employed as stimuli to elicit characteristic subjective reactions within interactants. Accordingly, our team pursued the following procedure for generating a sample of impact message items:

1. We used Lorr and McNair's (1967) 15 sets of items, adapted as 15 "pure" or prototypical paragraph descriptions, as stimulus presentations of the interpersonal behavior patterns found on the circumplex.

2. We presented each of the 15 respective paragraphs independently and consecutively to the six members of our team with the instruction that we imagine a live interaction with a person in our lives who characteristically enacts one of the 15 prototypical interpersonal patterns described in the paragraphs.

3. We then recorded (in response to the stem: "He makes me feel . . .") the emotional engagements and other impacts we individually fantasized in reaction to the 15 distinct interpersonal patterns, identified the common responses recorded by our group, and then constructed items to represent our generalized responses (in three subcategories: direct feelings, action tendencies, and perceived evoking messages). A finalized version of 259 items classified as descriptive covert reactions to one or another of the 15 paragraph descriptions constituted the initial form of the Impact Message Inventory (IMI-Form I).

4. We administered IMI-Form I to a large sample of normal undergraduates (subjects were assigned randomly to one of 15 groups, each of which received a different vignette as a stimulus). We wanted to determine empirically whether their ratings of the same 15 paragraphs, using our newly constructed item pool, would produce a two-factor circumplex solution in which the 15 IMI scales occupied circular locations isomorphic to those of the original 15 IBI scales.

5. Finally, data from the student sample were used to select items for inclusion in IMI-Form II. The goal of item analysis was the selection of the six best items for each of the 15 interpersonal scales, with two items each coming from the subcategories of direct feelings, action tendencies, and perceived evoking message. The major emphasis in item analysis was on identifying item sets that would yield a circular ordering in two-dimensional space. A second, and when possible equally important, consideration was the selection of items whose mean-rated applicability was highest for the keyed categories.

For each of the resulting 15 scales, two items measured the respondents' direct feelings (e.g., "he makes me feel cold"), two items measured action tendencies (e.g., "I want to put him down"), and two items measured perceived evoking messages (e.g., "he wants everyone to like him"). The respondent was asked to record on the IMI (on a 4-point scale) the extent to which each of the 90 items accurately reflected the impact a target person produced in him or her during a just completed interaction. The sum of the item ratings on a given scale indicated the relative strength of the target person's interpersonal behavior as communicated transactionally to the interactant respondent.

The result of this procedure was the Impact Message Inventory-Form IIA (Kiesler, 1987c; Kiesler, Anchin, et al., 1976, 1985; Perkins et al., 1979), which empirically anchored and offered initial confirmatory support for one of the key constructs in my communications theory of psychotherapy (Kiesler, 1973–1975, 1977, 1979; Kiesler, Bernstein, & Anchin, 1976). The measure provided an assessment of the domain of impact messages for the universe of late adolescent and adult normal and psychoneurotic individuals. The resulting 90-item IMI-Form IIA contained 6 items keyed to each of 15 prototypical interpersonal behavior patterns, with 30 items assessing each of three subscales of impact messages: direct feelings, action tendencies, and perceived evoking messages.

The initial IMI validation data offered some support for circumplex ordering of the 15 impact message categories, but somewhat poor confirmation that the 15 scales occupied a two-factor space around the axes of control and affiliation. Further, although the affiliation factor was strongly confirmed, the control dimension seemed to be reflected in two separate factors, dominance and submission.

Our initial validation study (Perkins et al., 1979) concluded that a particular encoder-person's impacts are indeed generalizable to a general population of decoder-interactants. (If, to summarize this study, we had used the terminology of interpersonal theory, we would have concluded that individuals' distinct patterns of interpersonal behavior evoke generalizable complementary responses from interactants; further, these complementary responses can be charted systematically on the interpersonal circumplex.) Because we had deliberately obscured decoder differences in our attempt to determine the common impact message, responses on the IMI had been averaged across subjects. The high internal consistency of each of the 15 categories of interpersonal impacts as well as our successful cross-validation of the factor structure on split-half samples confirmed our assumption that impact messages are generalizable. Further support for generalizability emerged from subsequent IMI studies as summarized in the Research Manual (Kiesler, 1987c). Reliability and validity evidence for the 15-category IMI are also summarized in the Manual (Kiesler, 1987c).

Wiggins (1982) observed that the emphasis of interpersonal circumplex measures other than the IMI is placed on what persons do to one another, on their observable actions. In contrast, the IMI is directed at the *intermediate impact link,* which can be distinguished conceptually from "subsequent actions . . . [an interactant] may take toward the original actor," in the chain of interpersonal actions and reactions (p. 198). He concluded that the focus of the IMI "upon the covert impact of a patient upon significant others provides a valuable source of clinical information that could not be derived from previous assessment devices" (p. 200). Wiggins (1982; see also Kiesler, 1983) also highlighted some of the structural psychometric problems with the IMI Form IIA measure.

More recently, a modified scoring procedure has been routinely recommended to obtain scores for 8 interpersonal circle octant scales, rather than the original 15 scales. The octant scales are *D:* Dominant, *HD:* Hostile-Dominant, *H:* Hostile, *HS:* Hostile-Submissive, *S:* Submissive, *FS:* Friendly-Submissive, *F:* Friendly, and *FD:* Friendly-Dominant. The octant version has demonstrated satisfactory circumplex and internal consistency reliability properties (Kiesler & Schmidt, 1993; Schmidt, Wagner, & Kiesler, 1994) and measures more closely, although in octant form, the most recent version of the interpersonal circle (Kiesler, 1983).

Table 5–1 presents examples of IMI octant version items that are keyed to (target the interpersonal behaviors of) the octant categories of the interpersonal circle. The

TABLE 5–1. Sample Items from the Impact Message Inventory, Octant Scoring Version

Octant Scale	Sample Item *"When I am with this person, she (he) makes me feel . . .*
Dominant (D)	bossed around."
Hostile-Dominant (HD)	that she thinks it every woman for herself."
Hostile (H)	distant from her."
Hostile-Submissive (HS)	that I should do something to put her at ease."
Submissive	I should tell her to stand up for herself."
Friendly-Submissive (FS)	that she trusts me."
Friendly (F)	welcome with her."
Friendly-Dominant (FD)	that she wants to be the charming one."

Inventory protocol and Research Manual (Kiesler & Schmidt, 1993) are available from the Mind Garden division of Consulting Psychologists Press, Palo Alto, CA.

Practicing clinicians can routinely use an additional training measure to develop expertise in identifying impact messages during psychotherapy sessions. Table 5–2 defines the four classes of impact messages that can be differentiated within an interactant's covert experience. Table 5–3 is a corresponding free-response therapist worksheet that clinicians can use to practice recording of their impacts to psychotherapy patients and to other target persons. These Therapist Worksheets have proved quite useful in training psychotherapists, both as an individual exercise and as a group exercise in which a client is viewed and rated, with group members subsequently sharing and validating their free-response impacts in a round-robin sequence.

The IMI was designed to identify and measure the distinctive central and repetitive ways in which we go about negotiating our transactions with others. It was designed to measure the relatively consistent interpersonal behavior pattern of one person as experienced through the covert reactions of other persons with whom he or she interacts.

Table 5–2.   Impact Messages. Definitions of the Four Subcategories: Direct Feelings, Action Tendencies, Perceived Evoking Messages, and Fantasies

An Impact Message refers to the various ways a particular person engages you internally as you are interacting with him or her. There are four major classes of Impact Messages: Direct Feelings, Action Tendencies, Perceived Evoking Messages, and Fantasies.

1. *Direct Feelings.*   While you are in the presence of a certain person, he or she arouses specific feelings in you—you are made to feel certain distinctive ways. This person pulls particular emotions, feelings, or attitudes from you—makes you experience them while he or she is present.

Examples

When I am with this person he or she makes me feel:

1. bored	**6.** put-down
2. angry	**7.** uneasy
3. complimented	**8.** distant from him
4. competitive	. . . and so on
5. admired	

2. *Action Tendencies.*   While you are in a person's presence you also experience definite urges to do something, or not do something, to him or her. These are behaviors or actions you want to direct toward the person when he or she is around—things you like doing or not doing when you're with that person.

Table 5–2. *(Continued)*

Examples

When I am with this person he or she makes me feel that:

1. I want to tell him off
2. I could tell her anything
3. I should leave him alone
4. I want to insult her

5. I can trust her
6. I can ask him to do anything
7. I should defend myself
   . . . and so on

3. *Perceived Evoking Messages.* When you're with a person, various ideas run through your head about what you think this person is trying to do to you, or what he or she is trying to get you to do. You're aware that the person seems to have some definite ideas about what he or she wants you to do or not do when you're present. Also, certain descriptions come to your mind about how this person sees your relationship to him or her—statements he or she might make to him- or herself about how he or she feels about you, what he or she thinks of you, generally what he or she may be saying to him- or herself about you.

Examples

When I am with this person it appears to me that he or she:

1. thinks I can't be trusted
2. doesn't care what I want
3. wants me to put him on a pedestal
4. wants to be the center of attention

5. is considerate of me
6. would rather be left alone
7. is determined to outdo me
   . . . and so on

4. *Fantasies.* Sometimes when you're with a person specific metaphors, images, or fantasies develop in your mind that seem to capture important aspects of your reactions to that person.

Examples

Sometimes when I am with this person it seems to me that:

1. we're playing poker with our cards clutched closely to our chests
2. often he drives a steamroller right over me
3. he's drowning in quicksand and can't bring himself to grab my hand
4. she's a fine glass figurine who must be handled delicately
   . . . and so on

TABLE 5–3. Impact Messages: Therapist Worksheet for Recording Direct Feelings, Action Tendencies, Perceived Evoking Messages, and Fantasies

Think of the particular person described to you. Or think of a person who seems to fit very closely the description you have received.

1. First, *imagine that you are in this person's presence,* in the process of interacting with him or her. Try to visualize what he or she looks like, what he or she would be doing and saying while with you.

2. Then, *focus on the impacts you would be feeling* with that person—the immediate reactions you would be experiencing. Keep in mind the four types of Impact Messages described to you.

3. Finally, fill in your answers *below* as to what your impacts are while interacting with this person. *Fill in what your predominant impact responses would be in each of the four groups.* For each group, write in your strongest response beside 1., your next strongest beside 2., and so on.

WHAT WE WANT ARE YOUR PERSONAL REACTIONS! Be sure to fill in at least one of your impact responses for each group.

Group 1: Direct Feelings (emotions the other person makes you feel)

When I am with this person he (she) makes me feel:

1. _____
2. _____
3. _____

Group 2: Action Tendencies (what you want to do or not to do to him or her)

When I am with this person he (she) makes me feel that:

1. _____
2. _____
3. _____

Group 3: Perceived Evoking Messages (what he or she wants you to do or not do, what he or she thinks of you)

When I am with this person it appears to me that he (she):

1. _____
2. _____
3. _____

Group 4: Fantasies (an image or metaphor that comes to mind as capturing your reactions to this person)

Sometimes when I am with this person it seems to me that:

1. _____
2. _____
3. _____

UNIQUE ADVANTAGES OF THE IMPACT MESSAGE INVENTORY

Although other interpersonal inventories (e.g., the ICL, the IAS-R, the IBI) are available for measuring the domain of interpersonal behaviors empirically charted on the Interpersonal Circle, the IMI is unique in assessing the covert reactions evoked during interpersonal transactions. *The IMI is a self-report transactional inventory designed to measure a target person's typical pattern of interpersonal behavior.* It measures the *self-reported* emotional, cognitive, and action-tendency internal engagements experienced by a second person during interactions with the target. The items are scored *transactionally* in that the second person's self-reported impacts or engagements are scored to characterize the target person's typical pattern of interpersonal behavior. As Wiggins (1982) concluded:

> The Impact Message Inventory is a much needed and welcome addition to the clinician's collection of methods for measuring dimensions of interpersonal behavior. The focus of the instrument upon the covert impacts of a patient upon significant others provides a valuable source of clinical information that could not be derived from previous assessment devices. (p. 200)

Because the IMI is both a self-report and transactional inventory, it is the first of its kind in the area of psychological measurement. The IMI is not a traditional self-report inventory since Person B's report of his or her internal engagements is *not* scored to provide characterizations of Person B's own interpersonal behavior. Rather, Person B's responses to the IMI items are scored to define the interpersonal behavior of Person A. The IMI is not a traditional rating instrument since Person B is *not* asked to judge, describe, or otherwise characterize A's overt behavior; rather, Person B *is* asked to report inner reactions and engagements experienced while interacting with A. Then, by use of empirical derived keys, the IMI is scored to characterize A's interpersonal behavior.

The IMI is designed to measure the interpersonal behavior of people as they go about their daily routine of establishing relationships with each other. Originally constructed to characterize primarily the patient-therapist interpersonal relationship in psychotherapy, it has proven useful for the study of any two-person late adolescent or adult interaction including that between husband-wife, friends, acquaintances, strangers, siblings, and other family members, and so on. The Inventory has wide applications to individual, marital, family, and group psychotherapy transactions, to analogue interviews and other laboratory dyadic situations, and to in situ transactions occurring daily in a person's life.

In particular, the IMI shows considerable promise for single-case and group studies of psychotherapy as well as for psychotherapy training and supervision. It may be used as an outcome measure by which the therapist, observers, and significant others record their changing interpersonal impacts to the patient over the course of therapy and follow-up periods. In marital and group therapy, it can serve as a repeatedly applied outcome measure filled out by spouses or group members on each other.

In the therapist training context, the Inventory can be used to sensitize therapists to the emotional and other engagements they experience with their patients, as well as to the patients' verbal and nonverbal behaviors that produce the impacts. It can also sensitize therapists to the impacts they regularly produce in their patients. Generally, the IMI can be used to assist therapists to broaden the range of their emotional sensitivity and response to a patient's nonverbal relationship messages.

Kiesler (1992; also see Chapter 9) illustrated in detail how interpersonal circle inventories, such as the IMI, can form an integral part of the conceptualization and assessment of important constructs that have derived from various psychotherapy theories—therapeutic alliance, social reinforcement, resistance and countercontrol, transference, and countertransference—and can also address other important issues such as therapist-patient matching, parallel process in psychotherapy and supervision, and assessment of personality disorders.

EMPIRICAL RESEARCH WITH THE IMPACT MESSAGE INVENTORY

The reader is referred to the *Research Manual for the Impact Message Inventory* (Kiesler, 1987c) for more detail regarding the more than 40 studies up to that time that had used the IMI to examine a wide range of clinical and other issues. Throughout the Manual, some of these studies are presented in detail to highlight specific issues, applications, or findings. Only brief descriptions of the 40 studies will be provided in this section.

The 40 studies fell into four broad categories: psychotherapy, maladjusted groups, personality, and health psychology.

Psychotherapy

Clinical Studies.   Five studies concentrated on patient-therapist dyads. Two studied the interpersonal impact of psychiatric outpatients, one in the context of the intake interview (Kiesler et al., 1982), the other within the context of group psychotherapy (Kivlighan et al., 1984). Three studied the interpersonal impact of therapists: one, of therapists with individual psychotherapy cases (Moras, Waterhouse, & Suh, 1981), one, of three eminent therapists during demonstration interviews (Zians, 1981), and the last, of clinical psychology versus psychodrama versus pastoral counseling interns during a role-played psychiatric interview (Hudgins & Chirico, 1982).

Analogue Studies.   Seven studies sought to understand the events of psychotherapy by analyzing single-session "analogue" interviews conducted with nonpatient undergraduate subjects. Anchin (1979) studied the effects of interviewer interpersonal behavior (obsessive vs. hysteroid) in combination with a stressful versus nonstressful condition (personal vs. impersonal questions) on the resulting impacts elicited by obsessive interviewees during an analogue session. Bale (1983) explored the effects of interviewer sex-role orientation (sex-typed or androgynous) as communicated nonverbally on female interviewees' level of self-disclosure and on their evaluations of interviewers in a one-session analogue situation. E. L. Cooley (1983) examined the effects of several factors (explanation vs. lack of explanation, presence vs. absence of positive "reframing") in the delivery of paradoxical symptom prescriptions on normal college students' ability to fall asleep. Wenzel (1980) investigated the effects of interviewer touch on interpersonal affiliation and control as perceived by androgynous versus sex-typed female interviewees. Wenzel (1984), in a follow-up study, studied the effects of interviewer touch by male and female interviewers, as it interacted with affiliative versus dominant nonverbal behavior, on the impacts experienced by interviewees exposed to these conditions. Thibodeau (1979) examined whether subjects exhibiting internal versus external locus of control would respond differently to complementary versus noncomplementary analogue therapists.

Maladjusted Groups

Clinical Studies.   Blumberg and Hokanson (1983) studied the effects of contrasting interpersonal behaviors on the reactions of depressed individuals. Subjects interacted with experimental confederates trained to portray different interpersonal roles (critical-competitive, supportive-cooperative, and helpless-dependent) during a laboratory procedure involving cooperative problem solving. Holliday (1983) examined interpersonal aspects of depression within the context of the marital relationship. Specifically, he tested whether the interpersonal behavior of depressive individuals is aversive to interactants and whether the aversiveness is partially mediated by the negative feelings of anxiety, guilt, and depression that are induced in interactants. Schreiber (1984) had listeners rate depressed individuals using the IMI and found that the depressed person scored in the submissive quadrants of the interpersonal circle. Kahn (1983; Kahn, Coyne, & Margolin, 1985) investigated how couples with a depressed partner evaluate their own behavior, their partner's behavior, and the relationship; how they cope with conflict in their relationship; and how they experience one another during a controlled interaction. Milestone (1984) explored the usefulness of the IMI, as filled out on each other by marital partners, for differentiation of distressed (dissatisfied) versus nondistressed (satisfied) marital couples. Goethe (1984) used the IMI as one of a battery of outcome measures in a comparative study of treatment procedures for persons with self-reported deficits in heterosocial skills. A. P. Nelson (1984) tested whether abnormal persons (male VA hospital patients) would demonstrate greater rigidity than normals in their interpersonal impacts across a series of brief interactions with stylistically different (hostile-dominant; submissive, neutral on affiliation; friendly, neutral on control) dyadic partners.

Analogue Studies.   Howes and Hokanson (1979) studied the reactions of persons interacting, in the context of waiting together for an experiment to begin, with a confederate portraying either a depressed, a normal, or a physically ill interpersonal role. Thornton (1984) tested the notion that typical responses to depressive behaviors follow a characteristic temporal sequence, such as initial sympathy followed by irritation and disappointment (Leary, 1957), or initial induced guilt and inhibited hostility followed by rejection and avoidance (Coyne, 1976a, 1976b). Chirico (1977) investigated perceptual/decoding differences between nonclinical groups of obsessive and hysteroid individuals. Undergraduates recorded their reactions to a simulated interview (either a silent videotape, a linguistically masked audiotape, or a typescript) in which the interviewer portrayed a dominant, and the interviewee a submissive, interpersonal style. Chirico (1980) replicated and extended his previous study by having obsessive and hysteroid individuals respond to the same interviewer-interviewee stimulus presentation in one of four communication channel conditions: face-only video, body-only video, audio only, or verbal only (typescript). Each subject also was subsequently presented the unedited all-channel videotape.

Kiesler and Federman (1978) used written descriptions of prototypic obsessive and hysteroid individuals as contrasting interpersonal stimuli to record the impacts the target descriptions evoked on the IMI from a sample of normal interactants. Greenwood (1979) studied the effects of a high- versus low-status interviewer on relationship impacts and on verbal expressions of doubt or uncertainty in groups of nonclinical obsessive and normal subjects. Federman (1980) set out to demonstrate the presence of a rigid interpersonal style among a group of dependent personality disorder individuals. Sequential analysis of the act-by-act behaviors of the dependent versus normal subjects, assigned to dyads who constructed team stories for Thematic Apperception Test (TAT) cards, was used to test the hypothesis that dependent subjects would impact their partners as behaving more submissively. Hudgins (1982) used Chirico's interviewer-interviewee presentations to study whether differences between Whitehorn and Betz's A versus B therapist types could be linked to perceptual-decoding preferences on the visual, audio, and linguistic channels of communication.

Personality

Chewning (1983) explored several factors (interpersonal distance, type and closeness of relationship, frequency of interaction, and interpersonal styles of interactants) that might influence the relationship between subjects and different classes of significant others. Schwaninger-Morse (1979) tested her prediction that a person's overt task behaviors would reflect primarily situational demands, while the person's interpersonal style (expressed through more subtle nonverbal behaviors) would be more consistent and generalizable across situations. She analyzed two speech measures, talk-time and turn-taking frequency, as each of her subjects enacted either a dominant or submissive role while engaging in either a positive or negative interaction with a partner. Simpson (1983) investigated the impact of social power, assertiveness, and race on interpersonal perception and influence. Subjects were assigned to either high or low power positions to work jointly on a series of tasks with assertive African American or white confederates who were assigned to the complementary power position. Saxby (1982) investigated how a perceiver's sex, a labeling (psychiatric vs. normal) assigned to the person being perceived, and the interpersonal behavior (dominant vs. submissive) of the person being perceived would affect how that person is actually perceived based on the interpersonal impacts registered by the perceiver. Kyle (1977) used the IMI to study person perception after a brief interaction between strangers (complementary vs. similar on FIRO-B Inclusion) in a naturalistic waiting-room setting. Cheek (1977) studied the effects of a fictional typescript interaction on an airplane between two opposite-sex strangers, with interactants varying according to sex, level of disclosure, and topic of disclosure. Castronova (1980) used the IMI to measure the distinctive interpersonal styles of adolescents characterized as high, medium, and low in moral judgment.

Three separate investigations focused on the interpersonal correlates of assertive behavior. Reagan (1978) had high versus low assertive females participate in experimental situations in which requests were made of them by a live role model. After viewing each role-played session, a group of observers independently recorded their impacts on the IMI, while a group of coders independently completed a behavioral coding sheet on each subject. Reagan (1979) extended and replicated her earlier study. This time, subjects high, low, or moderate in assertiveness participated in the role-playing procedure with the standard confederate; impacts and coding were again obtained from separate groups of observers. Labe-Sloan (1982) studied the effects of observer characteristics (high vs. low assertiveness) on IMI impacts recorded after observing four videotapes of assertive and nonassertive experimental portrayals.

Health Psychology

Three IMI studies by Auerbach and colleagues provide supportive evidence for the notion that interpersonal issues may be central to effective health care. Auerbach, Martelli, and Mercuri (1983) gave patients scheduled for dental extraction surgery either specific or general information about the impending surgery, delivered in either a personalized or relatively impersonal-businesslike fashion. Each patient filled out an IMI on the information-giver following the presurgical contact; also subsequently, while in the recovery room, each patient filled out an IMI on the dental surgeon who had performed the extraction. Auerbach, Meredith, Alexander, Mercuri, and Brophy (1984) studied the interpersonal behavior of a group of surgeons with their patients over the course of orthognathic (jaw) surgery (applied to correct dentofacial function and appearance) by having both patients and surgeons fill out IMIs on each other at various stages of the procedure. Penberthy (1982) studied the effects on patient adjustment and satisfaction of providing dental patients with different degrees of control over the procedure of denture-fitting by student dentists at a training hospital. Degree of control (maximum, minimum, and no-treatment group) was manipulated through a series of audiotapes that provided distinctly different levels of preparatory information, procedural choices, and expectancy sets of personal responsibility for decision making.

Other IMI Studies

More recent IMI studies are reported in detail elsewhere in this book and include Auerbach et al. (1994); Devens (1993); Dobson (1989); Gotlib (1986); Heffner (1993); LaFromboise (1992); Mancini (1995); Marcus and Holahan (1994); McCullough and Carr (1987); McCullough et al. (1994); Moras, Waterhouse, and Suh (1981); Murdock, Banta, Stromseth, Viene, and Brown (1995); Shean and Uchenwa (1990); Shuler (1994); Simon, Gaul, Friedlander, and Heatherington (1992); Strong, Hills, Kilmartin, et al. (1988); Swaney and Stone (1990); M. Werner (1984); and T. L. Wright and Ingraham (1986). One of these studies, because of its unusual scope, deserves more detailed summary in this final section.

In four separate studies, Strong, Hills, Kilmartin, et al. (1988) had 17 women confederates interact with 80 undergraduate women in pairs on a creative story construction task (the pairs were to construct together a story about two TAT cards). The confederates had been coached to perform one of eight different scripted roles that conformed with one of ICRS circle octant behaviors: leading, self-enhancing, critical, distrustful, self-effacing, docile, cooperative, and nurturant. The interactions were videotaped, and the responses of each participant were coded into ICRS octants. At the end of the procedure, subjects' perceptions of the confederates were measured using the IMI. In a series of analyses, the effect of the confederate's behavior on subject behavior was calculated.

ICRS ratings revealed that the interpersonal behavior that the confederate displayed toward the subject was significantly related to the subject's own behaviors in line with the principles of complementarity (leading encouraged docile, critical encouraged distrustful, cooperative encouraged leading) and anticomplementarity (docile discouraged cooperative, and self-enhancing discouraged leading). The authors also found significant relationships between the confederates' overt behaviors and the perceptions of that behavior as rated on the IMI:

> The Impact Message Inventory scales that reflected distinct perceptual impacts of the roles corresponded to the [ICRS] paragraph descriptions of the behaviors. For example, confederates who portrayed the nurturant role were perceived as significantly more nurturant, affiliative, and sociable than were confederates who portrayed the other roles; confederates who portrayed the critical role were perceived as significantly more competitive, dominant, hostile, and exhibitionistic and as less deferent, abasive, inhibited, succorant, and nurturant. (p. 805)

In summary, Strong, Hills, Kilmartin, et al. (1988) demonstrated that the confederates indeed acted in the prescribed complementary and anticomplementary manners as indicated by the ICRS ratings of the confederates' and subjects' actual behaviors; moreover, the ICRS ratings of the confederates' overt actions showed significant relationships also with the subjects' IMI perceptions of the confederates' behaviors. These findings provide strong confirmation of the validity of the IMI in that they show strong association of an interactant's covert engagements to a confederate's overt actions in a manner supportive of interpersonal complementarity theory.

CHAPTER 6

Maladjusted Interpersonal Behavior

General Principles and Formulations for Specific *DSM* Disorders

> *It is the self-system—the vast organization of experience which is concerned with protecting our self-esteem—which is involved in all inadequate and inappropriate living and is quite central to the whole problem of personality disorder and its remedy.*
>
> *(Sullivan, 1953b, p. 247)*

In Sullivan's (1953a, 1953b) theory, mental disorder referred to nothing more nor less than the distortion and complication of an individual's interpersonal relationships. Maladjusted behaviors were characterized as ineffective interpersonal relations or difficulties in living. Underlying all deviant behavior was the person's feeling that he or she is unworthy and incompetent in relationships with other people. Early unsatisfying relationships created a negative view of self, led to despair, resulted in a cessation of efforts to relate to others, and interrupted the process of consensual validation. With consensual validation suspended, autistic material became more and more a part of the person's experience and reflection.

In Sullivan's formulation also, no qualitative differences existed between normal and maladjusted individuals. In his famous *one-genus postulate,* he asserted "In most general terms, we are all much more simply human than otherwise, be we happy and successful, contented and detached, miserable and mentally disordered, or whatever" (Sullivan, 1953a, p. 16). He noted further, "There are no peculiarities shown by the morbid, there are only differences in degree—that is, in intensity and timing—of that which is shown by everyone" (Sullivan, 1953b, p. 305).

In the contemporary interpersonal model, difficulties in living are viewed primarily as problematic transactional patterns. During their interpersonal development, maladjusted individuals formed a constricted self-system that is manifested in their present rigid and extreme interpersonal behavior. In the current situation, they are functioning on the basis of "eidetic transactional patterns" (Van Denburg, 1991), the internalized-introjected early interactions between the client and significant others. In their early relationships, they became acutely aware of the exact covert experiences in themselves, inferred covert experiences of others, and overt transactional patterns that created anxiety and a threat to self-esteem in themselves and their transactional partners.

The general psychological literature offers several themes for defining abnormal behavior. By far, the most prominent characterization is referred to variously as *rigidity, indiscriminate responding,* or *consistent behavior across situations.* Wachtel (1973), for example, specified that the defining property of neurotic behavior is its rigidity, its inflexibility in the face of changing conditions. Mischel (1973) observed that "whereas discriminative facility is highly functional . . . diminished sensitivity to changing consequences (i.e., indiscriminative responding) may be a hallmark of an organism coping ineffectively" (p. 368). Moos (1968) conducted one of the earlier studies providing confirmation of this general proposition. Many personality theorists cite flexibility as being central to the healthy personality (e.g., Scott, 1968).

Pervin (1968) provided a second potentially defining characteristic of maladjusted behavior with his notion of *individual-environment fit.* Conceptualizing performance as a function of the interaction between the characteristics of the individual and those of the environment, Pervin asserted that for each individual there are environments (impersonal and interpersonal contexts) that more or less match the characteristics of a particular individual's personality. Importantly, a match or "best fit" of individual to environment is viewed by Pervin as expressing itself in high performance, satisfaction, and little stress in the system. In contrast, a "lack of fit," which also may typify abnormal individuals, is viewed as resulting in decreased performance, dissatisfaction, and stress in the system. Jahoda (1961) also emphasized the need for a best-fit concept between the values and beliefs of the individual and cultural environmental patterns.

A third notion is that maladjusted individuals, in contrast to normals, are *more image-maintaining* individuals who seemingly must defensively maintain a particular self-presentation (Bem, 1972). According to Bem, because defensive individuals appear to monitor their behavior to ensure a particular self-presentation, they may be unwilling or motivationally unable to alter that behavior to take advantage of shifting situational contingencies. Bem adds his notion of *cross-modality consistency* to the traditional notion of cross-situational consistency as the two basic processes of image-maintenance. Modality refers to the various categories of ongoing behavior including instrumental, expressive, projective, and physiological responses. Bem points out:

> The individual who is attempting to present or maintain a particular image probably monitors only those overt behaviors whose connotations are known to him and which are under his own functional control. Expressive behavior, projective behaviors, and physiological responses probably escape the monitoring process (Bem, 1972, p. 22).

In Bem's formulation, image-maintaining (more maladjusted) individuals should show cross-situational consistency but cross-modality inconsistency; whereas non-image-maintaining (more normal) individuals should show cross-situation inconsistency but cross-modality consistency.

Millon (1969) offered three criteria for differentiating abnormal from normal behavior. His first, *functional inflexibility,* designated that the alternative strategies the individual uses in transactions are not only few in number, but appear to be practiced rigidly. His second, a *tendency to foster vicious or self-defeating cycles,* identifies that the abnormal person's habitual cognitions, mechanisms, and behaviors are likely to perpetuate and intensify preexisting difficulties provoking reactions from others that reactivate earlier problems. This criterion is identical to the interpersonal notion of maladaptive transaction cycle mentioned in earlier chapters and which will be discussed in detail in this chapter (see Figures 6–1 and 6–2). Millon's (1969) third criterion, *structural instability,* referred to the abnormal individual's fragility or lack of resilience under conditions of subjective stress.

GENERAL INTERPERSONAL PRINCIPLES OF MALADJUSTED BEHAVIOR

Interpersonal Communication Theory

In interpersonal communication theory (Kiesler, 1979, 1988; Kiesler, Bernstein, & Anchin, 1976), abnormal behavior is defined as inappropriate or inadequate interpersonal communication. It occurs when one person, through verbal and nonverbal behavior, continually evokes or pulls from significant others a rigidly constricted range of intense and predominantly aversive impact responses for which the abnormal person assumes little responsibility because the negative consequences were unintended. The person's inability to detect and correct these self-defeating, interpersonally unsuccessful communications results in continual aversive-rejecting impact responses that others, in turn, countercommunicate directly or indirectly to the abnormal person. These aversive impact responses can vary greatly, reflecting the possible mixtures of evoking styles on the interpersonal circle.

These results are unintended, unwanted, unaccountable, and aversive consequences for the client. A person's particular inflexible abnormal style can be assessed through the distinctive and repetitive impact responses he or she pulls from significant persons in his or her life, including the therapist. From this perspective, *duplicitous communication* (Kaiser, in Fierman, 1965) is the universal symptom of abnormal behavior and consists of indirect, confusing, ambiguous, incongruous, and self-defeating messages encoded by the client during interactions with significant others.

The abnormal person operates from a selective inattention that ignores aspects of messages to and from others that are inconsistent with his or her constricted self-definition. The person ignores the ground of his or her experience, continual avoidance of which prevents both a holistic and integrated experience of self and consensually validated perception of self in relation to others. Fragmented and constricted experience of self leads to fragmented and constricted (duplicitous) communication to others.

For example, many obsessive-compulsive individuals present themselves to others as rational, logical, and self-controlled persons—all commendable attributes when not rigidly or extremely enacted. They exhibit these patterns in their very careful and cautious use of words, frequent qualifications of opinions and feelings, monotonous voice tone, and minimal range of body movements and other nonverbal behaviors. As a direct result of this behavior pattern, other persons tend to experience reciprocal impacts such as boredom, impatience, a feeling of being evaluated by the obsessive, much caution themselves in expressing their own opinions and feelings, and so on. Because of the predominant negative tone and chronic state of these reactions, others tend to withdraw from obsessive persons, or to countercommunicate in similarly unclear, cautious, and incongruous ways. The overall result over time is that obsessive persons come to feel isolated from others and lonely; they experience few if any intimate relationships and gradually develop the accumulated anxiety and depression of the abnormal person. And they don't understand at all how they have come to, or have any responsibility for, this miserable state of affairs.

Problems in living are directly but duplicitously expressed through a person's distinct evoking and impact messages. These constricted, extreme, and rigid evoking and impact messages (reflexes and complementary responses) *are* the problem!

Contemporary Interpersonal Theory

Maladjusted behavior, or problems in living, reside in the recurrent transactions of a person with others, especially significant others, in his or her life. Maladjusted behavior is defined as disordered, inappropriate, inadequate, and self-defeating interpersonal actions. It results originally and cumulatively from a person's not attending to (and not correcting) the self-defeating, interpersonally unsuccessful aspects of his or her interpersonal acts.

Extreme or Intense Interpersonal Behavior.   The abnormal individual imposes an extreme and intense force field on his or her interpersonal transactions. Recall that on the 1982 Interpersonal Circle depicted in Figure 1–1, the 16 circle radii represent a continuum of normal (near the midpoint) to abnormal (near the circumference) versions of each segment's interpersonal acts. That is, component actions subsumed by each segment vary in terms of their intensity or extremeness. The more extreme the act, the more maladjusted it is—the more aversive its effects on interactants.

Sullivan (1953a, 1953b) offered a sociological perspective for this notion that a quantitative and continuous dimension extends from normal to abnormal levels of interpersonal behavior. He conceptualized that an abnormal-extreme level of a particular category of interpersonal behaviors *represents a region at which a society suffers if all persons behave in this manner.* For example, a society cannot survive for long if many of its members insist on being domineering or dictatorial (extreme level); while the society may survive, indeed may prosper, if many of its members make a habit of taking charge of activities and becoming community or group leaders (mild-moderate level). Sullivan's notion also implies that successful functioning of any group of individuals (a society) results from a balanced adoption of different roles by group members. The categories of behavior found on the circumference of the interpersonal circle, in turn, represent a valid operationalization of the domain of interpersonal behavior that may be adopted to fulfill different societal roles such as leaders (segment A), judges and other legal enforcers (B, D), and social assistance agencies (L, M).

Carson (1969) emphasized that the essential factor in maladjusted behavior is public violation of the residual rules of a culture. Personality disorder is "the pursuit of a particular stable interpersonal position in relation to real or imagined others in ways that publicly violate the residual rules of a culture" (p. 239). The maladjusted person breaks residual rules "in such a spectacular and/or persistent way that it is impossible for others to ignore the rule-breaking; or to discover 'normal' reasons for its occurrence" (p. 228). Further, the social costs of such rule breaking do not seem to be matched at all by any apparent benefits of the disordered behavior to the rule breaker. Although the abnormal person gets trapped in the maintenance of a particular rigid interpersonal stance, his or her behavior represents the best outcome exchanges the person is able to manage with the environment.

Carson (1969) also suggested that the maladjusted person "is driven to break rules in the pursuit of particular interpersonal positions vis-à-vis others because any recognition by himself of his occupation of *other* positions would at the time constitute a serious violation of his self-system, exposing him to anxiety" (p. 237). What is implicit in this characterization is that for maladjusted persons the *Bad Me and Not Me personifications* have become rigid and extreme and reduce the individual's interpersonal strategies to a highly narrow range.

Rigid Interpersonal Behavior.   Besides being intense or extreme, the interpersonal acts of a maladjusted individual are characterized by a *rigidity* that constricts them to expressions of only a few segments of circle behaviors. The disturbed person consistently broadcasts a rigid and extreme self-presentation and simultaneously pulls for a rigid and constricted relationship from others. The individual imposes a rigid program on transactions that he or she is unwilling or unable to modify despite the initially varying interpersonal stances of others. As Wachtel (1977) described, deviant behavior "is brought about in the present, both by the patient's own behavior and by the behavior he evokes in others" (p. 43). He labels this process the "cyclical re-creation of interpersonal events," a process that emphasizes the ongoing behavior of interactants in perpetuating characterological patterns.

As a result, the maladjusted person lacks the flexibility to use the broad range of interpersonal behaviors (depicted around the circle circumference) that different interpersonal situations may warrant. Instead, the person continually enacts the same rigid and extreme interpersonal behaviors with virtually all significant persons. As Conway (1987) observed, the maladjusted person must maintain his or her restricted self-image, which is "maintained in part by cognitive-affective biasing and in part by maintaining an extreme and narrow interpersonal stance in relation to others" (p. 20).

For example, a patient receiving a *DSM-IV* diagnosis of Histrionic Personality Disorder (American Psychiatric Association [APA], 1994) tends to enact behaviors exclusively from categories O_1: spontaneous-demonstrative to O_2: impulsive-histrionic and from categories N_1: outgoing-responsive to N_2: monophobic-intrusive in Figures 1–2 and 1–3. He or she does not seem to be able to respond to others with mild-moderate or extreme actions from the 14 other segments.

The maladjusted person lacks the flexibility to use the broad range of interpersonal behaviors (depicted around the circle circumference) that different interpersonal situations may warrant. Instead, the person continually enacts the same rigid and extreme interpersonal behaviors with virtually all significant others.

In contrast, as Carson (1969) described, the more normal individual has a sufficiently broad style of interacting, reflecting a more flexible definition of himself and others. "We would expect reasonably well-adjusted persons to be capable, in appropriate circumstances and with modulated intensity, of displaying behaviors across the entire range of . . . [circle] categories" (Carson, 1969, p. 112). As Leary (1957) observed, "in the adjusted, well-functioning individual, the entire repertoire of interpersonal reflexes is operating spontaneously, flexibly, and appropriately—and when the survival situation demands aggression, he can aggress; when it calls for tenderness, he can be tender" (p. 118). Nevertheless, Leary and Carson both added that very few, if any, individuals can utilize with ease the entire range of interpersonal reactions; rather, the normal person tends to show a restricted set of responses that will "favor some segments of the circle more than others, thus giving his interpersonal behavior the distinctive coloration we ordinarily associate with the concept of personality" (Carson, 1969, p. 112).

Conway (1987) provided a further elaboration of the form normal interpersonal behavior might take, as follows:

> Often an individual's repertoire of typical interpersonal behaviors and an individual's sense of self will favor some portion of the circle and other portions may be behaviourally underrepresented and may be cognitively and affectively warded off, thus giving the person and his or her behaviour the distinctive colouration we might describe as his or her personality. (p. 20)

The normal person, thus, enacts varied sets of interpersonal acts appropriately tuned to the persons with whom he or she is interacting. In each new case, he or she is successful to various degrees in negotiating a mutually agreed on and satisfying definition of self and other, in response to the unique aspects of the particular interaction.

For the abnormal person, however, this ability to modify the definition of both self and other in line with situational factors seems strikingly absent. The rigid covert experiences of abnormal persons act as distorting filters, deactivating normative situational influences, and evoking actions that are, in fact, congruent with the maladjusted person's intrapsychic experience. What disordered persons are aware of and attend to are some aspects of their claims as to how to define self in important relationships, and some aspects of the interpersonal situation that are most relevant to those claims. What they are not aware of and do not attend to are other aspects of their interpersonal acts (especially nonverbal behaviors) and other aspects of the interpersonal situations that are quite relevant to the aversive interpersonal consequences they unintentionally produce. Their rigid construals, the result of distorting attentional and perceptual filters that override "real" situational influences, aggressively evoke complementary-impact responses that are, in fact, congruent with the maladjusted person's covert experience.

The Dynamism of Difficulty.   Sullivan (1953a, 1953b) named an individual's particular pattern of rigid and extreme behaviors the "dynamism of difficulty," by which he meant that limitations in development of the self-dynamism lead to limitations in the kinds of behavior the person presently emits, defining for that person a "course of avoidance." The result is that the person uses one form of interpersonal behavior exclusively in transactions with other persons; this, in turn, interferes with interpersonal spontaneity and flexibility. In Sullivan's (1954) words:

> Behavior that might be useful for something or other is used by [maladjusted persons] to meet problems for which it is singularly ineffective, or . . . [maladjusted persons] do something that every one of us does at some time during the day, but they do it almost all the time, and thereby seem very eccentric indeed. (p. 195)

Horney (1942) offered quite similar notions. In her formulation, the healthy person can shift easily from one need to another as circumstances change. The neurotic person, instead, is likely to do one of two things. He or she may adopt two or more interpersonal orientations at once (e.g., "moving against" and "moving toward"), causing inner conflict that the person is not flexible enough to handle. Or because of being inflexible in the use of these interpersonal needs in reacting to different situations, he or she may rely compulsively on only one of these needs (e.g., moving away from) to the exclusion of all others. This last possibility echoes strongly Sullivan's dynamism of difficulty. In Horney's view, the neurotic person makes one of the needs the indiscriminate strategy for all social interactions: "If it is affection that a person must have, he must receive it from friend and enemy, from employer and bootblack" (Horney,

1942, p. 39). For Horney, in short, needs are neurotic when a person makes one of them an insatiable way of life.

In the same tradition, Leary (1957) observed that the maladjusted individual

> tends to overdevelop a narrow range of one or two interpersonal responses. These are expressed intensely and often, whether appropriate to the situation or not. . . . [Further,] the more extreme and rigid the person, the greater his interpersonal "pull"—the stronger his ability to shape the relationship with others. (p. 126)

Leary felt also that the sicker an individual, "the more likely he is to have abandoned all interpersonal techniques except one—which he can handle with magnificent finesse" (p. 116).

Carson (1969) also observed that the abnormal individual gets "'hung up' in the maintenance of a particular interpersonal stance" (p. 230). Finally, Wiggins and Trapnell (in press) observed: "Difficulties in living may result when traits are expressed rigidly or excessively, or when they are *not* expressed in situations in which they would be clearly adaptive."

Transactional Escalation. Van Denburg (1989) and Van Denburg and Kiesler (1993) described how momentary increased extremeness and rigidity of interpersonal behavior can occur periodically for normal persons as well:

> We suggest that, *during periods of transitory relative "maladjustment" precipitated by perceived stress, an interpersonal process of "transactional escalation" can occur in which a person's prototypical interpersonal behaviours become more extreme (more intense) and rigid (available interpersonal behaviours decrease in range).* (Van Denburg & Kiesler, 1993, p. 15, italics added)

In other words, when a normal individual encounters a stressful or self-threatening context, the individual is likely to rely more on and escalate interpersonal behaviors that are most familiar and most automatically performed. For example, a person who typically enacts cooperative and helpful behaviors will, under perceived stress, tend to become placating and indulgent (more extreme or intense); moreover, he or she may be less able than usual to be critical, aloof, or mistrusting (the person's available interpersonal repertoire decreases in range).

Some support for transactional escalation can be found in the literature. Irritable and explosive men became even more so during the severe economic setbacks of the Great Depression (Elder & Caspi, 1988). The coping styles of entrepreneurs whose businesses suffered extensive damage during a natural disaster accentuated during the recovery period (Anderson, 1977). Similar behavioral escalation was observed during the Nazi revolution (Allport, Bruner, & Jandorf, 1941).

Van Denburg and Kiesler (1993) conducted the first experimental investigation of the new interpersonal proposition. Their CLOIT results revealed an increase in the intensity and rigidity of individuals' typical pattern of interpersonal behavior when subjected to a stressful interview. They concluded that the proposition of transactional escalation

> likely needs to be incorporated explicitly into contemporary interpersonal theory. In previous conceptualizations of abnormal behaviour, interpersonal theory has

focused primarily on one type of rigidity—that of interpersonal behaviour as manifest across situations. For the most part, it has not dealt explicitly with a second type of rigidity—that manifested by different intensities of behaviour within a subject's interpersonal profile. . . . In sum, to understand the impact a person has in relationships, it is necessary to investigate both the cross-situational and within-situational rigidity and intensity of the person's interpersonal behaviours. The proposition of transactional escalation includes both factors and is believed to be applicable to both normal and maladjusted persons. (Van Denburg & Kiesler, 1993, pp. 27–28)

Multilevel Inconsistency in Interpersonal Behavior.   Leary (1957) offered "two basic maladjustive factors" (p. 121): "rigidity" and "unstable oscillation," the latter referring to "an intense attempt to adjust to all aspects of the presented environment." Leary noted that both concepts "involve the multilevel organization and diagnosis of personality and must await publication in a subsequent volume" (p. 121). That volume, unfortunately, has not appeared.

What Leary (1957) did articulate was that a functional diagnosis of personality involved two basic dimensions: interpersonal behavior and variability. He especially emphasized that the variability in interpersonal behavior of an individual can be investigated, not only cross-situationally and transtemporally, but also "structurally" (p. 75) across the five levels of personality that he delineated (summarized in Chapter 3 of this book). One of the three diagnostic indices that the Kaiser project routinely used was the diagnostic profile of personality: "a diagrammatic and numerical summary of the patient's behavior at each level, and of his variability indices" (p. 211).

In the Kaiser system, summary totals of interpersonal measures were calculated for each of the five levels; then each, after being converted to standard scores and using the vector method, was charted onto a single summary diagram. Next, measurements could be obtained directly from the diagram to serve as "variability indices" (p. 86) of the degree of structure of personality organization (the kind and amount of conflict or rigidity present, and the agreement or conflict between the various levels of behavior). These variability indices "reflected in mathematical terms the tendency of any one level to duplicate or balance the inevitable distortions of the other levels of personality" (p. 86). Leary (1957) subsequently detailed 12 variability indices that could be calculated using his interpersonal diagnostic system.

A reader might be prone to conclude that these variability indices were considered to represent degree of maladjustment: The more inconsistency present among personality descriptions at the five levels for a particular individual (the higher the variability index), the more maladjusted that person would be. Leary (1957), however, took pains *not* to draw this conclusion. He did specify that the lower the variability indices (the more the data from the five levels consistently repeat the same themes), the more *stable* is the organization of personality. Conversely, the more conflict or oscillation among the levels, the more variation in personality can be expected over time (cf. p. 247). However, Leary, went on to point out that "stable" does not necessarily mean normal:

In order to understand the meaning and use of these indices in the interpersonal system, it is essential that two points be kept in mind: (1) these [variability] concepts are not [defense] mechanisms or dynamisms, but rather numerical indices of interlevel variation; as such they have no function. (2) They have no a priori value-loading as far as adjustment and maladjustment are concerned; they can describe flexibility and healthy ambivalence, or they can indicate pathological rigidity or maladaptive oscillation. . . . The level and amount of the conflict and its relationship to the over-all character structure determine the positive or negative interpretation. (p. 248)

It's safe to conclude that Leary (1957) would disagree steadfastly with any attempt to list interlevel discrepancy in personality description, as measured by any of the variability indices he offered, as an important criterion for differentiating abnormal from normal behavior. On the other hand, it's likely that future theory and research might reveal important relationships of multilevel variability to maladjustment.

For example, Summers (1980) found that spontaneous self-exploration in therapy was avoided most by individuals whose overt interpersonal behavior (based on the ICL) contradicted their TAT interpersonal fantasy expressions. That is, when a discrepancy was found to exist between the level of conscious self-perception (I) and the fantasy level (III), the individual during therapy was less likely to probe deeply within.

Romano (1960), in a case study of marital therapy, found that the husband and wife's Level I, Level II, and Level III descriptions showed face-valid discrepancies. For example, at Level II, one partner (wife) viewed herself in a way that contradicted her Level III self-descriptions (TAT fantasy measure), which, however, were entirely compatible with the husband's Level II ratings of his wife. Specifically, although the wife perceived her own actions as cooperative and affiliative, her TAT stories depicted heroes who were aggressive, hostile people who reacted violently to their environment; her husband, however, viewed her as a hostile aggressive person, similar to the wife's heroes. Romano (1960) found the same pattern for the husband's Level II self-ratings.

Summary

We are now ready to summarize interpersonal principles that govern maladjusted behavior. My summary will include the previously discussed principles developed by interpersonal theorists, but will add other indices that have been used or implied in interpersonal studies of maladjusted behavior.

Proposition 6–1.   Maladjusted behavior has at least seven important interpersonal characteristics:

a. *Extremeness.* The more extreme an interpersonal behavior, the more maladaptive it is, the more aversive its effects on interactants.

b. *Rigidity.* With varying interactants, a maladjusted individual's interpersonal acts are constricted to expressions of only a few classes of the total range of possible interpersonal behaviors. Hence, distinctive patterns of interpersonal behavior are expressed invariantly across situations, and other patterns of interpersonal behavior are not expressed in situations in which they would be clearly adaptive.

c. *Self-Other Perceptual Discrepancy.* The discrepancy can occur either in regard to an individual's self-perceived interpersonal behavior and its impact on others, or in regard to the overt interpersonal behavior of other persons and its interpretation by the abnormal individual.

d. *Cross-Channel Incongruity* or *Duplicitous Communication.* The complex of verbal and nonverbal messages that constitute the interpersonal acts of maladjusted individuals yield discrepant, mixed, and inconsistent information to interactants, in turn evoking from them discrepant, mixed, and inconsistent interpersonal reactions.

e. *Vicious Self-Defeating Cycles* or *Maladaptive Transaction Cycles.* The abnormal individual's rigid and extreme interpersonal behaviors evoke from interactants restricted interpersonal reactions that reinforce the maladjusted person's maladaptive pattern; the constricted complementary responses are progressively experienced as more aversive by interactants whose reactions increasingly encompass indirect—more rarely, direct—messages of rejection and abandonment.

f. *Tenuous Stability under Conditions of Stress.* Given the unavailability of the full range of alternative interpersonal behaviors to maladjusted persons, they are highly susceptible to the impact of difficulties or stressors that occur. Moreover, a different self-defeating vicious cycle is initiated through "transactional escalation" (Van Denburg & Kiesler, 1993): the tendency of individuals (in the present case, maladjusted) to escalate the extremeness and rigidity of their interpersonal behavior patterns under stress.

g. *A Higher Level of Interpersonal Distress* than is characteristic of normal subjects (e.g., Sheffield, Carey, Patenaude, & Lambert, 1995), as measured by the Inventory of Interpersonal Problems (IIP; L. M. Horowitz, Rosenberg, et al., 1988) or some other equivalent measure of interpersonal complaints or problems.

An important implication of these notions regarding abnormal behavior is that in the therapy context the patient's interpersonal actions of necessity will override the actions of the hopefully more normal therapist. Especially during their earlier sessions, the patient will exhibit greater interpersonal pull than the therapist and will demonstrate a stronger ability to shape the therapy relationship.

INTERPERSONAL MALADJUSTMENT: EMPIRICAL RESEARCH

Various researchers have attempted to evaluate one or more of these interpersonal indices of maladjustment including Campbell (1991); Devens (1993); Dinitz, Mangus, and Pasamanick (1959); Duke and Nowicki (1982); Federman (1980); A. P. Nelson (1984); Paulhus and Martin (1988); Pincus and Wiggins (1990); Segal, Adams, and Shaw (1992); Sheffield et al. (1995); Sim and Romney (1990); and Willner and Blackburn (1988).

Empirical support for the first three of these interpersonal indices was obtained in a study by Sim and Romney (1990). They directly tested the hypotheses that individuals with personality disorders have more intense and more rigid interpersonal behavior than normals, and that there is a greater discrepancy between their own ratings of their interpersonal behavior and ratings of their interpersonal behavior made by others. A sample of patients diagnosed by psychiatrists as personality disordered was given the Interpersonal Check List (ICL) and the Millon Clinical Multiaxial Inventory-II (MCMI; Millon, 1987); a control group of university students was given just the ICL. In addition, both groups were rated on the ICL by persons who interacted with them for a brief period. Results supported Sim and Romney's (1990) propositions that the interpersonal behavior of individuals with diagnosed personality disorders is more intense and rigid, and their self- versus others-ratings are more discrepant than those of normal individuals.

Devens (1993) hypothesized that the interpersonal maladjustment indices of intensity, rigidity, and discrepancy would predict severity of personality disorders as independently determined. Subjects were clients from a university counseling center who volunteered for a study using the IMI, the IIP-C, and the MMPI Scales for the DSM-III personality disorders (Morey, Waugh, & Blashfield, 1985). Findings from regression analyses revealed that, despite a few supportive trends, none of the MMPI personality disorders was predicted by either the severity of the two interpersonal indices (rigidity, intensity) or by the discrepancy variables, as measured from either interpersonal inventory.

Dinitz et al. (1959) used the ICL with a large sample of institutionalized mental patients. They found that the patients' self-concepts did not in general appreciably differ from the notions of them held by significant others. On the other hand, patients tended to view significant others differently from the way these persons viewed themselves. The authors concluded that the problem in maladjustment is the person's inability both to perceive others realistically and to play his or her roles in such a way to lead to a changing definition of self by him or herself and by others.

Segal et al. (1992) examined whether disturbed interpersonal relationships are associated with relapse in depression by comparing discrepancies in self-ratings provided by formerly depressed patients and their collateral informants. Segal et al. (1992) hypothesized that patient-collateral dyads displaying a greater discrepancy in interpersonal perception would have a higher risk of relapse than dyads who showed more agreement in their ratings. Results demonstrated that discrepancies in the perceptions of patients' life events were indeed associated with the duration of a relapse once it occurred; however, discrepancies were generally not related to the emergence of new episodes of depressive disorder.

Nelson (1984) used the IMI to test the hypothesis that abnormal persons would demonstrate greater rigidity in their interpersonal impacts across a series of brief interactions with stylistically different dyadic partners. Groups of male psychiatric patients and normal subjects participated serially in 5-minute videotaped interactions with three experimental confederates. The confederates had been trained in both verbal and nonverbal behaviors to exhibit one of three interpersonal patterns: hostile-dominant, submissive-neutral (neutral on affiliation), or friendly-neutral (neutral on control). Analyses focused on IMIs that subjects filled out on the confederates at the end of their interaction, and on IMIs filled out on subjects by two observers after viewing a videotape of the interaction.

Results showed, first, that while interacting with the hostile-dominant confederate, all subjects impacted observers as behaving more hostilely, less friendly, and more submissively than they did when interacting with either of the two other confederates. Second, in their interactions with all three confederates, patients, in contrast to normals, impacted observers as behaving more submissively and hostilely, and less friendly; that is, as exhibiting more extreme patterns of interpersonal behavior. In sum, analysis of the observers' protocols showed that both patients and normals impacted observers as enacting interpersonal behaviors that were complementary to the behaviors portrayed by the confederates; further, psychiatric patients (in contrast to the normals) impacted observers as demonstrating more extreme manifestations of hostile-submissive interpersonal behaviors.

Federman (1980) examined the workings of a rigid and extreme interpersonal style among groups of psychometrically defined dependent personalities and normals. Female subjects were randomly assigned to four dyadic group compositions, each dyad having the task of constructing a team story for a set of TAT cards. After the session, each subject filled out an IMI and a relationship inventory on her partner.

Sequential analyses of the act-by-act codings of the interactants' behaviors during the sessions showed that the dependent personalities were more likely to convey one-down, and were less likely to convey one-up, messages to the interacting partner. Also, dependent interactants elicited fewer one-down messages from their partners than did normal interactants. These results confirmed Federman's (1980) hypothesis that the more psychometrically deviant dependent personalities, in contrast to normals, were more rigid in their TAT story negotiations—were less responsive than normals to their partner's varying interpersonal presentations.

Campbell (1991), in a study of the relationship of interpersonal complementarity to marital satisfaction, obtained results that appear inconsistent with the cross-situational rigidity hypothesis. She found that marital partners whose inside-of-marriage and outside-of-marriage patterns of CLOIT interpersonal behaviors were similar reported higher marital satisfaction, higher security, and a lower avoidant attachment style. Conversely, partners who displayed more discrepant inside versus outside interpersonal styles reported lower marital satisfaction, lower security, and higher avoidant attachment. Campbell (1991) speculated that a partner's interactions with the spouse may not coincide with his or her image of self; but a partner displays the style because he or she feels constrained to do so. Consequently, "those whose 'inside' and 'outside' interpersonal styles are more consistent may be operating in a way more consistent with their self images, therefore more consistent with their security operations (Sullivan, 1953b)" (Campbell, 1991, pp. 74–75).

Willner and Blackburn (1988) tested the rigidity hypothesis by examining forensic psychiatric patients' self-ratings of their interpersonal behavior across eight threat and eight affiliation situations. Patients were diagnosed with either psychopathic disorder or general mental illness, and scored high versus low on psychopathy and social withdrawal measures. Results showed that although all patient groups varied their interpersonal behavior according to situation, the rank-ordering of "differences between them were maintained across situations, as demanded by the notion of interpersonal style" (Willner & Blackburn, 1988, p. 274). The latter rigidity pattern was also shown by significant cross-situational correlations respectively for the dominant, friendly, and avoidant interpersonal clusters measured.

Duke and Nowicki (1982) took exception to listing cross-channel incongruity as one of the indices of maladjustment. They argued that "not only may incongruence sometimes be 'normal' and appropriate, but that incongruence may actually be the prevalent mode of adult human interaction" (pp. 82–83). The effect of cross-channel incongruity depends crucially on situational parameters. In their view, the result is at least four categories of dyadic congruence-incongruence situational patterns: adaptive congruence, adaptive incongruence, maladaptive congruence, and maladaptive incongruence. They conclude that incongruence "must be viewed as associated with maladjustment only in certain situationally defined instances . . . failure to learn when, where, and with whom to be congruent or incongruent may have more to do with the development of maladjustment than with simple incongruence per se" (p. 83).

Pincus and Wiggins (1990) proposed that interpersonal problems are a useful way of operationalizing maladaptive and inflexible trait expression. Extrapolating from the major item classes in the IIP, Pincus and Wiggins proposed two ways in which personality traits could be expressed in a maladaptive and inflexible manner: (a) in behaviors one "does too much" and (b) in behaviors one consistently finds "hard to do." As they observed, rigid overt interpersonal responses involve at a minimum chronic behavioral excesses and inhibitions—interpersonal problems.

Paulhus and Martin (1988), after reviewing previous conceptualizations of interpersonal flexibility proposed a notion of adaptive *functional flexibility* that satisfied the two critical components of flexibility they had abstracted from the literature: a wide behavioral repertoire, and the ability to adjust to situational demands. Their notion of interpersonal functional flexibility referred to "the ability to adjust one's behavior to the interpersonal demands of a wide range of situations" (p. 91). "Functionally flexible persons possess a great many interpersonal capabilities: They have a large repertoire of social behaviors and can deploy these behaviors in situations they deem appropriate (Paulhus & Martin, 1988, p. 99).

Paulhus and Martin's definition involves both an individual's self-perceived trait pattern (as defined by interpersonal circle inventories) and self-perceived capability of enacting a particular pattern of interpersonal behavior when the occasion demands (as measured by the Battery of Interpersonal Capabilities, BIC; Paulhus & Martin, 1987). The BIC was developed by adapting the 16 interpersonal attributes measured by Wiggins's (1979a) IAS to a format in which respondents provide capability ratings (their rated potential for performing each of the 16 categories of behavior when the situation requires it). The BIC was scored to form a composite of capabilities, the *Functional Flexibility Index (FFI)*—the sum around the circumplex of the respondent's 16 capability ratings.

Consistent with their formulation, in a series of studies Paulhus and Martin (1988) found that trait versus capability self-ratings loaded on separate factor dimensions. Further, although the circumplex was replicated for standard trait ratings, the capability ratings revealed a dramatically different structure marked by the two orthogonal traits: nurturance and hostility (polar opposites on the same dimension for trait ratings). Paulhus and Martin (1988) noted that this new structure for the capability data indicates that "an individual who is capable of warm behavior will, as likely as not, be capable of cold behavior. Moreover, the individual who is incapable of warm behavior is not necessarily capable of cold behavior" (p. 91). Their findings also supported the validity of their FFI by showing substantial correlations with peer ratings of interpersonal flexibility. Finally, the FFI outperformed other flexibility measures in predicting psychological adjustment (an independent measure of self-esteem).

Andrews (1991) cautioned that the notion of functional flexibility, if carried to its logical conclusion, presents some problems: If a person were completely flexible, he or she could respond adaptively to the demands of each situation "without imposing a self-confirmational stamp on one's actions or expressions" (p. 48). Andrews (1991) offered an alternative concept, *stylistic elaboration,* according to which a normal person "has a distinctive identity style that is flexibly elaborated so that it enables him or her to cope with a range of human situations" (p. 48). This notion sustains an emphasis on functional individuality in that a person's behavior in more ambiguous or unstructured situations will reflect his or her preferred pattern of interpersonal behavior.

Sheffield et al. (1995) hypothesized a significant difference in level of interpersonal distress between a large sample of normal undergraduates in contrast to the sample of clinically maladjusted individuals (Horowitz, Rosenberg, et al., 1988) on which the IIP had been standardized. As predicted, the IIP successfully discriminated the normal undergraduates from the IIP normative group. Their results also produced correlations between total scores on the IIP and two measures of mental health in the expected negative direction, and of sufficient magnitude to suggest that low interpersonal distress is related to high self-actualization and interpersonal closeness. Sheffield et al. (1995) concluded that their results not only provide new evidence for the construct validity of the IIP but importantly "suggest that interpersonal functioning may be an important indicator of psychological health in general" (p. 954).

POSITIVE ILLUSION: MALADAPTIVE? OR NORMAL?

Contemporary interpersonal theorists assert that the rigid covert experiences of abnormal individuals act as *distorting filters* to deactivate normative situational influences and evoke actions that are, in fact, congruent with the personality-disordered person's intrapsychic experience. Recent research suggests that a more valid notion may be that it is the normal individual who wears distorting filters.

Positive Illusion and Depression

A series of studies set out to test various cognitive theories of depression by demonstrating the existence of a "negative bias" in depressive subjects. Depressives, who are generally low in self-esteem, had been described (and early research seemed to demonstrate) as having negative bias or distortion in their recall of information about the self—although not in their perception of information in general (DeMonbreun & Craighead, 1977).

A number of other researchers have found, however, that *it is the "normal" person who actually distorts information in a positive manner, whereas the depressed individual actually perceives it more accurately* (Ackermann & DeRubeis, 1991; Sackeim & Wegner, 1986; M. L. Snyder, Stephan, & Rosenfield, 1978; Taylor & Brown, 1988). Based on their findings regarding judgments of contingency, Alloy and Abramson (1979) described depressed subjects as "sadder, but wiser." Alloy and Abramson (1988) termed this phenomenon *depressive realism:* Depressives appear to be more realistic or accurate in their perceptions and appraisals, whereas nondepressed persons are found to employ cognitive illusions. Alloy and Abramson (1988) speculated that actually "depressed individuals may be suffering from the absence or breakdown of normal optimistic biases and distortions," that maladaptive symptoms of depression "may be consequences, in part, of the absence of healthy personal illusions."

Lewinsohn, Mischel, Chaplin, and Barton (1980), also finding that depressed individuals were more accurate in their self-perceptions, suggested, "Non-depressed people may thus be characterized with a halo or glow that involves an [illusory self-enhancement] in which one sees oneself more positively than others see one" (p. 210). Taylor and Brown (1988; see also Taylor & Brown, 1994), after a thorough review of the literature, concluded that positive illusion about oneself not only may be normal, but may be necessary to protect self-esteem.

Converging results, then, indicate that depressives have a more balanced view of negative and positive aspects of self; it is the normal individual who displays a bias in the recall and attribution of positive self-referent material. To explain the positive bias demonstrated for normal subjects in these studies, a number of researchers (Alloy & Abramson, 1988; M. L. Snyder et al., 1978; Zuckerman, 1979) have posited *the theory of self-esteem maintenance,* which suggests that *positive illusions about oneself may be a necessary means of protecting one's self-esteem.* According to this theory, an individual is motivated to perceive him- or herself optimistically, both separately and in relation to others, to maintain a high level of self-worth. The existence of "self-serving" biases and illusions is considered adaptive because it functions to protect the person against threats to self-esteem that may be elicited by an unbiased view of his or her actual situation (such as successes or failures, strengths or weaknesses). Given the focus on the internal process of self, perceptions of others would not be affected by this process. The tendency to take credit for good outcomes and deny blame for bad outcomes to enhance self-esteem has been called "attributional egotism" (M. L. Snyder et al., 1978) or "self-serving bias" (Ickes & Layden, 1978; Tennen & Herzberger, 1987; Tennen, Herzberger, & Nelson, 1987; Zuckerman, 1979).

R. E. Nelson and Craighead (1977) offered the view that "nondepressed individuals may filter out a certain amount of low-frequency, negative feedback in order to maintain a positive self-image." Lazarus (1983), based on his study of subjects' responses to stress, concluded that denial processes can have adaptive functions when attempting to deal with threatening events such as terminal illness. He concludes that "illusion is necessary for positive mental health"—humans need to maintain illusions to make life tolerable.

Positive Illusion and Other Psychopathological Groups

Studies of other nonpsychotic clinical groups besides depressives have similarly confirmed the fascinating notion of maladjusted individuals' superiority, in comparison with normal controls, in veridical perception and construal of environmental information. Confirmatory findings have been reported for general neurotics (Cunningham, 1977), for cases of anxiety and depression (Dalgleish & Watts, 1990; Dobson, 1989), for schizotypal college students (Raulin & Henderson, 1987), and even for paranoid patients (LaRusso, 1978).

Accordingly, Taylor and Brown (1988, 1994) challenged the notion that accurate perceptions of self and the world are essential for mental health. The authors argued instead that *people's perceptions of self and the world are positively biased and that these positive illusions promote psychological well-being.* They documented that normal mental functioning is characterized by self-aggrandizing positive biases: overly positive self-conceptions, an exaggerated perception of self-control, and overly optimistic assessments of the future. Further, these positive illusions appear to be associated with traditional criteria of mental health (Jahoda, 1958; Jourard & Landsman, 1980; Schulz, 1977): the ability to be happy and form social bonds, the capacity for creative and productive work, persistence in pursuit of goals, and the ability to adapt successfully to stressful events.

There seems to be substantial evidence to support the idea that humans generally maintain positive illusions—actively protect and enhance their personal theories of self—with many positive consequences resulting to the individual. These findings seriously challenge the assumption that an accurate perception of reality as it pertains to oneself is a key to mental health.

On the other hand, Colvin and Block (1994); see also Block & Colvin, 1994) examined the logic and relevant empirical evidence supportive of the positive illusion position and failed to substantiate Taylor and Brown's (1988) thesis. Colvin and Block

(1994) documented that close consideration of several assumptions underlying the positive illusion formulation raised further questions regarding its validity. They concluded that it remains unproven that positive illusions indeed foster mental health.

Social psychology research with normal people has also revealed important risks and dangers of illusions. A literature review of a dozen different self-defeating behavior patterns found that over a third of them seemed to involve misjudging the self or misjudging the social environment in some way (Baumeister & Scher, 1988). In light of this research, Baumeister (1989) argued:

> There is an optimal margin of illusions. The advantages of illusions seem to be associated with *small* illusions: seeing things as slightly better than they are, overestimating one's capabilities and self-worth slightly, and so forth. The disadvantages seem to be associated with larger distortions. There may be a certain bandwidth of illusion, within which the individual can generally reap the benefits of illusions while avoiding most of the negative consequences. (p. 182)

If this is the case, it's likely that a curvilinear relationship exists between the propensity to engage in positive illusion and maladaptive consequences (C. R. Snyder, 1989).

Janoff-Bulman (1989) suggested the similar importance of a dimension of core-to-peripheral-beliefs in determining the maladaptive effects of illusions. He postulated:

> The key to the "good life" would be to maintain illusions at the level of our most basic assumptions, but to strive for accuracy at the level of our lower-order postulates. . . . Most feedback we get relates specifically to beliefs at the level of lower-order postulates. Illusions are least likely to exist at the lower, more specific levels of our conceptual systems, primarily because of the numerous possibilities for direct behavioral feedback; yet those which are maintained at this level are apt to be most maladaptive . . . the ability to respond to feedback, to be self-critical and learn, is an important criterion for mental health. Yet such accuracy is not inconsistent with maintaining illusions. It is the level of the assumption that matters. People learn and grow, and this learning and growth are far more likely to occur at the level of our lower-order postulates than our higher-order ones. (pp. 170, 172)

Finally, Taylor, Collins, Skokan, and Aspinwall (1989) documented important distinctions between use of more normal illusions versus more abnormal defense mechanisms. They pointed out that illusions are simply overly positive subjective evaluations, whereas defense mechanisms result in the distortion of reality. Moreover, typically normal illusions are quite responsive to negative information and its implications for future well-being—a subtlety and patterning of reaction to negative information noticeably absent from defense mechanisms such as repression or denial.

Overall, then, it seems safe to conclude that some level (or bandwidth) of illusion, probably involving less central or basic assumptions and beliefs, is characteristic of normal functioning and may be positively associated with various criteria of mental health. On the other hand, it seems crucial to determine the degree of disregard of reality involved in either positive or negative directions, with larger distortions (up to and including delusions) and frequent use of defense mechanisms remaining characteristic of the behavior of maladjusted individuals. In short, although our illusions may be adaptive, real limits unquestionably apply.

THE MALADAPTIVE TRANSACTION CYCLE

The interpersonal circle provides the first essential conceptual model for diagnosis in interpersonal psychotherapy. However, the circle is not a model that might guide understanding of the sequence of transactions—the evolving momentary actions and reactions, moves and countermoves—that occur over a session between patient and therapist and, outside the sessions, between the patient and significant others.

What the circle offers is a static characterization, at a frozen moment in time, of the transactional behaviors exhibited by one or the other interactant. If measures of the behavior of both interactants are taken at intervals over an evolving relationship, the circle can provide some "macro" description of the emerging trends in the transaction. What the circle does not offer is a conceptual guide that predicts the specific components of the recurrent pattern of actions and reactions that define the patient's distinctive self-defeating maladaptive transactions with others. If a conceptual map were available that described the key steps in the patient's maladaptive sequence with others, the therapist could apply it by discovering the specific content for each component.

I introduced (Kiesler, 1986a, pp. 7–10) the Maladaptive Transaction Cycle (MTC) as a model that defines the essential components of the maladjusted person's action-reaction sequence with others; it is a conceptual guide that predicts the specific components of the recurrent pattern of actions and reactions that define the person's self-defeating maladaptive transactions with others. The model, together with complementarity predictions from the interpersonal circle, provides the framework for specifying the covert and overt aspects of the maladjusted person's behavior that are chained circularly to the covert and overt aspects of the interactant's reactions. It specifies, further, how the maladjusted individual's transactions with others typically move to "impasse": to recurrent enactment of the cycle of maladaptive self-fulfilling prophecy and behavior. The transactional result of the maladjusted person's extreme and rigid interpersonal behaviors is a two-stage vicious cycle of self-defeating interpersonal interactions with significant others.

Figure 6–1 depicts the Maladaptive Transaction Cycle constructed to model the essential components in this maladaptive action-reaction temporal sequence. At less rigid and extreme levels of interpersonal behavior, the MTC provides a dynamic theoretical depiction of the full range of overt and covert human behaviors involved in interpersonal transactions.

The squares to the far left of Figure 6–1 represent Person A (the patient) in a transaction. The squares to the far right represent Interactant B (significant other or the therapist). The arrows depict the direction of overriding influence between A and B—the flow of action and reaction and their causal interrelatedness. What is evident from the flow is that a major effect of B's reactions is to confirm or validate the cognitive, emotional, and other inner experience of Patient A and, in turn, to escalate A's repetition of the extreme and rigid actions originally enacted. Overall, what is depicted is the "vicious cycle" that characterizes maladaptive interpersonal behavior in which, mostly out of awareness, the patient produces and maintains his or her own maladaptive predicament.

In Figure 6–1, Stage 1 describes the earlier sequence in Patient A's transactions with a particular Interactant (B). In line with the principle of complementarity, B will be pulled to experience constricted covert reactions producing complementary overt actions that confirm A's expectancies, cognitions, emotions, and other inner experience. This confirmation leads to A's continued production of his or her original maladaptive

STAGE 1

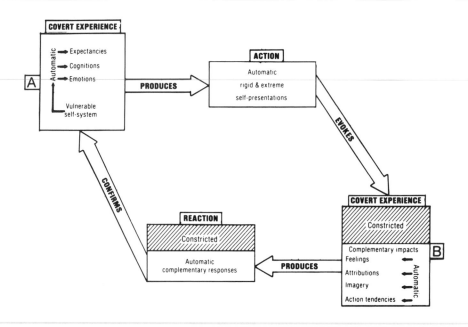

STAGE 2

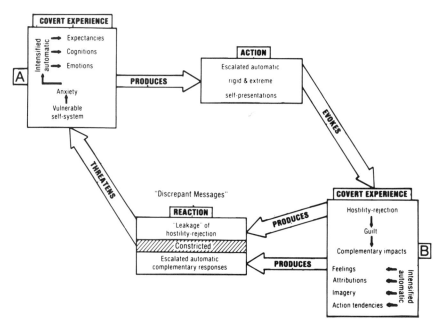

FIGURE 6–1. The Maladaptive Transaction Cycle. Copyright © 1985 by Donald J. Kiesler.

interpersonal behaviors. In this earlier stage of A and B's relationship, the complementary fit makes their transactions somewhat mutually satisfying and confirming.

The difficulty develops over time as the relationship continues. As they continue to replay the cycle, Interactant B increasingly experiences the aversive impacts that result from being "pushed around" by Patient A's superior and rigid power. Because of chronic vulnerability, Patient A cannot alter his or her behavior toward enactment of behaviors from other segments of the circle, but also now because B continues to confirm his or her expectancies and cognitions through enactment of complementary responses. On the other hand, B now begins to experience more hostile and rejecting impacts and, if possible, will escape from or avoid further encounters. If for a variety of reasons escape is not possible, B will continue to enact complementary responses, yet simultaneously will "leak" subtle messages of hostility and rejection. These rejecting cues will be picked up by Patient A's selectively attuned perceptual system and trigger anxiety in response to this threat to his or her self-system. Now more desperate, Patient A escalates enactment of the same interpersonal behaviors that form the constricted core of his or her maladaptive self-presentation. In Stage 2, then, the transaction between A and B is at an impasse; it is locked into recurrent enactment of the cycle of maladaptive self-fulfilling prophecy and behavior.

Watzlawick et al. (1967) provided some excellent examples of the reinforcement involved in the vicious cycle:

> A paranoid patient suspects the motives of others; this prompts the others to prove to him the honesty and sincerity of their intentions, which not only confirms but increases his suspicions; for, he argues, if they were not out to hurt him they would not be trying so hard to make him believe that they meant well. . . . [Again,] a depressed patient withdraws; his withdrawal worries those close to him; they try to help him by increasing their attention; on perceiving their concern and anxiety he feels doubly guilty for causing their emotional pain; on seeing his depression thus increase they try harder and at the same time feel more desperate for being unable to help him; which in turn compounds his depression to the point of considering suicide for being so "bad" to those who love him. (p. 65)

Johnson et al. (1989) used the SASB as a component of their "cyclical maladaptive pattern" assessment in psychotherapy. Their results supported use of the SASB-based procedure as a clinically relevant means of quantifying psychotherapeutic transference and rigidity of interpersonal style.

The therapist and other significant persons in Patient A's life initially cannot *not* be pulled into the patient's specific version of the Maladaptive Transaction Cycle. Unless they cease to be significant, others cannot avoid experiencing over time aversive feelings and reactions when transacting with the patient. The therapist also cannot avoid this aversive consequence unless he or she first detects the pattern of the cycle and then makes interventive moves to disrupt patient A's maladaptive pattern.

A TRANSACTIONAL CONCEPTUALIZATION OF *DSM* DYSTHYMIA

Figure 6–2 depicts application of the MTC to the chronic, moderately depressed dysthymic patient. Some of the components found in Figure 6–2 are adapted from Coyne's (1976a, 1976b) and Leary's (1957, p. 284) interpersonal analysis of depression.

STAGE 1

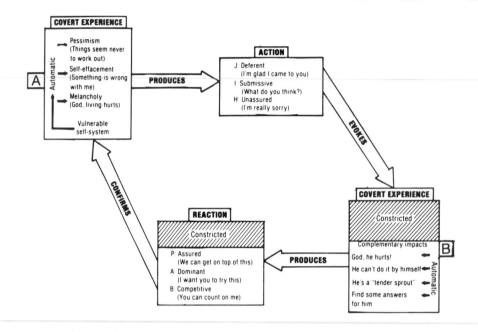

STAGE 2

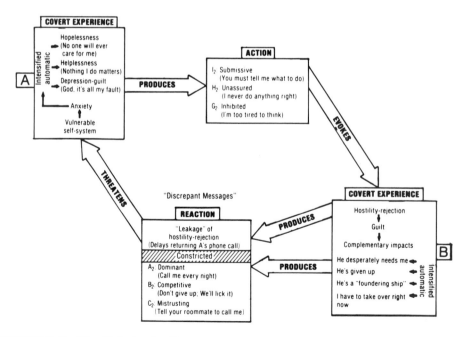

FIGURE 6–2. The Maladaptive Transaction Cycle for a *DSM* Patient with Dysthymia.

Leary (1957) analyzed the interpersonal behaviors of persons with psychoneurotic depression within the submissive-hate (hostile-submissive) quadrant of the circle, closer to the submissive than to the hate pole of the respective axes. He depicted the normal (premorbid) interpersonal style of the depressive individual as "adjustment through self-effacement," while he labeled the more extreme abnormal style the "masochistic personality." Anticipating later formulations, Leary (1957) noted that a two-stage "complementary response" or "impact" typically occurs inside a person interacting with the depressive individual: (a) initial sympathy, which subsequently evolves into (b) irritation, disapproval, and rejection (p. 284).

Coyne (1976a, 1976b) presented what has become a well-known interpersonal hypothesis for depression that generated a large amount of subsequent research. According to Coyne (1976b):

> Depressed persons and members of their environment become enmeshed in an emergent system of depressive symptom and response from others. The symptoms of depressed persons (a) are aversive yet powerful in the ability to arouse guilt in others and to inhibit any direct expression of annoyance and hostility from others. Members of the social environment (b) attempt to reduce the aversive behavior of depressed persons and alleviate guilt by manipulating them with nongenuine reassurance and support. At the same time, these same persons reject and avoid the depressed persons. As discrepancies between the reassurance of others and their actual behavior become apparent, (c) the depressed persons are confirmed in their suspicions that they are not accepted and that further interactions cannot be assured. To maintain their increasingly uncertain security and to control the behavior of others, depressed persons display more symptoms and convey more distress, thereby further stimulating the depressive social process. (pp. 186–187)

Coyne, thus, picked up on Leary's (1957) earlier theme and described the interpersonal consequences of the depressive's style as having both a double-message nature and a sequential phasing, as follows. First, an interactant is pulled to express genuine reassurance and support—concern and helpful intent—in response to the depressed person's dysphoric behaviors. Second, over time, as frustration and irritation accumulate since the depressed person refuses to experience a healthy response to the increased attention (and the dysphoric behavior continues), the interactant's reassurance and support are now expressed less genuinely. The interactant begins to feel angry and hostile, but is sidetracked from direct expressions of these feelings because of the vulnerability and suffering exhibited by the depressed person. The interactant is forced to respond with verbal assurances accompanied by nonverbal leakage of hostility, which the depressed person interprets as avoidance and rejection. Rather than risk criticism or abandonment, the depressed individual escalates his or her dysphoric behaviors. Finally, the interactant either avoids or eliminates contact with the depressed person, or the spiral continues as they get locked into a pattern of mutual manipulation.

Coyne (1976b) explicitly contrasted his model with popular cognitive theories of depression that emphasized the "cognitive distortions" found among depressed individuals. In contrast to cognitive explanations, Coyne's interpersonal model asserted that depressed individuals accurately perceive that they are being rejected by others. Indeed, as this chapter just reviewed, empirical studies of depressive realism and normality bias provide support for Coyne's contention. What depressed persons constantly ignore (selectively inattend) is that their rigid dysphoric behaviors actually produce the rejection they receive.

Coyne's hypothesis can be translated quite easily into the format of the Maladaptive Transaction Cycle. Depressive symptoms and behavior serve as messages that solicit and pull reassurance and support from others, as communications that probe and test for acceptance. As Figure 6–2 shows, the depressive's inner experiences consist of cognitions, memories, fantasies, emotions, and so forth characterized by low self-worth, sadness, self-effacing automatic thoughts, hopeless expectations, and the like. This phenomenological experience (reflecting a vulnerable self-system) leads the depressive to enact unassured, submissive, and deferent behaviors (circle segments H, I, J).

Application of the principle of complementarity reveals that significant others will be pulled to experience covert reactions of sympathy, concern, and responsibility that lead the others to enact behaviors of reassurance, support, advice giving, and taking charge (the complementary circle segments of B: competitive, A: dominant, and P: assured). In the earlier stage of their relationship, the friendlier components (A: dominant, P: assured) will predominate in B's reaction, and both parties, to some extent, will find their transactions satisfying and confirming.

The difficulty develops as the relationship continues. The bottom half of Figure 6–2 depicts this later stage. The basic problem is that the depressive's actions do not change or improve. Interactant B now begins to experience more hostile and rejecting impacts. The portion of B's reaction that "leaks" rejection intensifies the depressive negative cognitions, irrational expectancies, and other experience. Patient A who becomes increasingly vulnerable, is anxiously driven to evoke supportive and accepting reactions and desperately escalates the depressive maladaptive behavior pattern. J: deference now becomes less evident in Patient A's actions toward B, while G: inhibited becomes more prominent. In correspondence to A's shift, Interactant B's response now includes a new C: mistrusting element (in complementary response to A's new G: inhibited), while the P: assured components begin to subside.

Their interaction now is in a clear state of conflict for both participants. Patient A is increasingly vulnerable to B's potential rejection but perceives no options that might replace escalation of inhibited, dependent, and submissive behaviors. Interactant B now vacillates between anger and guilt. Direct expression of anger is inhibited by B's perception of the depressive's abject suffering and profound helplessness, and these same perceptions intensify B's guilt for having hostile and rejecting thoughts in the first place. Interactant B is now trapped into expression of discrepant or incongruous messages that simultaneously are supportive and reassuring yet subtly hostile and rejecting. Because of the depressive's low perceptual thresholds for cues of hostility, Patient A takes in primarily the messages of rejection and interprets B's reassurance and support as nongenuine. As a result, the depressive finds further confirmation of maladaptive beliefs and expectancies. The depressive's unique maladaptive transaction cycle is now complete, with A and B remaining at an impasse.

Research Investigating the Interactional Model

Over the past two decades, many studies inspired by Coyne's (1976a, 1976b) interactional model of depression have explored interpersonal aspects of depression with generally confirmatory results (Coyne, 1990; Coyne, Burchill, & Stiles, 1991; Gurtman, 1986, 1987; Marcus & Nardone, 1992; Segrin & Abramson, 1994; Segrin & Dillard, 1992; Youngren & Lewinsohn, 1980). Although this research convincingly demonstrates that depressed people elicit rejection from other people, (a) it often fails to demonstrate that depressed individuals induce a prior negative mood in their interactional partners and (b) it fails to demonstrate exactly what it is that depressed people do to prompt this rejection. The robust rejection effect may be moderated by sex of the depressed target, length of acquaintance with the depressed person, listener response style, length of the depressive episode, and both the physical attractiveness and self-esteem of the depressed target (Segrin & Abramson, 1994).

Segrin and Abramson (1994) reviewed the interactional literature on response of others to the depressed person as well as on social skill impairments associated with depression. They concluded that depressed people reliably experience rejection from those in their social environment and that depression generally is associated with impairments in social behavior. They concluded also that the research does not explain exactly what depressed people do to elicit rejection, or exactly why others react negatively to them. Segrin and Abramson (1994) suggest that the hostility and rejection depressed people encounter from others are the result of what appear to be social behavioral deficits: specifically, unresponsiveness to the social environment, an impoliteness that violates the desire for social approval on the part of their interpersonal partners, and violations of partners' expectations of nonverbal involvement. Depressed individuals become "caught in a vicious cycle in which they continue to regenerate their own depressive symptoms as a result of the negative life events caused by their social skill deficits" (Segrin & Abramson, 1994, p. 663).

This same research literature also provides some support for the more specific circle profile translations in Figure 6–2: Dependent, self-devaluating, and deferent (I, H, J circle segments combined with C: mistrusting) interpersonal behaviors are the ones that prompt rejection and strife during interpersonal transactions (Blumberg & Hokanson, 1983; Dobson, 1989; Hammen & Peters, 1978; Hokanson & Butler, 1992; Hokanson, Rubert, Welker, Hollander, & Hedeen, 1989; Howes & Hokanson, 1979). Howes and Hokanson (1979), for example, found that confederates who portrayed a depressed role impacted (IMI) subjects as being less agreeable, nurturant, and affiliative as well as more inhibited, submissive, succorance-seeking, detached and hostile than confederates who played physically ill or normal roles.

Another line of research provides additional confirmation of the I, H, J circle translations. The basic interpersonal style postulated by Leary (1957) for the Masochistic Personality consists of the ABA, SUB, SUC, and INH behaviors. It seems valid to extrapolate that a depressed person with this interpersonal pattern could be described quite accurately as functioning with minimal adaptive "assertiveness." To the extent that this inference is valid, any interpersonal findings regarding nonassertive individuals should produce results consistent with those described earlier. Two interpersonal studies of nonassertive individuals provide strong support for this extrapolation.

Reagan (1978) had four judges independently record their interpersonal engagements on the IMI while viewing videotaped role-playing sessions of 10 high and 10 low assertive subjects. The judges' IMI scores significantly differentiated the two groups of subjects. Low assertive subjects pulled significantly stronger impacts on the ABA, SUB, SUC, and INH Impact Message Inventory scales, whereas high assertive subjects elicited significantly stronger Sociable (SOC) impacts.

In a careful follow-up study, Reagan (1979) replicated and extended these findings. Using a conflict resolution inventory, she selected three groups of eight subjects each: high, moderate, and low assertive individuals. All subjects role-played four scenes designed to elicit refusal-assertive behavior. All portrayals were videotaped, and one group of judges coded verbal and nonverbal content, while a second group of judges independently reported their engagements on the IMI. Results showed that the ABA, SUB, SUC, and INH scales significantly differentiated all three groups, with less assertive subjects producing the stronger impacts on these scales. Also low assertive subjects elicited significantly stronger impacts on an IMI "composite hate" (MIS + DET) than did the two other groups. All three verbal content measures (capacity for refusal of requests, expression of personal responsibility, and requesting behavior change from the interpersonal partner) discriminated the groups, with high assertive individuals also receiving significantly higher IMI Dominance (DOM) and Affiliative (AFF) scores than did the other groups. Finally, significant positive correlations were found between IMI scores and behavioral measures of assertion "providing support for the convergent validity of the IMI as a measure of assertive behavior."

INTERPERSONAL CONCEPTUALIZATIONS OF OTHER
DSM DISORDERS

Contemporary interpersonal theory requires that the Maladaptive Transaction Cycle be applied concretely to the wide range of *DSM* disorders, especially to the Axis II personality disorders. Other seminal interpersonal conceptualizations have appeared that show considerable promise for this translation process. This section will review these formulations with the hope of facilitating renewed interest and research. Seminal comprehensive and creative interpersonal formulations for a wide range of DSM disorders, especially for the personality disorders, also can be found in Benjamin (1993), Leary (1957), and Sullivan (1956).

The contemporary interpersonal formulations and analyses to be reviewed in this section include the following groups of DSM mental disorders: (a) *Axis I symptom disorders:* agoraphobia (Bennum, 1986; M. M. Carter, Turovsky, & Barlow, 1994; Dobson, 1989; Shean & Uchenwa, 1990; Shuler, 1994), alcohol abuse and dependency (Gorad, McCourt, & Cobb, 1971; Heffner, 1993), bipolar disorder (Davenport, Adlind, Gold, & Goodwin, 1979; R. G. Fitzgerald, 1972; Janowsky, El-Yousef, & Davis, 1974; Janowsky, Leff, & Epstein, 1970), dissociative disorder (Celani, 1976; Slipp, 1977) dysthymic disorder or neurotic depression (Andrews, 1989c; Brokaw & McLemore, 1991; Coates & Wortman, 1980; Coyne, 1976a, 1976b; Gotlib & Colby, 1987; L. M. Horowitz et al., 1991; L. M. Horowitz & Vitkus, 1986; Kiesler, 1986a; McCullough et al., 1994; McLean, 1976; Whiffen et al., 1990; Wiener, 1989; Youngren & Lewinsohn, 1980), schizophrenia (Bateson, Jackson, Haley, & Weakland, 1956; Haley, 1959), and specific phobia (Andrews, 1966, 1991); (b) *Axis II personality disorders:* antisocial personality disorder (Foreman, 1989; Mackenzie, Rosenberg, Bergen, & Tucker, 1978; Rime, Bouvy, Leborgne, & Rouillon, 1978), avoidant personality disorder (Alden & Capreol, 1993), borderline personality disorder (Benjamin, 1987a, 1993; Benjamin & Wonderlich, 1994; Dawson, 1988), dependent personality disorder (Birtchnell, 1987); histrionic personality disorder (Andrews, 1984; Andrews & Moore, 1991; Bergner, 1977; Celani, 1976); obsessive compulsive personality disorder (Barnett, 1966, 1969, 1972; Kiesler, 1973–1975, 1977), paranoid personality disorder (Cameron, 1943, 1959; LaRusso, 1978; Lemert, 1962; Tyhurst, 1957); and (c) *Psychological Factors Affecting Medical Condition (psychophysiological disorders):* cancer (Wortman & Dunkel-Schetter, 1979), chronic pain (Mikail, Henderson, & Tasca, 1994), heart disease (Mancini, 1995; Smith, 1992; Smith & Pope, 1990), and weight loss (R. B. Stuart & Davis, 1978).

Axis I Symptom Disorders

Agoraphobia.   Bennum (1986) offered a composite formulation of agoraphobia in which he integrates three distinct perspectives: (a) Bowlby's attachment and misattribution, (b) Rachman's safety-signal, and (c) the role of the spouse and conflict in the interpersonal marital context.

According to M. M. Carter et al. (1994), belief in the importance of the interpersonal system in agoraphobia has led researchers to postulate two major tenets. First, successful treatment of agoraphobia will result in improvement in the extant interpersonal relationship. A corollary to this assumption is that agoraphobics in "bad" or "poor" relationships will fare less well in treatment than those in "good" relationships (Milton & Hafner, 1979). Second, given the impact of the disorder on the interpersonal system, inclusion of the partner in treatment efforts will result in greater treatment efficacy than will treating the client alone (Barlow, Mavissakalian, & Hay, 1981).

After their review of the empirical literature M. M. Carter et al. (1994) concluded that there appears to be mixed evidence regarding these two tenets. In light of this relatively inconsistent evidence:

> It seems prudent to conclude that there may be some interpersonal difficulties among agoraphobics. However, what the specific interpersonal dysfunction is and whether it plays a causal, moderator, or consequential role in agoraphobia remains unclear. (p. 28)

They recommended that future studies need to (a) explicate a specific dysfunctional interpersonal pattern, its relationship to agoraphobia, or its impact on the syndrome, and (b) develop and incorporate measures of relationship functioning with good psychometric properties.

Some researchers (e.g., Goldstein & Chambless, 1978) have observed that agorophobics tend to be women who exhibit stereotypic behaviors of unassertiveness, fearfulness, passivity, and dependence. Also, agoraphobia tends to occur in highly complementary relationships (Bergner, 1977; Fry, 1962; Goldstein & Chambless, 1978; Hafner, 1982) characterized by a caretaking strategy in which the husband is reinforced by the dependency of the patient (Agulnik, 1970; Webster, 1953).

In line with these reports, Shean and Uchenwa (1990) predicted that high-anxiety subjects would evidence more stereotypically feminine patterns of interpersonal behavior than low-anxiety subjects; that these patterns would be evidenced by higher scores on the self-effacing/obedient and docile/dependent octant scales of the ICL and on the unassured, submissive, and deferent scales of the CLOIT. Also, ratings of partners of high anxiety subjects were predicted to reflect the complementary patterns of ICL managerial/autocratic and self-confident/competitive as well as of CLOIT competitive, dominant, and assured scales respectively.

Subjects were undergraduates who obtained very high versus very low scores on a questionnaire designed to measure DSM-III panic experience and agoraphobic fears. In high and low pairs, subjects were instructed to get acquainted during a 10-minute period, after which they filled out self-characterization versions of the CLOIT and ICL, and also rated their partners using the IMI.

Findings for both males and females revealed that, as predicted, self-reports of agoraphobiclike anxiety experiences correlated positively with interpersonal behavior associated with the female sex role stereotype: unassured, submissive, and deferent behavior. Although not predicted, mistrusting and inhibited styles were also positively related to the anxiety scores. The authors also found significant negative relationships between high anxiety and a friendly-dominant interpersonal pattern (friendly-sociable and exhibitionistic-assured interpersonal behaviors as rated by interactants). Contrary to Shean and Uchenwa's (1990) predictions, subjects' ratings of their partners did not confirm a complementary pattern of interpersonal behavior during the acquaintance process. Shean and Uchenway (1990) concluded that their results "lend support to clinical reports that some individuals may be likely to develop agoraphobic problems because of the interaction between their interpersonal style and their relationship patterns" (p. 407).

Shuler (1994) examined whether interpersonal transactions (measured by the CLOIT and IMI) with significant others differed between people who experience panic attacks and people who experience anxiety but no panic attacks. She predicted that the interpersonal behavior of the person with panic: (a) as self-reported on the CLOIT would be more variable and more intense, reflecting the internal experience of loss of control and disintegration of self; (b) would reflect a nonintegrated self-concept (indicated by a discrepancy between the "actual" self-presentation to the significant other versus the self-presentation reported by the subject that would represent his or her "real" self); (c) would reflect greater incongruence between the subject's self-concept and actual behavior (difference between subject's self-reported behavior and significant other's ratings of the subject); and (d) would reflect an absence of complementarity (would show a pattern of noncomplementarity) between the subject and the significant other. Subjects consisted of samples of ADIS-R diagnosed nonclinical panic versus general anxiety female subjects who volunteered in response to media announcements. The panic subjects reported an average of at least three attacks within the month immediately prior to the study. The general anxiety subjects reported the current experience of worry diffused across a number of life situations, or with no apparent cause; worries endured for at least a month immediately prior to the study.

Results showed no significant differences between the two groups' profiles, number of peak scores, or average profile intensities of interpersonal transactions—the women in the panic group were remarkably similar to those in the anxiety group. Hence, the phenomenon of panic per se did not have a differential effect on interpersonal transactions with significant others. Also, no differences were found between the two groups for incongruency and complementarity. Contrary to prediction, it was the women in the general anxiety group who showed a significant discrepancy between the subject's actual impact on the significant other and the impact on the significant other reported by the subject if she were to show her "real self" to the other.

All high-anxiety (questionnaire) subjects reported more hostile-submissive and friendly-submissive—and, to a lesser degree also more dominant—interpersonal behaviors in transactions with their significant others. High levels of anxiety, then, were associated with a bipolar pattern of interpersonal behavior reflecting primarily submission, but at times also dominance.

Dobson (1989) measured interpersonal responses of recent-acquaintance interactants to anxious, depressed-anxious, and normal young women using the IMI. The only difference in impacts reported for the three groups of subjects was for warm-sociable interpersonal behavior: Interactants rated the depressed-anxious subjects as significantly less warm-sociable than the normal subjects. Further analyses revealed that, although no significant group differences were found for respondents' degree of rejection of the target subjects, the anxious and depressed groups both perceived more social rejection in the acquaintanceship setting.

Alcohol Abuse and Dependency.   Gorad et al. (1971) conceptualized drunken behaviors as interpersonal acts designed to have a dramatic effect on other persons. Drunkenness obtains its effects through indirect, responsibility-avoiding mechanisms (symptomatic acts), rather than through direct communications. This occurs through the simultaneous transmission of two messages. First, the drunken person broadcasts the message "I am drunk" by providing cues (e.g., staggering, slurred speech, glazed eyes) which together send the message. Once this message is established, the drunken person proceeds to send other messages (e.g., seductive moves, insults, etc.), all of which are now qualified by "I am drunk" and which command others not to hold the drunk responsible for what he or she says or does. The metacommunication underlying all this is a request (e.g., for nurturance), but responsibility for the request is denied by the drunken person. This puts the drunk in a position of unusual control: to be able to send a command but simultaneously to be able to deny that one is sending it.

Gorad et al. (1971) assumed further that all alcoholics share use of certain communicational maneuvers, whether drunk or sober, regardless of personality type. The alcoholic's transactional style consists of five components:

1. The primary feature is general avoidance of responsibility for communications. This is particularly observable in his or her verbal productions (choice of words, use or misuse of grammar, use of stress, and method of articulation). Statements typically are confounded by ambiguities, confusion-creation devices, retractions, and the excessive use of qualifiers.

2. Avoidance of responsibility can be observed also in nonverbal messages. The combination of subtle facial, trunk, and postural cues accompanying verbal statements often produces the feeling that the alcoholic does not really mean much of what he or she says.

3. Responsibility avoidance is also evident in a split between verbalizations of intentions and actions. Alcoholics shy away from taking decisive action. If pushed, they may come to verbally stated decisions, but they will not follow through.

4. Alcoholics communicate that they cannot help what they are doing by shifting responsibility to something or someone else. They externalize responsibility in the form of "field dependence" (relying more on external than internal perceptual cues) and by perceiving locus of control to be external rather than internal. Things happen to the alcoholic—he or she plays no active role in anything done including excessive drinking.

5. Through use of the preceding maneuvers, the alcoholic presents a self-picture that is highly variable, unpredictable, and confusing. This picture of elusiveness

commands interactants to be attention-giving and nurturant without retaliation or rejection. The pulled-for reaction is to engage oneself in the alcoholic's plight and to want to help him or her stop drinking. This reaction later is replaced by resentment, helplessness, and anger when the enormity of taking over someone else's life is realized.

According to Gorad et al. (1971), the alcoholic acts directly on self rather than directly on others; uses maneuvers designed to ensnare important others; externalizes control; and is ready to get others to assume responsibility. By use of this dependent pattern, the alcoholic seems to sacrifice an active, direct way of making his or her desires known and of satisfying them, in return for a higher probability of holding on to emotionally important others.

Gorad et al. (1971) also described the system elements present between the alcoholic, his or her spouse, and the immediate family. They assumed that the alcoholic's use of responsibility-avoidance is not only permitted or tolerated by the spouse, but is in some sense encouraged and agreed on by the spouse. The basic dyadic struggle is over who is to have control in the relationship. Escalations of the conflict over control, together with the alcoholic's perception that he or she is losing and is powerless to win the battle openly, frequently are the precipitants to the drinking bout. The alcoholic's drunken state, then, serves to restabilize the dyadic system to a familiar and recurrent equilibrium point.

The alcoholic's spouse is the most visibly powerful family member, the one in control of most rule-setting in the family. However, the one area in family events where the spouse cannot assert power, and where the alcoholic has complete control, is the alcoholic's drinking. If the spouse did not get upset at the alcoholic's drinking and did not try to control it, the drinking would lose its effectiveness as a control measure.

Gorad et al. (1971) suggested that family therapy is the obvious treatment choice for alcoholics. They do not, however, provide any systematic or explicit differential treatment program for the alcoholic family that might be derivable from their conceptualization of the problem.

Bipolar Disorder.   Davenport et al. (1979) detailed the characteristic transactional patterns between husband and wife that are present in families in which one mate has bipolar disorder. They document how these transactional patterns help maintain stability in the marriage and in the patient's clinical state. Specifically, family interactions become dominated by a suppression of affective expression, since expressiveness evokes fears of loss in both the disturbed and normal family members. The authors speculated whether this acquiesced in interpersonal rule takes the form of an etiological factor, a maintenance factor, or both.

R. G. Fitzgerald (1972) observed that manic symptoms are sometimes "provoked" by relatives during their interactions with the manic family member. He defined manic behaviors as constituting a message to family members that the manic individual is angry, frustrated, and wanting to individuate.

Janowsky et al. (1974) tested their hypothesis that a manic episode is characterized not only by certain symptoms (e.g., flight of ideas, grandiosity, etc.) but also by a certain style of relating interpersonally. Janowsky et al. (1970) had earlier specified that manic patients frequently manipulate the self-esteem of others, either building up or denigrating a person's sense of pride. Manics also show a remarkable perceptiveness to areas of vulnerability and conflict in others, and possess a keen ability to sense, reveal, and exploit areas of covert sensitivity. Finally, they often project responsibility onto others and engage in progressive limit testing and in so doing subtly extend externally imposed limits.

Janowsky et al. (1974) tested their formulation on a group of inpatients including DSM-II schizophrenics, schizoaffective patients excited type, and manic-depressive patients manic type. During their acute illness, each patient was rated daily by a team of nurses on Likert scale measures reflecting the "interpersonal-interactional" characteristics specified by Janowsky et al. (1970): testing of limits, projection of responsibility, sensitivity to others' soft spots, attempts to divide staff, flattering behavior, and ability to evoke anger in people. The sum of the scores on the six items constituted a total "manic interpersonal interaction scale (MIIS)" score.

Results were clearly supportive of Janowsky et al.'s (1974) "interpersonal-interactional" predictions. The manic patients obtained a significantly higher total MIIS score than both other patient groups and also obtained higher scores on each of the six scale items. Additionally, a sample of five manic patients were evaluated longitudinally with ratings while acutely ill and then following remission; both the total MIIS score and the six individual item scores for these subjects diminished dramatically as remission occurred.

Janowsky et al. (1974) concluded that their conceptualization is helpful for both understanding and designing interventions for the manic individual's interpersonal displays:

> Expecting the manic patient to divide staff members, assault self-esteem, progressively test limits, project responsibility, and distance himself from family members allows anticipation of these actions with the possibility of formulating concrete responses and plans. (p. 253)

Dissociative Disorder.   Celani (1976) offered an interpersonal formulation for dissociative states in which he suggested that dissociation is the result of persons who have a predisposition toward hysteria finding themselves in situations in which they are unable to elicit the type of response from others that confirms a basic sense of self. Feedback contradictory to the person's self-attitude increases anxiety and prompts the person to flee the conflict by switching roles. Celani argues that the perceptions of these persons screen out specific classes of stimuli. When roles are shifted, classes of perceived and nonperceived stimuli are shifted as well; the person shifts roles so that the perceived stimuli are no longer in conflict with self-attitudes.

Slipp (1977) discussed how Freud's original seduction theory of the etiology of hysteria emphasized both interpersonal and intrapsychic factors; but when Freud abandoned the theory, the emphasis in psychoanalysis was transferred to intrapsychic fantasies stemming from the patient's infantile sexuality. Slipp noted that recent developments in ego psychology and object relations returned a greater emphasis on adaptive functioning and human relationships. From the more contemporary perspective Slipp (1977) attempted to develop a typology of mental disorders—including hysteria, depression, and schizophrenia—that incorporated both interpersonal and intrapsychic factors. Within Slipps's formulation, seduction is conceived as an interpersonal power maneuver and a style of relating designed to manipulate and control others.

Dysthymic Disorder.   In addition to Coyne's (1976a, 1976b) model of depression described in detail earlier, other transactional conceptualizations have appeared in the literature. McLean (1976) offered an interpersonal disturbance model of depression that highlights "coercive communication patterns." Wiener (1989) interpreted depressive pathology as residing in psychosocial transactions. Gotlib and Colby (1987) detailed an interpersonal systems approach to the treatment of depression. Youngren and Lewinsohn (1980) provided a systematic analysis demonstrating the functional relation between depression and problematic interpersonal behavior.

Gotlib and Colby (1987) presented an interpersonal systems approach to depression and outlined family, marital, and individual intervention strategies and procedures based on their conceptualization. They adopted the position that an approach that integrates both intra- and interpersonal factors holds greater promise in providing a comprehensive conceptual model of depression than does either focus alone.

In their formulation, the first stage in the development of depression is an "event" or "stressor" that imposes a significant demand on the individual to make an adaptive change. The event can be interpersonal or intrapsychic, or both; it may be internal (e.g., biochemical changes) or may interact with other internal factors (e.g., maladaptive cognitions). Once the individual becomes depressed and begins to exhibit depressed symptoms, two interactive factors may converge to maintain or exacerbate the depression. The first factor is interpersonal and involves the nature and quality of the response of others in the depressive's social environment to the individual's symptomatic behavior (a pattern of aversive nonverbal and conversational behaviors)—an aversive interpersonal style to which others ultimately respond with negativity and rejection. The second factor involves the depressed individual's perceptions and interpretations of the reactions of others: The individual has a tendency or readiness to focus on or attend to negative aspects of the environment.

According to Gotlib and Colby (1987):

> When individuals become depressed, they exhibit depressive symptoms. This symptomatic behavior elicits negative or, at best, ambivalent responses from others in their social environment. Because of the depressed person's cognitive style, they attend closely to these negative responses. . . . This focus on the negative characteristics of the environment leads the depressed person to become even more depressed, more symptomatic. . . . These depressive behaviors lead others to become even more negative or to withdraw further. Because the depressed individual has little difficulty perceiving and focusing on these negative behaviors, the cycle worsens. (p. 35)

Finally, important individual and family differences serve as crucial moderating factors throughout the depressive process. Some individuals are better able to adapt to the demand of the precipitating stressor or event. Some families are better able to adapt to the aversive behaviors of the depressed individual:

> Healthy families who have an optimal balance of cohesiveness and adaptability will cope best. Members of these families may still become depressed; the families, however, will have a higher probability of being able to find solutions to the difficulties and help ameliorate the member's depression. They are also likely to tolerate the depression longer without exhibiting disruptive efforts. (Gotlib & Colby, 1987, p. 37)

In a series of three studies, L. M. Horowitz et al. (1991) tested their general proposition that self-derogations, so central in the dysthymic process, connote submissiveness together with neutrality in affiliation. Results showed that self-derogations are indeed judged to be submissive and, in accordance with the principle of complementarity, elicit dominating reactions from a partner. However, contrary to the principle of complementarity, the results also demonstrated that neutral submissiveness can elicit friendly dominance. The upshot is that people who seem friendly or hostile are more apt to seem self-assured or assertive, whereas people who seem submissive, helpless, or passive are more apt to seem neutral in affiliation.

Whiffen et al. (1990) explored the interpersonal patterns associated with Blatt's (1974) dependent versus self-critical depressive character structures. Hypothesizing that depression would be associated with marital relationship "complementarity," they had female university students complete measures of dependency, self-criticism, and depressed mood; the students also rated themselves and their boyfriend or spouse on the CLOIT. The authors found that the self-critical women described themselves as more cold, and their partners as more cold and more dominant, than did either the dependent or control subjects. A significant main effect also was obtained showing that the self-critical women reported the highest levels of depression; however, this main effect was mediated by the predicted interaction: Self-critical women reported greater feelings of depression when they perceived their partner's behavior to be complementary to their own behavior. Whiffen et al. (1990) concluded that the latter finding is consistent with Andrews' (1989c) view that depression is more likely to occur when the partner's behavior confirms a vulnerable person's self-concept.

Other interpersonal approaches also have examined the nature of depression (e.g., Brokaw & McLemore, 1991; L. M. Horowitz & Vitkus, 1985; Kiesler, 1986a; McCullough et al., 1994).

Schizophrenia.   Bateson et al. (1956) and Haley (1959) offered an early interactional description of schizophrenia within the framework of communications psychiatry (e.g., Ruesch & Bateson, 1951; Watzlawick et al., 1967). Haley (1959) documented how, as two people define their relationship with each other, they work out together what sort of communicative behavior is to take place in their relationship. From among all the possible messages, they select certain kinds that shall be included. "This agreement on what is and what is not to take place can be called a mutual definition of the relationship" (Haley, 1959, p. 322).

Haley then described the one way in which a person can avoid indicating what is to take place in a relationship, can avoid defining it, by negating what he says. "Even though he will be defining the relationship by whatever he communicates, he can invalidate this definition by using qualifications that deny his communications" (Haley, 1959, p. 325). Haley detailed four ways a person can avoid indicting what sort of relationship he is in: (a) by denying that he is speaking, (b) by denying that anything is said, (c) by denying that it is said to the other person, and (d) by denying that the interchange is occurring in this place at this time.

Haley (1959) continued, "It seems apparent that the list of ways to avoid defining a relationship is a list of schizophrenic symptoms" (p. 326). For example, schizophrenic patients may deny that they are the one doing the speaking (by using another name, or indicating that "voices" are saying these things). They may deny that the message is a real message (perhaps by busily spelling out each of the words). They may deny that their message is addressed to the other person, leading others to consider them delusional. They may deny their presence in the hospital by saying that they are in a castle or prison. In various ways, and at various times, schizophrenic patients may react incongruently, with inappropriate affect. And so on. By using one or more of these negating maneuvers, "the schizophrenic avoids indicating what behavior is to take place in his relationships and thereby avoids defining his relationships" (Haley, 1959, p. 328).

Specific Phobia.   Andrews (1966) offered one of the earliest interpersonal formulations of a specific DSM disorder and its treatment. His basic assumption was that what is learned in psychotherapy are new "central strategies" (rather than isolated habits) which, in turn, are closely related to the learning of social roles.

Andrews (1966) defined the phobic disturbance as consisting of two main elements: dependence and avoidance.

1. Dependence and immaturity, together with the fearfulness exhibited by such individuals, "tend to evoke from others the care and protection which is part of such dependency relationships" (p. 456).
2. As part of a pattern of avoidance, phobic individuals typically avoid any activity that involves independent, self-assertive handling of difficult and fear-arousing situations. "This is, of course, a description of how the phobic behaves when confronted by the phobic stimulus; but frequently this lack of self-assertion constitutes a broader pattern of response as well" (p. 459).

In Andrews' formulation, phobics respond to difficult and frightening experiences with an exaggerated tendency to avoid confronting and self-assertively mastering them. In addition, they tend to establish dependent relationships with strong, protective, and guiding individuals as a part of such avoidance. Phobics, and those they depend on, behave as though such dependency relationships are incompatible with any self-reliance on the phobic's part, either in the form of self-assertion within that relationship, or in the form of dealing directly with the outside world and its dangers.

Andrews (1966) offered a two-stage model of psychotherapy that articulated therapy processes targeting the phobic's essential problems of dependency and avoidance. A close relationship exists between the life strategies that define the problem and the therapeutic strategies Andrews uses to resolve it. The first element in therapeutic strategy is the support that the therapist needs to provide the phobic patient. For the therapy relationship to be tolerable for the phobic, the therapist must establish him- or herself in the directive-nurturant role "which is normally 'pulled' from others by the phobic's symptoms and other demonstrations of helplessness" (p. 463)—the role-complement of the dependency that characterizes such patients.

Within the context of this supportive relationship, however, the therapist introduces a very new element: The therapist begins to use the guiding, directing, helpful role to urge the patient to become more self-assertive and to deal with his or her fears directly. "The therapist does not reduce his support, but quite clearly indicates confidence in the patient and rather directively urges him to take steps toward self-reliance" (p. 463). To accomplish this, the therapist (a) encourages and accepts self-assertion within the therapy relationship itself, thus sanctioning it; (b) urges the patient to attempt confrontation of difficult situations, phobic and otherwise, in life outside the therapy relationship.

Andrew's (1966) two-stage intervention consists of establishment of a dependent rapport with the patient, followed by a rather directive effort to induce the patient to move directly against his or her fears. The therapist, thus, comes to represent a novel object in the phobic's world—someone who is something of a paradox: "a protective, directive person who nevertheless favors independence" (p. 475). Psychotherapeutic change involves a situation in which the therapist: (a) by embodying both support and encouragement, offers the patient an opportunity to learn new ways of interacting and, (b) by maintaining confidence in the patient's ultimate ability and desire to become more independent, offers the phobic a new conception of self.

Axis II Personality Disorders

Antisocial Personality Disorder.   Rime et al. (1978) studied psychopathic versus nonpsychopathic male adolescents living in a minimum security institution. The authors hypothesized that, inasmuch as psychopaths typically are unaware of subtle social cues (Hare, 1970), a greater amount of intrusive and troublesome behavior would be observed among psychopaths in the course of an interpersonal encounter. Subjects were interviewed in a face-to-face situation about their leisure activities; the interviews were videotaped and trained judges rated the subjects' and interviewers' nonverbal behaviors.

Results showed that, as predicted, psychopathic and nonpsychopathic nonverbal behavior patterns were different. Specifically, psychopathic subjects displayed more hand gestures and leaned forward more, thus reducing the distance between them and the interviewer. They also looked into the interviewer's eyes for much longer periods and tended to smile less than the nonpsychopaths. In general, the obtained nonverbal differences were consistent with the prediction that psychopaths would be more intrusive toward the interviewer.

Rime et al. (1978) also found that, when interacting with the psychopaths, interviewers spoke significantly less than with the nonpsychopaths. The authors speculated that the psychopath's greater intrusiveness in the interpersonal situation induced an increase of arousal and feelings of discomfort in the interviewers; the reduced amount of interviewer speech could well be one evoked reaction to this intrusive behavior.

Foreman (1989) used IAS-R self-descriptions and ratings by others to differentiate psychopathic and nonpsychopathic inmates from a federal medium security prison. Findings showed that, although self-ratings were not different, IAS-R ratings by staff members discriminated the psychopathic inmates as predicted.

Avoidant Personality Disorder.   Alden and Capreol (1993) examined the extent to which differences in a group of outpatients' problematic interpersonal behavior influenced treatment response. Patients meeting diagnostic criteria for avoidant personality disorder completed the IIP-C. Findings showed, as expected, that all avoidant PD patients reported problems with social avoidance and nonassertiveness. Further, those patients who also had interpersonal problems related to distrustful and angry behavior benefited from the behavioral intervention of graduated exposure, but not from skills training. Finally, patients who experienced interpersonal problems related to being coerced and controlled by others, in addition to avoidance and nonassertiveness, benefited from both graduated exposure and skills training.

Borderline Personality Disorder.   Benjamin (1987a, 1993) theorized that interpersonal relationships play a more prominent role than temperamental factors in the etiology of borderline personality. Specifically, she hypothesized that the borderline person experiences early interpersonal attack, neglect, and threats of abandonment (e.g., high levels of sexual and physical abuse; perception of their families as conflicted and nonempathic) which are not associated with nonborderline mood disorders. Benjamin and Wonderlich (1994) confirmed that borderline subjects were more likely than unipolar or bipolar subjects to see their parental relationships and selected current relationships as attacking and neglectful.

Dawson (1988) presented a conceptual model that borrows from and bridges self psychology and interpersonal theory. In his formulation, borderline individuals are those with deeply conflicted, unstable, or poorly boundaried self-systems who are inordinately dependent on here-and-now experience for self-definition. Their concept of self as being basically good or bad, thus is, to a significant degree, "context bound."

In the psychotherapy context, the borderline individual presents or displays to the therapist one side of the basic conflict between good and bad self. This opening move metacommunicates convincingly the message: "I am helpless/hopeless . . . not responsible . . . bad . . . sick . . . unlovable . . ." (p. 372). In response to the metacommunication, the therapist is pulled to convey, in one fashion or another, that he or she agrees or disagrees with the patient's proposition. "The patient may briefly accept the definition of self put forward by the therapist, nonverbally as well as verbally, but inevitably will reject it and/or be forced to display more vociferously the other side of the coin" (p. 372).

Dawson (1988) offered detailed relationship management guidelines and specific interventions for treatment of the borderline. His approach basically emphasizes the necessity of the therapist providing the patient a corrective experience. The borderline patient repeatedly attempts to distort the role of the therapist in a manner that will provide the patient with some imposed self-definition. Instead of responding to the evoked pressure, the therapist attempts to remain neutral. The therapist leaves the patient with conflicts

> but continuously, despite evidence she presents to the contrary, metacommunicates to her that she is a healthy, competent, intelligent, responsible, likeable adult. Her behavior and then her sense of self will gradually adopt this definition. The experience of interacting with someone who does not allow distortions will strengthen her own self-system boundaries. (p. 374)

Dependent Personality Disorder.   A considerable literature (Bornstein, 1992, 1993; Masling, 1986; Masling & Schwartz, 1979) indicates that dependent persons often behave in a passive, compliant manner, preferring to look to others for nurturance, guidance, and support rather than initiating tasks and activities on their own. Dependency has been found to predict help-seeing behavior, sensitivity to interpersonal cues, compliance with rules and authorities, and interpersonal yielding. It also seems to be a risk factor for certain forms of psychopathology (depression and agoraphobia) but not others (alcoholism). The child-rearing practices of parental overprotectiveness and/or authoritarianism, in turn, serve as risk factors for dependency in later childhood and adulthood.

Birtchnell (1987) offered a model for resolution of dependency in the depressed patient that, in fact, concentrated on the dependent personality disorder. According to Birtchnell, abnormally dependent people are childish; they are adults behaving like children, who exhibit the following characteristics: an excessive need to be loved, cherished, and made a fuss of; a general feeling of inadequacy and incompetence; a persistent need for guidance, reassurance, and approval; a tendency to take rather than to give; and an inclination to relate to others in a humble and apologetic manner from a lowly and submissive position. On the interpersonal circle, this pattern would be translated as falling at segments I: Submissive, H: Unassured, and J: Deferent (lazy).

The dependent individual can relate to others only as would a child to a parent, hence, needs to induce other adults to adopt a parentlike attitude toward him or her. That is, the dependent individual seeks out a relatively exclusive relationship with a "complementary personality type who needs to be needed and who prefers to play the dominant role in relationships" (1987, p. 2)—to coerce others into assuming a more subordinate role. On the circle, this complementary pattern would fall at segments A: Dominant and B: Competitive. In short, the depressed person's belief is that he or she is (and remains) helplessly dependent on another person who simultaneously is responsible for his or her present misery and the only possible source of rescue from it. Accordingly, the depressed person enters into a "bargain relationship" in which he or she denies self personal pleasures in return for nurturance from the dominant other.

Birtchnell (1987) offered an intervention plan in which the object of therapy is to correct, belatedly, the maturational deficiencies that define the dependent pattern. "That requires a kind of rerun of the patient's childhood, with the therapist inescapably taking on the role of alternative parent" (p. 4). A central related goal is to assist the dependent person to become more separate and autonomous, to establish a more secure identity, gradually building up an identity "that is recognizably his own." Strategies the therapist can use in pursuit of this goal include repeatedly inviting the patient to express his or her opinion and to make choices, as well as assisting the patient to "discover his likes and dislikes, to do those things he thinks would give him pleasure, and to fully experience the pleasure he derives from doing them" (p. 5).

Birtchnell (1987) described what is, in actuality, a two-stage model for the course of therapy. During the initial stage the therapist needs to resign him- or herself that it will be difficult to be anything other than relatively dominant to a patient who is behaving in a conspicuously submissive manner. During a subsequent stage, the therapist works to establish a relationship in which the therapist and patient interact on an adult-to-adult basis. To accomplish this, "the therapist must increasingly decline to respond to the patient's appeals for guidance and reassurance and instead treat him as though he were a competent and responsible adult" (p. 5). Therapist and patient move to break the vicious circle by helping the patient to take progressively more responsibility for self.

As a final distinct strategy with the dependent individual, Birtchnell (1987) recommended drawing the dominant significant other into the therapy sessions. The guiding rule in attempting to modify the relationship with the significant other is to prevent excessive anxiety in either member of the relationship; "when anxiety is aroused by the possibility of change, each member will dig in and adhere even more strongly to his present role" (p. 6). Progress can be made only by suggesting a series of small shifts in each partner's interpersonal behaviors.

Histrionic Personality Disorder.   Andrews (1984) provided a conceptualization of the hysteric personality and a plan of differential interpersonal treatment. His interpersonal analysis of the hysteric's personality centered on a self-presentational style characterized by excessive use of agreeable, affiliative, and overconventional behavior (the

NO segments of the 1982 Interpersonal Circle). He described a transactional cycle in which the hysteric sends conflicting and indirect messages to others. The messages combine both symbolic sexual overtones (to gain interest and attention) and simultaneous but subtle hostile messages (to keep the other person at a distance). No matter to which part of the hysteric's message an interactant responds—the interactant who shows disinterest is regarded as rejecting and mean; the interactant who reciprocates the advances is regarded as guilty of sexual exploitation—the effect is the same: confirmation and strengthening of the hysteric's overconventional self-image. In addition, the hysteric's cognitive experience is distinguished by his or her tendency to perceive in global, diffuse, and impressionistic ways (field dependence) and to exhibit a weak differentiation of self from the environment. The hysteric is oversensitive to external stimuli and confused as to what is external and internal.

The therapy package Andrews advocated consists of strategies and techniques designed to counteract the preceding stylistic components and attain the following objectives: symptom reduction, development of a clear sense of identity, acceptance of negative feelings, greater assertiveness, and enhanced cognitive differentiation.

The most important relationship issue posed for the therapist stems from the patient's eagerness for approval, which leads the hysteric to try to discover the therapist's attitudes, which are then used as an external guide for being a "good" patient. The aim is to gain the therapist's confirmation of the patient's self-image as an agreeable, nonhostile person. The therapist counters this ploy by using the ambiguity inherent in the free-association rule of psychoanalysis, insisting that the patient share all thoughts, feelings, and associations no matter how bizarre or unacceptable they may seem. What this ambiguous stance accomplishes is a paradoxical attack on the patient's facade of overconventionality. For if the hysteric religiously follows the rule (as might be expected from one who conforms to conventions, rules, and expectations), he or she inevitably will come up with censored hostile, sexual, and other troublesome feelings that contradict his or her self-presentation. On the other hand, for the hysteric to openly resist or deliberately censor thoughts introduces conflict or deceit that is equally incompatible with the agreeable self-image. Change will occur no matter what the patient does, since the only way to please the therapist is to bring up that which is unpleasant and conflictual about oneself. To accomplish this paradoxical attack, the therapist must establish and maintain a realistic middle ground between pleasing and disappointing the hysteric patient. Thus, the therapist maintains a neutral, steady, but flexible attitude by being willing to accept some of the hysteric's demands for dependency.

According to Andrews (1984), to enhance development of more discriminating cognitive skills, the therapist continually needs to provide reflective comments to the patient's spontaneous associations and self-disclosures. This labeling provides cognitive structure for the hysteric's inner experiences, facilitates conceptual clarity, and reinforces early steps toward cognitive control of emotionally laden internal experiences. Finally, the histrionic individual is helped to learn new communication skills, including how to express needs effectively even in the face of conflict, and how to be a more effective and less manipulative elicitor of attention.

Andrews' (1984; see also Andrews & Moore, 1991) interpersonal therapy directs the therapist to create a setting in which the hysteric's repeated efforts to elicit attention from the therapist by symptomatic and other manipulative maneuvers are not reinforced. Once this has been accomplished, the therapist fosters new ways for the hysteric to live with him- or herself and with others.

Obsessive Compulsive Personality Disorder.   In two unpublished papers (Kiesler, 1973–1975, 1977), I presented a transactional theory of the obsessive compulsive personality disorder, using the conceptual frameworks of the interpersonal circle and the meaning frames.

1. The obsessive's pattern of interpersonal behavior was defined as falling at the F: Detached and G: Inhibited circle segments within the hostile-submissive quadrant.

2. In addition, the pattern of "obsessive" communication (both syntactic stylistics and nonverbal) behaviors was defined as including (a) emotional nonexpressiveness, (b) hyperrationality, (c) perfectionism, (d) indecisiveness and uncertainty, (e) censoring and premonitoring, and (f) avoidance of the present by ruminating over past and future events. A set of corresponding indices for these stylistic communications characteristics (e.g., "isolators," "evaluators," "justifiers," "abstract words," "modifiers," and "retractors") were operationalized in a psycholinguistic scoring system for the obsessive personality (Kiesler, Moulthrop, & Todd, 1972). These distinct communication behaviors and indices defined "the discriminative cues by which an 'obsessive' individual encodes his distinctive connotative-relationship (evocative) messages (a) along the nonverbal channels including paralanguage, and (b) through . . . [specific] syntactic-stylistics on the speech channel" (1973–1975, p. 4).

3. The distinctive irrational assumptions that define the obsessive's cognitions were specified in detail (e.g., "It's unreasonable and weak to show important or strong feelings to others"; "It's important to have other people respect you as intelligent, rational, and in control of yourself and situations"; "It's extremely embarrassing and probably unforgivable to make a mistake in front of others, to 'fall on one's face' in public").

4. The two unpublished papers were inconsistent and inconclusive in defining the distinctive pattern of impact messages that are experienced by persons interacting with an obsessive individual. Interpersonal complementarity theory, as operationalized on the circumplex, would identify the complements of the obsessive's F: Detached and G: Inhibited interpersonal behaviors to be D: Cold (critical) and C: Mistrusting respectively.

Finally, an interpersonal communication intervention strategy was specified as follows:

> The goal of any modification strategy for the "obsessive" pattern of communication is to modify the various communication styles away from the extremes of the respective continua. Although the most effective and efficient strategies are yet to be systematically and reliably determined, it seems that they would involve, on the "therapeutic" Decoder's [therapist's] part: (a) first, metacommunication about the individual's "obsessive" communication styles, and (b) introduction of relearning techniques emphasizing communication style in "marked contrast" (Kelly, 1955) to those of the "obsessive" individual. (Kiesler, 1973–1975, p. 5)

Barnett (1966, 1969, 1972) discussed the role of interpersonal factors within his heavily cognitive conceptualization of the obsessive compulsive personality disorder and provided an intervention model that targeted the obsessive's dysfunctional thought processes. According to Barnett (1972), the primary difficulty in obsessional living lies in a dynamically produced cognitive defect in which the patient needs to maintain innocence. The goal of therapy is to search for and obtain comprehension and clarity of experience so as to undercut the cognitive mechanisms that maintain obscurity, vagueness, confusion, and refusal to think—all of which are entrenched in the obsessive's mental life in order to maintain innocence and faultlessness.

Barnett (1969) emphasized that the obsessive's cognitive system seeks to maintain innocence of hostility to others as well as of their hostility to the obsessive. This goal is accomplished by enacting aggression more or less covertly: "It is more often aggression by omission than commission" (p. 56). Probably the most common expression of the obsessive's hostility and aggression is through enactment of an inhibited pattern of behavior: noncommitment, withholding, withdrawing, thwarting operations, and passivity. Inhibition reflects the obsessive's perception of the environment as hostile, and counters that hostility by the refusal to be exposed to it:

> Because of his difficulties in drawing inferences about interpersonal events, he is able to maintain denial of his own hostile intentions, even in the face of conscious fantasies and ruminations about gross violence, and even when his impact on others is clearly destructive. . . . When confronted by others about his hostility, he is often bewildered and unable to understand how he can be accused of hostility when he has expressed no anger. This confusion between anger and hostility reflects his cognitive style of literalizing experience and avoiding the implications of interpersonal transactions. (p. 50)

This example of aggression highlights Barnett's (1972) notion that central to the dynamics of the obsessive patient are defects in interpersonal inference making that involve avoidance of the implications of his or her transactions. The patient substitutes static and stereotyped notions about self and others for more valid inferences he or she might draw about ongoing, in-the-moment interpersonal transactions.

Barnett (1972) concluded:

> In his massive avoidance of interpersonal inference-making, the patient remains largely unaware of the impact he makes on others and his own contribution to his interpersonal difficulties. This refusal to see that the behavior of others toward him is often responsive to his impact on them consolidates and magnifies the feelings of insignificance and helplessness so central to the early life experience of the obsessional. (p. 341)

Paranoid Personality Disorder.   In Cameron's (1943, 1959) conceptualization, paranoid persons are those whose inadequate social learning leads them, when confronted with situations of unusual stress, to perform incompetent social reactions. Based on perceptions selective of only fragments of the interpersonal behaviors of others, the paranoid person symbolically constructs and organizes a *pseudocommunity* whose members perform actions the paranoid perceives as focused on him or her. The paranoid's reactions to this supposed community bring him or her into open conflict with the actual community, resulting in the paranoid's temporary or permanent isolation from its affairs. Eventually, the real community, which is unable to share in the paranoid's attitudes and reactions, takes action through forcible restraint or retaliation, but does so only after the paranoid person bursts into defiant or vengeful activity.

Lemert (1962) provided an analysis of paranoid personality disturbance that built on, yet differed in significant respects from, Cameron's earlier formulation of the paranoid "pseudocommunity." In sharp contrast to Cameron's thesis, Lemert (1962) argued that the *paranoid community is real* rather than pseudo "in that it is composed of reciprocal relationships and processes whose net results are informal and formal exclusion [of the paranoid] and attenuated communication [with him or her]" (p. 18). Not only do paranoid patterns eventually lead to exclusion, but evoke real maneuvers by others to exacerbate development of paranoid patterns of behavior. As Lemert (1962) stated, "While the paranoid person reacts differentially to his social environment, it is also true that 'others' react differentially to him, and this reaction by others commonly if not typically involves covertly organized action and conspirational behavior in a very real sense. Further, these differential reactions are reciprocals of one another, being interwoven and concatenated at each and all phases [of the process of exclusion]" (p. 3). Delusions and associated paranoid behaviors, then, must be understood as partially the result of exclusion by others of the paranoid person, which produces disrupted relationships with and constricted communications to the paranoid.

According to Lemert (1962), the paranoid person originally exhibits more normal variants of behaviors characterized by arrogance, insults, presumption of privilege, and exploitation of weakness in others. Over time, these behaviors put strain on the paranoid's social relationships, especially in groups he or she encounters frequently. Slowly, an exclusionist "coalition" forms among these group members (co-workers, neighbors, family, etc.) leading to an organized reactive strategy "distinguished by patronizing, evasion, 'humoring,' guiding conversations onto selected topics, underreaction, and silence" (p. 8). In the paranoid person's presence, the group members enact "a whole repertoire of subtle expressive signs" such as huddled conversations about the paranoid, humming "signal" tunes when he or she approaches, carefully closing doors and lowering voices, going out of their way to arrange activities that exclude the paranoid, and so on. In short, others overtly avoid the paranoid who, in turn, excludes and isolates him- or herself even further from interactions. Part of what occurs in this reciprocal process is that the paranoid correctly perceives that he or she is being isolated and excluded by concerted interaction. In Lemert's view, it is far from being the case that the paranoid lacks insight, as is frequently claimed.

As channels of communication become increasingly closed to the paranoid, "he has no means of getting feedback on the consequences of his behavior, which is essential for correcting his interpretations of the social relationship . . . which he must rely on to define his status and give him identity" (p. 14). At this point the paranoid's reactions shift to more extreme behavioral expressions. In Lemert's (1962) view, the instances of "random aggression" (that Cameron described) enacted by the paranoid against the pseudocommunity are in fact sequels rather than an integral part of the paranoid pattern: "They are likely products of deterioration and fragmentation of personality appearing, when and if they do, in the paranoid person after long and intense periods of stress and complete social isolation" (p. 19).

Lemert (1962) argued that although the paranoid person's needs and disposition, as well as self-imposed isolation, are significant factors in perpetuating his or her delusional reactions, the shallow response, evasion, and distrust displayed by members of the "exclusion coalition" create a social environment of uncertainty and ambiguity, that also perpetuates and exacerbates the paranoid's delusional reactions.

Lemert's (1962) analysis provides a clearly transactional alternative to accounts of paranoia that exclusively emphasize intrapsychic or personal causal factors. Interpersonal treatments building on his account likely would include as central interventions strategically timed but frequent use of metacommunicative feedback by the therapist as a direct attempt to provide valid information on the consequences of the paranoid's behavior and to correct instances of faulty interpretation by the paranoid of his or her transactions with others, including those with the therapist.

Tyhurst (1957) critiqued the Freudian theory of paranoia as also relying too exclusively on intrapsychic processes. He argued that studies of a wide range of paranoid reactions suggested the importance not only of dispositional factors but also of characteristic kinds of interpersonal situations that in themselves might be crucial determinants. After an extensive review of social formulations of paranoia, Tyhurst detailed several important common emphases: (a) dependency of the individual on other persons for his or her development and existence, (b) development through social interaction of a self-system, (c) a paranoid self-system characterized by a deficiency in role-taking skills, a "we-insufficiency," and so on, and (d) paranoid symptom formation determined by a reorganization of the individual's perceptual field on the basis of predominant subjective elements.

Tyhurst (1957) added that precipitation of a paranoid disorder can result from any situation or event which "has either exposed the underlying disposition or placed the individual in such a situation that his total orientation, however adequate for some social contexts, becomes inadequate for interpretation or action in a new one" (p. 65). Paranoid symptoms would develop from the way in which perceptual and motor "sets" organize the organism-environment relationship through a particular selection of certain aspects and the neglect of others. This focus inevitably leads to development of delusions whose content is characterized by the special preoccupations of the individual.

In summary:

> It seems justifiable to label an interaction as paranoid when it is characteristically suspicious, hostile, and involves misinterpretation—whether or not we also call it pathological. It may appear as the form of interaction most appropriate for the society, or it may appear inappropriately in another society. . . . In the latter case, interaction that is typically distant, anxious, uncertain, and full of distrust would develop. Perceptions would become highly subjective, and then would develop a compulsive preoccupation with the "right" and "wrong" attitudes and responses in any relationship so as to reduce uncertainty and produce a type of contrived interpersonal communion and predictability. (Tyhurst, 1957, p. 66)

LaRusso (1978) tested the hypothesis that paranoid patients possess a special sensitivity to nonverbal cues. A group of hospitalized paranoid patients and a group of normal subjects were presented videotapes of a series of genuine versus simulated enactments of an individual actually about to be electrically shocked versus posed anticipations. Results showed that the paranoid subjects demonstrated higher accuracy than normals for detecting the genuine stimuli, while normals were more accurate than patients for the simulated stimuli. LaRusso (1978) concluded that his data provided support for the superior sensitivity of paranoid patients to nonverbal cues.

Psychological Factors Affecting Medical Condition: Psychophysiological Disorders

Chronic Pain.   Mikail et al. (1994) suggested that the focus of psychosocial assessment for chronic pain syndrome be extended beyond the current emphasis on coping and emotional functioning to include determination of (a) patients' attachment styles and (b) patterns within previous and current interpersonal relationships. The authors proposed a model in which chronic pain syndrome results from a dynamic interaction between biological alteration, intrapsychic factors, and external or systemic variables that are interpersonally based. Mikail et al. conceptualized that "components of the three levels of influence are intertwined in a pattern of cyclical causality, with biological alteration serving as the precipitating event in the development of chronic pain syndrome, while intrapsychic variables and the concomitant environmental context serve as vulnerability factors. Specificity of syndrome or condition is determined by the unique combination of a given biological change occurring within the context of a particular intrapsychic structure and the associated social context" (p. 7).

Mikail et al. (1994) felt that attachment theory provided a framework for conceptualizing the influence of intrapsychic and contextual variables. They argued further that a comprehensive model of pain needs to accommodate the diversity of responses to chronic pain—needs to identify potential patient subgroups that might emerge. They defined four attachment styles (secure, dismissing, fearful, and preoccupied) that they suggested should be differentially represented within the chronic pain population. Mikail et al. advocated examination of the relationship between the various styles and typical interpersonal functioning, hypothesizing the following patterns: that individuals with preoccupied attachment would be hostile toward self while friendly and dependent toward others; those with dismissing attachment would be hostile and independent as well as ignoring and neglectful; and those with fearful attachment would be hostile and withdrawn. The authors concluded that an adequate model should allow for a coherent integration of biological, intrapersonal, and interpersonal influences in explicating the etiology and course of chronic pain.

Heart Disease.   Various theories have attempted to specify mechanisms underlying the association between individual differences in hostility and incidence of heart disease (Smith, 1992). These include what have been called the constitutional vulnerability model, the health behavioral model, the psychophysiological reactivity model, the psychosocial vulnerability model, and the transactional model.

In the transactional model (Smith, 1992; Smith & Pope, 1990), hostile individuals are not seen as simply responding to stressors with increased cardiovascular and neuroendocrine reactivity, as the psychophysiological reactivity model asserts. Rather, they create through their own thoughts and actions more frequent, severe, and enduring contact with stressors. In Smith and colleagues' model:

1. Hostile people are likely to elicit and exacerbate interpersonal conflict by (a) anticipating mistreatment from others, (b) interpreting others' actions with hostile intent, (c) behaving antagonistically, and (d) mistrusting pervasively.
2. Within this context, social support is likely to be undermined by the person's own cognitive and behavioral style; once created, this negative social environment serves to reinforce these very cognitions and behaviors.
3. Finally, the proposed pathway that links hostility to illness lies in the repeated physiological insults caused by increased reactivity, not only to unavoidable stressors, but especially those that the person creates through his or her interactional style.

Mancini (1995) observed that, although in many studies hostility has been associated with an increased cardiovascular reactivity that can lead to cardiovascular-related disease, little research has been conducted on hostility-mediated racial differences in cardiovascular reactivity. He suggested that the problems African Americans face in coping with minority status and prejudice may make them strong candidates for increased stressor-related cardiovascular reactivity.

Mancini's (1995) in-process study evaluates the associations between hostility and cardiovascular reactivity, as well as the impact of discriminatory stimuli, on a sample of black females within the framework of Smith's (1992) transactional model. High versus low hostility subjects were assigned to either neutral or ethnically biased instructions (the latter noted an expected poor performance for blacks relative to whites). During an experimental task, cardiovascular reactivity was assessed using a set of psychophysiological measures, and at the end of the procedure, both subjects and experimenters filled out IMIs to assess their impacts on each other.

Mancini (1995) hypothesized that, in contrast to either low hostile subjects or subjects who received neutral instructions, the high hostile African American females who received the biased-prejudicial instructions would (a) demonstrate greater psychophysiological reactivity and (b) both rate, and be rated by, the experimenter as significantly more hostile. Data analyses and results are still in process.

Yarnold et al. (1987) examined the interpersonal implications of the assumption that social support serves as a buffer against coronary artery and heart disease (CAHD). They argued that if the assumption is valid, certain predictions from interpersonal complementarity theory should hold. "Type A's who are friendly should evoke friendliness, resulting in development of social support and lower risk for CAHD. Hostility, in contrast, could lead to poor interpersonal relations and increased risk" (p. 194). Further, if these predictions obtain, psychotherapeutic intervention might be targeted to reducing interpersonal hostility and increasing interpersonal friendliness.

Yarnold et al. (1987) found that Type A's scored higher than B's on the following IAS octants: AP (ambitious-dominant), BC (arrogant-calculating), and NO (gregarious-extraverted); Type B's scored higher on HI (lazy-submissive) and FG (aloof-introverted). The authors noted that their findings replicated their earlier studies (Yarnold & Grimm, 1986; Yarnold, Mueser, & Grimm, 1985) in which Types A's were found to exhibit greater interpersonal dominance and assertiveness than Type B's. Findings revealed also that, although Type A's were distributed significantly more frequently in the friendly-dominant quadrant than they were in any other quadrant, "males were infrequently observed in high-nurturance quadrants and frequently observed in the low-nurturance quadrants, whereas the opposite was true for females" (p. 194).

Yarnold et al. (1987) concluded that, rather than Type A serving as an independent risk factor for CAHD, it is a *subtype* of the Type A behavior pattern (high dominance + high hostility and low nurturance + male gender) that seems to constitute the actual high-risk profile.

As a postscript to this section, it needs to be noted that Wortman and Dunkel-Schetter (1979) offered an extensive theoretical analysis of the role of interpersonal relationships in the maintenance of cancer.

Weight Loss.   In their presentation of a behavioral control intervention model for obese patients, R. B. Stuart and Davis (1978) documented how the marital interaction serves maintenance functions for the overweight condition of the obese partner.

Specifically, both husbands and wives exhibit a number of behaviors that appear detrimental to the wife's weight-loss attempts.

Dental Treatment and Orthognathic Surgery.   Three studies by Auerbach and colleagues provide supportive evidence for the notion that interpersonal issues may be central to effective delivery of dental and orthognathic treatment. Auerbach et al. (1983) gave patients scheduled for dental extraction surgery either specific or general information about the impending surgery that was delivered in either a personalized or relatively impersonal-businesslike fashion. Each patient filled out an IMI on the information giver following the presurgical contact; also subsequently, while in the recovery room, each patient filled out an IMI on the dental surgeon who had performed the extraction. Results showed that when the information giver delivered information in an impersonal fashion, he or she impacted patients as being more hostile-dominant and less friendly. Unexpectedly, it was found also that the degree to which patients registered impacts from the information giver generalized to the impacts they experienced from the dental surgeon.

Auerbach et al. (1984) studied the interpersonal behavior of a group of surgeons with their patients over the course of orthognathic surgery (applied to correct dentofacial function and appearance) by having both patients and surgeons fill out IMIs on each other at various stages of the procedure. Analyses revealed that the strongest impact surgeons had on patients, at each of four stages of the surgery process, was friendly. At pretherapy, the patients as a group impacted their surgeons as predominantly friendly and submissive. Finally, it was found that the more a patient impacted the surgeon as being dominant, the higher the presurgery psychopathology of that patient, and the poorer that patient adjusted postsurgery as recorded by hospital ward ratings.

Penberthy (1982) studied the effects on patient adjustment and satisfaction of providing dental patients with different degrees of control over a denture-fitting procedure by student dentists at a training hospital. Degree of control was manipulated through a series of audiotapes that provided distinctly different levels of preparatory information, procedural choices, and expectancy sets of personal responsibility for decision making. At the end of treatment patients and dentists filled out IMIs on each other. Results showed that dentists who treated the minimum-control group impacted their patients as being more dominant than did dentists for the maximum-control and no treatment conditions. Also, regardless of group, external locus of control patients registered more dominant, hostile, and submissive impacts from their dentists than did internal patients. Finally, patient satisfaction measures obtained 7 to 10 days after treatment correlated significantly with the manner in which patients impacted their dentists. Patients who impacted their dentists as being more agreeable as well as less dominant and hostile reported greater satisfaction with treatment than did other patients.

CONCLUSION

It's important to note that none of these interpersonal formulations has been articulated with the level of specificity demonstrated for Dysthymic Disorder in Figure 6–2. Obviously much work remains for interpersonal therapists.

Diagnosis, Psychotherapy, and Supervision

Interpersonal Assessment and Diagnosis

Given that the process of diagnosis is largely a social one, that interpersonal effectiveness has been viewed as crucially important by [widely divergent] theorists . . . , that social behavior may be taken as a kind of common denominator of higher phylogenetic functioning, and that psychologists have accumulated an impressive body of literature on psychosocial functioning, it seems appropriate and timely for behavioral scientists to construct a comprehensive interpersonal taxonomy.

(McLemore & Benjamin, 1979, p. 32)

Various authors have argued that contemporary interpersonal theories of personality and psychopathology can provide taxonomies to guide assessment of the DSM mental disorders (Adams, 1964; Kiesler, 1986a, 1986b; Leary, 1957; Leary & Coffey, 1955; McLemore & Benjamin, 1979; McLemore & Brokaw, 1987; Plutchik & Conte, 1986; Schaefer & Plutchik, 1966; Widiger, 1991, 1993; Widiger & Frances, 1985, 1988, 1994; Widiger, Frances, Spitzer, & Williams, 1988; Widiger & Kelso, 1983; Wiggins, 1982). Schaefer and Plutchik (1966), for example, provided evidence that trait terms, emotion terms, and ratings of diagnostic labels share a common interpersonal factor space. McLemore and Benjamin (1979) argued that interpersonal behavior may be the most useful basis for a classification system for abnormal behavior and eventually can function as an alternative to the present *Diagnostic and Statistical Manual of Mental Disorders (DSM-IV)* (APA, 1994). These various interpersonal authors have proposed adoption of one or another version of the interpersonal circle to serve as a taxonomy of individual differences for the domain of normal to maladjusted adult interpersonal behavior.

Other authors have provided more in-depth analyses of principles and procedures of interpersonal diagnosis (Andrews, 1988, 1989a, 1989b, 1989d, 1991; Benjamin, 1984, 1986b, 1987b, 1993; Boghosian, 1982; D. M. Buss & Craik, 1986b, 1987; L. M. Horowitz, French, Lapid, & Weckler, 1982; L. M. Horowitz, Post, French, Wallis, & Siegelman, 1981; Horowitz & Vitkus, 1986; L. M. Horowitz, Weckler, & Doren, 1983; Kiesler, 1986a, 1986b; Leary, 1957; Safran, 1984a, 1990b; Safran et al., 1986; Widiger & Trull, 1987; Wiggins, 1982). Kiesler (1986b), for example, documented in detail how the interpersonal circle provides a theoretically derived and operationally anchored taxonomy that can provide both reliable diagnosis and differential therapy for the personality disorders.

A few authors have made a priori attempts to translate *DSM* characterizations of the personality disorders into prototypic patterns of maladaptive interpersonal behavior at distinctive segments or octants of the interpersonal circle (e.g., Kiesler, 1986b; Leary, 1957; McLemore & Brokaw, 1987; Wiggins, 1982). Studies that have empirically examined distinctive profiles of interpersonal behavior on samples of Axis I and Axis II disorders will be reviewed later in this chapter.

THE INTERPERSONAL CIRCLE: A CONCEPTUAL MAP FOR PSYCHIATRIC DIAGNOSIS

It should be clear by now that the interpersonal circle is a key conceptual map that guides interpersonal diagnosis (Kiesler, 1986b, 1991) and interpersonal psychotherapy (Kiesler, 1983, 1986a, 1988, 1992). As we saw in Chapter 1, a repertoire of interpersonal measures is available to obtain empirical scores that profile a given patient's interpersonal behavior at specific segments and levels of the circle. Wiggins (1982) and Kiesler (1983, 1991) provided earlier summaries and critiques of these measures.

By use of these measures, a therapist can assess the interpersonal behavior of a particular patient in one or all of several distinct ways. First, the therapist can administer to the patient directly the self-report versions of these circle inventories. Second, significant others in the patient's life can be asked (with the patient's permission) to rate the patient's interpersonal behavior at various points over the course of the patient's life and over the course of therapy. Alternatively, groups of observers can be shown videotaped samples of therapy sessions and asked to rate the patient's behavior from these transcriptions. Third, significant others, observers of videotaped sessions, and the therapist—through use of the unique self-report transactional measure, the IMI—can also be asked to report the internal, covert emotional and other experiences they identify in themselves when interacting with the patient. Further, application of any or all of these measures at sequential points of the treatment process permits direct measures of outcome or improvement in the patient's interpersonal problem behaviors.

It's evident, then, that these inventories have the advantage of allowing researchers to obtain interpersonal characterizations (using identical items) from multiple perspectives (e.g., patients, therapists, independent judges, significant others). Also, the administration time of these inventories is relatively brief, taking most individuals 10 to 15 minutes to complete. In addition, the inventories can be applied in observer ratings of therapist or patient behaviors from relatively brief samples (e.g., 5- to 10-minute segments) of therapy sessions or from the entire session. Finally, although to date the emphasis in applying these inventories has been to test one or more propositions of contemporary interpersonal theories of personality and psychotherapy, the inventories can also be used to assess underlying assumptions, as well as gauge the process and outcome, of other models of psychotherapy (see Chapter 9).

Although these measures are at various stages of psychometric development, work in progress is likely to provide increasingly reliable and valid versions. Administration of any one of these instruments permits assessment of the patient's pattern of interpersonal actions. This assessment, in turn, produces an exact profile of that patient's interpersonal behavior on the interpersonal circle—which permits precise prediction of conjunctive and disjunctive reactions of others (including the therapist) to the patient and of a range of effective interventions for facilitating change in the patient's maladaptive pattern of behavior.

These adult two-dimensional circle inventories are devised to measure the complete domain of interpersonal behavior as categorized on the various interpersonal circles. Although they have been designed to measure all 16 circle segments, in practice only 8-scale, octant versions (conceptually equivalent to collapsing adjacent 16ths) have attained the trigonometric ideal of circumplex structure that is needed, not only for interpersonal diagnosis, but also for precise tests of many propositions of contemporary interpersonal theory. Available two-dimensional circle octant inventories that satisfactorily meet these criteria include the IAS-R (Wiggins et al., 1988b), the IIP-C (Alden, Wiggins, & Pincus, 1990), and the IMI-IIA octant version (Kiesler & Schmidt, 1993). The remaining measures described in Chapter 1—ICL, IBI, and CLOIT-R (although for the CLOIT-R see Tracey & Schneider, 1995)—show certain circumplicial inadequacies that necessitate both careful analysis of octant scores and cautious interpretation of specific results.

SOME CIRCUMPLEX METHODOLOGICAL CONSIDERATIONS

"Interpersonal diagnosis involves the assignment of subjects to typological categories defined by the average directional tendencies of their interpersonal behaviors with reference to the coordinates of dominance and love" (Wiggins et al., 1989, p. 303).

In the interpersonal system of personality diagnosis, an individual may be classified as falling within one of the 8 (or 16) sectors of the interpersonal circle with reference to his or her average profile of scores on the constituent variables of the system. An individual's location within a sector of the circle (angular location) may be further characterized in terms of the distance of his or her location from the center of the circle (vector length).

Angle and vector length serve different purposes in diagnostic classification. *Angular location* is used to assign category membership. *Vector length* corresponding to a given individual's octant scores is basically an index of the standard deviation of those scores (Wiggins et al., 1989)—an index of the standard deviation of a circumplex profile.

As Wiggins and Pincus (1992) noted, vector length has been considered a measure of deviance in a psychiatric as well as statistical sense (e.g., Leary, 1957). However, vector length is not, in itself, considered to be a general measure of psychopathology; accordingly, "One would not expect vector length to be related to measures of interpersonal problems in a random sample of unclassified subjects" (Wiggins et al., 1989, p. 298). Rather, vector length *within* a particular sector of the circle is taken to be an index of the intensity or extremity with which that particular pattern of interpersonal dispositions is expressed. "For example, one might anticipate a relationship between vector length and general psychological discomfort (neuroticism) within a group of subjects who have all been classified as aloof-introverted types" (Wiggins et al., 1989, p. 298).

In testing this circumplex assumption of interpersonal theory, Wiggins et al. (1989) examined the correlations between vector length and measures of psychological dysfunction in a sample of undergraduates and in eight subgroups of the same sample, formed by classification of IAS-R profiles. They found that within the total sample, as predicted, vector length was unrelated to general measures of psychopathology and to more specific measures of interpersonal problems (IIP-C). However, meaningful patterns of correlations were found between vector length and scales from the aforementioned inventories *within* groups of subjects classified as falling in particular sectors of the interpersonal circle. They concluded that the sound geometric and psychometric properties of the IAS-R (one might also add, of the IIP-C and the IMI octant version) suggest that it may be applied fruitfully to the diagnosis of the personality disorders.

Overall, then, Wiggins et al. (1989) demonstrated that assignment of subjects to diagnostic categories indeed results in homogeneous groupings of subjects with respect to characteristic patterns of interpersonal behavior; further, vector length may be used as an index of the extremity of these characteristic patterns.

PSYCHIATRIC SYMPTOMS AND INTERPERSONAL PROBLEMS

L. M. Horowitz and Vitkus (1986) observed that, during first interviews, most patients report both psychiatric symptoms and interpersonal problems. Therapists, when concentrating on classification of disorders and evaluation of the severity of disorder, tend to think in terms of symptoms; but when doing the actual work of treatment, therapists typically focus on interpersonal events, conflicts, and goals. L. M. Horowitz and Vitkus (1986) advocated that researchers need to understand the relationship between symptoms and interpersonal problems.

They defined *a symptom* as a "complex subjective experience that consists of a network of interrelated cognitive, affective, and interpersonal elements" (p. 444). Horowitz and Vitkus (1986) advocated an investigatory procedure that involves identification of the most common elements in different people's experiences and use of those elements to construct an idealized form of the symptom—a theoretical ideal or prototype. Different people's experiences of the symptom would vary in the degree to which they approximate the ideal or prototype.

Importantly, a symptom prototype (e.g., depression, or loneliness) can reveal relevant constituent interpersonal problems. L. M. Horowitz and Vitkus (1986) emphasized that the interpersonal problems implied by a symptom predispose a person to particular types of interpersonal interactions that *sustain the symptom*. As an example, they cited depressed people who find it difficult to be assertive; they unwittingly invite others to assume an assertive role while they themselves accept the complementary unassertive role.

INTERPERSONAL CIRCLE DIAGNOSIS OF *DSM* PERSONALITY DISORDERS

At present, interpersonal diagnosis seems most clearly relevant to the *DSM* personality disorders. Future theory and research will determine the extent to which the circle might be useful for diagnosis of *DSM* Axis I symptom disorders (Widiger & Hyler, 1987). In this regard, seminal interpersonal formulations of Axis I and Axis II disorders have appeared, which were reviewed in Chapter 6.

Within interpersonal theory, individual differences in disordered communication represent the range of constricted and extreme styles on the interpersonal circle around

the axes of control and affiliation. The disordered person tenaciously holds to a restricted "slice" of the circle for self-definition and for expressing claims on others
through his or her evoking messages.

As mentioned earlier, a few authors have made a priori attempts to translate *DSM*
characterizations of the personality disorders into prototypic patterns of maladaptive interpersonal behavior at distinctive segments or octants of the interpersonal circle (e.g.,
Kiesler, 1986b; Leary, 1957; McLemore & Brokaw, 1987; Widiger & Kelso, 1983; Wiggins, 1982). Leary (1957) interfaced his circle with the *DSM-II* (APA, 1952), while
Kiesler (1986b), McLemore and Brokaw (1987) and Wiggins (1982) interfaced with
DSM-III (APA, 1980). Benjamin's (1993) volume documents in detail SASB diagnosis
(using her three diamonds model) of the 11 DSM personality disorders. Earlier and
more recent empirical studies have examined interpersonal relationships with a wide
range of the *DSM* versions, from *DSM-II* through *DSM-IV.*

The language that DSM *uses to define and discuss the personality disorders is saturated with interpersonal terms.* A personality disorder is "an enduring pattern of inner
experience and behavior that deviates markedly from the expectations of the individual's culture, is pervasive and inflexible, has an onset in adolescence or early adulthood,
is stable over time, and leads to stress or impairment" (APA, 1994, p. 629). Personality
disorders occur "when personality traits are inflexible and maladaptive and cause significant functional impairment or subjective distress" (p. 630). These maladaptive traits
represent "enduring patterns of perceiving, relating to, and thinking about the environment and oneself that are exhibited in a wide range of social and personal contexts"
(p. 630). The disorders begin in childhood or adolescence and are characteristic of most
of adult life. In contrast to the major symptom disorders on Axis I, psychiatric signs and
symptoms need not be clinically prominent at all. Finally, personality disorder features
may not be considered problematic by the individual and are often ego-syntonic; accordingly, any negative consequences need to be assessed carefully with supplemental information obtained from other informants.

Several cautions have been suggested (Kiesler, 1986b) in regard to attempts to build
conceptual and empirical bridges between the interpersonal circle and *DSM* personality
disorders. First, is it more useful to accept on an a priori basis the clinical validity and
"real" existence of the *DSM* personality disorders and then to focus our efforts on
translating *DSM* disorders onto corresponding segments or octants of the circle? Or
might it be much more useful in the long run, in light of the internally consistent theoretical structure of the circle, to first derive personality disorder possibilities from
the circle and then to search for clinical verification of these theoretical types? In
the latter case, launching our efforts from the solid structure of interpersonal theory
would avoid the atheoretical and descriptive "mixed bag" deficiencies of *DSM* (e.g.,
McLemore & Benjamin, 1979). In the former, starting from the base of observed, albeit
unsystematically, "live" clinical cases seems to ensure a continual anchoring of empirical efforts in existent patient problems in living. Likely, solid advantages exist for both
directions of attack.

Second, as a manifestation of their characteristic interpersonal pattern, some theoretically derivable circle disorders by definition avoid seeking help from others and, as
a result, would show up infrequently in clinical treatment settings. For example, persons
whose behaviors fall in the strongly dominant octants of the circle may be infrequent
clinical patrons since "the very essence of these maladjustments is a compulsive maintenance of autonomy, independence and domination—social techniques which preclude

the role of psychiatric patient" (Leary & Coffey, 1955, p. 119). In similar fashion, more extreme deferent and trusting styles in the bottom-right quadrant of the circle may also be underrepresented clinically, since their rigid patterns may fit more easily and subtly into traditionally acceptable societal roles. Generally, these and similar possibilities imply strongly that any analysis of the personality disorders that springs exclusively from existing clinical populations might necessarily overlook some individuals who possess extreme and rigid interpersonal patterns, but who confine the scope of their abnormality within everyday life situations in such a way that they seldom come to the attention of mental health practitioners.

Third, since Leary (1957) first observed the pattern, it still seems the case that *DSM* disorders are classified predominantly in the hostile (left) half of the interpersonal circle; further, they are underrepresented in the bottom-right (friendly-submissive) and extreme top-left (dominant-competitive) circle categories. These patterns of interpersonal behavior undoubtedly reflect interactive effects of societal preferences and values. These societal contributions, however, need to be both explicitly conceptualized and empirically demonstrated, before interpersonal diagnosis can provide a comprehensive paradigm for mental disorder.

SOME PRINCIPLES OF INTERPERSONAL CIRCLE DIAGNOSIS

Earlier (Kiesler, 1986b), I articulated six principles that seem necessary as guides for translating *DSM* personality disorders onto the interpersonal circle and, more generally, for an eventual interpersonal taxonomy of psychiatric disorders.

> *Proposition 7–1.* Interpersonal diagnosis using circle inventories typically focuses on assessment of overt social-interpersonal behaviors of abnormal persons. These observable actions include both verbal and nonverbal behaviors.

By far, the majority of empirical interpersonal studies of psychiatric patients ask patients to self-report their typical interpersonal behaviors; only a few have therapists, significant others, or observers rate the patients' interpersonal behavior. In either case, however, the target is the patient's overt, observable actions.

It is this restricted focus on overt behavior that provides a clear advantage of circle diagnosis over previous *DSM* descriptions of the personality disorders that combine descriptors of overt behaviors with symptomatic, anamnestic, physiological, affective, and cognitive events. The exclusive focus of circle diagnosis on observable behavior in and of itself promises superior interobserver reliability for circle assessments.

Kiesler (1983) emphasized, "Basic aspects of nonverbal communication need also to be integrated both with the interpersonal circle and with interpersonal theory more generally" (p. 211). Kiesler (1973–1975, 1977, 1979, 1982b, 1988; Kiesler, Bernstein, & Anchin, 1976) provided a theoretical integration of nonverbal behavior with interpersonal theory. Nowicki and colleagues have pursued a program of research examining the nonverbal and verbal correlates of interpersonal behavior (E. L. Cooley & Nowicki, 1989; McGovern, 1985; McLeod & Nowicki, 1985; Nowicki & Manheim, 1991; Oxenford & Nowicki, 1989), as have Perlmutter, Paddock, and Duke (1985) and Schmidt (1989). Nonverbal messages predominate in emotional and relationship communication;

predominate in the arena of interpersonal behavior. The factor structure underlying both domains is identical. Sets of specific nonverbal behaviors have been identified for control and affiliation relationship messages; these sets need to be interfaced with the traditional acts that define the interpersonal circle categories; they should become an essential part of assessment of interpersonal behavior.

On the other hand, what the Maladaptive Transaction Cycle makes abundantly evident is that comprehensive assessment of mental disorders will require, in addition to present interpersonal circle inventories targeting overt behavior, additional inventories or measures that target patients' *covert* behaviors and experiences (Kiesler, 1983, 1986a, 1986b; Widiger, Frances, & Trull, 1987). Ideally, models of covert events will be developed that permit predictions of one-to-one correspondence with the categories of overt behavior depicted on the interpersonal circle.

To date, this circular bridging work has occurred primarily in the area of emotion. Plutchik (1980) showed that circumplex models of personality traits can be mapped onto structural models of the emotion domain. Schaefer and Plutchik's (1966) factor analytic findings supported their hypothesis that circular configurations would be found for trait and emotion signs and for diagnostic constructs. They concluded that most of the variance of traits and emotions associated with psychiatric diagnostic categories falls within a two-dimensional space, so that trait and emotion terms can be plotted within the same semantic configuration. Russell (1980; Russell, Lewicka, & Niit, 1989) provided evidence of a clear circumplex structure in the domain of personal affect. Kiesler, Horner, Larus, and Chapman (1988) showed that (a) interpersonal acts located at the poles of the two 1982 Circle axes evoke distinctive patterns of emotion as measured by Russell's (1980) personal affect scales, and (b) Russell's list of affect adjectives exhibits a circumplex structure, equivalent to that found for personal affect, when used to measure the "evoked emotion" characteristic of interpersonal encounters.

Empirical studies of the traditional cognitive realm are necessary to determine whether similar circular models can be found for construal, perceptual, expectational and other cognitive events that provide covariate matches to the categories of overt behavior anchored on the circumference of the interpersonal circle. The available research was reviewed in detail in Chapter 3.

Finally, we need to remember that, although circle diagnosis typically has been restricted to overt interpersonal behaviors, it need not be. For example, one distinctive advantage of the IMI circle inventory, as we have seen, is that its items target the *covert* experiences (emotions, thoughts, action tendencies) of interactants. It, thus, can be used as part of a total interpersonal assessment battery to assess the two covert blocks of the Maladaptive Transaction Cycle (see Figures 6–1 and 6–2).

The Big Five Factors of Personality

Chapter 1 introduced the Big Five dimensions (e.g., Norman, 1963; Tupes & Christal, 1961) that emerge universally as higher order factors within the personality domain. Recent studies also demonstrate that the two circumplex dimensions are embedded within this Big Five structure (Hofstee, de Raad, & Goldberg, 1992; Saucier, 1992; Trapnell & Wiggins, 1990; Wiggins, in press; Wiggins & Trapnell, in press).

The Big Five factors are Dominance (extraversion), Agreeableness (nurturance), Neuroticism, Conscientiousness, and Openness to Experience. McCrae and Costa (1986) emphasized that the significance for clinicians and counselors is that "the five-factor model is a universal and comprehensive framework for the description of individual differences in personality" (p. 1001). Accordingly, in addition to other routine psychological assessments, clinicians should obtain additional information in regard to the individual's standing on each of the five factors: "The normative portrait formed can then be used as a basis for further idiographic elaboration and interpretation, based on whatever instruments the clinician feels are most appropriate" (McCrae & Costa, 1986, p. 1002).

Wiggins and Pincus (1992; Pincus & Wiggins, 1990, 1992) discussed implications of the recent recognition that the circumplex and five-factor representations are complementary rather than competing (e.g., Hofstee et al., 1992; McCrae & Costa, 1989; Trapnell & Wiggins, 1990). Two possibilities have been suggested:

1. The first two factors can be considered simple structure variants of the interpersonal personality dimensions (e.g., McCrae & Costa, 1989). From this perspective, the NEO-PI model provides a simple-structure representation of the factors of Extraversion and Agreeableness that differs by approximately 30 degrees from the orientation of the circumplex (e.g., IAS-R) dimensions of dominance and nurturance.

2. The interpersonal circle can be used to represent in circumplex structure the first two dimensions of the five-factor model (Pincus & Wiggins, 1990, 1992; Trapnell & Wiggins, 1990; Wiggins, 1988; Wiggins & Pincus, 1992; Wiggins & Trapnell, in press), as described in the "dyadic-interactional perspective" (Wiggins & Pincus, 1992; Wiggins & Trapnell, in press).

Pincus and Wiggins (1992) emphasized that interpersonal assessment can be interpreted more meaningfully within the five-factor model context:

> Two individuals whose circumplex profiles are similar will probably present with distinctive patterns of behavioral rigidity depending on their relative standings on emotional lability and distress (Neuroticism), impulse control, motivation, and responsibility (Conscientiousness), and conformity, tolerance, and imagination (Openness). (p. 94)

Trapnell and Wiggins (1990) extended the revised Interpersonal Adjective Scales (IAS-R; Wiggins et al., 1988b) to include the remaining three Big Five factors (IAS-R-B5). The result is a measure of a trait structure comprising one circumplex and three bipolar factor scales. The IAS-R-B5, therefore, constitutes an integration of the simple structure Big Five factors and the two dimensions of the interpersonal circle (Wiggins & Pincus, 1992; Wiggins & Trapnell, in press).

A series of studies have examined the relationship between measures of the Big Five factors of personality and various measures of psychopathology (Widiger & Trull, 1987) or *DSM* personality disorders (Costa & McCrae, 1990; M. J. Lyons, Merla, Ozer, & Hyler, 1990; Trull, 1992; Wiggins, 1987; Wiggins & Pincus, 1989, 1994). T. R. Miller (1991) provides a stimulating account of the manner in which the five-factor model, assessed with the NEO-PI, can facilitate the practice of psychotherapy. Others have examined applications of the five-factor model to clinical assessment (e.g., Costa & McCrae, 1992; McCrae, 1994a; McCrae & Costa, 1986), to personality and health psychology

(Booth-Kewley & Vickers, 1994; Marshall, Wortman, Vickers, & Kusulas, 1994; Muten, 1991), and to close relationships (D. M. Buss, 1992).

Trull (1992) and Shopshire and Craik (1994) replicated on clinical and other populations the earlier findings of Wiggins and Pincus (1989) and Costa and McCrae (1990) that showed substantive correspondence between the personality disorders and the five-factor model of personality. Trull summarized the trend as follows:

1. *Neuroticism* appears to be characteristic of most of the personality disorders, particularly borderline, dependent, and obsessive-compulsive.
2. Low levels of *Extraversion* are characteristic of schizoid and avoidant and, to a lesser degree, of schizotypal and obsessive-compulsive; high is characteristic of histrionic.
3. *Agreeableness* is negatively correlated with paranoid, schizotypal, antisocial, borderline, and passive-aggressive.
4. *Openness* is negatively correlated with schizoid personality disorder.
5. Low levels of *Conscientiousness* characterize antisocial personality and, to a lesser degree, dependent and passive-aggressive.

It seems, then, that the dimensions of Neuroticism, Extraversion, and Agreeableness and, to a lesser extent, Conscientiousness are most relevant to assessment of the *DSM* personality disorders.

Both *DSM* and interpersonal assessment can profit from interpretation utilizing the five-factor model context (e.g., Costa & McCrae, 1990; McCrae, 1994a, 1994b; Schmidt, Wagner, & Kiesler, 1993; Trull, 1992; Widiger, 1991, 1993; Wiggins & Pincus, 1989). It is likely, further, that routine five-factor model inventories de facto assess both overt (1: surgency, 2: agreeableness—the interpersonal *duo*) and covert (3: emotionality, 4: conscientiousness, 5: openness-creativity) aspects of a person's interpersonal behavior (Schmidt et al., 1993).

McCrae (1994a, 1994b) offered an alternative to the *DSM* system for the diagnosis of personality-related disorders based on the five-factor model. His conceptualization of personality disorders, both embedded in and extending the five-factor model, is based on the central assumption that when patients are said to have a personality disorder, "They in fact have not a pathologic personality, but a personality-related pathology" (McCrae, 1994a, p. 31).

According to McCrae (1994a), a *personality-related disorder* is "a set of life problems that (a) are characteristically related to the individual's personality traits, (b) cause the individual significant distress, and (c) are maintained by misperceptions of reality" (p. 34). In McCrae's model, an individual's traits can be characterized by the Big Five factors, whereas distress is distinctly measured by high scores on the Neuroticism factor. McCrae emphasized that all people have problems; problems become disorders only when they exceed the individual's ability to deal with them and become chronic (e.g., an abusive husband who cannot control his temper despite the likelihood of legal consequences). Finally, McCrae emphasized that the set of chronic life problems that constitute personality-related disorders are maintained by some form of cognitive distortion (disturbance in thinking, misperception of reality): "Borderlines have identity disturbances, histrionics have impressionistic thinking, narcissists have an inflated sense of self-importance, paranoids have groundless suspicions, schizoids are vague and absent-minded" (1994a, p. 33). According to McCrae's formulation, (a) all individuals have characteristic standings on the five factors; (b) those who also are high in Neuroticism and have impaired contact with reality are at risk for developing a personality-related disorder.

In the long run, it's clear that circle diagnosis will remain incomplete until it incorporates independent systematic assessments of the person's covert behaviors—including distinctive affective, perceptual, cognitive, fantasy, and other important internal experiences—which likely, in turn, correlate in lawful ways with the various overt styles that can be charted on circle profiles.

Proposition 7–2.   To provide reliable and valid characterizations, circle diagnosis must assess an abnormal person's behaviors by identifying (a) the exact circle segments or octants that define the person's transactions with others, and (b) the exact level (mild vs. moderate vs. extreme) on each segment that defines the extremeness and/or rigidity of the abnormal pattern.

For example, it is insufficient merely to locate behaviors of the dependent personality on 1982 segments IJ: Submissive-Deferent without specifying further whether the pattern falls at I_1: Docile or the more extreme I_2: Subservient, and whether at J_1: Respectful-Content or at the more extreme J_2: Ambitionless-Flattering.

Although it is theoretically possible that an abnormal person's interpersonal behaviors could be rigid (restricted to one or a few segments only) and also at mild levels, this does not seem a likely or frequent condition. What seems more probable is that any rigid pattern would be expressed by behaviors characterized at least at the moderate level and often at the extreme level. Further, it is entirely possible that an abnormal person's behaviors can be extreme on one segment and moderate to mild on adjacent segments. Hence, valid characterization of a particular personality disorder necessitates a profile statement that subsumes not only a given number of circle segments, but also the exact level of each constituent segment.

Proposition 7–3.   Interpersonal circle diagnosis combines both dimensional and typological assessment of interpersonal behaviors toward the goal of Roschian polythetic descriptions of each personality disorder.

What this means, as Wiggins (1982) documented, is that circle diagnosis will never be able to classify the personality disorders at mutually exclusive circle segments or octants. From a Roschian perspective (Rosch, 1975, 1978; Rosch & Mervis, 1975), the taxonomic descriptions of the circle segments—just as of personality traits (Cantor & Mischel, 1977, 1979) or *DSM* diagnostic categories (Cantor, Smith, French, & Mezzich, 1980)—do not identify sets of critical or categorically necessary defining elements, all of which must be present for a person's behavior to be classified at a particular segment. Instead, it is likely that circle segments operate as Roschian categories wherein the interpersonal behaviors defining a particular segment cluster around a prototype or exemplar, with less prototypic elements merging into the fuzzy boundaries of related adjacent segments.

Circle diagnosis provides a geometric representation of relationships between "fuzzy sets" in which membership is probabilistic and continuous (polythetic) rather than determinate and discrete. As a result, it is more valid to conceptualize interpersonal di-agnostic categories as "wedge-shaped segments of a circle, in which elements of a cate-gory (segment) are organized with reference to a prototype that falls near the center of the perimeter of a given wedge" (Wiggins, 1982, p. 204). There is no reason, then, to ex-pect a one-to-one correspondence between *DSM* categories and circle segments or oc-tants. Horowitz and his colleagues (L. M. Horowitz & French, 1979; L. M. Horowitz, French, & Anderson, 1982; L. M. Horowitz, French, Lapid, & Weckler, 1982; L. M. Horowitz, Post, et al., 1981; L. M. Horowitz, Wright, Lowenstein, & Parad, 1981) have provided detailed applications of prototype analysis in their long-range program of interpersonal research.

An important implication is that circle diagnosis offers the advantages of the com-bined dimensional and categorical approach that Millon (1981) and Widiger and Frances (1994), among others, advocate. The major diagnostic utility of the circle resides in des-ignating prototypical profiles of circle segments that define the various personality disorders, keeping in mind that no particular patient will ever match exactly the defini-tional exemplar. Having established each prototype, any individual patient's manifesta-tion of a particular personality disorder can be summarized as the empirical degree of fit between his or her behavior pattern and a particular prototypical circle profile.

Proposition 7–4. It seems highly probable that the various personality and/or symptom disorders will not be validly defined by prototypical circle profiles that contain isomorphic segmental structure.

The prototypical circle profile for a particular disorder may subsume elements from a single circle octant, whereas that for another may subsume a wider band of segments. Similarly, one disorder's profile might include the extreme level of one segment with moderate-level behaviors from an adjacent segment, whereas another disorder might peak at the extreme level of each of two adjacent segments. Further, for those more ex-treme personality disorders that show more complexity in their interpersonal patterns, valid diagnosis may require characterizations of behavior from octants highly dissimi-lar to one another, indeed falling in different circle quadrants. These possibilities are consistent with recent research which shows that individuals differ in the degree to which their behaviors show cross-situational consistency (Bem & Allen, 1974; S. Epstein, 1979; Mischel & Peake, 1982).

It seems quite probable that to capture the varying complexity of the various clini-cal personality (and other) disorders, circle prototypical diagnosis will need multiple patternings of circle segments and levels. Indeed, much of the work ahead of us is to validate the distinct concrete pattern or profile of circle segments for each of the per-sonality disorders.

Proposition 7–5. To establish reliable and valid diagnosis of the *DSM* personality disorders using the interpersonal circle, relevant correlated situations need to be specified and interfaced with the circle segments defining each particular prototype.

This principle states that interpersonal diagnosis must incorporate the well-estab-lished interactionist position (Endler & Magnusson, 1976; Kendrick & Funder, 1988) of identifying the interacting situation and person factors that are distinctly operative for a particular disorder. Valid diagnosis, then, would not only express in empirical terms the degree of fit of a particular patient to a defining prototype for that disorder (expressed as a distinctive profile of circle segments), but would also explicitly designate distinctive classes of situations and interpersonal contexts in which the prototypical behavior pattern is most likely to be expressed.

An important interpersonal tenet (as Chapter 6 discussed) is that the more abnormal a person, the more likely it is that his or her interpersonal behaviors will override environmental influences, remaining rigidly consistent across situations and interactants. What Principle 7–5 asserts, however, is that the degree and limits of the transsituational consistency operative for each of the personality disorders need to be carefully determined. The distinctive situational bandwidth most relevant to a particular personality disorder must be specified as an essential part of the diagnostic prototype.

Because it seems to be the case, as Chapters 3 and 4 documented, that each of us displays consistency primarily in those behaviors central to our self-definitions (e.g., Bem & Allen, 1974; Millon, 1981), classes of these core-reflective behaviors are likely more resistant to situational influences, whereas other more peripheral behaviors may be more readily influenced by environmental factors. Another possibility is that when the control or affiliation demands in persons' lives change, some individuals may adjust to the new situational demands by modifying expression of more peripheral interpersonal behaviors (e.g., on the circle, behaviors from a less characteristic quadrant). For example, a histrionic personality, if confronted with a new job situation exhibiting hostile overtones, might shift in that situation to deferent and trusting behaviors found in the bottom-right circle quadrant, momentarily abandoning the more prototypical gregarious and exhibitionistic top-right quadrant behaviors.

Another possibility is that some personality disorders may reveal their central prototypical patterns only over successive transactions with the same interactants. The sociopathic individual rarely affects others as manipulative after a single encounter; rather it is from repeated encounters that the maladaptive pattern begins to appear. In similar fashion, the borderline personality disorder is defined by extreme shifts from one maladaptive pattern to another, shifting over time between icy paranoia and antagonistic behavior (top-left quadrant) and trusting, adoring, and compliant behavior (bottom-right).

Also, interpersonal behavior and diagnosis need to be viewed from the perspective of relationship development. Duke and Nowicki (1982) proposed that relationships progress through four phases: choice, beginning, deepening, and termination. From their perspective, negotiation of relationship definition is not as essential during the earliest stages of a relationship, but becomes more important as the interaction continues over time.

If circle diagnosis is to contribute to a full understanding of the *DSM* personality disorders, assessment must systematically incorporate the important situational and temporal factors relevant to the expression of each maladaptive interpersonal pattern, including both central and peripheral components.

Proposition 7–6. For optimally useful interpersonal diagnosis, the prototypical pattern of interpersonal circle behavior defining a particular personality disorder needs to be related specifically to the distinctive situational influence of the therapist and the therapeutic context.

To be ultimately useful, interpersonal diagnosis needs to relate directly to the treatment situation. It can accomplish this by specifying precisely how behaviors typical of the therapist role are likely to influence expression of a particular patient's prototypical circle behavior as well as by specifying the distinctive complementary covert engagements the therapist can expect to experience with that client in their sessions.

Further, some facets of the interpersonal behavior of a disordered individual, rarely seen by others in the client's life, may be more uniquely available and apparent to the therapist. For example, in interacting with an avoidant personality, the therapist may observe self-doubting components that are carefully kept hidden from others. The therapist, being in the "helper" position, is more likely than others to be the object of at least a mild degree of self-dissatisfaction and negative self-worth. This moderate disclosure may temper the cold, aloof, disengaged impact that is generally experienced by other interactants.

Summary

Considerable conceptual and empirical work remains to be done before interpersonal diagnosis will compile anything like a sophisticated and comprehensive body of knowledge regarding the personality disorders. This is the case even if we ignore entirely the long-range issue of how these personality disorders might interface with (e.g., as primary or secondary conditions) Axis I symptomatic disorders. Elaboration of in-depth formulations of interpersonal diagnosis and therapy likely will result from intensive and restricted targeting by investigators of one or two personality disorders at a time—in contrast to attempts at wide-band coups.

Future theory and research will determine the extent to which interpersonal conceptualizations and measurement might be useful for diagnosis of *DSM* Axis I disorders (Widiger & Hyler, 1987). Also, as Kiesler et al. (1990) noted, self-report data are suspect as the sole basis for determining either diagnosis of personality disorder or profiles of interpersonal behavior because it is the pattern of a patient's overt behavior as assessed from interactants' or observers' ratings that produces the maladaptive aversive effects in others emphasized both by *DSM-IV* and by interpersonal theory. Trull (1992) emphasized that multiple methods of assessment are necessary to distinguish trait variance from method variance. He underscored:

> Assessments of the patients based on the report of significant others are important because they provide a more broadly based picture of the patient's personality and personality pathology. However, reports from significant others may also be subject to bias, and it is important to sample as many significant others as possible to arrive at a valid, accurate evaluation of the patient. (p. 559)

In conclusion, interpersonal theory, besides construing abnormal behavior in terms highly similar to those used by *DSM,* also offers an empirically based, internally consistent taxonomy for classification of interpersonal behavior in its normal and abnormal ranges. Most importantly, as we shall see in Chapters 10 and 11, once a patient's interpersonal behavior has been diagnosed as showing good fit to the defining prototype for a particular disorder (in terms of a distinctive profile of circle segments and designated situations), precise intervention possibilities are derivable from the circle and can be sequentially staged across the course of therapy using the principles of "complementarity," "acomplementarity," and "anticomplementarity," described in Chapter 4. The real promise of the circle is that, having identified prototypical segments that define a particular disorder, theoretically derivable interventions can be systematically designated.

AN INTERPERSONAL CIRCLE TRANSLATION OF THE *DSM-III* PERSONALITY DISORDERS

Inspection of the 1982 Interpersonal Circle (Figure 1–1), especially the Level 1 and Level 2 1985 Acts Versions (Figures 1–2 and 1–3) undoubtedly suggested to the clinically experienced reader corresponding locations at various circle segments and octants of the 11 *DSM* personality disorders. As a first-step, wide-band attempt, based on a careful content analysis of *DSM-III* (APA, 1980) criterial descriptors for the Axis II disorders, I (Kiesler, 1986b) earlier projected each disorder's primary loadings on one or more of the 16 categories (sectors) of the 1982 Interpersonal Circle. I examined each set of diagnostic criteria for the 11 disorders and summarized the profile of corresponding circle sectors for each disorder. Table 7–1 provides the summary profile translations (for similar profile translations, see Leary & Coffey, 1955; McLemore & Brokaw, 1987).

Several conclusions can be drawn from the circle descriptions provided in Table 7–1. First, the translations confirm Proposition 7–4, that the prototypes ultimately defining the clinical personality disorders will exhibit structures that are nonisomorphic in terms of number of circle segments, segment levels, and quadrant range. The table

TABLE 7–1. Diagnosis of the *DSM-III* Personality Disorders Using the 1982 Interpersonal Circle*

A. "Octant" Prototypes	
1. Histrionic	N_2O_2: Frenetically Gregarious/Histrionic
2. Narcissistic	O_2P_2: Histrionic/Arrogant-Rigidly Autonomous
3. Dependent	HI: Unassured/Submissive (levels unspecified)
4. Compulsive	F_1G: Aloof/Inhibited (level unspecified for G)
5. Passive-Aggressive	E_1F_1: Antagonistic-Harmful/Aloof
B. "Triad" Prototypes	
6. Paranoid	$C_2D_1E_1$: Rivalrous-Disdainful/Cold-Punitive/Antagonistic-Harmful
7. Avoidant	$F_1G_1H_1$: Aloof/Taciturn/Self-Doubting-Dependent
C. "Segment" Prototypes	
8. Antisocial	E: Hostile (level unspecified)
9. Schizoid	F_2: Escapistic (without F_{2c}: autistic-eccentric)
D. "Mixed Quadrant" Prototypes	
10. Schizotypal	C_1F: Suspicious-Resentful/Detached (level unspecified for F)
11. Borderline	$B_2 \leftrightarrow J_2$: Rivalrous-Disdainful $\leftrightarrow$ Ambitionless-Flattering and $E_2 \leftrightarrow M_2$: Rancorous-Sadistic $\leftrightarrow$ Devoted-Indulgent

*A–P = circle segments; $_{1,2}$ = segment levels.

shows that only 5 of the 11 *DSM-III* disorders (histrionic, narcissistic, dependent, compulsive, and passive-aggressive) can be located at a particular octant of the 1982 Circle; 2 of the 11 disorders (schizoid and antisocial) can be located at only one segment; two disorders (paranoid and avoidant) were defined by a triad of circle segments; and two disorders (schizotypal and borderline) were characterized by segments from different quadrants. A subsequent study analyzing ratings of seven prototypical cases (Kiesler et al., 1990) empirically confirmed the prediction that personality-disordered individuals may be identified by two or more peaks on segments of the interpersonal circle.

Second, also present in the circle translations in Table 7–1 is clear evidence that *DSM-III* descriptors for the various disorders target abnormal interpersonal behaviors of varying levels of intensity. Some disorders are described at mild-moderate levels of segment intensity (e.g., avoidant: $F_1G_1H_1$), others show mixed-level patterns (e.g., paranoid: $C_2D_1E_1$), while others define segment behaviors all at the extreme level (e.g., narcissistic: O_2P_2).

Third, circle diagnosis of the personality disorders reveals no patterns that would directly support the three clusters outlined in *DSM-III:* (a) "odd or eccentric" disorders (paranoid, schizoid, schizotypal), (b) "dramatic, emotional, or erratic" disorders (histrionic, narcissistic, antisocial, borderline), and (c) "anxious or fearful" disorders (avoidant, dependent, compulsive, passive-aggressive). Instead, the personality disorders are classified predominantly in the hostile (left) half of the 1982 Circle. Among them a few disorders show behaviors from the hostile-dominant (top-left) quadrant, but most fall in the hostile-submissive (bottom-left) quadrant. Only two disorders are found in the friendly hemisphere, narcissistic and histrionic, both in the friendly-dominant (top-right) quadrant. *DSM-III,* thus, offers no definitions of disorders classifiable in the friendly-submissive (bottom-right) quadrant, nor at the dramatically dominant octants (PA or AB). As discussed earlier, for various reasons these abnormal persons missing from *DSM-III,* but theoretically and empirically identifiable on the circle, seldom seem to appear in psychiatric treatment settings.

Fourth, inspection of Table 7–1 also reveals that some *DSM-III* criterial descriptors target behaviors that do not fall in the circle domain of overt interpersonal behaviors. Among these are descriptors targeting inferred motivational states (e.g., avoidant: B and D), inferred affective events (e.g., borderline: E and F), inferred cognitive events (e.g., schizotypal: A and B), and anamnestic events (e.g., borderline: G). Further, some disorders are defined almost exclusively by interpersonal descriptors (e.g., paranoid, histrionic), others provide a mix of interpersonal and other descriptors (e.g., passive-aggressive), while still others provide few, if any, interpersonal descriptors (e.g., antisocial). These observations underline Proposition 7–1 of circle diagnosis, which states that, in contrast to *DSM-III,* circle diagnosis focuses primarily on assessment of overt, observable interpersonal behaviors exhibited by abnormal persons.

Finally, it is evident from Table 7–1 that *DSM-III* descriptions of the personality disorders completely ignore Propositions 7–5 and 7–6 of circle diagnosis. Nowhere among the *DSM-III* (APA, 1980) or *DSM-IV* (APA, 1994) sections on the personality disorders can one find any discussion, much less specification, of either (a) the important classes of situations in which the various dysfunctional patterns will and will not be evident, or (b) the specific manner in which clients will present their respective abnormal patterns within the context of the therapy session. If future versions of *DSM* continue to ignore these vital contextual issues, users will continue to find it difficult to arrive at reliable diagnostic assessments or to derive differential treatment programs.

INTERPERSONAL EMPIRICAL FINDINGS

Interpersonal Diagnosis of *DSM* Axis I Disorders

Several investigators (Alden & Phillips, 1990; Lorr, Bishop, & McNair, 1965; Plutchik & Platman, 1977) have examined patterns of interpersonal behavior associated with various *DSM* symptomatic (Axis I) disorders.

Alden and Phillips (1990), using the interpersonal circumplex version of the IIP (IIP-C; Alden, Wiggins, & Pincus, 1990), examined the specificity of the interpersonal problems that are associated with the affective complaints of social anxiety and depression. Using standard questionnaires for measuring social avoidance and depression, a large sample of undergraduates were assigned to one of four groups: socially anxious, depressed, socially anxious and depressed, and control subjects (neither socially anxious nor depressed). The four groups were compared in terms of their subjective conceptualizations of their interpersonal problems as measured on the IIP-C.

Findings revealed several distinct patterns of social perceptions. First, *control subjects* reported few interpersonal problems. Second, individuals complaining of *both depression and anxiety* perceived themselves as having greater interpersonal difficulties than did either depressed or control subjects; as predicted, they characterized their social behavior as nonassertive and avoidant. Third, *socially anxious, nondepressed* individuals perceived themselves as cold or nonresponsive to others and related their interpersonal difficulties to an inability to experience or express warm and intimate feelings toward others. As predicted, their perceptions placed them closer to the cold pole of the interpersonal circle than either the depressed or control subjects. Finally, individuals who were *depressed, but not socially anxious*, were no different from control subjects in the self-perceptions of their social interactions. Alden and Phillips (1990) concluded that their results suggest that beliefs and self-perceptions concerning characteristic patterns of interpersonal behavior may be able to distinguish empirically individuals with various types of affective complaints.

The next two studies examined the interpersonal behavior of mixed diagnostic groups containing both clinical syndrome and personality disorder patients. Lorr et al. (1965) adopted the view that diagnoses of milder mental disorder (psychoneurosis and personality disorders) "should be based primarily on characteristic interpersonal behavior patterns. Associated neurotic symptoms and complaints should be regarded as secondary to maladaptive patterns of interpersonal adjustment" (p. 468).

Subjects were a large sample (212 men and 313 women patients; 116 psychotherapists) of nonpsychotic outpatient psychotherapy patients who had met for therapy sessions at least once a week for a minimum of 3 months. Using the IBI, the therapists were instructed to rate a sample of their case load as diverse as possible with respect to interpersonal behavior, occupation, and social class.

Profile analyses yielded basically four patient types among the various outpatient samples, as follows: Type I (inhibited, submissive, abasive; more likely to be labeled neurotic and to be accepted for psychotherapy); Type II (agreeable, nurturant, affectionate, sociable; more likely to be labeled hysteric); Type III (hostile, mistrusting, detached; ordinarily designated schizoid); and Type IV (exhibitionistic, dominant, competitive, hostile; more likely to be diagnosed passive-aggressive, aggressive, or compulsive). Findings also revealed significant occupational correlates for the four profile types: Type I (housewives), Type II (white-collar workers), Type III (unskilled and semiskilled blue-collar workers), and Type IV (managers, administrators, or professionals).

Lorr et al. (1965) concluded that their method of IBI interpersonal diagnosis "yields meaningful, mutually exclusive and replicable outpatient types . . . the approach and the findings show promise for a useful and fruitful system of patient classification" (p. 472).

Plutchik and Platman (1977) sought to identify personality traits that might be associated with psychiatric diagnostic labels such as paranoid, schizoid, hysterical, and cyclothymic. Twenty psychiatrists were given a list of diagnostic terms (seven *DSM-II* nonpsychotic personality disorders) and were asked to indicate, using the Emotions Profile Index (EPI; Kellerman & Plutchik, 1968; Plutchik & Kellerman, 1974), what personality traits typically were associated with them. The EPI consists of 12 personality trait terms that had been selected by factor analysis to sample all four quadrants of the interpersonal circle.

Plutchik and Platman (1977) found good interjudge agreement among psychiatrists on the personality traits they believe to be implied by the diagnostic terms. EPI results revealed, for example, the following characterizations: schizoid (shy, self-conscious, brooding), passive-aggressive (resentful, obedient, brooding), hysterical (sociable, impulsive, affectionate, adventurous). Factor analysis of the EPI ratings placed the diagnostic groups in the following circumplex quadrants: hostile-dominant (sociopath), hostile-submissive (paranoid, schizoid, passive-aggressive, compulsive), friendly-submissive (well-adjusted), and friendly-dominant (cyclothymic, hysterical).

Plutchik and Platman (1977) concluded that psychiatrists carry around in their heads a set of common images and connotations about the kinds of people to whom diagnostic labels are applied and that diagnosis can represent "implicit personality estimates of the likelihood of observing certain clusters of traits" (p. 421).

Interpersonal Diagnosis of *DSM* Axis II Disorders

A series of studies investigated the ability of the interpersonal circle to describe and discriminate *DSM* Axis II personality disorders: Benjamin (1987a); Benjamin and Wonderlich (1994); Blashfield, Sprock, Pinkston, and Hodgin (1985); De Jong, Van den Brink, Jansen, and Schippers (1989); Gurtman (1992b); Kerr et al. (1994); Kiesler et al. (1990); Mantano and Locke (1995); Morey (1985); Pincus and Wiggins (1990); Robbins and Dupont (1992); Romney and Bynner (1989, 1992); Sim and Romney (1990); Soldz, Budman, Demby, and Merry (1993); Tryer and Alexander (1979); Widiger, Trull, Hurt, Clarkin, and Frances (1987); and Wiggins and Pincus (1989). Generally, the studies have reported positive findings. They also report a failure of the circumplex to account for all the *DSM* disorders, suggesting instead that diagnosis of personality disorders involves more than assessment of simply disordered *overt* interpersonal behavior.

Tryer and Alexander (1979) used a structured interview schedule to record the personality traits of a large sample of psychiatric outpatients, half having a primary diagnosis of personality disorder, the other half having other psychiatric diagnoses. Factor analysis revealed a similar structure of personality variables in both groups of patients. Two main factors were found, termed sociopathic and passive-dependent, with a third dysthymia factor emerging in the non-personality-disorder group. The authors interpreted their findings as supporting the notion that the traits of patients with personality disorder differ only in degree from those of other psychiatric patients. A set of cluster analyses revealed five discrete categories into which their sample could be placed: sociopathic, passive-dependent, anankastic, schizoid, and a non-personality-disordered group. Two-thirds of the personality-disordered patients fell into the passive-dependent or sociopathic categories. Tryer and Alexander (1979) concluded that their findings, which revealed that the underlying structure of variables is similar in patients both with and without primary personality disorder, support "the concept of personality disorders as being at the extreme of a multidimensional continuum" (p. 166).

Blashfield et al. (1985), as part of their study examining the extent to which the prototype model fit the classification of *DSM-III* personality disorders, also analyzed interrelationships among the 11 personality diagnoses to determine how well they fit Wiggins's (1982) circumplex model. Printed case histories of personality disorders selected from various appropriate publications, were presented to a group of clinicians who assigned a *DSM-III* diagnosis to each. Results identified prototypic cases for 8 of the 11 personality disorder diagnoses. Multidimensional scaling (MDS) analysis yielded a clear circumplex ordering of the personality disorders, including predicted positioning of adjacent and opposite diagnostic groups, that offered confirmatory support for Wiggins's (1982) hypothesized orderings.

In an interpersonal analysis, Benjamin (1987a) reported that borderline personality inpatients were distinguished from other inpatient diagnostic groups by their greater likelihood of attacking other patients. Results also indicated that borderline persons were likely to perceive their fathers as friendly and controlling, and their mothers as actively attacking; they also reported consistent dislike for their mothers. Benjamin (1987a, p. 13) suggested that this latter finding may represent the social correlate of splitting: the borderline tendency either to idealize (fathers) or devalue (mothers). Benjamin (1987a) also reported that other SASB research confirms that borderline individuals suffer extremely self-oppressive self-concepts.

Gurtman (1992b) demonstrated that the circumplex could differentiate normal levels of trust from more extreme and maladaptive levels of gullibility and exploitability. He predicted that the problems of subjects low in trust generally would have the largest loading in the IIP vindictive (BC) interpersonal circle octant; that for those high in trust, problems would be greatest in the exploitable (JK) octant. Findings confirmed that low trust and increased hostility were associated with greater interpersonal distress. In contrast, subjects characterized by high trust and low levels of hostility reported little or no problems in any areas of the circumplex, and were at or below the mean for each of the eight octants. Gurtman (1992b) concluded that his findings demonstrate the ability of the circumplex to differentiate normal versus abnormal levels of interpersonal trust.

Robbins and Dupont (1992) studied whether broad patterns of interpersonal behavior within a sample of outpatient group therapy clients would relate to disturbances characterized within Kohut's (1971) grandiose-exhibitionistic or idealizing trends of self (Patton & Robbins, 1982). Canonical correlations were calculated between a measure of the Kohut trends and client CLOIT-R interpersonal scores (both self-reports and counselor ratings). Results indicated a clear convergence between client narcissistic needs and therapists' perceptions of the clients' interpersonal behaviors. Clients with strong Kohutian grandiose-exhibitionistic needs were viewed as manifesting primarily assured, dominant, and exhibitionistic behavior; clients with idealizing needs were viewed as manifesting primarily deferent and submissive behavior. In contrast, clients' self-reports of their interpersonal behavior were not differentiated by client narcissistic need type. Overall, the clients viewed themselves as exhibiting a wide range of interpersonal behaviors in a flexible manner; therapists, on the other hand, perceived these narcissistic clients as being primarily dominant and exhibitionistic. Robbins and Dupont (1992) concluded that the discrepancy between client and counselor perceptions supports the notion that narcissistic individuals engage in ego-defensive operations that disavow and/or slide the meaning of maladaptive behaviors (Patton & Robbins, 1982).

Kerr et al. (1994) examined the relationship between self-reported interpersonal behavior (measured by an adaptation of Strong, Hills, & Nelson's, 1988, ICRS) and narcissism (measured by five scales derived from Kohut's (1971) psychoanalytic theory of the self). Subjects were large samples of adolescents from junior high and high schools. Canonical correlation analyses revealed a relationship between self-reported interpersonal behavior and narcissistic vulnerability. Positive associations were obtained between (a) narcissistic idealizing tendency and interpersonal self-effacement, (b) between narcissistic vulnerability in the grandiose sector of the self and high-control/low-affiliation interpersonal behaviors, and (c) between a healthier level of narcissism and socially acceptable expressions of grandiosity through nurturant and leading interpersonal behaviors. Finally, results on a subsample of adolescents who had undergone psychotherapy revealed that treated, compared with nontreated adolescents, tended to display more narcissistic vulnerability, together with more distrustful and less cooperative interpersonal behaviors.

Sim and Romney (1990) tested the hypotheses that individuals with personality disorders, in contrast to normals, have more intense and more rigid interpersonal behavior than normals, and that a greater discrepancy can be found between their own ratings of their interpersonal behavior and ratings of their behavior by interactants. Self-reported and interactant-rated ICL scores were obtained on a clinical sample of diagnosed *(DSM-III-R)* personality disorder cases and a control group of university undergraduates. An MDS analysis confirmed that the control and affiliation dimensions underlay the ICL for both clinical and nonclinical samples using either self-ratings or others-ratings. Results also showed that the clinical subjects as a group were more intense, more rigid, and more discrepant (with respect to their self versus others ratings) than the nonclinical subjects. Finally, results also provided empirical support for postulated (Widiger & Kelso, 1983; Wiggins, 1982) correspondences between *DSM-III-R* Axis II disorders as measured by Millon's (1987) MCMI and interpersonal circumplex quadrants; however, a finer grained analysis examining octant placements revealed less consistent patterns.

Widiger, Trull, et al. (1987) assessed the presence of each of the symptom descriptors (individual diagnostic criteria) for the *DSM-III* personality disorders in a group of personality-disordered patients. The number of symptoms (criterial descriptors) of each of the personality disorders possessed by each patient was correlated across patients, and the correlations were subjected to multidimensional scaling analysis. MDS findings revealed a three-dimensional solution. The first dimension, social involvement, classified the schizoid and paranoid at one pole, and the dependent, avoidant, borderline, and histrionic at the other. The second dimension, assertiveness, seemed to reflect interpersonal power or dominance with the narcissistic and histrionic at one end, and the schizoid, passive-aggressive, avoidant, and dependent at the other. The third dimension ranged from anxious rumination at one end (schizotypal, compulsive, paranoid, and avoidant) to external behavioral expression at the other (antisocial, passive-aggressive, schizoid, and borderline). In sum, the first two of the three dimensions obtained could be aligned quite easily with the interpersonal circle axis dimensions. Widiger, Trull, et al. (1987) concluded:

> The current study found that the dimensions of social involvement (affiliation), assertion (dominance), and anxious rumination versus behavioral acting out may be useful to describe the similarities and differences among patients with personality disorder and among the personality disorders themselves. (p. 563)

De Jong et al. (1989) studied correlations between interpersonal octant scores obtained from ICL ratings and diagnoses obtained from the Structured Interview for the *DSM-III-R* Personality Disorders (SIDP; Pfohl, Stangl, & Zimmerman, 1983). They found that the amount of variance of SIDP diagnostic scores explained by ICL octant scores ranged from 25% for the schizotypal disorder to 66% for the dependent personality disorder.

Kiesler et al. (1990) conducted the first study to provide objective ratings (in contrast to self-report characterizations) of the interpersonal behavior of patients with personality disorder. The study used ratings of patients' interpersonal behavior by relatively large groups of clinical trainees and undergraduates to test Kiesler's (1986b) a priori classifications of prototypical *DSM-III* personality disorders onto the 1982 Interpersonal Circle. A sample of eight videotaped personality disorder patient interviews was obtained from two psychiatric training tape series. A panel of 10 clinical diagnosticians provided independent checks on the diagnosis assigned to the eight patients by the training series and also rated the degree of "prototypicality" each case exhibited. Interpersonal characterizations of the interview behavior of the eight patients were obtained from the ratings by the undergraduate and clinical trainee observers. Findings revealed that CLOPT interpersonal ratings significantly differentiated the interpersonal behavior of the sample of patients with principal diagnoses on DSM-III Axis II—confirming empirically that patterns of overt interpersonal behavior are indeed different for patients who have various personality disorders. Results also revealed that, at best, Kiesler's (1986b) circle translations in the form of peak octants or triads for the disorders were confirmed for only three cases; predictions for the other five cases were either confirmed only partially or not at all. The authors concluded that prototypic interpersonal profiles for the various personality disorders seem to be more complex and subtle than previous a priori translations, which focused on octant patterns, suggested—since findings of the study showed that important core features for a particular disorder may include three or more sectors, from more than one circle quadrant (Kiesler et al., 1990).

Morey (1985) studied a sample of hospitalized patients, virtually all of whom had *DSM-III* principal diagnoses on Axis I. He obtained *DSM-III* personality disorder scores for the patients from their responses to an earlier version of Millon's (1987) MCMI and also obtained their self-reports to LaForge and Suczek's (1955) ICL. Intercorrelations of the 11 Millon scales and the 16 ICL circle segments revealed relatively poor fit of the personality disorders to various a priori projections onto the circle. As Kiesler et al. (1990) observed, however, Morey's findings need to be viewed with caution for several reasons. First, clinical *DSM-III* diagnoses of the patients obtained from structured interviews were not used; rather, personality disorder diagnoses were obtained from a self-report inventory (MCMI) alone. Second, all interpersonal data were obtained from a self-report (ICL) inventory; in contrast, it is the pattern of a patient's overt interpersonal behavior as assessed from interactants' or observers ratings that produces the aversive effects on others. Third, by far the majority of Morey's sample had received hospital staff principal diagnoses on Axis I, with 74% diagnoses either affective disorder or schizophrenia; in contrast, interpersonal circle translations assume a principal diagnosis on Axis II.

Romney and Bynner (1989) used confirmatory factor analysis to test the goodness of fit of the circumplex pattern to empirical data that had been collected in two previous studies. They found that only five of the personality disorders could be diagnosed on the circle: dependent, histrionic, narcissistic, paranoid, and schizoid. In a follow-up study, Romney and Bynner (1992) sought to determine whether the relationships between the five personality disorders that could not be represented by a circular structure in their earlier analysis could in fact be explained by a simplex model. Results showed that the five other personality disorders (antisocial, avoidant, borderline, compulsive, and passive-aggressive) indeed fit a simplex model that provided a linear ordering of the five disorders along a single "cognitive style" dimension, impulsivity, with personality disorders ranging from most impulsive (antisocial), through borderline, avoidant, and passive-aggressive, to least impulsive (compulsive). Romney and Bynner (1992) concluded that a cognitive dimension can account for the clustering of 5 of the 10 personality disorders studied, and that those disorders with a strong cognitive component should not be included in interpersonal circumplex conceptualizations.

Soldz et al. (1993) studied a sample of outpatients in group therapy by correlating scores on the IIP, the Millon Clinical Multiaxial Inventory (MCMI-II; Millon, 1987), and the Personality Disorder Examination (PDE; Loranger, Susman, Oldham, & Russakoff, 1985). Avoidant, schizoid, and schizotypal personality disorders (as determined by PDE and MCMI-II scores) were located as expected near the FG (aloof-introverted) octant of the circle; histrionic and borderline disorders were located in the NO (gregarious-extraverted) octant; antisocial, passive-aggressive, and paranoid personality disorders clustered in interpersonal space from the PA (assured-dominant) to BC (arrogant-calculating) octants. The authors found, however, that the avoidant, schizoid, and compulsive personality disorders were not differentiated or represented well in circular space. Soldz et al. (1993) concluded that the interpersonal circumplex did not classify the various personality disorders clearly—that important aspects of the personality disorders are not measured by interpersonal circle inventories.

Mantano and Locke (1995) administered Millon's MCMI-II personality disorder scales and the IIP to a large sample of patients being treated for alcohol dependence. Results revealed that MCMI-II schizoid, avoidant, and negativistic patients reported problems with being too guarded and distant; narcissistic patients with being too domineering; compulsive patients with being too unassertive; antisocial and paranoid patients with being both guarded and domineering; histrionic patients with being both open and domineering; and dependent patients with being both open and unassertive.

Hence, three studies (Mantano & Locke, 1995; Pincus & Wiggins, 1990; Soldz et al., 1993) found reliable associations between octants of the IIP-C and measures of the *DSM* personality disorders. Across all three studies, antisocial or paranoid patients were generally placed in the cold-domineering (hostile-dominant) quadrant;

avoidant and schizoid subjects in the cold-nonassertive (hostile-submissive) quadrant; dependent subjects in the warm-nonassertive (friendly-submissive) quadrant; and narcissistic subjects at the domineering sector. As subjects, the three studies used students, personality-disordered patients without Axis I comorbidity, and alcoholics respectively, "suggesting that the types of interpersonal problems associated with different personality disorders are consistent across different populations" (Mantano & Locke, 1995, p. 66).

Wiggins and Pincus (1989) conducted a principal-components factor analysis of two self-report measures of the five-factor model and two self-report measures of personality disorder pathology. They found, first, that conceptions of personality disorders were strongly and clearly related to dimensions of normal personality traits. They found, second, that although the circumplex model illuminated conceptions of some of the disorders, the full five-factor model was required to capture and clarify the entire range of personality disorders. Specifically, six disorders were strongly related to the interpersonal circumplex: antisocial, avoidant, dependent, histrionic, narcissistic, and schizoid. The remaining five (borderline, compulsive, passive-aggressive, paranoid, and schizotypal) were better able to be classified using the five-factor model (the circle dimensions of control and affiliation are represented by the first two factors). These findings support an earlier speculation by Widiger and Frances (1985) that "the interpersonal circle might fail to adequately represent all the cognitive and affective variables that are integral to the concept of personality disorder" (p. 621).

Wiggins and Pincus (1989) obtained a five-factor solution that accounted for 63.5% of the variance, with loadings confirming a relationship between the five-factor model and self-reported personality disorder pathology. Disorders loading positively on the *Neuroticism* factor were borderline, avoidant, passive-aggressive, dependent, and compulsive; loading negatively were narcissistic and antisocial. Positive loadings on *Extraversion* were found for histrionic, narcissistic, and antisocial disorders; negative loading were found for schizoid and avoidant. A high positive loading on *Agreeableness* was found for dependent; loading negatively were antisocial, paranoid, and narcissistic. Loading positively on *Conscientiousness* was the compulsive disorder; loading negatively was passive-aggressive. Finally, schizotypal disorder loaded positively on the *Openness* factor. Wiggins and Pincus (1989) concluded that the five-factor model of personality provides a comprehensive model of both normal and abnormal personality.

Pincus and Wiggins (1990) documented how the five-factor model—in coordination with its two component dimensions (surgency and agreeableness) that form the interpersonal circumplex—can provide clarification of the finding that certain personality disorders, but not all, can be clearly anchored to octant within the circle. Pincus and Wiggins (1990) discussed the lack of representation on the circumplex by certain diagnostic groups, such as the borderline personality disorder. They also observed that some personality disorders, such as schizoid, are characterized by the more typical "interpersonal spaceship" profile, in which extreme scores in one octant gradually decrease in adjacent octants, until the lowest score is obtained in the octant opposite the peak octant. In contrast, other disorders, especially borderline, do not demonstrate a single interpersonal pattern and to date have eluded valid interpersonal classification (Kiesler, 1986b; Sim & Romney, 1990; Wiggins, 1987; Wiggins & Pincus, 1989).

Interpersonal studies generally establish that 6 of the 11 *DSM* personality disorders can be validly diagnosed using either interpersonal circle or interpersonal problem inventories.

Other Circumplex Studies of Psychiatric Disorders

Liggett (1993) examined the factors of shame, guilt, and childhood abuse as associated with self-reported (CLOIT-R) interpersonal behavior patterns of male spousal abusers who had been arrested for assaulting their domestic partner. She found that overall the predominant interpersonal style reported by the male spousal abusers was PA: Assured-Dominant. She pointed out that assured-dominant behavior is consistent with the literature that identifies control as the central issue in spouse abuse; it also is consistent with interpersonal circle diagnosis of the narcissistic personality disorder, an often-cited characteristic of abusive men. Second and third highest octant peaks obtained on the CLOIT-R circle profile were NO: Sociable-Exhibitionistic and BC: Competitive-Mistrusting. Analyses showed, further, that the highest three CLOIT-R octants (PA, NO, BC) were significantly related to the abusive subjects having been abused in childhood and with shame—but not with guilt. Liggett (1993) found that spouse abusers described themselves as exhibiting primarily dominant interpersonal behaviors, as being shame (but not guilt) prone, and as being heavy drug and alcohol users; they also admitted to a high rate of childhood abuse in their own background.

Kiesler et al. (1982) studied the impacts (IMI) of a group of psychiatric outpatients on intake interviewers in a training clinic over a 2-year period. The patients represented a wide range of Axis I and II *DSM* conditions. Analyses of the IMIs filled out by interviewers on patients after the intake interviews showed that the interpersonal behavior of the patient (in contrast to the normative undergraduate) sample was predominantly submissive and friendly. In the less frequent instances in which patients' behavior came across as more dominant, it was also registered by the interviewer as more hostile.

Reagan (1978) studied the interpersonal behavior of high versus low assertive skills individuals. Subjects in each group participated in four experimental situations in which requests were made of them by a live role model. After viewing each videotaped session, one set of observers filled out IMIs on each subject, while another set completed a behavioral coding sheet on each subject. Analyses revealed that low assertive subjects impacted the observers as being significantly more inhibited and submissive than did high assertive subjects. Also, high assertive subjects were perceived as being significantly more sociable. Finally, coders' ratings of subjects' tendencies to comply with or refuse the role model's requests correlated significantly with subjects' IMI submissive scores.

Reagan (1979) replicated her earlier study using an identical procedure except that individuals of moderate assertiveness were included with the high and low groups and found that inhibited and submissive IMI scores differentiated all three groups in the expected order. High assertive subjects also produced stronger dominant impacts than did both other groups, stronger competitive impacts than did the moderates, and stronger affiliative impacts than the low assertives. Both highs and moderates scored higher than did lows on the detached scale. Reagan (1979) concluded that the IMI can provide an important and unique source of validation of the outcome of assertiveness training, especially if scores are obtained from significant others in the person's life.

Labe-Sloan (1982) studied the effects of observer characteristics on impacts produced by actors trained to exhibit high versus low assertive behavior. Analyses showed, first, that assertive actors impacted all observers as being more friendly-dominant and less hostile-submissive, replicating once again Reagan's (1978, 1979) findings. Also male, in contrast to female, assertive actors impacted all observers as being more dominant. In contrast, both male and female unassertive actors scored strongest in submissive and friendly behavior; they also produced more hostile impacts in observers than did the assertive actors. Once again, submissive interpersonal behaviors were found to discriminate best between high and low assertive individuals.

Kiesler and Federman (1978) attempted an interpersonal circumplex diagnosis, in an analogue situation, of obsessive and histrionic personality disorders. Written personality descriptions of the two disorders (male and female versions) were constructed based on a review of the clinical literature, and were presented to normal subjects who recorded their IMI impacts in reaction to the paragraph descriptions. Findings supported Kiesler and Federman's prediction that the obsessive scenario, in contrast to the histrionic, would evoke stronger hostile and weaker sociable impacts. Female subjects alone reported stronger mistrusting and detached, and weaker affiliative, impacts to the obsessive description. Additional analyses showed that the obsessive scenario pulled stronger competitive impacts from all subjects, while the histrionic description engaged stronger affiliative and submissive impacts. Kiesler and Federman (1978) concluded, "The hypothesis that written descriptions of obsessive and hysteric behavior patterns would evoke impacts in subjects indicative of distinct clusters of stylistic behavior on the Interpersonal Circle was supported" (p. 11).

Summary

Empirical efforts toward conceptualization of *DSM* disorders using interpersonal circumplex methodologies have been abundant but have yielded mixed results. *Diagnostic studies using only the interpersonal circumplex dimensions of control and affiliation, have clarified and confirmed the interpersonal pathology of certain* DSM *personality disorders, but not others.* On the other hand, *the ability of the full five-factor model,* which subsumes the two interpersonal circle dimensions, *to describe and differentiate among the* DSM *personality disorders has been confirmed* in a series of factor analytic and other studies.

ASSESSMENT OF THE MALADAPTIVE TRANSACTION CYCLE

When using interpersonal assessment in counseling and psychotherapy, therapists should address all four components of the Maladaptive Transaction Cycle described in Chapter 6, using multiple sources or perspectives. The goal of this form of assessment is to obtain information regarding how clients and their significant others experience the clients' interpersonal functioning and problems.

As the Maladaptive Transaction Cycle showed (see Figures 6–1 and 6–2), the basic blocks of transactional behavior are four: person A's covert experience about B, A's overt behavior (action) toward B, person B's covert engagements (impacts) in response to A's action, and B's overt reaction to A. Any comprehensive study of interpersonal behavior, then, requires measurement of each of these four transactional blocks.

Interpersonal assessment, thus, can target any one or more of the following components of the MTC:

1. The covert experiences of the therapist registered as engagements pulled by the patient's actions (the therapist's impact messages).

2. The overt reactions of the therapist to the patient that comprise his or her discrepant reactions or incongruous messages.

3. The actions (patterns of overt verbal and nonverbal behaviors) of the patient toward the therapist during their sessions.

4. The thematic covert experience (thoughts, emotions, expectations, etc.) of the patient as inferred from the patient's verbalizations and nonverbal messages.

The reader can consult Chapter 6 for an in-depth presentation of the four MTC components.

Also, if our analysis focuses on the interpersonal behavior of A, we can extend our measurement to A's behavior, not only with B, but with various other persons with whom A interacts (or has interacted) in his or her life. Study of A's interactions with these other persons also will, ultimately, involve characterizations of the environmental contexts in which these interactions occur, the defined roles of both A and the others in each of these contexts, the interface of the various A-B dyadic units with larger interpersonal systems (e.g., family, group, subculture) in which the dyad is embedded, and so on.

No matter which of these four components is initially assessed by the therapist, the intent or purpose is to measure and understand these cyclically related patient-actions and therapist-reactions as lawfully related and codetermined aspects of a central thematic interpersonal problem for the patient. Further, this theme is exhibited not only with the therapist, but also with other significant persons in the patient's life. In sum, the therapist seeks to measure the patient's central Maladaptive Transaction Cycle— the patient's vicious cycle of abnormal interpersonal behavior, the patient's "self-fulfilling prophecy" of abnormal cognitions and expectancies.

The Therapist's Covert Experiences or
Impact Messages

In the beginning stages of therapy, the patient recurrently communicates his or her particular pattern of evoking messages and enacts his or her pattern of rigid and extreme interpersonal behaviors to the therapist. The patient's self-presentations have both intended and nonintended, aware and less aware, components. In turn, the therapist's emotional, cognitive, and fantasy covert responses are engaged as impact messages that mediate automatic countercommunications and complementary reactions that confirm the patient's vulnerable and incompetent self-image. During early sessions, these internal events in the therapist's experience can't help but trigger the therapist's overt complementary reactions to the patient.

In the interpersonal tradition, a person's actions can be understood only as they derive *conjoint* meaning from the historical and present interpersonal transactions in which they are embedded. A patient's actions, similarly, need to be understood as communicative "force fields" that influence, and simultaneously are influenced by, other "force fields" from present-day interactants in important lawfully reciprocal ways. To be fully cognizant of oneself or of another requires an observational stance offering a clear view of the sequence of events played out tenaciously and recurrently by a person or patient in encounters with significant others.

From this systems perspective, transferences (parataxic distortions) and countertransferences—although expressed and evoked rigidly and extremely by psychotherapy patients—are phenomena not at all unique to the therapy situation (see Chapter 9). Rather, their more or less rigid and extreme expressions by all persons constitute the essence of human living—the "stuff" of human relationships. Perhaps the most distinctive aspect of interpersonal therapy, in regard to both diagnosis and intervention, is its unswerving emphasis on these transference-countertransference sequences as they unfold between patient and therapist. A patient's central problems in living are played out "live" in the therapist's office and as they emerge must be counteracted by the therapist through use of multifaceted interventions.

Appropriately, then, interpersonal diagnosis requires that therapists continually monitor the inner experiences and overt reactions evoked from them by their patients during sessions. The important purpose of this monitoring process is to pinpoint and identify the patient's maladaptively rigid bids for self-confirmation. Likewise, in providing metacommunicative feedback (Chapter 11), therapists need to be able to label the interpersonal impacts they experience as a springboard to collaborative exploration with the patient of their self-defeating and "self-fulfilling prophecy" meanings.

The Therapist's Overt Reactions: The Discrepant Response

Impacts all occur internally, covertly in the therapist's experience. They lead to constricted overt responding by the therapist, initially in the form of the complementary response. For example, we may observe the therapist increasing his or her activity by asking more questions, giving more advice, or by more frequent interruptions. Or the therapist may decrease his or her activity, sitting much longer in silence, feeling cautious about any intervention, and choosing his or her words carefully. In another instance, we may notice more frequent light banter with a patient, with frequent laughter and spontaneous comments. The therapist may feel increasingly threatened, feeling more and more inadequate with a particular patient. Or we may see little or no emotional response to the patient. In another case, the therapist may become angrily sympathetic regarding the patient's reported mistreatment by a spouse or family member. Or the therapist may become increasingly depressed or overtly anxious with a particular patient.

These various therapist enactments of the complementary response result in the patient's continued enactment of his or her maladaptive interpersonal behaviors because the complementary response confirms or validates the patient's expectancies, cognitions, emotions, and other inner experience.

The Patient's Thematic Covert Experience

A third target of assessment consists of aspects of the patient's internal experience inferred by the therapist to be related thematically to the patient's maladaptive pattern of overt interpersonal behavior (to the patient's ED-evoking style). This component is first registered internally by the therapist as the cognitive attribution (perceived evoking message) class of impact messages. This impact component includes the therapist's automatic thoughts about what he or she thinks the patient is trying to do to him or her, or what he or she thinks the patient wants the therapist to do. More generally, the therapist infers what is going on inside the patient's head—what the patient's central expectations, construals, feelings, fantasies, and so on might be in regard to the therapist and their relationship. At a deeper or more core level, these covert experiences have thematic relevance to the patient's self-concept or self-esteem. In the language of contemporary cognitive psychology, these covert events refer to the patient scripts and schemas, including self-schemas, which serve as decoding and encoding filters in the realm of interpersonal relationships (see Chapter 3).

The Patient's Overt Maladaptive Pattern

A fourth essential component to target in assessment is some description of the patient's overt actions (verbal and nonverbal) pinpointed by the therapist as central in producing the impacts experienced with the patient. In identifying the specifics of the patient's maladaptive action pattern, the therapist provides the patient concrete instances of what the patient has done in their sessions to "make" the therapist react in the complementary manner.

THE INVENTORY OF INTERPERSONAL PROBLEMS

Horowitz and his colleagues (Bartholomew & Horowitz, 1991; L. Horowitz, 1979, 1988; L. M. Horowitz & French, 1979; L. M. Horowitz, French, & Anderson, 1982; L. M. Horowitz, French, Lapid, & Weckler, 1982; L. M. Horowitz et al., 1991; L. M. Horowitz, Post, et al., 1981; L. M. Horowitz, Rosenberg, et al., 1988; L. M. Horowitz, Rosenberg, & Bartholomew, 1993; L. M. Horowitz, Rosenberg, & Kalehzan, 1992; L. M. Horowitz, Rosenberg, Ureno, Kalehzan, & O'Halloran, 1989; L. M. Horowitz, Sampson, & Siegelman, 1978; L. M. Horowitz, Sampson, Siegelman, Weiss, & Goodfriend, 1988; L. M. Horowitz & Vitkus, 1986; L. M. Horowitz et al., 1983; Horowitz, Wright, et al., 1981) set out to investigate the relationships among three classes of complaints that bring patients into psychotherapy: symptoms, specific behavioral difficulties, and self-defeating thoughts. In the process, they examined complaints in the form of interpersonal problems (e.g., "I can't seem to make friends;" "I find it hard to say 'No' to my friends") gathered from samples of patients about to begin therapy. Observers viewed videotaped intake interviews and recorded each problem that began with the phrase "I find it hard to . . ." or with a synonym such as "I can't . . ."; as well as statements that began "I find it hard *not* to . . ." or with a synonym such as "I can't *stop* . . ." Nearly 200 problems were identified, and over three quarters were judged to be interpersonal in nature.

By various sorting and scaling procedures, three major problem dimensions were identified among the 200 problem statements: control, degree of psychological involvement, and nature of the involvement (friendly to hostile). A clustering procedure grouped the problems further into five thematic clusters concerning intimacy, aggression, compliance, independence, and socializing. A final analysis yielded a list of 127 problem statements scored under one of these five clusters. These 127 items represent the present version of the IIP (L. Horowitz, 1979, 1988; Horowitz, Rosenberg, et al., 1988; Horowitz et al., 1983). The circumplex version of the inventory (IIP-C; Alden et al., 1990) was reviewed in Chapter 1.

In filling out the IIP, each item is rated by a subject or patient on a 5-point scale ranging from "not at all" to "extremely." The inventory demonstrates acceptable test-retest reliability and convergent validity both with other interpersonal measures and with clinicians' ratings of patients' behaviors. The authors suggest that the IIP is a promising instrument that fills the need for a measure of distress due to interpersonal problems:

> Because interpersonal problems are among the most frequent complaints that patients bring to psychotherapy, this measure should help assess therapeutic gain. It may also help identify people who are particularly suitable for specific forms of treatment and allow us to examine the fate of different types of interpersonal problems during treatment. Finally, it may enable us to relate symptoms to particular types of interpersonal problems, thereby clarifying the role of interpersonal difficulties in psychopathology. (Horowitz, Rosenberg, et al., 1988, pp. 891–892)

The quality and nature of interpersonal relationships are viewed by many as indicators of psychopathology (e.g., Millon, 1981), a salient focus of therapeutic intervention (e.g., Klerman et al., 1984), and important predictors of therapeutic outcome (e.g., Piper, Azim, Joyce, McCallum, Nixon, & Segal, 1991). Comprehensive interpersonal assessment, thus, requires some form of inventory of interpersonal problems. As Alden et al. (1990) suggested, self-report interpersonal inventories ask an individual to describe his or her characteristic traits and do not specifically include statements of interpersonal problems; trait endorsements do not necessarily imply interpersonal problems. Study of interpersonal problems not only can provide an interpersonal translation of presenting complaints but also can illuminate the correspondence of patient presenting problems to clusters of overt interpersonal behaviors defined by the 16 segments of the interpersonal circle (e.g., Alden et al., 1990) and to various physical and mental disorders. The IIP shows considerable promise for serving these important functions as a standard component of an emerging battery of interpersonal measures.

A number of investigators have used the IIP and IIP-C *to map various interpersonal problems and psychiatric disturbances* (e.g., depression, social anxiety, personality disorder) *within circumplex space* (e.g., Alden & Phillips, 1990; Bartholomew & Horowitz, 1991; Gurtman, 1992a, 1992b; Pincus & Wiggins, 1990; Soldz et al., 1993; Wiggins et al., 1989). The inventory also has shown utility in *differentiating normal versus maladjusted individuals* (Sheffield et al., 1995; Youngren & Lewinsohn, 1980), in *predicting a positive working alliance and responsiveness to psychotherapy* (Alden & Capreol, 1993; L. M. Horowitz, Rosenberg, et al., 1988; L. M. Horowitz et al., 1992; L. M. Horowitz et al., 1989; Maling, Gurtman, & Howard, 1995; Muran, Samstag, Jilton, Batchelder, & Winston, 1992a, 1992b; Muran, Segal, Samstag, & Crawford, 1994; Piper et al., 1991), in *measuring change across the duration of treatment* (L. M. Horowitz, Rosenberg, et al., 1988; Maling et al., 1995), and in *discriminating patients with more versus less successful treatment outcome* (L. M. Horowitz, Rosenberg, et al., 1988; L. M. Horowitz et al., 1978; Mohr et al., 1990).

THE INTERACTION RECORD AND FUNCTIONAL ANALYSIS OF INTERPERSONAL BEHAVIOR

Peterson and colleagues have developed and applied several sequential analysis methods that are relevant to clinicians and researchers alike (Boals, Peterson, Farmer, Mann, & Robinson, 1982; Peterson, 1977, 1979a, 1979b, 1979c, 1982, 1989). A central method that Peterson and colleagues employ is the Interaction Record (IR: Peterson, 1979a,

1979b) and its accompanying manual (Peterson, 1979c), which has been applied primarily in studies of marital therapy. Peterson argues that the flow of actions and reactions that occurs as spouses meet, deal with one another, and then part must first be described at a very specific and concrete level. This is accomplished through administration of the IR to the couples. Only subsequently should the therapist attempt to understand this flow in terms of deeper relationship meanings.

On separate IR forms, both spouses describe the most important interaction they had on a given day. In their own words, and from their respective viewpoints, each independently describes in specific detail the conditions under which the exchange took place, how the interaction started, and what happened then. The third point is especially crucial in that the spouse is asked to write a fairly detailed account of the exchange from start to finish, including: Who did and said what to whom? What were you thinking and feeling as the action went on? What ideas and emotions did your partner seem to have? How did it all come out?

In interpreting interaction records, Peterson (1982) first identifies the major acts or moves that each person has made in the course of the exchange; then an interpersonal meaning or message is inferred for each act. Each message contains three kinds of meaning: a report of the emotion the person is feeling at the time, a report of the way the person construes the situation, and an expectation about the response of the other. Peterson reports that, despite the rather high level of inference required for these interpretations, clinicians agree fairly closely about them. He finds interesting differences between normal and disturbed couples regarding the kinds of affect, construal, and expectation they report with this procedure.

Peterson (1982) also advocated use of videotaped samples of "analogue interactions" between spouses for which they are directed to discuss conflicts, to plan vacations, and so on. Descriptions of recurrent interaction patterns can be derived from these videotapes by clinicians or other observers, who can then infer the causal governing regularities in interpersonal behavior between marriage partners or other dyads. Peterson uses the phrase, "functional analysis of interpersonal behavior" to designate this "cyclical process of describing interaction patterns, formulating ideas about the conditions that maintain the patterns, testing the propositions by planned interventions, and describing the interaction patterns that follow" to determine whether changes have or have not occurred. Changes "in predicted directions confirm hypotheses about the causes of the disorder. Persistence of the problem tends to disconfirm the hypothesis and requires conceptual reformulation" (Peterson, 1982, p. 164).

Peterson's modifications of behavioral procedures for study of interpersonal disorders have much to offer interpersonal assessment, especially in regard to discovery of specific components of Maladaptive Transaction Cycles prototypical of distinct individual, marital, and family psychiatric disturbances.

THE PROCESS OF INTERPERSONAL ASSESSMENT AND DIAGNOSIS

This section is adapted from an earlier presentation by Van Denburg et al. (1992). In the assessment of clients' interpersonal functioning, the first decision to be made concerns what components of their interpersonal functioning are to be targeted. If the assessment is to be relatively comprehensive, all four basic components of interpersonal behavior depicted in the Maladaptive Transaction Cycle should be targeted. Analysis of any one of these elements in isolation provides valuable information, but examination as complete covert-overt transactional sequences produces a synergistic body of information (Van Denburg et al., 1992). In addition to gaining information regarding these four basic elements of transaction cycles, it is also essential to obtain information from multiple sources or perspectives on each of the components, for example, measuring clients overt interpersonal behavior based on self-report and therapist characterizations.

During the initial assessment phase of therapy, it is suggested that information regarding the client's interpersonal functioning be collected from two readily available sources: the client and therapist. Self-assessments made by the client would ideally include evaluations of overt interpersonal behavior and perceived impact on others. These variables could be measured through self-report versions of the CLOIT, IAS-R, or IMI, respectively.

One of the precepts of the interpersonal model is that clients' behavior and experience with the therapist will resemble in many ways their behavior and experience with others. With that in mind, Van Denburg et al. (1992) recommended that the therapist characterize the client's overt interpersonal behavior as well as the therapist's covert reactions to that behavior. Therapist ratings of the client with the CLOIT: Transactant Version can be used to assess the former, whereas the IMI can be used to assess the latter. Assessment of the MTC can then be completed by having the client assess the overt interpersonal behavior of the therapist, as well as the covert impacts experienced when he/she interacts with the therapist. Client ratings of the therapist on the CLOIT: Transactant Version and the IMI can be used to measure these respective variables.

Van Denburg et al. (1992) recommended that a minimal interpersonal battery would include the Inventory of Interpersonal Problems, scored using Standard (IIP) and Circumplex (IIP-C) scales. This provides information regarding the type of interpersonal problems the client is experiencing, the level of discomfort associated with the problems, and a translation of the problems onto the interpersonal circle (IIP-C). Interpersonal problems identified by the IIP and IIP-C can be most meaningfully interpreted in light of the joint client-counselor mapping of the in-session transaction cycle described earlier. Together, ratings of these components of the transaction cycle and a summary of the types of interpersonal problems experienced can provide information regarding the client's baseline interpersonal functioning (Van Denburg et al., 1992).

Understanding of the client's interpersonal behavior can be further enhanced through assessment of the client from additional perspectives. For example, significant others can complete an IMI and CLOIT with the client serving as the targeted individual. There are two other alternative applications of the IMI and CLOIT that therapists may also wish to consider. To better understand the disjunctive-conjunctive nature of clients' relationships, clients can complete IMIs and CLOITs about specific problematic or satisfying relationships. To evaluate best-case (good me-you patterns; good self and object representations) and worst-case (bad me-you patterns; bad self and object representations) transactional patterns, clients can complete CLOITs and IMIs according to (a) dreaded, least preferred, worst, most repulsive transaction cycle; and (b) desired, most preferred, best, ideal transaction cycle. These are but a few of the many variations to which these tools can be applied in treatment (Van Denburg et al., 1992).

An interpersonal approach to psychotherapy assumes that a patient's central problems in living reside in maladaptive transaction cycles with significant others, including the therapist. The therapist's overriding diagnostic task is to identify the specific components of the self-defeating maladaptive pattern. The therapist's major interventive task is to disrupt the identified transaction cycle by various interpersonal moves that refuse to reinforce, that insist on exposing, and that push to alter the patient's self-defeating pattern both within and outside the therapy sessions.

Empirical Research on Psychological Assessment

Gonick (1987) studied the effects of interpersonal complementarity and clinician characteristics on clinical judgments of diagnostic severity and prognosis. A sample of clinicians viewed videotaped simulations of a psychotherapy intake interview; half the clinicians viewed a client whose interpersonal style was hostile-submissive, while the other half viewed a friendly-submissive client. After viewing the videotaped session, clinicians made clinical judgments concerning the diagnostic severity and prognosis of the client. Findings were several. First, for the entire sample, clinicians who liked the client more, who were less experienced, and who had a nonpsychodynamic orientation made less severe diagnostic, and more optimistic prognostic, judgments. Second, for the hostile-submissive client, male clinicians made more optimistic prognostic judgments than did female clinicians. Third, for clinicians who viewed the friendly-submissive client, female clinicians whose interpersonal (CLOIT/CLOPT) behavior toward the simulated client was more complementary made less severe diagnostic judgments. Four, nonpsychodynamic clinicians whose interpersonal behavior toward the client was more complementary made more optimistic prognostic judgments. Gonick (1987) concluded that although interpersonal complementarity was not found to be as strongly associated with clinical judgments of severity of diagnosis and prognosis as predicted, "The interaction of clinician sex $\times$ client interpersonal presentation $\times$ diagnostic severity does offer indirect support for the complementarity hypothesis" (p. 63).

ISSUES IN INTERPERSONAL DIAGNOSIS

It's important to realize that basic understanding of both interpersonal diagnosis and intervention requires use of *two* conceptual models: the interpersonal circle, and the Maladaptive Transaction Cycle. The interpersonal circle specifies the range of individual differences in normal and abnormal interpersonal behavior. Through use of the inventories described in Chapter 1, one can assess a patient's interpersonal behavior and precisely locate that behavior on the surface of the interpersonal circle. This placement, in turn, permits both exact specification of the patient's maladaptive pattern of living as well as precise prediction of various components of the optimal treatment program for the patient (Kiesler, 1983, 1988; see also Chapters 10 and 11). The second model, the Maladaptive Transaction Cycle, provides a framework for depicting the specific transactional pattern present in any patient's self-defeating interpersonal relationships. It also pinpoints covert (cognitive, emotional, etc.) and overt behavioral components that need to be targeted for intervention to disrupt the patient's pattern of maladaptive transactions.

Covert Interpersonal Assessment

What the Maladaptive Transaction Cycle makes abundantly evident is that comprehensive assessment of mental disorders will require, in addition to present interpersonal circle inventories that target overt behavior, additional inventories or measures that target patients' *covert* behaviors and experiences (Kiesler, 1983, 1986a, 1986b; Widiger, Frances, & Trull, 1987). Ideally, models of covert events will be developed that permit predictions of one-to-one correspondence with the categories of overt behavior depicted on the interpersonal circle. As we saw earlier in Chapter 3, this bridging work has occurred primarily in the area of emotion and with the IMI.

Empirical studies of the traditional cognitive realm are necessary to determine whether similar circular models can be found for construal, perceptual, expectational, and other cognitive events that provide covariate matches to the categories of overt behavior anchored on the circumference of the interpersonal circle.

Situational and Temporal Assessment

Also, if interpersonal diagnosis is to contribute to full understanding of mental disorders, its assessment must systematically incorporate the important situational and temporal factors relevant to expression of each disorder's prototypical maladaptive interpersonal pattern, including both central and peripheral components (see Chapter 3). An important move in this direction is the "act-frequency approach" of D. M. Buss (1985a, 1985b) and D. M. Buss and Craik (1980, 1981, 1983a, 1983b, 1983c, 1984, 1986a, 1986b, 1987; D. M. Buss et al., 1987), which provides an alternative to trait theory by conceptualizing patterns of interpersonal behavior as cognitive categories of acts that summarize general trends in behavior. Their prototypical (act-in-context) interpersonal descriptors anchor interpersonal assessment simultaneously in both overt behaviors and situations.

Also, interpersonal behavior and diagnosis need to be viewed from the perspective of relationship development. As we have seen, Duke and Nowicki (1982) proposed that relationships progress through four phases: choice, beginning, deepening, and termination. From their perspective, negotiation of relationship definition is not as essential during the earliest stages of a relationship, but becomes more important as the interaction continues.

Assessment of Nonverbal Behavior

As discussed earlier in the chapter, I (Kiesler, 1983) emphasized that "basic aspects of nonverbal communication need to be integrated both with the interpersonal circle and with interpersonal theory more generally" (p. 211). The next chapter includes a review of studies of nonverbal behavior and also will discuss in some detail my interpersonal communications formulation of nonverbal behavior.

Assessment of Significant Others

Duke and Nowicki's (1982) analysis and supportive research indicating that relationship definition becomes more important as an interaction continues was reviewed in detail in Chapter 2. This research supports the conclusion, emphasized by Kiesler (Kiesler,

Bernstein, & Anchin, 1976, p. 35), that significant others are crucial to the task of interpersonal diagnosis—that assessment of patients' maladaptive behavior must include transactant ratings by persons currently significant in each patient's life. Use of the Significant Other Inventory (SOI-R; Larus-McShane et al., 1990) and the Significant Other Inventory for Adolescents (SOI-R:A; Larus-McShane et al., 1993), which were reviewed in detail in Chapter 3, may provide one initial methodology for identification of these important interactants.

CHAPTER 8

A Vocabulary for Interpersonal Interventions
Interpersonal Communication, Nonverbal Behavior, and the Meaning Frames

> *The psychiatric interview is primarily a matter of vocal communication, and it would be a quite serious error to presume that the communication is primarily verbal. The sound accompaniments suggest what is to be made of the verbal propositions stated.*
>
> *(Sullivan, 1954, p. 7)*

Communication is defined differently depending on the empirical and theoretical perspective of a particular scientist. Generally, it is defined as the process of transmitting stimuli, conveying meaning, the signals that individuals send to each other, and so on.

INTERPERSONAL COMMUNICATION

For our purposes, *communication* refers to *the process of transmitting information (messages) from sender (encoder) to receiver (decoder), and the decoder's reciprocal response* (Kiesler, 1973–1975, 1979; Kiesler, Bernstein, & Anchin, 1976). Communication is a social event or interpersonal, in that when two or more persons are in perceptual contiguity they are constantly communicating; regardless what they do or don't do, they continuously send messages to each other. In communicating, the encoder produces stimuli that evoke cognitive or affective responses in the decoder. One loop of communication is completed when a response of an encoder is received or registered as a stimulus for the decoder. Hence, the "encoder" is the originator of the cognitive and/or affective message; the "decoder" is the active recipient of that message. A "message" is any encoder's response that functions as a stimulus for the decoder. Messages are sent by the encoder not only through words on the linguistic channel but also by simultaneous behaviors along the nonverbal channels. "Meaning" is transmitted when the encoder's communicative stimulus evokes cognitive and/or affective responses from the decoder.

It is crucial to keep a few points in mind about the words *encoder* and *decoder*. First, for conceptual purposes, it is often necessary to slice artificially the ongoing and reciprocal live process of interpersonal dyadic communication, to base analysis in a "stop-action" freeze of the communication process, which makes it possible to refer arbitrarily to one participant as encoder or sender and the other as decoder or receiver. In any live dyadic interaction, however, both participants simultaneously encode messages to and decode messages from the other, no matter who may be encoding at a given moment on the linguistic channel. Second, in the next three chapters, which concentrate on the relationship and psychotherapeutic intervention, in our "stop-action" slice of the therapy dyad, the encoder will refer to the client, the decoder to the therapist.

The messages, cues, or response-produced stimuli that an encoder generates during communication are not only linguistic (words and sentences on the speech channel) but include important nonverbal channels or response modalities as well. The nonverbal channels include paralanguage (tempo of talk, volume, pitch, pitch change, etc.); kinesics (gaze, facial expressions, limb movements, posture); proxemics or interpersonal distance; touch; odor; body display; and also stylistic individual differences on the linguistic channel. Figure 8–1 presents a visual summary of the communication process.

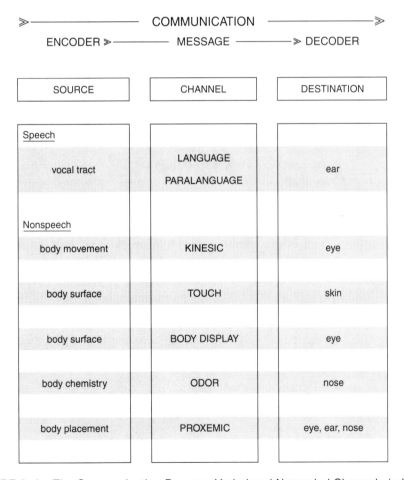

FIGURE 8–1. The Communication Process: Verbal and Nonverbal Channels (adapted from Markel, 1969, and from Scheflen, 1967).

Barnlund (1970) offered a list of defining characteristics of interpersonal communication: (a) two or more individuals are present in physical proximity; (b) some sort of perceptual engagement occurs; (c) reciprocity is present in that each interactant provides cues that are direct consequents of the cues supplied by the other—the behavior of each depends on that of the other; (d) a focused interaction occurs through an exchange of messages or meanings; (e) the most common context is vis-à-vis, in which all sense modalities can be utilized; and (f) the interpersonal setting most frequently is unstructured or spontaneous.

PRINCIPLES OF INTERPERSONAL COMMUNICATION

In an earlier monograph (Kiesler, Bernstein, & Anchin, 1976), I presented basic assumptions of my interpersonal communication approach, which are summarized briefly here.

Proposition 8–1.   Interpersonal communication represents the pervasive human condition.

Whenever another person is physically present and/or some form of perceptual engagement occurs, interpersonal communication is the dominant human behavioral event. In an interpersonal situation, all human actions or inactions have message value. This assumption is modified from Watzlawick et al. (1967), who state, "All behavior, not only speech, is communication and all communication—even the communicational cues inherent in an impersonal context—affects behavior" (p. 22).

Proposition 8–2.   Whereas a person may or may not act in an interpersonal situation, no matter how the person may try, he or she cannot *not* communicate.

Activity or inactivity, words or silence, all have message value. The messages influence other persons and these others, in turn, cannot not respond to these communications and are, thus, themselves communicating (Watzlawick et al., 1967, pp. 48–49).

Proposition 8–3.   The construct of interpersonal communication provides a maximally comprehensive and veridical base for assessment of human interpersonal behavior.

This is the case because the term, communication, incorporates patterned multichannel verbal and nonverbal behaviors.

Proposition 8–4.   Human communication not only conveys information but it simultaneously defines the relationship between the interpersonal interactants.

Any communication has meaning on two different levels. The representational level refers to the manifest symbolic content of communication, linguistic messages that are decoded by use of rules of semantics and syntaxics. The presentational level refers to the process by which an encoder imposes a condition of engagement on the decoder to respond as the encoder would like, in a manner that is confirmatory of the encoder self-definition. At this level, decoding targets the internal emotion or attitudinal states of either the decoder or encoder in respect to the other participant. This assumption represents a modification of Watzlawick et al.'s (1967) specification of the content and relationship levels of communication, which they termed the "report" and "command" levels of any communication.

> *Proposition 8–5.*   Any communication contains at least two aspects of relationship connotation that contribute to definition of a particular interpersonal dyad: (a) The encoder-encoder (EE) aspect is the part of the encoder's communication that connotatively defines the encoder him- or herself; the encoder-decoder (ED) component connotatively defines the encoder's feelings about, evaluation of, and wants from the decoder.

EE communication occurs primarily through the encoder's nonverbal messages that express feelings about, evaluation of, or construals of self. ED communication also occurs primarily along nonverbal channels, with messages that impose or command behavior and reactions from the decoder. The ED message, identical to what Beier (1966) described as the "evoking message," imposes a condition of emotional engagement on decoders, as a result of which decoders countercommunicate as an encoder wishes without being aware of their compliance. Encoders also are mostly unaware that they imposed a condition or sent a command message and, consequently, obtain responses from decoders for which they cannot account, even though they elicited them. Beier (1966) contrasted the evoking message to the persuasive message, which is identical except that in the latter the encoder *is aware* of what he or she wants from, or is imposing on, the decoder.

Beier (1966) asserted:

> The evoking message is probably one of the basic tools used by individuals to maintain their consistency of personality. With this message an individual can elicit responses without being aware that he is responsible for doing so. To a certain extent he can create his environment without feeling that he is accountable for the responses which come his way. . . . The person with emotional conflicts . . . creates a world in which he typically feels victimized by others, in which he experiences great unhappiness, though he has little awareness that he is often the creator of this world. (p. 13)

Beier's (1966) evoking message is related closely to Sullivan's (1953b) theorem of reciprocal emotion and to Leary's (1957) interpersonal reflex.

In contrast to the ED-evoking message, the EE (encoder to encoder) message primarily involves nonverbal expression of the encoder's self-concept, as emphasized earlier by Secord and Backman (1965). They assert that an individual actively employs overt and covert behavioral processes to maintain congruency among three components of his or her personality: (a) some aspect of his or her self-concept, (b) his or her perception or interpretation of his or her own behavior relevant to that aspect, and (c) his or her perceptions or beliefs about how other people behave and feel toward him or her with regard to that aspect of self. Secord and Backman's (1965) central postulate is that a "state of congruency exists when behavior of [self and others] imply definitions of self congruent with relevant aspects of [the person's] self-concept" (p. 529).

Proposition 8–6.   ED-evoking messages, which are contributed to by concurrent EE meanings, express relationship-to-interactant messages falling in two-factor space: the dimensions of control and affiliation.

This assumption brings together Beier's (1966) evoking message and the theory and research of interpersonal behavior. It defines the content domain of evoking messages as identical to that of the two-factor space represented by the interpersonal circle.

Proposition 8–7.   Presentational relationship messages (EE and ED-evoking messages) can be communicated directly on the linguistic channel, but much more frequently are transmitted on nonverbal channels and through syntactic stylistics on the speech channel.

This assumption will be elaborated in detail in Chapter 9, in discussion of the concept of relationship in psychotherapy.

Proposition 8–8.   An encoder's ED-evoking message elicits emotional and other engagements from the decoder that are termed DE-impact messages; the DE-impact message defines the momentary relationship command automatically sent by the encoder's evoking message, defining the decoder-to-encoder meaning of that moment.

The DE-impact message registered by the decoder interacts with the decoder's own self-concept and self-presentations (DD) simultaneously engaged to contribute to the decoder's reactions to the encoder.

Beier's (1966) definition of the evoking message includes both the ED and DE components. My conceptualization distinguishes between the two components, referring to them respectively as the evoking and impact messages. Hence, the evoking message refers only to that which the encoder sends as a relationship command to an interactant; the impact message refers only to that which the decoder receives or registers, to the elicited emotional and other engagement.

In addition to the DE-impact message, an encoder's ED-evoking message also elicits emotional and other aspects of the decoder's own self-evaluation; command messages typically have some implications for the decoder's own self-concept and self-presentation. The DD (decoder to decoder) aspects of the message refer to these simultaneously elicited meanings.

Proposition 8–9.   DE-impact messages, which are contributed to by the DD meaning components and which mediate the decoder's subsequent overt reaction, reflect relationship-to-encoder meanings falling in the identical two-factor space (control and affiliation) hypothesized for the ED-evoking message.

The Impact Message Inventory was designed to assess the momentary, dyadic emotional, cognitive, and behavioral engagements falling in this two-factor space that a given interactant registers from his or her dyadic partner.

Proposition 8–10.   An encoder's pattern of relationship communication (ED-evoking messages) at a given moment in time is the joint interactive consequence of (a) his or her history of previous interpersonal communications, (b) his or her cumulative prior interactions with the present interactant, (c) on his or her perceptions/construals of the interactant's characteristics, and (d) on impersonal contextual (situational) factors.

What this proposition advocates is an interactionist position (Endler & Magnusson, 1976) in regard to the influence of person and situation factors.

Proposition 8–11.   The most salient class of situational determinants for interpersonal communication is that of significant persons in an encoder's life, those persons the encoder construes as providing, or potentially providing, prepotent emotional satisfactions or positive reinforcements.

The most probable subclasses of significant other persons include members of the encoder's family of origin (parents, siblings), close friends of both sexes, and some work associates.

NONVERBAL BEHAVIOR

The power of a communications model increases dramatically when nonverbal channels are added to the linguistic channel (see Figure 8–1). The crucial implication for interpersonal behavior and psychotherapy is that the nonverbal channels seem directly and intimately related to transmission of emotional and relationship meanings. The burgeoning science of nonverbal communication (Knapp & Hall, 1992) also permits therapists to develop the assessments that can operationally anchor key concepts within the elusive domains of interpersonal relationship and psychotherapy.

Ekman and Friesen (1968) outlined what have come to be accepted as major assumptions of the science of nonverbal communication, as follows:

> (1) Nonverbal language can be considered a relationship language, sensitive to, and the primary means of signaling, changes in the quality of an ongoing relationship. . . . (2) It is the primary means of expressing or communicating emotion. . . . (3) Nonverbal behavior has special symbolic value, expressing in body language basic, perhaps unconscious, attitudes about the self or body image. . . . (4) It serves the metacommunicative function of providing qualifiers as to how verbal discourse should be interpreted. . . . (5) Nonverbal behavior is less affected than verbal behavior by attempts to censure communication. (pp. 180–181)

In summary, *the nonverbal system is the primary system for communicating emotional, relationship messages, including expressions of the encoder's attitudes about self and others—all of this being quite difficult for the encoder to distort or censor compared with his or her messages on the linguistic channel.*

Verbal and nonverbal messages normally complement each other, neither appearing sufficient in and of itself for adequate and complete communication. One system can accentuate, emphasize, qualify the other. Importantly, however, one system can be inconsistent with or contradict the other. A clenched fist can accentuate the linguistic message "Back off!" but it can negate the digital message, "Of course, I love my wife." Hence, the factor of congruency-incongruency of linguistic and nonverbal systems becomes a central concern within a communication model.

Mehrabian (1971, 1972) earlier surveyed factor analytic studies of nonverbal behavior measures and concluded that three dimensions summarize the domain. His first factor was a dimension (evaluation) by which the encoder communicates nonverbally his or her like-dislike for the decoder; the second factor (potency) differentiated dominant-controlling versus submissive-dependent attitudes of the encoder toward the decoder; the third (responsiveness) tapped the extent of the encoder's awareness of, and reaction to, the decoder—the extent to which the encoder finds the decoder important or salient. The first two dimensions are identical to those found for interpersonal behavior as organized on the interpersonal circle.

In this regard, basic aspects of nonverbal communication need to be integrated with both the interpersonal circle and interpersonal theory more generally. At some point, the interpersonal acts defining the 1982 (and any subsequent) Interpersonal Circle need to include the corresponding control (e.g., greater asymmetrical posture, visual dominance pattern, more frequent initiation of touch) and affiliation (e.g., more direct body orientation, reciprocal gaze and touch, closer interpersonal distance) nonverbal behaviors. Good preliminary sources for leads toward specification of these behaviors are Hall, Harrigan, and Rosenthal (1995); Harper, Wiens, and Matarazzo (1978); Henley (1977); Knapp and Hall (1992); LaFrance and Mayo (1978); Mehrabian (1971, 1972); Siegman and Feldstein (1978); and Waxer (1978).

In attempting to understand psychotherapy, therapists and researchers cannot ignore the nonverbal behavior of either therapist or client. Exclusive focus on the linguistic messages between client and therapist can result only in the observer missing most of the action. Restricted study of only one of the multiple channels of communication can produce only incomplete, misleading, inconclusive, or invalid results. Investigators need to move beyond transcripts (beyond content analysis), beyond audiotape recordings (linguistics and paralanguage), to either live observation or audio-video recordings of psychotherapy sessions. Only video representations can capture the important visual channels including kinesic, proxemic, and touch behaviors. And it is precisely these visual channel messages that nonverbal research points to as crucial for communication of emotional and relationship messages.

THE MEANING FRAMES

We can now add one more proposition:

> *Proposition 8–12.* The assessment task of a therapeutic decoder, that is of the therapist, is to decode the multiple messages and register the multiple levels of meaning being communicated by a client-encoder.

This means first that the therapist continually decodes both linguistic and nonverbal messages within client communications and analyzes them in terms of their report and command meanings. The therapist analyzes the client's messages according to the levels of meaning detailed in the earlier propositions.

Figures 8–2, 8–3, 8–4, and 8–5 outline a model of what I have referred to as "meaning frames" (Kiesler, 1982a). The more precise working terminology contained in Figure 8–2 represents the dyadic referential options the therapist has in responding to the explicit or implicit, content or relationship, meanings of clients's statements. As I use

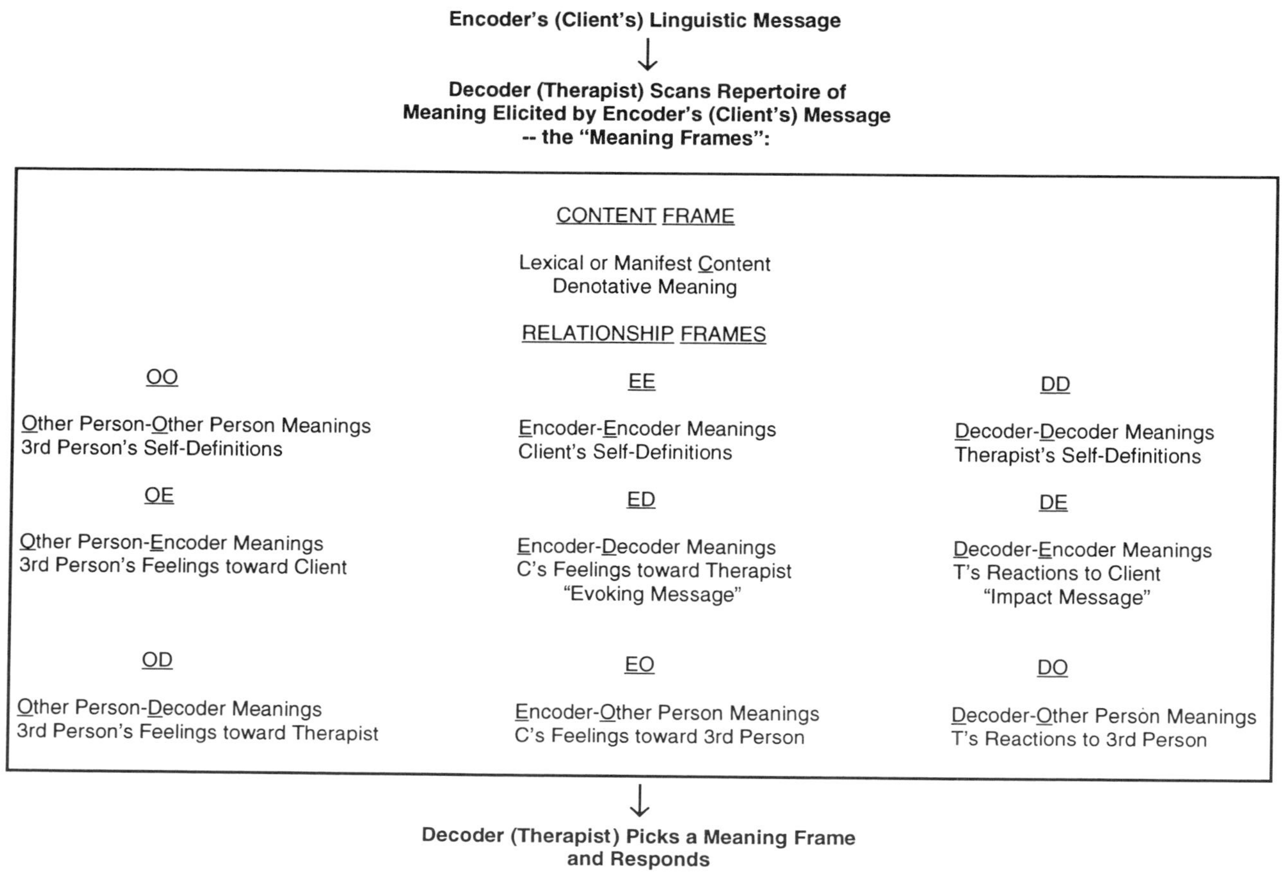

Encoder's (Client's) Linguistic Message

↓

**Decoder (Therapist) Scans Repertoire of
Meaning Elicited by Encoder's (Client's) Message
-- the "Meaning Frames":**

<u>CONTENT FRAME</u>

Lexical or Manifest Content
Denotative Meaning

<u>RELATIONSHIP FRAMES</u>

<u>EE</u>

Encoder-Encoder Meanings
Client's Self-Definitions

<u>ED</u>

Encoder-Decoder Meanings
C's Feelings toward Therapist
"Evoking Message"

<u>EO</u>

Encoder-Other Person Meanings
C's Feelings toward 3rd Person

<u>DD</u>

Decoder-Decoder Meanings
Therapist's Self-Definitions

<u>DE</u>

Decoder-Encoder Meanings
T's Reactions to Client
"Impact Message"

<u>DO</u>

Decoder-Other Person Meanings
T's Reactions to 3rd Person

<u>OO</u>

Other Person-Other Person Meanings
3rd Person's Self-Definitions

<u>OE</u>

Other Person-Encoder Meanings
3rd Person's Feelings toward Client

<u>OD</u>

Other Person-Decoder Meanings
3rd Person's Feelings toward Therapist

**Decoder (Therapist) Picks a Meaning Frame
and Responds**

↓

FIGURE 8-2. The Meaning Frames: A Model of Content and Relationship Meanings Implicit in a Particular En-coder (in Therapy, the Client) Response.

211

Client's (E's) Linguistic Message
What good is talking going to do?

→

Therapist (D) Scans Meaning Frames:

CONTENT FRAME

We're so close to our feelings, sometimes the more we think about them, the more confused we get. Someone who is more objective and trained to listen can be quite helpful.

RELATIONSHIP FRAMES

OO	EE	DD
Your mother seems to feel strongly that talking is a waste of time.	You feel you should be able to lick this problem by yourself somehow.	I wondered that myself when I first started seeing clients.

OE	ED	DE
Has anyone told you that talking won't help?	You're doubtful that I'll be able to help you?	I felt a tug -- like you want me to take responsibility for giving you the answers.

OD	EO	DO
Your mother seems convinced that whatever I have to say is pretty much useless.	You've tried talking to others and it hasn't helped.	I just had an image -- playing tug-of-war with your mother with the winner getting your soul.

Therapist Picks a Response

→

"You're doubtful that I'll be able to help you."

FIGURE 8–3. The Meaning Frames: Example 1.

Client's (E's) Linguistic Message

This guy I went to town with the other day told me I was no good to nobody... I just want to run away and die.

→

Therapist (D) Scans Meaning Frames:

CONTENT FRAME

Where would you go?

RELATIONSHIP FRAMES:

EE

Here's someone who meant something to you. "If he feels I'm no good to him, then that just proves I'm no good to anyone."

ED

Perhaps part of that applies to me.... Do I think you're worth anything?

EO

What did you say to him when he told you that?

DD

There was a time when I felt that way about myself.

DE

I would be quite sad if you killed yourself.

DO

I just had an image -- playing tug-of-war with your friend to win your affection.

OO

Perhaps he was feeling worthless himself when he said that to you.

OE

Do you think he really meant what he said about you?

OD

Do you think your friend resents me for being your therapist-friend?

→

Therapist Picks a Response

"I would be quite sad if you killed yourself"

FIGURE 8–4. The Meaning Frames: Example 2.

213

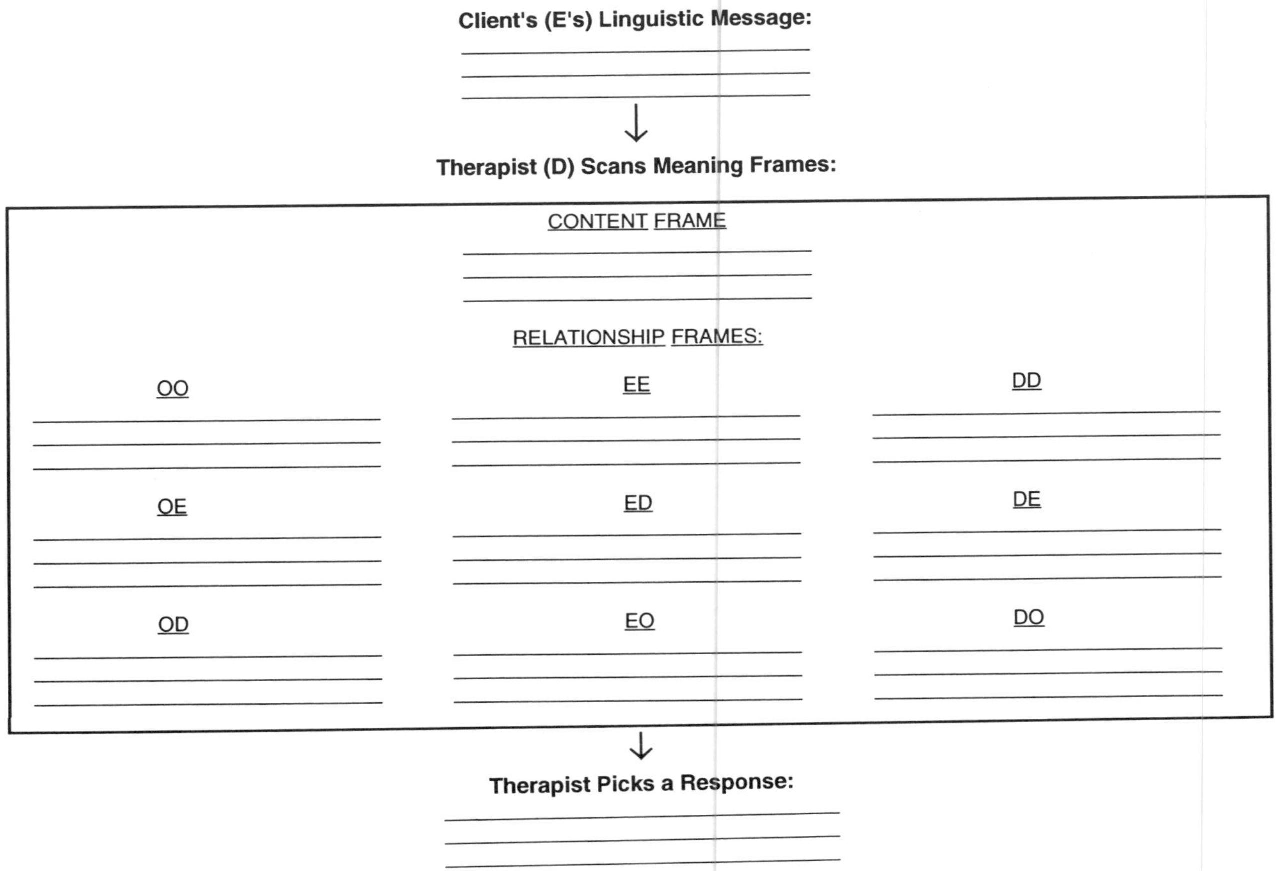

Client's (E's) Linguistic Message:

_____

→

Therapist (D) Scans Meaning Frames:

_____

CONTENT FRAME

_____

RELATIONSHIP FRAMES:

OO	EE	DD
___	___	___
QE	ED	DE
___	___	___
OD	EO	DO
___	___	___

Therapist Picks a Response:

_____

→

FIGURE 8–5. The Meaning Frames: Therapist Worksheet.

214

these terms in the therapy context, E (encoder or sender of the message) is the client, D (decoder or receiver of the message) is the therapist, and O (3rd person or person other than client or therapist) is some significant other in the client's life.

I used the capital letters "E" and "D" earlier in this chapter where we saw that any client statement or nonverbal behavior has both content and relationship meaning—any comment has both report and command, representational and presentational levels of meaning. Further, the relationship (command, presentational) level includes two separate components: the in vivo therapy relationship encompasses the client and the therapist; the *extended* therapy relationship contains the client, therapist, and other significant persons in the client's life (at any given moment of discourse, one significant other, SO, in the client's life). All content and relationship meanings are communicated not only by the statements the client makes, but especially by the distinctive pattern of nonverbal behavior that accompanies his or her words.

As can be seen in Figure 8–2, nine distinct possibilities of relationship meaning (nine distinct relationship meaning frames) are possible.

1. The *encoder-to-encoder (client-to-client)* aspect defines the encoder-client himself or herself; expresses feelings about, evaluations of, and attitudes toward him- or herself; constitutes the client's general self-presentation to others. In Figures 8–2 through 8–5, this aspect is designated *EE*.

2. The *encoder-to-decoder (client-to-therapist)* component expresses the encoder-client's feelings about, evaluations of, and attitudes toward the decoder-therapist; constitutes the client's self-presentation to the therapist. I call this half of the relationship the encoder-to-decoder message, which is very similar to Beier's (1966) "evoking message." In Figures 8–2 through 8–5, this aspect is referred to as *ED,* or the "evoking message" by which the encoder-client imposes or commands behavior from the therapist decoder.

3. The *encoder-to-other (client-to-SO)* component expresses the encoder-client's feelings about, evaluations of, and attitudes toward a particular SO in the client's life. In the figures, this aspect is referred to as *EO,* or the "evoking message" by which he or she imposes or commands behavior from the particular SO.

As an in vivo participant in the dyad, the therapist-decoder records three corresponding aspects of relationship messages:

4. The *decoder-to-decoder (therapist-to-therapist)* meanings are the therapist's feelings about, evaluations of, and attitudes toward him- or herself, meanings relevant to his or her own self-definition. These *DD* meanings are triggered from time to time within the therapist as he or she reacts to, associates to, the client's disclosures and comments.

5. The second half of relationship consists of the *decoder-to-encoder (therapist-to-client)* meanings registered covertly by the decoder or therapist in response to the ED messages. I call these emotional, cognitive, behavioral tendencies, and imaginal internal responses of the decoder or therapist the *DE* "impact messages." These DE meanings represent pulls to enactment of the complementary response in reaction to the client's ED-evoking messages—in reaction to the client's rigid and extreme self-presentations.

6. The *decoder-to-other (therapist-to-SO)* meanings are the therapist's internal reactions or *DO*-impact messages that he or she experiences in reaction to a particular significant other being discussed or commented on by the client.

The final three relationship frames designate possible meanings of clients's statements that target particular significant others in their life whom they are discussing or
describing:

7. *Other-to-Other (SO-to-SO)* meanings refer to a particular SO's feelings about,
evaluations of, and attitudes toward him- or herself, meanings relevant to his or her
own self-definition. These meanings are stated or implied in the client's discussion of
that SO, and are coded *OO.*

8. *Other-to-encoder (SO-to-client)* aspects express the SO's feelings about, evaluations of, and attitudes toward the client. In the figures, this aspect is referred to as *OE,*
or the evoking message by which the SO imposes or commands behavior from the client.

9. *Other-to-decoder (SO-to-therapist)* meanings are those stated or implied *OD*
messages from the SO to the therapist, as reported in the client's discourse.

Following any utterance or action by the client during a session, the therapist has the
following options: (a) to respond directly to the manifest content *(C)* of what the client
has just said; (b) to respond to one of the nine relationship aspects *(EE, ED, EO, DD, DE,
DO, OO, OE, OD);* (c) to change topics *(T:* Transitional meanings; meanings unrelated to
what the client has just said); or (d) not to respond verbally at all *(S:* silence). Which
meaning frame a therapist targets in his or her specific response depends on his or her
best guess at the moment as to the salient meaning in the client's experience, as well as
on what is most "figure" for the therapist at the moment. The therapist's choices are influenced by the total pattern of the client's previous communications, by the therapist's
conceptualizations of the central issues permeating the client's problems, and particularly by the degree of congruence evident at that moment between the client's verbal and
nonverbal messages.

*Whenever therapists address either the ED-evoking or DE-impact frames, they di-
rectly address the therapeutic relationship* (through "metacommunicative" interventions that will be defined and discussed in Chapter 11). Subsequent chapters will focus
on definitions of relationship in psychotherapy (Chapter 9) and on psychotherapeutic
maneuvers by which the therapist confronts the client-therapist relationship as conceptualized in the client's Maladaptive Transaction Cycle (Chapters 10 and 11). To facilitate understanding of these aspects of interpersonal communication psychotherapy,
you may find it helpful to keep in mind, and refer back from time to time to, the distinct meaning frames depicted in Figures 8–2 through 8–5.

CHAPTER 9

The Relationship in Psychotherapy

An Interpersonal Communication Analysis

Ultimately we only come to truly know and experience ourselves through the eyes, the thoughts, and the touch of others.

(Villard & Whipple, 1976, p. 176)

I have documented elsewhere (Kiesler, 1992) that contemporary interpersonal theory and interpersonal circle methodology can serve as major sources of pantheoretical integration and elaboration of key concepts of psychotherapy theory and research. The essential link conjoins the central concept of relationship in psychotherapy and the interpersonal dimensions of control and affiliation, which emerge as two of the Big Five factors permeating personality measurement (Wiggins, in press; Wiggins & Pincus, 1992).

The relationship between patient and therapist underlies various key concepts of psychotherapy. *Every event or intervention that occurs within psychotherapy does so with some aspect of the relationship serving either as its direct mechanism or its immediate context.* Interpersonal communication therapy considers relationship to be inevitable and pervasive in all human interactions, including those in psychotherapy.

Not surprisingly, in psychotherapy theory, research, and practice, relationship has remained a controversial and elusive construct (Lambert, 1983). Each therapy model provides its own formulation of what the relationship is and why it is (or is not) important and effective.

INTERPERSONAL RELATIONSHIPS

Definitions of relationship within social psychology subsume the essential properties of interpersonal behavior as detailed in Chapter 1. For example, relationship exists when two people's behaviors, emotions, and thoughts are mutually and causally interconnected (are interdependent)—when ongoing chains of mutual influence exist between two people (Kelley et al., 1983). For these same authors, a "close relationship" exists to the extent that ongoing chains of mutual influence between two people endure and involve strong, frequent and diverse causal interconnections.

For Peterson (1982), an interpersonal relationship refers to "a developing process of interdependent functioning characterized by recurrent patterns of interaction, the rules governing those patterns of interaction, and the relatively enduring emotional, cognitive, and behavioral dispositions of the people involved toward the people involved in the relationship" (p. 150). *Interdependent functioning* means that the actions and reactions of each interactant affect the actions and reactions of the others; *rules* indicates that each interactant develops normative expectations about the rights and obligations of both participants; finally, to describe and understand a relationship requires that one identify the recurrent patterns of interaction that take place between the interactants.

RELATIONSHIP IN PSYCHOTHERAPY: AN INTERPERSONAL COMMUNICATION ANALYSIS

In an earlier article (Kiesler, 1979), I provided an analysis of relationship in psychotherapy based on my "communications theory of psychotherapy," which was summarized in Chapter 8. The present chapter will now apply the analysis of Chapter 8 to specific relationship phenomena in psychotherapy.

My analysis is highly congruent with Villard and Whipple's (1976) definition of relationship as "the negotiation process by which two people determine the focus and boundary rules of their relationship, and thereby define those identities, behaviors, and activities that are to be included and excluded from that relationship" (p. 126). My analysis of relationship is organized around a list of propositions that are summarized in this chapter.

Proposition 9–1.   The question is not, *Is* relationship important in psychotherapy? Rather, the question is, *How* is relationship important in psychotherapy and behavior change?

Overtly, we have the option of acting or not acting, behaving or not behaving, talking or remaining silent. But in an interpersonal, social, or dyadic context, we do *not* have the option of communicating or not communicating (Watzlawick et al., 1967). Activity or inactivity, words or silence, all have message value. The messages influence other persons, and these others, in turn, cannot not respond to these communications and are, thus, themselves communicating.

Another important point is that in human communication there are always *two levels* of messages. One level is the manifest content, the informational content of our words on the linguistic channel—the "report" or representational level. The second level is the relationship engagement, the self-presentational impact, that occurs primarily along the nonverbal channels—the "command" or presentational level. At this level, a person's pattern of verbal and nonverbal behavior elicits or pulls from an interactant emotional, cognitive, and imaginal responses that represent the person's attempt to define a relationship in a manner congruent with his or her self-image.

Hence, human behavior (communication) not only conveys information on the representational level, but simultaneously defines the relationship between interactants on the presentational level. Of necessity, the same dual behavior (communication) levels, content and relationship, occur in the psychotherapy situation.

Relationship is inevitable and pervasive in interpersonal interaction; all human behavior (communication) is continuously reciprocal in terms of relationship; relationship occurs primarily on the nonverbal channels; relationship involves a claim placed
on the interactant to accept a person (or client's) self-presentation.

Proposition 9–2.   Relationship is the momentary and cumulative result of the reciprocal messages, primarily nonverbal, exchanged between two interactants.

The first half of relationship consists of the linguistic and nonverbal messages sent
by an encoder to the decoder-interactant expressing the encoder's relationship claim
(the "command" message). This is the "encoder-to-decoder" (or "ED") message, which
is identical to Beier's (1966) "evoking message." With this command message, the encoder imposes a condition of emotional, cognitive, and imaginal engagement on the decoder, which pulls the decoder to respond or countercommunicate as the encoder wishes
(without either the encoder or decoder being clearly aware of the process).

Translated to psychotherapy, the client continually sends ED-evoking messages that
command the therapist by imposing a particular condition of engagement on the therapist. As a result of the client's ED messages, the therapist is "pulled" to respond or countercommunicate as the client wishes (without either the client or therapist being clearly
aware of the process).

The second half of relationship consists of decoder-to-encoder messages (DE) registered covertly by the decoder or therapist in response to the person or client's ED messages. These emotional, cognitive, and fantasy responses compose the "impact" message
described in detail in Chapter 5, which represents the receiving end of relationship communication. Most interactants ordinarily do not attend directly to the DE-impact responses elicited by a partner, but with training and experience, the therapist becomes
facile at attending to and identifying these highly automatic covert events.

Relationship is the result of the reciprocal evoking-impact messages, primarily nonverbal, exchanged between a particular encoder-decoder dyad, including the client-
therapist dyad. Decoders can reliably register or covertly detect the relationship
command messages being sent by a given encoder, including a client in psychotherapy.
Relationship is in the engagement or covert-pull of the beholder.

Proposition 9–3.   Relationship can be operationalized or reliably measured.

Relationship need not be either mystical or ephemeral. Assessment of relevant relationship behaviors is in the public arena and hence in the domain of science.

1. The most crucial place to search for relationship is in the nonverbal behavior of
   the interactants. Nonverbal communication is the language of emotion and relationship. Hence, the total available methodology of assessment for paralanguage,
   kinesics, proxemics, touch, gaze, and so on, is centrally relevant for assessment
   of relationship factors. Further, the research reviewed in Chapter 8 suggests that
   operationalized sets of nonverbal indices can be constructed for codings of the
   two central interpersonal dimensions, affiliation and status/control.
2. Given assessment of nonverbal channels, it is possible to tap another crucial
   index of relationship: the degree of congruency, consistency, or redundancy

present among messages on both verbal and nonverbal channels. For example, nonverbal positive affiliation contributes significantly to the efficacious effects of applied social reinforcements; congruence across communication channels (or the absence of inconsistent or contradictory leakage) represents a major determinant of the credibility of a particular instance of social reinforcement.

3. One can shift the focus of nonverbal assessment from the individual in a dyad to the sequentially interacting (act-react-act-react, etc.) dyad. The degree of affiliative relationship, for example, between two interactants can be measured by the degree, direction, and speed of "interactional synchrony" or "nonverbal tracking" occurring in their exchanges over time (Hall et al., 1995; Harper et al., 1978; Siegman & Feldstein, 1978). More generally, to be comprehensive, study of relationship needs to incorporate at some point sequential (stochastic) analysis of encoder-decoder or client-therapist exchanges.

4. A fourth place to target assessment of relationship is the DE-impact messages of the therapist. The Impact Message Inventory (see Chapter 5) was designed for that assessment.

5. A fifth place to look for indices of relationship is among stylistic factors on the linguistic channel (e.g., Kiesler et al., 1972). Individuals and clients differ significantly in the way in which they put words together into spoken sentences and sequences of sentences. These stylistic differences (e.g., frequent use of abstract words, long reaction silences, frequent qualifications and retractions, and the like) are important components of the person's ED-evoking style and elicit distinctive impact messages from interactants.

6. The final place to assess relationship is among the instances (less frequent than other communication behaviors) in which interactants, including client and therapist, state their feelings about each other to each other. It is obviously important to code these overt statements about relationship, and this has been the focus of the bulk of psychotherapy process research (Kiesler, 1973; L. S. Greenberg & Pinsof, 1986).

Thus, relationship can be operationalized or reliably measured. The central constructs are the ED-evoking and DE-impact message. The behavioral domains are the nonverbal channels, including congruency-incongruency and interactional synchrony, impact messages reported by interactants, coding of linguistic style, and codings of explicit relationship statements.

Proposition 9–4.   Persons interacting with each other are continually negotiating two major interpersonal or relationship issues: affiliation (love or hate, friendliness or hostility) and control (dominance or submission, high vs. low status).

When we are interacting with someone, our nonverbal behavior continually expresses messages as to how friendly and kind we want to be with him or her and how much in charge or in control we want to be.

If we describe behavior in terms of the interpersonal circle, the relationship behavior of a particular person peaks at one of 16 interpersonal segments, while also including aspects of behavior from segments immediately adjacent on the circle. Hence, the ED-evoking and DE-impact messages characteristic of a particular person can be described as a mixture of the two relationship issues as resolved in a specific cluster of several adjacent categories on the interpersonal circle.

In therapy, any client stakes claim to the relationship he or she wants with the therapist along the same two dimensions: how friendly and intimate the client wants to become and to what extent the client is willing to give up control to the therapist. The therapist, in turn, will register the client's predominant interpersonal pattern through the DE-impact messages he or she experiences during therapy sessions with the client.

In psychotherapy, to the extent that the therapist represents or becomes a significant person to the client, he or she will experience impact responses similar to those experienced by other persons in the client's life. The client's ED-evoking messages to the therapist are representative of the client's self-defeating style with other significant persons in his or her life. The therapist's emotional and other engagements, then, represent vital cues for targeting the self-defeating patterns of the client's particular problematic interpersonal behavior.

Summary

The question is not, *Is* relationship important in psychotherapy? Rather, the question is, *How* is relationship important in psychotherapy and behavior change? Relationship is inevitable and pervasive in human interactions and in psychotherapy. Relationship occurs through verbal and (especially) nonverbal messages by which a person invokes a claim on the interactant to accept the person's self-presentation.

Relationship is the momentary and cumulative result of the reciprocal ED-DE or evoking-impact messages exchanged between two interactants, including a client-therapist dyad. Decoders and therapists can reliably receive, register, or covertly detect the relationship or command messages being sent by a given person, including a client in psychotherapy.

Relationship can be operationalized or reliably measured. The constructs to be tapped are the ED-evoking message and the DE-impact message. Assessment focuses on the nonverbal channels, including the amount of congruency-incongruency and interactional synchrony of the messages sent; on the impact messages reportable by the interpersonal participants (measurable by the Impact Message Inventory); on codings of linguistic style, and on codings of explicit relationship statements. The relevant indices of relationship, thus, are in the public domain.

Persons interacting with each other are continually negotiating two major relationship issues: affiliation and control. The characteristic relationship pattern of a particular person peaks at one of 16 circle categories of interpersonal behavior and includes aspects of behavior immediately adjacent on the circle.

Events, therefore, referred to by Sullivan (1953a, 1953b) as *"parataxic distortions"* and by psychoanalysts as transference and countertransference—*redefined by interpersonal communication theory as reciprocal behaviors communicating ED-evoking and DE-impact messages—are integral and pervasive components of human interaction and of the therapeutic encounter.*

The underlying interpersonal communication constructs are derived from Sullivan's interpersonal psychiatry and its derivatives in interpersonal personality, and from communications psychiatry. When these relationship events are described (a) as pervasive aspects of all human interactions, (b) as not exclusive by-products of the psychotherapy transaction, and (c) as not restricted at all to derivatives of aggressive and sexual impulses, it's clear that metacommunication is being rooted much more closely in Sullivan's, rather than Freud's, tradition (Chrzanowski, 1973; Gill, 1983; Hoffman, 1983; Wachtel, 1977, 1982a).

DISTINCT RELATIONSHIP EVENTS IN PSYCHOTHERAPY

It has become increasingly evident that the relationship between client and therapist encompasses several classes of phenomena. The roles of at least three such constructs as (a) the *working alliance,* (b) the *transference-countertransference* (just redefined as ED-DE evoking-impact messages), and (c) the *real relationship* have been carefully elaborated by authors such as Greenson (1978), Bordin (1979), and Gelso and Carter (1985, 1994). In addition to specifying the three separate constructs, Gelso and Carter (1985) drew on the theoretical and research literature to offer 19 propositions about how these three relationship components interact with one another, how each operates across the course of psychotherapy, and how they affect the treatment in both brief and long-term therapies. Gelso and Carter (1994) extended their earlier presentation by offering additional relationship propositions.

The Working Alliance

In the search for effective ingredients common to all psychotherapies, researchers have identified the therapeutic (helping, working) alliance (Zetzel, 1956) as a central aspect of the patient-therapist relationship. A positive working alliance, measured in early sessions, has shown positive associations with posttherapy outcome in therapy dyads composed of a wide range of patient and therapist demographic characteristics as well as of therapeutic approaches (Bordin, 1985; Gelso & Carter, 1985; Hartley & Strupp, 1983; Horvath & Greenberg, 1994; Luborsky & Auerbach, 1985; Safran & Muran, 1995a).

Zetzel (1956) was the first to use the terms "working alliance" and "therapeutic alliance." He defined the underlying construct as that part of the analytic relationship that is stable, realistic, and cooperative. Greenson (1978) included in the alliance concept the *non*transferential and realistic aspects of the patient-analyst relationship. He emphasized the necessity for therapists to differentiate, as separate from the transference, patient perceptions of the therapist that are realistic. In its most general meaning, then, the therapeutic alliance refers to the realistic relationship that exists between patient and therapist apart from the maladaptive (transferential, parataxic) elements that patients bring into the sessions.

Bordin (1979) translated the psychoanalytic notion of the alliance into a transtheoretical conceptualization. He distinguished three components of the alliance: (a) mutual bonds of caring, liking, and trusting between patient and therapist; (b) their mutual agreement on the goals of treatment; and (c) their mutual understanding of the tasks necessary to accomplish the therapeutic goals. Bordin (1985) further emphasized that different kinds of therapy require different alliances because some goals require a greater depth of relationship.

Interpersonal complementarity (reviewed in detail in Chapter 4) addresses a component of the patient-therapist relationship—distinct from the therapeutic alliance—that consists of the degree of fit of the interpersonal transactions between client and therapist (the degree of reciprocity between the ED-evoking and DE-impact messages and reactions). As we just saw, the therapeutic alliance refers to a central component of the conscious and realistic relationship between therapist and client. In contrast, interpersonal complementarity articulates the automatic, relatively unaware, and distorted therapy relationship resulting primarily, but not exclusively, from the patient's rigid and extreme parataxic distortions (Sullivan, 1953a, 1953b) or transferences.

Based on these complementarity notions, I (Kiesler, 1983, 1986a, 1988) offered interpersonal propositions operative within the individual psychotherapy context. In the earliest stage of therapy, the therapist becomes "hooked" into providing the complementary response to the patient's rigid and extreme maladaptive behavior:

> The therapist inevitably is pulled to provide the complementary response because the patient is more adept, more expert in his distinctive, rigid, and extreme game of interpersonal encounter. . . . The therapist cannot not be hooked temporarily into providing the complementary response to the patient. Indeed, getting hooked probably is necessary for establishment of a working therapeutic alliance. It also permits the therapist to experience firsthand the aversive interpersonal consequences of the patient's maladaptive transactions. (Kiesler, 1986a, p. 14)

The following proposition is in line with this conceptualization:

Proposition 9–5.   A high degree of interpersonal complementarity between patient and therapist in their early therapy sessions should be associated with a strong patient-therapist working alliance.

A complementary transactional pattern between patient and therapist operates as a mediating mechanism for establishment of a positive therapeutic alliance. The rationale is that the client needs to experience some level of acceptance and endorsement of his or her self-definition (self-presentation) by the therapist, as expressed through the therapist's continuing complementary responses, as a prerequisite for alliance formation. Hence, in dyads characterized by closer fit to interpersonal complementarity, clients should perceive stronger levels of positive therapeutic alliance.

Kiesler and Watkins's (1989) study was the first to examine this hypothesized relationship between the therapeutic alliance and interpersonal complementarity. After the third therapy session, 36 pairs of patients and therapists from a variety of outpatient settings recorded their perceptions of the therapeutic alliance and rated each other's therapy behaviors using an interpersonal circle inventory (CLOIT). Results revealed positive associations between patient-therapist interpersonal complementarity (especially on the hostile half of the circle) and both patients' and therapists' perceptions of the alliance. These findings suggested that compatible interpersonal behaviors within the hostile hemisphere of the circle may be crucial for development of a positive working alliance as perceived by either patient or therapist. Within the psychotherapy context, therefore, complementarity principles appear much more relevant to the patient-therapist matchup of hostile-side behaviors than of friendly-side behaviors. In other words, the valence of interpersonal behaviors from the hostile versus friendly hemispheres may not be equivalent. How the patient and therapist match on the hostile half of the circle seems important for development of a positive working alliance; how they match on the friendly half may be relatively irrelevant—at least during early therapy sessions. This issue will be discussed in detail in Chapter 10.

Another principle in regard to the association between interpersonal complementarity and the therapeutic alliance can be stated:

Proposition 9–6.   For dyads in which a client's interpersonal behavior is especially rigid and extreme, the client initially will perceive a weaker positive alliance than for dyads in which a patient's behavior is less rigid and extreme.

This proposition is based on the assumption that a client's overt behavioral rigidity reflects a corresponding covert perceptual rigidity (selective attention and inattention) that prevents the client from responding to the unique and real aspects of the therapist's behavior that constitute the therapeutic alliance. Accordingly, the more extreme and rigid a patient's overt behavior, the more likely the patient will *mis*perceive the real aspects of the positive alliance offered by his or her therapist.

The Kiesler and Watkins (1989) study also directly tested this second proposition. Findings were confirmatory, again only when interpersonal behavior within the hostile hemisphere was considered. Pearson correlations between patients' perceptions of working alliance and the extremeness of patients' hostile-side behavior were significant for all therapeutic alliance scales, with r ranging between $-.351$ and $-.423$. These coefficients indicate that the more extreme a patient's behavior within the hostile half of the circle, the less strong is the working alliance perceived by that patient. These findings seem to suggest that the more extreme the patient's overt behavior, the more likely it is that the patient may selectively unattend or misperceive the positive aspect of the therapist's helping behavior—or may selectively attend and be responsive to any negative aspects of the therapist's alliance behaviors. More parsimoniously, these findings indicate that establishment of a strong working alliance is more difficult and requires more time for cases in which a patient's behavior presents more maladaptively (is more categorically extreme).

Interestingly, analyses of therapists' self-reported alliance scores did not reveal similar relationships. The extremeness of a therapist's behavior was essentially unrelated to the therapist's or patient's perception of the helping alliance. On the other hand, a very strong association was found between the extremeness of patients' behavior and therapists' perceptions of the helping alliance. The more extreme a patient's behavior within either or both circle hemispheres, the less strong the working alliance perceived by his or her therapist.

Overall, then, the Kiesler and Watkins (1989) findings show that both patients and therapists perceive a stronger helping alliance when the patient's hostile-side interpersonal behavior is less extreme. In contrast, extremeness of the therapist's interpersonal behavior is essentially unrelated to either the patient or the therapist's perceptions of the working alliance. Hence, degree of maladjustment or extremeness of a patient's interpersonal behavior (but not that of the therapist) seems to operate as an important moderator variable for both the patient's and the therapist's perceptions of the working alliance.

Muran, Segal, Samstag, and Crawford (1994) examined pretreatment predictors of the quality of therapeutic alliance as measured early in a 20-session protocol of cognitive therapy. Specifically, they examined the relationship of patient pretreatment interpersonal functioning (as measured by the IIP and the Millon Clinical Multiaxial Inventory) to the therapeutic alliance (as measured by a patient self-report version of the Working Alliance Inventory. They found that hostile-dominant behaviors predicted a poor alliance and that friendly-submissive behaviors predicted a good alliance, suggesting that friendly-submissive patients more readily accept and comply with the structure and requirements of cognitive therapy.

Muran, Samstag, Jilton, Batchelder, and Winston (1992a, 1992b) examined patient and therapist interpersonal transactions within sessions sampled across a 40-session protocol of dynamic psychotherapy, as measured from a third-party perspective. They found that patient and therapist friendliness was positively related to a helping alliance; but it was patient and therapist hostility that was negatively related to both alliance and ultimate outcome. Additional analyses revealed that the control (dominant-submissive) axis, rather than the affiliation (friendly-hostile) axis of the circle, was most predictive of outcome. Reciprocal shifts upward on therapist control. and downward on patient control, were more characteristic of good outcome cases. From the set of three studies, Muran (1993) concluded, "A didactic interaction against a stable backdrop of friendliness represents productive interpersonal process" (p. 70).

Based on a conceptualization of a dysfunctional cognitive-interpersonal cycle, Safran (1990a), Safran and Segal (1990), and Safran, McMain, Crocker, and Murray (1990) viewed problems or ruptures in the therapy alliance as a unique opportunity for assessing the patient's pathogenic beliefs. J. H. Wright and Davis (1994) concluded that "the therapeutic relationship is an essential interactive component of cognitive-behavioral therapy" (p. 42).

Safran and Muran (1995a) outlined a scheme for conceptualizing the range of possible strategies available for working with problems in the alliance, including the use of therapeutic metacommunication. In their scheme, alliance interventions are categorized into those that are direct and indirect. Within each of these two categories, the therapist can distinguish between interventions that address the bond component of the alliance versus those that address the task and goal components. Finally, the two subcategories are further differentiated into eight specific intervention types.

In presenting their own integrative approach, Safran and Muran (1995a) noted that the exploration and resolution of therapeutic alliance ruptures provide an important corrective emotional experience for the client. The experience of working through an alliance rupture can play an important role in helping the client to develop an interpersonal schema that represents the self as capable of attaining relatedness to others as potentially available emotionally. A central theme involves helping clients learn that they can express their needs and assert themselves without destroying the therapeutic relationship. Safran and Muran (1995a) presented a four-stage model of the processes involved in resolving alliance ruptures, (a) attending to the ruptured alliance, (b) exploration of ruptured experience, (c) exploration of avoidance, and (d) self-assertion.

Resistance and Countercontrol

According to Sullivan (1954):

> *The interviewee's self-system is at all times, but in varying degrees, in opposition to achieving the purpose of the interview.* This is an elaborate but fairly correct way of saying what might be said casually as: The self-system of the stranger is always viewing the other person as an enemy and taking due precautions against the other person on that basis. (p. 139)

Kiesler, Bernstein, and Anchin (1976) analyzed the behavioral construct of treatment noncompliance or "countercontrol" from the interpersonal communication perspective. The concept of countercontrol has many features that overlap with the psychodynamic construct of patient "resistance." It refers to instances when the patient directly or indirectly, obviously or subtly, sabotages or opposes the task of the therapy sessions, however the task might be structured by the therapist and construed by the patient.

Kiesler, Bernstein, and Anchin (1976) documented that a major issue of resistance is interpersonal: Countercontrol is an expression of the cumulative emotional relationship of the client and therapist up to the moment of a given oppositional behavior by the patient. A thread of negative feelings runs through oppositional patient behaviors and these feelings are directed to and felt by the therapist in varying degrees.

Van Denburg and Kiesler (1996) have provided an expanded analysis. Within an individualistic framework, resistance can be described as referring to the effects on the psychotherapy task and process of the client's specific maladaptive pattern of interpersonal behavior. From a transactional interpersonal viewpoint, however, *resistances* are viewed as:

Moments during sessions when the patient and therapist are interacting with one another in a way that keeps the patient from becoming aware of any covert experiences or transactional patterns that are conflictual and anxiety provoking; or

Moments during or between sessions when the patient's interpersonal behaviors sabotage the therapeutic alliance and task.

During sessions it takes both the patient and therapist to create a barrier between the unaware anxiety-tinged components of the patient's experience and the conscious components to which the patient and therapist are currently attending. Between sessions, the patient can enact interpersonal maneuvers that constitute a threat to the therapeutic relationship; for example, the patient may cancel or reschedule appointments, avoid consideration of identified themes, and forget to complete homework assignments. According to Van Denburg and Kiesler (1996), whether actually present within the sessions, or symbolically present between sessions, the therapist conjointly participates in the patient's interpersonal behaviors in his or her role as a participant observer.

Resistance is not seen as an adversarial process, wherein sometimes the patient is being a "good" patient and sometimes being a "bad" patient. Instead, the patient is constantly communicating to the therapist, albeit indirectly, anxiety-provoking aspects of self by interpersonally communicating his or her desire for the therapist to confirm the self-definitional bids by providing the complementary response.

Resistance can be *realistic and conscious* if the therapist has not provided clear structure and expectations for the therapy task, or if the patient does not have the abilities or characteristics necessary to pursue the task after it has been clearly structured. *Automatic or unconscious* resistance can be separated into either state or trait manifestations. *State resistances* occur at specific moments within a session in which the patient experiences signal anxiety triggered by a threat to his or her self-system emanating during exploration with the therapist of a particular topic or issue. Newly emerging thoughts or feelings within the patient may trigger momentary anxiety that the therapist will react negatively to the emerging contents, or the anxiety may reflect a particular relation matrix between the patient and therapist. *Trait (or character) resistances* occur repeatedly during therapy sessions at moments in which the patient's maladaptive pattern of interpersonal behavior and the therapist's response interfere with the task or process of therapy. At these moments, in reaction to the patient's off-task maneuvers, the therapist experiences some level of negative emotion and cognition toward the patient that, if not identified and then confronted through empathic or other interventions on the therapist's part, cumulates and moves the patient-therapist interaction toward a state of impasse that bogs down the therapy task.

Van Denburg and Kiesler (1996) speculated further as to the empirical indices of the presence of resistance during psychotherapy. Realistic and conscious resistance typically leads to unilateral premature termination of therapy by the patient. The patient sensibly realizes that what the therapist is providing does not meet his or her needs or is beyond his or her capacity.

State resistances are telegraphed primarily by momentary instances of patient overt anxiety displayed through the patient's nonverbal behavior (facial expression, self-touches, vocal changes in pitch, etc.). What occurs are clear instances of "shifts from baseline" (momentary deviations from the patient's usual communication pattern during the sessions). At these moments, the patient has some level of awareness that the experience of anxiety is imminent and that some shift away from or avoidance of the therapy task is occurring. A shift that frequently occurs is what we have termed *transactional escalation* (Van Denburg & Kiesler, 1993). This is an escalation in the intensity and rigidity of the patient's baseline interpersonal style in response to perceived threat or stress. The function of this interpersonal maneuver is to put more pressure on the therapist (or other interactants) to provide the complementary response, thereby decreasing anxiety by reinstating the familiar and relatively secure relational pattern. The therapist, on noticing the shift from baseline, begins to identify the precipitating circumstances and topics, and wonders if what the patient is feeling has any relationship to the patient's expectations regarding the therapist's possible response.

Trait or character resistances are displayed through the patient's distinctive pattern of interpersonal behavior—through the patient's typical baseline of intimate communication with significant others, including the therapist. The possibilities are multiple, depending on the patient's particular form of personality organization as shown in the specific categorization of the patient's interpersonal behavior on the interpersonal circle. A histrionic pattern, for example, recurrently interferes with the task of therapy by entertaining the therapist and distracting the process away from threatening introspection. An obsessive-compulsive pattern, in contrast, consistently derails the therapy task by intellectual circumlocution that distracts the therapist away from helping the patient to experience threatening clarity or action. Generally, trait resistances emanate from processes that, although maladaptive, are ego-syntonic; hence, their recurrent manifestations tend to be automatic and less available to the patient's awareness. These trait resistances pull complementary responses from the therapist in the form of generalizable impacts (objective countertransference) that similarly occur relatively automatically in the therapist's experience and are less available to the therapist's awareness. If undetected, these impacts gradually take on a negative emotional quality for the therapist (the aversive result of the patient's maladaptive pattern) and cumulate as the therapist's contribution to the therapy impasse.

Trait resistance, then, is an expression of the cumulative emotional relationship between the patient and therapist. A thread of negative feelings runs through instances of resistance and these feelings are directed to and felt by the therapist in varying degrees. At these moments of resistance, the patient's evoking messages to the therapist represent various combinations of dislike (anger, boredom, fear, disappointment, disrespect, etc.) on the affiliation axis of the interpersonal circle, and of dominance-submission struggles (competitiveness, rivalry, assertion, one-upmanship, passivity, etc.) on the control axis. Hence, a central component to the study of resistance consists of measurement, using interpersonal circle inventories, of the ongoing relationship behaviors occurring between patient and therapist.

Van Denburg and Kiesler (1996) pointed out that a therapist's experience of participation in given instances of resistance with patients will vary widely and invariably will include reactions that are outside the therapist's level of awareness. For a therapist to avoid or resolve moments of resistance requires that the therapist first notice and identify any negative impacts occurring toward the patient as well as pinpoint the pattern of patient transactions that evoked this objective countertransference. Through the labeling disengagement or unhooking process, the therapist regains the empathic freedom subsequently to respond to the patient with other interventions that can facilitate productive therapeutic work. If successful, these interventions reinforce the patient's gradual movements away from his or her erstwhile pattern of resistance.

If considerable complementarity exists between the interpersonal behavior of a patient during moments of resistance and the therapist's baseline (preferred) interpersonal behavior, it may be more difficult for the therapist to identify and disengage from the patient's pull. This is the case because the therapist—to interrupt the patient's pattern of resistance—must diverge from his or her comfortable and preferred interpersonal pattern. At the other extreme, when little or no complementarity exists between the therapist's baseline interpersonal style and the interpersonal behavior of the patient during periods of resistance, the therapist may experience heightened anxiety during therapy inasmuch as the patient is pulling for reactions that constitute the therapist's Not Me, thereby considerably threatening his or her own sense of self.

Finally, Van Denburg and Kiesler (1996) emphasized that a therapist is more likely to engage in counterresistance when his or her psychological vulnerabilities match those aspects of the patient's self-system that the patient is determined to avoid confronting. If the therapist assists the patient to experience conflictual elements of the patient's self-system, the therapist risks experiencing his or her own vulnerabilities—horns of a dilemma indeed. For example, a therapist with narcissistic vulnerabilities may be less likely to help the patient with a narcissistic personality disorder explore and understand conflicts associated with bottom-line rage and entitlement.

Although the possible elements are multiple (Wachtel, 1982b), a central component to the study of patient oppositional and resistance behaviors consists of measurement of the relationship behaviors occurring between patient and therapist. This assessment can use interpersonal circle inventories either (a) individualistically, to measure the patient's interpersonal self-presentations as both a component and a context for specific oppositional behaviors or (b) transactionally, to measure the pattern or mix of patient-action/therapist-reaction that serves as the context for specific countercontrol or resistance maneuvers.

Parataxic Distortion and Transference

Sullivan (1953a, 1953b) offered a more distinctly interpersonal conception of transference in which individuals are assumed to develop particular personifications of themselves and others (both good and bad) and particular dynamisms characterizing the interplay between self and other. In his model, when so-called transference occurs, whether in a treatment context or in daily life, its content reflects the interpersonal dynamics that link self and other representations together in memory, which are displaced onto a new person. Sullivan referred to the process as *parataxic distortion,* rather than transference, to indicate that its content does not evolve out of psychosexual drives, but instead evolves out of interpersonal needs and experiences (J. R. Greenberg & Mitchell, 1983).

Contemporary interpersonal theorists (e.g., Kiesler, Bernstein, & Anchin, 1976; see also Lineham, 1988) have documented how various therapeutic approaches have overlooked or minimized the important possibility that patients' self-defeating interpersonal behaviors enacted with their therapists can be representative of patients' central self-defeating interactions with other significant persons in their lives. As a comprehensive assessment of these behaviors, the interpersonal circle can serve as an empirical model of individual differences in transference patterns of psychotherapy patients.

Patient resistance or countercontrol struggles with the therapist actually have two relationship components that sometimes overlap (Kiesler, Bernstein, & Anchin, 1976). The first, the resistance component just described, reflects the interpersonal implications of the therapy situation, task, or therapist for the patient's self-definition.

The second, the transference dimension, reflects the implications of the therapist's interactions as another example of a significant other in the patient's life. That is, the therapist evokes the patient's typical interpersonal self-presentation, which can include both obvious and paradoxical expressions (e.g., extreme compliance) of oppositional behaviors. It is this second aspect of resistance or countercontrol that reflects the patient's transference pattern—the particular style of rigid and extreme self-presentation identified through location of the patient's behavior patterns on the interpersonal circle.

Kiesler, Bernstein, and Anchin (1976) reviewed in detail earlier arguments that the emotional engagements occurring between patient and therapist are not essential to the therapeutic process. They show that, by rejecting constructs such as transference and parataxic distortion as valid features of psychotherapy, the therapist can take the unfortunate position of not looking for or detecting, and certainly not assessing as samples of the patient's more general interpersonal problems, the actual patient behaviors enacted with the therapist that express these same problems.

Apfelbaum's (1958) study, although he did not use an interpersonal circle inventory, illustrated clearly the applicability of interpersonal patterns to the concept of transference. Before therapy started, he asked each of 100 patients in a university psychiatric clinic to *Q*-sort statements describing various role behaviors they expected their prospective therapists to manifest. (One of the interpersonal circle inventories could have been used instead to rate the expected interpersonal behaviors of their prospective therapists.) Cluster analysis revealed three types of therapist role-behavior. The *Nurturant* therapist was rated as supportive, protective, and willing to guide the patient, actively helping him or her in problem areas. The *Model* therapist was described as an interested and tolerant listener who tends to be permissive and nonjudgmental, and is perceived by patients as being well adjusted, interested, but not highly responsive. The *Critical* therapist was rated as being judgmental and as expecting patients to show a high level of responsibility; this type was seen as the least benign, largely lacking in permissiveness or supportiveness.

Apfelbaum (1958) found that those patients who expected to work with a Model therapist demonstrated the lowest dropout rates; patients expecting Nurturant therapists, if they remained in therapy, stayed the longest. Finally, patients with both Nurturant and Critical expectations started psychotherapy with higher MMPI maladjustment scores and more distress than those with Model therapist expectations.

Apfelbaum's study illustrates a methodology that can be used to assess precontact transference. In line with other systems that attempt to assess transference constellations, such as Horowitz's role-relationship models (RRMs; M. Horowitz, 1988) and Luborsky's core conflictual relationship theme (CCRT; Luborsky, 1984), the interpersonal circle inventories can be applied to obtain typical self and other transactional patterns, or the instructional sets can be modified to obtain "desired" and "dreaded" (Van Denburg & Holifield, 1993) and other transactional patterns.

Counter-Parataxic-Distortion and Countertransference

Modern psychoanalytic theory (e.g., L. Epstein & Feiner, 1979) makes the crucial distinction between "subjective" and "objective" countertransference. *Subjective countertransference* (Spotnitz, 1969) refers to the defensive and irrational reactions and feelings a therapist experiences with a particular patient. These feelings and attitudes represent the residual effects of the therapist's own irrational transference resulting from his or her own developmentally induced conflicts and anxieties.

In contrast, *objective countertransference* (Winnicott, 1949) refers to the constricted feelings, attitudes, and reactions of a therapist, that are induced primarily by the patient's behavior and that are generalizable to other therapists and to other significant persons in the patient's life. This countertransference registers the objective effects of the patient's central transference feelings and conflicts as they continue to be expressed in present-day interactions with significant others, including the therapist. In line with this distinction, modern psychoanalytic therapy emphasizes the therapist's use of objective countertransference to understand the patient's conflicts and problems and to guide interpretive intervention.

As I've detailed elsewhere (Kiesler, 1979, 1982b, 1983, 1988), the therapist experiences live within the sessions a patient's distinctive interpersonal problems. The therapist, at his or her end of the feedback loop, registers the patient's distinctive style with the impact messages he or she experiences with the patient—impacts complementary to a distinctive cluster of categories on the interpersonal circle:

> Interpersonal theory redefines countertransference to include recent analytic emphasis on *all* the therapist's emotional, cognitive, and fantasy engagements experienced from the client. Therapist impact responses are by no means restricted to irrational responses. Rather, many impacts experienced by the therapist are shared by others in the client's life, serve as important cues to the client's unsuccessful style, and are important feedback to the client in resolving his interpersonal problems. (Kiesler, 1982b, p. 17)

In interpersonal theory, the equivalent of objective countertransference is the complementary response being pulled for so expertly and tenaciously by the patient during their sessions. The generalizable pattern of interpersonal reaction by significant others and therapists constitutes the objective countertransference for a particular patient.

One interpersonal procedure for measurement of objective countertransference is for therapists (and therapeutic observers) to fill out Impact Message Inventories on their patients. As previously noted, impact messages "refer to all internal events a therapist experiences as predominantly produced or elicited by a particular patient during their transactions . . . emotions, action tendencies, cognitive attributions, and metaphors or fantasies (Kiesler, 1988, p. 40). The average circle category scores obtained from IMIs filled out by the therapist and a sample of therapeutic observers become estimates of the patient's objective (generalizable) countertransferential reaction.

Assessment of subjective (irrational, neurotic) *countertransference* traditionally has focused on identification of occurrence within therapy sessions of moments of therapist anxiety, of a therapist's rigid approach or avoidance behavior in regard to certain topics being discussed by the patient, or of a therapist's continual avoidance of transference interpretations in response to various aspects of the patient's discourse. Interpersonal assessment of subjective countertransference would add the identification of a significantly different and idiosyncratic pattern of reaction to the patient by the therapist in contrast to (a) the generalizable objective countertransference found for other interactants or observers as a group or (b) the therapist's typical pattern of reaction to most other patients.

Cutler (1958) provided one of the earliest interpersonal inventory studies of subjective countertransference. Cutler identified conflict areas in two therapists by first having them rate their own interpersonal behavior using a circle inventory; second, nine or more judges who were well acquainted with the two therapists rated them using the same inventory. *Those circle categories on which there was a significant discrepancy between the therapist's and the judges' ratings were assumed to be indicative of conflict.*

Cutler's (1958) findings showed that the therapist was much less accurate in reporting behavior of self and of patient during psychotherapy when the topics being discussed were related to the therapist's own personality conflicts; there was a significantly greater discrepancy between the self-report and the judges' report of what had occurred. Further, when the therapist was working with the patient on issues that were also a problem for the therapist, interventions were judged to be significantly less effective than when the therapist was working with neutral material. Thus, the interpersonal circle can serve also as an empirical model of the domain of subjective countertransference behaviors therapists can enact with their patients during psychotherapy.

Eisenthal (1992) summarized and contrasted *three contemporary approaches to countertransference* that reflect different aspects of current changes in the meaning of the concept: one based on *psychoanalytic object relations theory* developed by Tansey and Burke (1989); one based on *interpersonal object relations theory* developed by Cashdan (1988); and one based on *the interpersonal communications approach* (Kiesler, 1979, 1982a, 1988). According to Eisenthal (1992), the three approaches present contrasting ways of understanding and responding to countertransference. Tansey and Burke illuminate the empathic processing of countertransference. Kiesler's approach clarifies metacommunication strategies for disengagement from the countertransference pressure. Cashdan presents a confrontative strategy from disengagement that incorporates the concepts of projective identification and its underlying metacommunication.

In Tansey and Burke's (1989) paradigm, the interplay between the patient's projective identifications and the therapist's identification responses constitutes the critical interactive unit for analysis. It is in the medium of the countertransference that the therapist experiences the impact of the projective identification. Because of the intense affective pressures that can disrupt the process, the challenge is to proceed empathically through the three phases of receiving, processing, and communicating the interpersonal significance of this exchange.

The equivalent of objective countertransference in my conceptualization (Kiesler, 1979, 1982a, 1988; Kiesler & Van Denburg, 1993) is the therapist's impact messages. The objective of interpersonal communication psychotherapy, as Eisenthal (1992) noted, is to identify and then modify the patient's self-defeating evoking style of interaction with others, especially with the therapist. This process occurs in two stages from the therapist's perspective: the "engaged" or "hooked" stage, and the "disengaged" or "squirmed loose" phases. Therapist disengagement requires recognizing the state of being hooked, or deciphering the impact message. The objective is to identify the patient's evoking style, embedded in the impact message, in order to disengage from the reciprocal response and to metacommunicate about the relationship.

According to Eisenthal (1992), key concepts in Cashdan's (1988) object relations therapy are projective identification, metacommunication, and affective confrontation. Projective identifications, resulting from disturbed early interpersonal relationships with the mother, generate coercive and manipulative interpersonal tactics that carry patient metacommunications. Cashdan believes that modifying projective identifications is the keystone to essential therapeutic change. He developed a schema of relevant interpersonal diagnosis that describes four major projective identifications: dependence, power, sex, and ingratiation. The therapist's recognition and response to countertransference depends on the treatment stage involved. In the middle stage, the patient's projective identification enters the process; only when it has drawn the therapist into the desired role can the therapist be aware that a countertransference has occurred. In this process of reacting to the patient's inductions, strong and often overpowering affects are aroused. During the essential confrontation stage, the therapist communicates directly about the patient's projective identification and its underlying metacommunication. Cashdan believes that this reactive approach obliges the patient to drop manipulative and coercive interpersonal tactics for a more direct and honest style of relationship.

In concluding his comparative summary and analysis, Eisenthal (1992) laconically wondered "when there will be an exchange of information between the psychoanalytic and interpersonal communication approaches. This absence of communication is a disquieting metacommunication" (p. 161).

RELATIONSHIP: A CONTEXT FOR THE EFFECTIVENESS OF PSYCHOTHERAPY INTERVENTIONS

DeVogue and Beck (1978), Kiesler (1979), Kiesler, Bernstein, and Anchin (1976), Safran (1990a), Safran and Segal (1990), and Andrews (1991) review empirical findings demonstrating that relationship factors contribute to the effectiveness of various behavior therapy interventions.

Lambert (1983) concluded that both technique and relationship variables contribute to positive results in psychotherapy. Butler and Strupp (1986) challenged the traditional distinction between specific and nonspecific factors in psychotherapy. They argued that, unlike treatment by medication in which biochemical action can be separated conceptually from the symbolic meaning of the treatment, psychological interventions are intrinsically linked to the interpersonal context of their application. Butler and Strupp (1986) amplified that "the complexity and subtlety of psychotherapeutic processes cannot be reduced to a set of disembodied techniques because techniques gain their meaning and, in turn, their effectiveness from the particular interaction of the individuals involved" (p. 33; see also Henry, Schacht, & Strupp, 1986).

Schaffer (1982) detailed his view that, if we are to study therapeutic interventions validly, we need to obtain simultaneous "multidimensional" measures of three aspects of therapist behavior: *type of activity, skillfulness of activity,* and *interpersonal manner.* He documented convincingly that in most earlier psychotherapy studies, one or more of the three therapist dimensions had been neglected. He suggested that at least two (preferably all three) of these therapist dimensions need to be assessed in any particular study, with hypotheses stated and results discussed at all times from this multidimensional perspective.

Interpersonal circle measures provide state-of-the-art options for assessment of the therapist's "interpersonal manner," whether applied individualistically or transactionally (Kiesler, 1991, 1992). For example, we may want to study the effectiveness of a session-length intervention such as psychodramatic doubling (Hudgins & Kiesler, 1987) in facilitating the patient's level of experiencing (Klein, Mathieu-Coughlan, & Kiesler, 1986) during psychotherapy. We develop a manual to operationalize application of the doubling intervention and, as an experimental check, perform ratings of therapists' adherence to the manual while with their patients. We solicit experienced therapists to rate the level of expertise of each doubling intervention. We then have a group of observers rate the therapist's interpersonal manner, using one of the interpersonal circle inventories.

An "individualistic" interpersonal hypothesis might be that skillful therapist doubling will facilitate greater patient experiencing only when the therapist's interpersonal manner peaks at friendly octants (does *not* peak at dominant, submissive, or hostile octants). A "transactional" interpersonal hypothesis might be that skillful therapist doubling will facilitate greater patient experiencing only when the therapist-patient dyad is manifesting a particular complementary pattern; for example, the patient's behavior is friendly-submissive, the therapist's behavior is friendly-dominant.

LaFromboise (1992) examined the relationship impact of three types of specific counselor interventions used frequently in the initial stage of counseling: counselor affinity (discloses personal information about self), clarification (asks questions, summarizes information about perceptions, feelings, and thoughts), and helpful comments (making suggestions or offering advice). Five vignettes were composed to describe typical problems in American Indian families; each included a brief description of the client, the client's problem, and a few lines of the initial dialogue between the client and a counselor. The therapeutic intent of each type of counselor intervention was rated both by panels of therapists and of undergraduates. American Indian undergraduates were asked to read each vignette-response combination and imagine themselves in the role of the client described in each case. Using the IMI, participants then rated the impact on them of each specific counselor's intervention. Analyses focused on comparing the impact of counselor's interventions on the analogue clients with the (rated) therapeutic intention that had originally prompted use of that particular response.

LaFromboise's (1992) results demonstrated that differential interpersonal impacts were evoked by the three counseling interventions. Affinity interventions were perceived by the analogue clients as reflecting affiliative, agreeable, and nurturant counselor actions, and clarifications as reflecting agreeable and nurturant counselor behaviors. In contrast, in the clients' perceptions, helpful interventions characterized the counselor as dominant, mistrusting, competitive, and hostile. Generally, complementarity (correspondence) effects were obtained for the affinity and clarification counselor responses; whereas the American Indian clients perceived the intent of counselor helpful (friendly) responses as noncorrespondent (hostile). LaFromboise (1992) concluded that the interpersonal model "provides an effective paradigm for capturing the difference between counselor intentions and the communication conveying those intentions and the perceptions of the recipient. . . . [Further, the IMI] shows promise for obtaining culture-specific and universal information about communication barriers in cross-cultural counseling" (p. 285).

Muran, Safran, and colleagues (Muran, 1993; Safran & Muran, 1994) have used interpersonal circumplex measures to assess both personality and interpersonal process as part of the Beth Israel Brief Psychotherapy Research Project. The project is a comparative study of manualized, time-limited treatment trials of cognitive-behavioral and psychodynamic therapies for personality disorders.

OTHER INTERPERSONAL RESEARCH ON THE PSYCHOTHERAPY RELATIONSHIP

Moras, Waterhouse, and Suh (1981) used the IMI to study patient-therapist interactions within the Vanderbilt Psychotherapy Research Project (Strupp & Hadley, 1979). A large group of observers viewed videotaped segments of the third therapy session for a sample of cases drawn from the larger project, after which they filled out IMIs on the therapist. Based on factor analysis of the IMI data, they constructed a set of nine IMI therapist scales to discriminate among the four therapists of their study. Analyses showed that eight of the nine scales significantly differentiated the therapists' interpersonal behavior during their sessions. Moras et al. (1981) concluded that their findings consistently confirmed the value of the IMI as an observer-rated process measure of therapist relationship variables.

Studies by Brokaw (1983), Kiesler and Goldston (1988), and Zians (1981) used various interpersonal circle inventories to demonstrate stylistic differences of Rogers, Perls, and Ellis's interactions with the same client, Gloria. Andrews (1988, 1991) documented that the techniques used by these respective therapists are important components of the therapist interpersonal styles being conveyed. For example, Andrews observed that Rogers's core conditions "are far from neutral with respect to the complementary patterns codified in the interpersonal circle. In descriptions of these relationship conditions one repeatedly encounters words like *safe, trusting,* and *empathic,* and such qualities fall consistently into the friendly and friendly-dominant sectors of the [Leary] circle" (Andrews, 1991, p. 276). Andrews concluded that "the therapist's and the client's respective self-confirmation endeavors affect each other and shape the course of therapy" by providing a context for the specific interventions of the therapist (p. 206).

Hudgins and Chirico (1982) studied the interpersonal behavior of psychotherapy interns from three different training backgrounds (clinical psychology, psychodrama, pastoral counseling). Each of the interns participated in a 15-minute interview with an actor trained to portray a patient presenting symptoms of paranoid schizophrenia. A group of observers filled out IMIs on the interns after viewing 5-minute segments extracted from the interviews. Results showed that the interpersonal behavior of all three groups was most characterized by the observers as first friendly and then submissive.

Also, the psychodrama interns were rated by observers as significantly more abasive than the other two intern groups.

Murdock et al. (1995) investigated variables that related to counselors' choices of theoretical orientation. Participants completed measures of philosophical assumptions, interpersonal style (the "generalized other" self-report form of the IMI octant version), and level of counselor development. The counselors who were studied fell into five theoretical groups: psychoanalytic, cognitive behavioral, interpersonal/systems, person centered, and existential/gestalt. The IMI results revealed that counselor self-reported dominance was the only personality dimension significantly associated with theoretical orientation. Psychoanalytic respondents characterized themselves as the most interpersonally dominant; the cognitive behavioral and interpersonal/systems counselors described themselves as the least dominant of all orientations. The counselors' scores on the affiliation axis did not significantly predict their theoretical orientation; the authors suggest that this might have resulted from a restricted range of affiliation scores in that all the counselors described themselves as moderately affiliative. Murdock et al. (1995) cautioned that results were based on the counselors' self-reports and might have shown different patterns had they been based on the counselor's actual in-session transactions.

CHAPTER 10

Interpersonal Communication Interventions
Interpersonal Complementarity Principles

A diagnostic system that only describes *is of very limited value. . . . To be of more than minor use, a diagnosis must carry with it specific implications for what to do—it must* prescribe. *The principal benefit of an operationalized interpersonal psychology is that it specifies "treatment."*

(McLemore & Brokaw, 1987, p. 274)

AN ENCAPSULATION

Interpersonal Communication (IC) psychotherapy has both "task" and "transaction" components. The task involves the patient's efforts, with the therapist's help, to self-disclose and explore his or her problems and experience. The transaction entails the patient's interpersonal communications as the therapist experiences them during their therapy sessions.

The patient begins the task by disclosing a "rehearsed story" of his or her problems and concerns. This rehearsed story is the product of the patient's previous mental replays of aspects of experience that he or she judged relevant to the problem—with no resolution. "The Answer" to the patient's problem cannot reside in this rehearsed story since the patient knows that story better than anyone and has not found any solutions. It follows that answers to the patient's problems have to be found in the "unrehearsed story": in aspects of the patient's experience and actions that he or she selectively ignores or unattends.

The therapist's job is to help the patient attend to, identify, and clarify "missing elements" of the rehearsed story. Missing elements are of two sorts:

1. *Task elements.* Aspects of experience (cognitions, feelings, fantasies) and action (words and nonverbal behavior) ignored or deemphasized in the patient's delivery of the rehearsed story.

2. *Transactional elements.* Automatic, habitual relationship messages and actions by which the patient induces others including the therapist to respond with restricted "complementary responses" classifiable on the interpersonal circle.

If the therapist continues to comply with the patient's relationship commands, the patient will maintain his or her self-defeating, maladjusted pattern of interactional communication with the therapist and with significant others. Hence, while continuing to help the patient clarify missing elements of his or her story, the therapist recurrently provides transactional feedback to the patient through various "metacommunication" maneuvers and offers interventions designed specifically to alter the patient's interactional communication pattern.

The therapist begins to say good-bye when the patient's continuing story shows entrenched and noticeable shifts from rehearsed to unrehearsed components; when the covert complementary responses (impact messages) the therapist experiences with the patient show stable and noticeable shifts to less extreme engagements from more quadrants of the interpersonal circle.

PROLOGUE

Principles of interpersonal therapy have been presented in detail by Anchin (1982a), Carson (1969), and Kiesler (1979, 1982a, 1982b, 1983, 1986a, 1988, 1992), Kiesler, Bernstein, and Anchin (1976), Leary (1957), and Strong (1987a, 1987b, 1987c). Earlier summaries of various approaches to interpersonal therapy can be found in Anchin and Kiesler (1982) and Kiesler (1986a, 1991). Recent therapeutic volumes include works by Andrews (1991), Benjamin (1993), Kiesler (1988), Safran and Segal (1990), and Teyber (1992). Also, formulations of object relations therapy (Cashdan, 1988), of brief dynamic psychotherapy (Luborsky, 1984; Strupp & Binder, 1984), and of psychodynamic interpersonal psychotherapy (Klerman & Weissman, 1992; Klerman et al., 1984; Weissman, Klerman, Rounsaville, Chevron, & Neu, 1982; Weissman & Markowitz, 1994) focus to a large extent on interpersonal relationships between the patient and significant others.

Yalom's (1985) theory and practice of *group psychotherapy* is embedded in interpersonal transactional notions. Perhaps most central is his notion of the "social microcosm," which means that "given enough time, every patient will begin to be himself or herself: one will interact with the group members as one interacts with others in one's social sphere, will create in the group the same interpersonal universe one has always inhabited" (p. 30).

The approach of Segraves (1982) to *couples therapy* is based on the assumption that marital transactions tend to confirm each spouse's interpersonal schema regarding members of the opposite sex. This confirmation occurs through a cyclical process that sequentially includes distortion of the spouse's behavior to fit with prior schemas, elicitation of confirmatory behavior from the spouse, and establishment of homeostasis-maintaining self-fulfilling prophecies. In Romano's (1960) marital formulation, ailing marriages result from a mutual failure in consensual validation: Husband and wife fail to agree on the interpersonal intent of their own and their spouse's marital behavior. Romano advocates and illustrates use of the circumplex system of diagnosis to define the discrepancies that occur in the way each of the partners perceives himself and the other at various levels of awareness.

Interpersonal approaches to *child or adolescent therapy* have also appeared (Colm, 1966; Green, 1972; Paddock, Woodruff, & Pate, 1984; Spiegel, 1989). According to Green (1972), "The interpersonal approach points out that the infant is not utterly help-less or dependent, but rather is an agent of an interpersonal transaction, who gives cues and signals indicating to the mother his wants and needs" (p. 540). Colm (1966) applied Sullivan's theory to the child-psychiatrist transactional experience. In her formulation, the analytic situation is merely a human situation in which the responses of both the an-alyst and the patient express the same human involvement with their pasts. The analyst, however, is better able to distinguish what is present involvement; he or she does not react parataxically, nor does the analyst undefensively accept the patient's suspicions and ac-cusations that the analyst is not realistically involved. Rather, the analyst engages in self-scrutiny. For Colm, appearance of countertransference in the analytic situation with the child was a way to investigate the mutual interaction.

Within individual psychotherapy, the goal of interpersonal therapy is for the therapist and client to identify, clarify, and establish alternatives to the rigid and self-defeating evoking style of the patient. Their task is to replace constricted, extreme transactions with more flexible and clear communications adaptive to the changing realities of spe-cific encounters. The therapist's priority task is to stop responding in kind, in comple-mentary fashion, to the client's duplicitous communications—*not* to respond in the same way as have others in the client's life.

The essential therapeutic task, then, is to disrupt the patient's vicious circle of self-defeating actions depicted in the Maladaptive Transaction Cycle. To accomplish this task, therapists can use important components of intervention that are derivable from the interpersonal circle. Although interpersonal therapists have yet to articulate comprehen-sive treatment packages applying these principles to specific disorders, some important first steps have been taken.

Contemporary interpersonal conceptualizations part company with Sullivan's pre-scriptions for psychotherapy. Sullivan defined psychotherapy as "a two-group in which there is an expert-client relationship, the expert being defined by the culture." The es-sential mechanism of change was insight, which is accomplished by uncoverings and interpretations that focus on the patient's personifications and parataxic distortions. The therapist's basic task is to convince the client that these personifications (eidetic people) are from the past, are the root of his or her interpersonal problems, but no longer exist.

On the other hand, contemporary interpersonal therapy is quite consistent with Car-son's (1969) view of therapy as "a two-person professional relationship in which one of the members uses the *relationship* in a planned attempt to alter the disordered behavior of the other" (p. 265). The therapist's basic task is to change the client's self-other per-sonifications, making them more encompassing, permeable, and flexible. The *cardinal therapeutic tactic* is "non-confirmation of the client's constricted self. The therapist must be the one person in the client's life who does *not* yield to the client's pressure to confirm his or her "crippled self" (Carson, 1969, pp. 277–280). In Halpern's (1965) words, the therapist must avoid ensnarement in the *"disturbance-perpetuating maneu-vers of the patient"* (p. 117).

Contemporary psychotherapy formulations also are highly congruent with the concept of *corrective emotional experience* offered by F. A. Alexander (1963) and F. A. Alexander and French (1946) as documented by Wallerstein (1990). According to Alexander's concept, which he saw as the heart of psychotherapeutic change, the analyst deliberately responds to the patient in a way that is different from the parents' usual responses. In this way, the transference is manipulated, the ego is freed from old patterns, and continued enactment by the patient of the old transference pattern becomes blatantly analogous to "one-sided shadow boxing" (Wallerstein, 1990, p. 290). The corrective emotional experience, thus, allows the patient intellectually and affectively to experience the difference from, and the irrationality of, his or her self-defeating interpersonal enactment. For Alexander, the reward of the corrective experience was development of less conflictual relationships, first with the therapist, then with the environment, and finally with the self.

TARGETING THE MALADAPTIVE TRANSACTION CYCLE

Basically, interpersonal interventions target the central, recurrent, and thematic relationship issues occurring between client and therapist during their therapy sessions. Interventions, thus, can encompass any one or more of the following components of the Maladaptive Transaction Cycle (Figures 6–1 and 6–2): (a) the covert experience of the therapist registered as engagements pulled by the patient's actions (the therapist's impact messages); (b) the overt reactions of the therapist to the patient which comprise the therapist's discrepant reactions or incongruous messages; (c) the thematic covert experience (thoughts, emotions, expectations, etc.) of the patient as inferred from the patient's verbalizations and nonverbal messages; (d) the actions (patterns of overt verbal and nonverbal behaviors) of the patient toward the therapist during their sessions.

No matter which of these four components is initially addressed by the therapist's interventions, *the intent or purpose is to explore and validate these cyclically related patient-actions and therapist-reactions as lawfully related and codetermined aspects of a central thematic interpersonal problem for the patient.* This theme is exhibited not only with the therapist but also with other significant persons in the patient's life. The therapist seeks to put on the table and discuss with the patient his or her central Maladaptive Transaction Cycle—the patient's vicious cycle of abnormal interpersonal behavior, the patient's "self-fulfilling prophecy" of abnormal cognitions and expectancies.

The Therapist's Covert Experiences or Impact Messages

In the beginning stages of therapy, the patient recurrently communicates his or her particular pattern of evoking messages and enacts his or her pattern of rigid and extreme interpersonal behaviors to the therapist. The patient's self-presentations have both intended and nonintended, aware and less aware, components. In turn, the therapist's emotional, cognitive, and fantasy covert responses are engaged as impact messages that generate automatic countercommunications and complementary reactions that confirm the patient's vulnerable and incompetent self-image. In short, these internal events mediate the therapist's overt complementary reactions to the patient.

The Therapist's Overt Reactions: The Discrepant Response

Impacts all occur internally, covertly in the therapist's experience. From the first session with a patient, however, they lead to constricted overt responding by the therapist, initially in the form of the complementary response. For example, we may observe the therapist increasing his or her activity by asking more questions, giving more advice, or by more frequent interruptions. Or the therapist may decrease his or her activity, sitting much longer in silence, feeling cautious about any intervention, and choosing his or her words carefully. In another instance, we may notice more frequent light banter with a patient, with frequent laughter and spontaneous comments. The therapist may feel increasingly threatened, feeling more and more inadequate with a particular patient. Or we may see little or no emotional response to the patient. In another case, the therapist may become angrily sympathetic regarding the patient's reported mistreatment by a spouse or family member. Or the therapist may become increasingly depressed or overtly anxious with a particular patient.

These various therapist enactments of the complementary response result in the patient's continued enactment of his or her maladaptive interpersonal behaviors since the complementary response confirms or validates the patient's expectancies, cognitions, emotions, and other inner experience. In the earlier stage of the Maladaptive Transaction Cycle, as we have seen, the patient-therapist complementary fit makes their transactions somewhat mutually satisfying and confirming. But difficulty develops as the relationship continues. As the cycle is replayed, the therapist increasingly experiences the aversive or negative impacts that result from being "pushed around" by the patient's superior and rigid power. The therapist thus now experiences more hostile and rejecting impacts. In turn the therapist, in addition to continuing to enact complementary responses, simultaneously "leaks" subtle messages of hostility and rejection. These rejecting cues are picked up by the patient as the discrepant part of the therapist's reaction, trigger patient anxiety in response to this threat to his or her self-esteem, and further disrupt the self-disclosure process.

The Patient's Thematic Covert Experience

A third interventive target consists of aspects of the patient's internal experience inferred by the therapist to be related thematically to the patient's maladaptive overt interpersonal behavior (to the patient's ED-evoking style). This component is first registered internally by the therapist as the cognitive attribution (perceived evoking message) class of impact messages. This impact component includes the therapist's automatic thoughts about what he or she thinks the patient is trying to do to him or her, or what he or she thinks the patient wants the therapist to do. More generally, the therapist infers what is going on inside the patient's head—what the patient's central expectations, construals, feelings, and fantasies might be in regard to the therapist and their relationship. At a deeper or more core level, these covert experiences have thematic relevance to the patient's self-concept or self-esteem; they refer to the patient "scripts" and "schemas," including self-schemas, which serve as decoding and encoding filters in the realm of interpersonal relationships.

An essential part of the interventive task, then, is that the therapist makes statements incorporating his or her guesses about the content of these patient covert experiences as they relate to the targeted central problems in living. These statements often take the following form: "When you do that, it seems to me that . . ." Examples of these therapist statements are: "You want to do this all by yourself"; "You're not interested in what I have to say"; "You look to me for all the answers"; "You wait for me to decide what we will talk about"; "It's important for you to impress me with your accomplishments";

"It's vital for you not to show any weakness to me"; "You expect that I will criticize you"; "You assume that what you do won't make any difference anyway"; "You're testing whether I will exploit you also."

Carson (1982) emphasized:

> A major task of the psychotherapist is that of explicit identification of the client's habitual, disorder-related, parataxic distortions of social cognition, an examination of their sources, and a comprehensive analysis of the manner in which they affect the client's behavior, particularly in its maladaptive aspects. In the typical instance, much of the task can be accomplished through a detailed analysis of events that occur *within* the therapeutic relationship. (pp. 67–68)

Safran and Segal (1990) emphasized that, by empathically exploring the patient's expectations, beliefs, and appraisals of the therapy situation as it unfolds, the therapist "helps patients see how their own cognitive processes shape their experiences. They thus begin to distinguish between reality and reality as they construe it. They begin to regard their perceptions as hypotheses that can be tested" (p. 148). Safran and Segal (1990) suggested further that the therapist needs to encourage the patient to test dysfunctional expectations and perceptions both within and outside the therapy relationship.

The Patient's Overt Maladaptive Pattern

A fourth essential target for intervention is a specific description of the patient's overt actions (verbal and nonverbal) pinpointed by the therapist as central in producing the impacts the therapist experiences with the patient. In pinpointing the specifics of the patient's maladaptive action pattern, the therapist provides the patient concrete instances of what the patient has done in their sessions to "make" the therapist react in the complementary manner.

A precondition of effective therapist pinpointing is repeated occurrence over their sessions of the patient's pattern with the therapist. The effect of pinpointing is that the patient begins to highlight components of his or her actions that previously were selectively ignored. Once the action pattern with its communicational incongruities is clearly identified—once the nonverbal and less aware "game" is put on the verbal "table"—it is extremely difficult for the patient (or therapist) to continue to remain ignorant about what the patient is doing with others. Hence, even if alternative, more adaptive actions are not yet clear, pinpointing has the power, in and of itself, to interrupt or stop the patient's overt maladaptive pattern. The patient may have no idea initially of what to do instead but is clear about what he or she wants to stop doing.

In targeting any of the four components of the MTC, *statements offered by either the therapist or client to clarify the client's living patterns are at best hypotheses or guesses* that vary in their usefulness to facilitate changes for the client. Validation of these hypotheses comes from changes in the client's pattern of communication behavior both with the therapist and with others. These changes can be mediated by any combination of interventions targeting the client's emotional experience, cognitive expectancies or beliefs, or overt verbal and nonverbal behaviors. But the priority intervention targets the evoking-impact messages manifest within and outside the therapy transaction. The client needs new, more consensually validated hypotheses about living, new and more consensually validated communication and behavior strategies.

Validation of therapeutic hypotheses comes from the therapist's, the client's, and others' perceptual experience of changes in the client's transactional patterns. Adaptive client changes should be evident in more adaptive transactions with the therapist in their sessions. Further, client changes of necessity imply changes in the dyadic system, so that both therapist and client should change away from the transactional baseline evident in their earlier sessions.

The point that hypotheses are the best we can do in verbal therapy transactions follows from interpersonal theory's emphasis on the psychological environment. Useful therapy transactions are those that facilitate change in the client's experiential-perceptual world. Inferences are all that we have in explaining another person's private world or, for that matter, in intuiting our own.

A therapist speaks most validly when reporting his or her own impacts as a basis for clarification and understanding of the client's interactional patterns. The therapist is the only valid reporter of his or her own internal states as he or she experiences them. Therapists speak least validly when presenting inferences about the client as having a truth-value that cannot be questioned. Virtually every therapist statement should take on a tentative, "let's explore the usefulness of this statement," flavor. In short, the therapist's interventions are based on tentative formulations and should be expressed in the same fashion. This hypothetical quality, if communicated clearly, can easily lead to participatory exploration with the client of the value of any given intervention and is the ideal context for the client's adaptation and growth.

INTERPERSONAL CIRCLE PRINCIPLES OF INTERVENTION

To reiterate, in interpersonal therapy the therapist's essential task is to disrupt the patient's vicious cycle of self-defeating actions depicted in the Maladaptive Transaction Cycle. In attempting to accomplish this task, the therapist has available important components of intervention that are derivable from the interpersonal circle (Kiesler, 1983, 1988). Having identified prototypic segments on the circle that define a particular patient's disordered pattern, theoretically derivable interventions can be systematically designated, including (a) the goal of therapy, (b) the precise overt and covert reactions (objective countertransference) that will be "pulled" from the therapist in early transactions, (c) the therapist's shift to therapeutic "asocial" responses (Beier, 1966) to effect cognitive ambiguity and uncertainty as the first step toward disrupting the patient's maladaptive style, and (d) the specific "anticomplementary" responses the therapist can initiate to exert the greatest pressure for positive change in the patient. I earlier provided an unpublished pictorial summary of this *Interpersonal Treatment Plan* as a clinical guide for psychotherapy applications. Figure 10–1 depicts the worksheet version to be filled in by the therapist. Figure 10–2 illustrates a worksheet completed on a client with dependent personality disorder.

Although interpersonal therapists have yet to articulate comprehensive treatment packages applying these principles to specific disorders, some important first steps have been taken (Andrews, 1966, 1977, 1984, 1989c, 1991; Benjamin, 1982, 1987a, 1993; Coyne, 1976a, 1976b; Coyne & Segal, 1982; Kiesler, 1973–1975, 1977, 1988; McLemore & Hart, 1982; Safran & Segal, 1990; Wachtel, 1977, 1982a; Young & Beier, 1982). Earlier summaries of many of these various approaches to interpersonal therapy can be found in Anchin and Kiesler (1982) and Kiesler (1986a).

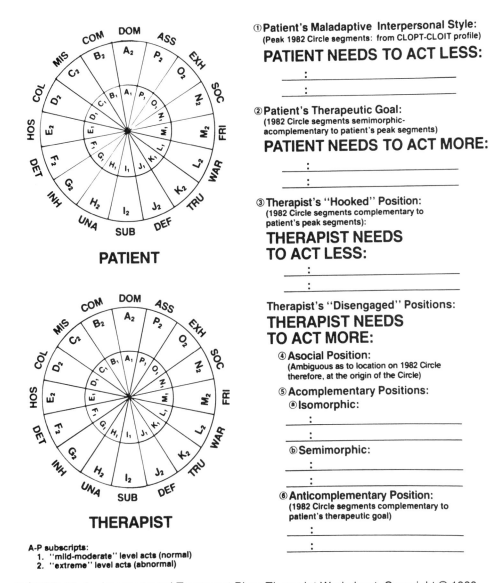

FIGURE 10–1. Interpersonal Treatment Plan: Therapist Worksheet. Copyright © 1988 by Donald J. Kiesler.

Available, then, as guides to interpersonal intervention are a series of basic principles that will be presented in this chapter, each of which is derivable and specifiable from the interpersonal circle (Kiesler, 1983). Underlying all these propositions is the assumption that to disrupt a patient's maladaptive transaction cycle, the therapist must respond to the patient in a manner markedly different from others in the patient's life. That is, the therapist must respond to the patient with something other than complementary responses. If the patient is permitted to restrict the therapist's reactions to only complementary responses, the therapist simply continues to confirm or reinforce (as do others) the patient's maladaptive cognitions and behaviors.

Another embarrassing possibility is evident at the point of impasse, which occurs in the later stage of the Maladaptive Transaction Cycle. During impasse, the therapist

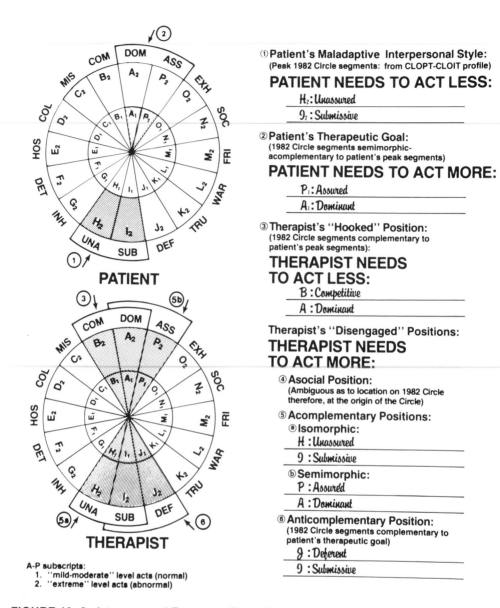

① **Patient's Maladaptive Interpersonal Style:**
(Peak 1982 Circle segments: from CLOPT-CLOIT profile)

PATIENT NEEDS TO ACT LESS:

H_2: *Unassured*

9_2 : *Submissive*

② **Patient's Therapeutic Goal:**
(1982 Circle segments semimorphic-
acomplementary to patient's peak segments)

PATIENT NEEDS TO ACT MORE:

P_1: *Assured*

A_1: *Dominant*

③ **Therapist's "Hooked" Position:**
(1982 Circle segments complementary to
patient's peak segments):

THERAPIST NEEDS TO ACT LESS:

B : *Competitive*

A : *Dominant*

Therapist's "Disengaged" Positions:

THERAPIST NEEDS TO ACT MORE:

④ **Asocial Position:**
(Ambiguous as to location on 1982 Circle
therefore, at the origin of the Circle)

⑤ **Acomplementary Positions:**
ⓐ **Isomorphic:**

H : *Unassured*

9 : *Submissive*

ⓑ **Semimorphic:**

P : *Assured*

A : *Dominant*

⑥ **Anticomplementary Position:**
(1982 Circle segments complementary to
patient's therapeutic goal)

9 : *Deferent*

9 : *Submissive*

PATIENT

THERAPIST

A-P subscripts:
1. "mild-moderate" level acts (normal)
2. "extreme" level acts (abnormal)

FIGURE 10–2. Interpersonal Treatment Plan: Example for a Client with *DSM* Dependent Personality Disorder. Copyright © 1988 by Donald J. Kiesler.

sends incongruent messages (enacts discrepant behaviors) expressing the unrecognized conflict that the patient's maladaptive pattern evokes. The general form of the therapist's conflict consists of hostile-rejecting feelings and cognitions toward the patient. The therapist then experiences guilt about these feelings and cognitions that are so much at variance with the role of an accepting and nurturant caregiver. The extreme of these hostile-rejecting feelings and their concomitant threat to the therapist have been vividly described by object relations theorists characterizing the treatment process with borderline and narcissistic personalities. In interpersonal therapy, the preeminent objective is to avoid this impasse, which represents the extreme of unhelpful "treat-ment" by a therapist.

Proposition 10–1.   The goal of therapy is to facilitate an increased frequency and intensity of interpersonal actions with significant others from segments *opposite* on the circle to the segments that define the patient's pattern of maladaptive interper-sonal behavior.

As noted in Chapter 3, Sullivan's Not Me is designated on the interpersonal circle at segments directly across the diameter from the patient's peak segment or octant score. The Not Me opposite categories represent a range of interpersonal behaviors that the maladjusted person avoids at all costs. This avoidance, in turn, is primarily responsible for the lack of flexibility (rigidity) that characterizes the maladjusted person's self-defeating interpersonal pulls. Emphasizing the cognitive components of this process, Carson (1969) asserts, "The role of the therapist is to provide his client with experiences that result in an expansion and loosening of the client's Image of Self . . . rendering it more encompassing, permeable, and flexible" (pp. 272, 275).

The direct effects of attainment of this goal are reductions of (a) the extremeness of the patient's maladaptive behaviors with others by pulling him or her toward the center of the circle, and (b) the rigidity of the patient's behavior by increasing the range of acts (around the circumference of the circle) available to the patient in transactions with oth-ers. Both reductions make the patient more "normal"—better able to adjust his or her actions more appropriately to different interpersonal situations. These new options pro-vide the patient a much better opportunity to attain the intimacy with others that is es-sential for genuine self-esteem and for satisfaction of basic interpersonal needs.

To illustrate, if a patient is diagnosed as *DSM* obsessive compulsive personality dis-order, interpersonal measures might profile the patient at the FG octant of the 1982 Circle (see Figures 1–1 thru 1–3, Tables 1–2 and 1–3, and Table 7–1). The therapeutic goal, then, is to facilitate an increased frequency and intensity of patient actions from octant NO, which is directly opposite to FG on the circle. Improvement for the obses-sive compulsive patient results from helping him or her interact with others in a man-ner more like that of a normal histrionic individual. Specifically, where F: detachment and G: inhibition prevail, more N: sociable and O: exhibitionistic behavioral possibili-ties with others need to be introduced. The hopeful outcome is that by facilitating greater occurrence and ego-syntonicity of sociable and exhibitionistic behaviors, the obsessive patient will enjoy greater options of being detached or not, inhibited or not, based on real characteristics of an interactant and his or her significance to the patient.

Once a patient's interpersonal behavior is precisely diagnosed on the circle, the goal of therapy for that patient is specifically determined.

Proposition 10–2.   In early therapy sessions especially, the patient will evoke or pull covert and overt responses from the therapist that are precisely characterized at segments of the circle that are *complementary* to those that define the patient's mal-adaptive interpersonal style.

Continuing the case of the FG obsessive-compulsive patient, this means that the therapist inevitably will be hooked or pulled to enact behaviors from the DC: cold-mistrusting octant of the circle. The therapist quickly will begin to experience an objective countertransference manifested by actions that are cold, stern, and strict/punitive (segment D) as well as vigilant, suspicious/jealous, cunning, resentful, and covetous/stingy (segment C).

Through statements and nonverbal behaviors, the patient sends evoking messages that shape the therapist to respond from a narrow portion of his or her inner experience and behavioral repertoire. The therapist inevitably is pulled to provide the complementary response because the patient is more adept, more expert in this distinctive, rigid, and extreme game of interpersonal encounter. The position the patient pushes the therapist to adopt is one that is least threatening to, and most confirming of, roles central to the patient's self-definition. By eliciting the complementary role from the therapist, the patient continues to validate a crippled self-definition and hangs on to the self-in-world view that maladaptively organizes his or her experience and behavior.

As the therapist becomes hooked, he or she experiences greater or lesser intensities of the various classes of "impact messages": feelings, action tendencies, cognitive attributions, and fantasies. The therapist who does not disengage from these impacts in effect unwittingly reinforces the maladaptive behavior of the patient. As their sessions continue, the therapist will increasingly feel more negative feelings such as boredom, anxiety, frustration, irritation, and depression. The Maladaptive Transaction Cycle shows that as the therapist continues to be unaware of the hooking, his or her experience of these feelings is inevitably communicated to the patient through a package of the therapist's own discrepant acts. These events not only compound the transactional impasse but, by his own incongruent communications, the therapist is placed in the embarrassing position of modeling maladaptive communication for the patient.

The therapist cannot *not* be hooked temporarily into providing the complementary response to the patient. Indeed, getting hooked eventuates in positive consequences. Becoming hooked probably is necessary for establishment of a working therapeutic alliance; it also permits the therapist to experience firsthand the aversive interpersonal consequences of the patient's maladaptive transactions.

Proposition 10–3.   The first therapeutic priority is for the therapist to *disengage* from the complementary covert and overt responses being pulled from him by the patient.

Since relationship messages mostly are automatic and outside the direct awareness of both participants, the therapist of necessity experiences feelings and other internal engagements before noticing or labeling them. Accordingly, the first task in the disengagement process is for the therapist *to detect, attend to, and label the engagements being evoked* by a given patient. From the first session, the therapist must ask some essential questions about his or her internal reactions: What is this patient trying to do to me? What am I feeling when I'm with this patient? What do I want to do or not to do with this patient? The Impact Message Inventory provides a useful format for this self-exploratory process.

A second disengagement maneuver available to the therapist is *to discontinue the complementary response.* The therapist who has been enticed to provide answers and advice must withhold these responses. When the therapist has been pulled to be entertained, he or she must stop enjoying the entertainment. When pushed into feeling cautious and constricted, the therapist must find a way to be more spontaneous. When trapped into protecting the patient from more intense emotion, the therapist must begin to help the patient face the feared feelings.

A third disengagement option for the therapist is *to use various techniques to help the patient interrupt his or her distinctive pattern of interpersonal behavior.* When the obsessive compulsive patient uses abstractions and qualifications to describe problems, the therapist can push for concrete elaborations through pinpointing and situational analysis procedures. When the histrionic patient entertains the therapist with anecdotes and dramatic displays, the therapist can reflect the patient's feelings of fragility and encourage him or her to attend to and elaborate the feelings being avoided.

Through the process of disengagement, the therapist prevents the relationship from ending in alienation. Unlike most others with whom the patient interacts, the therapist hangs in supportively to help the patient face tuned-out aspects of experience. The patient avoids these aspects to keep his or her self-definition and esteem from being devastated—to avoid emerging naked and vulnerable in a totally unpredictable new world. Finally, through disengagement, the therapist regains options to act therapeutically toward the patient and to use a more varied repertoire of interventions.

Proposition 10–4. The therapist can produce cognitive ambiguity and uncertainty for the patient, as the first step toward disrupting the patient's maladaptive style, by shifting from complementary responses to therapeutic *asocial* (Beier, 1966) responses.

The therapist responds to the patient in an asocial or disengaged way whenever he or she withholds the customary, preferred, or expected complementary response. As a direct first result, the patient experiences a sense of "beneficial uncertainty" (Beier, 1966) since the patient's preferred style does not produce the expected and familiar interpersonal consequences.

Murrell (1971) described how

> the burden for initiating change lies primarily with the therapist. To effect change he must introduce new information, or negative feedback, to the patient. . . . This means, first, that the therapist must respond to the patient in a way that is significantly different from the customary responses the patient receives in his social system. (p. 213)

In the case of our obsessive compulsive patient, asocial therapist responses would require that (a) the therapist in no way provide the DC: cold-mistrusting complementary response bid for so vigorously by the FG: detached-inhibited compulsive patient and (b) that any therapist response have ambiguous meaning in the sense that the compulsive patient cannot pinpoint a position on the circle from which the therapist is responding. As examples of therapeutic asocial responses, Young and Beier (1982) list delay responses such as long therapist silences, reflection of content and feeling, labeling the patient's interaction style, and use of therapeutic paradox.

Kiesler (1979, 1982a, 1988; Kiesler, Bernstein, & Anchin, 1976; Kiesler & Van Denburg, 1993) emphasizes that the asocial response of metacommunicative feedback (or therapist impact disclosure) has interventive priority throughout the course of therapy. Metacommunication means that the therapist talks directly to the patient about the transactional engagements transpiring between them and refers directly to the evoking or impact messages he or she experiences. Since it is far from the norm that persons talk directly to each other about their subtle relationship messages, metacommunication is very much an asocial response. With maladjusted individuals who have problems, others most frequently take the easiest way out by simply leaving the scene. Even those who do not flee usually stay with the implicit agreement that talking about what they might be doing to each other is forbidden. Generally metacommunication remains a remote option in everyday affairs because of the threat that it can eventuate in rejection, withdrawal of affection, various forms of punishment, or social isolation—that it might lead to dramatic disconfirmation of the person's identity.

In the case of our obsessive patient, the therapist might feed back to the patient the following kinds of internal engagements: "I'm trying to figure out why it is that I feel so emotionally distant from you—feel that you have to do all this by yourself without any help from me." "You know, often when you talk, it's difficult for me to follow your train of thought—you start off in one direction, shift to another, then another; and all the time I'm wondering where you're going and whether you're going to bring it back to the original topic." "Often I find myself being cautious and careful about what I'm going to say to you—as if, if I'm not careful, you will disapprove of what I say and lose respect for me."

The therapist not only disrupts the patient's maneuvers with a surprising asocial response that addresses the relationship directly, but importantly provides the patient with new information about the undesirable effects the patient has on others. Open feedback focuses both patient and therapist on the relationship issues occurring between them and interfering with the self-exploratory task and permits pinpointing of the distinctive patterns these maneuvers have taken. Through collaborative exploration of each other's contribution to the transactional effects experienced by the therapist, therapist and patient begin to clarify the patient's central maladaptive patterns with others—to detail the content of the patient's particular MTC. The therapist, by being willing to address the patient-therapist relationship openly, also models a powerful technique for the patient to use with significant others outside sessions.

The success of metacommunication depends crucially on the commitment of the therapist to open, direct, unambiguous communication to the patient about the therapist's feelings, fantasies, and pulls as well as on the skill with which the therapist can provide feedback in a manner that is simultaneously confrontative and protective of the patient's self-esteem. To be assimilated by the patient, feedback first must be heard. Hence, in using impact messages the therapist must always consider, in addition to his own possible subjective countertransference, the potential threat to the patient's shaky conception of self. The advantages of metacommunication, as well as principles that guide its use in therapy, will be discussed in detail in the next chapter.

Proposition 10–5.   In later sessions, the therapist can exert the greatest pressure for change in the patient's interpersonal behavior (for increasing the frequency and intensity of actions from opposite segments of the circle) by initiating responses that are *anticomplementary* on the circle to the patient's maladaptive interpersonal profile.

In enacting an anticomplementary response, the therapist is rejecting both components (control and affiliation) of the patient's self-presentation. That is, the therapist's response is both nonreciprocal on the control axis and noncorresponding on the affiliation axis. Anticomplementary responses come from the opposite vertically divided half of the circle and from the same horizontally divided half. The anticomplement to friendly-dominant behavior is hostile-dominant action, to friendly-submissive behavior is hostile-submissive action, and vice versa. Anticomplementary segments on the circle are depicted in Figure 4–3.

Because the anticomplementary response represents total rejection of the patient's self-presentation, its use early in therapy would likely result in the patient's rejection of treatment and/or premature termination. These patient reactions would represent very sensible responses to a threatening and aversive situation. It seems probable, then, that effective use by the therapist of anticomplementary responses can occur only in later stages of the therapy transaction. The therapist must first hook the patient—establish a working therapeutic alliance—by reacting with some components of the complementary response, so that later injections of the anticomplementary response do not elicit the strong and disruptive patient anxiety that is probable in earlier sessions.

In the case of the obsessive compulsive patient, the therapist would provide responses anticomplementary to the patient's maladaptive FG: detached-inhibited behaviors whenever the therapist responds from the KL: trusting-warm octant. By these actions, the therapist offers a stance characterized as unguarded, trusting, innocent, forgiving, and generous (segment K) as well as warm, gentle, and lenient/pardoning (segment L). These acts are bipolar opposites to the complementary responses the compulsive is working so hard to pull from the therapist—vigilant, suspicious/jealous, cunning, resentful, and covetous/stingy (segment C) and cold, stern, and strict/punitive (segment D). To provide the anticomplementary response, then, the therapist must struggle to find a way to enact behaviors diametrically opposite to the complementary acts being pulled so relentlessly by a patient.

The most powerful response available to the interpersonal therapist requires use of actions from circle segments anticomplementary to those that define the patient's rigid and extreme maladaptive style. Effective use of these responses probably occurs only after a working therapeutic alliance has been established.

Proposition 10–6.   In moving away from complementary responses for a particular patient to implement therapeutically desirable anticomplementary responses—in moving away from the segment on the interpersonal circle that is complementary to the patient's maladaptive pattern to the anticomplementary segment position—the therapist must avoid ever staying long in segment E: Hostile, must avoid being pulled chronically to enact responses that are antagonistic and harmful to the patient. To assure attainment of this goal, when the complementary segment the therapist is locked into falls within the dominant hemisphere of the circle, the therapist needs to advance toward the anticomplementary segment by moving in the clockwise direction; when the complementary segment the therapist is locked into with a particular patient falls within the submissive hemisphere of the circle, the therapist needs to move in the counterclockwise direction.

The rationale for this principle is (a) that the therapist seeks to avoid automatic enactments of Segment E: Antagonistic/Harmful behaviors toward the patient; (b) that the therapist of necessity seeks to confine most response time within the friendly hemisphere of the circle. Both strategies seem necessary for maintenance of a positive therapeutic alliance with the patient.

Proposition 10–6 is offered tentatively and will likely be modified or rejected by subsequent theory and research. It may not apply to all patient groups; it may not apply to any patient group. Winnicott (1949), for example, emphasized the crucial therapeutic importance of the patient's experiencing, within a holding environment, the full impact of the therapist's hate as validly experienced in the countertransference. This suggests that the therapist, in the process of disclosing the hateful feelings to the patient, needs to include credible features of the therapist's real emotion.

Moreover, alternatively credible circle strategies are available to guide the therapist's movements away from the complementary segment to the anticomplementary segment; these need at the very least also to be considered. One alternative is for the therapist simply to jump somewhat randomly between segments located in all four quadrants, thereby making it impossible for the patient to ascertain what the therapist's modal response might be or where on the circle it might fall. This alternative basically constitutes another possible form of the "asocial" response described in Proposition 10–4.

A second alternative is that the therapist move first to either one of the segments of the circle that are acomplementary (isomorphic or semimorphic) to the patient's peak segment. The rationale in this case is that the therapist would continue to provide the complementary response to the patient on at least one axis (e.g., affiliation) but would be denying the patient's bid on the other axis (e.g., control). This change would represent a halfway point between either continuing to confirm the patient's bid on both axes (complementary segment) or rejecting the patient's bid on both axes (anticomplementary).

A third possibility takes the form of a modification of this second alternative. It directs that the therapist move to the semimorphic acomplementary circle segment first (to the segment directly opposite, at the other end of the diameter from, the patient's peak segment). The rationale here is that the therapist not only would still be confirming the patient's bid on one of the circle axes, but would also be *modeling* behaviors that constitute the goal of therapy for that patient.

A fourth alternative is that the therapist move in the direction (clockwise or counterclockwise) that entails the "least resistance," that is, in the direction that discontinues confirmation of the circle axis having the weaker loading in regard to the patient's problematic pattern. Accordingly, except for the cases where the patient's peak segment (and its complement) falls exactly midway in one of the quadrants, the therapist would move from the complementary segment toward the closer axis that has the smaller weighting on the sum vector point (e.g., if the complement is segment L, the therapist would move first in a counterclockwise direction to segment M). The therapist, thus, would always move from the complementary segment toward the closest axis pole on the circle. This movement challenges the patient's bid first on the weaker vector, rather than attempting to challenge the patient first on the stronger vector.

Other important questions need to be addressed in considering the most desirable therapeutic alternatives. Should the therapist's responses ever remain long at the "extreme" level of the circle segments? Once disengaged, should the therapist ensure that his or her responses, whatever they may be, remain always at the "mild-moderate" level? In moving toward, arriving at, and responding from the *anti*complementary segment position (thereby putting maximum pressure on the patient to move to circle segments that represent his or her therapy goal), is it more important that the therapist's responses be "rigid" at mild-moderate levels, than ever to be "extreme"?

A different perspective on the desirability of therapists responding to clients' problematic behaviors from the various quadrants of the interpersonal circle was offered by Crowder (1972). Using the framework provided by the Kaiser Permanente group's interpersonal circumplex (Leary, 1957), Crowder postulated that "ideal" therapist responding is defined by consistent therapist response in the "support-interpretive" mode (the

FD quadrant of the 1982 Circle). He elaborated that a therapist's responding to a client in any other interpersonal response mode—Leary's support-seeking, hostile-competitive, or passive-resistant (F-S, H-D, and H-S quadrants of the 1982 Circle)—is most correctly construed as an expression of the therapist's "subjective" or irrational countertransference reactions and, thus, is detrimental to the course and outcome of therapy. As a dyadic corollary, Crowder (1972) implied that therapeutically appropriate client behavior should be characterized by consistent responding in Leary's support-seeking (for the 1982 Circle, friendly-submissive) mode; that client behavior in any other response mode constitutes a client transference reaction, which may be detrimental to the positive therapy outcome.

Benjamin (1980) offered some interesting notions regarding sequential timing of the anticomplementary response in therapy, based on her three-surface SASB Intrex model. "With more disturbed individuals, one usually cannot move directly to the antithetical (anticomplementary) point and have much impact" (1980, p. 25). Instead, she offered what she calls the Shaurette principle to guide prior interventions leading to eventual use of the anticomplementary response: "The milieu must 'connect' first with the patient by taking the complementary posture (with a constructive thrust) and then moving in a counterclockwise direction toward the final goal specified by the antithesis principle" (p. 25).

Berzins (1977) suggested similar therapeutic possibilities in his review of research on therapist-patient matching:

> It would seem that a complementary therapist could be readily provided. Anticomplementary pairing could be avoided since, under anticomplementary pairing conditions, therapeutic communication would be difficult to establish and dropouts may occur. On the other hand, given initially satisfactory (complementary) pairing conditions, the therapist's subsequent task is to *avoid prolonged complementary reciprocation* of the patient's interpersonal overtures since doing so would "confirm" the patient's rigid or constricted self-concept and little therapeutic change could be expected. (p. 225)

As Carson (1969) earlier suggested, the generally effective therapist is one who is able to move to any quadrant of the interpersonal circle in response to the presenting maladaptive styles of particular patients.

DeVogue and Beck (1978) pointed out that persons preferring to engage the therapist from a position of friendly submission should make ideal clients for therapy because they respond best to praise and approval. Furthermore, "these people should be most able to assume nonaversively a compliant role with a dominant other" (DeVogue & Beck, 1978, p. 234). They noted further that most therapists tend to interact in a friendly-dominant manner regardless of a patient's interactional style. An unfortunate consequence is that the therapist's friendly-dominant stance provides initial disconfirmation (non-complementarity) to all patient interpersonal styles except friendly-submissive (its complement).

Summary

These six interpersonal circle intervention principles provide only the skeleton of an ultimately comprehensive treatment package for a psychotherapy patient. Many additional components are necessary, including guidelines for analysis of situational manifestations of the patient's maladaptive pattern; specification of interventions that target cognitive, affective, and other covert events lawfully associated with the client's overt interpersonal style; specific rules that would guide the therapist's metacommunicative use of covert complementary impacts; and rules that would govern optimal sequencing over sessions of asocial, acomplementary, and anticomplementary therapist responses.

These six principles, however, represent a significant addition to what is predictively available in other discussions of the personality disorders, and especially when compared with the absence in the *DSM* of anything like differential treatment prescriptions.

OTHER PRESENTATIONS OF CONTEMPORARY INTERPERSONAL INTERVENTIONS

Andrews (1988, 1989d, 1991) offered an extensive presentation of his interpersonal "self-confirmation" model as a system for personality assessment and psychotherapy. The central therapeutic interventions he detailed are organized around the goals of fostering awareness and experimentation, creating a safe therapeutic environment, enhancing the client's self-responsibility, offering corrective experiences within the therapeutic interaction, and using targeted interventions to help the client alter specific self-confirmation processes.

Andrews (1991) demonstrated how the therapist-client relationship can be used as a vehicle for intervention in five principal ways: to foster greater awareness and insight, to send messages of disengagement from the client's evoking messages, to provide a corrective emotional experience involving the evocation of new interpersonal responses, to create in the therapeutic setting a laboratory for experimentation, and to offer the client an experience of acceptance and reparenting.

Benjamin (1982, 1992, 1993) systematically detailed her "brief SASB-directed reconstructive learning therapy." Her key proposition is that each of the *DSM* mental disorders is hypothetically associated with specific SASB-codable interpersonal and intrapsychic patterns. The SASB model also provides pathogenic hypotheses about specific associated interpersonal learning experiences presumed to contribute to a disorder. Her analysis has specific implications for psychotherapeutic learning experiences needed to change the patterns characteristic of the respective *DSM* personality disorders. Her "reconstructive therapy" seeks to help the patient learn to identify his or her interaction patterns, where they came from, and what they are for.

Benjamin (1993) detailed six features that are essential to the therapeutic intervention process: collaboration, use of "free form" to track the patient's unconscious, the assumption that the patient makes sense, interpersonal specification, avoidance of affirming destructive patterns, and quick correction of interviewer errors. She then outlined and illustrated for each of the 11 *DSM* personality disorders five categories of "correct treatment interventions." These interventions:

1. Facilitate collaboration between the patient and therapist.
2. Help the patient recognize present and past patterns and the relationships between them.
3. Block maladaptive patterns.

4. Strengthen the patient's will to give up destructive wishes and fears.

5. Help the patient learn new, more adaptive patterns.

Weiss, Sampson, and the Mount Zion Psychotherapy Research Group (1987) conceptualized that neurotic problems arise from pathogenic beliefs about interpersonal relationships (e.g., I will by rejected by the therapist if I reveal my basic doubts and fears). These beliefs develop as a result of traumatic experiences with significant others. The Group speculated that patients routinely (and unconsciously) submit their therapists to "transference tests" to ascertain whether the therapist will confirm their pathogenic beliefs. Crucially, it's only when the therapist successfully passes the transference test that real therapeutic progress can occur.

L. M. Horowitz and Vitkus (1986) provided an in-depth discussion of therapeutic intervention in interpersonal psychotherapy. They base their analysis on their earlier work showing that many symptoms and syndromes like depression include among their ingredients severe problems with assertiveness, as part of which the depressed individual expresses complaints involving the self and other people, with the complaints conveying to others a sense of helplessness. As a reciprocal response, the listener tends to regard the complaint "as a bid for help and, as predicted by the interpersonal circle, reacts by offering advice. Yet the offer of advice is precisely the wrong type of reaction for helping the distressed person overcome the symptom since it fails on [several] counts to enhance the person's sense of efficacy" (L. M. Horowitz & Vitkus, 1986, p. 466).

Their general paradigm asserts that in psychotherapy interactions Person A (the troubled or maladjusted person) complains to Person B (the therapist) about Person C. They noted that in some cases Person C can be the same as the Speaker A (patient) or the Listener B (therapist). They, then, highlight three frequent within-session paradigms as follows:

1. A talks to B against C (e.g., "My mother-in-law is always criticizing me in subtle ways").

2. A talks to B against A (e.g., "You know, I think I'm actually long-winded and boring").

3. A talks to B against B (e.g., "I think it's best to level with you: Sometimes I think the treatment is doing me more harm than good").

L. M. Horowitz and Vitkus (1986) analyzed six common therapist responses for each paradigm by evaluating each in light of two essential criteria. The first criterion is whether the therapist's (B's) response sustains the relationship—sustains the friendly collaboration (therapeutic alliance). The second criterion is whether the content of B's response enhances A's (the patient's) position in the C-A relationship—whether it enhances A's self-esteem, improves A's sense of competence, and reduces A's symptom.

L. M. Horowitz and Vitkus (1986) applied these evaluative criteria to six common types of responses from B (the therapist) for each of the three paradigms. The types of responses were:

1. B directly disagrees with A's premise.

2. B offers advice to solve the problem.

3. B simply acknowledges A's problem.

4. B investigates the conditions of the problem by probing for more information.

5–6. B makes a comment on the C-A relationship that reinterprets the problem.

The six response types comprised a sample of the therapist's (B's) possible responses; for instance, they do not include responses that shift the focus of attention from the patient to the therapist (e.g., therapist self-disclosure or impact-disclosure), nor responses that shift the focus of attention from the content of A's remark to the process of A's communication.

L. M. Horowitz and Vitkus (1986) analyzed the six types of intervention as they might occur in each of the three paradigms. Disagreements and advice-giving (Responses 1 and 2) failed to satisfy both of their evaluative criteria (hence are generally nontherapeutic). Therapist responses that acknowledge the problem (Response 3) or investigate the problem (Response 4) satisfy the first evaluative criterion (sustains the alliance) but not the second (enhances the patient's self-esteem and position with C). Responses 5 and 6, however, plausible relationship reinterpretations of the patient's premise, satisfied both evaluative criteria.

Finally, L. M. Horowitz and Vitkus (1986) illustrated the last two therapist responses for each of the three paradigms. In Paradigm 1, to the patient's statement, "My mother-in-law is always criticizing me in subtle ways," therapist Response 5 is, "Is it possible that she's jealous of you being married to her son?"; Response 6 is, "I have an idea that you could be pretty tough with her if you wanted to, but you prefer to let her feel as though she's in charge." In Paradigm 2, to the patient's statement, "You know, I think I'm actually long-winded and boring," therapist Response 5 is, "Maybe it makes you feel uncomfortable to have the floor and spotlight to yourself"; Response 6 is, "I'd describe you as verbally fluent, but I have an idea that there are special reasons why you've come to regard yourself so pejoratively." In Paradigm 3, to the patient's statement, "Sometimes I think the treatment is doing me more harm than good," Response 5 is, "I've had the impression that you dislike having the attention always focused on yourself"; Response 6 is, "I have the impression that you had wanted me to say more, and you feel displeased that I haven't done so."

L. M. Horowitz and Vitkus (1986) cautioned that reinterpretive responses by the therapist always involve a risk. If it doesn't seem plausible to the patient, an interpretation may arouse A's suspicions and perhaps disrupt the alliance. If it make sense to the patient, however, "it can have the greatest therapeutic impact of all; it can modify A's self-image and permit A to experiment with bolder patterns of interaction" (p. 466).

INTERPERSONAL STAGE MODELS OF PSYCHOTHERAPY

The basic interpersonal circle propositions presented in this chapter need to be further elaborated into treatment packages, consisting of distinct stages, which are tailored for specific psychiatric disorders. This section summarizes attempts by therapists to articulate the distinct stages within the process of interpersonal therapy.

Cashdan's (1971) stage-process notions provide a useful framework for organizing these stage model attempts. According to Cashdan (1971), a psychotherapy process is "essentially a miniature theory that specifies how therapist operations are sequenced [and that] predicts what changes can be expected in the patient as therapy progresses" (pp. 3–4). *Process, thus, represents a series of "stages," each of which is composed of a set of "rules" for the therapist to follow, as well as specified corresponding behavioral shifts for the patient.* Rules for a given stage are principles that guide the therapist's "technique" [the concrete responses of the therapist].

Most of the following process conceptualizations offer models that articulate the sequential stages of intervention occurring over the course of interpersonal therapy. As will be evident, however, these models vary considerably in providing the precise detail advocated by Cashdan.

Interactional/Object Relations Psychotherapy

Cashdan's (1971, 1982) original interactional therapy dictated five stages of transaction between therapist and client. His earlier model was modified substantially in a subsequent publication (Cashdan, 1988). I will summarize only his later formulation.

Cashdan's (1988) object relations therapy was presented in four stages. In Stage 1, *engagement,* the therapist fosters therapeutic bonding to ensure that the patient stays in treatment early on and as a relational foundation for the threatening confrontation by the therapist that is to occur later. This goal is fostered by the therapist's use of "emotional linking," humor, offering suggestions and advice, and similar interventions.

Stage 2 is referred to as *emergence of projective identification* in which the patient's characteristic projective identification (Cashdan focuses on four: dependency, sexuality, power, and ingratiation) manifests itself within the session. In this stage, the therapist's goal is to make this devious pattern public and interpersonally accessible—needs to obtain a clear expression of the metacommunication associated with the patient's projective identification before the therapy can move ahead. The therapist attempts to highlight the interactional nature of their sessions, probes for more direct expressions, and refuses to offer whatever is being demanded by the patient's metacommunication.

In Stage 3, *confrontation,* the goal is for patients to begin to realize that their maladaptive ways of relating to the therapist are no longer viable and to learn that open, honest relationships are possible. Instead of using interpretations, the therapist directly and forcefully follows one strategy: to refuse to concede to the patient's metacommunicative demand while continuing to affirm the relationship with the client.

Stage 4 is termed *termination.* Toward the end of Stage 3 instances of projective identification become less frequent and less intense. The therapist now provides the patient some appreciation and understanding of his or her projective patterns and how they affect others. The therapist accomplishes this by providing interpersonal feedback to the patient as to how the patient affects the therapist, by interpretations of early childhood and current experiences. Finally, the therapist addresses issues relating to termination. The goal is to ensure that the patient is actively engaged in the separation experience, which the therapist accomplishes through discussion and disclosure of his or her own feelings and thoughts.

Interpersonal Behavior Therapy

DeVogue and Beck (1978) offered a four-stage process model in which interpersonal and behavior therapy strategies are integrated. In Stage 1, the therapist tries to avoid any interpersonal actions that would be classified as intense or extreme on any of the circle segments. As a result of this tactic, the patient will begin to use his or her preferred interpersonal tactic to initiate a comfortable form of intimacy with the therapist.

In Stage 2, the therapist invites the patient directly into a conversation about their "here-and-now" relationship. In Stage 3, the therapist refuses to enact any behavior that is complementary to the patient's preferred interpersonal stance. Instead, he or she launches an unemotional and logical attack against the patient's position, while providing the patient with a clear message of the therapist's desire to continue the relationship.

Finally, at Stage 4, various behavioral techniques such as social skills and assertiveness training are instituted.

Interpersonal-Cognitive Therapy

Carson (1969, 1982) has written convincingly about the cognitive components of interpersonal therapy. He noted, "By far the most important cause of persistently maladaptive behavior is the tendency of the interpersonal environment to confirm the expectancies mediating its enactment" (1982, p. 64). In Carson's view, and as depicted in the Maladaptive Transaction Cycle, an unbroken causal loop exists among the patient's social perceptions or cognitions, behavioral enactments, and reactions of interactants that confirm the patient's maladaptive cognitions or expectancies.

From Carson's interpersonal-cognitive viewpoint:

> A major task of the psychotherapist is that of explicit identification of the client's habitual, disorder-related, parataxic distortions of social cognition, an examination of their sources, and a comprehensive analysis of the manner in which they affect the client's behavior, particularly in its maladaptive aspects. (1982, p. 67)

Further, the therapy relationship itself is the major arena in which corrective experiences occur. In addressing specific parataxic distortions projected by the patient onto the therapist, the therapist encourages a nondefensive and participatory exploration of the patient's more problematic "person-schematas" by undertaking a "thorough examination of the evidential basis of the characteristics assigned to him, and repeatedly asserts his willingness to be put to *fair* tests, having *explicit* criteria, concerning his personal attitudes and commitments" (1982, p. 67).

For Carson, the therapist's basic task is to change the client's self-other personifications, making them more encompassing, permeable, and flexible. In two therapeutic stages, the therapist first concentrates on "relationship enhancement," becoming an important and valued person in the client's life, while simultaneously avoiding provision of the complementary response. The second stage holds the "cardinal therapeutic tactic": nonconfirmation of the client's constricted self. The therapist must be the one person in the client's life who does *not* yield to the client's pressure to confirm his or her "crippled self" (Carson, 1969, pp. 277–280).

Safran (1984a, 1984b, 1990a, 1990b; Safran & Segal, 1990) amplified Carson's notions regarding the cognitive components of interpersonal therapy and argued convincingly for a rapprochement between cognitive-behavioral and interpersonal therapies. He (1984a) detailed a number of ways in which Sullivan's concepts are compatible with the contemporary cognitive behavioral tradition. He also detailed specific ways in which incorporation of interpersonal principles can broaden and enrich its theoretical and practical scope. Interpersonal theory provides a systematic framework for understanding and dealing with problems in therapeutic compliance and for understanding what variables can lead to problems in therapeutic maintenance, and at the same time allows cognitive behavior therapists to broaden their conceptualization of the role of emotions in psychotherapy.

Safran (1984b), like Carson, argued that "cognitive activities, interpersonal behaviors, and repetitive interactional or *me-you patterns* are linked together and maintain one another in an unbroken causal loop" (p. 342). Expanding on Kiesler's metacommunicative principles (Kiesler, 1982a, 1988; also see Chapter 11), Safran emphasized

> In addition to pinpointing and providing feedback to the patient about the interpersonal impact of dysfunctional behavior, the process of pinpointing dysfunctional interpersonal behaviors can provide the cognitive therapist with markers indicating the need for cognitive exploration. (p. 342)

This process involves the therapist-led exploration of the automatic thoughts accompanying or preceding the behaviors. Once some of the automatic thoughts and beliefs have been identified, the therapist can assign a variety of homework tasks described in detail by Safran.

Safran (1984b) suggested:

> A full assessment in the context of a *cognitive-interpersonal* therapy requires that the therapist conduct a comprehensive exploration of both the specific interpersonal behaviors and *me-you patterns* that impair the client's interpersonal relations, and the particular cognitive activities that are linked to them. (pp. 345–346)

Safran (1990a) outlined a systematic conceptualization that can guide use of the therapeutic relationship in cognitive therapy and clarify the relationship between cognitive and interpersonal processes in problem maintenance and change. Central to his framework are the concepts of *interpersonal schema* and *cognitive-interpersonal cycle*. Safran documented how dysfunctional interpersonal schemas constitute the cognitive component of cognitive-interpersonal cycles in which dysfunctional interpersonal transactions are shaped by and maintain dysfunctional cognitive structures.

Safran (1990b), building on the theoretical framework outlined in Safran (1990a), offered a number of suggestions for systematically integrating therapeutic concepts and intervention strategies derived from contemporary interpersonal theory into the practice of cognitive therapy. He argued that current cognitive behavioral writers, although increasingly recognizing the importance of the relationship, still tend to view a good therapeutic relationship as more of a necessary condition for change, rather than a mechanism of change. Safran (1990b) concluded:

> By "unpacking" the concept of the therapeutic relationship, my intention has been to show how every cognitive intervention inevitably impacts on the therapeutic relationship and how any "relationship act" is ultimately a cognitive intervention. (p. 119)

Safran and Segal's (1990) volume considerably expanded, in a comprehensive and systematic format, Safran's earlier cognitive-interpersonal formulations. It also summarized the distinguishing principles of Safran and Segal's approach and outlined relevant research directions.

Relational Psychotherapy

McLemore and Hart (1982) described a "relational psychotherapy" consisting of five process stages. In Stage 1, *inquiry,* the therapist gathers information about the patient and the presenting problems primarily through use of open-ended questions.

In Stage 2, *stabilization,* the therapist and client establish the transactional rhythm into which they both settle for joint exploration of the patient's life. During this stage, the patient is encouraged to take the lead, with the goal being "emotional immersion," which the therapist encourages through use of "triadic reflection" responses.

Stage 3, *assimilation,* involves the therapist's use of free-association technique to explore the patient's mental representations of significant others. Jointly, they clarify the patient's powerful introjects or personifications, and the therapist helps the patient to accept aspects of an introject that the patient deems desirable and to reject the rest.

In Stage 4, *confrontation,* the therapist directly helps the patient to extend learnings about introjects to ongoing relationships in the patient's life. As a major means of accomplishing this goal, McLemore and Hart (1982) used an intervention they call "the disclosure," which consists of bringing into the therapy session at the same time the patient and one or more significant others. This focal intervention has the purpose of assisting the patient

> at the appropriate time, and in the appropriate manner, to inform his or her significant other(s) of what the patient thinks and feels about some private "something." This is done with the therapist present to ensure clear communication, to encourage benevolence, and to prevent the patient from getting stuck or diverted. (p. 234)

Finally, Stage 5, *transition,* leads to a discontinuance of regular therapy sessions, but with the clear understanding that patients may consult the therapist later at any point in their lives. A careful analysis is also conducted of the degree to which the patient's goals have been reached as the patient's visits gradually decrease in frequency.

A Brief Strategic Therapy

Coyne and Segal (1982) extended and systematized the brief strategic therapy developed by Watzlawick and colleagues (Watzlawick et al., 1967; Watzlawick & Weakland, 1977) at the Palo Alto Mental Research Institute. Coyne and Segal offered detailed descriptions and examples of five basic maladaptive "metapatterns of interpersonal solutions." These metapatterns include attempts to be spontaneous deliberately; attempts to have others behave in a desired fashion even while requiring that they do so spontaneously; the seeking of a nonrisk method where some risk is inevitable; attempts to reach accord through argument; and efforts to attract attention by attempting to be left alone.

Coyne and Segal (1982) detailed five stages of their version of brief strategic therapy. In Stage 1, *pretreatment,* a concerted effort is made to identify the members of an interpersonal problem situation who are most committed to change. If the person calling for an appointment fails to meet this criterion, they use a number of strategies either to increase that person's motivation for therapy or to identify a more appropriate point of intervention in the system.

In Stage 2, *obtaining a problem description,* the therapist gathers concrete information that comprehensively describes the ongoing interactions characterizing a problem in the interpersonal system.

In Stage 3, *describing attempted solutions,* the emphasis is on obtaining behaviorally relevant descriptions of specific interactions that characterize the patient's attempts to handle or resolve the identified problem. In this stage, the therapist looks for commonalities in what the patient is trying to accomplish and how he or she goes about doing this.

In Stage 4, *eliciting a goal statement,* the therapist seeks from the patient a clear behavioral description of the kind of interaction that could signify that the problem has been resolved. Attempts are made to have the goal stated in terms of the occurrence of a positive event that involves a small but strategic change.

Stage 5, *strategic planning,* involves the therapist's attempts to influence the patient "to take a new tack that is not a variation of the basic solution so that the behaviors perpetuating the problem are abandoned" (p. 257). This final stage is accomplished through use of reframing interventions that change the meaning attributed to the problem situation, and therefore its consequences, but not the concrete facts. The particular reframing that is chosen is carefully constructed to reflect the patient's values, beliefs, and attitudes.

An Interpersonal Process Approach

Teyber (1992) developed a therapeutic model that synthesized concepts from interpersonal theory, object relations theory (and the attachment literature that developed from it), and family systems theory. Several major points are central to his "interpersonal process approach." First, problems are interpersonal in nature. Second, family experience is the most important source of learning about ourselves and others. When certain basic developmental tasks are not completed in the client's family of origin, conflicts often occur along the separateness-relatedness continuum. Third, the therapist-client relationship can be used to resolve problems: "Clients do not just talk with therapists about their problems in an abstract manner: rather they actually recreate and act out in their relationship with the therapist the same conflicts that have led them to seek treatment" (Teyber, 1992, p. 15).

Teyber (1992) developed a five-stage model of psychotherapy intervention. In Stage 1, the therapist establishes a working alliance with the client, sets expectations for how they are going to work together, and provides the client an experience of working together on his or her problems. The therapist's strategies include exploring expectations, fostering independence by sharing control, demonstrating empathic understanding, and identifying a "superordinate theme, conflict, or affect" that recurs throughout the client's presentations.

In Stage 2, the therapist helps the client to adopt an "internal focus for change"— to explore and clarify his or her own internal and interpersonal processes. Among the strategies the therapist employs are focusing the client inwardly, helping the client be an active agent in the change process, and responding receptively to the full range and intensity of feelings aroused. More centrally, the therapist approaches the client's primary affect and expands, elaborates, and intensifies it toward the goals of highlighting the client's predominant or characterological affect and working with the "three-tiered" constellation of feelings (anger-sadness-guilt) that make up the client's emotional conflict.

The goal of Stage 3 is to facilitate resolution and change in the client's central conflicts within the live interchange with the therapist. Essential to this stage is that the client must enact a resolution of his or her conflict in the current relationship with the therapist. Although the therapist and client explore the content of the client's dynamics, they also play out these same dynamics in their interpersonal process. The therapist's strategies include tracking the client's anxiety (in a four-step sequence detailed by Teyber) and using the process dimension to resolve conflict (the therapist makes process comments that describe or inquire about what is going on between them in their present interaction).

In Stage 4, the goal is to reenact central conflict themes over and over again in the therapeutic relationship and to generalize the experience of change beyond the therapy setting. Among strategies the therapist employs are giving the client permission to try out new ways of responding within the therapy relationship; helping the client "work through" the central conflict first with current relationships and then in family-of-origin relationships; and helping the client explore his or her "dream" (an image of the kind of life the client ideally wants).

In Stage 5, the final stage of Teyber's (1992) approach, the major rule is that the therapist must accept both sides of the client's feelings about ending—must take pleasure in the client's independence, but not be burdened or disappointed if the client wants to return later. The therapist pursues this rule by acknowledging the reality of the ending, by discussing the client's emotional reactions and acknowledging the client's unfinished business, by discussing how each perceives positive change in the client, and by the therapist's sharing of his or her own feelings about the client.

Interpersonal Communication Psychotherapy

Kiesler (1982a) offered a two-stage process model detailing the optimal sequence that objective countertransference events should take over the course of therapy. In the first, *engaged or hooked,* stage, the therapist invariably is pulled into enactment of covert and overt complementary reactions to the patient. A side effect of this engagement is that it permits the therapist to experience the interpersonal consequences of the patient's maladaptive behavior and also to "hook" the patient into a working therapeutic alliance wherein the therapist attains "significant other" status.

The second, *disengaged,* stage requires that the therapist prevent his or her objective countertransference responses from building to intense levels. As the therapist experiences intense covert reactions to the patient, it is easy for subjective, irrational countertransferences to engage full-blown, blocking any possibility of therapeutic intervention. Further, by becoming intensely trapped in the patient's maladaptive style, the therapist's reactions dramatically reconfirm and reinforce the patient's maladaptive cognitions and behavior. I have detailed methods of disengagement the therapist can use to avoid transactional impasses with patients (Kiesler, 1982a, 1988). Chapter 11 will elaborate these issues in considerable detail.

Interpersonal Stage Models: A Critique

From an interpersonal circle viewpoint, *what is conspicuously absent from stage descriptions of psychotherapy is specification of the transactional patterns between patient and therapist that may constitute central relationship rules for a given stage*—patterns that represent necessary preconditions for the effectiveness of the therapist interventions specified for that stage. Within a particular transactional pattern at one stage, a given intervention will likely be effective; within a different transactional pattern at another stage, the "identical" intervention will likely be ineffective.

Based on complementarity notions, various interpersonal theorists (e.g., Cashdan, 1988; Dietzel & Abeles, 1975; Kiesler, 1983, 1986a, 1988) have specified a necessary sequence of effective transactional patterns over the stages of therapy. Common to all these conceptualizations is a first stage in which the therapist cannot *not* be hooked into providing the complementary response to the patient's maladaptive interpersonal behaviors. Importantly, during this first stage in which the therapist's interpersonal behavior is, in effect, providing confirmation of the patient's maladaptive self-presentation, any intervention designed to change the patient's problematic behaviors is unlikely to be effective. Instead, the most appropriate interventions are those addressed specifically to facilitation of the therapeutic alliance. A second stage of interpersonal therapy has been variously defined by interpersonal theorists but has as a central feature the notion that the therapist now must cease to provide the complementary reaction and/or provide responses that disconfirm the patient's maladaptive self-presentation.

Obviously, additional stages can be specified from various theoretical frameworks. However, it should be clear that "identical" events occurring between therapist and patient during the first and second stages just described are likely to have dramatically different effects. The identical therapist interpretation that "falls flat on its face" during the first stage may be assimilated and applied vigorously during the early part of the second stage.

As Chapter 9 discussed, *it seems highly probable that individual and/or transactional interpersonal behaviors serve as important moderators for the effectiveness of any intervention applied both (a) within a particular psychotherapy session and (b) within a particular stage of the therapy process.*

COMPLEMENTARITY PATTERNS OVER THE STAGES OF PSYCHOTHERAPY: FORMULATIONS AND RESEARCH

Various interpersonal and interactional writers have conceptualized and/or researched successful versus unsuccessful patterns of patient-therapist complementarity across the stages of psychotherapy (Brokaw, 1983; Carson, 1969; Coulter, 1993; Dietzel & Abeles, 1975; Kiesler, 1982a, 1983, 1988; Kiesler & Watkins, 1989; Laird & Vande Kemp, 1987; Tasca, 1988; Tasca & McMullen, 1993; Tracey, 1986, 1987; Tracey & Ray, 1984). Carson (1969) was the first to suggest that the initial complementarity between patient and therapist that is required to establish a working alliance must change during the middle, working portion of therapy.

The resulting transactional prediction offered almost unanimously by interpersonal theorists is as follows: *In the case of successful psychotherapy, the patient and therapist will move from rigid and extreme complementary transaction early in therapy, to non-complementary positions in the change-oriented middle phases of therapy, to a later transactional pattern that exhibits mild and flexible complementarity.* In contrast, in unsuccessful therapy, the patient-therapist relationship will remain bogged down in various degrees of complementarity throughout the entire therapy course.

Dietzel and Abeles (1975) hypothesized that "the therapeutic timing of complementary levels is crucial to facilitate constructive client change" (p. 271). Their pioneering study examined 20 therapy cases selected from Michigan State University Counseling Center's research project by having observers rate on the ICL the interpersonal behaviors of clients and therapists during early, middle, and late therapy sessions. They found no differences in degree of patient-therapist complementarity during the early stage. In the middle/working stage of therapy, a lower level of complementarity was discovered for successful cases than for unsuccessful ones. During the late therapy sessions, the successful therapists reverted to more complementary patterns that were not different from the patterns of the unsuccessful therapists.

Tracey and Ray (1984) offered a highly similar stage formulation based on relational control conceptions of complementarity or symmetry (see Chapter 4). They observed that "as represented by the complementarity construct, three relatively distinct stages of the counseling relationship could be delimited: (a) an initial stage of high complementarity, (b) a middle stage of lower complementarity (greater symmetry), and (c) a final stage of high complementarity" (p. 15). Initially, the therapist establishes rapport and a working alliance and follows the client's definition of the relationship. In the middle stage, to induce change, it is important for the therapist to alter his or her behavior away from the client's initial expectations toward behavior that fits less well. Accordingly, a moderate amount of relationship conflict (high symmetry) is therapeutic, and would be reflected in lower complementarity. In the third stage, complementarity returns.

> As the client becomes more aware of his or her unrealistic expectations and tries out new behaviors, both the client and counselor are better able to negotiate what form their relationship should take so as to realistically meet the needs of each. (Tracey & Ray, 1984, p. 16)

Tracey (1987) and Tracey and Ray's (1984) findings confirmed that their hypothesized general stage model was associated with positive therapy outcome. Also, Tracey (1986) found that failure to achieve high levels of complementarity early in therapy was related to premature termination.

Tasca (1988; Tasca & McMullen, 1993) examined therapist-client interactions from early, middle, and late sessions for eight therapy cases (one successful and one unsuccessful from each of four therapists) drawn from Strupp's (1980a, 1980b, 1980c) Vanderbilt I research project. Using SASB codings (Benjamin et al., 1981) of within-session transactions, Tasca found that for the successful cases the pattern of complementarity was as predicted: more complementary interactions in the early and late stages of therapy, and significantly less complementarity in the middle sessions. Also, most of the complementary exchanges in successful cases were friendly, with the therapists behaving dominantly and the clients submissively. In the case of the more noncomplementary exchanges during the middle sessions, the therapists were more submissive and clients were more dominant; the more noncomplementary client-therapist exchanges were primarily F-D/F-D and F-S/F-S. For unsuccessful cases, the amount of complementarity remained constant from early through middle to late sessions, as expected. More important, however, in distinguishing successful from unsuccessful cases was the substantial amount of hostile complementarity in unsuccessful cases—typically, a client's hostile-submission was complemented with hostile-dominance from the therapist. Further, and totally unexpectedly, there were significantly more noncomplementary exchanges throughout therapy with *unsuccessful* cases (for example, therapists responding to hostile-submission with friendly-submission). Obviously, noncomplementarity did not improve the outcome for these unsuccessful cases. Tasca and McMullen (1993) concluded that even experienced therapists sometimes attempt to change clients' hostile-submission with friendly-submissive reactions and sometimes respond in kind to their clients' hostility.

Coulter (1993) used an analogue design to explore the effects of therapist experience and interpersonal style on therapist response complementarity in the middle stage of counseling (the stage in which the theoretically effective therapist needs to have shifted to noncomplementary reactions). Coulter offered an important clarification that, during the middle phase of therapy, a therapist should not always respond with the anticomplement to a client's statement. Coulter observed that global anticomplementary responding to all client statements regardless of their similarity to the client's problematic style would likely result in angering or confusing the client, and would constitute a global rejection of the client. She argued instead for the necessity of considering client problematic interpersonal style as a central variable in determining the appropriateness of therapist complementarity levels during the middle stage:

> Therapists should demonstrate the least complementarity in response to statements that are consistent with the problematic style of the patient. In order to discourage such behavior, the therapist should respond with anticomplementarity. Conversely, therapists should offer complementary communications in response to client statements that represent the opposite of their identified problematic style, in order to encourage these types of behaviors [the goal of interpersonal therapy]. Further, statements emitted by the client that are acomplementary to the client's interpersonal style (similar to the client's style on either the control or affiliation dimension but different on the other dimension) should be met with acomplementary responding geared toward complementing the style-deviant aspect of the patient's communication and challenging the style-characteristic aspects of the patient's communication. For example, in middle stages of counseling with a hostile-dominant client, the therapist's complementarity of response ideally should be lowest in response to hostile-dominant client statements, greatest in response to friendly-submissive client statements and at intermediate levels with either hostile-submissive or friendly-dominant client statements. (p. 9)

Coulter (1993) hypothesized that, during the middle stage of therapy, therapists with greater experience and with more flexible interpersonal styles would offer the lowest levels of complementarity to client interpersonal style. She showed a videotape (developed by Gonick, 1987) portraying a client with either a hostile-submissive or hostile-dominant interpersonal style to 90 therapist subjects (30 each at beginning, intern and professional levels of experience). She then gave the therapists 16 client statements and instructed them to respond to those statements as they would if the statements were being made to them by that client during the middle stage of counseling. The 16 client statements represented the range of interpersonal behaviors, with four statements characterizing hostile-dominant, hostile-submissive, friendly-dominant, and friendly-submissive behaviors respectively. Classification of client statements and therapist responses were coded using Strong, Hills, and Nelson's (1988) Interpersonal Communication Rating Scale (ICRS).

Findings indicated that therapist experience level did not affect the degree of noncomplementarity that therapists offered to problematic aspects of client interpersonal style. Therapists indeed did offer different levels of complementarity to different types of client statements—complementarity to F-S client statements was greater than complementarity to F-D and H-S client statements, which in turn was greater than complementarity to H-D client statements. Obtained patterns suggested that therapists offered the same pattern of complementarity to client statements across different client interpersonal styles. That is, regardless of type (quadrant) of interpersonal statement, therapists relied most heavily on friendly-dominant responding, with the effect that they actively encouraged friendly-submissive client behaviors and actively discouraged hostile-dominant client behaviors. Coulter (1993) found that although therapists responded to H-D clients with high levels of appropriate F-D anticomplementarity, they responded to H-S clients also with F-D (instead of F-S anticomplementary) responses.

Using Benjamin's SASB, Laird and Vande Kemp (1987) conducted a microanalysis of one of Salvador Minuchin's successful family therapy cases. Interactions (20 minutes each) from videotapes sampled from early, middle, and late stages of therapy were observed and coded. Analysis of SASB codings revealed that level of therapist complementarity vis-à-vis the identified patient (adolescent child) was significantly greater in the early and later stages than in the middle stages. Further, level of therapist complementarity was significantly correlated with the changes occurring for all family members. Laird and Vande Kemp (1987) observed:

> Although Minuchin maintained a supportive and moderately directive interactional stance, he showed much flexibility in the types of transactions utilized. . . .
> In the middle, working stage, Minuchin utilized 12 of the 16 possible types of interaction. These data suggest that, while a therapist can maintain a uniform stance throughout therapy, the combination of this stance—which will be acomplementary to the client at times—and responses that are *not* typical of the therapist, are meshed in order to produce and sustain client change. (p. 135)

Finally, Brokaw (1983) found a strong association between complementary therapist responses and stable client behavior, and between noncomplementary therapist responses and changed client behavior.

Positive versus Negative Interpersonal Behavior over the Stages of Psychotherapy

A series of studies indicated that the meaning and relevance to outcome of therapist-patient interpersonal behavior that occurs during early, middle, or late stages of the psychotherapy course depends crucially on whether the behaviors occur in the right (friendly) versus left (hostile) hemispheres of the interpersonal circle. Studies include Campbell (1991), Campbell and Brown (1990), Celani (1974), Crowder (1972), Henry et al. (1986), Kiesler and Watkins (1989), Muran (1993), Muran et al. (1992a, 1992b), Muran et al. (1994), Saltzman, Luetgert, Roth, Creaser, and Howard (1976), and Svartberg and Stiles (1992).

As we saw in Chapter 9, Kiesler and Watkins's (1989) study, which examined the relationship between the therapeutic alliance and interpersonal complementarity, found positive associations between patient-therapist interpersonal complementarity (especially on the hostile half of the circle) and both patient's and therapist's perceptions of the alliance. Their findings suggested that compatible interpersonal behaviors within the hostile hemisphere of the circle may be crucial for development of a positive working alliance as perceived by either patient or therapist. They found also that the more extreme a patient's behavior within the hostile half of the circle, the less strong was the working alliance perceived by the patient. Overall, in testing interpersonal theory within the psychotherapy context, it was crucial to differentiate patient-therapist matchup of hostile-side versus friendly-side behaviors.

Kiesler and Watkins (1989) suggested that one possible explanation for the differential valence in favor of the hostile-side circle behaviors considers the role definitions of the therapy participants: therapist as friendly-dominant caregiver, patient as friendly-submissive supplicant. Since this role matchup pulls so strongly for interpersonal behaviors from the friendly side of the circle, their compatible occurrence between patient and therapist may be selectively unattended or deemphasized by both. Within this context, further, occurrence of hostile-side behaviors may produce high salience, especially in terms of their complementary (or not) matchup.

C. C. Wagner (1995) suggested another possibility when he speculated:

> What has been interpreted as the ill-effects of high complementarity of hostile behaviors in early psychotherapy sessions may instead be limited to ill-effects of hostile complementarity *only* in patients with typically high baseline friendly behaviors and low baseline hostile behaviors, that is, for patients to whom hostile behaviors are unusual, uncomfortable and threatening. (p. 21)

Henry et al. (1986) also found different relationships to therapeutic outcome for the friendly versus hostile hemispheres of the circle (as measured by the SASB), but in a direction apparently opposite to the Kiesler and Watkins (1989) CLOIT-R results. While agreeing with the interpersonal principle that noncomplementary therapist responses are therapeutic, Henry et al. (1986) added the qualification that affiliative therapist behaviors have a more therapeutic valence in the therapy context than do hostile ones. They differentiated "negative" complementarity (a hostile and controlling client-therapist exchange) from "positive" complementarity (a friendly and autonomy-enhancing exchange). Generally, as Tracey (1994) observed, negative complementarity refers to complementarity given hostile antecedent behavior; positive refers to complementarity given friendly antecedent behavior.

Henry et al. (1986) found, as did Svartberg and Stiles (1992), that positive complementarity (in contrast to negative, or mixed communication) was associated with positive therapy process and desirable patient change. Negative complementarity or mixed communication was actually disruptive of desirable therapy process and outcome. In the case of mixed communication, Henry et al. (1986) suggested that therapists should attempt to respond in complementary fashion only to the positive portion of the patient's message.

In a similar vein, results from a series of investigations of the interpersonal process in a dynamic-cognitive psychotherapy, suggested that control has a stronger relationship to outcome than does affiliation (Muran et al., 1992a, 1992b). In an overview of this research program, (Muran, 1993) noted that friendliness between patient and therapist was positively related to the quality of the alliance, but hostility was negatively related to both the alliance and outcome. An analysis of changes within sessions revealed that reciprocal shifts toward a moderate level of therapist control and patient compliance were characteristic of good outcome cases. Muran (1993) concluded that the most productive interpersonal process in psychotherapy can be characterized as "a didactic interaction against a stable backdrop of friendliness" (p. 70). A replication study using cognitive-behavioral treatment is apparently underway.

Muran et al. (1994) examined patient interpersonal functioning as it relates to the development of the therapeutic alliance. Specifically, they examined the relationship of patient pretreatment interpersonal functioning (as measured by the IIP-C and by

Millon's (1987) MCMI) to the therapeutic alliance measured early in treatment by a patient self-report inventory. Findings from the IIP-C revealed that friendly-submissive interpersonal problems were positively related, while hostile-dominant problems were negatively related, to development of a strong therapeutic alliance early in short-term cognitive therapy.

Crowder (1972) studied successful versus unsuccessful therapy cases by sampling 15-minute segments from early, middle, and late therapy sessions. Almost 10,000 interaction units from these segments were then coded, using the ICL, into one of the four quadrants of the interpersonal circle. Crowder defined "transference" behavior as client behavior rated in any quadrant but F-S (friendly-submissive, support-seeking) and defined "countertransference" (CT) behavior as any therapist behavior rated in any quadrant but F-D (friendly-dominant, supportive-interpretive). Results showed that successful therapists displayed a lower proportion of CT behaviors only in the later therapy sessions. Relative to the present discussion, during early sessions the successful therapists showed more hostile-competitive and less passive-resistant CT behaviors. Also, successful clients showed a lower proportion of transference behavior only in the early and middle stages of therapy. Again, in relation to the present discussion, in early sessions successful clients were hostile-competitive and less passive-resistant and supportive-interpretive; during middle sessions, however, unsuccessful clients continued to show more passive-resistant transference behavior.

Celani (1974) used the ICL to classify the interview behaviors of 10 psychotherapists. He found that friendly-dominance was the overwhelmingly predominant therapist interpersonal behavior. In terms of the present discussion, he also found that therapists were least successful in deliberately evoking patient behavior opposite on the circle from the patient's peak style—the "goal" of interpersonal therapy (see Proposition 10–1)—when such behavior involved hostile-dominant categories. In other words, clients were reluctant to be assertively critical with their therapists. Celani observed that interactions of this kind, if long continued, would dissolve the therapeutic relationship. Finally, Celani (1974) found that when therapists were trained to shift toward behaviors less complementary with their client's, the client also shifted so as to complement the new therapist behavior.

Saltzman et al. (1976) found that the patient's awareness of having emotional reactions focused on the therapist was a distinguishing characteristic for subsequent successful outcome. Interestingly, the patient's awareness of feelings not focused on the therapist (such as hostility, anxiety, depression) was unrelated to outcome.

Campbell (1991; Campbell & Brown, 1990) examined the relationship of interpersonal complementarity to marital satisfaction and security within a large sample of married couples. "Objective" complementarity was assessed using the spouses' CLOIT self-reports of their interpersonal behavior when interacting with each other. "Perceived" complementarity was assessed using an index calculated from a spouse's (A's) self-report of his or her own behavior together with A's perception of the marital partner's (B's) interpersonal behavior during their transactions. Also, the difference in CLOIT interpersonal patterns manifested by the spouses within and outside their marriage was also calculated.

Campbell and Brown's (1990) results provided support for the complementarity hypothesis in that both objective and perceived complementarity showed a significant positive relationship with marital satisfaction and security. Also, the greater the departure from complementarity in the couple, the higher was the avoidant attachment style within the marital relationship. In regard to the current issue of focus, results in the hostile hemisphere of the circle showed stronger support for the complementarity hypothesis. For a secure, satisfactory marital relationship, complementarity was more important in marital interactions that occurred within the hostile hemisphere. Campbell (1991) speculated:

> This indicates that the presence of reciprocity on the Control dimension appears to be more important in the Hostile hemisphere than in the Friendly hemisphere. . . . Complementary interactions in the Friendly hemisphere may not be as necessary in order to achieve a friendly, affectionate relation. (p. 72)

Thus, findings from a series of studies suggest that in the psychotherapy context the valence of interpersonal behaviors from the hostile versus friendly halves of the interpersonal circle is not equivalent. It may be that how the patient and therapist match on the hostile half of the Circle is important for development of a positive working alliance; how they match on the friendly half may be relatively irrelevant—at least during early therapy sessions. Future studies need to concentrate on this important circle hemisphere complementarity issue.

DIFFERENTIAL INTERPERSONAL TREATMENTS

The interpersonal stage models reviewed earlier offered guides for a therapist's efforts with the "unspecified" psychotherapy patient. Few had much to offer in regard to the types of patients with whom a given stage model is more or less effective. Two exceptions—Andrews' (1966) two-stage model of interpersonal therapy for specific phobia and Birtchnell's (1987) two-stage therapy model for dependent personality disorder—were reviewed in Chapter 6. Few described any principles that might guide differential applications to the various psychiatric disorders.

The distinctive power of interpersonal therapy derives from its potential for concrete specification of distinctive maladaptive cognitions and behaviors corresponding both to the maladaptive transactions cycle and to distinctive profiles on the interpersonal circle. This power can be realized only as differential treatment programs are constructed for patients prototypical of various *DSM* disorders or for patient exhibiting prototypical profiles of circle interpersonal behaviors. We glimpsed this power in Chapter 6's contemporary interpersonal analysis of *DSM* dysthymia (see Figure 6–2). At present, attempts at systematic differential interpersonal treatments of this sort are few and far between.

Interpersonal Psychotherapy of Depression

Klerman et al. (1984) provide a detailed description of a comprehensive interpersonal treatment program for patients with *DSM* major depressive disorder. Their interpersonal psychotherapy (IPT) of depression is a time-limited treatment that focuses on interpersonal behavior rather than on intrapsychic phenomena. It concentrates on the patient's current life situations and is directed toward alleviation of one or two problem areas by changing the way the patient thinks, feels, and acts in current problematic relationships. In IPT, the therapist first identifies one of four problem areas that depressed patients commonly encounter: grief reactions, interpersonal disputes with a significant other, role transitions, and interpersonal deficits resulting in isolation and loneliness.

The strategies of IPT are applied in three stages of the treatment process. During Phase 1, the depression is diagnosed within a medical model and the disorder is explained in some detail to the patient. Initial sessions are devoted to identification of the major problem areas associated with the onset of depression and to establishment of a treatment contract. Also, a primary problem area is defined to identify and clarify the most recent stress with which the patient is trying to cope. The defined problem area then becomes the focus of the therapy sessions.

In Phase 2, the *intermediate* phase, the therapist and patient begin the hard work on the defined major current interpersonal problem area. The therapist's main tasks are to help the patient discuss topics pertinent to the problem while constantly attending to the patients's affective state and to the therapeutic relationship. These tasks are necessary to maximize the patient's intimate self-disclosure and to prevent the patient from sabotaging the treatment. Exploration of the problem area entails general exploration of the problem, a focus on the patient's expectations and perceptions, an analysis of possible alternative ways to handle the problem, and attempts at new behavior.

In Phase 3, *termination,* two to four sessions are devoted to discussing the patient's feelings about termination, to reviewing progress, and to outlining the work remaining to be done. Areas of potential difficulty are discussed, the therapist guides the patient in exploring possible ways to handle various contingencies and emphasizes the importance of the patient's ability to judge when he or she needs to seek help again.

The volume by Klerman et al. (1984) serves as an IPT training manual that standardizes the strategies and techniques therapists should follow when treating depressed patients. It provides detailed instructions and guidelines for the actual conduct of the treatment, a list of operationalized techniques from which the therapist can choose, detailed outlines of strategies for approaching the patient's interpersonal problem depending on which of the four problem areas is being presented, a set of guidelines for handling specific issues that usually arise in the sessions, instructions about the sequence of events to be followed in the various stages of therapy, and descriptions of the defining features of the relationship the IPT therapist attempts to form with the patient. A recent volume (Klerman & Weissman, 1992) and a journal article (Weissman & Markowitz, 1994) detail additional applications of interpersonal psychiatry to other disorders.

As Chapter 1 observed, Klerman and colleagues' conceptualizations are interpersonal primarily in the individualistic (rather than transactional) sense. Their formulations are not "contemporary interpersonal" as defined in the Preface—they are not based on either the interpersonal circle or the interpersonal transaction cycle. We hope that future attempts at integration of the individualistic and transactional perspectives for depressed and other patients will appear.

Interpersonal Psychotherapy of the Histrionic Personality

Andrews (1984; Andrews & Moore, 1991) provided a conceptualization of the hysteric (*DSM* histrionic) personality disorder and a plan of differential interpersonal treatment. His interpersonal analysis of the hysteric's personality was presented in Chapter 6, but will be repeated briefly here. It centered on a self-presentation style characterized by excessive use of agreeable, affiliative, and overconventional behavior (equivalent to the N: Agreeable and O: Exhibitionistic segments of the 1982 Interpersonal Circle). Andrews described a transactional cycle in which the hysteric sends conflicting and indirect messages to others. The messages combine both symbolic sexual overtones (to gain interest and attention) and simultaneous but subtle hostile messages (to keep the other person at a distance). No matter to which part of the hysteric's message an interactant responds—the interactant who shows disinterest is regarded as rejecting and mean; the interactant who reciprocates the advances is regarded as guilty of sexual exploitation—the effect is the same: confirmation and strengthening of the hysteric's overconventional self-image. In addition, the hysteric's cognitive experience is distinguished by the tendency to perceive in global, diffuse, and impressionistic ways (field dependence) and to exhibit a weak differentiation of self from the environment. The hysteric is oversensitive to external stimuli and confused as to what is external and internal.

The therapy package Andrews (1984) advocated for the hysteric patient consisted of strategies and techniques designed to counteract the preceding stylistic components. They are designed to attain the following objectives: symptom reduction, development of a clear sense of identity, acceptance of negative feelings, greater assertiveness, and enhanced cognitive differentiation.

The most important relationship issue posed for the therapist stems from the patient's eagerness for approval, which leads the hysteric to try to discover the therapist's attitudes, which are then used as an external guide for being a "good" patient. The aim is to gain the therapist's confirmation of the patient's self-image as an agreeable, non-hostile person. The therapist counters this ploy by using the ambiguity inherent in the free-association rule of psychoanalysis, insisting that the patient share all thoughts, feelings, and associations no matter how bizarre or unacceptable they may seem. What this ambiguous stance accomplishes is a paradoxical attack on the patient's facade of overconventionality. The hysteric who religiously follows the rule of free association (as might be expected from one who conforms to conventions, rules, and expectations) inevitably will come up with censored hostile, sexual, and other troublesome feelings that contradict the self-presentation. On the other hand, for the hysteric to openly resist or deliberately censor thoughts introduces conflict or deceit that is equally incompatible with the agreeable self-image. Change will occur no matter what the patient does because the only way to please the therapist is to bring up that which is unpleasant and conflictual about oneself.

To accomplish this paradoxical attack, the therapist must establish and maintain a realistic middle ground between pleasing and disappointing the hysteric patient. Thus, the therapist maintains a neutral, steady, but flexible attitude by being willing to accept some of the hysteric's demands for dependency. To enhance development of more discriminating cognitive skills, the therapist continually provides reflective comments to the patient's spontaneous associations and self-disclosures. This labeling provides cognitive structure for the hysteric's inner experiences, facilitates conceptual clarity, and reinforces early steps toward cognitive control of emotionally laden internal experiences. Finally, the hysteric is helped to learn new communication skills, including how to express needs effectively even in the face of conflict, and how to be a more effective and less manipulative elicitor of attention.

The interpersonal therapy of Andrews (1984) directs the therapist to create a setting that does not reinforce the hysteric's repeated efforts to elicit attention from the therapist by symptomatic and other manipulative maneuvers. Once this has been accomplished, new ways of living with him- or herself and with others are fostered.

EMPIRICAL INTERPERSONAL RESEARCH ON PSYCHOTHERAPY

Therapist-Patient Matching

A group of studies investigated the utility of using interpersonal variables for optimal therapist-patient matching in psychotherapy, including Andrews (1991), Berzins (1977), P. L. K. Rice (1970), S. Stuart et al. (1992), and Talley et al. (1990).

Unquestionably, the most extensive interpersonal study of patient-therapist matching was that of the Indiana Matching Project reported by Berzins (1977), which sought to identify optimal patient-therapist pairings for short-term, crisis-intervention oriented psychotherapy. The 4-year study examined 751 patients, each randomly assigned to 1 of 10 project therapists. The therapists saw from 29 to 145 patients each (mean = 75.1), typically for about 3 weeks. Measures of patients' role orientations (avoidance of others, turning against the self, dependency on others, and turning toward others) were obtained pretherapy and related to measures of therapist activity within the sessions. Findings indicated favorable therapist pairings for the first three patient role orientations, suggesting dyadic complementarity along a superordinate dominance-submission dimension:

> Favorable pairings generally conjoined submissive, inhibited, passive patients with dominant, expressive, active, cue- and structure-emitting therapists, and sometimes vice versa, suggesting that improvement in brief psychotherapy was facilitated by pairing patients with therapists whose personalities embodied ingredients that complemented the patients' needs, deficits, expectations, or interpersonal stances. (Berzins, 1977, p. 243)

Andrews (1991) reported findings that suggest another possibility of optimal interpersonal matching. Using the ICL, he characterized a sample of randomly assigned patient-therapist dyads as high (anticomplementary), moderate (acomplementary), and low (complementary) in "interpersonal challenge." Recall that anticomplementarity defines the situation in which the patient and therapist's behaviors deny each other's self-presentational claims on both axes; in acomplementarity, they confirm on one axis and deny on the second. In line with McClelland's (1951) discrepancy hypothesis, Andrews (1991) predicted that very high levels of anticomplementarity or interpersonal challenge would produce anxiety and threat, and hence inhibit growth; conversely, low levels of challenge would be unstimulating and unmotivating. In the middle or acomplementary range, however, affective response would be positive and the opportunity for growth would be greatest. In Andrews' study, at several stages of therapy patients and therapists filled out rating instruments characterizing their contemporary in-therapy moods (e.g., tense, angry, excited, challenged, indifferent, uninvolved). Andrews found a positive correlation between higher levels of dyadic challenge and both (a) moods of tension and positive arousal and (b) positive outcome—providing support for the discrepancy hypothesis.

Stuart et al. (1992) examined the effects of security of attachment and interpersonal style on the patient-therapist match in psychotherapy as it related specifically to early in-therapy behavior and dropout. Patients and therapists were evaluated using a semistructured interview for interpersonal relations. Using attachment profiles developed and modified from Bowlby (1969, 1979), patients were found to be

(a) less securely attached than therapists and (b) more dependent in personality style. These profiles correlated well with the in-therapy behavior displayed by patients. Using the CLOIT-R, therapists consistently described the in-therapy behavior of their patients as more warm and sociable when the patient had been rated also as more dependent in personality type. Also, patients' perceptions of their therapists were affected by the patients' personality styles, with dependent (in contrast to autonomous) patients rating their therapists more dominant and inhibited. Finally, evaluation of patient and therapist security of attachment suggested a pattern of early dropout (prior to seven sessions) from therapy. Matches of insecurely attached patients and less securely attached therapists had a high rate of dropout; dependent patients who were paired with autonomous therapists also had a high rate of early termination.

Talley et al. (1990) used the SASB to test hypotheses regarding therapist-client matching in psychotherapy. Their findings suggested that treatment outcome differs as a function of patients' and therapists' self-concepts as assessed by the interpersonal circle. They also found that greater degrees of noncomplementarity between the therapist's self-concept and the therapist's perception of patient behaviors is associated with less clinical improvement. In contrast, greater degrees of noncomplementarity between the patient's self-concept and the patient's perception of the therapist's behaviors is associated with the patient's perceptions of therapeutic improvement. Talley et al. concluded: "The more noncomplementary a behavior is to one's self-concept, the more likely it is to disrupt the self-system. With therapists it seems undesirable to have such disruptions occurring, but with patients, it is generally regarded as a necessary part of change" (p. 187).

P. L. K. Rice (1970) coached three advanced clinical psychology trainees to assume managerial, docile, and ambiguous interpersonal roles. A sample of self-effacing veterans were assigned to interviews in which the trainee-therapist assumed one of the three roles. During the interviews, a baseline of client interpersonal behavior was obtained prior to the therapists' assuming their coached role. Two observers then rated both client and therapist on the ICL and on an anxiety rating scale. P. L. K. Rice's (1970) results were strongly supportive of interpersonal complementarity. Clients of managerial therapists became more dominant and friendly, showed greater flexibility at shifting to the reciprocal role (submissiveness), and were the only subjects to experience a reduction in their anxiety level. In contrast, clients of the docile therapists became more dominant and more hostile. Finally, clients of ambiguous-role therapists showed no significant changes in the observer ratings of their interpersonal behavior.

Overall, interpersonal conceptualization and circle assessment of patient-therapist matchings seem to offer promising results. *In future studies, it seems essential that the initial matching of therapist and patient in regard to degree of complementarity has to be evaluated successively through middle and late stages of the therapy encounter.*

Predicting Responsiveness to Psychotherapy

Other studies have investigated the ability of interpersonal variables to predict responsiveness to psychotherapy, including Alden and Capreol (1993); L. M. Horowitz, Rosenberg, et al. (1988); L. M. Horowitz et al. (1992); L. M. Horowitz et al. (1989); Maling et al. (1995); and Mohr et al. (1990).

L. M. Horowitz, Rosenberg, et al. (1988) examined the possibility that various interpersonal problem clusters may not be equivalent in their response to psychotherapy.

The authors evaluated patient changes in assertiveness and intimacy problems over the course of brief psychotherapy (also see Horowitz et al., 1993). Patients were evaluated at selected sessions (1, 10, and 20); in each case, therapist and patient discussed and jointly rated improvement on the problems using a special version of the IIP. Results showed that, in contrast to intimacy problems, assertiveness problems both were focused on much more strongly in therapy and were judged as more improved following treatment.

Maling et al. (1995) examined change in level of interpersonal problems over the course of outpatient psychotherapy by comparing endorsement patterns for distress related to interpersonal problems for patient ($n = 307$) and nonpatient ($n = 1,093$) samples. For the patient sample, a 26-item version of the IIP was administered at intake and at selected sessions of psychotherapy. Three factors were identified in the patient sample:

1. *Controlling* (e.g., It is hard to accept another person's authority over me; I try to control people too much).
2. *Detached* (e.g., It is hard to feel comfortable around people; I keep other people at a distance too much).
3. *Self-Effacing* (e.g., I am too sensitive to rejection; I worry too much about disappointing other people).

First, the patient and nonpatient groups were compared in regard to their report of interpersonal problems. The two groups reported relatively few problems in the Controlling area and differed little overall. However, on both the Detached and Self-Effacing scales, the two groups were significantly different, with the patient groups reporting significantly more problems in both areas. Second, analyses showed that for all three factor scales the greatest change occurred from intake to Session 4. For the Controlling scale, the dose-response curve (Howard, Kopta, Krause, & Orlinsky, 1986) inflected at Session 10, and from that point, showed a monotonic increase in improvement up to Session 37. For the Detached scale, inflection occurred at Session 17, with subsequent monotonic increase to Session 37. The Self-Effacing scale did not show any response to treatment. In sum, Maling et al. (1995) found (a) significantly different report of problems on two of the three IIP factor scales; (b) that outpatients report greater distress in some, but not all, areas of interpersonal functioning; and (c) that interpersonal problems respond to therapy differentially, and in a manner inverse to their apparent importance to patients.

L. M. Horowitz et al. (1992) hypothesized that one predictor of a patient's success in brief dynamic psychotherapy was the relative salience of interpersonal over noninterpersonal distress in the patients' initial self-reports. Since the formats and psychometrics of the two measures are similar, they first obtained from a psychiatric symptom checklist (SCL-90-R) a mean score across all items that they labeled "S" (symptomatic distress); and from their own interpersonal problem inventory (IIP) a mean score across all items that they labeled "I" (interpersonal distress). For each patient in their studies, they determined a difference score (I-S) as a way of describing the relative salience of interpersonal over noninterpersonal (symptomatic) distress. For most patients in their samples, the I-S difference score was positive (patients reported more interpersonal distress); for about 20% of subjects the difference scores were negative. The authors assumed that the difference score measured the patient's interpersonal orientation in describing his or her distress.

Previous studies by the research group had shown that patients who completed the full 20 sessions of brief dynamic therapy obtained substantially higher I-S difference scores (exhibited relatively more interpersonal distress) than patients who had dropped out of treatment before reaching 20 sessions. Also, patients with high I-S difference scores obtained a more positive treatment outcome. Horowitz et al. (1992) speculated that patients with low or negative I-S scores express real interpersonal problems indirectly, in a noninterpersonal form; because they think less about other people, they possess less detailed cognitive representations of other persons and are less able to describe other persons clearly. They hypothesized that patients with low I-S scores lack the words, language, or concepts to describe other people clearly, perhaps because they lack clear internal representations of other people to begin with.

Their first study tested the hypothesis by examining each patient's capacity to describe other people clearly. Descriptions that patients had provided of their mothers and fathers during the initial evaluation interview were presented to naive undergraduate students, who subsequently were directed to recall the descriptions and rate their clarity. The descriptions were judged to be clearer for patients with relatively greater interpersonal than noninterpersonal distress; patients with low I-S scores were not able to describe other people very well, and they did so using such vague images that listeners could not comprehend, paraphrase, or recall their descriptions very well.

Horowitz et al. (1992) second study tested their hypothesis that patients with relatively greater interpersonal distress tend to become overly involved with other people, so their interpersonal problems reflect difficulties disengaging from other persons. In contrast, patients with greater noninterpersonal distress tend to remain uninvolved with others, so their interpersonal problems more often reflect their reluctance to become involved in the first place. More specifically, patients' interpersonal problems were characterized by different patterns on the interpersonal circle: subjects with high I-S scores (who describe other people clearly) would be more likely to express difficulties in being too submissive and passive; whereas people with low I-S scores (who describe other people less clearly) would be more likely to express difficulties trusting and relaxing control over other people.

To test their hypothesis, they examined patients' self-reported interpersonal problems on the IIP-C and found that, as predicted, patients with negative and low I-S scores had relatively higher scores in the upper octants of the circle (vindictive, domineering, and intrusive); patients with high I-S scores had relatively higher scores in the lower octants (socially avoidant, nonassertive, exploitable). Horowitz et al. (1992) concluded:

> People whose interpersonal problems reflect difficulties becoming psychologically involved with others seem to be less able to describe other people clearly and it is possible that interpersonal concepts are less available to those people, so their presenting complaints are less often expressed in interpersonal form. If so, these patients may not be best served by those procedures of brief dynamic psychotherapy that involve intense focus on interpersonal processes. (p. 49)

Horowitz et al. (1989) provided evidence indicating that patients with primarily interpersonal (as opposed to symptomatic) problems are better candidates for brief dynamic psychotherapy. Similarly, Mohr et al. (1990) reported that the IIP was useful in discriminating nonresponders from positive and negative responders in psychotherapy. They concluded that interpersonal problems and distress activate the individual to seek change in psychotherapy.

Alden and Capreol (1993) examined the extent to which differences in outpatients' problematic interpersonal behavior influenced treatment response. Patients meeting diagnostic criteria for avoidant personality disorder completed the IIP-C. Findings showed, as expected, that all avoidant PD patients reported problems with social avoidance and nonassertiveness. Further, those patients who also had interpersonal problems related to distrustful and angry behavior benefited from the behavioral intervention of graduated exposure, but not from skills training. Finally, patients who experienced interpersonal problems related to being coerced and controlled by others, in addition to avoidance and nonassertiveness, benefited from both graduated exposure and skills training.

Client Improvement in Psychotherapy

Emerging "change process" research (L. S. Greenberg, 1986; L. N. Rice & Greenberg, 1984) is a new paradigm that emphasizes study of miniature change events that occur during a single or few therapy sessions, to determine how these miniature (proximal, intermediate) changes relate to the subsequent major distal outcomes of therapy (documented at termination and follow-up). In a similar spirit:

> An interpersonal perspective challenges any compartmentalization of the "process" and the "outcome" of psychotherapy. Client-therapist transactions should be simultaneously relevant to outcome as well as to process.
>
> If the client shows adaptive changes, these should be evident in more adaptive transactions with the therapist in their sessions. In turn, these client changes of necessity imply changes in the dyadic system, so that both therapist and client should change away from the transactional baseline of their earlier sessions. (Kiesler, 1982b, p. 17)

Further, patient transactions with significant others outside therapy should demonstrate movement from pretherapy rigid and extreme patterns to posttherapy mild and flexible patterns. Validation of therapeutic intervention, then, needs to assess changes in the patient's pattern of interpersonal communication and behavior both with the therapist and with others.

A series of studies has investigated use of interpersonal variables to evaluate client improvement in psychotherapy, including Feldman (1985); Henry et al. (1986, 1990); L. M. Horowitz, Rosenberg, et al. (1988); L. M. Horowitz et al. (1978); Kivlighan et al. (1984); Kivlighan et al. (1992); McCullough and Carr (1987); McMullen and Conway (1994); Moras and Strupp (1982); Muran (1993); Muran and Safran (1990); Muran et al. (1994); Piper et al. (1991); Rudy et al. (1985); Safran, Muran, and Winston (1992); Schopler (1959); Strupp (1980c); and Weinstock-Savoy (1986).

One interpersonal circle prediction is as follows: *In successful psychotherapy, the patient should show in transactions with the therapist (a) reduction in his or her original rigid and extreme interpersonal behavior pattern ("peak" octants) and (b) an increase in the originally deficient behaviors ("nadir" octants) falling at diagonally opposite circle categories* (Kiesler, 1983). McCullough and Carr (1987), in a single-case analysis of psychotherapy with a dysthymic disorder patient, demonstrated a decrease over the course of therapy in the patient's original peak IMI hostile-submissive interpersonal pattern (as well as a simultaneous increase in the patient's friendly-dominant nadir behaviors) with the therapist. Kivlighan et al. (1984), in an evaluation of timed and structured intervention information in group psychotherapy, demonstrated that group members' peak styles decreased over therapy and their nadir styles increased, as determined from external observers' CLOIT ratings. L. M. Horowitz, Rosenberg, et al. (1988) reported that problems of assertiveness (versus problems of intimacy) changed more in brief dynamic psychotherapy. L. M. Horowitz et al. (1978) found that interpersonal complaints, phrased on the IIP in terms of "I can't (do something)" or "I have to (do something)" declined in frequency over the course of successful psychotherapy.

Muran and Safran (1990) attempted to identify central "within session" outcome factors that might serve as intermediate links between more molecular process events and ultimate outcome. Obtaining patient and therapist postsession ratings of cognitive shift, problem resolution, session helpfulness, and therapeutic alliance, Muran and Safran determined that an alliance index, as rated by the patient, was the most significant link to ultimate outcome. In a more recent project, Safran et al. (1992) attempted to target potential treatment failures in terms of problematic alliances, as measured early in treatment by patient, therapist, and third-party observers.

Muran and colleagues (Muran, 1993) measured change in the self over psychotherapy by using several circumplex measures as repeated outcome measures. They also used an assessment strategy called interpersonal scenarios (Muran et al., 1992; Muran & Segal, 1992; Muran, Segal, & Samstag, 1994), which was described in detail in Chapter 3. Change in the self-schemas over therapy sessions are used as an interpersonal index of therapeutic outcome.

In their research program, after each therapy session the patient rates the two most clinically relevant scenarios on eight parameters: frequency of recent occurrence, degree of concern, accessibility to imagination, accuracy of self-other representation, chronicity of scenario in the patient's life, availability of alternative scenarios, confidence in ability to enact alternatives, and recent enactment of alternative scenarios. These multiple variables have been found to be relevant to cognitive activity (Muran, 1991) and have demonstrated differential predictability of short- versus long-term change in reaction to time-limited cognitive therapy (Muran, Segal, & Samstag, 1992).

McMullen and Conway (1994) followed up an earlier study by McMullen (1989) which concluded that many of the figurative, metaphoric expressions produced by clients in psychotherapy are representations of their views of self, others, and the self-in-relation to others. McMullen and Conway (1994) set out to determine the utility of employing an interpersonal coding scheme to organize the meanings of client's figurative expressions in therapy. They hypothesized that in cases of better outcome the clients' perceptions of self and/or others as represented in figurative language would be less rigid (distributed more evenly around the segments of the interpersonal circle); in contrast, the metaphors for self or others produced by clients with poorer outcomes would be more rigidly located on the circle, with metaphors clustered at a few segments. They also expected that more of the figurative language of clients with poorer outcomes would be coded on the hostile half of the circumplex.

Subjects were cases of depression, anxiety, and mixed personality disorder drawn from the Vanderbilt II psychotherapy research project, a 5-year study of time-limited dynamic psychotherapy (Strupp & Binder, 1984). Each of 471 audiotaped psychotherapy sessions were audited and every therapy-related instance of figurative language used by clients that pertained to the client's actions with others was identified. Some typical examples were: "There's a brick wall; I'll go so far and that's it. Don't get too close"; "I felt like that I had sort of brushed her [friend] aside." Each of these instances of "acts of self" ($n = 2,243$) and "acts of other" ($n = 1,611$) were then coded, with very good interrater reliability, using Kiesler's (1985) Acts Version of the 1982 Interpersonal Circle. On the basis of these codings, each of the 3,854 instances of figurative language was placed first in 1 of the 16 segments of the 1982 Circle, then in one of the eight circle octants.

McMullen and Conway (1994) found that the interpersonal meanings of the clients' metaphors, particularly those metaphors of the self, as coded on the interpersonal circumplex were generally quite consistent with the predictions in three areas:

1. The most frequent codes assigned to the figurative expressions of the clients as a whole were those in the hostile-submissive quadrant; octants HI, FG, and DE contained 67.9% of the metaphors of self actions (and 63.2% of the metaphors of others' actions).

2. Compared with high-change clients, the metaphors of self actions of clients with poorer outcomes tended to fall primarily on the hostile half of the circumplex and to be less evenly distributed around the octants of the circumplex.

3. The self metaphors of the high-change clients fell primarily in the dominant to friendly-dominant portion of the circumplex and were more evenly distributed around the octants; this latter pattern was present both early and late in therapy.

The authors concluded, "The results of the present project indicated that employing the interpersonal circumplex as a way of organizing clients' figurative expressions of self and others' actions can be quite useful" (p. 55).

Rudy et al. (1985) measured the extent to which progress in psychotherapy can be predicted from the interpersonal styles of therapists and clients. They made a number of predictions in which they expected progress in therapy to be related to perceived therapist interpersonal behaviors, to perceived client interpersonal behaviors, or to the "match" between the two. Therapists and clients drawn from two outpatient clinics rated self and the other, at a time point reflecting a wide range of completed sessions, on versions of the SASB Intrex questionnaires. Progress in therapy was assessed from a pre-post measure of symptomatology completed by the client, the client's subjective evaluation of success, and the therapist's rating of the client's outcome-to-date.

Findings revealed that when clients rated their therapists as affiliative and freeing, clients reported more satisfaction with therapy and their therapists rated therapy as more successful. Clients also reported more progress when they saw their therapists as helping and protecting. However, neither symptom reduction (HSCL) nor therapist-rated change in the client was significantly related to these pleasant-friendly behaviors of the therapist. On the other hand, therapist hostility was found to be clearly detrimental to good outcome. "Specifically, even small amounts of rejection, blaming, belittlement, accusation, or suspiciousness related negatively to symptom improvement (HSCL)" (Rudy et al., 1985, p. 278). Findings revealed also that unfavorable self-concept ratings by therapists and therapist ratings of clients as helping or protecting (which suggests role reversal) were negatively associated with symptom amelioration. Rudy et al. (1985) suggested that the latter role reversal might serve as an operational definition of troubling (subjective) countertransference within psychotherapy. Finally, results suggested that when therapist and client described each other as affiliative (complementarily "correspondent"), both therapist and client rated therapy as more successful; however, once again, correspondence was not a robust predictor of symptom amelioration or therapist-rated client change.

Weinstock-Savoy (1986) used the CLOIT/CLOPT and IAS to study psychotherapy outpatients. Her analysis revealed that high patient-therapist (CLOPT and IAS) complementarity during *initial* sessions was positively associated with successful patient outcome. Outcome was assessed by posttreatment evaluations by the patient, therapist, and independent raters as well as by change in target problem behaviors. Her finding, however, was related primarily to complementarity that occurred on the friendly-hostile axis.

Based on intensive analysis of the data from the Vanderbilt I study, Strupp (1980c) concluded that a major characteristic of poor outcome cases was a tendency for therapists to respond to patient negativism and hostility with counterhostility. Strupp observed:

> In the Vanderbilt Project, therapists—even highly experienced ones and those who had undergone a personal analysis—tended to respond to such patients with counterhostility that not uncommonly took the form of coldness, distancing, and other forms of rejection. Needless to say, to the patient such response become self-fulfilling prophecies leading to a dissolution of the therapeutic relationship, early termination, and poor outcome. (1980c, p. 953)

Henry et al. (1986) demonstrated a method for operationalizing the therapeutic relationship that allowed the therapist's relationship contribution to be conceptualized as a specific technique in itself. Moment-by-moment transactions between therapist and patient were measured with Benjamin's SASB and were compared across good versus poor outcome cases seen by the same therapists. Findings showed that disaffiliative and complex (mixed message) interpersonal transactions occurring between patient and therapist were strongly related to subsequent clinical outcome. Specifically, therapists in poor outcome cases exercised more hostile control and were less prone to grant friendly autonomy, while their patients responded with a reduced level of affiliative autonomy and greater hostile separation.

Henry et al. (1990) used Benjamin's SASB system to study the interpersonal process between patient and therapist during the third session of 14 therapeutic dyads. Dyads were first grouped into good and poor outcome cases on the basis of the amount of change in the patient's "introject" as measured by the INTREX Introject Questionnaire. The basic principle of introject theory is that people learn to treat themselves as they have been treated by others (Henry et al., 1990). Healthy individuals evidence introjects that are relatively friendly (self-accepting, self-nurturing) most of the time. Maladjusted individuals, in contrast, tend to have hostile introjects that are recurrently self-critical, self-destructive, and self-neglectful. According to introject theory, a therapist's interpersonal behavior serves either to perpetuate problematic introject states (leading to poor outcome) or to ameliorate them through experiential disconfirmation. Further, therapists whose introjects are self-accepting should engage their patients in accepting and supportively helpful transactions; therapists with hostile introjects should behave in a relatively more critical or neglectful manner with their patients (Henry et al., 1990, pp. 768–769).

Findings provided strong support for Henry et al.'s (1990) hypotheses. First, poor outcome cases (no introject change) were typified by interpersonal behaviors of the therapist (belittling and blaming, ignoring and neglecting) that confirmed a negative patient introject. Second, in the poor outcome group, both patients and therapists exhibited higher levels of complex communications (mixed messages) and acted with significantly greater hostility. Third, the number of therapists' statements that were subtly hostile and controlling was highly correlated with the number of self-blaming and critical statements uttered by the patients. Finally, therapists with disaffiliative introjects tended to engage in a much higher level of problematic interpersonal processes (e.g., treating their patients in a disaffiliative manner) that have been associated with poor outcome. Overall, there was a significant relationship between therapists' interpersonal behaviors and the ways in which the patients acted toward themselves: "Patients whose introjects showed marked improvements engaged in therapeutic interactions that were almost completely devoid of disaffiliative therapist behaviors, whereas therapists of those patients showing no introject change (or deterioration) engaged in hostile blaming, ignoring, and separating sequences" (Henry et al., 1990, pp. 772–773). The authors conclude that the role of the patient-therapist relationship in fostering therapeutic change through its effect on the patient's introject structure constitutes "a common change mechanism of central importance" (p. 774).

Moras and Strupp (1982) studied interpersonal predictors of outcome for a major psychotherapy study comparing the effectiveness of highly experienced therapists and untrained college professors as therapists with college men presenting symptoms of depression, anxiety, and social introversion. On the basis of semistructured pretherapy interviews, they assessed interpersonal functioning in the areas of current social relationships (friendships, peer relations, relations with elders), family relationships (parents and siblings), and prominence of hostile and resentful attitudes toward others.

Analysis showed that patients judged to have basically adequate interpersonal relationships were likely to form collaborative, positively toned therapeutic alliances. These assessments of interpersonal relations were highly comparable with pretherapy assessments of psychological health and adaptive functioning as predictors of positive alliance. Finally, pretherapy evaluations of interpersonal relations were related to several indexes of outcome from the patient's and an independent clinician's perspectives. However, the magnitude of these associations was generally lower than for associations between pretherapy interpersonal relations and alliance, suggesting that pretherapy assessments of relationships may not, in themselves, be especially good predictors of a person's ability to benefit from time-limited therapy.

Piper et al. (1991) used an unstructured interview to assess patients' lifelong patterns of quality of object relationships at one of five levels: mature, triangular, controlling, searching, and primitive. Results revealed that a higher quality of a patient's object relations was a significant predictor of a positive therapeutic alliance and of posttherapy improvement in general symptomatology and dysfunction and of both posttherapy and follow-up improvement in the specific problems that brought the patient to therapy. In contrast to measures of recent interpersonal functioning (primarily six areas of social adjustment), quality of object relations proved to be a superior predictor of therapeutic alliance and outcome. The one exception was that recent interpersonal functioning with a marital partner emerged as almost equivalent in predictive power to quality of object relations.

Kivlighan et al. (1992) selected good and bad sessions from three short-term personal growth groups on the basis of group members' ratings of session depth and engagement. For each good and bad session, speaking turns were determined by summing the number of times one speaker (member or leader) directed a comment to another (member or leader). Speaking turns among the group members and leader were converted to proportions (the number of speaking turns for each dyad as a proportion of the total interaction for that interview). Multidimensional scaling was used to provide a map of the latent structure of the speaking turns within these sessions. A two-dimensional solution provided the best fit for the data for each of the six (a good and a bad session for each of the three groups) sessions examined. Based on CLOPT-R, ratings of each session by groups of observers that correlated very highly with the two MDS dimensions (control axis scores correlated .78–.96 with the turn-taking X-axis; affiliation axis scores .82–.92 with the Y-axis), the two dimensions were interpreted as control (dominant vs. submissive) and affiliation (friendly vs. hostile). Further analyses revealed that the leader's position in the good sessions was less extreme (more moderate) on the control and affiliation dimensions, which suggested greater interpersonal flexibility of the leader during good sessions. The authors elaborated:

> During the good sessions, the leader's behavior seemed more variable. He/she would sometimes direct (dominant) and at other times sit back (submissive). Likewise, he/she would at times challenge (unfriendly) and at other times support (friendly). Not only did the leaders exhibit this flexibility across the group members, he/she also interacted flexibly with the same member at different times during a single session. (Kivlighan et al., 1992, p. 506)

Findings also revealed that during bad sessions the group leader occupied a more extreme position on the two dimensions. The authors speculated that in these instances the leaders may have remained hooked in extreme and rigid enactments to group members' maladjusted interpersonal behaviors; as a result, the leader abdicated his or her responsibility to use the group as the medium for change. Also, in the bad sessions the leaders interacted with only one or a few members, and their interactions involved only a narrow range of behavior. The authors concluded that "leaders could be aware of when they are communicating in only one manner and work to incorporate other styles of interacting" (p. 507).

Werner (1984) used a German translation of the IMI to study a group of clients who presented problems in the areas of assertiveness and social competence. Friends, partners, and relatives of the clients filled out IMIs on the clients before and after psychotherapeutic treatment. Results showed that the client sample as a whole showed significant reductions, pre- to posttherapy, in their submissive and inhibited interpersonal behaviors.

Finally, Feldman's (1985) formulation of marital therapy, which integrates interpersonal and intrapsychic components, documented that interventions targeting both sets of components have been supported by positive outcome data.

Interpersonal circle inventories using similar methodologies can be used also in the investigation of therapeutic impasses, premature terminations, unsuccessful outcomes, and other negative events (Strupp, Hadley, & Gomes-Schwartz, 1977). For example, they can be used to confirm or disconfirm certain patient-therapist relationship patterns that are theorized to lead to premature terminations in therapy (Van Denburg & Van Denburg, 1992).

Other Interpersonal Research on Psychotherapy

In two therapy analogue studies, Buranyi (1989) examined the effectiveness of a paradoxical intervention for resistant hostile-dominant therapy clients. He developed a transcript and then a videotape in which a hostile-dominant therapy client is given a paradoxical intervention by his therapist—basically, the therapist reframed the client's hostile-dominant behavior and then prescribed more of it outside therapy. In two studies, he selected, using IAS scores, groups of moderate (flexibles) and extreme (inflexibles) hostile-dominant males. In Study 1, half the subjects read the transcript (in Study 2 watched the videotape) with the paradoxical ending present, and the other half without the paradoxical ending present. In Study 1, Buranyi found that inflexible hostile-dominant subjects who had read the paradoxical therapy transcript subsequently described themselves as less dominant than did the inflexible H-D subjects who had not been presented the paradoxical therapy; the subjects seem to have resisted the paradox by describing themselves as less dominant. In contrast, the flexible H-D subjects behaved oppositely by describing themselves as more dominant than those who had not read the paradoxical therapy script; the moderate-flexible hostile-dominant subjects seemed actually to have followed the directive in the paradox. In Study 2, inflexible (extreme) hostile-dominant subjects who had viewed the paradoxical intervention subsequently delivered significantly less punishment to a confederate in a laboratory situation than did the H-D subjects who had not viewed the paradox. Buranyi (1989) concluded that paradox may have its desired effects only with patients of extreme, inflexible interpersonal behavior patterns; it may be contraindicated for patients exhibiting more moderate patterns who may be more likely actually to follow the paradoxical directive than to resist it as therapeutically desired.

Simon et al. (1992) examined the degree to which client gender and sex role orientation are predictors of counselors' initial interpersonal impressions of clients after the first session (as measured by the IMI) and specific treatment expectancies. They found that university counseling center clients impacted their counselors as being primarily friendly-submissive (more submissive than dominant, more friendly than hostile). They also obtained significant relationships between gender and sex role orientation of clients and their counselors' initial impressions and expectancies. Specifically, regardless of actual gender, client masculine and feminine sex role characteristics were predictors of counselors' higher social skills' evaluations and more successful expected treatment outcomes. The authors concluded that neither gender nor sex role orientation was a factor in determining counselors' impressions of the interpersonal impacts of their clients.

Andrews (1989a, 1991) used the interpersonal circle to systematize the existential philosophies underlying various schools of psychotherapy, in the hope of facilitating integration among the schools. He assigned an existential "vision of reality" that underlies the values and theories inherent in psychotherapeutic schools, corresponding to each of the eight octants of the interpersonal circle.

A series of studies has examined the interpersonal style of three well-known therapists (Rogers, Ellis, Perls) as they interacted sequentially with the same client, Gloria.

Zians (1981) had groups of undergraduate observers rate each therapist after viewing a film using the IMI. Kiesler and Goldston (1988) used the CLOIT; Brokaw (1983) analyzed the transcripts using the SASB; and Andrews (1988, 1989d, 1991) used his own 18-category measure of therapist intervention styles. The IMI and CLOIT findings generally portray Rogers as friendly-submissive, Ellis as dominant-neutral, and Perls as dominant-hostile. Andrews (1991) provides a detailed discussion and comparison of these studies.

Benjamin has applied the SASB to helpful and unhelpful instances of emotional catharsis in psychotherapy (Benjamin, 1990), to analyses of chronic schizophrenics' relationships with their hallucinated voices (Benjamin, 1989), to family therapy (Benjamin, 1977), and to the free associative therapeutic process (Benjamin, 1986a).

CHAPTER 11

Interpersonal Communication Interventions

Therapeutic Metacommunication

The special power of the interpersonal approach to therapy . . . is that the thera-
peutic relationship itself, in all of its immediacy to observation and its possibility of
permitting controlled input to the client, becomes the arena in which the major cor-
rective experiences occur.

(Carson, 1982, p. 74)

The rock-bottom assumption of contemporary interpersonal psychotherapy is that *the*
client-therapist interaction, despite its unique characteristics, is similar in major ways
to any other human transaction. The therapist is just as much a participant as the client
despite the one-sided linguistic focus. In Sullivan's terms, the therapist can be nothing
other than a "participant observer."

It follows from this assumption that the client will communicate to the therapist in
the same duplicitous way that he or she communicates with other important persons in
his or her life—will send the same rigid and extreme evoking messages to the therapist
that he or she sends to others. As a result, the therapist will experience "live" in the
sessions the client's distinctive interpersonal problems. The therapist, at one end of the
feedback loop, registers the client's distinctive style with the impact messages he or
she experiences with the client. These impacts are complementary to a distinctive sector or pie-slice of the interpersonal circle.

The important *diagnostic* task of the interpersonal therapist is to attend to, identify, and assess the client's distinctive evoking style as it unfolds during the client-
therapist transactions. A major component of this assessment includes the therapist's
own emotional and other felt engagements or "pulls" experienced during these transactions. The therapist's prepotent assessment tool involves his or her own internal responses to the client. The therapist must attend to the ground of the communication
process more than to the "figure" of linguistic content. The ground subsumes the
client's and therapist's nonverbal messages as well as the therapist's covert experiences or engagements. Attending to the ground, however, can be threatening to the
therapist as well as to the client. Interpersonal diagnosis, then, requires that therapists continually monitor the inner experiences and overt reactions evoked from them

by their patients within the sessions. The important purpose of this monitoring process is to pinpoint and identify the patient's maladaptively rigid bids for self-confirmation.

The essential *therapeutic* task is for the therapist to metacommunicate with the client about the client's evoking style and its self-defeating consequences. Therapists need to provide metacommunicative feedback that labels the interpersonal impacts they experience, as a springboard to collaborative exploration with the patient of their self-defeating and "self-fulfilling prophecy" meanings. The client's abnormal behavior patterns need to be altered as they operate in important contexts with significant others, including the therapist. Levenson (1973) noted: "One might say that the patient improves because of a new experience, an authentic exchange with a therapist who responds honestly and openly" (p. 166).

Perls (1976) described the essential therapeutic task in similar language:

> The neurotic's problem is not that he cannot manipulate, but that his manipulations are directed toward preserving and cherishing his handicap, rather than getting rid of it. . . . When the patient becomes aware that he is manipulating his environment in a fashion that, no matter how intricate, is self-defeating, and when he becomes aware of these manipulating techniques themselves, he will be able to make changes. (pp. 46–47)

Goldfried and Davison (1976) observed that the therapist could provide direct feedback primarily to help the client realize how his or her maladaptive behavior manifests itself. They noted further:

> In construing the therapeutic relationship as providing a sample of the client's interaction, it is important for the therapist to focus on his own reactions during the therapeutic sessions. The therapist should continually observe his own behavior and emotional reactions, and question what the client may have done to bring about such reactions. Provided the therapist is in relatively good contact with reality, such a seemingly paranoid stance can offer important clues about how other individuals in the client's natural environment may be reacting toward him. (pp. 57–58)

An interpersonal approach to psychotherapy assumes that a patient's central problems in living reside in maladaptive transaction cycles with significant others, including the therapist. The therapist's overriding diagnostic task is to identify the specific components of the self-defeating maladaptive pattern. The therapist's major interventive task is to disrupt the identified transaction cycle by various interpersonal moves, especially metacommunication, that refuse to reinforce, that insist on exposing, and that push to alter the patient's self-defeating pattern both within and outside the therapy sessions.

My *interpersonal communication therapy* (Kiesler, 1988) *seems distinct in emphasizing among therapist's interventions the priority of the therapist's use of metacommunicative feedback throughout individual psychotherapy* (cf. Anchin, 1982b). Interpersonal communication therapy *emphasizes the therapist's actual disclosure of "objective"* (Winnicott, 1949) *countertransference feelings and reactions throughout the course of therapy.* The most demanding work of therapy involves this metacommunicative task.

Although modern psychoanalytic therapy has evolved to the point of emphasizing the therapist's use of countertransference responses, that use almost universally is restricted to conceptualizations of the patient that can guide transference and other interpretations offered to the patient. With few exceptions, modern psychoanalysts continue to preclude any direct disclosure to the patient of the therapist's actual countertransference reactions (Kiesler & Van Denburg, 1993). In contrast, interpersonal communication therapy emphasizes the importance and centrality of therapists' disclosure to their patients whatever it is they experience that their patients are evoking, pulling, or commanding from them. *Of course, the effectiveness of feedback interventions needs to be guided by therapeutic principles,* which this chapter will elaborate.

Metacommunicative feedback is one of the most powerful asocial responses in the therapist's repertoire. Recall that the therapist responds to the patient in an asocial or disengaged way whenever the therapist withholds the customary, preferred, or expected (by the patient) complementary response. As a direct first result of metacommunication, then, the patient experiences a sense of "beneficial uncertainty" (Beier, 1966) because the patient's preferred style does not produce the expected and familiar interpersonal consequences.

This chapter will illuminate the metacommunicative process and the principles that underlie and guide its applications by the therapist. It will be based primarily on my book (Kiesler, 1988), which attempted an earlier systematic theoretical statement. In that volume, the therapeutic relationship was viewed as a microcosm of the Maladaptive Transaction Cycle in which the patient pulls a restricted range of responses from significant others, which in turn tend to reinforce the patient's rigidly held self-view. The intervention model I proposed relied heavily on metacommunicative feedback to the patient concerning the interpersonal impact he or she is having on the therapist.

METACOMMUNICATION DEFINED

Metacommunication occurs whenever the patient's pattern of verbal and nonverbal communication itself becomes the topic of communication between therapist and patient. *Therapeutic metacommunication* or *metacommunicative feedback* refers to any instance in which the therapist provides to the patient verbal feedback that targets the central, recurrent, and thematic relationship issues occurring between them in their therapy sessions (Kiesler, 1988, p. 39). The feedback can address any one or more of the various components of the Maladaptive Transaction Cycle.

The therapist's intent in providing feedback is to explore and validate with the patient these cyclically related and codetermined aspects of the patient's central thematic interpersonal problems. Instead of reliving and confirming the patient's maladaptive expectations, feelings, and fantasies about relationships, the therapist places the transactional cycle occurring automatically and unawarely between them on the verbal table for conjoint, collaborative exploration, validation, and understanding.

A more limited category of metacommunicative feedback targets the covert experiences of the therapist registered as engagements or impact messages pulled by the patient's actions. *Impact disclosure* refers to those instances where "therapists reveal to patients their inner, covert reactions (feelings, thoughts, fantasies, action tendencies) which they experience as directly evoked by the patient's recurrent behaviors during psychotherapy" (Kiesler, 1988, pp. 1–2).

Relative to the anticomplementary response, a therapist can exert the next greatest pressure for change in a patient's rigid and extreme interpersonal behaviors by emitting actions from the class of asocial responses—especially by offering metacommunicative feedback to the patient that describes the patient's style and its self-defeating interpersonal consequences. The therapist's metacommunicative act relates to the interpersonal circle in one or more of three possible ways: (a) by falling at the midpoint (origin) of the circle and, hence, being neutral in regard to both control and affiliation, (b) by constituting a mild or more ambiguous form of the anticomplementary response, or (c) by falling altogether outside the domain of the circle on some plane defining a metalevel of interpersonal activity. Regardless, its basic function is to disrupt the patient's rigid and extreme interpersonal style, first by not providing the complementary response bid for by the patient; second, by pursuing conjoint exploration and validation of the automatic and unaware transactional game occurring between patient and therapist.

In Villard and Whipple's (1976) analysis, metacommunication occurred in those instances when "the relationship members actually 'communicate about their communication' and specifically about the relationship communication by which they have been unsuccessfully attempting to hammer out an acceptable relationship definition" (p. 132). In their view, metacommunication attempts to impose some control and direction in the relational process by employing the more precise verbal communication channel.

The uniqueness of metacommunicative feedback is that it makes therapeutically available to the patient "a kind of independent reality check that is difficult to make alone" (Morran et al., 1985, p. 57). It seems highly probable that a person's (especially a maladjusted person's) "intended" versus "actual" impacts on others are often quite different. Gottman (1979), for example, assessed distressed and nondistressed couples ongoing evaluations of their interactions and found differences between a spouse's stated intent and the subjective impact of the communication on the partner. H. H. Blumberg (1972) found that trait evaluations were communicated freely to other friends, but tended to be withheld from the person being evaluated. Dorris and Wertheim (1976), noting the existence of strong cultural norms against the explicit expression of interpersonal evaluations, observed that evaluative feedback is usually communicated implicitly through nonverbal means, or indirectly through verbal hints, indirect references, and circumlocutions.

Since it is far from the norm for persons to talk directly to each other about what is transpiring between them at the nonverbal relationship level, metacommunication is very much an asocial response, especially with individuals who have problems in living. Others most frequently take the easiest way out by simply leaving the scene. Even those who do not flee usually stay with the implicit agreement that talking about what they are really doing to each other is verboten. Generally, metacommunication remains a remote option in everyday affairs because of the threat that it can eventuate in rejection, withdrawal of affection, and isolation—the disconfirmation of one's self-presentation or identity.

A major result of these everyday implicit pacts is that relationships with significant others continue to be defined exclusively along nonverbal channels. Analogic, iconic, or nonverbal signs are powerful, but they often also are imprecise, especially when they include incongruous messages. An unfortunate result is that nonverbal relationship messages between persons are too often susceptible to misinterpretation. Most frequently, we actually prefer these ambiguous nonverbal messages to more precise linguistic encodings, since the latter can result in clear, unwanted, and feared responses such as rejection, disapproval, and withholding of love.

The *advantages of metacommunication,* however, are evident. As Villard and Whipple (1976) emphasized, metacommunication produces several distinctly favorable interpersonal outcomes:

1. It reduces the likelihood of problems resulting from inaccurate communication or from misinterpretations, by moving toward a negotiated validation of the actual relationship messages being sent between two persons.

2. Metacommunication brings ambiguities, difficulties, and uncertainties between two parties to a conscious level of awareness so that the parties have the opportunity to clarify together what is happening between them. This negotiated validation labels the intents of both parties so that possible future areas of confrontation and misunderstanding can be avoided more easily.

3. This explicit definition of relationship makes it less likely that the parties will continue to maneuver covertly, nonverbally, with each other to obtain what they want. Instead, in concrete momentary instances, it is more possible to state wants directly.

4. Finally, metacommunication increases tolerance for personal differences in that the parties clarify for each other their basic identities. Even during impasses, discussion and elucidation of basic wants and fears provide a perspective for understanding that is difficult to arrive at solely by inferences from nonverbal messages.

By metacommunicating with his or her patient, the therapist provides a very powerful asocial response. Most importantly, through metacommunication, the patient begins to identify and understand his or her basic maladaptive transactional pattern with others as the first step toward healthier interpersonal alternatives. As Sullivan (1953a) noted, "One achieves mental health to the extent that one becomes aware of one's interpersonal relations" (p. 207). By addressing their relationship directly, the therapist also models for the patient a powerful and unusual technique for communicating with those persons who are significant in the patient's life. Further, metacommunication can provide the same advantages for the patient's relationship to the therapist that it can provide for his or her relationships outside therapy. It makes inaccurate communication or misunderstanding less likely between therapist and patient. It brings the attention and labeling of both therapist and patient to the relationship issues that are developing between them, permitting pinpointing of the distinctive patterns these maneuvers have taken; this, in turn, makes it easier for both parties to notice and label subsequent issues as they emerge. It interferes with any continued unintended and predominantly nonverbal maneuvers in the therapy dyad. Finally, it facilitates increased mutual tolerance and understanding by therapist and patient, making it easier for the uniqueness of each party to be preserved, with mutual respect for continuing differences. Unquestionably, these are constructive consequences, and their implementation in the therapy process provides a unique and powerful human experience.

A TWO-STAGE MODEL

Before the therapist can effectively pursue the general metacommunicative task, a previous sequence of two sets of events must have occurred. These two previous stages require that the therapist first be engaged (or hooked), and second become disengaged (or unhooked). Only after having disengaged from the patient's powerful command or presentational messages can the therapist effectively proceed to the third stage of metacommunication or impact disclosure.

The Hooked or Engaged Stage

From the moment the patient first enters the therapist's office, the therapy dyad is off and running. Already the therapist is being pushed into a constricted, narrow range of responding to the patient. The therapist cannot *not* be hooked or sucked in by the patient, because the patient is more adept, more expert in his or her distinctive, rigid, and extreme game of interpersonal encounter.

The patient tells the therapist his or her rehearsed story about complaints and problems, but since it has led to neither understanding nor change, the story has significant omissions or blind spots as well as under- and overemphases. Along with the story comes a rehearsed, overpracticed, automatic pattern of nonverbal messages that push other persons, including the therapist, into adoption of complementary roles vis-à-vis the patient. The adoption of these roles in turn confirms the patient's own role definition or identity.

In the hooked stage, therefore, the patient's ED-evoking style pulls a distinct pattern of covert impacts and overt complementary responses from the therapist. The therapist cannot prevent this hooking because the patient, at least initially, is superior to the therapist in shaping the direction of their relationship.

It's crucial, however, to underline that the therapist's hooked stage can just as validly be referred to as the patient's hooked stage. The therapist hooks the patient by giving the patient the reaction he or she expects or wants—the complementary response.

By the process of the therapist's being hooked, the patient derives some important therapeutic benefits. First, becoming hooked permits the therapist to experience firsthand the aversive interpersonal consequences of the patient's maladaptive transactions with others. Second, the therapist's empathic attempts to understand the covert experience of the patient (his or her pain, expectations, intentions, fears, etc.) lead to the therapist's active bonding with the positive aspects and strengths of the patient's personality. Importantly, this bonding, together with the validating effects of the therapist's complementary responses, is necessary for establishment of a working therapeutic alliance with the patient. In short, the therapist cannot *not* be hooked in this first stage of the relationship; moreover, it is fortunate and facilitative that the therapist becomes hooked so as to be able, in turn, to hook the patient into a working alliance.

The Unhooked or Disengaged Stage

As the therapist is hooked, he or she experiences greater or lesser intensities of the various classes of covert impact messages (feelings, action tendencies, cognitive attributions, fantasies) and continues to enact versions of the complementary response. As Levenson (1973) observed, "Any therapist working with a practicing masochist will become sadistic. This is not [subjective] countertransference, a failure of analysis or moral fiber, but a realistic consequence of entering the other person's world" (p. 160).

If the therapist continues to be hooked, does not squirm loose, he or she is in effect unwittingly reinforcing the maladaptive style of the patient. From another viewpoint, Murrell (1971) observed, "If the therapist duplicates the customary [social] system responses and thereby fails to introduce new information, then he is in effect signaling positive feedback which would only serve to amplify the patient's current problematic phenomena" (p. 213).

Over their sessions, the therapist will experience the cumulative impact of the patient's maladaptive evoking style by increasingly feeling some combination of negative feelings such as anxiety, frustration, irritation, depression, and so on (see Figures 6–1 and 6–2). The therapist who continues to be unaware of being hooked automatically countercommunicates to the patient the experience of these negative feelings usually through a package of the therapist's own ambiguous, negative, and incongruent verbal and nonverbal messages. Not only do these occurrences compound the transactional stalemate, the therapist—through ambiguous and incongruent communications—finds him- or herself in the embarrassing position of modeling maladaptive communication for the patient!

Mackenzie et al. (1978) illustrated the importance of disengagement for both physicians and psychiatrists in working with what often comes to be labeled the "manipulative" patient. As a group, these patients are described as having a strident quality, presenting with dramatic complaints, seizures, heart attacks, anorexia, suicide, or psychotic behavior. In Mackenzie et al.'s (1978) analysis, initially the manipulative patient steps outside the patient role by asking more from the caretaker than he or she feels prepared to give. In addition, the patient rejects or refuses to recognize the contextual cues the therapist provides as to what is expected of the patient in the role of patient. The therapist may react to this rule violation with a sense of outrage and fear; because of expecting to be in charge, the therapist feels at sea when the sense of therapeutic control slips and thus denies the patient's request. The patient then accuses the therapist of incompetence or neglect; the failure of treatment (e.g., attempted suicide) is publicly placed on the therapist's doorstep. The upshot is that the patient comes to represent basic and primitive fears the helper may have about his or her work. The patient is experienced as overwhelmingly needful and dangerous. The therapist fears that capitulation to the patient's needs will lead to entrapment in a situation that will be totally draining and devouring. The resulting anxiety contributes to the therapist's desire to be free of the patient and to feel righteous about the withdrawal. Basically, the therapist seeks to regain control of the interpersonal situation by censuring the patient's behaviors.

According to Mackenzie et al. (1978), the first step in this process is applying the label "manipulative" to the patient:

> In failing to identify the patient's dependency fusion with his symptoms as part of the psychopathology, the therapist denies his responsibility. He asserts that the patient is willfully and deliberately demanding what the therapist has decided he cannot give. . . . By labeling the patient as manipulative, the therapist places the onus of breakdown [of treatment] on the patient's behavior. The helper confers absolution on himself should treatment come to a bad end. (p. 270)

In their view, then, use of the term manipulative to describe a patient often signifies that the relationship has shifted from therapeutic to adversarial grounds. The initial step toward repairing the therapeutic dyad

> is to acknowledge that one is identifying the patient as the exclusive source of the breakdown. . . . Once the process is recognized as evolving from a threat to [the therapist's] self esteem [and competence], alternative solutions to the impasse become available. Only then does the behavior which was labeled manipulative cease to be the characteristic of an unworthy patient, but an integral part of the psychopathological interactional style. (Mackenzie et al., 1978, pp. 270–271)

Phenomenonologically, the extreme experience of the hooked stage is a bad place for therapists to be. On the one hand, they perceive their role with patients to be that of an accepting, understanding, and nurturant caregiver. On the other hand, they increasingly experience boredom, dread, anxiety, incompetence, irritation, and other feelings during the therapy sessions. These negative feelings obviously can threaten a therapist's self-system by precipitating negative self-statements. One way to prevent this negative occurrence is for the therapist to initiate his or her own ED-evoking game with the patient through what often becomes a power struggle initiated to protect the therapist's identity. This maladaptive possibility on the therapist's part underscores the necessity of the therapist's arriving at the second stage of disengagement.

Since the therapist cannot *not* be pulled in by the patient, the therapist of necessity experiences feelings and other engagements with the patient *before* he or she ever notices or labels them:

> *Proposition 11–1.*   The first essential step in the disengagement process, then, is that the therapist notice, attend to, and subsequently label the engagements being pulled from him or her by a given patient.

Until the therapist notices what is happening internally, he or she is caught in the patient's transactional game.

In pursuing this task, it's likely that a maximally effective therapist will experience the same stages in reacting to the impact messages registered with a particular client that children do in developmentally experiencing affect: (a) acting out the feeling, (b) symbolizing the feeling in fantasy, and (c) symbolizing the feeling with a label. Accordingly, from the first session the therapist must address these essential questions: How has my baseline of responsiveness changed with this particular client? What kind of fantasies or dreams have I experienced since initiating therapy with this client? What is this patient trying to do to me? What am I feeling when I'm with this patient? What do I feel pulled to do or not to do with this patient?

In this identification task, the major cue the therapist employs is the emerging outline of a *repetitive pattern* to his or her internal responses—the general feeling that whatever is happening is *recurrent* with this patient, that the same feelings and tendencies appear over repeated instances. Other important cues are instances where the therapist notices the therapy task bogging down, when the patient seems to abandon his or her previous immersion in productive self-disclosure and exploration. Or, if things had started to get better for the patient, they stop. Or if homework is suggested or assigned, it isn't done. In various ways, the patient interrupts his or her previous baseline of pursuing understanding and change.

Other cues available to the therapist to detect hooking are instances of incongruity where he or she says things to the patient that are not really meant, or uses nonverbal expressions that don't seem to fit. Or the therapist may notice herself way off her own usual baseline in therapy—talking more or less than usual, liking or disliking a patient more intensely, feeling particularly brilliant or dull with a given patient, and so on. The therapist may find herself tending to avoid or to emphasize certain topics regardless of the patient's interest. Or the therapist may notice her own anxiety at particular moments with the patient.

By whatever means, the therapist notices or attends to the distinctive transactional milieu experienced internally, makes figure out of what was previously ground, he or she takes the initial, crucial step of disengagement. By identifying what is happening to him or her, by perceiving his or her personal consequences as one more instance of how the patient engages others, the therapist regains a level of understanding and objectivity that permits use of alternative interventions designed to help the patient also see and experience the pattern.

Proposition 11–2.   The second disengagement maneuver available to the therapist is to discontinue the complementary response.

When therapists realize they have been pulled to give answers and advice, they must withhold these responses. If they have been pulled to be entertained, they must cease enjoying the entertainment. Therapists who have been feeling cautious and constricted must find a way to become more spontaneous. If they have been protecting the patient from more intense emotion, they must help the patient face the feared feelings.

Proposition 11–3.   A third disengagement option for the therapist is, through use of appropriate technique, to help the patient interrupt his or her distinctive ED-evoking style.

If the patient uses abstractions and qualifications in disclosing problems and concerns, the therapist can consistently push for concrete elaborations through pinpointing and situational analysis. If the patient entertains the therapist with anecdotes and histrionic displays, the therapist can reflect the patient's feelings of fragility and vulnerability, and encourage the individual to attend to and elaborate the scary feelings being avoided. In other words, by selective use of technique, the therapist can assist the patient to tune in on aspects of internal experience he or she is ignoring, under-, or overemphasizing, which underlie the constricted self-presentation that eventually alienates others in the patient's life. By disengaging, the therapist also prevents alienation from the patient. Unlike others with whom the patient interacts, the therapist hangs in supportively to help the patient face tuned-out aspects of his or her experience, which the patient is evading so as to preserve self-definition—to avoid emerging naked and vulnerable in a totally unpredictable world.

Proposition 11–4.   The last and most powerful disengagement option in the therapist's arsenal is for the therapist to talk directly to the patient about the engagements that are transpiring between them: The therapist metacommunicates with the patient by referring directly to the ED-evoking or DE-impact relationship messages occurring between them.

PRINCIPLES OF METACOMMUNICATION

We have seen that effective metacommunicative feedback targets all four components of the Maladaptive Transaction Cycle. Obviously, the therapist cannot give feedback about all four components at one time. Instead, feedback must be phased and the therapist must decide what is the most efficient and effective place to start. To accomplish its goals, however, therapist feedback must, over time, discuss and validate all four components until their cyclical regularity is overwhelmingly apparent to the patient. As the crucial first step in discovering more adaptive interpersonal alternatives, the therapist and patient collaboratively "etch in marble" the vicious cycle that represents the patient's central problem in living.

This section will discuss and summarize the major principles that seem necessary for successful, supportive, and growth-enhancing use of therapeutic metacommunication. It is based on my previous presentations (Kiesler, 1982a; 1988).

Proposition 11–5.   The success of the therapist's metacommunication depends crucially on the extent to which he or she can provide feedback in a manner that is confrontative as well as supportive and protective of the patient's self-esteem.

In using feedback, the therapist must always consider the level of potential threat and disruption to the patient's conception of self (the central role the patient assumes in dealing with his or her interpersonal world). In interpersonal theory, threat of disruption of the self-system is the basic source of anxiety—the more the threat, the greater the anxiety. Accordingly, effective delivery of feedback assumes some level of perceived safety by the patient within the therapy context, as well as the presence of some level of established positive therapeutic alliance between patient and therapist.

Proposition 11–6.   The therapist's facilitative attitude and intent are crucial to the effectiveness of the feedback, leading to its being heard and usefully explored by the patient.

A facilitative attitude on the therapist's part is communicated by nonverbal messages of positive affiliation; by a tentative presentation of the feedback; and by an attitude of participatory exploration wherein both therapist and patient pursue the validity of what the therapist has said to understanding and changing the patient's approach to life. Like any other hypothetical statements, metacommunicative feedback may be shown to be invalid or in need of modification. Indeed, invalidating clarification can be just as useful for understanding and change as the case where the therapist's feedback seems to fit precisely.

This principle emphasizes that the purpose of feedback is to provide new information that will help the patient understand and change ineffective and self-defeating interactional patterns. To accomplish this goal, it is critical that the patient perceive the feedback as being offered for his or her benefit, by someone concerned enough for the patient's welfare to say things that are to some extent risky to the teller. It is important, then, that the therapist's feedback not manifest a "win or lose" flavor, or evolve into a contest of power or put-down of the patient. To the extent that this kind of power struggle results, the therapist is pursuing his or her own maladaptive game by attempting to force the patient into a role that supports the therapist's constricted definition of him- or herself.

Proposition 11–7.   The success of metacommunication depends crucially on the commitment of the therapist to open, direct, unambiguous communication to the patient about the therapist's inner engagements or pulls, and also by the therapist's willingness to explore (and to admit where accurate) his or her own contributions to the patient-therapist transactional cycle.

It is this demand that makes the feedback process risky and sometimes scary for the therapist. By openly examining with the patient all the evidence relevant to the feedback given, the therapist's own blind spots or less aware patterns may become exposed, with a resulting loss of the therapist's own self-esteem.

From their study of interpersonal feedback in the group therapy context, Morran et al. (1985) made the highly relevant observation that "the exchange of negative feedback is typically accompanied by anxiety and mixed emotion on the part of both the giver and receiver" (p. 64). Accordingly, it is unrealistic, unfair, and counterproductive for a therapist to assume that "owning up" or confessing will always be a one-sided event. If the patient perceives incongruent denial on the therapist's part, the facilitative metacommunicative process is disrupted, if not finished.

Proposition 11–8.   In reporting impact messages to the patient, it is essential that the therapist communicate both the positive and negative polarity of his or her covert engagements.

The patient needs a confrontation, but it must simultaneously communicate support and endorsement of the patient's self-concept. Patients need to be told of the negative effects they produce in others; but if it is to be useful, they must first hear the feedback. The patient cannot become open to honest exploration of the validity of the feedback if his or her world, his or her identity, is drastically challenged or dramatically disrupted. None of us can let go of the familiar, least of all the ineffective and self-defeating familiar, until the hope of an alternative is provided. The familiar, even when unsatisfactory, is predictable, somewhat comfortable, and clearly preferable to the panic of sudden unpredictability. Hence, it is vital for the therapist to judge beforehand the resultant impact on the patient, especially the level of disruptive anxiety, of any feedback he or she may provide. This empathic judgment by the therapist presupposes an understanding and respect for the real anxiety and pain involved in the patient's growth process.

The therapist incorporates positive-negative polarity in metacommunications in two ways. The first and most frequent manner is the situation in which the therapist's linguistic messages carry the negative feedback while concomitant nonverbal messages signal positive affiliation and respect; the therapist states the negative while nonverbally displaying the positive.

We have all experienced this verbal-nonverbal mixture at various times in our lives. Person A and Person B may give us identical verbal feedback: In the case of A we don't hear it and go to war, whereas with B we hear it and assimilate it. We may dislike

A or perceive A simultaneously communicating ridicule, disrespect, or contempt. On the other hand, we respect and like B, and read B as generally respecting us, caring enough to tell us something that is difficult both for him to say and for us to hear. Because of the positive nonverbal messages that accompany B's feedback, we hear and, it is hoped, learn. In contrast, because of the predominantly negative messages coming from A, we tune him out and counterattack.

Our patients are no different in this respect, except that their self-definitions and ED-presentational styles are more extreme and more rigid. Therapists are naive to expect that their feedback will be heard and integrated regardless of the patient-therapist relationship context or concurrent nonverbal presentations. Instead, it is vital that therapists, through their gaze, posture, distance, and paralanguage, communicate a clear positive message of respect and concern for the patient, for the patient's approach to life, and for his or her struggle to change. When the patient-therapist alliance is strong and predictable, when the therapist shows empathy for the patient's tolerance for pain and anxiety, the therapist can effectively confront the patient, sometimes with incredible frankness, about the invalidity of some of the patient's labelings, assumptions, and overt behaviors with significant others in his or her life.

A second avenue for effective confrontation is to feed back to the patient the positive aspect of his or her presentational style (targeting his or her intent in what he or she is doing with others) in combination with its negative aspects (the aversive consequences for others of his or her presentational style, of which he or she remains relatively ignorant). For example, a therapist might say: "It frustrates me that every time we get close to exploring something important, you immediately run away from it. The message I get from you is that you're very fragile, and I must be very careful not to upset you further by asking you to keep your focus there. But although it's frustrating to me, I realize also that you're trying to protect yourself from discovering some things about yourself that might be painful, or that might make you feel more vulnerable with me." The first part of this statement reflects the therapist's exasperation with the patient's presentational message, "I'm fragile; treat me with kid gloves," which over time pushes the therapist and others away. The second part verbalizes the therapist's realization that this protective maneuver makes sense, that it is a form of avoiding pain and anxiety that any of us might use to maintain self-respect and identity. The combined statement, therefore, helps the patient both to retain self-esteem as well as to begin to discriminate strengths and weaknesses in his or her approach to living. It facilitates the important learning that valid self-esteem is built on honest confrontation of one's weaknesses as well as strengths—that weakness is a component of living for us all.

A third way to incorporate polarity in feedback is to help the patient understand that the very strengths he or she values and exhibits with others represent, at the other poles, his or her interpersonal blind spots and weaknesses. This is the case since an individual's valued actions, when flexible and moderate, are attractive and admirable to others; however, the same valued actions, when rigid and extreme, become unattractive and aversive. As a result, the very strengths that patients identify and value in themselves and exhibit to others, when carried to an extreme, constitute weaknesses that provoke self-defeating consequences within others. A therapist typically provides this kind of polarity feedback in the following general form: "One of the things I admire in you is . . . but, the other side of that same thing is that at times it . . . ." For example, a therapist might say, "I really admire how you think carefully before you say something in here, how you try to be so fair and to consider all your feelings before you blurt something out impulsively. But the other side of that same thing is that often I feel frustrated that you can't trust your first response, and distanced that you seem to have to figure it all out by yourself, that you won't let me help you clarify what's happening inside you."

By one or all of these polarity communications, the therapist softens the threat value, reduces the anxiety of loss of self-esteem for the patient so that the feedback can be received—the necessary first step before further exploration and validation can occur. Effective therapist metacommunication thus communicates both negative and positive engagements from the patient, thereby expressing the polarity of the impact complex.

The findings from group therapy research strongly support this emphasis on including both positive and negative components of the impact complex. For example, Morran et al. (1985) found:

> Positive feedback was more effectively given than negative feedback regardless of the session of delivery. Additionally, recipients rated positive feedback as more accurate than negative feedback, regardless of when received. These findings add support to a growing empirical data base pointing to valence as the major factor influencing the giving and receiving of feedback messages. . . . Positive feedback tends to arouse little threat or anxiety and, thus, is easier to give in a straightforward manner and easier to receive and process. Negative feedback, on the other hand, tends to arouse strong feelings of threat and anxiety. . . . Research has also suggested that feedback may be more accepted and utilized by recipients when delivered in a positive-negative sequence. (pp. 58, 65)

Proposition 11–9.   For effective metacommunication, it is not sufficient for the therapist to report his or her elicited impacts or overt complementary responses; additionally the therapist must pinpoint instances of the patient's actions that elicited these responses and state inferences about the covert experiences (expectations, intentions, feelings, thoughts, etc.) of the patient that precipitated these maladaptive actions.

The evidence regarding interpersonal feedback in group therapy supports the importance of the specificity and concreteness of feedback statements, especially negative ones. As Morran et al. (1985) observed:

> The exchange of negative feedback is typically accompanied by anxiety and mixed emotion on the part of both giver and receiver. . . . This situation, in turn, arouses strong tendencies to veil the negative message in a cloak of generalities and qualifications and, thus, to lessen the impact on the receiver and the degree of risk assumed by the giver. Unfortunately, this may also tend to decrease the usefulness of the message for the recipient. (p. 64)

They go on to suggest that interpersonal feedback should be most effective and most readily accepted when it focuses on observable behaviors, is unqualified, refers to specific and concrete events, and is nondirective. They define a nondirective statement as one that is completely descriptive with no stated or implied message that demands or requests future changes of the recipient.

In Proposition 11–9, pinpointing "instances of the patient's specific actions" refers to giving the patient concrete examples specifying in detail the patient's overt pattern of verbal and nonverbal behaviors that triggered the therapist's impacts and overt reactions. Pinpointing presumes the repeated occurrence of an aspect of the patient's presentational style to which the therapist automatically provided the complementary response. By identifying and labeling the pattern during the hooked stage, the therapist becomes sensitized to future occurrences and gradually can rehearse a precise statement to the patient of the identified pattern. For example, the therapist might offer the following: "I realize it's important for you to be cautious and rational in what you do or say to others, and I agree that it is important in many situations. Yet in our sessions, you sometimes seem to send messages you don't intend as a result of this caution. For example, you often show long, silent pauses with me after I've said something to you, and frequently a quick smile flashes on and off. Several times when you did that I felt you were really disagreeing with what I was saying, or were thinking that my comment was a little stupid. But I found out later that wasn't the case, that actually you were feeling a little stupid about yourself . . . I wonder if others might misread you sometimes in the same way, feeling that you are disapproving of them, which is not your intent at all."

The pinpointed portion of this statement is "you often show long, silent pauses with me . . . and frequently a quick smile flashes on and off." This is a concrete specification of one aspect of the patient's overt communication pattern. If the patient uses that pattern repetitively with his spouse, parents, friends, and other significant persons, it is likely that it produces negative engagements in them of a similar form: "He really thinks what I said is stupid, but he won't tell me that"; "He's looking down his nose at me." Accompanying these attributions are varying intensities of irritation and anger toward the patient and a tendency to pull back from any further disclosing or spontaneous response. The patient tends to push away persons with whom he wants to be close by an unintended, disdainful, and negatively evaluative nonverbal display. If this is a valid description of what this patient does both to the therapist and to others, it seems crucial that the patient should know about it, and get on with discovering what it is that keeps him from communicating more clearly with others.

As a second part of the pinpointing process described in Proposition 11–9, the therapist states inferences or pursues exploration in regard to the patient's covert experiences (expectations, intentions, feelings, thoughts, etc.) that precipitate a particular pattern of maladaptive action. Safran (1984a) used the preceding feedback example to show how a therapist might facilitate exploration of this patient's associated covert experiences. He observed:

> The process of pinpointing dysfunctional interpersonal behaviors can provide . . . markers indicating the need for cognitive exploration. . . . In the above illustration, for example, the therapist who has pinpointed the behavior that has the negative impact could interrupt the interaction the moment the client becomes silent and smiles, and say: "I'm aware that when I asked you that question, a smile flashed on and off your face very quickly. What was going through your mind when that happened?" If the client is not immediately aware of the relevant cognitive activity, the therapist can have the client intentionally engage in the relevant behavior, in order to provide himself with behavioral cues that may trigger the associated cognitions. In the above situation, if the client appears to be registering disapproval or condescension on his face, it is probable that some aspect of his cognitive activity corresponds to his communicative behavior. In other words, it is unlikely that experiencing a sense of foolishness has arbitrarily become paired with looking scornful. . . . One hypothesis would be that the client does indeed

experience a scornful feeling toward the therapist, but that this is at least in part a security operation, which functions to raise his self-esteem when he feels foolish. The best way to evaluate the veracity of such an hypothesis is to explore the client's cognitive processes in collaboration with the client, in as nonthreatening a fashion as possible. (p. 342)

Safran and Segal (1990) elaborated further that a major purpose of the therapist conveying his or her feelings to patients is to "probe for the patient's internal experience" (p. 151). Similarly, the major goals of pinpointing patients' interpersonal behaviors during the session are to help patients become aware of their role in the interaction, and to use the pinpointed interpersonal events "as a juncture for cognitive/affective exploration."

Another key piece of evidence that can help a therapist infer a patient's covert processes resides in the class of impact messages referred to as cognitive attributions or the perceived evoking message. By identifying the various thoughts that run through the therapist's head about what he or she thinks the patient is trying to do to him or her, or what the patient wants him or her to do, the therapist gets an initial idea of one important aspect of the patient's experience that is relevant to the patient's Maladaptive Transaction Cycle.

Proposition 11–10. Maximum effectiveness of metacommunicative feedback requires that the therapist and patient conjointly explore, elaborate, and validate the specified Maladaptive Transaction Cycle by "shuttling" around and between the four essential components (a) as they are relevant to the patient-therapist relationship in their sessions and (b) as they are relevant outside the session in the patient's relationships to significant others.

This principle reflects the basic interpersonal assumption that the patient's ED-presentational style, as played out with the therapist, mirrors the patient's central problems in living manifest with other important persons in his or her life. Further, since the therapist's labelings of the essential components of the Maladaptive Transaction Cycle represent hypotheses or empathic guesses, they need to be consensually validated with the patient. The crucial, ultimate validation involves the generality of occurrence of the maladaptive pattern with other significant persons.

Murrell (1971) argued that a crucial step for patient change requires accommodation of a patient's social system to any improvements in a patient's behavior that occur with the therapist:

If the social system is able to accommodate this new input and make corresponding changes that will further support and consolidate patient changes, then enduring patient change is probable. If, however, the social system acts to reject the new inputs and actively works to extinguish patient changes, then enduring patient changes are unlikely; or between these two alternatives it may allow certain changes but not others, or it may allow only a certain degree of change. (p. 214)

It is vital that the therapist, with the patient's participation, validate the pinpointed in-therapy maladaptive patient patterns by exploring their occurrence in extratherapy encounters with significant others. Shuttling among and between the essential components of the Maladaptive Transaction Cycle within and without therapy is necessary to establish the validity of the patient's maladaptive patterns as a framework for discovering more adaptive and satisfying alternatives in living for the patient.

> *Proposition 11–11.*   In the actual delivery of feedback to the patient regarding his or her Maladaptive Transaction Cycle, optimal sequencing of the four essential components varies with the strength of the working alliance, with the particular characteristics of a particular patient and presenting problem, and with the particular patient-therapist stylistic matchup.

For one patient, effective and efficient participatory exploration may result from the therapist's initial disclosure of his or her impact response (e.g., "Your refusal to take a stand frustrates me and makes me feel helpless"). With another patient it may be more effective for the therapist to lead with an inference about the patient's covert experience (e.g., "You seem to want to avoid taking a stand at all costs"). With another case, the therapist may first introduce his or her complementary overt reaction (e.g., "I've been noticing how frequently I laugh in our sessions"). Finally, with another patient, the therapist might label or draw attention to the patient's overt action (e.g., "Did you notice how you just looked at me: expectantly and waiting for me to give you the answer?").

> *Proposition 11–12.*   The earlier in their sessions the therapist detects and labels his or her impact responses to a patient, the easier it is for the therapist to disengage from the associated emotion and be able to pursue identification of the patient's Maladaptive Transaction Cycle and facilitative metacommunication with the patient.

Effective metacommunication seems to require mild to moderate levels of affective intensity in the therapist, whereas strong levels of therapist emotion make metacommunication quite difficult and problematical.

This principle directly reflects the effect of strong emotion on humans, which is primarily to disrupt perceptual, cognitive, and motor activity. The consequences of strong emotion ensure that the therapist cannot perform in an efficient, objective, and detached manner to use his or her feelings as corrective feedback for useful exploration with the patient. Instead, the therapist is to some extent, at least temporarily, lost in associative fantasies, thoughts, and action tendencies. Generally, the least disruptive action for the therapist at these points is to stall through the remainder of the session, and to disengage between sessions by supervisory consultation, by personal analysis of the disruptive events, or by the various interpersonal supervisory disengagement exercises that will be described in the next chapter.

Intense feelings are not frequent occurrences for most therapists, but seem to be universal happenings at some times for all therapists. Their occurrence reflects that therapists cannot always be maximally efficient, that patients are more adept at their distractive games than therapists, and that some patient-therapist matchups present more problems for a given therapist than do others. They also reflect the therapist's potential for introducing his or her own hang-ups into the relationship, with certain more threatening patients and/or topics triggering the therapist's own automatic presentational responses during the therapy session. All of this underscores the continuing importance of the therapist's monitoring of his or her own idiosyncratic input into the relationship issues that develop with patients. This possibility is what makes therapy a continual opportunity for both personal growth and personal threat for the therapist.

Beier (1966) noted that the therapist is also capable of responding to stimuli that are quite independent of the patient's messages and, as a result, may distort the client's message. He goes on to add:

> To obtain accurate information, the therapist must not only know his own contribution but must also develop the capability to disengage from the emotional climate the patient has prepared for him and look at the patient's message from the outside—from a different viewpoint altogether. . . . It is probably unavoidable for the therapist to learn about the patient first by reacting to him emotionally, before disengaging and recognizing the covert meaning of the messages. . . . A therapist can give a disengaged therapeutic response only after he has withdrawn from the emotional climate the patient imposed on him. (pp. 34–35)

The importance of detecting and labeling therapist impact responses as early as possible in psychotherapy sessions also reflects another basic process. It is highly likely that all human feelings that remain unlabeled or unacted-on tend to incubate. Incubation has been empirically established for the emotion of fear and is probably equally applicable to anger and other emotions. By incubation, the intensity of unlabeled or unacted-on emotion tends to increase with the passage of time, apparently through some form of a cognitive rehearsal process. This phenomenon would lead us to predict that the level of undetected therapist affect should increase in intensity over sessions. In addition, the enactment by the patient of repeated instances of his or her presentational style during their sessions ensures cumulative repetitive elicitings of the therapist's impacts. Both these processes again underscore the conclusion that earlier disengagement, by detection and labeling, is easier.

A final consideration leads to the same conclusion. From a transactional perspective, the earlier the therapist detects any level of recurrent impact response in sessions with a patient, the more likely it is that the patient is *not* responding to the particular characteristics of the therapist, but is responding to the therapist in a generalized role. The earlier in their encounter this occurs, the more likely it is that the patient's actions triggering the therapist's impacts are parataxic distortions or transferences that push the therapist into a restricted, overprogrammed role to protect and validate the patient's identity. As Singer (1970) noted, the earlier this occurs, the more likely it is that the patient is responding to the therapist in a "disrespectful" manner, as a generalized other carried over from the past; the less likely it is that the patient is discriminating the unique presentations of the therapist in their sessions. The sooner a therapist can detect and label distinctive impacts from his or her patient, the more confident he or she is that the therapist's own idiosyncratic characteristics are being ignored by the patient, and that his or her impacts represent the objective countertransference induced by the patient.

It does not follow from Proposition 11–12 that the therapist can metacommunicate more effectively with his or her patient in earlier than in later sessions. Application of Proposition 11–12 needs to be balanced with other principles. Effective metacommunication presumes some level of established positive therapeutic alliance (Proposition 11–5), the patient's perception of a respectful, on-task attitude and intent from the therapist (Proposition 11–6), the openness of the therapist to examination of his or her own contributions to the relationship (Proposition 11–7), successful communication by the therapist of both positive and negative polarities of internal engagements (Proposition 11–8), and availability of specific pinpointed examples of recurrent patterns (Proposition 11–9). Since some time usually is necessary to ensure these preconditions, effective metacommunication is not a highly probable event in early sessions. What Proposition 11–12 does assert, however, is that the earlier the therapist can detect and label his or her impact responses, the easier will be the task of disengagement and the more easily will the therapist be able to defuse higher intensities of affect. In earlier sessions this labeling also can immediately begin to guide appropriate technique by the therapist to begin to alter the patient's presentational style in the sessions themselves.

Proposition 11–13. During the hooked stage of reacting to what the patient "wants"—of reacting to the patient's command or ED-evoking response—the therapist can identify the specific reaction that the patient expects or wants from the therapist by labeling as accurately as he or she can the "perceived evoking message" component of the impact messages the therapist has been experiencing.

This principle asserts that the therapist can most readily pinpoint the patient's specific expectations for the therapeutic relationship by concentrating on identifying the "perceived evoking message" component of his or her internal engagements experienced during the session.

Proposition 11–14. Among the four classes of impact messages, the one that is least threatening to disclose to the patient is fantasy or metaphor—in contrast to direct feeling, action tendency, or perceived evoking message.

By its very nature, metaphor embodies ambiguity or imprecision in the meanings conveyed. This ambiguity of the therapist's metaphor provides the patient freedom to select particular implied meanings that are least threatening or anxiety inducing. As a result, the patient and therapist can approach central or core aspects of the Maladaptive Transaction Cycle by successive approximations, with the patient controlling the level of discomfort that is tolerable at a given moment. However, the other side of the fantasy coin is that its very concreteness and vividness makes it a difficult-to-ignore-or-forget representation of the patient's central problem. This makes it much easier for either the patient or therapist to refer to it, resurrect it, amplify it, or modify it as additional evidence emerges. For example, the therapist might interrupt the patient as follows: "I just had an image about us—that we were playing poker together, with a green-shaded light hanging down between us, with both of us wearing sunglasses, and holding our cards very close to our chests."

Fantasy or metaphor, thus, represents a subtle probe that initially is quite safe for the patient; over time, however, it can lead to emergence of unexpected, surprising, and scary meanings for the patient. Its maximum usefulness, further, depends on both the patient and therapist's facility in its use as a well-practiced and prepotent channel of representational meaning. To the extent that these conditions are present, a therapist's impact disclosure in the form of fantasy or metaphor is an initially safe, but powerful, mode of metacommunicative feedback. The relative threat value of the three other classes of impact messages likely can be rank-ordered (from less to more threatening) as perceived evoking messages, direct feelings, and action tendencies.

Andrews (1991, p. 192) prefers to present feedback to the client through role-playing. He first provides the patient a verbal lead-in which is followed by Andrews' enactment, often humorously exaggerated, of the posture that is complementary to the patient's bid. Andrews (1991) also uses role reversal, in which Andrews enacts the client's typical style so that the client, as interactant, can experience firsthand the impact on self of his or her own interpersonal problem.

> *Proposition 11–15.*   Whenever the therapist is referentially but implicitly included in a patient's statements about relationships with others, the therapist's priority is to explore explicitly with the patient the implications a statement has for their therapeutic or working alliance.

This exploration is particularly crucial in early sessions, but remains a metacommunicative priority throughout therapy. If in a first session a patient states, "I really led my former therapist around by the nose," it behooves the therapist soon to inquire regarding the implications that statement has for their own sessions. If a female patient states to her male therapist, "I have trouble relating to men," the therapist needs to inquire into the meaning for their own therapy relationship. Other similar patient statements are "I really have trouble trusting people"; "Other persons don't understand me"; "I have trouble taking responsibility with people"; and the like.

In each of these instances, the patient is using indirect and generalized, rather than direct and concrete, language to refer to a relationship issue. Class-membership words are used (therapist, men, people), and although the therapist is an obvious member of that class, the direct translation is avoided. Patients much more frequently use this indirect language instead of talking directly and unambiguously (e.g., "I'm not sure I can relate to you since you are a man"; "I probably will have trouble trusting you"; "I doubt that you will be able to understand me either").

If the therapist does not respond to and explore with the patient the ED implications of this kind of statement, he or she participates in avoiding direct and clear communication. But more relevant to the working alliance, he or she avoids clarification of a relationship issue that can continue to interfere with the basic therapy task of honest and complete self-disclosure. On the other hand, by addressing the issue directly and explicitly, the therapist demonstrates his or her empathic expertise and can negotiate explicitly with the patient strategies for addressing these issues in their subsequent sessions.

The therapist's inquiry can take this form of "I wonder how that (e.g., your leading your former therapist around by the nose; your having trouble relating to men) relates to me"; or "I wonder what that means for our relationship." Or in a later session when the patient obviously is irritated or angry, the therapist can inquire: "You're obviously pissed off about something today. I wonder if you're pissed at me."

Summary

To metacommunicate effectively, the therapist must successfully disengage from the complementary response into which he or she has become hooked. Disengagement requires occurrence of the following events: (a) that the therapist notice, attend to, and subsequently label the engagements being pulled from him or her by the patient (Proposition 11–1); (b) that the therapist discontinue the complementary response (Proposition 11–2); (c) that the therapist, through appropriate technique, attempt to help the patient interrupt his or her distinctive ED-evoking style (Proposition 11–3); and (d) that the therapist metacommunicate with the patient by referring directly to the ED-evoking and DE-impact relationship messages occurring between them (Proposition 11–4).

Effective therapeutic metacommunication, then, *presumes the patient's perception of* (a) some level of perceived safety within the therapy context as well as some level of established positive therapeutic alliance with the therapist (Proposition 11–5), (b) a respectful and on-task attitude and intent from the therapist (Proposition 11–6), and (c) the therapist's commitment to examination and ownership of his or her own contributions to their relationship (Proposition 11–7).

Effective delivery of metacommunicative feedback *requires that the therapist* (a) successfully communicate both the positive and negative polarities of his or her covert engagements in reaction to the patient (Proposition 11–8), (b) pinpoint instances of the patient's actions that evoked his or her impact responses and state inferences about the patient's covert experiences that instigated these actions (Proposition 11–9), and (c) together with the patient conjointly explore, elaborate, and validate the identified Maladaptive Transaction Cycle by shuttling around and between the four essential components both as they are relevant to the patient-therapist relationship and to the patient's relationships with significant others outside (Proposition 11–10). Optimal sequencing of feedback regarding the four essential components varies with the strength of the working alliance, with the particular characteristics of the individual patient and presenting problem, and with the specific patient-therapist stylistic matchup (Proposition 11–11).

The earlier in their relationship the therapist detects and labels his or her own impact responses to a patient, the easier it is for the therapist (a) to disengage from his or her associated emotional reactions and (b) to obtain the objectivity necessary for facilitative communication and clarification with the patient of the latter's central Maladaptive Transaction Cycle (Proposition 11–12). During the hooked stage, the therapist can most readily pinpoint the patient's specific expectations for their relationship by concentrating on identifying the "perceived evoking message" component of his or her internal engagements (Proposition 11–13). Among the four classes of impact messages, the one that is least threatening to disclose to the patient is fantasy or metaphor—in contrast to direct feelings, action tendencies, or perceived evoking messages (Proposition 11–14). Finally, throughout the course of therapy, the therapist's intervention priority is to explore explicitly with the patient any implications the patient's statements or actions have for the (a) real, (b) therapeutic alliance, or (c) parataxic distortion aspects of their relationship (Proposition 11–15).

Epilogue

In their discussion of metacommunication, Villard and Whipple (1976) specified that, if metacommunication is to be facilitative, supportive, and growth producing, it needs to incorporate six important features:

1. It must be *descriptive* (rather than evaluative).
2. *Empathetic* (rather than neutral).
3. *Problem-centered* (rather than control-centered).
4. *Spontaneous* (rather than strategic).

5. *Maximizing equality* (rather than superiority).
6. *Provisional* (rather than absolute).

Morran et al. (1985) offered a similar formulation that when interpersonal feedback is facilitative, its content is:

1. *Publicly observable* (rather than referring to inferences and other unobservable personal reactions).
2. *Unqualified* (rather than a statement using qualified words such as "a little," "somewhat," "kind of," and the like, which minimize the impact of the feedback).
3. *Specific* (describes specific, rather than general/global, behaviors or events).
4. *Nondirective* (the statement is completely descriptive, rather than implicitly or directly demanding future changes of the recipient).

Morran et al. (1985) provided 7-point Likert scales for rating interpersonal feedback on each of these four criteria.

EMPIRICAL STUDIES OF IMPACT DISCLOSURE

Individual Psychotherapy

One group of social psychology studies presents subjects with feedback and measures its impact on the subjects' self-concept. Shrauger (1975) reviewed this extensive literature and concluded that such explicit feedback usually leads subjects to modify their self-descriptions. Shrauger (1975) listed various factors that seemed to enhance the change effect, including (a) the presence of objective evidence for the feedback, (b) larger discrepancies between self-description and feedback whenever the feedback source is very credible, (c) consensual validation for the feedback, (d) favorableness of feedback if subjects have high self-esteem, and (e) subject characteristics such as susceptibility to social influence.

Only a few studies are presently available to guide the use of metacommunicative feedback in individual psychotherapy. Critelli and Neumann (1978) conducted a study contrasting the interpersonal effects of "self-disclosure" (telling another person about one's own traits) and "feedback disclosure" (telling another about one's perception of the other's traits). A sizable sample of male and female undergraduates indicated the extent to which they had disclosed positive and negative trait information, as self-disclosure or as feedback disclosure, to each of three friends in the course of their relationships. Critelli and Neumann conceptualized and identified two interpersonal disclosure clusters: dominant (positive self-disclosure and negative feedback disclosure) and friendly (negative self-disclosure and positive feedback disclosure). Results showed that subjects disclosed more to their dating friends, next to their same-sex friends, and least to their nondating opposite-sex friends. Feedback disclosure occurred more frequently than self-disclosure; females disclosed more frequently than males. However, type of disclosure interacted with positive versus negative information, occurring more frequently in the following order: positive feedback disclosure, negative self-disclosure, negative feedback disclosure, positive self-disclosure. A follow-up analysis confirmed that the authors' friendly cluster (negative self-disclosure, positive feedback) occurred significantly more often than did their dominant cluster, suggesting that close peer relationships are characterized more by affiliative than by dominant responding in terms of self-disclosure and feedback. Critelli and Neumann (1978) concluded that their results support the utility of distinguishing among the four types of disclosure: "Conceptually, they appear to serve differing functions in interpersonal communication" (p. 176).

Swaney and Stone (1990) attempted to identify factors related to therapist awareness of impact messages—important sources of interpersonal diagnostic information. They hypothesized that amount of supervision, personal relevance (the therapist's positive attitude toward the usefulness of processing covert reactions), and expressed knowledge (the therapist's ability cognitively to process covert reactions) would be positively related to therapist awareness of interpersonal impacts. Four brief (4 minutes) client monologues were videotaped depicting two female clients engaged primarily in dominant behavior and two female clients engaged primarily in submissive behavior. The authors used the IBI to demonstrate that the actress client had succeeded in enacting clearly dominant versus submissive overt interpersonal behaviors. A group of therapist trainees from various mental health settings then viewed the videotapes, were instructed to imagine they were the counselor or therapist, present in the room with the client on the videotape but not participating in the dialogue, and to fill out IMIs on the observed client. Swaney and Stone's (1990) results showed that all trainees reported impacts that significantly differentiated the dominant versus submissive clients. In other words, the trainees generally responded to both dominant and submissive client behaviors with complementary internal affective and cognitive IMI impacts. Findings also showed that therapist trainees who view their covert reactions as "relevant" to therapy, or who have more "expressed knowledge" of the important role of these reactions in therapy, displayed greater impact awareness.

Goldfried and colleagues (Goldfried, 1991) developed the Coding System of Therapeutic Feedback (CSTF; Goldfried, Newman, & Hayes, 1989) to assess various aspects of metacommunicative feedback, including feedback on the patient's thoughts and feelings, the connection between thoughts and feelings, the impact the patient has on another person, and so on). The goal of their process studies was to determine those aspects of therapist feedback that are common and unique to different orientations, by shedding light first on both the common and unique factors associated with cognitive-behavior therapy and psychodynamic-interpersonal therapy.

Goldfried (1991) summarized the findings from three preliminary studies comparing these different therapeutic orientations. One study, for example, found that both therapies used more *inter*personal than *intra*personal feedback "links" and showed no differences in their emphasis on the two categories. However, a follow-up study of the same group of therapy cases showed that only in the case of psychodynamic-interpersonal therapy was a positive correlation obtained between the focus on interpersonal links and improvement in social adjustment and self-esteem. Goldfried (1991) concluded: "Thus, although the two therapies may not have differed in their emphasis on interpersonal links, . . . this focus had more of a therapeutic impact in the psychodynamic-interpersonal conditions" (p. 20).

Goldsamt, Goldfried, Hayes, and Kerr (1992) compared demonstration sessions of cognitive therapy (Beck), cognitive behavior therapy (Meichenbaum), and short-term psychodynamic therapy (Strupp) with the same patient, Richard. Videotapes were analyzed using the Coding System of Therapeutic Focus (Goldfried et al., 1989). Results showed that, in comparison with the other therapists, Beck focused more on the cognitive triad of Richard's thoughts about self, world, and future. Although all three therapists placed a comparable emphasis on the impact that other people had on the patient, both Meichenbaum and Strupp, more than Beck, focused on the impact Richard may have had on others. In other words, "both Strupp and Meichenbaum probed more for what Richard might have done to create difficulties in his relationships with others" (Goldsamt et al., 1992, p. 174). The authors speculated that, "taken together, these findings suggest that cognitive therapy may emphasize the impact that other people have on the patient, rather than what the patient may be doing to contribute to the problem" (p. 174).

Goldfried's research program may yield additional findings that illuminate the operation of metacommunicative feedback interventions within various psychotherapies. Also, his coding system is likely to be expanded to pinpoint the effects of the more specific metacommunicative category of impact disclosure, as the latter intervention is applied more frequently and routinely by therapists of various theoretical orientations.

Group Psychotherapy

By far, the majority of relevant studies have looked at "interpersonal feedback" in group psychotherapy or in small-group research. The results of these studies provide confirming support to several of the metacommunication propositions offered in this chapter. The following major reviews or studies offer more detail: Bednar and Kaul (1978), J. P. Campbell and Dunnette (1968), Kaul and Bednar (1986), Kivlighan (1985), Lamphere (1993), Morran et al. (1985), Morran and Stockton (1985), and Yalom (1985).

Morran et al. (1985) expressed one of the major conclusions of the group studies of interpersonal feedback: "There is, in fact, considerable support for viewing feedback as one of the most important dimensions of the therapeutic group process" (p. 57). Feedback has been found to be positively related (a) to behavior change within the group itself, including greater in-group sensitivity and increased group cohesion, (b) to change in actions and emotional expression outside the group as rated by self and others, and (c) to improved self-insights. Yalom (1985) reported that both successful group therapy patients and group leaders identify feedback as an essential therapeutic factor. Kaul and Bednar (1986), recognizing feedback as theoretically key to almost all forms of therapy, concluded: "there appears to be unanimity of opinion that clients' interests will be well served by the appropriate kinds of feedback given under the correct conditions" (p. 695).

Of the various components of interpersonal feedback, *valence* has been most extensively researched. Results indicate that positive feedback tends to be rated as more credible, more desirable, more impactful, more cohesion promoting, and less threatening than negative feedback. In contrast, negative feedback arouses anxiety and mixed emotions in both giver and receiver and is often general and qualified, thereby reducing its usefulness for the recipient (Morran et al., 1985). A second consistent finding of valence studies is that maximum therapeutic change tends to be associated with feedback that incorporates *both* positive and negative components. Disproportionately high amounts of positive feedback have been associated with diminished therapeutic outcomes. Also, feedback seems to be more accepted and utilized by recipients when delivered in a positive-negative sequence (Morran et al., 1985). These findings provide support for Proposition 11–8, which stated that metacommunicative feedback needs to include both positive and negative components of the impact message complex.

In a series of studies, Andrews (1973, 1974–1975, 1990) tested, in dyadic interactions, McClelland's (1951) discrepancy hypothesis, which asserts that moderate discrepancies from expectation evoke exploratory behavior, whereas extreme discrepancies produce anxiety and avoidance. His findings were consistently supportive: Moderate discrepancy in feedback provided by group members produces excitement and interest, large discrepancies generated tension, and small discrepancies were experienced by group members as unstimulating.

Most of the studies to date have focused on various dimensions of the message itself, such as valence, sequence, emotionality level, and degree of behavioral specificity. Kivlighan (1985) provided a model that adds two other determinants affecting receiver acceptance and use of feedback: *characteristics of the feedback deliverer* (e.g., closeness, expertness, trustworthiness, reliability), and *characteristics of the feedback receiver* (e.g., level of self-esteem, degree of defensiveness). A transactional approach would insist on adding a fourth determinant: the *nature of the relationship present between the deliverer and receiver.*

Studies have made clear progress in beginning to clarify the nature and efficacy of interpersonal feedback in group psychotherapy. Available findings tend to be supportive of several of the propositions of metacommunicative feedback offered in this chapter. Available findings also suggest that more concentrated empirical study of feedback in individual psychotherapy might yield equally promising results.

IMPACT DISCLOSURE IN CONTEMPORARY PSYCHOANALYTIC PSYCHOTHERAPY

As reviewed in detail by Kiesler and Van Denburg (1993), some contemporary psychoanalytic formulations emphasize that the therapist's countertransference reactions, far from hindering the therapy transaction, actually contain important information and, if carefully examined, can shed important light on the patient's defenses and their dynamics. This "totalistic" viewpoint on countertransference, as distinguished from the "classical" viewpoint (Kernberg, 1965), emphasizes reference to *all* the therapist's emotional, cognitive, and fantasy engagements experienced from the patient.

Modern psychoanalytic theory (L. Epstein & Feiner, 1979; Meyers, 1986; Tansey & Burke, 1989; Wolstein, 1988) makes an additional crucial distinction between subjective and objective countertransference (see Chapter 9). "Subjective" countertransference (Spotnitz, 1969) refers to the defensive and irrational reactions and feelings a therapist experiences with a particular patient—the narrow definition of countertransference advocated by classicists. In contrast, "objective" countertransference (Winnicott, 1949) refers to the constricted feelings, attitudes, and reactions of a therapist that are induced primarily by the "actual personality and behavior of the patient, based on objective observation" (p. 195), and that are generalizable to other therapists and to significant others in the patient's life. This countertransference registers the objective effects of the patient's central transference feelings and conflicts as they continue to be expressed in present-day interactions with significant others, including the therapist.

In terms of identifiable therapist behaviors, *interpersonal impact disclosure is equivalent to the therapist's disclosure of objective countertransference feelings and attitudes to the patient during psychotherapy* (Kiesler, 1992; Kiesler & Van Denburg, 1993). A therapist's impact messages can include both irrational (subjective) and generalizable (objective) countertransference components. Use of metacommunication as an effective intervention requires delivery of feedback that maximizes the objective, and minimizes the subjective, countertransference components. As discussed earlier, this underscores the necessity that therapists continually monitor their own idiosyncratic inputs into the therapeutic relationship and work to achieve a level of disengagement that permits their objective use of interventive options. Techniques and suggestions to therapists for accomplishing the disengagement process and for obtaining consensual validation of their impacts within the therapy and supervisory situations were provided earlier in this chapter and will be elaborated in Chapter 12.

Kiesler and Van Denburg (1993) also emphasized that, similar to interpersonal advocates of impact disclosure, analytic proponents of countertransference disclosure *do not advocate subjective or irrational countertransferences as legitimate content for therapeutic metacommunication.* Spotnitz (1969), for example, cautions that "countertransference cannot be utilized with complete confidence unless it has been purged of its subjective element." When irrational countertransference is directly, impulsively enacted or discharged, the therapist is simply acting out his or her unresolved issues and conflicts at the expense of the patient. Also, inasmuch as, even in the best of circumstances, part of the therapist's functioning remains unconscious, it is not being implied that all of the objective countertransference reactions the therapist experiences result solely from the patient's evoking style. This extreme stance would merely recapitulate the analytic "blank screen" emphasis. What interpersonal communication theory advocates as therapeutically essential in all instances of impact disclosure is that the therapist be able to pinpoint recurrent behavior patterns of the patient that are evoking his or her particular experiences, while at all times being empathically sensitive to the consequences that impact disclosure can have on the patient's self-esteem. Finally, the therapist remains open at all times to his or her own unique contributions to the patient-therapist relationship as the patient's self-defeating patterns continue to be explored both within and outside therapy.

Kiesler and Van Denburg (1993) concluded:

> It took analysts repeated experiences of extreme negative feelings towards their patients to permit them to begin to shake loose from the taboo against using countertransference in therapeutic ways. What further experiences will be required before they routinely recognize the therapeutic importance of less intense, more subtle, but much more commonplace manifestations of the same countertransference phenomenon? Why would it not be the case that subtle, moderate therapist countertransference reactions are equally useful—albeit demanding that the therapist bring considerably more sensitivity and acumen to bear for their identification, interpretation and metacommunication? (p. 10)

CONCLUSION

The therapist intervention of impact disclosure has an increasingly prominent place in contemporary interpersonal theories of psychotherapy. Psychoanalytic writers as well are encouraging experimentation with and therapeutic use of countertransference disclosure. Systematic theoretical statements of impact disclosure have emerged as well as practical clinical guidelines. A growing body of research on interpersonal feedback in group psychotherapy has appeared, and initial empirical forays have occurred into individual psychotherapy.

Serious programmatic studies of applications of impact disclosure in individual psy-chotherapy are needed to expand further the empirical base of this therapist interven-tion. Process change (L. S. Greenberg, 1986; L. N. Rice & Greenberg, 1984) studies are needed to investigate the effectiveness, and limitations, of impact disclosure and other applications of metacommunicative feedback within therapy sessions and over sequences of sessions. Studies also are needed to identify the important patient, thera-pist, interactional, and contextual conditions that combine to effect the results ob-tained (Kiesler, 1992). Still other studies are required to demonstrate the relationship of therapist impact disclosure during sessions to subsequent proximal and ultimate case outcomes. And so on. It is likely that impact disclosure, alone or (more likely) in combination with other interventions, can be systematized into a brief-psychotherapy format (e.g., Kiesler, 1990), the therapeutic effects of which can be investigated with different patient groups and problems in clinical trials designs.

CHAPTER 12

Interpersonal Communication Supervision and the Parallel Process

> *The art of therapy [and of supervision] is not in avoiding engagement, but in recognizing engagement and accomplishing disengagement.*
>
> *(Young & Beier, 1982, p. 194)*

Of necessity, the practice of supervision is based on the supervisor's conceptualization, explicit or not, of psychotherapy. The present chapter offers a model for supervision of individual, adult psychotherapy derived from my interpersonal communication viewpoint.

TASK AND TRANSACTION COMPONENTS

A central interpersonal communication (IC) assumption is that psychotherapy, like any other human interaction, occurs at two levels of communication: a report, content, or representational level; and a command, relationship, or presentational level. Within the context of therapy (or supervision), the former can be called the Task level, the latter the Transactional level. *The Task* involves the patient's efforts, with the therapist's help, to self-disclose and explore the meanings of his or her problems and experiences. *The Transaction* entails the patient's concomitant interpersonal behaviors or communications as the therapist experiences them during their sessions. The therapist's job is to help the patient attend to, identify, and clarify (a) "missing" Task elements—aspects of the patient's experience (cognitions, expectations, feelings, fantasies, etc.) and actions (words and nonverbal behaviors) that are overlooked or deemphasized in the patient's self-exploration; and (b) unattended to Transactional elements—automatic and habitual relationship messages or actions by which the patient repeatedly induces others, including the therapist, to respond with constricted complementary reactions.

Supervision, just like psychotherapy or any other human interaction, is an interpersonal transaction. The process of supervision, then, is symmetrical to the process of psychotherapy and is governed by the same principles. Accordingly, *IC supervision,* just as IC psychotherapy, has both Task and Transaction components. The *Task elements* consist of the therapist's disclosure (words, videotapes, etc.) during supervisory sessions of his or her case conceptualizations and of the specific therapeutic interventions applied to patients in therapy sessions. The *Transaction elements* comprise the automatic interpersonal action-reaction sequences concomitantly occurring at the relationship level between therapist and supervisor. Just as in psychotherapy, impasses also can occur during the supervisory process. That is, periods can occur during which relationship or command issues surface at undetected and unresolved levels between therapist and supervisor to the point that effective collaborative work is interrupted, pursuit of the supervisory Task proper bogs down, supervisory interventions become ineffective, and the supervisor and therapist remain hooked or trapped into actions complementary to each other's evoking behavior and into more intense negative emotions toward each other.

At the Task level, the basic work of the interpersonal supervisor is to monitor and facilitate the therapist's application of an interpersonal treatment plan based in systematic and ongoing interpersonal diagnosis and assessment. In IC supervision, the therapist is asked continually to apply various interpersonal circle measures summarized in Chapter 1. These measures, filled in by the therapist (or observers) on the patient, and by the patient (or observers) on the therapist, permit placement of the patient's and/or therapist's pattern of interpersonal behavior on the 1982 Interpersonal Circle (Figures 1–1 to 1–3). As we discussed, this circle diagnosis guides therapists in specifying an interpersonal treatment plan based on the propositions summarized in Chapter 10. Figure 10–2 illustrates an interpersonal treatment plan, applied to a patient with a *DSM-IV* diagnosis of Dysthymia with Dependent Personality Disorder. These measures also permit the therapist to begin to fill in the essential features of the patient's Maladaptive Transaction Cycle (MTC) (cf. Figures 6–1 and 6–2).

The IC supervisor addresses the Task level by ensuring that the therapist has learned contemporary interpersonal and IC psychotherapy. Although Task supervision is crucial for facilitating understanding and application of interpersonal treatment plans, the necessary concepts and skills are relatively easily mastered through didactic discussion, concrete applications, and corrective feedback. On the other hand, periods of impasse are frequent occurrences in therapy sessions and sabotage interpersonal interventions designed to return the patient and therapist to more collaborative and open pursuit of change. The result is that, unless these relationship issues are targeted directly by the therapist or supervisor, the impasses continue to emasculate other therapist interventions.

At the Transaction level the basic work of the IC supervisor is to facilitate therapeutic communication and a therapeutic relationship, both between patient and therapist and between therapist and supervisor. The IC supervisor not only participates in the therapist's interpersonal treatment of the patient but also collaborates with the therapist to monitor and change the relationship present within, and between, both sets of dyads (patient-therapist, therapist-supervisor). At all times, the IC supervisor gives interventive priority to the metacommunication occurring (or not occurring) between patient and therapist and between therapist and supervisor.

PARALLEL PROCESS: AN INTERPERSONAL ANALYSIS

The distinctively unique aspects of IC supervision derive from the supervisor's constant attention to the Transaction level of the therapy and supervisory dyads and especially to impasses that occur in both. What seems necessarily operative is another version of the interpersonal transaction cycle which might be labeled "the patient-therapist-supervisor transaction cycle." Indeed, the literature suggests that an important lawful interface exists between therapy and supervisory transactions, referred to as the *parallel process* (Doehrman, 1976; Ekstein & Wallerstein, 1958).

Searles (1955) was among the first to observe:

> The emotions experienced by the supervisor—including even his private, "subjective" feeling experiences and his personal feeling about the supervisee—often provide valuable clarification of processes currently characterizing the relationship between the supervisee and the patient. In addition, these processes are often the very ones which have been causing difficulty in the therapeutic relationship and, because heretofore unrecognized by the supervisee, have not been consciously, verbally reported by him to the supervisor. (p. 135)

Searles named these therapy-to-supervision interfaces the *reflection process:* "One may say that the supervisor's emotion is a reflection of something which has been going on in the therapist-patient relationship and, in the final analysis, in the patient" (p. 136).

At the most general level, parallel process refers to the similarity between the processes occurring in a given therapy relationship and those occurring in the corresponding supervisory relationship. Only a few empirical studies have addressed this phenomenon (Alpher, 1991; Clavere, 1982; Doehrman, 1976; Forsleff, 1967; Friedlander, Siegel, & Brenock, 1989; McNeil & Worthen, 1989; Pollock, 1990). To explain parallel process, various writers have attributed differing underlying mechanisms: unconscious identification (Hora, 1957; Searles, 1955), role oscillation as an expression of the duality of ego function (Arlow, 1963), "problems about learning" reflecting the characters of therapist and supervisor (Ekstein & Wallerstein, 1958), or transference dispositions of both the therapist and supervisor (Doehrman, 1976). Pollock (1990) was the first to define parallel process in interpersonal terms as follows: "Given a therapy relationship and a corresponding supervision relationship, parallel process refers to the recapitulation in one of the relationships of a pattern of interpersonal behaviors and/or their impacts occurring in the other relationship" (p. 19).

Searles (1955) specified also that parallel (reflection) process could occur either by the therapist "identifying" with the patient's defenses (e.g., a therapist's feeling of confusion reflects directly the patient's confusion), or by the therapist's adoption of a position "complementary" to the patient's defenses (e.g., a therapist feels accused and guilty in response to the patient's subtle accusations). Doehrman (1976) emphasized that the parallel process can move in the supervision-to-therapy direction as well: The supervisor can induce an emotional state in the therapist who then acts out this supervisory identification with his or her patients.

My interpersonal analysis of what occurs in the parallel process is as follows. Within the psychotherapy transaction, especially during early sessions, the therapist is pulled to provide the complementary response to the patient. As the therapist becomes and remains hooked, a period of impasse develops in which the therapist's increasing negative emotions toward the patient raise the therapist's level of anxiety. Unable to disengage, the therapist, during supervision, expresses anxiety automatically and indirectly (acts out) by adopting a pattern of behavior identical to that of the patient. The enactment serves as a vicarious attempt by the therapist to find a solution to the patient-therapist impasse. The therapist's enactment, in turn, pulls from the supervisor complementary responses identical to those pulled from the therapist by the patient. The supervisory interaction, thus, recapitulates the exact ineffective transactional pattern evident in the psychotherapy interaction. If the supervisor remains hooked into providing complementary reactions to the therapist, supervision also moves quickly to impasse. The supervisor, unable to disengage, increasingly experiences negative emotions toward the therapist that raise the level of the supervisor's (and the therapist's) anxiety.

When parallel process moves in the other direction, the supervisor enacts rigid and extreme interpersonal behaviors toward the therapist. In the supervisory transaction, the therapist is pulled to provide the complementary response to the supervisor. As therapist and supervisor remain hooked, a period of impasse develops in which each participant's increasing negative emotions toward the other raise the anxiety level of both. Unable to disengage, the therapist, during the psychotherapy sessions, expresses anxiety automatically and indirectly (acts out) by adopting a pattern of behavior toward the patient identical to that of the supervisor. The enactment represents a vicarious attempt by the therapist to find a solution to the therapist-supervisor impasse. This enactment, in turn, pulls from the patient complementary responses identical to those pulled from the therapist by the supervisor. This reversed-direction parallel process results basically from the supervisor's superior power position among the triad of supervisory participants. The self-defeating consequence is that the therapy transaction recapitulates the exact ineffective transactional pattern evident in the supervisory interaction and therapy also moves quickly to impasse.

Essentially, unresolved therapy and supervisory impasses are characterized by reverberating waves of anxiety and other negative emotions moving in all directions between and among the patient, therapist, and supervisor interactants. To be successful, then, the IC supervisor must at all times be sensitive to and direct interventions toward therapy and supervisory impasses that are operative within the parallel process.

TRANSACTIONAL SUPERVISORY INTERVENTIONS

Basic impediments to open pursuit of supervisory work are transactional maneuvers, motivated by avoidance of or escape from anxiety, which can be contributed to by any one of the triad of interactants: patient, therapist, or supervisor. To greater or lesser degrees, our humanity makes all of us susceptible to disruptive anxiety. Greben, Markson, and Sadavoy (1973) noted that "common to both therapy and supervision is the fact that growth is a painful process. There is an unavoidable assault on a previously accepted self-image and style of performance, which can be humiliating and anxiety-provoking" (p. 478). Other authors have similarly detailed the many sources of anxiety for the therapist-supervisee. But the supervisor also is not spared anxiety and is vulnerable in ways similar to the supervisee (e.g., Benedek, 1954; Langs, 1980; Rioch, 1980). Supervisors can fear their supervisee's knowledge and perceptiveness, can fear that they will expose weaknesses and mistakes, and can fear that their supervisory efforts will be totally ineffective for either the therapist or patient.

In a particular supervisory situation, the degree of parataxic residue in therapist or supervisor generally is significantly less than that in the patient. Also, because of more experience and continued growth, the supervisor has a discriminable edge on the therapist-supervisee. Regardless, supervision, just as therapy, of necessity offers therapeutic side effects to both participants. Especially with novice supervisees and supervisors, parataxic residuals may rear their heads unintentionally in therapy and supervisory sessions. Further, if we keep in mind the experiential and interpersonal blind spots that result from periodic stresses and anxieties in the supervisee's and supervisor's personal lives, we have additional reason to highlight transactional components of the supervisory relationship that intermittently inhibit effective and efficient pursuit of the supervisory Task proper.

Supervision is able to be effective and efficient only if both supervisor and therapist admit up front, at least to self, that anxiety is unavoidable in their conjoint process. This admission, in turn, places on each the participatory effort of detecting occurrences of their respective anxieties and of discussing the personal and other meanings of these anxieties as they relate to the supervisory and therapy processes.

THE METACOMMUNICATIVE PRIORITY

Supervisory Impasses

At all times, the IC supervisor's most important job is to detect emergence of therapist-supervisor impasses (embedded or not in the parallel process) so that metacommunicative interventions may be applied. Hence, while pursuing with the therapist the Task level that concentrates on patient-therapist interactions, at another level the supervisor monitors the subtle relationship negotiations occurring between him- or herself and the therapist.

Open metacommunication is far from being a typical or easy supervisory happening since its occurrence depends on the willingness of both parties to tolerate and explore their respective anxieties. As Langs (1980) emphasized:

> The detection of countertransference expressions in the direct supervisory interaction itself, from either the supervisor or supervisee, is a difficult matter. For the supervisor, it calls for an openness to examining his possible contribution to any source of tension between himself and the supervisee, and to any moment of acute disturbance or stalemate in the supervised treatment situation. (pp. 109–110)

Greben et al. (1973) added, "Inevitably, both resident and supervisor encounter difficulties in working together, and these must be dealt with openly or the necessary alliance for mutual learning is endangered" (pp. 475–476). Cohen (1980) noted:

> How free the student therapist feels to express satisfaction, dissatisfaction, frustration, rage, and so on at the supervisor for fulfilling or not fulfilling the student's expectations in carrying out therapy is of paramount importance to the student's experience of supervision, and ultimately to the success or failure of the treatment being conducted by the supervisee. . . . Supervisees are quick to appreciate a climate where they can see their own anxiety on the wane because their feelings are tolerated, accepted, and solicited as useful. They begin to see such an environment

as useful in itself, by analogy, in the treatment situation in which they are so much involved. (pp. 80–81)

Inevitably, therapy impasses also seem to produce supervisory impasses. The former cannot be untangled without unraveling the latter, for several reasons. First, intense emotion experienced toward the patient threatens the supervisee's image as a therapist and, to varying degrees, threatens his or her more general self-definition. As therapists, it is difficult for us to juxtapose intense feelings of anger, disgust, rivalry, sexual fantasy, seductive behavior, and the like toward patients with our conception of self as "good" therapist. Second, to the extent that periods of nonmovement or stalemate imply failure and defeat—as always is the case, but especially so for novice supervisees and supervisors—the threat can lead to questioning our competence more generally as persons. To argue otherwise seems naive.

It's important to caution that, in IC supervision, *the purpose of open metacommunication is elucidation of issues related to the treatment process—not the personal therapy of the therapist (or supervisor)*, although personal side effects invariably accrue.

For supervision to be effective, both participants, but especially the supervisor, need constantly to assess the supervisory transaction. The supervisor's job is to detect the impact messages repetitively registered within while interacting with the therapist. Through clarification of these covert complementary responses, the supervisor pinpoints the specific command self-presentation of the supervisee and the position on the interpersonal circle where the supervisee's pattern is located. The supervisor asks him- or herself continually: What am I pulled to feel or do when I am with this supervisee? Is my supervisee presenting as friendly-dominant, hostile-dominant, friendly-submissive, or hostile-submissive? How extremely and rigidly?

Also, before supervision starts, the IC supervisor is careful to inform the supervisee that they both have responsibility for continuing assessment of their relationship and of their individual as well as dyadic communication baselines. Early in supervision, the dyadic baseline typically reflects a cooperative, task-oriented interplay within the context-appropriate roles of friendly-dominant supervisor and friendly-submissive supervisee. As supervision progresses, these role behaviors progressively are contaminated by the characteristic interpersonal behaviors of both participants. Especially when impasses occur, both fall back easily on their respective evoking styles as overlearned ways of handling threat; "transactional escalation" (Van Denburg, 1989; Van Denburg & Kiesler, 1993) occurs under stressful conditions and the dyad shifts away from the originally cooperative and friendly baseline. For all these reasons, both therapist and supervisor share responsibility for assessing their respective and dyadic baselines, detecting baseline shifts, and for metacommunicating to each other in regard to their respective contributions to impasses.

Avoiding or ignoring this pivotal work emasculates subsequent supervision. Rioch (1980) cogently noted: "The 'you are up; I am down' situation is not likely to obtain for very long. The balance is untenable. Something has to be done to bring things into equality" (p. 70). She described how supervisees quickly learn subtle maneuvers to "right" the situation, such as reporting that the supervisor's suggestions didn't work or that a patient about whom the therapist is pessimistic is improving dramatically; "or the supervisee does not change in any way, shape, or manner during the supervision. This last is perhaps the best way of all to bring him down, for the supervisor, being human, likes to think he is having an effect" (p. 71). In contrast, during successful supervision, just as in successful therapy, relationship develops toward greater flexibility in the interpersonal positions of both parties, with both being able to shift more freely to behaviors from the various circle quadrants.

Invariably, periods of impasse develop in supervision reflecting both therapist impasses with patients and clashes of interpersonal styles of therapist and supervisor. At these periods, pursuit of the supervisory Task proper is sabotaged. The IC supervisor bears the major responsibility for assessing the presence of these supervisory impasses and for metacommunication with the supervisee. The detailed clinical guidelines for therapeutic metacommunication presented in Chapter 11 apply equally validly to the supervisory situation.

Therapy Impasses

Therapy impasses refer to *periods wherein relationship or command issues surface at undetected levels between patient and therapist to the point that effective collaborative work is interrupted, pursuit of the therapy Task bogs down, the therapist's interventions are ineffective, and the therapist remains hooked or trapped into actions complementary to the patient's evoking behaviors and into more intense negative emotion toward the patient.* Safran and Segal (1990; see also Safran, McMain, et al., 1990) referred to an "alliance rupture" or "point in the interaction between therapist and patient when the quality of the therapeutic alliance is strained or impaired" (p. 88). Safran and Muran (1995a) argued that, in resolving problems or ruptures in the working alliance, a major intervention is for the therapist to invite "the client to take a step back and join with the therapist in a process of examining or metacommunicating about what is currently going on between them. The therapist's task is to identify his or her own feelings and to use these as a point of departure for collaborative exploration" (Safran & Muran, 1995a, p. 86).

The IC supervisor also gives priority to detection of these inevitable periods of patient-therapist impasse. Although assessment is a joint responsibility, it falls more heavily on the supervisor, who has a defined role that implies maturer skills and who is less likely to be emotionally involved with the patient. *As the next step, the supervisor helps the therapist "disengage" from the more intense affect toward the patient that is limiting intervention options.* As Young and Beier (1982) cogently pointed out, "The art of therapy is not in avoiding engagement, but in recognizing engagement and accomplishing disengagement" (p. 194).

Phenomenonologically, the extreme experience of the hooked stage is very unpleasant. On the one hand, therapists perceive their role as an accepting, understanding, and nurturant caregiver for patients. Yet they increasingly experience boredom, dread, anxiety, incompetence, irritation, and other negative feelings during the therapy sessions. Such feelings can threaten a therapist's self-system by precipitating negative self-statements. One security operation is for the therapist to initiate a rigid evoking game with the patient through what often becomes a power struggle to protect the therapist's identity. This possible maladaptive strategy by the therapist further underscores the necessity of achieving a state of disengagement.

By disengaging, the therapist also avoids becoming alienated from the patient. Unlike others with whom the patient interacts, the therapist perseveres in a supportive fashion to help the patient face aspects of experience that he or she has tuned out to prevent destruction of self-definition and to keep from emerging stripped and vulnerable in a totally unpredictable world.

DISENGAGEMENT INTERVENTIONS IN INTERPERSONAL COMMUNICATION SUPERVISION

Specific IC supervisory interventions are available to identify, and help the therapist disengage from, the hooked state occurring during periods of impasse with his or her patients. In addition to continual use of metacommunication and analysis of parallel process, other IC supervisory interventions can be applied, many of which were suggested earlier by Mintz (1972) from a psychoanalytic framework, but which fit snugly within the IC perspective. Several function best within team supervision, but most can be effectively used in individual supervision sessions as well.

The purpose of these interventions is to help supervisees first to identify the impact messages or covert complementary responses being pulled from them by a patient as well as to identify their own contributions to these reactions. Second, they are designed to help supervisees to disengage from being hooked so as to regain the option of more flexible interventions. These disengagement interventions are initiated by the supervisor (or, in a team format, by another supervisee acting as a supervisor) when it becomes apparent that a therapist is at an impasse with a patient, which, by definition, means being engulfed in strong emotion toward the patient.

In the first disengagement intervention, *the supervisee is asked to "role-play the patient" or to show a videotaped segment from the most recent therapy session.* The role-play takes the form of a monologue in which the supervisee mimics as closely as possible the patient's style of disclosure in therapy. At the end of either the monologue or videotape, *the supervisor reports the predominant impact messages he or she experienced as "therapist" while interacting with "the patient."* The supervisee is then asked to validate whether he or she has been experiencing the same command messages from the patient that the supervisor reported. This intervention helps the supervisee to pinpoint the patient's maladaptive self-presentational acts through labeling of the covert complementary responses heretofore undetected by the supervisee. Labeling is the first necessary step along the road to therapist disengagement.

A second supervisory intervention is similar to the preceding one. *Again, the supervisee is asked to role-play* the patient in monologue or to show a videotaped segment from a recent therapy session. At the conclusion, *the supervisor reports the fantasies he or she experienced while observing the patient.* Preferably, these fantasies are wild, primitive, and no-holds-barred. The purpose of this intervention is identical to that of the preceding; in addition, fantasy often presents dramatic, but safer, metaphors that condense the essential features of the impasse. Through raw expression of fantasies, the supervisor models for the therapist that it is not only helpful, but acceptable, to contact intense inner feelings.

A third intervention is called *"empty-chair raw dialogue"* and is an IC adaptation of gestalt therapy technique. The supervisor interrupts the supervisee's presentation of a particular patient and asks him or her to imagine the patient sitting in an empty chair in the room. The supervisor then says: "I want you to tell your patient exactly what you feel about him [her]. Don't hold back. Forget about being polite or tactful or empathic. Instead, relate your feelings in as raw, undisguised, blunt, primitive, no-holds-barred way as you possibly can!"

These instructions permit the supervisee to wax primitively, and most frequently it leads to a crescendo of complaints, disappointments, irritations, and frustrations. With support, challenge, and applause from the supervisor, the supervisee recounts these negative impacts, including what the patient does to produce them, until he or she arrives at the most succinct summary statement possible. Once this has been accomplished, the supervisor asks the supervisee to talk again to the empty-chair patient, this time expressing only feelings from the opposite pole: "Now I want you to tell your patient all the positive feelings, and only the positive ones, that you have for him [her]. Tell your patient what you admire and respect, what part you really enjoy sharing!"

The first part of the exercise permits the supervisee to label and, with supervisor support, to disengage from the strong emotional engagement interfering with objectivity toward the patient. The second part rekindles the supervisee's appreciation of the real pain and anxiety motivating the patient's self-protective security maneuvers and resistances. Having accomplished catharsis in a safe milieu, the supervisee is now more ready to return to objective metacommunication and to other intervention options with the patient.

All three of the preceding interventions typically are accompanied by the more systematic assessment provided by the use of circumplex inventories. To accomplish this, the supervisor independently completes IMIs or CLOPT-Rs, for example, on a particular patient and summarizes and profiles the patient's scores. The supervisee then reacts to and validates the patient's maladaptive self-presentational style thus measured. All three interventions may also be used within a team supervisory format in which one or more other supervisees play the role of therapist. In this role, team members frequently provide alternative metacommunicative and other interventions that can help the therapist to move beyond a particular impasse.

A fourth disengagement intervention seems to require the safer milieu of individual supervision because its purpose is to facilitate some resolution of the therapist's acting out with a patient of "subjective countertransference" (Spotnitz, 1969) feelings. *When a therapy impasse emerges primarily from the therapist's personal issues, the supervisor's intervention may be simply to ask the supervisor: "Does your patient remind you of anyone in your own background?"* Another form, suggested by Ross and Kapp (1962), directs the supervisee to concentrate on visual images that emerge when listening to the patient's imagery, metaphors, or dreams during sessions. These evoked images serve as starting points for the supervisee's own associations either during or after the session. By this process, images related to the supervisee's own past frequently are discovered, and awareness of them can help clarify the supervisee's own contributions to the feelings experienced with a particular patient.

These latter personal-disclosure forms of disengagement are designed for the rare impasses in which the therapist's contributions seem as much as or more than the patient's—in which the therapist's anxiety seems strongly present. To the extent that these interventions facilitate emotional elaboration and exploration of the identified parataxic themes, *the individual supervisory session momentarily becomes therapy for the supervisee. The limits of this task shift need to be controlled by the supervisor,* who constantly brings the discussions back to the relevance of personal themes to the specific impasse with the patient.

A fifth disengagement intervention, suggested by Safran and Segal (1990), consists simply of *watching (or listening) to a recording of a recent or problematic therapy session, either alone or with a colleague or supervisor present.* They noted that without the demand of responding to the immediate situation that the live transaction posed, the therapist is freer to concentrate on monitoring his or her ongoing inner feelings and action tendencies. With this freedom comes the possibility of discovery. *By attending to bodily felt sensations and feelings, the therapist gradually contacts a felt sense,* which subsequently can be abstracted as a conceptual meaning that clarifies the impasse.

SUMMARY

The most effective intervention of the IC supervisor is the manner in which he or she models the IC system during supervisory sessions. *The explicit priority given to metacommunication in each and every context, including supervision itself, makes it much more difficult for either therapist or supervisor to hide behind their defined roles and to continue to avoid resolution of impasses resulting from subtle evoking-command maneuvers on either's part.* At all times, both share responsibility for achieving clear, open, direct, and unambiguous communication. Similarly, both share responsibility for occurrence of impasses or communication failures. In avoiding blame of either for failures, the IC framework facilitates a safe climate for both therapist and supervisor to take risks and to continue to grow as professionals and as persons.

This also helps a supervisor cast outcome expectations in a realistically optimistic light. As a supervisor, at best I can help a therapist to achieve a few enduring shifts in the way he or she (a) self-presents to patients (and to others), (b) experiences and shares patients' (and others') misery and greatness, (c) confronts, and helps patients to "own," missing elements within their private and interpersonal experience, and (d) confronts supervisors (and other significant persons) to effect more participatory and meaningful transactions.

PARALLEL PROCESS: EMPIRICAL RESEARCH

A small but important series of studies has examined the parallel process in psychotherapy and supervision: Alpher (1991), Clavere (1982), Doehrman (1976), Forsleff (1967), Friedlander et al. (1989), McNeil and Worthen (1989), and Pollock (1990).

Apparently, the first recorded empirical study of the parallel process was that of Doehrman (1976). Using a clinical analysis of interview data, Doehrman studied eight sets of concurrent therapy-supervision processes: eight patients, four therapist trainees, and two supervisors. Each therapist-supervisor pair was interviewed jointly for 20 consecutive weeks; a summary interview was conducted at the end of 20 weeks, and a follow-up interview was done at 3 months. The interviews were designed to assess the current therapeutic situation, transference and countertransference issues in the therapy, and the dynamics of the supervision relationship. Patients were interviewed following most of their therapy sessions to determine the patient's perspective on the affective quality of the therapeutic relationship, therapeutic progress, and the therapist's level of skill.

Based on her analysis of the clinical data, Doehrman (1976) found substantial evidence for the existence of parallel process. In every case, there was evidence of "the therapist behaving with their patients in the same (or opposite) way that they experience their supervisors as behaving towards them" (p. 199). She also found, "All four therapists made a temporary identification with one of their patients, acting out with their supervisors the patient's impulse-defense patterns" (p. 214). Finally, she noted that the research involvement itself became an element in the parallel process. She concluded that her findings indicated "that the parallel process phenomenon occurs and recurs in a remarkable multiplicity of directions" (Doehrman, 1976, p. 217).

Clavere (1982) studied 10 triads (patient, therapist, supervisor). Every 2 weeks, every subject was administered alternate forms of an interpersonal attractiveness measure. The attractiveness scores were used to compute correlations between the level of attraction in therapy and the level of attractiveness in supervision. Clavere found that as the level of attraction between the patient and therapist increased, the level of attraction between the therapist and supervisor either decreased or increased. He concluded that one fourth of the variance in the level of interpersonal attractiveness in the therapy relationship could be explained by level of interpersonal attractiveness in the supervision relationship, and vice versa. Finally, Clavere (1982) believed the impact of the supervisory relationship was greater on the therapy relationship than the reverse case, but did not cite his reasoning.

In an early interpersonal study using the ICL, Forsleff (1967) confirmed his hypothesis that there is consistency of feeling-verbalization made by a counselor in counselor-client and counselor-supervisor relationships.

Friedlander et al. (1989) examined the theoretical model of parallel process by applying social psychological theories of self-presentation and interpersonal influence in an in-depth case study (one client, one therapist, one supervisor) of the naturally developing therapeutic and supervisory relationships. A variety of measures pointed to the characterization of both relationships as supportive and friendly overall. The trainee's profile of the value of the supervisory sessions was strikingly similar to her profiled evaluations from the counseling sessions. The client was more favorably disposed than was the counselor toward the counseling sessions; the counselor rated the supervisory sessions somewhat more favorably than did her supervisor. The client viewed the counselor as somewhat more attractive and trustworthy than he was expert; the trainee rated the supervisor as considerably more attractive and interpersonally sensitive than task-oriented. Analysis of verbal communication showed that the predominant self-presentational pattern in both dyads was complementary; the supervisor used mostly leading self-presentations, with the trainee mainly cooperating. The same pattern was found in the counseling dyad, with the counselor leading and the client cooperative. Finally, the relational control data showed relatively little struggle for control (competitive symmetry) in either relationship. There were indications, however, of critical points during the course at which the directionality of relational control shifted. This shift, in turn, was associated with a change in the therapist's attitude toward the supervisor and toward the research investigators and a decline in the quality of the therapist-supervisor relationship. Friedlander et al. (1989) concluded that the behavioral patterns identified in their study were consistent with the parallel process view of supervision;

at the very least, the patterns indicate that supervision and counseling are reciprocal and interlocking processes.

Alpher (1991) examined parallel process in supervised short-term dynamic psychotherapy using an intensive case study method. SASB was used to measure and track perceptions of interpersonal process by patient, therapist, and supervisor throughout a 25-session treatment. Results showed that perceptions of interdependence (SASB autonomy-giving) of therapist and supervisor in supervision were associated with interdependence of therapist and client in therapy. For example, during one period of therapy, "The therapist responds to the supervisor with high interdependence, and treats the patient that way—she, in turn, begins to treat herself that way (SASB introjection)" (Alpher, 1991, p. 228). The author also found that shifts in the interdependent patterns between therapist and supervisor that occurred throughout the treatment seemed to "indicate responses to events occurring at critical points" (p. 228). Alpher (1991) concluded that "research is now beginning to augment our understanding of the place of the supervisor in an interpersonal framework. . . . One could envision at some point the possibility of [interpersonal] ratings being used by supervisors and trainees to understand the total interpersonal network in which patient, therapist, and supervisor function" (p. 229).

Pollock (1990) provided the first analysis of parallel process from the perspective of contemporary interpersonal theory. He argued that the theoretical consensus indicated that an adequate investigation of parallel process required that the constructs of interpersonal behavior, interpersonal impact, and relationship anxiety be operationally defined. Paddock argued, further, that circumplex measurement provided a method for operationally defining interpersonal behavior and interpersonal impact. In addition, he felt that interpersonal theory could provide a conceptualization of the equally important construct of relationship anxiety.

Three hypotheses were tested in Pollock's (1990) study: (a) a significant positive correlation would be found between therapists' ratings of the patient's interpersonal behavior and supervisors' ratings of the therapist's interpersonal behavior (as measured by an interpersonal circumplex inventory); (b) the occurrence of parallel process would increase as the experience of relationship anxiety increased; and (c) as the degree of complementarity decreased in the therapy or supervision relationship, the probability of occurrence of parallel process would increase.

Thirty client-therapist-supervisor triads were studied from three training sites. Each subject in a triad first completed a self-report version of the CLOIT. Then, at the close of a sampled therapy session, the patient and the therapist completed a state anxiety scale; the therapist also used the CLOIT to rate the interpersonal behavior manifested by the patient during the targeted therapy session. Finally, at the end of the next scheduled supervision session, the therapist and supervisor completed a state anxiety scale; the supervisor also used the CLOIT to rate the interpersonal behavior manifested by the therapist during that just completed supervision session.

A first index of parallel process *(identical behaviors)* was obtained by *correlating the therapist's CLOIT ratings of the patient's behavior during the therapy session with the supervisor's CLOIT ratings of the therapist during the supervisory session.* A second index of parallel process *(opposite behaviors)* was obtained by *correlating the same two sets of CLOIT scores, but with the supervisor's ratings aligned to opposite categories* (e.g., the score received by the patient in sector A was correlated with the score received by the therapist in the opposite sector I).

Analyses confirmed the presence of a significant relationship between the behaviors manifested by the patient during the therapy session and the behaviors manifested by the supervisee during the supervisory session; the test for opposite behaviors, however, was not significant. The correlation between the patients' state-anxiety scores and patient-therapist complementarity demonstrated a tendency toward significance, but in the direction opposite to that predicted; the correlation between the state-anxiety therapists' scores and complementarity was not significant. A regression analysis indicated that the combined contribution of the state-anxiety scores for the participants of both relationships accounted for 11% of the variance in parallel process, which was not significant. Finally, a two-way ANOVA (patients vs. therapist by four quadrant scores) with repeated measures showed that patients had significantly higher scores than the supervisees; also all subjects obtained higher scores on the friendly quadrants than they obtained on the hostile quadrants.

Pollock (1990) concluded:

> The effort to validate parallel process occurrence was successful. Across all tri-ads, 20 percent of the variation in patient behavior during the targeted therapy session could be accounted for by the variation is supervisee behavior during the targeted supervision session . . . The paralleling of opposite behaviors was not confirmed. (p. 55)

However, the study failed to find a relationship between relationship anxiety and parallel process occurrence. Finally, "The proposed inverse relationship between complementarity and relationship-anxiety received only limited support. The supportive evidence that did exist occurred in the supervision relationship" (p. 58).

Before closing this chapter, it's important to describe a study by Tracey and Sherry (1993) that, although unrelated to parallel process, studied the process of therapist-supervisor complementarity as related to client therapeutic outcome. Tracey and Sherry (1993) examined the interaction sequence within six supervision dyads (three supervisors, each meeting with one more-successful and one less-successful trainee) over the course of supervision. Examining Kiesler's (1982a) hypothesized high-low-high pattern of complementarity over time during successful supervision, the researchers categorized each speaking turn into one of the interpersonal circumplex quadrants, with the sequence of these quadrant responses subsequently being examined using loglinear analysis. Tracey and Sherry (1993) found no support for the hypothesized three-stage complementarity model of successful supervision but obtained differences in supervisor responding to trainee hostility across outcome. They discussed their results with respect to the definition and utility of the construct of complementarity to the supervisory process.

CHAPTER 13

Conclusion

> *Perhaps nothing could be more laudatory than to say that after almost thirty [now more than fifty] years, Sullivan's theoretical scheme is still able to accommodate most of the facts accumulated in the study of interpersonal relationships within that time.*
>
> *(Swensen, 1973, p. 47)*

Although the earlier works of Sullivan and Leary were remarkably innovative and provocative and interpersonal theory had pervasive subterranean influence on psychology and psychiatry, until recently few sustained or systematic theoretical or empirical follow-ups appeared. This book demonstrates that this era of sporadic and abortive interpersonal startups has come to an end. Sustained momentum is now established, and exciting theoretical and empirical work is proliferating.

Systematic interpersonal diagnosis is an increasingly viable and practicable option. A comprehensive battery of psychometrically sophisticated interpersonal inventories, each a structurally valid representation of the interpersonal circle, is a real probability for the near future. Continuing attempts to chart the covert behavioral domains of interactants may gradually provide conceptual bridges to the categories of overt behavior organized on the interpersonal circle; these bridges also link together lawfully the covert and overt blocks of interactants' behaviors conceptualized in the Maladaptive Transaction Cycle. Horowitz and colleagues' Interpersonal Problem Inventory is directly relevant to diagnosis and treatment and already has shown important relationships to interpersonal circle categories. Preliminary methods for assessment of significant others (Larus-McShane, Kiesler and Murray's Significant Other Inventory, Klerman and colleagues's Interpersonal Inventory method) offer opportunities both for assessing significant others' perceptions of the interpersonal behavior of patients as well as charting patient improvement over the course of treatment. Most importantly, as we develop more sophisticated sequential analysis applications of interpersonal coding systems, we will evolve perhaps the most powerful methods for assessing the crucial maladaptive transaction cycles that are at the heart of various interpersonal psychopathologies.

Admittedly, we have little reliable information regarding the limits of applicability of interpersonal theory to the totality of abnormal behavior. Interpersonal theorists have concentrated their efforts on *DSM* Axis II personality disorders. However, the extent to which interpersonal therapy needs to be modified or expanded to address the multiple interactive factors operative among major or minor Axis I disorders is unknown and can be determined only through future theoretical and empirical efforts.

The most potent feature of interpersonal therapy resides in the close theoretical and empirical hookup it offers between psychodiagnosis and intervention. Its central models of individual differences in psychopathology, the interpersonal circle and the maladaptive transaction cycle, offer conceptual and empirical guides to the design of distinct treatment programs for various psychiatric disorders. Although as yet differential process-stage models have not been articulated systematically and in detail, the potential is there and creative first attempts have emerged.

Finally, what interpersonal theory also provides is a conceptual structure for explanations of psychopathology and psychotherapy that is sufficiently comprehensive to subsume and integrate concepts and methodologies from other treatment approaches. In turn, other orientations can offer much toward filling in gaps found in current interpersonal approaches. For one, interpersonal therapy needs a systematic developmental theory! Developmental conceptualizations from ego psychology, cognitive psychology, and object relations have much to offer. Likewise, current interpersonal therapy lacks any systematic and comprehensive theory explaining the cognitive, affective, and other covert events associated with, or isomorphic in structure to, overt interpersonal actions depicted on the interpersonal circle. Still other gaps exist and need to be filled in by integrative efforts with other disciplines.

Much remains to be done. Nonetheless, the unifying possibilities of the interpersonal paradigm for the fields of personality, psychopathology, and psychotherapy seem staggering and warrant serious contributory efforts by all concerned at this unusually propitious point in the field's scientific and clinical development.

References

Ackermann, R., & DeRubeis, R. J. (1991). Is depressive realism real? *Clinical Psychology Review, 11,* 565–584.

Adamopoulos, J. (1982a). Analysis of interpersonal structures in literary works of three historical periods. *Journal of Cross-Cultural Psychology, 13,* 157–168.

Adamopoulos, J. (1982b). The perception of interpersonal behavior: Dimensionality and importance of the social environment. *Environment and Behavior, 14,* 29–44.

Adamopoulos, J. (1984). The differentiation of social behavior: Toward an explanation of universal interpersonal structures. *Journal of Cross-Cultural Psychology, 15,* 487–508.

Adamopoulos, J., & Bontempo, R. N. (1986). Diachronic universals in interpersonal structure: Evidence from literary sources. *Journal of Cross-Cultural Research, 17,* 169–189.

Adams, H. B. (1964). "Mental illness" or interpersonal behavior? *American Psychologist, 19,* 191–197.

Agulnik, P. L. (1970). The spouse of the phobic patient. *British Journal of Psychiatry, 117,* 59–67.

Albrecht, T. L., & Adelman, M. B. (1987). *Communicating social support.* Newbury Park, CA: Sage.

Alden, L. E., & Capreol, M. J. (1993). Avoidant personality disorder: Interpersonal problems as predictors of treatment response. *Behavior Therapy, 24,* 357–376.

Alden, L. E., & Phillips, N. (1990). An interpersonal analysis of social anxiety and depression. *Cognitive Therapy and Research, 14,* 499–513.

Alden, L. E., Wiggins, J. S., & Pincus, A. L. (1990). Construction of circumplex scales for the Inventory of Interpersonal Problems. *Journal of Personality Assessment, 55,* 521–536.

Alexander, F. A. (1963). The dynamics of psychotherapy in the light of learning theory. *American Journal of Psychiatry, 120,* 440–448.

Alexander, F. A., & French, T. (1946). *Psychoanalytic therapy.* New York: Ronald.

Alexander, J. F. (1970, April). *Videotaperecorded family interaction: A systems approach.* Paper presented at the annual meeting of the Western Psychological Association, Los Angeles, CA.

Alimaras, P. E. (1967). Ambivalence in situations of negative interpersonal attitudes. *Journal of Psychology, 65,* 9–13.

Alloy, L. B., & Abramson, L. Y. (1979). Judgment of contingency in depressed and nondepressed students: Sadder but wiser? *Journal of Experimental Psychology: General, 108,* 441–485.

Alloy, L. B., & Abramson, L. Y. (1988). Depressive realism: Four theoretical perspectives. In L. B. Alloy (Ed.), *Cognitive processes in depression* (pp. 223–265). New York: Guilford.

Allport, G. W., Bruner, J. S., & Jandorf, E. M. (1941). Personality under social catastrophe: Ninety life histories of the Nazi revolution. *Character and Personality, 10,* 1–22.

Alpher, V. S. (1988). Structural Analysis of Social Behavior. In D. J. Keyser & R. C. Sweetland (Eds.), *Test critiques* (Vol. 7, pp. 541–556). Kansas City, MO: Test Corporation of America.

Alpher, V. S. (1991). Interdependence and parallel processes: A case study of Structural Analysis of Social Behavior in supervision and short-term dynamic psychotherapy. *Psychotherapy, 28,* 218–231.

Alpher, V. S., & France, A-C. (1993). Interpersonal complementarity and appeasement in relationships with initiators of childhood psychosocial trauma. *Psychotherapy, 30,* 502–511.

Altrocchi, J. (1959). Dominance as a factor in interpersonal choice and perception. *Journal of Abnormal and Social Psychology, 59,* 303–308.

American Psychiatric Association. (1952). *Diagnostic and statistical manual of mental disorders* (2nd ed.). Washington, DC: Author.

American Psychiatric Association. (1980). *Diagnostic and statistical manual of mental disorders* (3rd ed.). Washington, DC: Author.

American Psychiatric Association. (1987). *Diagnostic and statistical manual of mental disorders* (3rd ed., rev.). Washington, DC: Author.

American Psychiatric Association. (1994). *Diagnostic and statistical manual of mental disorders* (4th ed.). Washington, DC: Author.

Anchin, J. C. (1979). The effects of interpersonal stress upon the impact messages generated by the "obsessive personality." *Dissertation Abstracts International, 40,* 437B.

Anchin, J. C. (1982a). Interpersonal approaches to psychotherapy: Summary and conclusions. In J. C. Anchin & D. J. Kiesler (Eds.), *Handbook of interpersonal psychotherapy* (pp. 313–330). Elmsford, NY: Pergamon.

Anchin, J. C. (1982b). Sequence, pattern, and style: Integration and treatment implications of some interpersonal concepts. In J. C. Anchin & D. J. Kiesler (Eds.), *Handbook of interpersonal psychotherapy* (pp. 95–131). Elmsford, NY: Pergamon.

Anchin, J. C., & Kiesler, D. J. (1982). *Handbook of interpersonal psychotherapy.* Elmsford, NY: Pergamon.

Anderson, C. R. (1977). Locus of control, coping behaviors and performance in a stress setting: A longitudinal study. *Journal of Applied Psychology, 62,* 446–451.

Andrews, J. D. W. (1966). Psychotherapy of phobias. *Psychological Bulletin, 66,* 455–480.

Andrews, J. D. W. (1973). Interpersonal challenge: A source of growth in laboratory training. *Journal of Applied Behavioral Science, 9,* 514–533.

Andrews, J. D. W. (1974–1975). Interpersonal challenge workshop: A way to enhance laboratory experience. *Interpersonal Development, 5,* 26–36.

Andrews, J. D. W. (1977). Personal change and intervention style. *Journal of Humanistic Psychology, 77,* 41–63.

Andrews, J. D. W. (1984). Psychotherapy with the hysterical personality: An interpersonal approach. *Psychiatry, 47,* 211–232.

Andrews, J. D. W. (1988). Self-confirmation theory: A paradigm for psychotherapy integration: Part I. Content analysis of therapeutic styles. *Journal of Integrative and Eclectic Psychotherapy, 7,* 359–384.

Andrews, J. D. W. (1989a). Integrating visions of reality: Interpersonal diagnosis and the existential vision. *American Psychologist, 44,* 803–817.

Andrews, J. D. W. (1989b). Integrative languages in therapeutic practice and training: Promises and pitfalls. *Journal of Integrative and Eclectic Psychotherapy, 8,* 291–302.

Andrews, J. D. W. (1989c). Psychotherapy of depression: A self-confirmation model. *Psychological Review, 96,* 576–607.

Andrews, J. D. W. (1989d). Self-confirmation theory as a paradigm for psychotherapy integration. Part II. Integrative rescripting of therapy transcripts. *Journal of Integrative and Eclectic Psychotherapy, 8,* 23–40.

Andrews, J. D. W. (1990). Interpersonal self-confirmation and challenge in psychotherapy. *Psychotherapy, 27,* 485–504.

Andrews, J. D. W. (1991). *The active self in psychotherapy: An integration of therapeutic styles.* New York: Gardner.

Andrews, J. D. W., & Moore, S. (1991). Social cognition in the histrionic/overconventional personality. In P. Magaro (Ed.), *Cognitive bases of mental disorder. Annual review of psychopathology* (Vol. 1, pp. 11–76). Newbury Park, CA: Sage.

Apfelbaum, B. (1958). *Dimensions of transference in psychotherapy.* Berkeley: University of California Publications.

Argyle, M. (1972). *The psychology of interpersonal behaviour.* Harmondsworth, England: Penguin.

Arlow, J. (1963). The supervisory situation. *Journal of the American Psychoanalytic Association, 11,* 576–594.

Arnold, M. B. (1960a). *Emotion and personality: Vol. 1, Psychological aspects.* New York: Columbia University Press.

Arnold, M. B. (1960b). *Emotion and personality: Vol. 2, Neurological and physiological aspects.* New York: Columbia University Press.

Auerbach, S. M., Kiesler, D. J., Strentz, T., Schmidt, J. A., & Serio, C. D. (1994). Interpersonal impacts and adjustment to the stress of simulated captivity: An empirical test of the Stockholm Syndrome. *Journal of Social and Clinical Psychology, 13,* 207–221.

Auerbach, S. M., Martelli, M. F., & Mercuri, L. G. (1983). Anxiety, information, interpersonal impacts, and adjustments to a stressful health care situation. *Journal of Personality and Social Psychology, 44,* 1284–1296.

Auerbach, S. M., Meredith, J., Alexander, J. M., Mercuri, L. G., & Brophy, C. (1984). Psychological factors in adjustment to orthognathic surgery. *Journal of Oral and Maxillofacial Surgery, 42,* 435–440.

Averill, J. R. (1980). A contructivist view of emotion. In R. Plutchik & H. Kellerman (Eds.), *Emotion: Theory, research, and experience. Vol. 1: Theories of emotion* (pp. 305–339). New York: Academic Press.

Backman, C. (1985). Interpersonal congruency theory revisited: A revision and extension. *Journal of Social and Personal Relationships, 2,* 489–505.

Bakan, D. (1966). *The duality of human existence: Isolation and communion in Western man.* Boston: Beacon Press.

Bale, P. (1983). *Nonverbal communication of sex-role orientation: Effects of client perceptions and disclosure.* Unpublished master's thesis, Virginia Commonwealth University, Richmond.

Bandura, A., Lipsher, D., & Miller, P. (1960). Psychotherapists' approach–avoidance reactions to patients' expressions of hostility. *Journal of Consulting Psychology, 24,* 1–8.

Barlow, D. H., Mavissakalian, M., & Hay, L. R. (1981). Couples treatment of agoraphobia: Changes in marital satisfaction. *Behavior Research and Therapy, 19,* 245–255.

Barnett, J. (1966). On cognitive disorders in the obsessional. *Contemporary Psychoanalysis, 2,* 122–134.

Barnett, J. (1969). On aggression in the obsessional neuroses. *Contemporary Psychoanalysis, 6,* 48–57.

Barnett, J. (1972). Therapeutic intervention in the dysfunctional thought processes of the obsessional. *American Journal of Psychotherapy, 26,* 338–351.

Barnlund, D. C. (1970). *Interpersonal communication: Survey and studies.* Boston, MA: Houghton Mifflin.

Bartholomew, K., & Horowitz, L. M. (1991). Attachment styles among young adults: A test of a four-category model. *Journal of Personality and Social Psychology, 61,* 226–244.

Bateson, G. (1958). *Naven.* Stanford, CA: Stanford University Press.

Bateson, G., Jackson, D. D., Haley, J., & Weakland, J. (1956). Toward a theory of schizophrenia. *Behavioral Science, 1,* 251–264.

Baumeister, R. F. (1982). A self-presentational view of social phenomena. *Psychological Bulletin, 91,* 3–26.

Baumeister, R. F. (1989). The optimal margin of illusion. *Journal of Social and Clinical Psychology, 8,* 176–189.

Baumeister, R. F., & Scher, S. J. (1988). Self-defeating behavior patterns among normal individuals: Review and analysis of common self-destructive tendencies. *Psychological Bulletin, 104,* 3–22.

Baumrind, D. (1960). An analysis of some aspects of the interpersonal system. *Psychiatry, 23,* 395–402.

Beck, A. T. (1976). *Cognitive therapy and the emotional disorders.* New York: International Universities Press.

Becker, W. C., & Krug, R. S. (1964). A circumplex model for social behavior in children. *Child Development, 35,* 371–396.

Becker, W. C., Peterson, D. R., Luria, Z., Shoemaker, D. J., & Hellmer, L. A. (1962). Relations of factors derived from parent interview ratings to behavior problems of five-year-olds. *Child Development, 33,* 509–553.

Bednar, R. L., & Kaul, T. J. (1978). Experimental group research: Current perspectives. In S. L. Garfield & A. E. Bergin (Eds.), *Handbook of psychotherapy and behavior change* (2nd ed., pp. 769–816). New York: Wiley.

Beery, J. W. (1970). Therapists' responses as a function of level of therapist experience and attitude of the patient. *Journal of Consulting and Clinical Psychology, 34,* 239–243.

Beier, E. G. (1966). *The silent language of psychotherapy: Social reinforcement of unconscious processes.* Chicago: Aldine.

Bem, D. J. (1972). Constructing cross-situational consistencies in behavior: Some thoughts on Alker's critique of Mischel. *Journal of Personality, 40,* 17–26.

Bem, D. J., & Allen, A. (1974). On predicting some of the people some of the time: The search for cross-situational consistencies in behavior. *Psychological Review, 81,* 506–520.

Bem, S. L. (1974). The measurement of psychological androgyny. *Journal of Consulting and Clinical Psychology, 42,* 155–162.

Benedek, T. (1954). Countertransference in the training analyst. *Bulletin of the Menninger Clinic, 18,* 12–16.

Benjafield, J., & Carson, E. (1985). An historico-developmental analysis of the circumplex model of trait descriptive terms. *Canadian Journal of Behavioral Science, 17,* 339–345.

Benjafield, J., & Muckenheim, R. (1989). A further historicodevelopmental study of the interpersonal circumplex. *Canadian Journal of Behavioral Science, 21,* 83–93.

Benjamin, L. S. (1974). Structural analysis of social behavior. *Psychological Review, 81,* 392–425.

Benjamin, L. S. (1977). Structural analysis of a family in therapy. *Journal of Abnormal Psychology, 45,* 391–406.

Benjamin, L. S. (1979a). Use of Structural Analysis of Social Behavior (SASB) and Markov chains to study dyadic interactions. *Journal of Abnormal Psychology, 88,* 303–319.

Benjamin, L. S. (1979b). Structural analysis of differentiation failure. *Psychiatry, 42,* 1–23.

Benjamin, L. S. (1980). *Validation of Structural Analysis of Social Behavior (SASB).* Unpublished manuscript, Wisconsin Psychiatric Institute, Madison, WI.

Benjamin, L. S. (1982). Use of Structural Analysis of Social Behavior (SASB) to guide intervention in psychotherapy. In J. C. Anchin & D. J. Kiesler (Eds.), *Handbook of interpersonal psychotherapy* (pp. 190–212). Elmsford, NY: Pergamon.

Benjamin, L. S. (1983). *Intrex questionnaires.* Madison, WI: Intrex Interpersonal Institute.

Benjamin, L. S. (1984). Principles of prediction using Structural Analysis of Social Behavior (SASB). In R. A. Zucker, J. Aronoff, & A. J. Rabin (Eds.), *Personality and the prediction of behavior* (pp. 121–173). New York: Guilford.

Benjamin, L. S. (1986a). Operational definition and measurement of dynamics shown in the stream of free associations. *Psychiatry, 49,* 104–129.

Benjamin, L. S. (1986b). Using SASB to add social parameters to Axis I of DSM-III. In T. Millon & G. L. Klerman (Eds.), *Contemporary issues in psychopathology: Toward the DSM-IV* (pp. 599–638). New York: Guilford.

Benjamin, L. S. (1987a). Commentary on the inner experience of the borderline self-mutilator. *Journal of Personality Disorders, 1,* 334–339.

Benjamin, L. S. (1987b). An interpersonal approach. *Journal of Personality Disorders, 1,* 334–339.

Benjamin, L. S. (1987c). *Intrex Short Form Questionnaires.* Madison, WI: Intrex Interpersonal Institute.

Benjamin, L. S. (1988a). *Intrex Shortform Users Manual.* Madison, WI: Intrex Interpersonal Institute.

Benjamin, L. S. (1988b). Personal communication: List of published studies, theses and dissertations using SASB. University of Utah, Salt Lake City.

Benjamin, L. S. (1989). Is chronicity a function of the relationship between the person and the auditory hallucination? *Schizophrenia Bulletin, 15,* 291–310.

Benjamin, L. S. (1990). Interpersonal analysis of the cathartic model. *Emotion, 5,* 209–229.

Benjamin, L. S. (1992). Brief SASB-directed reconstructed learning therapy. In P. Crits-Christoph & J. Barber (Eds.), *Handbook of short-term dynamic therapy.* New York: Guilford.

Benjamin, L. S. (1993). *Diagnosis and treatment of personality disorders: A structural approach.* New York: Guilford.

Benjamin, L. S. (1994). SASB: A bridge between personality theory and clinical psychology. *Psychological Inquiry, 5,* 273–316.

Benjamin, L. S., Foster, S. W., Giat-Roberto, L., & Estroff, S. E. (1986). Breaking the family code: Analyzing videotapes of family interactions by Structural Analysis of Social Behavior. In L. S. Greenberg & W. M. Pinsof (Eds.), *The psychotherapeutic process: A research handbook* (pp. 391–438). New York: Guilford.

Benjamin, L. S., Giat, L., & Estroff, S. E. (1981). *Manual for coding social interactions in terms of Structural Analysis of Social Behavior.* Madison: University of Wisconsin.

Benjamin, L. S., & Wonderlich, S. A. (1994). Social perceptions and borderline personality disorder: The relation to mood disorders. *Journal of Abnormal Psychology, 103,* 610–624.

Bennum, I. (1986). A composite formulation of agoraphobia. *American Journal of Psychotherapy, 40,* 177–188.

Bergner, R. M. (1977). The marital system of the hysterical individual. *Family Process, 16,* 85–96.

Bermann, E., & Miller, D. R. (1967). The matching of mates. In R. Jessor & S. Feshbach (Eds.), *Cognition, personality and clinical psychology.* San Francisco: Jossey-Bass.

Berzins, J. I. (1977). Therapist–patient matching. In A. S. Gurman & A. M. Razin (Eds.), *Effective psychotherapy: A handbook of research* (pp. 222–251). Elmsford, NY: Pergamon.

Bierman, R. (1969). Dimensions of interpersonal facilitation in psychotherapy and child development. *Psychological Bulletin, 72,* 338–352.

Billings, A. (1979). Conflict resolution in distressed and nondistressed married couples. *Journal of Consulting and Clinical Psychology, 47,* 368–376.

Bingi, R. B. (1994). *International students' perceptions of counselor credibility and willingness to self-disclose as a function of the counselor's interpersonal style.* Unpublished doctoral dissertation, Texas Tech University, Lubbock.

Birtchnell, J. (1987). Attachment–detachment, directiveness–receptiveness: A system for classifying interpersonal attitudes and behaviour. *British Journal of Medical Psychology, 60,* 17–27.

Birtchnell, J. (1990). Interpersonal theory: Criticism, modification, and elaboration. *Human Relations, 43,* 1183–1201.

Birtchnell, J. (1993). *How humans relate: A new interpersonal theory.* Westport, CT: Greenwood Press.

Birtchnell, J. (1994). The interpersonal octagon: An alternative to the interpersonal circle. *Human Relations, 47,* 511–529.

Blashfield, R., Sprock, J., Pinkston, K., & Hodgin, J. (1985). Exemplar prototypes of personality disorder diagnoses. *Comprehensive Psychiatry, 26,* 11–21.

Blatt, S. (1974). Levels of object representation in anaclitic and introjective depression. *Psychoanalytic Study of the Child, 29,* 107–157.

Block, J. (1957). A comparison between ipsative and normative ratings of personality. *Journal of Abnormal and Social Psychology, 54,* 50–54.

Block, J., & Colvin, C. R. (1994). Positive illusions and well-being revisited: Separating fiction from fact. *Psychological Bulletin, 116,* 28.

Bluhm, C., Widiger, T. A., & Miele, G. M. (1990). Interpersonal complementarity and individual differences. *Journal of Personality and Social Psychology, 58,* 464–471.

Blumberg, H. H. (1972). Communication of interpersonal evaluations. *Journal of Personality and Social Psychology, 23,* 157–162.

Blumberg, S. R., & Hokanson, J. E. (1983). The effects of another person's response style on interpersonal behavior in depression. *Journal of Abnormal Psychology, 92,* 196–209.

Blyth, D. A., Hill, J. P., & Thiel, K. S. (1982). Early adolescents' significant others: Grade and gender differences in perceived relationships with familial and nonfamilial adults and young people. *Journal of Youth and Adolescence, 11,* 425–451.

Boals, G. F., Peterson, D. R., Farmer, L., Mann, D. F., & Robinson, D. L. (1982). The reliability, validity, and utility of three data modes in assessing marital relationships. *Journal of Personality Assessment, 46,* 85–96.

Bochner, A. P., Kaminski, E. P., & Fitzpatrick, M. A. (1977). The conceptual domain of interpersonal communication behavior: A factor-analytic study. *Human Communication Research, 3,* 291–302.

Boghosian, J. (1982). Interpersonal dimensions of mental health. *Dissertation Abstracts International, 43*, 397A.

Bohn, M. J. (1965). Counselor behavior as a function of counselor dominance, counselor experience and client type. *Journal of Counseling Psychology, 12*, 346–352.

Bohn, M. J. (1967). Therapist responses to hostility and dependency as a function of training. *Journal of Consulting and Clinical Psychology, 31*, 195–198.

Booth-Kewley, S., & Vickers, R. R., Jr. (1994). Associations between major domains of personality and health behavior. *Journal of Personality, 62*, 281–298.

Bordin, E. S. (1979). The generalizability of the psychoanalytic concept of the working alliance. *Psychotherapy: Theory, Research and Practice, 16*, 252–260.

Bordin, E. S. (1985, June). *Research on the therapeutic alliance.* Paper presented at the annual meeting of the Society for Psychotherapy Research, Dallas, TX.

Borgatta, E. F. (1960). Rankings and self-assessments: Some behavioral characteristics replication studies. *Journal of Social Psychology, 52*, 297–307.

Borgatta, E. F. (1964). The structure of personality characteristics. *Behavioral Science, 9*, 8–17.

Borgatta, E. F., Cottrell, L. S., Jr., & Mann, J. M. (1958). The spectrum of individual interaction characteristics: An interdimensional analysis. *Psychological Reports, 4*, 279–319.

Borgen, F. H. (1985). Review of the Impact Message Inventory, Form II. In J. V. Mitchell (Ed.), *Ninth mental measurements yearbook* (Vol. 1, pp. 678–679). Lincoln, NE: Buros Institute of Mental Measurements.

Borkenau, P., & Ostendorf, F. (1987). Fact and fiction in implicit personality theory. *Journal of Personality, 55*, 415–443.

Bornstein, R. F. (1992). The dependent personality: Developmental, social and clinical perspectives. *Psychological Bulletin, 112*, 3–23.

Bornstein, R. F. (1993). *The dependent personality.* New York: Guilford.

Bowlby, J. (1969). *Attachment and loss: Vol. 1. Attachment.* New York: Basic Books.

Bowlby, J. (1975). *Attachment and loss: Vol. 2. Separation, anxiety and anger.* London: Penguin.

Bowlby, J. (1979). *The making and breaking of affectional bonds.* New York: Methuen.

Bowlby, J. (1981). *Attachment and loss: Vol. 3. Loss, sadness and depression.* London: Penguin.

Brokaw, D. W. (1983). Markov chains and master therapists: An interpersonal analysis of psychotherapy process. *Dissertation Abstracts International, 44*, 1585–B.

Brokaw, D. W., & McLemore, C. W. (1983). Toward a more rigorous definition of social reinforcement: Some interpersonal clarifications. *Journal of Personality and Social Psychology, 44*, 1014–1020.

Brokaw, D. W., & McLemore, C. W. (1988). *Markov chains and master therapists: An interpersonal analysis of psychotherapy process.* Unpublished manuscript, Relational Dynamics Institute, Pasadena, CA.

Brokaw, D. W., & McLemore, C. W. (1991). Interpersonal models of personality and psychopathology. In D. G. Gilbert & J. J. Connolly (Eds.), *Personality, social skills, and psychopathology: An individual differences approach* (pp. 49–83). New York: Plenum.

Brown, J. D., & McGill, K. L. (1989). The cost of good fortune: When positive life events produce negative health consequences. *Journal of Personality and Social Psychology, 57*, 1103–1110.

Brown, R. (1965). *Social psychology.* New York: Free Press.

Browne, M. W. (1992). Circumplex models for correlation matrices. *Psychometrika, 57*, 469–497.

Bruner, J. S., & Tagiuri, R. (1954). The perception of people. In G. Lindzey (Ed.), *Handbook of social psychology* (Vol. 2, pp. 634–654). Reading, MA: Addison-Wesley.

Buranyi, G. (1989). Paradoxical interventions and flexibility in interpersonal style. *Dissertation Abstracts International, 49*, 4529–4530B.

Buss, A. H. (1989). Personality as traits. *American Psychologist, 44*, 1378–1388.

Buss, D. M. (1985a). The act frequency approach to the interpersonal environment. *Perspectives in Personality, 1*, 173–200.

Buss, D. M. (1985b). The temporal stability of acts, trends, and patterns. In C. Spielberger & J. N. Butcher (Eds.), *Advances in personality assessment* (Vol. 5, pp. 165–196). Hillsdale, NJ: Erlbaum.

Buss, D. M. (1992). Manipulation in close relationships: Five personality factors in interactional context. *Journal of Personality, 60*, 477–499.

Buss, D. M., & Barnes, M. (1986). Preferences in human mate selection. *Journal of Personality and Social Psychology, 50*, 559–570.

Buss, D. M., & Craik, K. H. (1980). The frequency concept of disposition: Dominance and prototypically dominant acts. *Journal of Personality, 48*, 379–392.

Buss, D. M., & Craik, K. H. (1981). The act frequency analysis of interpersonal dispositions: Aloofness, gregarious, dominance, and submissiveness. *Journal of Personality, 49*, 175–192.

Buss, D. M., & Craik, K. H. (1983a). The act frequency approach to personality. *Psychological Review, 90*, 105–126.

Buss, D. M., & Craik, K. H. (1983b). Act prediction and the conceptual analysis of personality scales: Indices of act density, bipolarity, and extensivity. *Journal of Personality and Social Psychology, 45*, 1081–1095.

Buss, D. M., & Craik, K. H. (1983c). The dispositional analysis of everyday conduct. *Journal of Personality, 51*, 393–412.

Buss, D. M., & Craik, K. H. (1984). Acts, dispositions, and personality. In B. A. Maher & W. B. Maher (Eds.), *Progress in experimental personality research: Normal personality processes* (Vol. 13, pp. 241–301). New York: Academic Press.

Buss, D. M., & Craik, K. H. (1986a). The act frequency approach and the construction of personality. In A. Angleitner, A. Furnham, & G. Van Heck (Eds.), *Personality psychology in Europe* (pp. 141–156). Lisse, The Netherlands: Stwets & Zeitlinger.

Buss, D. M., & Craik, K. H. (1986b). Acts, dispositions, and clinical assessment: The psychopathology of everyday conduct. *Clinical Psychology Review, 6*, 387–406.

Buss, D. M., & Craik, K. H. (1987). Act criteria for the diagnosis of personality disorders. *Journal of Personality Disorders, 1*, 73–81.

Buss, D. M., Gomes, M., Higgins, D. S., & Lauterbach, K. (1987). Tactics of manipulation. *Journal of Personality and Social Psychology, 52*, 1219–1229.

Butler, S. F., & Strupp, H. H. (1986). Specific and nonspecific factors in psychotherapy: A problematic paradigm for psychotherapy research. *Psychotherapy, 23*, 30–40.

Cameron, N. (1943). The paranoid pseudocommunity. *American Journal of Sociology, 46*, 33–38.

Cameron, N. (1959). The paranoid pseudocommunity revisited. *American Journal of Sociology, 65*, 52–58.

Campbell, J. (1980). Complementarity and attraction: A reconceptualization in terms of dyadic behavior. *Representative Research in Social Psychology, 11*, 74–95.

Campbell, J. P., & Dunnette, M. D. (1968). Effectiveness of T-group experiences in managerial training and development. *Psychological Bulletin, 70*, 73–104.

Campbell, S. R. (1991). The relationship of interpersonal complementarity to marital satisfaction and security. *Dissertation Abstracts International, 52,* 1051–B.

Campbell, S. R., & Brown, R. A. (1990, August). *The relationship of interpersonal complementarity to marital satisfaction and security.* Paper presented at the 98th annual convention of the American Psychological Association, Boston, MA.

Cantor, N., & Mischel, W. (1977). Traits as prototypes: Effects on recognition memory. *Journal of Personality and Social Psychology, 35,* 38–48.

Cantor, N., & Mischel, W. (1979). Prototypes in person perception. In L. Berkowitz (Ed.), *Advances in experimental social psychology* (Vol. 12, pp. 3–52). New York: Academic Press.

Cantor, N., Smith, E. E., French, R. D., & Mezzich, J. (1980). Psychiatric diagnosis as prototype categorization. *Journal of Abnormal Psychology, 89,* 181–193.

Carson, R. C. (1969). *Interaction concepts of personality.* Chicago: Aldine.

Carson, R. C. (1971). Disordered interpersonal behavior. In W. A. Hunt (Ed.), *Human behavior and its control.* Cambridge, MA: Schenkman.

Carson, R. C. (1979). Personality and exchange in developing relationships. In R. L. Burgess & T. L. Huston (Eds.), *Social exchange in developing relationships* (pp. 247–269). New York: Academic Press.

Carson, R. C. (1982). Self-fulfilling prophecy, maladaptive behavior, and psychotherapy. In J. C. Anchin & D. J. Kiesler (Eds.), *Handbook of interpersonal psychotherapy* (pp. 64–77). Elmsford, NY: Pergamon.

Carson, R. C. (1991). The social-interactional viewpoint. In M. Hersen, A. E. Kazdin, & A. S. Bellack (Eds.), *The clinical psychology handbook* (2nd ed., pp. 185–199). New York: Pergamon.

Carson, R. C., & Shapiro, J. H. (1985). *Mood, gender-typing, and interpersonal orientation: On "masculine" imperturbability.* Unpublished manuscript, Duke University, Durham, NC.

Carter, L. F. (1954). Evaluating the performance of individuals as members of small groups. *Personnel Psychology, 7,* 477–484.

Carter, M. M., Turovsky, J., & Barlow, D. H. (1994). Interpersonal relationships in Panic Disorder with Agoraphobia: A review of empirical evidence. *Clinical Psychology: Science and Practice, 1,* 25–34.

Cashdan, S. (1971). *Interactional psychotherapy: Stages and strategies in behavioral change.* New York: Grune and Stratton.

Cashdan, S. (1982). Interactional psychotherapy: Using the relationship. In J. C. Anchin & D. J. Kiesler (Eds.), *Handbook of interpersonal psychotherapy* (pp. 215–226). Elmsford, NY: Pergamon.

Cashdan, S. (1988). *Object relations therapy: Using the relationship.* New York: Norton.

Caspi, A., & Bem, D. J. (1990). Personality continuity and change across the life course. In L. A. Pervin (Ed.), *Handbook of personality: Theory and research* (pp. 549–575). New York: Guilford.

Caspi, A., Bem, D. J., & Elder, G. H., Jr. (1989). Continuities and consequences of interactional styles across the life course. *Journal of Personality, 57,* 375–406.

Caspi, A., Elder, G. H., Jr., & Bem, D. J. (1987). Moving against the world: Life-course patterns of explosive children. *Developmental Psychology, 23,* 308–313.

Castronova, N. R. (1980). The relationship between levels of moral judgment and self-actualizing personality variables and self-perceived styles of interpersonal interaction in late adolescence. *Dissertation Abstracts International, 41,* 1103–B.

Cattell, R. B. (1944). Psychological measurement: Ipsative, normative and interactive. *Psychological Review, 51,* 292–303.

Celani, D. P. (1974). *The complementarity hypothesis: An exploratory study.* Unpublished doctoral dissertation, University of Vermont, Montpelier.

Celani, D. P. (1976). An interpersonal approach to hysteria. *American Journal of Psychiatry, 133,* 1414–1418.

Chance, E. (1966). Content analysis of verbalizations about interpersonal experience. In L. A. Gottschalk & A. H. Auerbach (Eds.), *Methods of research in psychotherapy* (pp. 127–145). New York: Appleton-Century-Crofts.

Chapman, R. C. (1987). *A multidimensional scaling analysis of the 1982 Interpersonal Circle.* Unpublished master's thesis, Virginia Commonwealth University, Richmond.

Chartier, B. M., & Conway, J. B. (1984, August). *A psychometric comparison of the Leary and Wiggins Interpersonal Scales.* Paper presented at the meeting of the American Psychological Association, Toronto, Canada.

Cheek, C. E. (1977). *The effects of level of disclosure and sex of discloser on the positiveness of impact on observers.* Unpublished master's thesis, Virginia Commonwealth University, Richmond.

Chewning, M. F. (1983). *Interpersonal distance, interaction frequency, and the nature of relationship as a function of locus of control orientation and three classes of others.* Unpublished master's thesis, Virginia Commonwealth University, Richmond.

Chewning, M. F. (1991). A comparison of adolescent male sex offenders with juvenile delinquents and nonreferred adolescents. *Dissertation Abstracts International, 51,* 3557–B.

Chirico, B. M. (1977). *Decoding of visual and verbal communication by obsessives and hysterics.* Unpublished master's thesis, Virginia Commonwealth University, Richmond.

Chirico, B. M. (1980). Decoding of verbal and nonverbal communication by the obsessive and hysteric personality. *Dissertation Abstracts International, 41,* 3568–B.

Chrzanowski, G. (1973). Implications of interpersonal theory. In E. G. Witenberg (Ed.), *Interpersonal explorations in psychoanalysis* (pp. 132–146). New York: Basic Books.

Clark, T. L., & Taulbee, E. S. (1981). A comprehensive and indexed bibliography of the Interpersonal Check List. *Journal of Personality Assessment, 45,* 505–525.

Clark-Lempers, D. S., & Lempers, J. D. (1991). Early, middle, and late adolescents' perceptions of their relationships with significant others. *Journal of Adolescent Research, 6,* 296–315.

Clavere, S. (1982). Parallel processes in therapy and supervision. *Dissertation Abstracts International, 43* (6–A), 1833.

Coates, D., & Wortman, C. B. (1980). Depression maintenance and interpersonal control. In A. Baum & J. Singer (Eds.), *Advances in environmental psychology* (Vol. 2, pp. 149–182). Hillsdale, NJ: Erlbaum.

Cohen, L. (1980). The new supervisee views supervision. In A. K. Hess (Ed.), *Psychotherapy supervision: Theory, research and practice* (pp. 78–94). New York: Wiley.

Colm, H. (1966). *The existentialist approach to psychotherapy with adults and children.* New York: Grune and Stratton.

Colvin, C. R., & Block, J. (1994). Do positive illusions foster mental health? An examination of the Taylor and Brown formulation. *Psychological Bulletin, 116,* 3–20.

Conte, H. R., & Plutchik, R. (1981). A circumplex model for interpersonal personality traits. *Journal of Personality and Social Psychology, 40,* 701–711.

Conway, J. B. (1980). *Biases in cognitive–affective processing across interpersonal styles and stress.* Unpublished manuscript, University of Saskatchewan, Saskatoon, Canada.

Conway, J. B. (1983). *Individual differences in biased interpersonal construal of self and others.* Unpublished manuscript, Univeristy of Saskatchewan, Saskatoon, Canada.

Conway, J. B. (1987, November). *A clinical interpersonal perspective for personality and psychotherapy: Some research examples.* Paper presented to Department of Psychology, University of British Columbia, Vancouver, British Columbia, Canada.

Cooley, C. H. (1902). *Human nature and the social order.* New York: Scribners.

Cooley, E. L. (1983). *Explanation of intent and positive interpretation in the delivery of paradoxical messages to improve sleep onset latency of normal subjects.* Unpublished master's thesis, Emory University, Atlanta, GA.

Cooley, E. L., & Nowicki, S., Jr. (1989). Discrimination of facial expressions of emotion by depressed subjects. *Genetic Psychology Monographs, 115,* 449–465.

Costa, P. T., & McCrae, R. R. (1985). *The NEO Personality Inventory manual.* Odessa, FL: Psychological Assessment Resources.

Costa, P. T., & McCrae, R. R. (1990). Personality disorders and the five factor model of personality. *Journal of Personality Disorders, 4,* 362–371.

Costa, P. T., & McCrae, R. R. (1992). Normal personality assessment in clinical practice: The NEO Personality Inventory. *Psychological Assessment: A Journal of Consulting and Clinical Psychology, 4,* 5–13.

Coulter, L. P. (1993). *Effects of therapist experience and interpersonal style on complementarity of responses.* Unpublished doctoral dissertation, University of North Carolina, Chapel Hill.

Coyne, J. C. (1976a). Depression and the response of others. *Journal of Abnormal Psychology, 85,* 186–193.

Coyne, J. C. (1976b). Toward an interactional description of depression. *Psychiatry, 39,* 28–40.

Coyne, J. C. (1990). Interpersonal processes in depression. In G. I. Keitner (Ed.), *Depression and families: Impact and treatment* (pp. 31–53). Washington, DC: American Psychiatric Press.

Coyne, J. C., Burchill, S. A., & Stiles, W. B. (1991). An interactional perspective on depression. In C. R. Snyder & D. R. Forsyth (Eds.), *Handbook of social and clinical psychology* (pp. 327–349). Elmsford, NY: Pergamon.

Coyne, J. C., & Segal, L. (1982). A brief, strategic interactional approach to psychotherapy. In J. C. Anchin & D. J. Kiesler (Eds.), *Handbook of interpersonal psychotherapy* (pp. 248–261). Elmsford, NY: Pergamon.

Critelli, J. W., & Neumann, K. F. (1978). An interpersonal analysis of self-disclosure and feedback. *Social Behavior and Personality, 6,* 173–177.

Crowder, J. E. (1972). Relationship between therapist and client interpersonal behaviors and psychotherapy outcome. *Journal of Counseling Psychology, 19,* 68–75.

Crowley, R. M. (1985). Cognition in interpersonal theory and practice. In M. J. Mahoney & A. Freeman (Eds.), *Cognition and psychotherapy* (pp. 291–312). New York: Plenum.

Cunningham, M. R. (1977). Personality and the structure of the nonverbal communication of emotion. *Journal of Personality, 45,* 564–584.

Cutler, R. L. (1958). Countertransference effects in psychotherapy. *Journal of Consulting Psychology, 22,* 349–356.

Dalgleish, T., & Watts, F. N. (1990). Biases of attention and memory in disorders of anxiety and depression. *Clinical Psychology Review, 10,* 589–604.

D'Andrade, R. G. (1965). Trait psychology and componential analysis. *American Anthropologist, 67,* 215–228.

D'Andrade, R. G. (1974). Memory and the assessment of behavior. In H. Blalock (Ed.), *Measurement in the social sciences.* Chicago: Aldine.

Danziger, K. (1976). *Interpersonal communication.* Elmsford, NY: Pergamon.

Darley, J. M., & Fazio, R. H. (1980). Expectancy confirmation processes arising in the social interaction sequence. *American Psychologist, 35,* 867–881.

Davenport, Y. B., Adlind, M. C., Gold, P. W., & Goodwin, F. K. (1979). Manic–depressive illness: Psychodynamic features of multi-generational families. *American Journal of Orthopsychiatry, 49,* 24–35.

Davison, M. L. (1983). Introduction to multidimensional scaling and its applications. *Applied Psychological Measurement, 7,* 373–379.

Dawson, D. F. (1988). Treatment of the borderline patient: Relationship management. *Canadian Journal of Psychiatry, 33,* 370–374.

De Jong, C. A. J., Van den Brink, W., Jansen, J. A. M., & Schippers, G. M. (1989). Interpersonal aspects of DSM-III Axis II: Theoretical hypotheses and empirical findings. *Journal of Personality Disorders, 3,* 135–146.

Delgado, O. F. (1990). Interpersonal complementarity: A study of the predictive validity of the Structural Analysis of Social Behavior (SASB). *Dissertation Abstracts International, 50,* 2428–A.

DeMonbreun, B. G., & Craighead, W. W. (1977). Distortion of perception and recall of positive and neutral feedback in depression. *Cognitive Therapy and Research, 1,* 311–329.

Denzin, N. K. (1966). The significant others of a college population. *The Sociological Quarterly, 7,* 298–310.

De Raad, B. (1995). *Interpersonal language: Structural evidence from three psycho-lexical taxonomies.* Unpublished manuscript, University of Groningen, The Netherlands.

De Soto, C., & Kuethe, J. L. (1959). Subjective probabilities of interpersonal relationships. *Journal of Abnormal and Social Psychology, 59,* 290–294.

Devens, M. (1993). *Degree of severity of Axis II pathology and the interpersonal indices of rigidity, intensity, and discrepancy.* Unpublished master's thesis, Virginia Commonwealth University, Richmond.

DeVogue, J. T., & Beck, S. (1978). The therapist–client relationship in behavior therapy. In M. Hersen, R. M. Eisler, & P. M. Miller (Eds.), *Progress in behavior modification* (Vol. 6, pp. 203–248). New York: Academic Press.

Dietzel, C. S., & Abeles, N. (1975). Client–therapist complementarity and therapeutic outcome. *Journal of Counseling Psychology, 22,* 264–272.

Digman, J. M. (1990). Personality structure: Emergence of the five-factor model. *Annual Review of Psychology, 41,* 417–440.

Dinitz, S., Mangus, A. R., & Pasamanick, B. (1959). Integration and conflict in self-other conceptions as factors in mental illness. *Sociometry, 22,* 44–55.

Dobson, K. S. (1989). Real and perceived interpersonal responses to subclinically anxious and depressed targets. *Cognitive Therapy and Research, 13,* 37–47.

Dodge, K. A., & Somberg, D. R. (1987). Hostile attributional biases among aggressive boys are exacerbated under conditions of threats to the self. *Child Development, 58,* 213–224.

Dodge, K. A., & Tomlin, A. M. (1987). Utilization of self-schemas as a mechanism of interpretational bias in children. *Social Cognition, 5,* 280–300.

Doehrman, M. J. G. (1976). Parallel process in supervision and psychotherapy. *Bulletin of the Menninger Clinic, 40,* 1–20, 78–84.

Dorris, J. W., & Wertheim, A. (1976). An attribution approach to investigating the perception of implicit communications of evaluation. *Journal of Personality, 44,* 410–432.

Duke, M. P. (1978, May). *A new method for measuring the circumplex.* Paper presented at the Southeastern Psychological Association meeting, Atlanta, GA.

Duke, M. P. (1987). The situational stream hypothesis: A unifying view of behavior with special emphasis on adaptive and maladaptive behavior patterns. *Journal of Research in Personality, 21,* 239–263.

Duke, M. P., & Ekstrand, M. (1980). *Differential effects of dyadic complementarity/anticomplementarity in cooperative versus competitive tasks.* Unpublished manuscript, Emory University, Atlanta, GA.

Duke, M. P., & Mendelson, A. (1980). *Interpersonal style, complementarity, and interactional preferences.* Unpublished manuscript, Emory University, Atlanta, GA.

Duke, M. P., & Nowicki, S., Jr. (1982). A social learning theory analysis of interactional theory concepts and a multi-dimensional model of human interaction constellations. In J. C. Anchin & D. J. Kiesler (Eds.), *Handbook of interpersonal psychotherapy* (pp. 78–94). Elmsford, NY: Pergamon.

Edquist, M. H. (1973). Interpersonal choice and social attraction among four interpersonal types. *Dissertation Abstracts International, 34,* 1722B.

Eisenthal, S. (1992). Recognition of and response to counter-transference: Psychoanalytic and interpersonal communication approaches. In J. S. Rutan (Ed.), *Psychotherapy for the 1990s* (pp. 139–165). New York: Guilford.

Ekman, P., & Friesen, W. V. (1968). Non-verbal behavior in psychotherapy research. In J. M. Shlien (Ed.), *Research in psychotherapy* (Vol. 3, pp. 179–216). Washington, DC: American Psychological Association.

Ekstein, R., & Wallerstein, R. (1958). *The teaching and learning of psychotherapy.* New York: Basic Books.

Ekstrand, M. (1980). *Differential effects on interpersonal comfort of competition and cooperation among college students with varying interpersonal styles.* Unpublished undergraduate honors thesis, Emory University, Atlanta, GA.

Elder, G. H., Jr., & Caspi, A. (1988). Economic stress: Developmental perspectives. *Journal of Social Issues, 44,* 25–45.

Emmons, R. A., & Diener, E. (1986). An interactional approach to the study of personality and emotion. *Journal of Personality, 54,* 371–384.

Emmons, R. A., Diener, E., & Larsen, R. J. (1986). Choice and avoidance of everyday situations and affect congruence: Two models of reciprocal interactionism. *Journal of Personality and Social Psychology, 51,* 815–826.

Endler, N. S., & Magnusson, D. (Eds.). (1976). *Interactional psychology and personality.* Washington, DC: Hemisphere.

Epstein, L., & Feiner, A. H. (Eds.). (1979). *Countertransference: The therapist's contribution to the therapeutic situation.* New York: Jason Aronson.

Epstein, S. (1979). The stability of behavior: I. On predicting most of the people much of the time. *Journal of Personality and Social Psychology, 37,* 1097–1126.

Erdelyi, M. H. (1974). A new look at the new look: Perceptual defense and vigilance. *Psychological Review, 81,* 1–25.

Erdelyi, M. H., & Goldberg, B. (1979). Let's not sweep repression under the rug: Toward a cognitive psychology of repression. In J. F. Kihlstrom & F. J. Evans (Eds.), *Functional disorders of memory* (pp. 355–402). Hillsdale, NJ: Erlbaum.

Estroff, S. D., & Nowicki, S., Jr. (1992). Interpersonal complementarity, gender of interactants, and performance on puzzle and word tasks. *Personality and Social Psychology Bulletin, 18,* 351–356.

Federman, E. J. (1980). Unraveling interaction: A sequential analysis of the controlling behavior of the submissive personality. *Dissertation Abstracts International, 40,* 5403–B.

Feldman, L. B. (1985). Integrative multi-level therapy: A comprehensive interpersonal and intrapsychic approach. *Journal of Marital and Family Therapy, 11*, 357–372.

Felker, D. (1974). *Building positive self-concepts.* Minneapolis, MN: Burgess.

Fierman, L. B. (Ed.). (1965). *Effective psychotherapy: The contribution of Hellmuth Kaiser.* New York: Free Press.

Filak, J., Abeles, N., & Norquist, S. (1986). Clients' pretherapy interpersonal attitudes and psychotherapy outcome. *Professional Psychology: Research and Practice, 17*, 217–222.

Fineberg, B. L., & Lowman, J. (1975). Affect and status dimensions of mental adjustment. *Journal of Marriage and the Family, 37*, 155–160.

Fiore, J. (1975). *Preference for complementary versus anticomplementary personalities in male undergraduates.* Unpublished master's thesis, Emory University, Atlanta, GA.

Fisher, G. A. (1983). *Coefficients of agreement for circular data.* Unpublished manuscript, Indiana University, Bloomington.

Fisher, G. A., Heise, D. R., Bohrnstedt, G. W., & Lucke, J. F. (1985). Evidence for extending the circumplex model of personality trait language to self-reported moods. *Journal of Personality and Social Psychology, 49*, 233–242.

Fiske, A. P. (1991). *Structures of social life: The four elementary forms of social relationship.* New York: Free Press.

Fiske, A. P. (1992). The four elementary forms of sociality: Framework for a unified theory of social relations. *Psychological Review, 99*, 689–723.

Fitzgerald, J. M. (1978). Actual and perceived sex and generational differences in interpersonal style: Structural and quantitative issues. *Journal of Gerontology, 33*, 394–401.

Fitzgerald, R. G. (1972). Mania as a message: Treatment with family therapy and lithium carbonate. *American Journal of Psychotherapy, 26*, 547–555.

Foa, U. G. (1961). Convergences in the analysis of the structure of interpersonal behavior. *Psychological Review, 68*, 341–353.

Foa, U. G. (1964). Cross-cultural similarity and difference in interpersonal behavior. *Journal of Abnormal and Social Psychology, 68*, 517–522.

Foa, U. G., & Foa, E. B. (1974). *Societal structures of the mind.* Springfield, IL: Thomas.

Foreman, M. E. (1989). Interpersonal assessment of psychopathy. *Dissertation Abstracts International, 49*, 5517–B.

Forgas, J. P. (1979). *Social episodes: The study of interaction routines.* New York: Academic Press.

Forsleff, L. P. (1967). A study of counselor supervisor and counselor-client dyadic relationships. *Dissertation Abstracts International, 28*, 1677A.

Freedman, M. B. (1985). Symposium: Interpersonal circumplex models: 1948–1983. *Journal of Personality Assessment, 49*, 622–625.

Freedman, M. B., Leary, T. F., Ossorio, A. G., & Coffey, H. S. (1951). The interpersonal dimension of personality. *Journal of Personality, 20*, 143–161.

Freedman, S. M., & Hurley, J. R. (1979). Maslow's needs: Individual perceptions of helpful factors in growth groups. *Small Group Research, 10*, 335–367.

Freeman, G. (1971). Gaps in doctor–patient communication: Doctor–patient interaction analysis. *Pediatric Research, 5*, 298–311.

Frey, D. (1981). The effect of negative feedback about oneself and cost of information on preferences for information about the source of this feedback. *Journal of Experimental Social Psychology, 17*, 42–50.

Frey, D. (1986). Recent research on selective exposure to information. In L. Berkowitz (Ed.), *Advances in experimental social psychology* (Vol. 19, pp. 41–80). New York: Academic Press.

Friedlander, M. L. (1993a). Does complementarity promote or hinder client change in brief therapy? A review of the evidence from two theoretical perspectives. *The Counseling Psychologist, 21,* 457–486.

Friedlander, M. L. (1993b). When complementarity is uncomplimentary and other reactions to Tracey (1993). *Journal of Counseling Psychology, 40,* 410–412.

Friedlander, M. L., Siegel, S. M., & Brenock, K. (1989). Parallel processes in counseling and supervision. *Journal of Counseling Psychology, 36,* 149–157.

Friedman, H. S., & Di Matteo, M. R. (1979). Health care as an interpersonal process. *Journal of Social Issues, 35,* 1–11.

Friedman, H. S., & Di Matteo, M. R. (Eds.). (1982). *Interpersonal issues in health care.* New York: Academic Press.

Frijda, N. H. (1986). *The emotions.* New York: Cambridge University Press.

Fry, W. (1962). The marital context of an anxiety syndrome. *Family Process, 1,* 245–252.

Funder, D. C. (1991). Global traits: A neo-Allportian approach to personality. *Psychological Science, 2,* 31–39.

Furman, W., & Buhrmester, D. (1992). Age and sex differences in perceptions of networks of personal relationships. *Child Development, 63,* 103–115.

Gaelick, L., Bodenhause, G. V., & Wyer, R. S. (1985). Emotional communication in close relationships. *Journal of Personality and Social Psychology, 49,* 1246–1265.

Gaffin, G. L. (1981). Client-therapist complementarity as it relates to process and outcome of psychotherapy. *Dissertation Abstracts International, 42*(4), 1603B.

Gamsky, N. R., & Farwell, G. F. (1966). Counselor verbal behavior as a function of client hostility. *Journal of Counseling Psychology, 13,* 184–190.

Gascoyne, S. R. (1985). Interpersonal perceptions as a function of personality styles. *Dissertation Abstracts International, 46,* 1730–B.

Gelso, C. J., & Carter, J. A. (1985). The relationship in counseling and psychotherapy: Components, consequences, and theoretical antecedents. *The Counseling Psychologist, 13,* 155–244.

Gelso, C. J., & Carter, J. A. (1994). Components of the psychotherapy relationship: Their interaction and unfolding during treatment. *Journal of Counseling Psychology, 41,* 296–306.

Gergen, K. J. (1987). *Exploration of emotional scenarios.* Unpublished project description, Swarthmore College, Swarthmore, PA.

Gifford, R. (1991). Mapping nonverbal behavior on the Interpersonal Circle. *Journal of Personality and Social Psychology, 61,* 279–288.

Gifford, R., & O'Connor, B. (1987). The interpersonal circumplex as a behavioral map. *Journal of Personality and Social Psychology, 52,* 1019–1026.

Gill, M. M. (1983). The interpersonal paradigm and the degree of the therapist's involvement. *Contemporary Psychoanalysis, 19,* 200–237.

Gillespie, J. (1961). *Aggression in relation to frustration, attack, and inhibition.* Unpublished doctoral dissertation, University of Pittsburgh.

Goethe, K. E. (1984). The outcome of two treatments for heterosocial dysfunction. *Dissertation Abstracts International, 44,* 3195–B.

Goffman, E. (1959). *The presentation of self in everyday life.* Garden City, NY: Doubleday Anchor.

Goffman, E. (1961). *Encounters.* Indianapolis, IN: Bobbs-Merrill.

Goldberg, L. R. (1981). Language and individual differences: The search for universals in personality lexicons. In L. Wheeler (Ed.), *Review of personality and social psychology* (Vol. 2, pp. 141–165). Beverly Hills, CA: Sage.

Goldberg, L. R. (1990). An alternative "description of personality": The Big-Five factor structure. *Journal of Personality and Social Psychology, 59,* 1216–1229.

Goldberg, L. R. (1992). The development of markers of the Big-Five factor structure. *Psychological Assessment, 4,* 26–42.

Golden, B. R. (1989). Mechanisms of change in a model of short-term dynamic psychotherapy. *Dissertation Abstracts International, 49,* 4538–B.

Goldfarb, D. (1980). *Comfortable interpersonal distance as a reflection of complementarity and anticomplementarity of interpersonal styles.* Unpublished honors thesis, Emory University, Atlanta, GA.

Goldfried, M. R. (1991). Research issues in psychotherapy integration. *Journal of Psychotherapy Integration, 1,* 5–25.

Goldfried, M. R., & Davison, G. C. (1976). *Clinical behavior therapy.* New York: Holt, Rinehart & Winston.

Goldfried, M. R., Newman, C. F., & Hayes, A. M. (1989). *The coding system of therapeutic focus.* Unpublished manuscript, SUNY at Stony Brook, Stony Brook, NY.

Golding, S. L. (1977). Individual differences in the construal of interpersonal interactions. In D. Magnusson & N. Endler (Eds.), *Personality at the crossroads: Current issues in interactional psychology* (pp. 401–408). New York: Wiley.

Golding, S. L. (1978). Toward a more adequate theory of personality: Psychological organizing principles. In H. London (Ed.), *Personality: A new look at metatheories* (pp. 69–95). Washington, DC: Hemisphere.

Golding, S. L., & Knudson, R. M. (1975). Multivariable-multimethod convergence in the domain of interpersonal behavior. *Multivariate Behavioral Research, 10,* 425–448.

Golding, S. L., Valone, K., & Foster, S. W. (1980). Interpersonal construal: An individual differences framework. In N. Hirschberg (Ed.), *Multivariate methods in the social sciences: Applications* (pp. 163–193). Hillsdale, NJ: Erlbaum.

Goldsamt, L. A., Goldfried, M. R., Hayes, A. M., & Kerr, S. (1992). Beck, Meichenbaum, and Strupp: A comparison of three therapies in the dimension of therapist feedback. *Psychotherapy, 29,* 167–176.

Goldstein, A. J., & Chambless, D. L. (1978). A reanalysis of agoraphobia. *Behavior Therapy, 9,* 47–59.

Goldston, C. S. (1990). The Checklist of Psychotheapy Transactions as a self-report measure of covert and overt interpersonal complementarity. *Dissertation Abstracts International, 50,* 3695–B.

Gonick, J. (1987). The effects of interpersonal complementarity and clinician characteristics on clinical judgments of diagnostic severity and prognosis. *Dissertation Abstracts International, 48,* 1512–B.

Gorad, S. L., McCourt, W. F., & Cobb, J. C. (1971). A communications approach to alcoholism. *Quarterly Journal of Studies in Alcoholism, 32,* 651–668.

Gormly, J., & Edelberg, W. (1974). Validity in personality trait attribution. *American Psychologist, 29,* 189–193.

Gotlib, I. H. (1986, April). *Depression and marital interaction: A longitudinal perspective.* Paper presented at the Third International Conference on Personal Relationships, Tel Aviv, Israel.

Gotlib, I. H., & Colby, C. A. (1987). *Treatment of depression: An interpersonal systems approach.* Elmsford, NY: Pergamon.

Gottman, J. M. (1979). *Marital interaction: Experimental investigation.* New York: Academic Press.

Greben, S. E., Markson, E. R., & Sadavoy, J. (1973). Resident and supervisor: An examination of their relationship. *Canadian Psychiatric Association Journal, 18,* 473–479.

Green, M. (1972). The interpersonal approach to child therapy. In B. B. Wolman (Ed.), *Handbook of child psychoanalysis* (pp. 514–566). New York: Van Nostrand-Reinhold.

Greenberg, J. R., & Mitchell, S. A. (1983). *Object relations in psychoanalytic theory.* Cambridge, MA: Harvard University Press.

Greenberg, J. R., Pyszczynski, T., & Solomon, S. (1986). The causes and consequences of a need for self-esteem: A terror management theory. In R. Baumeister (Ed.), *Public self and private self* (pp. 189–212). New York: Springer-Verlag.

Greenberg, L. S. (1986). Change process research. *Journal of Consulting and Clinical Psychology, 54,* 4–9.

Greenberg, L. S., & Pinsof, W. M. (Eds.). (1986). *The psychotherapeutic process: A research handbook.* New York: Guilford.

Greenberg, L. S., & Safran, J. D. (1987). *Emotion in psychotherapy.* New York: Guilford.

Greenson, R. (1978). *Explorations in psychoanalysis.* New York: International Universities Press.

Greenwood, V. B. (1979). The effect of the interviewer's status upon the linguistic style and impact messages generated by the "obsessive" personality. *Dissertation Abstracts International, 39,* 3513–B.

Guidano, V. (1987). *Complexity of the self.* New York: Guilford.

Guidano, V. (1991). *The self in process.* New York: Guilford.

Gurtman, M. B. (1986). Depression and the response of others: Reevaluating the reevaluation. *Journal of Abnormal Psychology, 95,* 99–101.

Gurtman, M. B. (1987). Depressive affect and disclosures as factors in interpersonal rejection. *Cognitive Therapy and Research, 11,* 87–100.

Gurtman, M. B. (1991). Evaluating the interpersonalness of personality scales. *Personality and Social Psychology Bulletin, 17,* 670–677.

Gurtman, M. B. (1992a). Construct validity of interpersonal measures: The interpersonal circumplex as a nomological net. *Journal of Personality and Social Psychology, 63,* 105–118.

Gurtman, M. B. (1992b). Trust, distrust, and interpersonal problems: A circumplex analysis. *Journal of Personality and Social Psychology, 62,* 989–1002.

Gurtman, M. B. (1993). Constructing personality tests to meet a structural criterion: Application of the interpersonal circumplex. *Journal of Personality, 61,* 237–263.

Gurtman, M. B. (1994). The circumplex as a tool for studying normal and abnormal personality: A methodological primer. In S. Strack & M. Lorr (Eds.), *Differentiating normal and abnormal personality* (pp. 243–263). New York: Springer.

Gurtman, M. B. (in press). Studying personality traits—The circular way. In R. Plutchik & H. R. Conte (Eds.), *Circumplex models of personality and emotion.* Washington, DC: American Psychological Association.

Gurtman, M. B., Kiesler, D. J., Schmidt, J. A., & Wagner, C. C. (1994). *Interpersonal complementarity and the interpersonal circle: An integrative approach to testing complementarity in interpersonal transactions.* Unpublished manuscript, University of Wisconsin, Parkside, Kenosha.

Guttman, L. (1954). A new approach to factor analysis: The radex. In P. R. Lazarsfeld (Ed.), *Mathematical thinking in the social sciences* (pp. 258–348). Glencoe, IL: Free Press.

Hafner, R. J. (1982). The marital context of the agoraphobic syndrome. In D. L. Chambless & A. J. Goldstein (Eds.), *Agoraphobia* (pp. 241–267). New York: Wiley.

Haley, J. (1959). An interactional description of schizophrenia. *Psychiatry, 22,* 321–332.

Haley, J. (1963). *Strategies of psychotherapy.* New York: Grune & Stratton.

Hall, J. A., Harrigan, J. A., & Rosenthal, R. (1995). Nonverbal behavior in clinician-patient interaction. *Applied and Preventive Psychology, 4,* 21–37.

Halpern, H. M. (1965). An essential ingredient in successful psychotherapy. *Psychotherapy: Theory, Research and Practice, 2,* 177–180.

Hamilton, D. L. (1971). A comparative study of five methods of assessing self-esteem, dominance, and dogmatism. *Educational and Psychological Measurement, 31,* 441–452.

Hammen, C. L., & Peters, S. D. (1978). Interpersonal consequences of depression: Responses to men and women enacting a depressed role. *Journal of Abnormal Psychology, 87,* 322–332.

Hare, R. D. (1970). *Psychopathy: Theory and research.* New York: Wiley.

Harper, R. G., Wiens, A. N., & Matarazzo, J. D. (1978). *Nonverbal communication: The state of the art.* New York: Wiley.

Harter, S. (1990). Developmental differences in the nature of self-representation: Implications for understanding assessment and treatment of maladaptive behavior. *Cognitive Therapy and Research, 14,* 113–142.

Hartley, D. E. (1985). Research on the therapeutic alliance in psychotherapy. In American Psychiatric Association (Ed.), *Psychiatry update: Annual Review* (Vol. 4, pp. 532–549). Washington, DC: American Psychiatric Association Press.

Hartley, D. E., & Strupp, H. H. (1983). The therapeutic alliance: Its relationship to outcome in brief psychotherapy. In J. Masling (Ed.), *Empirical studies of analytic concepts* (Vol. 1, pp. 1–37). Hillsdale, NJ: Analytic Press.

Haslam, N. (1994). Mental representation of social relationships: Dimensions, laws, or categories? *Journal of Personality and Social Psychology, 67,* 575–584.

Heffner, K. P. (1988). *The effects of help-seeker role labels on subjects' recognition memory and perceptions of interpersonal behaviors.* Unpublished master's thesis, Virginia Commonwealth University, Richmond.

Heffner, K. P. (1993). Alcohol expectancies and self-perceived interpersonal behaviors attributed to drinking for interactions with same-sexed peers. *Dissertation Abstracts International, 53,* 6551–6552B.

Helgeson, V. S. (1994). Relation of agency and communion to well-being: Evidence and potential explanations. *Psychological Bulletin, 116,* 412–428.

Heller, K., Myers, R. A., & Kline, L. V. (1963). Interviewer behavior as a function of standardized client roles. *Journal of Consulting Psychology, 27,* 117–122.

Henderson, S., Duncan-Jones, P., Byrne, D. G., & Scott, R. (1980). Measuring social relationships: The interview schedule for social interaction. *Psychological Medicine, 10,* 723–734.

Henley, N. M. (1977). *Body politics: Power, sex, and nonverbal communication.* Englewood Cliffs, NJ: Prentice-Hall.

Henry, W. P., Schacht, T. E., & Strupp, H. H. (1986). Structural Analysis of Social Behavior: Application to a study of interpersonal process in differential psychotherapeutic outcome. *Journal of Consulting and Clinical Psychology, 54,* 27–31.

Henry, W. P., Schacht, T. E., & Strupp, H. H. (1990). Patient and therapist introject, interpersonal process, and differential psychotherapy outcome. *Journal of Consulting and Clinical Psychology, 58,* 768–774.

Hertel, R. K. (1972). Application of stochastic process analysis to the study of psychotherapeutic processes. *Psychological Bulletin, 77,* 421–430.

Hill, C., & Safran, J. D. (1994). Assessing interpersonal schemas: Anticipated responses of significant others. *Journal of Social and Clinical Psychology, 13,* 366–379.

Hoffman, I. Z. (1983). The patient as interpreter of the analyst's experience. *Contemporary Psychoanalysis, 19,* 389–422.

Hofstee, W. K. B., de Raad, B., & Goldberg, L. R. (1992). Integration of the big five and circumplex approaches to trait structure. *Journal of Personality and Social Psychology, 63,* 146–163.

Hogan, R. (1983). A socioanalytic theory of personality. In M. M. Page (Ed.), *1982 Nebraska symposium on motivation: Personality—Current theory and research* (pp. 58–89). Lincoln: University of Nebraska Press.

Hogan, R., Jones, W. H., & Cheek, J. M. (1985). Socioanalytic theory: An alternative to armadillo psychology. In B. R. Schlenker (Ed.), *The self and social life* (pp. 175–178). New York: McGraw-Hill.

Hokanson, J. E., & Butler, A. C. (1992). Cluster analysis of depressed college students' social behaviors. *Journal of Personality and Social Psychology, 62,* 273–280.

Hokanson, J. E., Hummer, J. T., & Butler, A. C. (1991). Interpersonal perceptions by depressed college students. *Cognitive Therapy and Research, 15,* 443–457.

Hokanson, J. E., Rubert, M. P., Welker, R. A., Hollander, G. P., & Hedeen, C. (1989). Interpersonal concomitants and antecedents of depression among college students. *Journal of Abnormal Psychology, 98,* 209–217.

Holland, J. L. (1973). *Making vocational choices: A theory of careers.* Englewood Cliffs, NJ: Prentice-Hall.

Holland, J. L. (1985a). *The self-directed search manual.* Odessa, FL: Psychological Assessment Resources.

Holland, J. L. (1985b). *The Vocational Preference Inventory manual.* Odessa, FL: Psychological Assessment Resources.

Holliday, S. L. (1983). Depression in marriage: Husbands' responses to depressed wives. *Dissertation Abstracts International, 44,* 310–B.

Holton, B., & Pyszczynski, T. (1989). Biased information search in the interpersonal domain. *Personality and Social Psychology Bulletin, 15,* 42–51.

Hora, T. (1957). Contribution to the phenomenology of the supervisory process. *American Journal of Psychotherapy, 11,* 769–773.

Horney, K. (1942). *Self-analysis.* New York: Norton.

Horowitz, L. M. (1979). On the cognitive structure of interpersonal problems treated in psychotherapy. *Journal of Consulting and Clinical Psychology, 47,* 5–15.

Horowitz, L. M. (1988). *Inventory of Interpersonal Problems: Scoring procedures.* Unpublished manuscript, Stanford University, Stanford, CA.

Horowitz, L. M., & French, R. deS. (1979). Interpersonal problems of people who describe themselves as lonely. *Journal of Consulting and Clinical Psychology, 57,* 762–764.

Horowitz, L. M., French, R. deS., & Anderson, C. A. (1982). The prototype of a lonely person. In L. Peplau & D. Perlman (Eds.), *Loneliness: A sourcebook of current theory, research, and therapy* (pp. 183–205). New York: Wiley.

Horowitz, L. M., French, R. deS., Lapid, J. S., & Weckler, D. A. (1982). Symptoms and interpersonal problems: The prototype as an integrating concept. In J. C. Anchin & D. J. Kiesler (Eds.), *Handbook of interpersonal psychotherapy* (pp. 168–189). Elmsford, NY: Pergamon.

Horowitz, L. M., Locke, K. D., Morse, M. B., Walkar, S. V., Dryer, D. C., Tarrow, E., & Ghannam, J. (1991). Self-derogations and the interpersonal theory. *Journal of Personality and Social Psychology, 61,* 68–79.

Horowitz, L. M., Post, D. L., French, R. deS., Wallis, K. D., & Siegelman, E. Y. (1981). The prototype as a construct in abnormal psychology: 2. Clarifying disagreement in psychiatric judgements. *Journal of Abnormal Psychology, 90,* 575–585.

Horowitz, L. M., Rosenberg, S. E., Baer, B. A., Ureno, G., & Villasenor, V. S. (1988). The Inventory of Interpersonal Problems: Psychometric properties and clinical applications. *Journal of Consulting and Clinical Psychology, 56,* 885–892.

Horowitz, L. M., Rosenberg, S. E., & Bartholomew, K. (1993). Interpersonal problems, attachment styles, and outcome in brief dynamic psychotherapy. *Journal of Consulting and Clinical Psychology, 61,* 549–560.

Horowitz, L. M., Rosenberg, S. E., & Kalehzan, B. M. (1992). The capacity to describe other people clearly: A predictor of interpersonal problems and outcome in brief dynamic psychotherapy. *Psychotherapy Research, 2,* 37–51.

Horowitz, L. M., Rosenberg, S. E., Ureno, G., Kalehzan, B. M., & O'Halloran, P. (1989). Psychodynamic formulation, consensual response method, and interpersonal problems. *Journal of Consulting and Clinical Psychology, 57,* 599–606.

Horowitz, L. M., Sampson, H., & Siegelman, E. Y. (1978). Cohesive and dispersal behaviors: Two classes of concomitant change in psychotherapy. *Journal of Consulting and Clinical Psychology, 46,* 556–564.

Horowitz, L. M., Sampson, H., Siegelman, E. Y., Weiss, J., & Goodfriend, S. (1988). Cohesive and dispersal behaviors: Two classes of concomitant change in psychotherapy. *Journal of Consulting and Clinical Psychology, 46,* 556–564.

Horowitz, L. M., & Vitkus, J. (1986). The interpersonal basis of psychiatric symptoms. *Clinical Psychology Review, 6,* 443–469.

Horowitz, L. M., Weckler, D. A., & Doren, R. (1983). Interpersonal problems and symptoms: A cognitive approach. In P. Kendall (Ed.), *Advances in cognitive-behavioral research and therapy* (pp. 81–125). London: Academic Press.

Horowitz, L. M., Wright, J. C., Lowenstein, E., & Parad, H. W. (1981). The prototype as a construct in abnormal psychology: 1. A method for deriving prototypes. *Journal of Abnormal Psychology, 90,* 568–574.

Horowitz, M. J. (1988). *Introduction to psychodynamics: A new synthesis.* New York: Basic Books.

Horvath, A. O., & Greenberg, L. S. (Eds.). (1994). *The working alliance: Theory, research, and practice.* New York: Wiley.

Howard, K. I., Kopta, S. M., Krause, M. S., & Orlinsky, D. E. (1986). The dose-effect relationship in psychotherapy. *American Psychologist, 41,* 159–164.

Howes, M. J., & Hokanson, J. E. (1979). Conversational and social responses to depressive interpersonal behavior. *Journal of Abnormal Psychology, 88,* 625–634.

Hubert, L. J., & Arabie, P. (1987). Evaluating order hypotheses within proximity matrices. *Psychological Bulletin, 102,* 172–178.

Hudgins, M. K. (1982). *Decoding differences on the verbal and nonverbal channels among "A" and "B" types.* Unpublished master's thesis, Virginia Commonwealth University, Richmond.

Hudgins, M. K., & Chirico, B. M. (1982). *Interpersonal therapist styles as related to theoretical orientation among first year interns.* Unpublished study, Virginia Commonwealth University, Richmond.

Hudgins, M. K., & Kiesler, D. J. (1987). Individual experiential psychotherapy: An analogue validation of the intervention module of psychodramatic doubling. *Psychotherapy, 24,* 245–255.

Humphrey, L. L. (1989). Observed family interactions among subtypes of eating disorders using Structural Analysis of Social Behavior. *Journal of Consulting and Clinical Psychology, 57,* 206–214.

Humphrey, L. L., & Benjamin, L. S. (1986). Using Structural Analysis of Social Behavior to assess critical but elusive family processes: A new solution to an old problem. *American Psychologist, 41,* 979–989.

Hurley, J. R. (1976). Two prepotent interpersonal dimensions and the effects of trainers on T-groups. *Journal in Small Group Behavior, 7,* 77–98.

Hurley, J. R. (1980). Two interpersonal dimensions relevant to group and family therapy. In L. R. Wolberg & M. L. Aronson (Eds.), *Group and family therapy, 1980* (pp. 65–78). New York: Brunner/Mazel.

Hurley, J. R. (1990). Does FIRO-B relate better to interpersonal or intrapersonal behavior? *Journal of Clinical Psychology, 46,* 454–459.

Ickes, W. J., & Layden, M. A. (1978). Attributional styles. In J. Harvey, W. Ickes, & R. Kidd (Eds.), *New directions in attribution research* (Vol. 2, pp. 119–152). Hillsdale, NJ: Erlbaum.

Ingraham, J. L., & Wright, T. (1987). A social relations model test of Sullivan's anxiety hypothesis. *Journal of Personality and Social Psychology, 52,* 1212–1218.

Jackson, D. D. (1959). Family interaction, family homeostasis, and some implications for conjoint family therapy. In J. H. Masserman (Ed.), *Individual and familial dynamics* (pp. 122–141). New York: Grune and Stratton.

Jackson, D. N., & Helmes, E. (1979). Personality structure and the circumplex. *Journal of Personality and Social Psychology, 37,* 2278–2285.

Jackson, D. N., & Paunonen, S. V. (1980). Personality structure and assessment. *Annual Review of Psychology, 31,* 503–551.

Jahoda, M. (1958). *Current concepts of positive mental health.* New York: Basic Books.

Jahoda, M. (1961). A social-psychological approach to the study of culture. *Human Relations, 14,* 23–30.

Janoff-Bulman, R. (1989). The benefit of illusions, the threat of disillusionment, and the limitations of inaccuracy. *Journal of Social and Clinical Psychology, 8,* 158–175.

Janowsky, D. S., El-Yousef, M. K., & Davis, J. M. (1974). Interpersonal maneuvers of manic patients. *American Journal of Psychiatry, 131,* 250–255.

Janowsky, D. S., Leff, M., & Epstein, R. S. (1970). Playing the manic game. *Archives of General Psychiatry, 22,* 252–261.

Johnson, M. E., Popp, C., Schacht, T. E., Mellon, J., & Strupp, H. H. (1989). Converging evidence for identification of recurrent relationship themes: Comparison of two methods. *Psychiatry, 52,* 275–288.

Jones, R. A. (1977). *Self-fulfilling prophecies: Social, psychological, and physiological effects of expectancies.* Hillsdale, NJ: Erlbaum.

Jourard, S. M., & Landsman, T. (1980). *Healthy personality: An approach from the viewpoint of humanistic psychology* (4th ed.). New York: Macmillan.

Juhasz, A. M. (1989). Significant others and self-esteem: Methods for determining who and why. *Adolescence, 24,* 581–595.

Jussim, L. (1986). Self-fulfilling prophecies: A theoretical and integrative review. *Psychological Review, 93,* 429–445.

Kahn, J. (1983). Depression in the marital context. *Dissertation Abstracts International, 43,* 3734–B.

Kahn, J., Coyne, J. C., & Margolin, G. (1985). Depression and marital disagreement: The social construction of despair. *Journal of Social and Personal Relationships, 2,* 447–461.

Kaul, T. J., & Bednar, R. L. (1986). Experiential group research: Current perspectives. In S. L. Garfield & A. E. Bergin (Eds.), *Handbook of psychotherapy and behavior change* (3rd ed., pp. 671–714). New York: Wiley.

Kell, B. L., & Mueller, W. J. (1966). *Impact and change: A study of counseling relationships.* New York: Appleton-Century-Crofts.

Kellerman, H., & Plutchik, R. (1968). Emotion-trait interrelations and the measurement of personality. *Psychological Reports, 23,* 1107–1114.

Kelley, H. H., Berscheid, E., Christensen, A., Harvey, J. H., Huston, T. L., Levinger, G., McClintock, E., Peplau, L. A., & Peterson, D. R. (1983). *Close relationships.* New York: Freeman.

Kelley, H. H., & Stahelski, A. J. (1970). The social interaction basis of cooperators' and competitors' beliefs about others. *Journal of Personality and Social Psychology, 16,* 66–91.

Kelly, G. A. (1955). *The psychology of personal constructs* (Vols. I & II). New York: Norton.

Kelly, G. A. (1969). The strategy of psychological research. In B. A. Maher (Ed.), *Clinical psychology and personality: The selected papers of George Kelly* (pp. 114–132). New York: Wiley.

Kemper, T. D. (1966). Self-conceptions and the expectations of significant others. *Sociological Quarterly, 7,* 323–344.

Kemper, T. D. (1978a). *A social interactional theory of emotions.* Melbourne, FL: Krieger.

Kemper, T. D. (1978b). Toward a sociology of emotions: Some problems and some solutions. *American Sociologist, 13,* 30–40.

Kendrick, D. T., & Funder, D. C. (1988). Profiting from controversy: Lessons from the person-situation debate. *American Psychologist, 43,* 23–34.

Kenny, D. A., & La Voie, L. (1984). The social relations model. *Advances in Experimental Social Psychology, 18,* 141–182.

Kerckhoff, A. C., & Davis, K. E. (1962). Value consensus and need complementarity in mate selection. *American Sociological Review, 27,* 295–303.

Kernberg, O. (1965). Notes on countertransference. *Journal of the American Psychoanalytic Association, 13,* 38–56.

Kerr, A. E., Patton, M. J., Lapan, R. T., & Hills, H. I. (1994). Interpersonal correlates of narcissism in adolescents. *Journal of Counseling and Development, 73,* 204–210.

Kiesler, D. J. (1973). *The process of psychotherapy: Empirical foundations and systems of analysis.* Chicago: Aldine.

Kiesler, D. J. (1973–1975). *A communications approach to modification of the "obsessive" personality—An initial formulation.* Unpublished manuscript, Emory University, Atlanta, GA.

Kiesler, D. J. (1977). *Communications assessment of interview behavior of the "obsessive" personality.* Unpublished manuscript, Virginia Commonwealth University, Richmond.

Kiesler, D. J. (1979). An interpersonal communication analysis of relationship in psychotherapy. *Psychiatry, 42,* 299–311.

Kiesler, D. J. (1982a). Confronting the client-therapist relationship in psychotherapy. In J. C. Anchin & D. J. Kiesler (Eds.), *Handbook of interpersonal psychotherapy* (pp. 274–295). Elmsford, NY: Pergamon.

Kiesler, D. J. (1982b). Interpersonal theory for personality and psychotherapy. In J. C. Anchin & D. J. Kiesler (Eds.), *Handbook of interpersonal psychotherapy* (pp. 3–24). Elmsford, NY: Pergamon.

Kiesler, D. J. (1982c). *The 1982 Interpersonal Circle: A taxonomy for complementarity in human transactions.* Richmond: Virginia Commonwealth University.

Kiesler, D. J. (1983). The 1982 Interpersonal Circle: A taxonomy for complementarity in human transactions. *Psychological Review, 90,* 185–214.

Kiesler, D. J. (1984). *Check List of Psychotherapy Transactions (CLOPT) and Check List of Interpersonal Transactions (CLOIT).* Richmond: Virginia Commonwealth University.

Kiesler, D. J. (1985). *The 1982 Interpersonal Circle: Acts Version.* Unpublished manuscript, Virginia Commonwealth University, Richmond.

Kiesler, D. J. (1986a). Interpersonal methods of diagnosis and treatment. In R. Michels & J. O. Cavenar, Jr. (Eds.), *Psychiatry* (Vol. 1, pp. 1–23). Philadelphia: Lippincott.

Kiesler, D. J. (1986b). The 1982 Interpersonal Circle: An analysis of DSM-III personality disorders. In T. Millon & G. L. Klerman (Eds.), *Contemporary directions in psychopathology: Towards the DSM-IV* (pp. 57–59). New York: Guilford.

Kiesler, D. J. (1987a). *Check List of Psychotherapy Transactions–Revised (CLOPT–R) and Check List of Interpersonal Transactions–Revised (CLOIT–R).* Richmond: Virginia Commonwealth University.

Kiesler, D. J. (1987b). Complementarity: Between whom and under what conditions? *Clinician's Research Digest: Supplemental Bulletin, 5*(20).

Kiesler, D. J. (1987c). *Research manual for the Impact Message Inventory.* Palo Alto, CA: Consulting Psychologist Press.

Kiesler, D. J. (1988). *Therapeutic metacommunication: Therapist impact disclosure as feedback in psychotherapy.* Palo Alto, CA: Consulting Psychologist Press.

Kiesler, D. J. (1990). *Intensive metacommunicative psychotherapy: A treatment manual.* Unpublished manuscript, Virginia Commonwealth University, Richmond.

Kiesler, D. J. (1991). Interpersonal methods of assessment and diagnosis. In C. R. Snyder & D. R. Forsyth (Eds.), *Handbook of social and clinical psychology: The health perspective* (pp. 438–468). Elmsford, NY: Pergamon.

Kiesler, D. J. (1992). Interpersonal circle inventories: Pantheoretical applications to psychotherapy research and practice. *Journal of Psychotherapy Integration, 2,* 77–79.

Kiesler, D. J., Anchin, J. C., Perkins, M. J., Chirico, B. M., Kyle, E. M., & Federman, E. J. (1976). *The Impact Message Inventory: Form II.* Richmond: Virginia Commonwealth University.

Kiesler, D. J., Anchin, J. C., Perkins, M. J., Chirico, B. M., Kyle, E. M., & Federman, E. J. (1985). *The Impact Message Inventory: Form II.* Palo Alto, CA: Consulting Psychologist Press.

Kiesler, D. J., Bernstein, A. B., & Anchin, J. C. (1976). *Interpersonal communication, relationship, and the behavior therapies.* Richmond: Virginia Commonwealth University.

Kiesler, D. J., & Chapman, R. C. (1988). *A multidimensional scaling analysis of the 1982 Interpersonal Circle.* Unpublished manuscript, Virginia Commonwealth University, Richmond.

Kiesler, D. J., & Federman, E. J. (1978). *Anchoring obsessive and hysteric personalities to the interpersonal circle.* Unpublished manuscript, Virginia Commonwealth University, Richmond.

Kiesler, D. J., & Goldston, C. S. (1988). Client-therapist complementarity: An analysis of the Gloria films. *Journal of Counseling Psychology, 35,* 127–133.

Kiesler, D. J., Goldston, C. S., Paddock, J. M., & Van Denburg, T. F. (1986). *An initial validation of the Check List of Interpersonal Transactions.* Unpublished study, Virginia Commonwealth University, Richmond.

Kiesler, D. J., Goldston, C. S., & Schmidt, J. A. (1991). *Manual for the Check List of Interpersonal Transactions–Revised (CLOIT–R) and the Check List of Psychotherapy Transactions–Revised (CLOPT–R)*. Richmond: Virginia Commonwealth University.

Kiesler, D. J., Horner, M. S., Larus, J. P., & Chapman, R. C. (1988). *Measurement of evoked emotion in interpersonal transactions*. Unpublished manuscript, Virginia Commonwealth University, Richmond.

Kiesler, D. J., Moulthrop, M. A., & Todd, T. S. (1972). *A psycholinguistic scoring system for the obsessive personality*. Atlanta, GA: Emory University.

Kiesler, D. J., & Schmidt, J. A. (1993). *The Impact Message Inventory: Form IIA Octant Scale Version*. Palo Alto, CA: Mind Garden.

Kiesler, D. J., Schmidt, J. A., & Larus, J. P. (1988). *Internal consistency and test-retest reliability of the self-report version of the Check List of Interpersonal Transactions (CLOIT)*. Unpublished study, Virginia Commonwealth University, Richmond.

Kiesler, D. J., Schmidt, J. A., & Larus, J. P. (1989). *The Interpersonal Adjective Scales (IAS) and the Check List of Interpersonal Transactions (CLOIT): Convergent validity evidence*. Unpublished study, Virginia Commonwealth University, Richmond.

Kiesler, D. J., Schmidt, J. A., & Wagner, C. C. (in press). A circumplex inventory of impact messages: An operational bridge between emotion and interpersonal behavior. In R. Plutchik & H. R. Conte (Eds.), *Circumplex models of personality and emotions*. Washington, DC: American Psychological Association.

Kiesler, D. J., & Van Denburg, T. F. (1993). Therapeutic impact disclosure: A last taboo in psychoanalytic theory and practice. *Clinical Psychology and Psychotherapy, 1,* 3–13.

Kiesler, D. J., Van Denburg, T. F., Sikes-Nova, V. E., Larus, J. P., & Goldston, C. S. (1990). Interpersonal behavior profiles of eight cases of DSM-III personality disorder. *Journal of Clinical Psychology, 46,* 440–453.

Kiesler, D. J., & Watkins, L. M. (1989). Interpersonal complementarity and the therapeutic alliance: A study of relationship in psychotherapy. *Psychotherapy, 26,* 183–194.

Kiesler, D. J., Wenzel, C. K., Chewning, M. C., & Davidson, K. M. (1982). Impacts of patients on intake interviewers in a mental health outpatient clinic. Unpublished study, Virginia Commonwealth University, Richmond.

Kihlstrom, J. F. (1987). The cognitive unconscious. *Science, 237,* 1445–1452.

Kihlstrom, J. F. (1990). The psychological unconscious. In L. A. Pervin (Ed.), *Handbook of personality: Theory and research* (pp. 445–464). New York: Guilford.

Kinch, J. W. (1968). Experiments on factors related to self-concept change. *Journal of Social Psychology, 74,* 251–258.

Kivlighan, D. M., Jr. (1985). Feedback in group psychotherapy. *Journal in Small Group Behavior, 16,* 373–385.

Kivlighan, D. M., Jr., & Angelone, E. O. (1992). Interpersonal problems: Variables influencing participants' perception of group climate. *Journal of Counseling Psychology, 38,* 25–29.

Kivlighan, D. M., Jr., & Goldfine, D. C. (1991). Endorsement of therapeutic factors as a function of stage of group development and participant interpersonal attitudes. *Journal of Counseling Psychology, 38,* 150–158.

Kivlighan, D. M., Jr., Marsh-Angelone, M., & Angelone, E. O. (1994). Projection in group counseling: The relationship between members' interpersonal problems and their perception of the group leader. *Journal of Counseling Psychology, 41,* 99–104.

Kivlighan, D. M., Jr., McGovern, T. V., & Corazzini, J. G. (1984). Effects of content and timing of structuring interventions on group therapy process and outcome. *Journal of Counseling Psychology, 31,* 363–370.

Kivlighan, D. M., Jr., & Mullison, D. D. (1988). Participants' perception of therapeutic factors in group counseling: The role of interpersonal style and stage of group development. *Journal in Small Group Behavior, 19,* 452–468.

Kivlighan, D. M., Jr., Mullison, D. D., Flohr, D. F., Proudman, S., & Francis, A. M. R. (1992). The interpersonal structure of "good" versus "bad" group counseling sessions: A multiple-case study. *Psychotherapy, 29,* 500–508.

Klein, M. H., Mathieu-Coughlan, P., & Kiesler, D. J. (1986). The Experiencing Scales. In L. S. Greenberg & W. M. Pinsof (Eds.), *The psychotherapeutic process: A research handbook* (pp. 21–71). New York: Guilford.

Klerman, G. L., & Weissman, M. M. (Eds.). (1992). *New applications of interpersonal psychotherapy.* Washington, DC: American Psychiatric Press.

Klerman, G. L., Weissman, M. M., Rounsaville, B. J., & Chevron, E. S. (1984). *Interpersonal psychotherapy of depression.* New York: Basic Books.

Klinger, E. (1971). *Structure and function of fantasy.* New York: Wiley.

Klinger, E. (1977a). *Meaning and void: Inner experience and the incentives in people's lives.* Minneapolis: University of Minnesota Press.

Klinger, E. (1977b). The nature of fantasy and its clinical use. *Psychotherapy: Theory, Research, and Practice, 14,* 223–231.

Knapp, M. L., & Hall, J. A. (1992). *Nonverbal communication in human interaction* (3rd ed.). Ft. Worth, TX: Holt, Rinehart & Winston.

Knight, T. A. (1992). Client role preferences, complementarity and attraction in the initial psychotherapy session. *Dissertation Abstracts International, 53,* 565–B.

Knudson, R., & Golding, S. (1974). Comparative validity of traditional versus S-R format inventories of interpersonal behavior. *Journal of Research in Personality, 8,* 111–127.

Kohut, H. (1971). *The analysis of the self.* New York: International Universities Press.

Krantz, S. E. (1985). When depressive cognitions reflect negative realities. *Cognitive Therapy and Research, 9,* 595–610.

Kuhn, M. H. (1964). The reference group reconsidered. *Sociological Quarterly, 5,* 5–24.

Kyle, E. M. (1977). Evaluation of a stranger in a brief dyadic situation as a function of the inclusion score of the interactants: An attempt to measure impact messages. *Dissertation Abstracts International, 37,* 3616–B.

Labe-Sloan, E. H. (1982). *The influence of assertive characteristics of raters on perceived assertiveness in others.* Unpublished master's thesis, Virginia Commonwealth University, Richmond.

Ladd, M., Nowicki, S., Jr., & Duke, M. (1979). *Interpersonal congruence as a function of degree of importance of relationship and importance of situation.* Unpublished manuscript, Emory University, Atlanta, GA.

LaForge, R. (1977). *Using the ICL: 1976.* Unpublished manuscript, Mill Valley, CA.

LaForge, R. (1985). The early development of the Freedman-Leary-Coffey Interpersonal System. *Journal of Personality Assessment, 49,* 613–621.

LaForge, R., Freedman, M. B., & Wiggins, J. S. (1985). Interpersonal circumplex models: 1948–1983 (Symposium). *Journal of Personality Assessment, 49,* 613–631.

LaForge, R., Leary, T., Naboisek, H., Coffey, H. S., & Freedman, M. B. (1954). The interpersonal dimension of personality: II. An objective study of repression. *Journal of Personality, 23,* 129–153.

LaForge, R., & Suczek, R. F. (1955). The interpersonal dimensions of personality: III. An interpersonal check list. *Journal of Personality, 24,* 94–112.

LaFrance, M., & Mayo, C. (1978). *Moving bodies: Nonverbal communication in social relationships*. Monterey, CA: Brooks/Cole.

LaFromboise, T. D. (1992). An interpersonal analysis of affinity, clarification, and helpful responses with American Indians. *Professional Psychology: Research and Practice, 23,* 281–286.

Laird, H., & Vande Kemp, H. (1987). Complementarity as a function of stage in therapy: An analysis of Minuchin's structural family therapy. *Journal of Marital and Family Therapy, 13,* 127–137.

Lambert, M. (Ed.). (1983). *Psychotherapy and patient relationships*. Homewood, IL: Dorsey.

Lamphere, R. A. (1993). *Effects of interpersonal feedback on self-conceptions and self-presentations*. Unpublished doctoral dissertation, Virginia Commonwealth University, Richmond.

Langs, R. J. (1980). Supervision in the bipersonal field. In A. K. Hess (Ed.), *Psychotherapy supervision: Theory, research and practice* (pp. 103–125). New York: Wiley.

Larus, J. P. (1989). *Significant Other Inventory: Towards charting the nature of significant others*. Unpublished master's thesis, Virginia Commonwealth University, Richmond.

Larus, J. P., & Kiesler, D. J. (1988). *Significant Other Inventory (SOI)*. Richmond: Virginia Commonwealth University.

Larus-McShane, J. P. (1993). *The Revised Significant Other Inventory: Exploring the positive and negative qualities of significant others*. Unpublished doctoral dissertation, Virginia Commonwealth University, Richmond.

Larus-McShane, J. P., Kiesler, D. J., & Murray, C. M. (1990). *Significant Other Inventory–Revised (SOI–R)*. Richmond: Virginia Commonwealth University.

Larus-McShane, J. P., Kiesler, D. J., Murray, C. M., Dowdy, B. B., & Kliewer, W. L. (1993). *Significant Other Inventory–Revised for Adolescents (SOI–R:A)*. Richmond: Virginia Commonwealth University.

LaRusso, L. (1978). Sensitivity of paranoid patients to nonverbal cues. *Journal of Abnormal Psychology, 87,* 463–471.

Lazarus, R. S. (1983). The costs and benefits of denial. In S. Breznitz (Ed.), *The denial of stress* (pp. 1–30). New York: International Universities Press.

Lazarus, R. S., & Averill, J. R. (1972). Emotion and cognition: With special reference to anxiety. In C. D. Spielberger (Ed.), *Anxiety: Current trends in theory and research* (Vol. 2, pp. 241–283). New York: Academic Press.

Lazarus, R. S., & Folkman, S. (1984). *Stress, appraisal and coping*. New York: Springer.

Lazarus, R. S., Kanner, A. D., & Folkman, S. (1980). Emotions: A cognitive–phenomenological analysis. In R. Plutchik & H. Kellerman (Eds.), *Emotion: Theory, research, and experience: Vol. 1. Theories of emotion* (pp. 189–217). New York: Academic Press.

Leary, T. F. (1955). The theory and measurement methodology of interpersonal communication. *Psychiatry, 18,* 147–161.

Leary, T. F. (1957). *Interpersonal diagnosis of personality*. New York: Ronald.

Leary, T. F., & Coffey, H. S. (1954). The prediction of interpersonal behavior in group psychotherapy. *Group Psychotherapy, 7,* 7–51.

Leary, T. F., & Coffey, H. S. (1955). Interpersonal diagnosis: Some problems of methodology and validation. *Journal of Abnormal and Social Psychology, 50,* 110–124.

Leary, T. F., & Harvey, J. S. (1956). A methodology for measuring personality changes in psychotherapy. *Journal of Clinical Psychology, 12,* 123–132.

Leary, T. F., Lane, H., Apfelbaum, A., Croppa, M. D., & Kaufmann, C. (1956). *Multilevel measurement of interpersonal behavior: A manual for the use of the interpersonal system of personality*. Berkeley, CA: Psychological Consultation Service.

Lecky, P. (1945). *Self-consistency.* New York: Island Press.

Lederer, W. J., & Jackson, D. D. (1968). *The mirages of marriage.* New York: Norton.

Lees-Halet, P. R. (1981). College norms for the Leary Interpersonal Checklist. *Journal of Consulting and Clinical Psychology, 49,* 302–303.

Lein, L., & Sussman, M. (Eds.). (1983). *The ties that bind: Men and women's social networks.* New York: Haworth.

Lemert, E. M. (1962). Paranoia and the dynamics of exclusion. *Sociometry, 25,* 2–20.

Lerner, H. E. (1983). Female dependency in context: Some theoretical and technical considerations. *American Journal of Orthopsychiatry, 53,* 697–705.

Levenson, E. A. (1973). Psychotherapy of the young adult: The fallacy of understanding. In E. G. Witenberg (Ed.), *Interpersonal explorations in psychoanalysis* (pp. 151–168). New York: Basic Books.

Lewicki, P. (1986). *Nonconscious social information processing.* New York: Academic Press.

Lewinsohn, P. M., Mischel, W., Chaplin, W., & Barton, R. (1980). Social competence and depression: The role of illusory self-perceptions. *Journal of Abnormal Psychology, 89,* 203–212.

Liggett, A. (1993). *Shame, guilt and childhood abuse as factors in interpersonal behavior style of male spouse abusers.* Unpublished doctoral dissertation, Fielding Institute, Santa Barbara, CA.

Lineham, M. M. (1988). Perspectives on the interpersonal relationship in behavior therapy. *Journal of Integrative and Eclectic Psychotherapy, 7,* 278–290.

Lochman, J. E. (1987). Self- and peer-perceptions and attributional biases of aggressive and nonaggressive boys in dyadic interactions. *Journal of Consulting and Clinical Psychology, 55,* 404–410.

Longabaugh, R. (1966). The structure of interpersonal behavior. *Sociometry, 29,* 441–460.

Lonner, W. J. (1980). The search for psychological universals. In H. C. Triandis & W. W. Lambert (Eds.), *Handbook of cross-cultural psychology: Perspectives* (Vol. 1, pp. 143–204). Boston: Allyn and Bacon.

Loranger, A. W., Susman, V. L., Oldham, J. M., & Russakoff, L. M. (1985). *Personality disorder examination (PDE): A structured interview for DSM-III-R personality disorders.* White Plains, NY: New York Hospital—Cornell Medical Center.

Lorr, M. (1986). *Interpersonal Style Inventory (ISI) manual.* Los Angeles: Western Psychological Services.

Lorr, M. (1990). Social role and interpersonal behavior as assessed by the Interpersonal Style Inventory. In P. McReynolds, J. C. Rosen, & G. J. Chelune (Eds.), *Advances in psychological assessment* (Vol. 7, pp. 39–63). New York: Plenum.

Lorr, M., Bishop, P. F., & McNair, D. M. (1965). Interpersonal types among psychiatric patients. *Journal of Abnormal Psychology, 70,* 468–472.

Lorr, M., & DeJong, J. (1986). A short form of the interpersonal style inventory (ISI). *Journal of Clinical Psychology, 42,* 466–469.

Lorr, M., & McNair, D. M. (1963). An interpersonal behavior circle. *Journal of Abnormal and Social Psychology, 67,* 68–75.

Lorr, M., & McNair, D. M. (1965). Expansion of the interpersonal behavior circle. *Journal of Personality and Social Psychology, 2,* 823–830.

Lorr, M., & McNair, D. M. (1966). Methods relating to evaluation of therapeutic outcome. In L. A. Gottschalk & A. H. Auerbach (Eds.), *Methods of research in psychotherapy* (pp. 573–594). New York: Appleton-Century-Crofts.

Lorr, M., & McNair, D. M. (1967). *The Interpersonal Behavior Inventory, Form 4.* Washington, DC: Catholic University of America.

Lorr, M., & Strack, S. (1990). Wiggins Interpersonal Adjective Scales: A dimensional view. *Personality and Individual Differences, 11,* 423–425.

Lorr, M., & Suziedelis, A. (1969). Modes of interpersonal behavior. *British Journal of Social and Clinical Psychology, 8,* 124–132.

Lorr, M., & Suziedelis, A. (1990). Distinctive personality profiles of the Interpersonal Style Inventory. *Journal of Personality Assessment, 54,* 491–500.

Lorr, M., Suziedelis, A., & Kinnane, J. F. (1973). Modes of interpersonal response to peers. *Multivariate Behavioral Research, 8,* 427–438.

Lorr, M., & Youniss, R. P. (1986). *The Interpersonal Style Inventory.* Los Angeles, CA: Western Psychological Services.

Lovejoy, M. C., & Busch, L. M. (1993). Emotional and behavioral responses to aversive interpersonal behaviors. *Journal of Abnormal Psychology, 102,* 494–497.

Luborsky, L. (1984). *Principles of psychoanalytic psychotherapy: A manual for supportive-expressive (SE) treatment.* New York: Basic Books.

Luborsky, L., & Auerbach, A. H. (1985). The therapeutic relationship in psychodynamic psychotherapy: The research evidence and its meaning for practice. In American Psychiatric Association (Ed.), *Psychiatry update: Annual review* (Vol. 4, pp. 550–561). Washington, DC: American Psychiatric Association Press.

Lyons, J., Hirschberg, N., & Wilkinson, L. (1980). The radex structure of the Leary interpersonal behavior circle. *Multivariate Behavioral Research, 15,* 249–257.

Lyons, M. J., Merla, M. E., Ozer, D. J., & Hyler, S. E. (1990, August). *Relationship of the "Big-Five" factors to DSM-III personality disorders.* Paper presented at the annual meeting of the American Psychological Association, Boston, MA.

Mackenzie, T. B., Rosenberg, S. D., Bergen, B. J., & Tucker, G. J. (1978). The manipulative patient: An interactional approach. *Psychiatry, 41,* 264–271.

Madison, J. K., & Paddock, J. R. (1983). Assessing variability in circumplex models of personality. *Journal of Personality Assessment, 47,* 390–395.

Magnusson, D., & Endler, N. S. (Eds.). (1977). *Personality at the crossroads.* Hillsdale, NJ: Erlbaum.

Mahalik, J. R., Hill, C. E., O'Grady, K. E., & Thompson, B. J. (1993). Rater characteristics influencing rating on the Checklist of Psychotherapy Transactions–Revised. *Psychotherapy Research, 3,* 47–56.

Mahalik, J. R., Hill, C. E., Thompson, B. J., & O'Grady, K. E. (1989). *Predicting rater bias: Variables affecting ratings on Kiesler's Interpersonal Circle.* Unpublished manuscript, University of Maryland, College Park.

Mahoney, M. J. (1991). *Human change processes.* New York: Basic Books.

Maling, M. S., Gurtman, M. B., & Howard, K. I. (1995). The response of interpersonal problems to varying doses of psychotherapy. *Psychotherapy Research, 5,* 63–75.

Mancini, A. M. (1995). *The effects of discrimination and hostility on cardiovascular reactivity: A test of the transactional model.* Unpublished doctoral dissertation (in progress), Virginia Commonwealth University, Richmond.

Mantano, R. A., & Locke, K. D. (1995). Personality disorder scales as predictors of interpersonal problems of alcoholics. *Journal of Personality Disorders, 9,* 62–67.

Marcus, D. K., & Holahan, W. (1994). Interpersonal perception in group therapy: A social relations analysis. *Journal of Consulting and Clinical Psychology, 62,* 776–782.

Marcus, D. K., & Nardone, M. E. (1992). Depression and interpersonal rejection. *Clinical Psychology Review, 12,* 433–449.

Mardia, K. V. (1972). *Statistics of directional data.* New York: Academic Press.

Markel, N. N. (1969). *Psycholinguistics: An introduction to the study of speech and personality.* Homewood, IL: Dorsey.

Marks, I. M., & Herst, E. R. (1970). A survey of 1200 agoraphobics in Britain. *Social Psychiatry, 5,* 16–24.

Markus, H. (1977). Self-schemas and processing information about the self. *Journal of Personality and Social Psychology, 35,* 63–78.

Markus, H. (1990). Unresolved issues of self-representation. *Cognitive Therapy and Research, 14,* 241–253.

Markus, H., & Cross, S. (1990). The interpersonal self. In L. A. Pervin (Ed.), *Handbook of personality: Theory and research* (pp. 576–608). New York: Guilford.

Markus, H., & Nurius, P. (1986). Possible selves. *American Psychologist, 41,* 954–969.

Markus, H., & Zajonc, R. (1985). The cognitive perspective in social psychology. In G. Lindzey & E. Aronson (Eds.), *Handbook of social psychology* (3rd ed., Vol. 1, pp. 137–230). New York: Random House.

Marshall, G. N., Wortman, C. B., Vickers, R. R., & Kusulas, J. W. (1994). The five-factor model of personality as a framework for personality-health research. *Journal of Personality and Social Psychology, 67,* 278–286.

Masling, J. M. (1986). Orality, pathology and interpersonal behavior. In J. M. Masling (Ed.), *Empirical studies of psychoanalytic theories* (Vol. 2, pp. 73–106). Hillsdale, NJ: Erlbaum.

Masling, J. M., & Schwartz, M. A. (1979). A critique of research in psychoanalytic theory. *Genetic Psychology Monographs, 100,* 257–307.

McAdams, D. P. (1985). *Power, intimacy and the life story: Personological inquiries into identity.* New York: Guilford.

McAdams, D. P. (1993). *The stories we live by: Personal myths and the making of self.* New York: Morrow.

McCarthy, P. R. (1985). Impact Message Inventory. In D. J. Keyser & R. C. Sweetland (Eds.), *Test critiques* (Vol. 3, pp. 349–357). Kansas City, MO: Test Corporation of America.

McClelland, D. C. (1951). *Personality.* New York: Dryden.

McCormick, C. C., & Kavanagh, J. A. (1981). Scaling interpersonal checklist items to a circular model. *Applied Psychological Measurement, 5,* 421–447.

McCrae, R. R. (1994a). Psychopathology from the perspective of the five-factor model. In S. Strack & M. Lorr (Eds.), *Differentiating normal and abnormal personality* (pp. 26–39). New York: Springer.

McCrae, R. R. (1994b). A reformulation of Axis II: Personality and personality-related problems. In P. T. Costa, Jr., & T. A. Widiger (Eds.), *Personality disorders and the five-factor model of personality* (pp. 303–309). Washington, DC: American Psychological Association.

McCrae, R. R., & Costa, P. T., Jr. (1986). Clinical assessment can benefit from recent advances in personality psychology. *American Psychologist, 41,* 1001–1003.

McCrae, R. R., & Costa, P. T., Jr. (1989). The structure of interpersonal traits: Wiggins' circumplex and the five-factor model. *Journal of Personality and Social Psychology, 56,* 586–595.

McCrae, R. R., & Costa, P. T., Jr. (1990). *Personality in adulthood.* New York: Guilford.

McCrae, R. R., & John, O. P. (1991). An introduction to the five-factor model and its applications. *Journal of Personality, 60,* 175–215.

McCullough, J. P., & Carr, K. F. (1987). Stage process design: A predictive confirmation structure for the single case. *Psychotherapy, 24,* 759–768.

McCullough, J. P., McCune, K. J., Kaye, A. L., Braith, J. A., Friend, R., Roberts, W. C., Belyea-Caldwell, S., Norris, S. L. W., & Hampton, C. (1994). Comparison of a community dysthymia sample at screening with a matched group of nondepressed community controls. *Journal of Nervous and Mental Disease, 182,* 402–407.

McGovern, S. R. (1985). *Degree of congruence between verbal and nonverbal behavior, expressed personality correlates, and interpersonal functioning.* Unpublished master's thesis, Emory University, Atlanta, GA.

McLean, P. D. (1976). Therapeutic decision-making in the behavioral treatment of depression. In P. O. Davidson (Ed.), *The behavioral management of anxiety, depression, and pain* (pp. 54–90). New York: Brunner/Mazel.

McLemore, C. W., & Benjamin, L. S. (1979). Whatever happened to interpersonal diagnosis? A psychosocial alternative to DSM-III. *American Psychologist, 34,* 17–34.

McLemore, C. W., & Brokaw, D. W. (1987). Personality disorders as dysfunctional interpersonal behavior. *Journal of Personality Disorders, 1,* 270–285.

McLemore, C. W., & Hart, P. P. (1982). Relational psychotherapy: The clinical facilitation of intimacy. In J. C. Anchin & D. J. Kiesler (Eds.), *Handbook of interpersonal psychotherapy* (pp. 227–247). Elmsford, NY: Pergamon.

McLeod, M., & Nowicki, S., Jr. (1985). Interpersonal style and cooperative behavior in preschool age children. *Journal of Personality, 117,* 85–96.

McMullen, L. M. (1989). Use of figurative language in successful and unsuccessful cases of psychotherapy: Three comparisons. *Metaphor and Symbolic Activity, 4,* 203–225.

McMullen, L. M., & Conway, J. B. (1994). Dominance and nurturance in the figurative expressions of psychotherapy clients. *Psychotherapy Research, 4,* 43–57.

McNair, D. M., & Lorr, M. (1965). Differential typing of psychiatric outpatients. *The Psychological Record, 15,* 33–41.

McNeel, S. P., & Messick, D. M. (1970). A Bayesian analysis of subjective probabilities of interpersonal relationships. *Acta Psychologia, 34,* 311–321.

McNeil, B. W., & Worthen, V. (1989). The parallel process in psychotherapy supervision. *Professional Psychology: Research and Practice, 20,* 329–333.

Mead, G. H. (1934). *Mind, self and society.* Chicago: University of Chicago Press.

Meddin, J. (1982). Cognitive therapy and symbolic interactionism: Expanding clinical potential. *Cognitive Therapy and Research, 6,* 151–165.

Mehrabian, A. (1971). *Silent messages.* Belmont, CA: Wadsworth.

Mehrabian, A. (1972). *Nonverbal communication.* Chicago: Aldine.

Meichenbaum, D., & Gilmore, J. B. (1984). The nature of unconscious processes: A cognitive-behavioral perspective. In K. Bowers & D. Meichenbaum (Eds.), *The unconscious reconsidered.* New York: Wiley.

Meredith, J. M. (1986). Perception of therapists: Influences of perceiver and therapist interpersonal styles. *Dissertation Abstracts International, 47,* 2175–2176B.

Merenda, P. F. (1987). Toward a four-factor theory of temperament and/or personality. *Journal of Personality Assessment, 51,* 367–374.

Merton, R. K. (1948). The self-fulfilling prophecy. *The Antioch Review, 8,* 193–210.

Merton, R. K. (1957). *Social theory and social structure.* London: Collier-MacMillan.

Meyers, H. C. (Ed.). (1986). *Between analyst and patient: New directions in countertransference and transference.* Hillsdale, NJ: Analytic Press.

Mikail, S. F., Henderson, P. R., & Tasca, G. A. (1994). An interpersonally based model of chronic pain: An application of attachment theory. *Clinical Psychology Review, 14,* 1–16.

Milestone, S. F. (1984). The relationship between interpersonal impacts of spouses and marital satisfaction. *Dissertation Abstracts International, 45,* 1293–B.

Miller, D. T., & Turnbull, W. (1986). Expectancies and interpersonal processes. *Annual Review of Psychology, 37,* 233–256.

Miller, G. A., Galanter, E., & Pribram, K. H. (1960). *Plans and the structure of behavior.* New York: Holt, Rinehart & Winston.

Miller, T. R. (1991). The psychotherapeutic utility of the five-factor model of personality: A clinician's experience. *Journal of Personality Assessment, 57,* 415–433.

Millon, T. (1969). *Modern psychopathology: A biosocial approach to maladaptive learning and functioning.* Philadelphia, PA: Saunders.

Millon, T. (1981). *Disorders of personality. DSM: Axis II.* New York: Wiley.

Millon, T. (1987). *Millon Clinical Multiaxial Inventory-II: Manual for the MCMI-II.* Minneapolis, MN: National Computer Systems.

Milton, F., & Hafner, J. (1979). The outcome of behavior therapy for agoraphobia in relation to marital adjustment. *Archives of General Psychiatry, 36,* 807–811.

Mintz, E. (1972). Group supervision: An experiential approach. *International Journal of Group Psychiatry, 28,* 467–479.

Mischel, W. (1968). *Personality and assessment.* New York: Wiley.

Mischel, W. (1973). Toward a cognitive social learning reconceptualization of personality. *Psychological Review, 80,* 252–283.

Mischel, W., & Peake, P. K. (1982). Beyond *deja vu* in the search for cross-situational consistency. *Psychological Review, 89,* 730–755.

Mohr, D. C., Beutler, L. E., Engle, D., Shohan-Solomon, V., Bergan, J., Kaszniak, A. W., & Yost, E. B. (1990). Identification of patients at risk for nonresponse and negative outcome in psychotherapy. *Journal of Consulting and Clinical Psychology, 58,* 622–628.

Monts, J. K., Zurcher, L. A., & Nydegger, R. V. (1977). Interpersonal self-deception and personality correlates. *The Journal of Social Psychology, 103,* 91–99.

Moos, R. H. (1968). Situational analysis of a therapeutic community milieu. *Journal of Abnormal Psychology, 73,* 49–61.

Moos, R. H., & Speisman, J. C. (1962). Group compatibility and productivity. *Journal of Abnormal and Social Psychology, 65,* 190–195.

Moras, K., & Strupp, H. H. (1982). Pretherapy interpersonal relations, patients' alliance, and outcome in brief therapy. *Archives of General Psychiatry, 39,* 405–409.

Moras, K., Waterhouse, G. J., & Suh, C. (1981, June). *Toward a standard, pantheoretical measure of therapist relationship variables: The Impact Message Inventory.* Paper presented at the annual conference of the Society for Psychotherapy Research, Aspen, CO.

Morey, L. C. (1985). An empirical comparison of interpersonal and DSM-III approaches to classification of personality disorders. *Psychiatry, 48,* 358–364.

Morey, L. C., Waugh, M. H., & Blashfield, R. K. (1985). MMPI scales for DSM-III personality disorders: Their derivation and correlates. *Journal of Personality Assessment, 49,* 245–251.

Morran, D. K., Robinson, F. F., & Stockton, R. A. (1985). Feedback exchange in counseling groups: An analysis of message content and receiver acceptance as a function of leader versus member delivery, session, and valence. *Journal of Counseling Psychology, 32,* 57–67.

Morran, D. K., & Stockton, R. A. (1985). Perspectives on group research programs. *Journal for Specialists in Group Work, 10,* 163–174.

Moskowitz, D. S. (1982). Coherence and cross-situational generality in personality: A new analysis of old problems. *Journal of Personality and Social Psychology, 43,* 754–768.

Moskowitz, D. S. (1986). Comparison of self-reports, reports by knowledgeable informants, and behavioral observation data. *Journal of Personality, 54,* 294–317.

Moskowitz, D. S. (1988). Cross-situational generality in the laboratory: Dominance and friendliness. *Journal of Personality and Social Psychology, 54,* 829–839.

Moskowitz, D. S. (1990). Convergence of self-reports and independent observers: Dominance and friendliness. *Journal of Personality and Social Psychology, 58,* 1096–1106.

Moskowitz, D. S. (1993). Dominance and friendliness: On the interaction of gender and situation. *Journal of Personality, 61,* 387–409.

Moskowitz, D. S. (1994). Cross-situational generality and the interpersonal circumplex. *Journal of Personality and Social Psychology, 66,* 921–933.

Moskowitz, D. S., & Cote, S. (1995). Do interpersonal traits predict affect? A comparison of three models. *Journal of Personality and Social Psycholgy, 69,* 915–924.

Moskowitz, D. S., Suh, E. J., & Desaulniers, J. (1994). Situational influences on gender differences in agency and communion. *Journal of Personality and Social Psychology, 66,* 753–761.

Mueller, W. J. (1969). Patterns of behavior and their reciprocal impact in the family and psychotherapy. *Journal of Counseling Psychology Monographs, 16,* 1–25.

Mueller, W. J., & Dilling, C. A. (1968). Therapist-client interview behavior and personality characteristics of therapists. *Journal of Projective Techniques and Personality Assessment, 32,* 281–288.

Mueller, W. J., & Dilling, C. A. (1969). Studying interpersonal themes in psychotherapy research. *Journal of Counseling Psychology, 16,* 50–58.

Mulford, H. A. (1955). *Toward an instrument to identify the self, significant others, and alcohol in the symbolic environment: An empirical study.* Unpublished dissertation, Iowa State University, Ames.

Mungas, D. M., Trontel, E. H., & Winegardner, J. (1981). Multivariable-multimethod analysis of the dimensions of interpersonal behavior. *Journal of Research in Personality, 15,* 107–121.

Muran, J. C. (1991). A reformulation of the ABC model: Implications for assessment and theory. *Clinical Psychology Review, 11,* 399–418.

Muran, J. C. (1993). The self in cognitive-behavioral research: An interpersonal perspective. *The Behavior Therapist, 16,* 69–73.

Muran, J. C., & Safran, J. D. (1990, November). *Measuring session change and predicting outcome in cognitive therapy.* Poster presented at the annual meeting of the Association for Advancement of Behavior Therapy, San Francisco, CA.

Muran, J. C., Samstag, L. W., Jilton, R., Batchelder, S., & Winston, A. (1992a). *Measuring patient–therapist interactions across time from a third-party perspective.* Unpublished manuscript, Beth Israel Medical Center, New York, NY.

Muran, J. C., Samstag, L. W., Jilton, R., Batchelder, S., & Winston, A. (1992b). *Relation of interpersonal behavior and transactions to alliance and outcome over time in short-term psychotherapy.* Unpublished manuscript, Beth Israel Medical Center, New York, NY.

Muran, J. C., Samstag, L. W., Segal, Z. V., & Winston, A. (1992). *Procedural manual for interpersonal scenarios.* Pittsburgh, PA: Behavioral Measurement Database Services.

Muran, J. C., & Segal, Z. V. (1992). The development of an idiographic measure of self-schemas: An illustration of the construction and use of self-scenarios. *Psychotherapy, 29,* 524–535.

Muran, J. C., Segal, Z. V., & Samstag, L. W. (1994). Self-scenarios as a repeated measure outcome measurment of self-schemas in short-term cognitive therapy. *Behavior Therapy, 25,* 255–274.

Muran, J. C., Segal, Z. V., Samstag, L. W., & Crawford, C. E. (1994). Patient pretreatment interpersonal problems and therapeutic alliance in short-term cognitive therapy. *Journal of Consulting and Clinical Psychology, 62,* 185–190.

Murdock, N. L., Banta, J., Stromseth, J., Viene, D., & Brown, T. M. (1995). *Joining the club: Factors related to choice of theoretical orientation.* Unpublished manuscript, University of Missouri-Kansas City.

Murray, H. A. (1951). Toward a classification of interaction. In T. Parsons & E. A. Shils (Eds.), *Toward a general theory of action* (7th ed., pp. 434–464). Cambridge, MA: Harvard University Press.

Murrell, S. A. (1971). An open system model for psychotherapy evaluation. *Community Mental Health Journal, 7,* 209–217.

Muten, E. (1991). Self-reports, spouse ratings, and psychophysiological assessment in a behavioral medicine program: An application of the five-factor model. *Journal of Personality Assessment, 57,* 449–464.

Nelson, A. P. (1984). Rigidity in the interpersonal functioning of psychiatric patients and normals. *Dissertation Abstracts International, 44,* 2902–B.

Nelson, R. E., & Craighead, W. E. (1977). Selective recall of positive and negative feedback, self-control behaviors, and depression. *Journal of Abnormal Psychology, 86,* 379–388.

Nisbett, R., & Ross, L. (1980). *Human inference: Strategies and shortcomings of social judgment.* Englewood Cliffs, NJ: Prentice-Hall.

Norman, W. T. (1963). Toward an adequate taxonomy of personality attributes: Replicated factor structure in peer nomination personality ratings. *Journal of Abnormal and Social Psychology, 66,* 574–583.

Nowicki, S., Jr., & Manheim, S. (1991). Interpersonal complementarity and time of interaction in female relationships. *Journal of Research in Personality, 25,* 322–333.

O'Connell, T. J. (1979). Interpersonal interactions: Social situational and personality determinants. *Dissertation Abstracts International, 40,* 1869–B.

O'Dell, J. W. (1967). Group size and emotional interaction. *Dissertation Abstracts International, 27,* 3094–3095A.

O'Dell, J. W. (1968). Group size and emotional interaction. *Journal of Personality and Social Psychology, 8,* 75–78.

Oden, T. C. (1976). *TAG: Transactional awareness game.* New York: Harper & Row.

Okiyama, S. L., & Vande Kemp, H. (1991). *The complementarity principle: Interpersonal status as an intervening variable.* Unpublished manuscript, Fuller Theological Seminary, Pasadena, CA.

Olson, D. H. (1986). Circumplex Model VII: Validation studies and FACES III. *Family Process, 25,* 337–351.

Olson, D. H., Russell, C. S., & Sprenkle, D. H. (1983). Circumplex model of marital and family systems: Theoretical update. *Family Process, 22,* 69–83.

Olson, D. H., Sprenkle, D. H., & Russell, C. S. (1979). Circumplex models of marital and family systems: Cohesion and adaptability dimensions, family types, and clinical applications. *Family Process, 18,* 3–28.

Olsson, J. E. (1968). The influence of the personality of the perceiver upon perception of hostility in other persons. *Dissertation Abstracts International, 28,* 2629B.

Orford, J. (1986). The rules of interpersonal complementarity: Does hostility beget hostility and dominance, submission? *Psychological Review, 93,* 365–377.

Orford, J. (1994). The interpersonal circumplex: A theory and method for applied psychology. *Human Relations, 47,* 1347–1375.

Oxenford, C., & Nowicki, S., Jr. (1989). The relation of hostile nonverbal communication styles and popularity in pre-adolescent children. *Journal of Genetic Psychology, 150,* 39–44.

Paddock, J. R., & Nowicki, S. (1986). The circumplexity of Leary's interpersonal circle: A multidimensional scaling perspective. *Journal of Personality Assessment, 50,* 279–289.

Paddock, J. R., & Nowicki, S. (1987). An examination of the Leary circumplex through the Interpersonal Check List. *Journal of Research in Personality, 20,* 107–144.

Paddock, J. R., Potts, M. A., Kiesler, D. J., & Nowicki, S. P., Jr. (1986, May). *Ipsative scoring of interpersonal circle measures.* Paper presented at the annual Southeastern Psychological Association meeting, Kissimmee, FL.

Paddock, J. R., Woodruff, D. L., & Pate, C. (1984). Examining nonspecific relationship factors in the behavioral treatment of seriously emotionally disturbed (SED) adolescents: An interpersonal communications approach. *Journal of Clinical Child Psychology, 13,* 74–80.

Palmer, J., & Byrne, D. (1970). Attraction toward dominant and submissive strangers: Similarity versus complementarity. *Journal of Experimental Research in Personality, 4,* 108–115.

Pande, S. K., & Gart, J. J. (1968). A method to quantify reciprocal influence between therapist and patient in psychotherapy. In J. M. Shlien (Ed.), *Research in psychotherapy* (Vol. 3, pp. 395–413). Washington, DC: American Psychological Association.

Pasciuti, F. M. (1982). An analysis of psychotherapy supervision on the dimensions of complementarity, process interaction, and perceived relationship. *Dissertation Abstracts International, 43,* 531–B.

Passini, F. T., & Norman, W. T. (1966). A universal conception of personality structure? *Journal of Personality and Social Psychology, 4,* 44–49.

Patterson, G. R. (1976). The aggressive child: Victim and architect of a coercive system. In L. A. Hamerlynck & L. C. Handy (Eds.), *Behavior modification and families: I. Theory and research* (pp. 267–311). New York: Brunner/Mazel.

Patterson, G. R. (1982). *Coercive family process.* Eugene, OR: Castaglia.

Patton, M., & Robbins, S. B. (1982). Kohut's self-psychology as a model for college student counseling. *Professional Psychology, 13,* 876–888.

Paulhus, D. L., & Martin, C. L. (1987). The structure of personality capabilities. *Journal of Personality and Social Psychology, 52,* 354–365.

Paulhus, D. L., & Martin, C. L. (1988). Functional flexibility: A new conception of interpersonal flexibility. *Journal of Personality and Social Psychology, 55,* 88–101.

Paunonen, S. V., Jackson, D. N., Trzebinski, J., & Forsterling, F. (1992). Personality structure across cultures: A multimethod evaluation. *Journal of Personality and Social Psychology, 62,* 447–456.

Penberthy, A. R. (1982). Perceived control, interpersonal impacts, and adjustment to a longterm, invasive health procedure. *Dissertation Abstracts International, 43,* 882–B.

Perkins, M. J., Kiesler, D. J., Anchin, J. C., Chirico, B. M., Kyle, E. M., & Federman, E. J. (1979). The Impact Message Inventory: A new measure of relationship in counseling/psychotherapy and other dyads. *Journal of Counseling Psychology, 26,* 363–367.

Perlmutter, K. B. (1980). Perception of interpersonal style as a function of mode of stimulus presentation in college males. *Dissertation Abstracts International, 41,* 1520B.

Perlmutter, K. B., Paddock, J. R., & Duke, M. P. (1985). The role of verbal, vocal, and nonverbal cues in the communication of evoking message styles. *Journal of Research in Personality, 19,* 31–43.

Perls, F. (1976). *The gestalt approach and eye witness to therapy.* New York: Bantam.

Pervin, L. A. (1968). Performance and satisfaction as a function of individual-environment fit. *Psychological Bulletin, 69,* 56–68.

Peterson, D. R. (1977). A functional approach to the study of person–person interactions. In D. Magnusson & N. S. Endler (Eds.), *Personality at the crossroads: Current issues in interactional psychology* (pp. 305–313). Hillsdale, NJ: Erlbaum.

Peterson, D. R. (1979a). Assessing interpersonal relationships by means of interaction records. *Behavioral Assessment, 1,* 221–236.

Peterson, D. R. (1979b). Assessing interpersonal relationships in natural settings. *New Directions for Methodology of Behavioral Science, 2,* 33–54.

Peterson, D. R. (1979c). *Instructions for collecting and interpreting interaction records.* New Brunswick, NJ: Rutgers State University.

Peterson, D. R. (1982). Functional analysis of interpersonal behavior. In J. C. Anchin & D. J. Kiesler (Eds.), *Handbook of interpersonal psychotherapy* (pp. 149–167). Elmsford, NY: Pergamon.

Peterson, D. R. (1989). Interpersonal goal conflict. In L. A. Pervin (Ed.), *Goal concepts in personality and social psychology* (pp. 327–361). Hillsdale, NJ: Erlbaum.

Pfohl, B., Stangl, D., & Zimmerman, M. (1983). *Structured interview for DSM-III-R personality disorders (SIDP).* Iowa City: University of Iowa Department of Psychiatry.

Phelps, R. E., & Slater, M. A. (1985). Sequential interactions that discriminate high- and low-problem single mother–son dyads. *Journal of Consulting and Clinical Psychology, 53,* 684–692.

Phillips, N. (1983). *Selection of items with circumplex properties.* Unpublished manuscript, University of British Columbia, Vancouver, Canada.

Pilkonis, P. (1988). Personality prototypes among depressives: Themes of dependency and autonomy. *Journal of Personality Disorders, 2,* 144–152.

Pincus, A. L. (1994). The interpersonal circumplex and the interpersonal theory: Perspectives on personality and its pathology. In S. Strack & M. Lorr (Eds.), *Differentiating normal and abnormal personality* (pp. 114–136). New York: Springer.

Pincus, A. L., & Wiggins, J. S. (1990). Interpersonal problems and conceptions of personality disorders. *Journal of Personality Disorders, 4,* 342–352.

Pincus, A. L., & Wiggins, J. S. (1992). An expanded perspective on interpersonal assessment. *Journal of Counseling and Development, 71,* 91–94.

Piper, W. E., Azim, H. F., Joyce, A. S., McCallum, M., Nixon, G. W., & Segal, P. S. (1991). Quality of object relations versus interpersonal functioning as predictors of therapeutic alliance and psychotherapy outcome. *Journal of Nervous and Mental Disease, 179,* 432–438.

Plutchik, R. (1962). *The emotions: Facts, theories, and a new model.* New York: Random House.

Plutchik, R. (1980). *Emotion: A psychoevolutionary synthesis.* New York: Harper & Row.

Plutchik, R. (1991). *The emotions* (Rev. ed.). Lanham, MD: University Press of America.

Plutchik, R., & Conte, H. R. (1986). Quantitative assessment of personality disorders. In R. Michels & J. O. Cavenar, Jr. (Eds.), *Psychiatry* (Vol. 1, pp. 1–13). Philadelphia: Lippincott.

Plutchik, R., & Conte, H. R. (Eds.). (in press). *Circumplex models of personality and emotion.* Washington, DC: American Psychological Association.

Plutchik, R., & Kellerman, H. (1974). *Emotions Profile Index manual.* Los Angeles: Western Psychological Services.

Plutchik, R., & Platman, S. R. (1977). Personality connotations of psychiatric diagnosis: Implications for a similarity model. *Journal of Nervous and Mental Disease, 165,* 418–422.

Pollock, T. E. (1990). *Parallel process: An empirical investigation.* Unpublished doctoral dissertation, Virginia Consortium for Professional Psychology, William & Mary University, Williamsburg, VA.

Pond, J. H. (1985). Psychological androgyny and adjustment: An interpersonal conceptualization of the adaptive consequences of sex-role orientation. *Dissertation Abstracts International, 46,* 1698–B.

Powers, M. J., Champion, L. A., & Aris, S. J. (1988). The development of a measure of social support: The Significant Others Scale (SOS). *British Journal of Clinical Psychology, 27,* 349–358.

Pyszczynski, T. T., Greenberg, J., & LaPrelle, J. (1985). Biased search for social comparison information after success and failure. *Journal of Experimental Social Psychology, 21,* 195–211.

Radecki-Bush, C. (1989). *On the nature of interpersonal problems: Instrumental and expressive traits, needs, and behaviors.* Unpublished manuscript, Virginia Commonwealth University, Richmond.

Raulin, M. L., & Henderson, C. A. (1987). Perception of implicit relationships between personality traits by schizotypic college students: A pilot study. *Journal of Clinical Psychology, 43,* 463–467.

Raush, H. L. (1965). Interaction sequences. *Journal of Personality and Social Psychology, 2,* 487–499.

Raush, H. L., Dittman, A., & Taylor, T. (1959). The interpersonal behavior of children in residential treatment. *Journal of Abnormal and Social Psychology, 58,* 9–26.

Raush, H. L., Farbman, I., & Llewellyn, L. (1960). Person, setting, and change in social interaction: II. A normal-control study. *Human Relations, 13,* 305–332.

Reagan, S. A. (1978). *The Impact Message Inventory: An interpersonal measure of assertive behavior.* Unpublished master's thesis, Virginia Commonwealth University, Richmond.

Reagan, S. A. (1979). The interpersonal and behavioral dimensions of assertive refusal. *Dissertation Abstracts International, 40,* 5416–B.

Reid, J. B. (1968). Reciprocity in family interaction. *Dissertation Abstracts International, 29,* 378–379B.

Rice, L. N., & Greenberg, L. S. (1984). *Patterns of change: Intensive analysis of psychotherapeutic process.* New York: Guilford.

Rice, P. L. K. (1970). The modification of interpersonal roles. *Dissertation Abstracts International, 30,* 4797B.

Rime, B., Bouvy, H., Leborgne, B., & Rouillon, F. (1978). Psychopathy and nonverbal behavior in an interpersonal situation. *Journal of Abnormal Psychology, 87,* 636–643.

Rinn, J. L. (1965). Structure of phenomenal domains. *Psychological Review, 72,* 445–466.

Rioch, M. J. (1980). The dilemmas of supervision in dynamic psychotherapy. In A. K. Hess (Ed.), *Psychotherapy supervision: Theory, research and practice* (pp. 68–77). New York: Wiley.

Robbins, S. B., & Dupont, P. (1992). Narcissistic needs of the self and perceptions of interpersonal behavior. *Journal of Counseling Psychology, 39,* 462–467.

Roe, A. (1956). *The psychology of occupations.* New York: Wiley.

Roe, A. (1957). Early determinants of vocational choice. *Journal of Counseling Psychology, 4,* 212–217.

Rogers, C. R. (1959). A theory of therapy, personality, and interpersonal relationships, as developed in the client-centered framework. In S. Koch (Ed.), *Psychology: A study of science: Vol. 3. Formulations of the person and the social context* (pp. 184–256). New York: McGraw-Hill.

Rogers, T., Kuiper, N., & Kirker, W. (1977). Self-reference and the encoding of personal information. *Journal of Personality and Social Psychology, 35,* 677–688.

Rollins, B. C., & Thomas, D. L. (1979). Parental support, power, and control techniques in the socialization of children. In W. R. Burr, R. Hill, F. I. Nye, & I. L. Reiss (Eds.), *Contemporary theories about the family* (Vol. 1, pp. 317–364). New York: Free Press.

Romano, R. L. (1960). The use of the interpersonal system of diagnosis in marital counseling. *Journal of Counseling Psychology, 7,* 10–18.

Romney, D. M., & Bynner, J. M. (1989). Evaluation of a circumplex model of DSM-III personality disorders. *Journal of Research in Personality, 23,* 525–538.

Romney, D. M., & Bynner, J. M. (1992). A simplex model of five DSM-III personality disorders. *Journal of Personality Disorders, 6,* 34–39.

Rosch, E. (1975). Cognitive reference points. *Cognitive Psychology, 7,* 532–547.

Rosch, E. (1978). Principles of categorization. In E. Rosch & B. B. Lloyd (Eds.), *Cognition and categorization* (pp. 27–71). Hillsdale, NJ: Erlbaum.

Rosch, E., & Mervis, C. (1975). Family resemblances: Studies in the internal structure of categories. *Cognitive Psychology, 7,* 573–605.

Rosenberg, M. (1979). *Conceiving the self.* New York: Basic Books.

Rosenfeld, H. M. (1967). Nonverbal reciprocation of approval: An experimental analysis. *Journal of Experimental Social Psychology, 3,* 102–111.

Rosenthal, R. (1973). On the social psychology of the self-fulfilling prophecy: Further evidence for Pygmalion effects and their mediating mechanisms. *MSS Modular Publications, 53,* 1–28.

Rosenthal, R., & Rubin, D. (1978). Interpersonal expectancy effects: The first 345 studies. *The Behavioral and Brain Sciences, 3,* 377–415.

Ross, D., & Kapp, F. T. (1962). A technique for self-analysis of countertransference: Use of the psychoanalyst's visual images in response to the patient's dreams. *Journal of the American Psychoanalytic Association, 10,* 645–657.

Rotter, J. B. (1954). *Social learning and clinical psychology.* New York: Prentice-Hall.

Rottschafer, R., & Renzaglia, G. (1962). The relationship of dependent-like verbal behaviors to counselor style and induced set. *Journal of Consulting Psychology, 26,* 172–177.

Rudy, J. P., McLemore, C. W., & Gorsuch, R. L. (1985). Interpersonal behavior and therapeutic progress: Therapists and clients rate themselves and each other. *Psychiatry, 48,* 264–281.

Ruesch, J., & Bateson, G. (1951). *Communication: The social matrix of psychiatry.* New York: Norton.

Russell, J. A. (1980). A circumplex model of affect. *Journal of Personality and Social Psychology, 39,* 1161–1168.

Russell, J. A., Lewicka, M., & Niit, T. (1989). A cross-cultural study of a circumplex model of affect. *Journal of Personality and Social Psychology, 57,* 848–856.

Sackheim, H. A., & Wegner, A. Z. (1986). Attributional patterns in depression and euthymia. *Archives of General Psychiatry, 43,* 553–560.

Safran, J. D. (1984a). Assessing the cognitive interpersonal cycle. *Cognitive Therapy and Research, 8,* 333–348.

Safran, J. D. (1984b). Some implications of Sullivan's interpersonal theory for cognitive therapy. In M. A. Reda & M. J. Mahoney (Eds.), *Cognitive psychotherapies: Recent developments in theory, research and practice* (pp. 251–272). Cambridge, MA: Ballinger.

Safran, J. D. (1990a). Towards a refinement of cognitive therapy in light of interpersonal theory: I. Theory. *Clinical Psychology Review, 10,* 87–105.

Safran, J. D. (1990b). Towards a refinement of cognitive therapy in light of interpersonal theory: II. Practice. *Clinical Psychology Review, 10,* 107–121.

Safran, J. D. (1993). The therapeutic alliance rupture as a transtheoretical phenomenon: Definitional and conceptual issues. *Journal of Psychotherapy Integration, 3,* 33–49.

Safran, J. D., & Greenberg, L. S. (1987). Affect and the unconscious: A cognitive perspective. In J. Stern (Ed.), *Theories of the unconscious* (pp. 191–212). Hillsdale, NJ: Analytic Press.

Safran, J. D., & Greenberg, L. S. (1988). Feeling, thinking and acting: A cognitive framework for psychotherapy integration. *Journal of Cognitive Psychotherapy: An International Quarterly, 2,* 109–130.

Safran, J. D., & Hill, C. (1989). *The Interpersonal Schema Questionnaire.* Toronto, Canada: Clarke Institute of Psychiatry.

Safran, J. D., McMain, S., Crocker, P., & Murray, P. (1990). Therapeutic alliance rupture as a therapy event for empirical investigation. *Psychotherapy, 27,* 154–165.

Safran, J. D., & Muran, J. C. (1994). Toward a working alliance between research and practice. In P. F. Talley, H. H. Strupp, & S. M. Butler (Eds.), *Psychotherapy research and practice: Bridging the gap* (pp. 206–226). New York: Basic Books.

Safran, J. D., & Muran, J. C. (1995a). Resolving therapeutic alliance ruptures: Diversity and integration. *In Session: Psychotherapy in Practice, 1,* 81–92.

Safran, J. D., & Muran, J. C. (Eds.). (1995b). Special issue: The therapeutic alliance. *In Session: Psychotherapy in Practice, 1,* 1–92.

Safran, J. D., Muran, J. C., & Winston, A. (1992, September). *Resolving problems in the therapeutic alliance* (Grant proposal 1R03MH50246-01). National Institute of Mental Health, Washington, DC.

Safran, J. D., & Segal, Z. V. (1990). *Interpersonal process in cognitive therapy.* New York: Basic Books.

Safran, J. D., Segal, Z. V., Hill, C., & Whiffen, V. (1990). Refining strategies for research on self-representations in emotional disorders. *Cognitive Therapy and Research, 14,* 143–160.

Safran, J. D., Vallis, T. M., Segal, Z. V., & Shaw, B. F. (1986). Assessing core cognitive processes in cognitive therapy. *Cognitive Therapy and Research, 10,* 509–526.

Saltzman, C., Luetgert, M. J., Roth, C. H., Creaser, J., & Howard, T. (1976). Formation of a therapeutic relationship: Experiences during the initial phase of psychotherapy as predictors of treatment duration and outcome. *Journal of Consulting and Clinical Psychology, 44,* 546–555.

Salzman, C., Shader, R., Scott, D. A., & Bonstock, W. (1970). Interviewer anger and patient dropout in a walk-in clinic. *Comprehensive Psychiatry, 11,* 267–273.

Sarason, B. R., Sarason, I. G., & Pierce, G. R. (1990). *Social support: An interactional view.* New York: Wiley.

Sarason, B. R., Shearin, E. N., Pierce, G. R., & Sarason, I. G. (1987). Interrelations of social support measures: Theoretical and practical implications. *Journal of Personality and Social Psychology, 52,* 813–832.

Saucier, G. (1992). Benchmarks: Integrating affective and interpersonal circles with the Big-Five personality factors. *Journal of Personality and Social Psychology, 62,* 1025–1035.

Saxby, S. P. (1982). An investigation into the effects of rater sex and cognitive styles and ratee labels and interpersonal styles on the perception of interpersonal styles. *Dissertation Abstracts International, 43,* 1306–B.

Schachtel, E. G. (1959). *Metamorphosis.* New York: Basic Books.

Schaefer, E. S. (1959). A circumplex model for maternal behavior. *Journal of Abnormal and Social Psychology, 59,* 226–235.

Schaefer, E. S. (1961). Converging conceptual models for maternal behavior and for child behavior. In J. G. Glidewell (Ed.), *Parental attitudes and child behavior* (pp. 124–146). Springfield, IL: Thomas.

Schaefer, E. S. (1965). A configurational analysis of children's report of parent behavior. *Journal of Consulting Psychology, 29,* 552–557.

Schaefer, E. S., & Plutchik, R. (1966). Interrelationships of emotions, traits, and diagnostic constructs. *Psychological Reports, 18,* 399–410.

Schaffer, N. D. (1982). Multidimensional measures of therapist behaviors as predictors of outcome. *Psychological Bulletin, 92,* 670–681.

Scheff, T. J. (1966). *Being mentally ill: A sociological theory.* Chicago, IL: Aldine/Atherton.

Scheflen, A. E. (1967). On the structuring of human communication. *American Behavioral Scientist, 10,* 8–12.

Scheiner, S. B. (1969). Differential perception of personality characteristics in cross-cultural interaction. *Dissertation Abstracts International, 30,* 477B.

Schlosberg, H. S. (1952). The description of facial expressions in terms of two dimensions. *Journal of Experimental Psychology, 44,* 229–237.

Schmidt, J. A. (1989). *Interpersonal ratings of channel incongruence of normal versus personality disordered individuals.* Unpublished master's thesis, Virginia Commonwealth University, Richmond.

Schmidt, J. A. (1994). *Revision of the Impact Message Inventory: Reconstruction to a circumplex criterion.* Unpublished doctoral dissertation, Virginia Commonwealth University, Richmond.

Schmidt, J. A., Wagner, C. C., & Kiesler, D. J. (1993). DSM-IV Axis II: Dimensional ratings? "Yes"; Big Five? "Perhaps later." *Psychological Inquiry, 4,* 119–121.

Schmidt, J. A., Wagner, C. C., & Kiesler, D. J. (1994). *The Impact Message Inventory Octant Scales: Initial evaluation of structural and psychometric characteristics.* Unpublished manuscript, Virginia Commonwealth University, Richmond.

Schopler, J. H. (1959). The relation of patient–therapist personality similarity to the outcome of psychotherapy. *Dissertation Abstracts International, 19,* 2659.

Schreiber, R. D. (1984). *Reactions to depressed individuals: An analogue study.* Unpublished doctoral dissertation, Pacific Graduate School of Psychology, Palo Alto, CA.

Schuldt, W. (1966). Psychotherapists' approach–avoidance responses and clients' expressions of dependency. *Journal of Counseling Psychology, 13,* 178–183.

Schulz, D. (1977). *Growth psychology: Models of the healthy personality.* New York: Van Nostrand-Reinhold.

Schutz, W. C. (1958). *FIRO: A three-dimensional theory of interpersonal behavior.* New York: Holt, Rinehart & Winston.

Schwaninger-Morse, F. (1979). The consistency of interpersonal impact style. *Dissertation Abstracts International, 40,* 4507–B.

Schwartz, D. (1980). *An application of Leary's circumplex model of personality to the question of roommate compatibility.* Unpublished master's thesis, Emory University, Atlanta, GA.

Schwartz, K. M. (1980). Self-disclosure and interpersonal style: A communications analysis. *Dissertation Abstracts International, 41,* 1525B.

Scott, W. A. (1968). Conceptions of normality. In E. F. Borgatta & W. W. Lambert (Eds.), *Handbook of personality theory and research* (pp. 974–1006). Chicago, IL: Rand McNally.

Searles, H. (1955). The informational value of the supervisor's emotional experiences. *Psychiatry, 18,* 135–146.

Secord, P. F., & Backman, C. W. (1961). Personality theory and the problem of stability and change in individual behavior: An interpersonal approach. *Psychological Review, 68,* 21–32.

Secord, P. F., & Backman, C. W. (1965). An interpersonal approach to personality. In B. A. Maher (Ed.), *Progress in experimental personality research* (Vol. 2, pp. 91–125). New York: Academic Press.

Segal, Z. V. (1988). Appraisal of the self-schema construct in cognitive models of depression. *Psychological Bulletin, 103,* 147–162.

Segal, Z. V., Adams, K. E., & Shaw, B. F. (1992). Do discrepancies in interpersonal perception predict relapse? A comparison of remitted depressed patients and collaterals. *Cognitive Therapy and Research, 16,* 437–450.

Segal, Z. V., & Muran, J. C. (in press). Self-representation in depression: A cognitive perspective. In Z. V. Segal & S. Blatt (Eds.), *Self-representation in emotional disorders: Cognitive and psychodynamic perspectives.* New York: Guilford.

Segraves, R. (1982). *Marital therapy.* New York: Plenum.

Segrin, C., & Abramson, L. Y. (1994). Negative reactions to depressive behaviors: A communications theories analysis. *Journal of Abnormal Psychology, 103,* 655–668.

Segrin, C., & Dillard, J. P. (1992). The interactional theory of depression: A meta-analysis of the research literature. *Journal of Social and Clinical Psychology, 11,* 43–70.

Shafer, R. B., & Keith, P. M. (1985). A causal model approach to the symbolic interactionist view of the self-concept. *Journal of Personality and Social Psychology, 48,* 963–969.

Shannon, J., & Guerney, B., Jr. (1973). Interpersonal effects of interpersonal behavior. *Journal of Personality and Social Psychology, 26,* 142–150.

Shean, G., & Uchenwa, U. (1990). Interpersonal style and anxiety. *The Journal of Psychology, 124,* 403–408.

Sheffield, M., Carey, J., Patenaude, W., & Lambert, M. (1995). An exploration of the relationship between interpersonal problems and psychological health. *Psychological Reports, 76,* 947–956.

Shevrin, H., & Dickman, S. (1980). The psychological unconscious: A necessary assumption for all psychological theory? *American Psychologist, 35,* 421–434.

Shoeneman, T. J., & Olson, R. (1984). Undergraduates' perceptions of social evaluators: Another look at orientational and role-specific others. *Representative Research in Social Psychology, 14,* 41–47.

Shopshire, M. S., & Craik, K. H. (1994). The five factor model of personality and the DSM-III-R personality disorders: Correspondence and differentiation. *Journal of Personality Disorders, 8,* 41–52.

Shrauger, J. S. (1975). Responses to evaluation as a function of initial self-perceptions. *Psychological Bulletin, 82,* 581–596.

Shrauger, J. S., & Schoeneman, T. J. (1979). Symbolic interactionist view of self-concept: Through the looking glass darkly. *Psychological Bulletin, 86,* 549–573.

Shuler, A. (1994). *Interpersonal transactions and the experience of panic: A study of membership.* Unpublished doctoral dissertation, Virginia Commonwealth University, Richmond.

Shulman, N. (1975). Life cycle variants in patterns of close relationships. *Journal of Marriage and the Family, 37,* 813–821.

Shweder, R. A. (1975). How relevant is an individual difference theory of personality? *Journal of Personality, 43,* 455–485.

Shweder, R. A. (1980). Factors and fictions in person perception: A reply to Lamiell, Foss, and Cavanec. *Journal of Personality, 48,* 74–81.

Shweder, R. A. (1982). Fact and artifact in trait perception: The systematic distortion hypothesis. In B. A. Maher & W. B. Maher (Eds.), *Progress in experimental personality research* (Vol. 11, pp. 65–100). San Diego, CA: Academic Press.

Shweder, R. A., & D'Andrade, R. G. (1979). Accurate reflection or systematic distortion? A reply to Block, Weiss, and Thorne. *Journal of Personality and Social Psychology, 37,* 1075–1084.

Siegman, A. W., & Feldstein, S. (Eds.). (1978). *Nonverbal behavior and communication.* Hillsdale, NJ: Erlbaum.

Sikes-Nova, V. E. (1990). *The relationship between needs and interpersonal problems of women in four interpersonal categories.* Unpublished doctoral dissertation, Virginia Consortium for Professional Psychology, William & Mary University, Williamsburg, VA.

Sim, J. P., & Romney, D. M. (1990). The relationship between a circumplex model of interpersonal behaviors and personality disorders. *Journal of Personality Disorders, 4,* 329–341.

Simon, L., Gaul, R., Friedlander, M. L., & Heatherington, L. (1992). Client gender and sex role: Predictors of counselors' impressions and expectations. *Journal of Counseling and Development, 71,* 48–52.

Simpson, A. W. (1983). Power, assertiveness, and race: Effects on influence and perceptions. *Dissertation Abstracts International, 44,* 1282–B.

Singer, E. B. (1970). *Key concepts of psychotherapy.* New York: Basic Books.

Slater, P. E. (1962). Parent behavior and the personality of the child. *Journal of Genetic Psychology, 101,* 53–68.

Slipp, S. (1977). Interpersonal factors in hysteria: Freud's seduction theory and the case of Dora. *Journal of the American Academy of Psychoanalysis, 5,* 359–376.

Small, S. A., Zeldin, L. R. S., & Savin-Williams, R. C. (1983). In search of personality traits: A multimethod analysis of naturally occurring prosocial and dominance behavior. *Journal of Personality, 51,* 1–16.

Smelser, W. T. (1961). Dominance as a factor in achievement and perception in cooperative problem solving interactions. *Journal of Abnormal and Social Psychology, 62,* 535–542.

Smith, T. W. (1992). Hostility and health: Current status of a psychosomatic hypothesis. *Health Psychology, 11,* 139–150.

Smith, T. W., & Pope, M. K. (1990). Cynical hostility as a health risk: Current status and future directions. *Journal of Social Behavior and Personality, 5,* 77–88.

Snyder, C. R. (1989). Reality negotiation: From excuses to hope and beyond. *Journal of Social and Clinical Psychology, 8,* 130–157.

Snyder, M. L. (1981). On the influence of individuals on situations. In N. Cantor & J. Kihlstrom (Eds.), *Personality, cognition and social interaction* (pp. 309–332). Hillsdale, NJ: Erlbaum.

Snyder, M. L., & Gangestad, S. (1981). Hypothesis-testing processes. In J. H. Harvey, W. J. Ickes, & R. F. Kidd (Eds.), *New directions in attribution research* (Vol. 3, pp. 171–196). Hillsdale, NJ: Erlbaum.

Snyder, M. L., & Ickes, W. (1985). Personality and social behavior. In G. Lindzey & E. Aronson (Eds.), *Handbook of social psychology* (3rd ed., Vol. 2, pp. 883–947). New York: Random House.

Snyder, M. L., Stephan, W. G., & Rosenfield, D. (1978). Attributional egotism. In J. H. Harvey, W. Ickes, & R. F. Kidd (Eds.), *New directions in attribution research* (Vol. 2, pp. 91–117). Hillsdale, NJ: Erlbaum.

Soldz, S., Budman, S., Demby, A., & Merry, J. (1993). Representation of personality disorders in circumplex and five-factor space: Explorations with a clinical sample. *Psychological Assessment, 5,* 41–52.

Solomon, M. (1981). Dimensions of interpersonal behavior: A convergent validation within a cognitive interactionist framework. *Journal of Personality, 49,* 15–26.

Sox, K. A. (1983). Reciprocity in interpersonal perception and behavior: An analysis based on the circumplex model. *Dissertation Abstracts International, 44,* 329–330B.

Spence, J. T., Helmreich, R. L., & Holahan, C. K. (1979). Negative and positive components of psychological masculinity and femininity and their relationships to self-reports of neurotic and acting out behaviors. *Journal of Personality and Social Psychology, 37,* 1673–1682.

Spiegel, S. (1989). *An interpersonal approach to child therapy: The treatment of children and adolescents from an interpersonal point of view.* New York: Columbia University Press.

Spotnitz, H. (1969). *Modern psychoanalysis of the schizophrenic patient.* New York: Grune and Stratton.

Sprenkle, D. H., & Olson, D. H. L. (1978). Circumplex model of marital systems: An empirical study of clinic and non-clinic couples. *Journal of Marriage and Family Counseling, xx,* 59–74.

Steinmetz, S. K. (1979). Disciplinary techniques and their relationship to aggressiveness, dependency, and conscience. In W. R. Burr, R. Hill, F. I. Nye, & I. L. Reiss (Eds.), *Contemporary theories about the family* (Vol. 2, pp. 405–438). New York: Free Press.

Stern, D. N. (1985). *The interpersonal world of the infant.* New York: Basic Books.

Stern, G. G. (1970). *People in context: Measuring person–environment congruence in education and industry.* New York: Wiley.

Stoller, F. H. (1968). Focused feedback with videotape: Extending the group's function. In G. M. Gazda (Ed.), *Innovations to group psychotherapy.* Springfield, IL: Thomas.

Strack, S. (Ed.). (1996). Special series: Interpersonal theory and the interpersonal circumplex: Timothy Leary's legacy. *Journal of Personality Assessment, 66,* 211–307.

Strack, S., & Lorr, M. (1990). Three approaches to interpersonal behavior and their common factors. *Journal of Personality Assessment, 54,* 782–790.

Strong, S. R. (1985). Review of the Impact Message Inventory. In J. V. Mitchell (Ed.), *The ninth mental measurements yearbook* (Vol. 1, pp. 679–681). Lincoln: University of Nebraska Press.

Strong, S. R. (1987a). Interpersonal change processes in therapeutic interactions. In J. Maddux, C. Stoltenberg, & R. Rosenwein (Eds.), *Social processes in clinical and counseling psychology* (pp. 68–82). New York: Springer-Verlag.

Strong, S. R. (1987b). Interpersonal influence theory as a common language for psychotherapy. *Journal of Integrative and Eclectic Psychotherapy, 6,* 173–184.

Strong, S. R. (1987c). Interpersonal influence theory and therapeutic interactions. In F. J. Dorn (Ed.), *Social influence processes in counseling and psychotherapy* (pp. 17–30). Springfield, IL: Thomas.

Strong, S. R. (in press). Interpersonal influence theory: The situational and individual determinants of interpersonal behavior. In R. V. Dawis & D. Lubinski (Eds.), *Assessing individual differences in human behavior: New concepts, methods, and findings.* Thousand Oaks, CA: Sage.

Strong, S. R., & Claiborn, C. D. (1982). *Change through interaction: Social psychological processes of counseling and psychotherapy.* New York: Wiley.

Strong, S. R., Hills, H. I., Kilmartin, C. T., DeVries, H., Lanier, K., Nelson, B. N., Strickland, D., & Meyer, C. W., III. (1988). The dynamic relations among interpersonal behaviors: A test of complementarity and anticomplementarity. *Journal of Personality and Social Psychology, 54,* 798–810.

Strong, S. R., Hills, H. I., & Nelson, B. N. (1988). *Interpersonal Communication Rating Scale (Revised).* Richmond: Virginia Commonwealth University.

Strupp, H. H. (1980a). Success and failure in time limited psychotherapy: A systematic comparison of two cases (Comparison 1). *Archives of General Psychiatry, 37,* 595–603.

Strupp, H. H. (1980b). Success and failure in time limited psychotherapy: A systematic comparison of two cases (Comparison 2). *Archives of General Psychiatry, 37,* 708–716.

Strupp, H. H. (1980c). Success and failure in time limited psychotherapy: Further evidence (Comparison 4). *Archives of General Psychiatry, 37,* 947–954.

Strupp, H. H., & Binder, J. L. (1984). *Psychotherapy in a new key: A guide to time-limited dynamic psychotherapy.* New York: Basic Books.

Strupp, H. H., & Hadley, S. W. (1979). Specific versus nonspecific factors in psychotherapy: A controlled study of outcome. *Archives of General Psychiatry, 36,* 1125–1136.

Strupp, H. H., Hadley, S. W., & Gomes-Schwartz, B. (1977). *Psychotherapy for better or worse.* New York: Aronson.

Stryker, S., & Statham, A. (1985). Symbolic interaction and role theory. In G. Lindzey & E. Aronson (Eds.), *Handbook of social psychology* (3rd ed., Vol. 1, pp. 311–378). New York: Random House.

Stuart, R. B., & Davis, B. (1978). *Slim chance in a fit world: Behavioral control of obesity.* Champaign, IL: Research Press.

Stuart, S., Pilkonis, P., Heape, C., Smith, K., & Fisher, B. (1992, June). *The patient–therapist match in psychotherapy: Effects of security of attachment and personality style.* Paper presented at the annual meeting of the Society for Psychotherapy Research Denver, CO.

Sullivan, H. S. (1953a). *Conceptions of modern psychiatry.* New York: Norton.

Sullivan, H. S. (1953b). *The interpersonal theory of psychiatry.* New York: Norton.

Sullivan, H. S. (1954). *The psychiatric interview.* New York: Norton.

Sullivan, H. S. (1956). *Clinical studies in psychiatry.* New York: Norton.

Summers, F. (1980). Focusing and defensiveness: An empirical study. *Psychotherapy: Theory, Research and Practice, 17,* 74–78.

Svartberg, M., & Stiles, T. (1992). Predicting patient change from therapist competence and patient–therapist complementarity in short-term anxiety-provoking psychotherapy: A pilot study. *Journal of Consulting and Clinical Psychology, 60,* 304–307.

Swaney, K. B., & Stone, G. L. (1990). Therapist awareness of covert reactions to client interpersonal behavior. *Journal of Social and Clinical Psychology, 9,* 375–389.

Swann, W. B., Jr. (1983). Self-verification: Bringing social reality into harmony with the self. In J. Suls & A. G. Greenwald (Eds.), *Psychological perspectives on the self* (Vol. 2, pp. 33–66). Hillsdale, NJ: Erlbaum.

Swann, W. B., Jr. (1985). The self as architect of social reality. In B. R. Schlenker (Ed.), *The self and social life* (pp. 100–125). New York: McGraw-Hill.

Swann, W. B., Jr. (1987). Identity negotiation: Where two roads meet. *Journal of Personality and Social Psychology, 41,* 119–128.

Swann, W. B., Jr., & Hill, C. A. (1982). When our identities are mistaken: Reaffirming self-conceptions through social interaction. *Journal of Personality and Social Psychology, 43,* 59–66.

Swann, W. B., Jr., & Read, S. J. (1981a). Acquiring self-knowledge: The search for feedback that fits. *Journal of Personality and Social Psychology, 41,* 119–128.

Swann, W. B., Jr., & Read, S. J. (1981b). Self-verification process: How we sustain our self-conceptions. *Journal of Experimental Social Psychology, 17,* 351–372.

Swensen, C. H., Jr. (1967). Psychotherapy as a special case of dyadic interaction: Some suggestions for theory and research. *Psychotherapy: Theory, Research and Practice, 4,* 7–13.

Swensen, C. H., Jr. (1973). *Introduction to interpersonal relations.* Glenview, IL: Scott Foresman.

Talley, P. F., Strupp, H. H., & Morey, L. C. (1990). Matchmaking in psychotherapy: Patient–therapist dimensions and their impact on outcome. *Journal of Consulting and Clinical Psychology, 58,* 182–188.

Tansey, M. J., & Burke, W. F. (1989). *Understanding counter-transference: From projective identification to empathy.* Hillsdale, NJ: Analytic Press.

Taplin, J. R. (1968). Interpersonal expectancies of newly hospitalized psychiatric patients. *Dissertation Abstracts International, 28,* 2634B.

Tasca, G. A. (1988). *Complementarity in the psychotherapeutic relationship.* Unpublished doctoral dissertation, University of Saskatchewan, Saskatoon, Canada.

Tasca, G. A., & McMullen, L. M. (1993). Interpersonal complementarity and antitheses within a stage model of psychotherapy. *Psychotherapy, 29,* 515–523.

Taulbee, E. S., & Clark, T. L. (1982). *A comprehensive annotated bibliography of selected psychological tests: Interpersonal Check List, MMPI short forms, the Blacky pictures.* Troy, NY: Whitson.

Taylor, S. E., & Brown, J. D. (1988). Illusion and well-being: A social psychological perspective on mental health. *Psychological Bulletin, 103,* 193–210.

Taylor, S. E., & Brown, J. D. (1994). Positive illusions and well-being revisited: Separating fact from fiction. *Psychological Bulletin, 116,* 21–27.

Taylor, S. E., Collins, R. L., Skokan, L. A., & Aspinwall, L. G. (1989). Maintaining positive illusions in the face of negative information: Getting the facts without letting go of you. *Journal of Social and Clinical Psychology, 8,* 114–129.

Tellegen, A. (1991). Personality traits: Issues of definition, evidence, and assessment. In D. Cicchetti & W. Grove (Eds.), *Thinking clearly in psychology: Essays in honor of Paul Everett Meehl: Vol. 2. Personality and psychopathology* (pp. 10–35). Minneapolis: University of Minnesota Press.

Tennen, H., & Herzberger, S. (1987). Depression, self-esteem and the absence of self-protective attributional biases. *Journal of Personality and Social Psychology, 52,* 72–80.

Tennen, H., Herzberger, S., & Nelson, H. F. (1987). Depressive attributional style: The role of self-esteem. *Journal of Personality, 55,* 631–660.

Teyber, E. (1992). *Interpersonal process in psychotherapy: A guide for clinical training* (2nd ed.). Pacific Grove, CA: Brooks/Cole.

Teyber, E. C., Meese, L. A., & Stollak, G. E. (1977). Adult responses to child communications. *Child Development, 48,* 1577–1582.

Thibaut, J. W., & Kelley, H. H. (1959). *The social psychology of groups.* New York: Wiley.

Thibodeau, J. R. (1979). Responses to an anticomplementary personality as a function of locus of control in college males. *Dissertation Abstracts International, 39,* 3542–B.

Thompson, B. J., Hill, C. E., & Mahalik, J. R. (1991). A test of the complementarity hypothesis in the interpersonal theory of psychotherapy: Multiple case comparisons. *Psychotherapy, 28,* 572–579.

Thorne, A. (1986, August). *Toward an interpersonology.* Paper presented at the annual convention of the American Psychological Association, Washington, DC.

Thorne, A. (1987). The press of personality: A study of conversations between introverts and extraverts. *Journal of Personality and Social Psychology, 53,* 718–726.

Thornton, A. L., Jr. (1984). Dyadic interactions with depressives: Temporal tracking of induced depression and personal rejection. *Dissertation Abstracts International, 44,* 3210–B.

Tracey, T. J. (1986). Interactional correlates of premature termination. *Journal of Consulting and Clinical Psychology, 54,* 784–788.

Tracey, T. J. (1987). Stages differences in the dependencies of topic initiation and topic following behavior. *Journal of Counseling Psychology, 34*, 123–131.

Tracey, T. J. (1993). An interpersonal stage model of the therapeutic process. *Journal of Counseling Psychology, 40*, 396–409.

Tracey, T. J. (1994). An examination of the complementarity of interpersonal behavior. *Journal of Personality and Social Psychology, 67*, 864–878.

Tracey, T. J., & Guinee, J. P. (1990). Generalizability of interpersonal rating scale ratings across presentation modes. *Journal of Counseling Psychology, 37*, 330–336.

Tracey, T. J., & Hays, K. (1989). Therapist complementarity as a function of experience and client stimuli. *Psychotherapy, 26*, 462–468.

Tracey, T. J., & Ray, P. B. (1984). Stages of successful time-limited counseling: An interactional examination. *Journal of Counseling Psychology, 31*, 13–27.

Tracey, T. J., & Schneider, P. L. (1995). An evaluation of the circular structure of the Checklist of Interpersonal Transactions and the Checklist of Psychotherapy Transactions. *Journal of Counseling Psychology, 42*, 496–507.

Tracey, T. J., & Sherry, P. (1993). Complementary interaction over time in successful and less successful supervision. *Professional Psychology: Research and Practice, 24*, 304–311.

Trapnell, P., & Wiggins, J. S. (1990). Extension of the Interpersonal Adjective Scales to include the Big Five dimensions of personality. *Journal of Personality and Social Psychology, 59*, 781–790.

Triandis, H. C. (1977). *Interpersonal behavior.* Monterey, CA: Brooks/Cole.

Triandis, H. C. (1978). Some universals of social behavior. *Personality and Social Psychology Bulletin, 4*, 1–16.

Triandis, H. C. (1990). Cross-cultural studies of individualism and collectivism. In J. J. Berman (Ed.), *1989 Nebraska symposium on motivation: Cross-cultural perspectives* (Vol. 37, pp. 41–133). Lincoln: University of Nebraska Press.

Trull, T. J. (1992). DSM-III-R personality disorders and the five-factor model of personality: An empirical comparison. *Journal of Abnormal Psychology, 101*, 553–560.

Tryer, P., & Alexander, J. (1979). Classification of personality disorder. *British Journal of Psychiatry, 135*, 163–167.

Tupes, E. C., & Christal, R. W. (1961). *Recurrent personality factors based on trait ratings* (USAF ASD Technical Report No. 61–97). Lackland Air Force Base, TX: U.S. Air Force.

Turner, J. L., Foa, E. B., & Foa, U. G. (1971). Interpersonal reinforcers: Classification, interrelationship, and some differential properties. *Journal of Personality and Social Psychology, 19*, 168–180.

Tyhurst, J. S. (1957). Paranoid patterns. In A. H. Leighton, J. A. Clausen, & R. N. Wilson (Eds.), *Explorations in social psychiatry* (pp. 31–66). New York: Basic Books.

Vallacher, R. R. (1980). An introduction to self theory. In D. M. Wegner & R. R. Vallacher (Eds.), *The self in social psychology* (pp. 3–30). New York: Oxford University Press.

Valone, K. E. (1982). Complementarity in interpersonal construal. *Dissertation Abstracts International, 43*, 890–B.

Van Denburg, T. F. (1989). Transactional escalation in rigidity and intensity of interpersonal behavior under stress. *Dissertation Abstracts International, 49*, 4069–4070B.

Van Denburg, T. F. (1991). *Interpersonal behavior: Development, transactional anxiety, and projection.* Unpublished manuscript, University of Kentucky, Lexington.

Van Denburg, T. F., & Holifield, J. (1993). *Typical, desired, and dreaded self and others: Patterns of complementarity and anticomplementarity.* Unpublished manuscript, University of Kentucky, Lexington.

Van Denburg, T. F., & Kiesler, D. J. (1993). Transactional escalation in rigidity and intensity of interpersonal behaviour under stress. *British Journal of Medical Psychology, 66,* 15–31.

Van Denburg, T. F., & Kiesler, D. J. (1996). An interpersonal communication perspective on resistance in psychotherapy. *In Session: Psychotherapy in Practice, 2,* 55–66.

Van Denburg, T. F., Kiesler, D. J., Wagner, C. C., & Schmidt, J. A. (1994). Not a completed bridge, but several solid spans. *Psychological Inquiry, 5,* 326–329.

Van Denburg, T. F., Schmidt, J. A., & Kiesler, D. J. (1992). Interpersonal assessment in counseling and psychotherapy. *Journal of Counseling and Development, 71,* 84–90.

Van Denburg, T. F., & Van Denburg, E. J. (1992). Premature termination in the midst of psychotherapy: Three psychoanalytic perspectives. *Psychotherapy, 29,* 183–190.

Villard, K. L., & Whipple, L. J. (1976). *Beginnings in relational communication.* New York: Wiley.

Wachtel, P. L. (1973). Psychodynamics, behavior therapy and the implacable experimenter: An inquiry into the consistency of personality. *Journal of Abnormal Psychology, 82,* 324–334.

Wachtel, P. L. (1977). *Psychoanalysis and behavior therapy.* New York: Basic Books.

Wachtel, P. L. (1982a). Interpersonal therapy and active intervention. In J. C. Anchin & D. J. Kiesler (Eds.), *Handbook of interpersonal psychotherpy* (pp. 46–63). Elmsford, NY: Pergamon.

Wachtel, P. L. (1982b). *Resistance: Psychodynamic and behavioral approaches.* New York: Plenum.

Wagner, B. C. (1984). Interpersonal complementarity and marital adjustment. *Dissertation Abstracts International, 44,* 3184–B.

Wagner, C. C. (1995). *A constructivist test of interpersonal complementarity: A comparison of self and peer ratings of interpersonal behavior.* Unpublished doctoral dissertation, Virginia Commonwealth University, Richmond.

Wagner, C. C., Kiesler, D. J., & Schmidt, J. A. (1995). Assessing the interpersonal transaction cycle: Convergence of action and reaction interpersonal circumplex measures. *Journal of Personality and Social Psychology, 69,* 938–949.

Wallerstein, R. (1990). The corrective emotional experience: Is reconsideration due? *Psychoanalytic Inquiry, 10,* 288–324.

Ward, C. O., Zanna, M. P., & Cooper, J. (1974). The nonverbal mediation of self-fulfilling prophecies in interracial interaction. *Journal of Experimental Social Psychology, 10,* 109–120.

Warner, R. M., Kenny, K. A., & Stoto, M. (1979). A new round robin analysis of variance for social interaction. *Journal of Personality and Social Psychology, 37,* 1742–1757.

Watzlawick, P., Beavin, J. H., & Jackson, D. D. (1967). *Pragmatics of human communication.* New York: Norton.

Watzlawick, P., & Weakland, J. H. (Eds.). (1977). *The interactional view.* New York: Norton.

Waxer, P. H. (1978). *Nonverbal aspects of psychotherapy.* New York: Praeger.

Webster, A. S. (1953). The development of phobias in married women. *Psychological Monographs, 67*(Whole No. 367).

Webster, M., & Sobieszek, B. I. (1974). *Sources of self-evaluation: A formal theory of significant others and social influence.* New York: Wiley.

Weinstock-Savoy, D. E. (1986). The relationship of therapist and patient interpersonal styles to outcome in brief dynamic psychotherapy. *Dissertation Abstracts International, 47,* 2638–B.

Weiss, D. S., & Mendelsohn, G. A. (1986). An empirical demonstration of the implausibility of the semantic similarity explanation of how trait ratings are made and what they mean. *Journal of Personality and Social Psychology, 50,* 595–601.

Weiss, J., Sampson, H., & the Mount Zion Psychotherapy Research Group. (1987). *The psychoanalytic process: Theory, clinical observation and empirical research.* New York: Guilford.

Weissman, M. M., Klerman, G. L., Rounsaville, B. J., Chevron, E. S., & Neu, C. (1982). Short-term interpersonal psychotherapy (IPT) for depression: Description and efficacy. In J. C. Anchin & D. J. Kiesler (Eds.), *Handbook of interpersonal psychotherapy* (pp. 296–310). Elmsford, NY: Pergamon.

Weissman, M. M., & Markowitz, J. C. (1994). Interpersonal psychotherapy: Current status. *Archives of General Psychiatry, 51,* 599–606.

Wenzel, C. K. (1980). *Interactive effects of psychological androgyny and touch on females' evaluation of their interviewers.* Unpublished master's thesis, Virginia Commonwealth University, Richmond.

Wenzel, C. K. (1984). Effects of affiliation versus dominance and touch on females' evaluation of their interviewer. *Dissertation Abstracts International, 44,* 2910–B.

Werner, C. M., & Haggard, L. M. (1985). Temporal qualities of interpersonal relationships. In M. L. Knapp & G. R. Miller (Eds.), *Handbook of interpersonal communication* (pp. 59–99). Beverly Hills, CA: Sage.

Werner, M. (1984). *Das Impact Message Inventory: Ein interpersonaler personlich keitsfragebogen von Donald J. Kiesler (1976). Uebersetzung aus dem Amerikanischen und erste validierungen.* Unpublished doctoral dissertation, University of Bern, Switzerland.

Wetter, M. W. (1984). A comparison of responses evoked by four major categories of interpersonal behavior. *Dissertation Abstracts International, 45,* 1300B.

Whiffen, V. E., Dudley, D., & Sasseville, T. (1990). *Interpersonal relations and vulnerability to depresssion.* Unpublished manuscript, University of Ottawa, Ontario, Canada.

Whitaker, D. S., & Lieberman, M. A. (1964). Assessing interpersonal behavior in group psychotherapy. *Perceptual and Motor Skills, 18,* 763–764.

White, G. M. (1980). Conceptual universals in interpersonal language. *American Anthropologist, 82,* 759–781.

Widiger, T. A. (1991). Personality disorder dimensional models proposed for DSM-IV. *Journal of Personality Disorders, 5,* 386–398.

Widiger, T. A. (1993). The DSM-III-R categorical personality disorder diagnoses: A critique and an alternative. *Psychological Inquiry, 4,* 75–90.

Widiger, T. A., & Frances, A. (1985). The DSM-III personality disorders: Perspectives from psychology. *Archives of General Psychiatry, 42,* 615–623.

Widiger, T. A., & Frances, A. J. (1988). Personality disorders. In J. Talbott, R. Hales, & S. Yudofsky (Eds.), *The American Psychiatric Press textbook of psychiatry* (pp. 621–648). Washington, DC: American Psychiatric Association Press.

Widiger, T. A., & Frances, A. J. (1994). Toward a dimensional model for the personality disorders. In P. T. Costa, Jr. & T. A. Widiger (Eds.), *Personality disorders and the five-factor model of personality* (pp. 19–39). Washington, DC: American Psychological Association.

Widiger, T. A., Frances, A. J., Spitzer, R. L., & Williams, J. B. W. (1988). The DSM-III-R personality disorders: An overview. *American Journal of Psychiatry, 145,* 786–795.

Widiger, T. A., Frances, A. J., & Trull, T. J. (1987). A psychometric analysis of the social-interpersonal and cognitive-perceptual items for the schizotypal personality disorder. *Archives of General Psychiatry, 44,* 741–745.

Widiger, T. A., & Hyler, S. (1987). Axis I/Axis II interactions. In R. Michels & J. O. Cavenar, Jr. (Eds.), *Psychiatry.* Philadelphia: Lippincott.

Widiger, T. A., & Kelso, K. (1983). Psychodiagnosis of Axis II. *Clinical Psychology Review, 3,* 491–510.

Widiger, T. A., & Shea, T. (1991). The differentiation of Axis I and Axis II disorders. *Journal of Abnormal Psychology, 100,* 399–406.

Widiger, T. A., & Trull, T. J. (1987). Behavioral indicators, hypothetical constructs, and personality disorders. *Journal of Personality Disorders, 1,* 82–87.

Widiger, T. A., Trull, T., Hurt, S., Clarkin, J., & Frances, A. (1987). A multidimensional scaling of the DSM-III personality disorders. *Archives of General Psychiatry, 44,* 557–563.

Wiener, M. (1989). Psychosocial transactional analysis of psychopathology: Depression as an exemplar. *Clinical Psychology Review, 9,* 295–321.

Wiggins, J. S. (1979a). A psychological taxonomy of trait-descriptive terms: The interpersonal domain. *Journal of Personality and Social Psychology, 37,* 395–412.

Wiggins, J. S. (1979b). *Taxonomy of interpersonal trait-descriptive terms.* Unpublished manuscript, University of British Columbia, Vancouver, Canada.

Wiggins, J. S. (1980). Circumplex models of interpersonal behavior. In L. Wheeler (Ed.), *Review of personality and social psychology* (Vol. 1, pp. 265–294). Beverly Hills, CA: Sage.

Wiggins, J. S. (1981). *Revised Interpersonal Adjective Scales.* Vancouver, Canada: University of British Columbia.

Wiggins, J. S. (1982). Circumplex models of interpersonal behavior in clinical psychology. In P. C. Kendall & J. N. Butcher (Eds.), *Handbook of research methods in clinical psychology* (pp. 183–221). New York: Wiley.

Wiggins, J. S. (1984). *Affective Reactions Questionnaire.* Vancouver: University of British Columbia.

Wiggins, J. S. (1985a). Interpersonal circumplex models: 1948–1983. *Journal of Personality Assessment, 49,* 626–631.

Wiggins, J. S. (1985b). Symposium: Interpersonal circumplex models: 1948-1983 (Commentary). *Journal of Personality Assessment, 49,* 626–631.

Wiggins, J. S. (1987, September). How interpersonal are the MMPI personality disorder scales? In R. L. Greene (Chair), *Current research on MMPI personality disorder scales.* Symposium conducted at the annual meeting of the American Psychological Association, New York, NY.

Wiggins, J. S. (1988). *Interpersonal Adjective Scales, Form IASR-B5.* Vancouver: University of British Columbia.

Wiggins, J. S. (1991a). Agency and communion as conceptual coordinates for the understanding and measurement of interpersonal behavior. In W. Grove & D. Cicchetti (Eds.), *Thinking clearly about psychology: Essays in honor of Paul Everett Meehl: Vol. 2. Personality and psychopathology* (pp. 89–113). Minneapolis: University of Minnesota Press.

Wiggins, J. S. (1991b). *The Interpersonal Adjective Scales (IAS) manual.* Odessa, FL: Psychological Assessment Resources.

Wiggins, J. S. (1994). Shoring up the SASB bridge between personality theory and clinical psychology. *Psychological Inquiry, 5,* 333–335.

Wiggins, J. S. (Ed.). (in press). *The five-factor model of personality: Theoretical perspectives.* New York: Guilford.

Wiggins, J. S., & Broughton, R. (1985). The Interpersonal Circle: A structural model for the integration of personality research. In R. Hogan & W. H. Jones (Eds.), *Perspectives in personality* (Vol. 1, pp. 1–48). Greenwich, CT: JAI Press.

Wiggins, J. S., & Broughton, R. (1991). A geometric taxonomy of personality scales. *European Journal of Personality, 5,* 343–365.

Wiggins, J. S., & Holzmuller, A. (1978). Psychological androgyny and interpersonal behavior. *Journal of Consulting and Clinical Psychology, 46,* 40–52.

Wiggins, J. S., & Holzmuller, A. (1981). Further evidence on androgyny and interpersonal flexibility. *Journal of Research in Personality, 15,* 67–80.

Wiggins, J. S., Phillips, N., & Trapnell, P. (1989). Circular reasoning about interpersonal behavior: Evidence concerning some untested assumptions underlying diagnostic classification. *Journal of Personality and Social Psychology, 56,* 296–305.

Wiggins, J. S., & Pincus, A. L. (1989). Conceptions of personality disorders and dimensions of personality. *Psychological Assessment: A Journal of Consulting and Clinical Psychology, 1,* 305–316.

Wiggins, J. S., & Pincus, A. L. (1992). Personality structure and assessment. *Annual Review of Psychology, 43,* 473–504.

Wiggins, J. S., & Pincus, A. L. (1994). Personality structure and the structure of personality disorders. In P. T. Costa, Jr. & T. A. Widiger (Eds.), *Personality disorders and the five-factor model of personality.* Washington, DC: American Psychological Association.

Wiggins, J. S., Steiger, J. H., & Gaelick, L. (1981). Evaluating circumplexity in personality data. *Multivariate Behavioral Research, 16,* 263–289.

Wiggins, J. S., & Trapnell, P. D. (1994). Personality structure: The return of the Big Five. In R. Hogan, J. H. Johnson, & S. R. Briggs (Eds.), *Handbook of personality psychology.* Orlando, FL: Academic Press.

Wiggins, J. S., & Trapnell, P. D. (in press). A dyadic-interactional perspective on the five-factor model. In J. S. Wiggins (Ed.), *The five-factor model of personality: Theoretical perspectives.* New York: Guilford.

Wiggins, J. S., Trapnell, P., & Phillips, N. (1988a). *The measurement of affective reactions to interpersonal stimuli.* Unpublished manuscript, University of British Columbia, Vancouver, Canada.

Wiggins, J. S., Trapnell, P., & Phillips, N. (1988b). Psychometric and geometric characteristics of the revised Interpersonal Adjective Scales (IAS-R). *Multivariate Behavioral Research, 23,* 517–530.

Wilkie, C. F. (1987). *Interpersonal complementarity in dyadic interaction.* Unpublished master's thesis, University of Saskatchewan, Saskatoon, Canada.

Wilkie, C. F., & Conway, J. B. (1988, June). *Does the theory of interpersonal complementarity adequately describe nonclinical dyads?* Paper presented at the Canadian Psychological Association annual convention, Montreal, Canada.

Willner, A. H., & Blackburn, R. (1988). Interpersonal style and personality deviation. *British Journal of Clinical Psychology, 27,* 273–274.

Winch, R. F. (1958). *Mate-selection: A study of complementary needs.* New York: Harper & Row.

Winnicott, D. W. (1949). Hate in the countertransference. *International Journal of Psycho-Analysis, 30,* 69–75.

Wish, M., Deutsch, M., & Kaplan, S. J. (1976). Perceived dimensions of the interpersonal domain. *Journal of Personality and Social Psychology, 33,* 409–420.

Woelfel, J. D. (1969). Significant others, roles, and the educational and occupational attainment process: Results of a preliminary administration of the Wisconsin Significant Other Battery. *Dissertation Abstracts International, 29,* 4109–4110B.

Wolstein, B. (1988). *Essential papers on countertransference.* New York: New York University Press.

Word, C. O., Zanna, M. P., & Cooper, J. (1974). The nonverbal mediation of self-fulfilling prophecies in interracial interaction. *Journal of Experimental Social Psychology, 10,* 109–120.

Wortman, C. B., & Dunkel-Schetter, C. (1979). Interpersonal relationship and cancer: A theoretical analysis. *Journal of Social Issues, 3,* 120–155.

Wright, J. H., & Davis, D. (1994). The therapeutic relationship in cognitive-behavioral therapy: Patient perceptions and therapist responses. *Cognitive and Behavioral Practice, 1,* 25–45.

Wright, T. L., & Ingraham, L. J. (1986). A social relations model test of the interpersonal circle. *Journal of Personality and Social Psychology, 50,* 1285–1290.

Wyer, R. S., & Gordon, S. E. (1984). The cognitive representation of social information. In R. S. Wyer & T. K. Srull (Eds.), *Handbook of social cognition* (Vol. 2, pp. 73–150). Hillsdale, NJ: Erlbaum.

Wyrick, R. A. (1979). Interpersonal perceptual congruence during group psychotherapy. *The International Journal of Group Psychotherapy, 29,* 139–148.

Yalom, I. D. (1985). *Theory and practice of group psychotherapy* (3rd ed.). New York: Basic Books.

Yarnold, P. R., & Grimm, L. G. (1986). Interpersonal dominance and coronary-prone behavior. *Journal of Research in Personality, 20,* 420–433.

Yarnold, P. R., Grimm, L. G., & Lyons, J. S. (1987). The Wiggins interpersonal behavior circle and the Type A behavior pattern. *Journal of Research in Personality, 21,* 185–196.

Yarnold, P. R., & Lyons, J. S. (1987). Norms for college undergraduates for the Bem Sex-Role Inventory and the Wiggins Interpersonal Behavior Circle. *Journal of Personality Assessment, 51,* 595–599.

Yarnold, P. R., Mueser, K. T., & Grimm, L. G. (1985). Interpersonal dominance of Type As in group discussions. *Journal of Abnormal Psychology, 94,* 233–236.

Young, D. M., & Beier, E. G. (1982). Being asocial in social places: Giving the client a new experience. In J. C. Anchin & D. J. Kiesler (Eds.), *Handbook of interpersonal psychotherapy* (pp. 262–273). Elmsford, NY: Pergamon.

Youngren, M. A., & Lewinsohn, P. M. (1980). The functional relation between depression and problematic interpersonal behavior. *Journal of Abnormal Psychology, 89,* 333–341.

Zetzel, E. (1956). Current concepts of transference. *International Journal of Psycho-Analysis, 37,* 369–376.

Zians, J. K. (1981). *Broadening the Impact Message Inventory for use by an uninvolved rater.* Unpublished manuscript, Vanderbilt University, Department of Psychology, Nashville, TN.

Zuckerman, M. (1979). Attribution of success and failure revisited, or: The motivational bias is alive and well in attribution theory. *Journal of Personality, 42,* 245–287.

Author Index

Abeles, N., 49, 51, 101, 103, 108, 261
Abramson, L. Y., 7, 138, 146, 147
Ackermann, R., 138
Adamopoulos, J., 8
Adams, H. B., 171
Adams, K. E., 134, 135
Adelman, M. B., 81
Adlind, M. C., 148, 152
Agulnik, P. L., 149
Albrecht, T. L., 81
Alden, L. E., 23, 28, 29, 148, 157, 173, 186, 197, 198, 271, 274
Alexander, F. A., 238, 239
Alexander, J., 24, 123, 167, 187, 188
Alimaras, P. E., 59, 66
Allen, A., 181, 182
Alloy, L. B., 138
Allport, G. W., 131
Alpher, V. S., 29, 30, 59, 62, 103, 310, 317, 319
Altrocchi, J., 59, 60
Anchin, J. C., xiii, 3, 5, 7, 25, 28, 45, 46, 51, 52, 53, 71, 74, 83, 112, 114, 120, 127, 176, 202, 203, 204, 206, 226, 229, 232, 237, 242, 247, 283
Anderson, C. A., 181, 197
Anderson, C. R., 131
Andrews, J. D. W., xiii, 3, 56, 73, 85, 86, 87, 91, 97, 100, 103, 137, 148, 155, 156, 157, 159, 160, 171, 232, 234, 237, 242, 252, 267, 268, 269, 270, 280, 281, 299, 300, 305
Angelone, E. O., 27, 59, 64, 65
Apfelbaum, A., 3, 16, 23
Apfelbaum, B., 229
Arabie, P., 31, 101
Argyle, M., 7
Aris, S. J., 81
Arlow, J., 310
Arnold, M. B., 72
Aspinwall, L. G., 140
Auerbach, A. H., 222
Auerbach, S. M., 101, 102, 123, 167
Averill, J. R., 72
Azim, H. F., 198, 274, 278

Backman, C., 58, 85, 86, 109
Baer, B. A., 28, 134, 137, 197, 198, 271, 274, 275
Bakan, D., 9
Bale, P., 120
Bandura, A., 103

Banta, J., 123, 235
Barlow, D. H., 148, 149
Barnes, M., 26
Barnett, J., 148, 161, 162
Barnlund, D. C., 206
Bartholomew, K., 197, 198, 272
Barton, R., 138
Batchelder, S., 198, 225, 265
Bateson, G., 88, 148, 155
Baumeister, R. F., 86, 140
Baumrind, D., 16
Beavin, J. H., 88, 89, 143, 155, 206, 207, 218, 258
Beck, A. T., 69
Beck, S., 51, 232, 251, 255
Becker, W. C., 8
Bednar, R. L., 304
Beery, J. W., 103
Beier, E. G., 207, 208, 215, 218, 242, 247, 284, 298, 308, 314
Belyea-Caldwell, S., 123, 148, 155
Bem, D. J., 91, 126, 181, 182
Bem, S. L., 42
Benedek, T., 311
Benjafield, J., 8, 13
Benjamin, L. S., xiii, 3, 8, 12, 29, 30, 39, 43, 59, 62, 109, 148, 158, 171, 175, 187, 188, 237, 242, 251, 252, 262, 281
Bennum, I., 148, 149
Bergan, J., 198, 271, 273
Bergen, B. J., 148, 288, 289
Bergner, R. M., 148, 149
Bermann, E., 8
Bernstein, A. B., 5, 45, 46, 51, 52, 83, 114, 127, 176, 202, 203, 204, 206, 226, 229, 232, 237, 247
Berscheid, E., 6, 74, 88, 217
Berzins, J. I., 8, 103, 251, 270
Beutler, L. E., 198, 271, 273
Bierman, R., 8, 103
Billings, A., 39
Binder, J. L., 73, 237, 275
Bingi, R. B., 27
Birtchnell, J., 8, 9, 10, 148, 158, 159, 267
Bishop, P. F., 8, 25, 113, 186, 187
Blackburn, R., 134, 136
Blashfield, R., 135, 187, 188
Blatt, S., 155
Block, J., 32, 109, 139, 140
Bluhm, C., 102

Blumberg, H. H., 8, 285
Blumberg, S. R., 103, 121, 147
Blyth, D. A., 75, 76, 78
Boals, G. F., 198
Bochner, A. P., 8
Bodenhause, G. V., 8, 103
Boghosian, J., 171
Bohn, M. J., 103
Bohrnstedt, G. W., 32, 33
Bonstock, W., 103
Bontempo, R. N., 8
Booth-Kewley, S., 179
Bordin, E. S., 222
Borgatta, E. F., 8, 9
Borgen, F. H., 28
Borkenau, P., 37
Bornstein, R. F., 158
Bouvy, H., 148, 157
Bowlby, J., 69, 77, 270
Braith, J. A., 123, 148, 155
Brenock, K., 310, 317, 318
Brokaw, D. W., 29, 39, 51, 53, 102, 103, 105, 148,
    155, 171, 172, 175, 184, 234, 236, 261, 264, 281
Brophy, C., 123, 167
Broughton, R., 11, 26, 30, 34, 36, 37
Brown, J. D., 86, 138, 139
Brown, R., 8, 27, 103, 264, 266
Brown, T. M., 123, 235
Browne, M. W., 33
Bruner, J. S., 87, 131
Budman, S., 187, 191, 198
Buhrmester, D., 77, 78
Buranyi, G., 26, 280
Burchill, S. A., 146
Burke, W. F., 231, 305
Busch, L. M., 103
Buss, A. H., 39
Buss, D. M., 26, 40, 171, 179, 202
Butler, A. C., 59, 65, 147
Butler, S. F., 232
Bynner, J. M., 187, 191
Byrne, D., 81, 103

Cameron, N., 148, 162
Campbell, J., 102, 304
Campbell, S. R., 27, 103, 134, 136, 264, 266, 267
Cantor, N., 180
Capreol, M. J., 148, 157, 198, 271, 274
Carey, J., 134, 137, 138, 198
Carr, K. F., 123, 274
Carson, E., 8, 13
Carson, R. C., xi, xiii, 3, 8, 11, 27, 42, 45, 46, 47,
    53, 58, 59, 60, 61, 62, 69, 73, 83, 84, 87, 90,
    91, 100, 105, 109, 128, 129, 131, 237, 238,
    241, 245, 251, 256, 261, 282
Carter, J. A., 222
Carter, L. F., 9
Carter, M. M., 148, 149
Cashdan, S., 231, 232, 237, 254, 255, 261

Caspi, A., 91, 131
Castronova, N. R., 122
Cattell, R. B., 32, 109
Celani, D. P., 103, 148, 153, 264, 266
Chambless, D. L., 149
Champion, L. A., 81
Chance, E., 103
Chaplin, W., 138
Chapman, R. C., 13, 31, 177
Chartier, B. M., 24
Cheek, C. E., 122
Cheek, J. M., 341
Chevron, E. S., 7, 73, 77, 82, 198, 237, 267, 268
Chewning, M., 27, 42, 45, 76, 78, 120, 122, 193
Chirico, B. M., 7, 25, 28, 53, 59, 63, 64, 71, 112,
    114, 120, 121, 234
Christal, R. W., 9, 177
Christensen, A., 6, 74, 88, 217
Chrzanowski, G., 222
Claiborn, C. D., 24
Clark, T. L., 23
Clark-Lempers, D. S., 77
Clarkin, J., 187, 189, 190
Clavere, S., 310, 317, 318
Coates, D., 148
Cobb, J. C., 148, 151, 152
Coffey, H. S., 3, 7, 8, 11, 12, 24, 39, 40, 56, 57,
    112, 171, 176, 184
Cohen, L., 312
Colby, C. A., 148, 154
Collins, R. L., 140
Colm, H., 238
Colvin, C. R., 139, 140
Conte, H. R., xiii, 3, 4, 8, 171
Conway, J. B., 24, 27, 87, 90, 97, 103, 104, 129,
    130, 274, 275, 276
Cooley, C. H., 73, 74, 75
Cooley, E. L., 120, 176
Cooper, J., 88, 372
Corazzini, J. G., 27, 120, 274, 275
Costa, P. T., Jr., 8, 9, 10, 26, 36, 37, 39, 177, 178,
    179
Cote, S., 45, 47, 48, 49, 86
Cottrell, L. S., Jr., 9
Coulter, L. P., 49, 51, 103, 261, 263, 264
Coyne, J. C., 121, 143, 145, 146, 148, 154, 242,
    258
Craighead, W., 138, 139
Craik, K. H., 40, 171, 179, 202
Crawford, C. E., 198, 224, 274
Creaser, J., 264, 266
Critelli, J. W., 302, 303
Crocker, P., 225, 314
Croppa, M. D., 3, 16, 23
Cross, S., 351
Crowder, J. E., 103, 250, 251, 264, 266
Crowley, R. M., 333
Cunningham, M. R., 139
Cutler, R. L., 231

Dalgleish, T., 139
D'Andrade, R. G., 35, 36, 37
Danziger, K., 3, 5, 99
Darley, J. M., 87, 88
Davenport, Y. B., 148, 152
Davidson, K. M., 42, 45, 120, 193
Davis, B., 149, 166
Davis, D., 225
Davis, J. M., 148, 152, 153
Davis, K. E., 103
Davison, G. C., 283
Davison, M. L., 31
Dawson, D. F., 148, 158
De Jong, C. A. J., 187, 190
DeJong, J., 25
Delgado, O. F., 103
Demby, A., 187, 191, 198
DeMonbreun, B. G., 138
Denzin, N. K., 74, 75, 76, 78
de Raad, B., 8, 9, 10, 177, 178
DeRubeis, R. J., 138
Desaulniers, J., 42, 43, 45, 47
De Soto, C., 59, 65
Deutsch, M., 8
Devens, M., 123, 134, 135
DeVogue, J. T., 51, 232, 251, 255
DeVries, H., 24, 103, 123, 124
Dickman, S., 69
Diener, E., 49
Dietzel, C. S., 49, 51, 101, 103, 108, 261
Digman, J. M., 9
Dillard, J. P., 146
Dilling, C. A., 103
Di Matteo, M. R., 103
Dinitz, S., 134, 135
Dittman, A., 103
Dobson, K. S., 123, 139, 147, 148, 151
Dodge, K. A., 59, 66
Doehrman, M. J. G., 310, 317, 318
Doren, R., 171, 197
Dorris, J. W., 285
Dowdy, B. B., 81, 203
Dryer, D. C., 103, 106, 108, 148, 155, 197
Dudley, D., 27, 103, 148, 155
Duke, M. P., 5, 24, 45, 46, 47, 49, 50, 103, 105, 106, 134, 136, 176, 182, 202
Duncan-Jones, P., 81
Dunkel-Schetter, C., 148, 166
Dunnette, M. D., 304
Dupont, P., 27, 187, 188, 189

Edelberg, W., 37
Edquist, M. H., 103
Eisenthal, S., 231, 232
Ekman, P., 209
Ekstein, R., 310
Ekstrand, M., 103, 106
Elder, G. H., Jr., 91, 131
El-Yousef, M. K., 148, 152, 153

Emmons, R. A., 49
Endler, N. S., 46, 181, 209
Engle, D., 198, 271, 273
Epstein, L., 230, 305
Epstein, R. S., 148, 152, 153
Epstein, S., 181
Erdelyi, M. H., 68, 69
Estroff, S., 29, 30, 39, 42, 43, 103, 262

Farbman, I., 103
Farmer, L., 198
Farwell, G. F., 103
Fazio, R. H., 87, 88
Federman, E. J., 7, 25, 28, 53, 71, 105, 112, 114, 122, 134, 135, 136, 194
Feiner, A. H., 230, 305
Feldman, L. B., 274, 279
Feldstein, S., 210, 220
Felker, D., 86
Fierman, L. B., 127
Filak, J., 103
Fineberg, B. L., 8
Fiore, J., 103
Fisher, B., 27, 77, 270
Fisher, G. A., 32, 33
Fiske, A. P., 66
Fitzgerald, J. M., 42, 43, 44
Fitzgerald, R. G., 148, 152
Fitzpatrick, M. A., 8
Flohr, D. F., 27, 274, 279
Foa, E. B., 8, 51, 53, 100, 105
Foa, U. G., 6, 8, 51, 53, 100, 105
Folkman, S., 72
Foreman, M. E., 148, 157
Forgas, J. P., 8, 47, 59
Forsleff, L. P., 310, 317, 318
Forsterling, F., 37
Foster, S. W., 29, 39, 59, 60
France, A-C., 29, 59, 62, 103
Frances, A., 171, 177, 181, 187, 189, 190, 192, 202
Francis, A. M. R., 27, 274, 279
Freedman, M. B., 3, 7, 8, 11, 12, 24, 39, 40, 56, 57, 112
Freedman, S. M., 65
Freeman, G., 103
French, R. D., 180
French, R. deS., 171, 181, 197
French, T., 238
Frey, D., 59, 65
Friedlander, M. L., 89, 109, 123, 280, 310, 317, 318
Friedman, H. S., 103
Friend, R., 123, 148, 155
Friesen, W. V., 209
Frijda, N. H., 72
Fry, W., 149
Funder, D. C., 37, 39, 46, 53, 54, 181
Furman, W., 77, 78

Gaelick, L., 8, 11, 23, 25, 26, 31, 103
Gaffin, G. L., 103
Galanter, E., 58
Gamsky, N. R., 103
Gangestad, S., 87
Gart, J. J., 103
Gascoyne, S. R., 26, 59, 62, 63
Gaul, R., 123, 280
Gelso, C. J., 222
Gergen, K. J., 6
Ghannam, J., 103, 106, 108, 148, 155, 197
Giat, L., 29, 30, 39, 43, 262
Giat-Roberto, L., 29, 39
Gifford, R., 26, 36, 37
Gill, M. M., 222
Gillespie, J., 103
Gilmore, J. B., 69
Goethe, K. E., 42, 45, 121
Goffman, E., 46, 84, 85, 91
Gold, P. W., 148, 152
Goldberg, B., 68
Goldberg, L. R., 8, 9, 10, 177, 178
Golden, B. R., 27
Goldfarb, D., 65, 103
Goldfried, M. R., 283, 303, 304
Golding, S. L., 38, 59, 60
Goldsamt, L. A., 303, 304
Goldstein, A. J., 149
Goldston, C. S., 26, 27, 39, 55, 90, 97, 101, 103,
    183, 185, 187, 190, 234, 281
Gomes, M., 26, 202
Gomes-Schwartz, B., 279
Gonick, J., 27, 42, 45, 103, 201, 263
Goodfriend, S., 197
Goodwin, F. K., 148, 152
Gorad, S. L., 148, 151, 152
Gordon, S. E., 67
Gormly, J., 37
Gorsuch, R. L., 30, 103, 274, 276
Gotlib, I. H., 123, 148, 154
Gottman, J. M., 285
Greben, S. E., 311, 312
Green, M., 238
Greenberg, J., 59, 65, 86, 229
Greenberg, L. S., 69, 72, 220, 222, 274, 307
Greenson, R., 222
Greenwood, V. B., 122
Grimm, L. G., 26, 166
Guerney, B., Jr., 39, 51, 103, 108
Guidano, V., 69
Guinee, J. P., 106
Gurtman, M. B., 11, 12, 13, 23, 30, 32, 33, 34,
    102, 146, 187, 188, 198, 271, 272
Guttman, L., 8, 11, 30, 31

Hadley, S. W., 234, 279
Hafner, J., 149
Hafner, R. J., 149
Haggard, L. M., 49
Haley, J., 88, 89, 148, 155, 156

Hall, J. A., 209, 210, 220
Halpern, H. M., 103, 238
Hamilton, D. L., 38
Hammen, C. L., 147
Hampton, C., 123, 148, 155
Hare, R. D., 157
Harper, R. G., 210, 220
Harrigan, J. A., 210, 220
Hart, P. P., 242, 258
Harter, S., 68
Hartley, D. E., 222, 340
Harvey, J., 3, 6, 74, 88, 217
Haslam, N., 59, 66, 67
Hay, L. R., 149
Hayes, A. M., 303, 304
Hays, K., 103
Heape, C., 27, 77, 270
Heatherington, L., 123, 280
Hedeen, C., 147
Heffner, K. P., 27, 123, 148
Heise, D. R., 32, 33
Helgeson, V. S., 42
Heller, K., 103
Hellmer, L. A., 8
Helmes, E., 35, 36, 37
Helmreich, R. L., 42
Henderson, C. A., 139
Henderson, P. R., 149, 164, 165
Henderson, S., 81
Henley, N. M., 210
Henry, W. P., 29, 39, 103, 233, 264, 265, 274,
    277, 278
Herst, E. R., 351
Hertel, R. K., 103
Herzberger, S., 139
Higgins, D. S., 26, 202
Hill, C., 27, 53, 70, 86, 103, 360
Hill, J. P., 75, 76, 78
Hills, H. I., 24, 27, 39, 103, 123, 124, 187, 189,
    263
Hirschberg, N., 24, 31
Hodgin, J., 187, 188
Hoffman, I. Z., 222
Hofstee, W. K. B., 9, 10, 177, 178
Hogan, R., 8, 341
Hokanson, J. E., 59, 65, 103, 121, 147
Holahan, C. K., 42
Holahan, W., 41, 42, 107, 123
Holifield, J., 103, 230
Holland, J. L., 8
Hollander, G. P., 147
Holliday, S. L., 121
Holton, B., 59, 65
Holzmuller, A., 26, 42
Hora, T., 310
Horner, M. S., 177
Horney, K., 130, 131
Horowitz, L. M., 28, 29, 103, 106, 108, 134, 137,
    148, 155, 171, 174, 181, 197, 198, 230, 253,
    254, 271, 272, 273, 274, 275

Horowitz, M. J., 342
Horvath, A. O., 222
Howard, K. I., 198, 271, 272
Howard, T., 264, 266
Howes, M. J., 121, 147
Hubert, L. J., 31, 101
Hudgins, M. K., 59, 64, 120, 122, 233, 234
Hummer, J. T., 59, 65
Humphrey, L. L., 29
Hurley, J. R., 8, 9, 65, 89
Hurt, S., 187, 189, 190
Huston, T. L., 6, 74, 88, 217
Hyler, S., 174, 178, 183

Ickes, W., 46, 86, 139
Ingraham, J. L., 41, 55
Ingraham, L. J., 41, 42, 103, 107, 123

Jackson, D., 35, 36, 37, 38, 88, 89, 143, 148, 155, 206, 207, 218, 258
Jahoda, M., 126, 139
Jandorf, E. M., 131
Janoff-Bulman, R., 140
Janowsky, D. S., 148, 152, 153
Jansen, J. A. M., 187, 190
Jilton, R., 198, 225, 265
John, O. P., 39, 46
Johnson, M. E., 29, 30, 143
Jones, R. A., 87
Jones, W. H., 341
Jourard, S. M., 139
Joyce, A. S., 198, 274, 278
Juhasz, A. M., 76
Jussim, L., 87

Kahn, J., 121
Kalehzan, B. M., 197, 198, 271, 272, 273
Kaminski, E. P., 8
Kanner, A. D., 72
Kaplan, S. J., 8
Kapp, F. T., 316
Kaszniak, A. W., 198, 271, 273
Kaufmann, C., 3, 16, 23
Kaul, T. J., 304
Kavanagh, J. A., 32
Kaye, A. L., 123, 148, 155
Keith, P. M., 75
Kell, B. L., 103
Kellerman, H., 187
Kelley, H. H., 6, 58, 66, 74, 88, 217
Kelly, G. A., 35, 161
Kelso, K., 171, 175, 189
Kemper, T. D., 8, 72
Kendrick, D. T., 37, 181
Kenny, D. A., 41, 55, 107, 108
Kerckhoff, A. C., 103
Kernberg, O., 305
Kerr, A. E., 27, 187, 189
Kerr, S., 303, 304

Kiesler, D. J., xi, xiii, 3, 4, 5, 7, 8, 11, 12, 13, 14, 15, 16, 19, 21, 22, 23, 24, 25, 26, 27, 28, 30, 31, 32, 33, 34, 39, 40, 41, 42, 45, 46, 47, 49, 50, 51, 52, 53, 58, 67, 70, 71, 72, 73, 74, 75, 78, 79, 81, 82, 83, 90, 91, 94, 98, 99, 101, 102, 103, 104, 105, 108, 109, 112, 114, 115, 116, 119, 120, 122, 123, 127, 131, 132, 134, 141, 142, 148, 155, 161, 171, 172, 173, 175, 176, 177, 179, 183, 184, 185, 187, 190, 192, 193, 194, 199, 200, 201, 202, 203, 204, 206, 210, 217, 218, 220, 223, 224, 226, 227, 228, 229, 230, 231, 232, 233, 234, 237, 242, 243, 244, 247, 257, 260, 261, 264, 265, 274, 276, 281, 283, 284, 285, 291, 305, 306, 307, 313, 320
Kihlstrom, J. F., 69
Kilmartin, C. T., 24, 103, 123, 124
Kinch, J. W., 74
Kinnane, J. F., 25
Kirker, W., 67
Kivlighan, D. M., Jr., 27, 59, 64, 65, 120, 274, 275, 279, 304, 305
Klein, M. H., 233
Klerman, G. L., 7, 73, 77, 82, 198, 237, 267, 268
Kliewer, W. L., 81, 203
Kline, L. V., 103
Klinger, E., 191
Knapp, M. L., 209, 210
Knight, T. A., 103
Knudson, R. M., 38, 59, 60
Knudson, R., 38
Kohut, H., 188, 189
Kopta, S. M., 272
Krantz, S. E., 347
Krause, M. S., 272
Krug, R. S., 8
Kuethe, J. L., 59, 65
Kuhn, M. H., 75
Kuiper, N., 67
Kusulas, J. W., 179
Kyle, E. M., 7, 25, 28, 53, 71, 112, 114, 122

Labe-Sloan, E. H., 123, 193
Ladd, M., 103
LaForge, R., 3, 8, 12, 23, 24, 33, 38, 101, 112, 113, 190
LaFrance, M., 210
LaFromboise, T. D., 123, 233, 234
Laird, H., 30, 103, 261, 264
Lambert, M., 134, 137, 138, 198, 217, 232
Lamphere, R. A., 304
Landsman, T., 139
Lane, H., 3, 16, 23
Langs, R. J., 311, 312
Lanier, K., 24, 103, 123, 124
Lapan, R. T., 27, 187, 189
Lapid, J. S., 171, 181, 197
LaPrelle, J., 59, 65
Larsen, R. J., 49

Larus, J. P., 26, 27, 74, 78, 79, 177, 183, 185, 187, 190
Larus-McShane, J. P., 75, 79, 81, 82, 203
LaRusso, L., 139, 148, 164
Lauterbach, K., 26, 202
La Voie, L., 41, 55, 107, 108
Layden, M. A., 139
Lazarus, R. S., 72, 139
Leary, T. F., xi, xiii, 3, 4, 6, 7, 8, 10, 11, 12, 16, 23, 24, 29, 39, 40, 51, 53, 56, 57, 58, 73, 83, 90, 109, 112, 121, 129, 131, 132, 133, 143, 145, 147, 148, 171, 172, 173, 175, 176, 184, 207, 237, 250, 251
Leborgne, B., 148, 157
Lecky, P., 85
Lederer, W. J., 89
Lees-Halet, P. R., 23
Leff, M., 148, 152, 153
Lein, L., 81
Lemert, E. M., 148, 162, 163
Lempers, J. D., 77
Lerner, H. E., 42
Levenson, E. A., 283, 287
Levinger, G., 6, 74, 88, 217
Lewicka, M., 8, 177
Lewicki, P., 69
Lewinsohn, P. M., 138, 146, 148, 154, 198
Lieberman, M. A., 9
Liggett, A., 27, 193
Lineham, M. M., 229
Lipsher, D., 103
Llewellyn, L., 103
Lochman, J. E., 59, 66
Locke, K. D., 103, 106, 108, 148, 155, 187, 191, 192, 197
Longabaugh, R., 8
Lonner, W. J., 8
Loranger, A. W., 191
Lorr, M., 8, 12, 16, 23, 24, 25, 26, 28, 31, 112, 113, 186, 187, 364
Lovejoy, M. C., 103
Lowenstein, E., 181, 197
Lowman, J., 8
Luborsky, L., 73, 222, 230, 237
Lucke, J. F., 32, 33
Luetgert, M. J., 264, 266
Luria, Z., 8
Lyons, J., 24, 26, 31, 166
Lyons, M. J., 178

Mackenzie, T. B., 148, 288, 289
Madison, J. K., 57
Magnusson, D., 46, 181, 209
Mahalik, J. R., 27, 103
Mahoney, M. J., 69
Maling, M. S., 198, 271, 272
Mancini, A. M., 123, 149, 166
Mangus, A. R., 134, 135
Manheim, S., 24, 49, 50, 51, 103, 108, 176

Mann, D. F., 198
Mann, J. M., 9
Mantano, R. A., 187, 191, 192
Marcus, D. K., 41, 42, 107, 123, 146
Mardia, K. V., 33
Margolin, G., 121
Markel, N. N., 205
Markowitz, J. C., 237, 268
Marks, I. M., 351
Markson, E. R., 311, 312
Markus, H., 67, 68, 85, 351
Marsh-Angelone, M., 27, 59, 65
Marshall, G. N., 179
Martelli, M. F., 123, 167
Martin, C. L., 134, 137
Masling, J. M., 158
Matarazzo, J. D., 210, 220
Mathieu-Coughlan, P., 233
Mavissakalian, M., 149
Mayo, C., 210
McAdams, D. P., 8
McCallum, M., 198, 274, 278
McCarthy, P. R., 28
McClelland, D. C., 270, 305
McClintock, E., 6, 74, 88, 217
McCormick, C. C., 32
McCourt, W. F., 148, 151, 152
McCrae, R. R., 8, 9, 10, 26, 36, 37, 39, 46, 177, 178, 179, 180
McCullough, J. P., 123, 148, 155, 274
McCune, K. J., 123, 148, 155
McGill, K. L., 86
McGovern, S. R., 176
McGovern, T. V., 27, 120, 274, 275
McLean, P. D., 148, 154
McLemore, C. W., 29, 30, 39, 51, 53, 102, 103, 105, 148, 155, 171, 172, 175, 184, 236, 242, 258, 274, 276
McLeod, M., 176
McMain, S., 225, 314
McMullen, L. M., 27, 49, 51, 103, 261, 262, 274, 275, 276
McNair, D. M., 8, 12, 16, 23, 24, 25, 28, 31, 112, 113, 186, 187
McNeel, S. P., 59, 65
McNeil, B. W., 310, 317
Mead, G. H., 68, 74, 75
Meddin, J., 58, 59
Meese, L. A., 103
Mehrabian, A., 210
Meichenbaum, D., 69
Mellon, J., 29, 30, 143
Mendelsohn, G. A., 37
Mendelson, A., 103
Mercuri, L. G., 123, 167
Meredith, J., 59, 123, 167
Merenda, P. F., 8
Merla, M. E., 178
Merry, J., 187, 191, 198

Merton, R. K., 87
Mervis, C., 180
Messick, D. M., 59, 65
Meyer, C. W., III, 24, 103, 123, 124
Meyers, H. C., 305
Mezzich, J., 180
Miele, G. M., 102
Mikail, S. F., 149, 164, 165
Milestone, S. F., 121
Miller, D., 8, 87
Miller, G. A., 58
Miller, P., 103
Miller, T. R., 178
Millon, T., 126, 127, 134, 181, 182, 189, 190,
    191, 198, 266
Milton, F., 149
Mintz, E., 315
Mischel, W., 46, 48, 49, 98, 126, 138, 180, 181
Mitchell, S. A., 229
Mohr, D. C., 198, 271, 273
Monts, J. K., 59
Moore, S., 148, 160, 268
Moos, R. H., 103, 126
Moras, K., 120, 123, 234, 274, 278
Morey, L. C., 30, 135, 187, 190, 270, 271
Morran, D. K., 285, 292, 294, 304
Morse, M. B., 103, 106, 108, 148, 155, 197
Moskowitz, D. S., 42, 43, 45, 47, 48, 49, 86, 106
Moulthrop, M. A., 161, 220
Muckenheim, R., 8
Mueller, W. J., 103
Mueser, K. T., 166
Mulford, H. A., 76
Mullison, D. D., 27, 65, 274, 279
Mungas, D. M., 38
Muran, J. C., 53, 70, 71, 198, 222, 224, 225, 234,
    264, 265, 274, 275, 314
Murdock, N. L., 123, 235
Murray, C. M., 79, 81, 82, 203
Murray, H. A., 6
Murray, P., 225, 314
Murrell, S. A., 247, 288, 296
Muten, E., 179
Myers, R. A., 103

Naboisek, H., 3
Nardone, M. E., 146
Nelson, A. P., 103, 121, 134, 135
Nelson, B. N., 24, 39, 103, 123, 124, 189, 263
Nelson, H. F., 139
Nelson, R. E., 139
Neu, C., 237
Neumann, K. F., 302, 303
Newman, C. F., 303
Niit, T., 8, 177
Nisbett, R., 69
Nixon, G. W., 198, 274, 278
Norman, W. T., 9, 36, 177
Norquist, S., 103

Norris, S. L. W., 123, 148, 155
Nowicki, S. P., Jr., 5, 23, 24, 31, 42, 43, 45, 46,
    47, 49, 50, 51, 103, 105, 106, 108, 109, 134,
    136, 176, 182, 202
Nurius, P., 68
Nydegger, R. V., 59

O'Connell, T. J., 103
O'Connor, B., 26, 36, 37
O'Dell, J. W., 24
Oden, T. C., xiii
O'Grady, K. E., 27
O'Halloran, P., 197, 198, 271, 273
Okiyama, S. L., 103
Oldham, J. M., 191
Olson, D. H., 8
Olson, R., 76, 78
Olsson, J. E., 59, 61
Orford, J., 40, 51, 82, 100, 102, 103, 104, 105, 108
Orlinsky, D. E., 272
Ossorio, A. G., 3, 7, 8, 11, 12, 24, 39, 40, 56, 57,
    112
Ostendorf, F., 37
Oxenford, C., 176
Ozer, D. J., 178

Paddock, J., 23, 24, 26, 31, 57, 109, 176, 238
Palmer, J., 103
Pande, S. K., 103
Parad, H. W., 181, 197
Pasamanick, B., 134, 135
Pasciuti, F. M., 59
Passini, F. T., 36
Pate, C., 238
Patenaude, W., 134, 137, 138, 198
Patterson, G. R., 91, 103
Patton, M., 27, 187, 188, 189
Paulhus, D. L., 134, 137
Paunonen, S. V., 37, 38
Peake, P. K., 181
Penberthy, A. R., 123, 167
Peplau, L. A., 6, 74, 88, 217
Perkins, M. J., 7, 25, 28, 53, 71, 112, 114
Perlmutter, K. B., 59, 176
Perls, F., 234, 283
Pervin, L. A., 126
Peters, S. D., 147
Peterson, D. R., 6, 8, 7, 50, 74, 88, 198, 199, 217,
    218
Pfohl, B., 190
Phelps, R. E., 24
Phillips, N., 11, 13, 23, 25, 26, 28, 29, 30, 31, 32,
    173, 174, 178, 186, 198
Pierce, G. R., 81
Pilkonis, P., 27, 77, 270
Pincus, A. L., 9, 10, 23, 26, 28, 29, 49, 50, 53, 85,
    105, 110, 134, 136, 173, 178, 179, 186, 187,
    191, 192, 197, 198, 217
Pinkston, K., 187, 188

Pinsof, W. M., 220
Piper, W. E., 198, 274, 278
Platman, S. R., 186, 187
Plutchik, R., xiii, 3, 4, 8, 72, 171, 177, 186, 187
Pollock, T. E., 27, 310, 317, 319, 320
Pond, J. H., 30, 42, 43
Pope, M. K., 149, 163
Popp, C., 29, 30, 143
Post, D. L., 171, 181, 197
Potts, M. A., 109
Powers, M. J., 81
Pribram, K. H., 58
Proudman, S., 27, 274, 279
Pyszczynski, T., 59, 65, 86

Radecki-Bush, C., 27, 42, 44
Raulin, M. L., 139
Raush, H. L., 6, 51, 103, 108
Ray, P. B., 49, 261, 262
Read, S. J., 86
Reagan, S. A., 122, 123, 147, 193
Reid, J. B., 103
Renzaglia, G., 103
Rice, L. N., 274, 307
Rice, P. L. K., 103, 270, 271
Rime, B., 148, 157
Rinn, J. L., 8
Rioch, M. J., 311, 313
Robbins, S. B., 27, 187, 188, 189
Roberts, W. C., 123, 148, 155
Robinson, D. L., 198
Robinson, F. F., 285, 292, 294, 304
Roe, A., 8
Rogers, C. R., 85, 234
Rogers, T., 67
Rollins, B. C., 8
Romano, R. L., 133, 237
Romney, D. M., 134, 187, 189, 191, 192
Rosch, E., 180
Rosenberg, M., 74, 75, 85, 86
Rosenberg, S., 28, 134, 137, 148, 197, 198, 271, 272, 273, 274, 275, 288, 289
Rosenfeld, H. M., 87, 103
Rosenfield, D., 138, 139
Rosenthal, R., 87, 88, 210, 220
Ross, D., 316
Ross, L., 69
Roth, C. H., 264, 266
Rotter, J. B., 359
Rottschafer, R., 103
Rouillon, F., 148, 157
Rounsaville, B. J., 7, 73, 77, 82, 198, 237, 267, 268
Rubert, M. P., 147
Rubin, D., 87, 88
Rudy, J. P., 30, 103, 274, 276
Ruesch, J., 155
Russakoff, L. M., 191
Russell, C. S., 8
Russell, J. A., 8, 177

Sackheim, H. A., 138
Sadavoy, J., 311, 312
Safran, J. D., xi, xiii, 3, 51, 52, 53, 58, 69, 70, 72, 105, 171, 222, 225, 232, 234, 237, 241, 242, 256, 257, 274, 275, 295, 296, 314, 317, 360
Saltzman, C., 103, 264, 266
Sampson, H., 197, 198, 253, 274, 275
Samstag, L. W., 53, 70, 71, 198, 224, 225, 264, 265, 274, 275
Sarason, B. R., 81
Sarason, I. G., 81
Sasseville, T., 27, 103, 148, 155
Saucier, G., 9, 177
Savin-Williams, R. C., 37
Saxby, S. P., 59, 64, 122
Schacht, T. E., 29, 30, 39, 103, 143, 233, 264, 265, 274, 277, 278
Schachtel, E. G., 69
Schaefer, E. S., 8, 29, 112, 171, 177
Schaffer, N. D., 233
Scheff, T. J., 88
Scheflen, A. E., 205
Scheiner, S. B., 42, 59, 63
Scher, S. J., 140
Schippers, G. M., 187, 190
Schlosberg, H. S., 8
Schmidt, J. A., 11, 12, 23, 26, 27, 30, 31, 32, 33, 34, 53, 71, 72, 73, 83, 101, 102, 105, 112, 115, 116, 123, 173, 176, 179, 199, 200
Schneider, P. L., 23, 26, 27, 31, 32, 101, 102, 103, 173
Schoeneman, T. J., 74, 75
Schopler, J. H., 103, 274
Schreiber, R. D., 121
Schuldt, W., 103
Schulz, D., 139
Schutz, W. C., 89, 109, 112
Schwaninger-Morse, F., 45, 47, 121
Schwartz, D., 103
Schwartz, K. M., 103
Schwartz, M. A., 158
Scott, D. A., 103
Scott, R., 81
Scott, W. A., 126
Searles, H., 310
Secord, P. F., 58, 85, 109
Segal, L., 242, 258
Segal, P. S., 198, 274, 278
Segal, Z. V., xiii, 3, 51, 52, 53, 68, 69, 70, 71, 134, 135, 171, 198, 224, 225, 232, 237, 241, 242, 256, 257, 264, 265, 274, 275, 296, 314, 317, 360
Segraves, R., 237
Segrin, C., 7, 146, 147
Serio, C. D., 101, 102, 123
Shader, R., 103
Shafer, R. B., 75
Shannon, J., 39, 51, 103, 108
Shapiro, J. H., 27, 42

Shaw, B. F., 51, 52, 135, 171
Shea, T., 370
Shean, G., 27, 103, 123, 148, 149, 150
Shearin, E. N., 81
Sheffield, M., 134, 137, 138, 198
Sherry, P., 49, 103, 320
Shevrin, H., 69
Shoemaker, D. J., 8
Shoeneman, T. J., 76, 78
Shohan-Solomon, V., 198, 271, 273
Shopshire, M. S., 179
Shrauger, J. S., 74, 75, 302
Shuler, A., 27, 123, 148, 150
Shulman, N., 76
Shweder, R. A., 35, 36, 37
Siegel, S. M., 310, 317, 318
Siegelman, E. Y., 171, 181, 197, 198, 274, 275
Siegman, A. W., 210, 220
Sikes-Nova, V. E., 26, 27, 59, 61, 183, 185, 187,
    190
Sim, J. P., 134, 187, 189, 192
Simon, L., 123, 280
Simpson, A. W., 121
Singer, E. B., 298
Skokan, L. A., 140
Slater, M. A., 24
Slater, P. E., 363
Slipp, S., 148, 153
Small, S. A., 37
Smelser, W. T., 59, 103
Smith, E. E., 180
Smith, K., 27, 77, 270
Smith, T. W., 149, 163, 164
Snyder, C. R., 140
Snyder, M. L., 46, 86, 87, 88, 138, 139
Sobieszek, B. I., 74, 75
Soldz, S., 187, 191, 198
Solomon, S., 8, 86
Somberg, D. R., 59, 66
Sox, K. A., 103
Speisman, J. C., 103
Spence, J. T., 42
Spiegel, S., 238
Spitzer, R. L., 171
Spotnitz, H., 230, 305, 306, 316
Sprenkle, D. H., 8
Sprock, J., 187, 188
Stahelski, A. J., 66
Stangl, D., 190
Statham, A., 74
Steiger, J. H., 11, 23, 25, 26, 31
Steinmetz, S. K., 8
Stephan, W. G., 138, 139
Stern, D. N., 68
Stern, G. G., 24, 112
Stiles, T., 103, 264, 265
Stiles, W. B., 146
Stockton, R. A., 285, 292, 294, 304
Stollak, G. E., 103

Stoller, F. H., 364
Stone, G. L., 103, 123, 303
Stoto, M., 41
Strack, S., 3, 26, 364
Strentz, T., 101, 102, 123
Strickland, D., 24, 103, 123, 124
Stromseth, J., 123, 235
Strong, S. R., 24, 28, 39, 103, 123, 124, 189, 237,
    263
Strupp, H. H., 29, 30, 39, 73, 103, 143, 222, 232,
    233, 234, 237, 262, 264, 265, 270, 271, 274,
    275, 277, 278, 279
Stryker, S., 74
Stuart, R. B., 149, 166
Stuart, S., 27, 77, 270
Suczek, R. F., 3, 8, 23, 24, 38, 112, 113, 190
Suh, C., 120, 123, 234
Suh, E. J., 42, 43, 45, 47
Sullivan, H. S., xi, xiii, 3, 6, 7, 38, 53, 54, 56, 59,
    68, 69, 70, 73, 74, 83, 84, 85, 88, 89, 105,
    125, 128, 130, 136, 148, 204, 207, 221, 222,
    223, 225, 228, 229, 238, 245, 256, 286
Summers, F., 133
Susman, V. L., 191
Sussman, M., 81
Suziedelis, A., 8, 25
Svartberg, M., 103, 264, 265
Swaney, K. B., 103, 123, 303
Swann, W. B., Jr., 86
Swensen, C. H., Jr., 53, 103, 321

Tagiuri, R., 87
Talley, P. F., 30, 270, 271
Tansey, M. J., 231, 305
Taplin, J. R., 59
Tarrow, E., 103, 106, 108, 148, 155, 197
Tasca, G. A., 49, 51, 103, 149, 164, 165, 261, 262
Taulbee, E. S., 23
Taylor, S. E., 138, 139, 140
Taylor, T., 103
Tellegen, A., 39, 46, 53
Tennen, H., 139
Teyber, E., 103, 237, 259, 260
Thibaut, J. W., 58
Thibodeau, J. R., 103, 121
Thiel, K. S., 75, 76, 78
Thomas, D. L., 8
Thompson, B. J., 27, 103
Thorne, A., 6, 103, 111
Thornton, A. L., Jr., 121
Todd, T. S., 161, 220
Tomlin, A. M., 59, 66
Tracey, T. J., 23, 26, 27, 31, 32, 49, 101, 102,
    103, 105, 106, 107, 108, 173, 261, 262, 264,
    320
Trapnell, P., 8, 9, 10, 11, 13, 23, 25, 26, 28, 29,
    30, 31, 32, 131, 173, 174, 177, 178
Triandis, H. C., 8
Trontel, E. H., 38

Trull, T., 171, 177, 178, 179, 183, 187, 189, 190, 202
Tryer, P., 187, 188
Trzebinski, J., 37
Tucker, G. J., 148, 288, 289
Tupes, E. C., 9, 177
Turnbull, W., 87
Turner, J. L., 51
Turovsky, J., 148, 149
Tyhurst, J. S., 148, 164

Uchenwa, U., 27, 103, 123, 148, 149, 150
Ureno, G., 28, 134, 137, 197, 198, 271, 273, 274, 275

Vallacher, R. R., 74
Vallis, T. M., 51, 52, 171
Valone, K., 59, 60, 103
Vande Kemp, H., 30, 103, 261, 264
Van den Brink, W., 187, 190
Van Denburg, E. J., 280
Van Denburg, T. F., 11, 12, 26, 27, 30, 83, 103, 108, 125, 131, 132, 134, 183, 185, 187, 190, 199, 200, 226, 227, 228, 230, 232, 247, 280, 284, 305, 306, 313
Vickers, R. R., 179
Viene, D., 123, 235
Villard, K. L., 73, 85, 88, 97, 217, 218, 285, 286, 301
Villasenor, V. S., 28, 134, 137, 197, 198, 271, 274, 275
Vitkus, J., 148, 155, 171, 174, 197, 253, 254

Wachtel, P. L., 84, 90, 126, 129, 222, 228, 242
Wagner, B. C., 103
Wagner, C. C., 11, 12, 30, 32, 33, 34, 53, 71, 72, 73, 83, 94, 102, 103, 105, 107, 115, 179, 265
Walkar, S. V., 103, 106, 108, 148, 155, 197
Wallerstein, R., 238, 239, 310
Wallis, K. D., 171, 181, 197
Ward, C. O., 88
Warner, R. M., 41
Waterhouse, G. J., 120, 123, 234
Watkins, L. M., 27, 49, 51, 101, 103, 223, 224, 261, 264, 265
Watts, F. N., 139
Watzlawick, P., 88, 89, 143, 155, 206, 207, 218, 258
Waugh, M. H., 135
Waxer, P. H., 210
Weakland, J., 89, 148, 155, 258
Webster, A. S., 149
Webster, M., 74, 75
Weckler, D. A., 171, 181, 197
Wegner, A. Z., 138
Weinstock-Savoy, D. E., 26, 27, 101, 103, 274, 277
Weiss, D. S., 37
Weiss, J., 197, 253

Weissman, M. M., 7, 73, 77, 82, 198, 237, 267, 268
Welker, R. A., 147
Wenzel, C. K., 42, 44, 45, 120, 121, 193
Werner, C. M., 49
Werner, M., 123, 279
Wertheim, A., 285
Wetter, M. W., 103
Whiffen, V. E., 27, 103, 148, 155, 360
Whipple, L. J., 73, 85, 88, 97, 217, 218, 285, 286, 301
Whitaker, D. S., 9
White, G. M., 8
Widiger, T. A., 102, 171, 174, 175, 177, 178, 179, 181, 183, 187, 189, 190, 192, 202, 370
Wiener, M., 148, 154
Wiens, A. N., 210, 220
Wiggins, J. S., xiii, 3, 4, 8, 9, 10, 11, 12, 13, 23, 24, 25, 26, 27, 28, 29, 30, 31, 32, 33, 34, 36, 37, 42, 53, 73, 100, 105, 109, 112, 115, 119, 131, 134, 136, 137, 171, 172, 173, 174, 175, 177, 178, 179, 180, 181, 186, 187, 188, 189, 191, 192, 197, 198, 217
Wilkie, C. F., 27, 39, 103
Wilkinson, L., 24, 31
Williams, J. B. W., 171
Willner, A. H., 134, 136
Winch, R. F., 8, 103
Winegardner, J., 38
Winnicott, D. W., 230, 249, 283, 300
Winston, A., 53, 70, 198, 225, 265, 274, 275
Wish, M., 8
Woelfel, J. D., 76, 78
Wolstein, B., 305
Wonderlich, S. A., 29, 59, 62, 148, 158, 187
Woodruff, D. L., 238
Word, C. O., 372
Worthen, V., 310, 317
Wortman, C. B., 148, 166, 179
Wright, J., 181, 197, 225
Wright, T., 41, 42, 55, 103, 107, 123
Wyer, R. S., 8, 67, 103
Wyrick, R. A., 103

Yalom, I. D., 64, 237, 304
Yarnold, P. R., 26, 166
Yost, E. B., 198, 271, 273
Young, D. M., 242, 247, 308, 314
Youngren, M. A., 146, 148, 154, 198
Youniss, R. P., 25

Zajonc, R., 67, 85
Zanna, M. P., 88, 372
Zeldin, L. R. S., 37
Zetzel, E., 222
Zians, J. K., 120, 234, 281
Zimmerman, M., 190
Zuckerman, M., 138, 139
Zurcher, L. A., 59

Subject Index

Abasive-helpless, 20
Abstract words, 161, 247
Acomplementarity:
    interpersonal circle diagnosis and, 183
    1982 Interpersonal Circle, 95
    personalities, 94, 96
    therapist-patient matching, 270
Acquaintance, relationship stage, 50
Act-by-act sequential analyses, 50, 107
Act-in-context, 202
Action impulses, 72
Action-reaction, study of, 6
Action tendencies, 53, 71–72, 112, 116–117, 317
Actor-focused studies, 40–41
Actual relationships, 6
Adjective items, 40
Adjustment, psychological, 8
Adolescents:
    interpersonal styles of, 122–123
    personality disorder diagnosis in, 175
    therapy for, 238
Adult interpersonal behavior, 8
Affective Reactions Questionnaire (ARQ),
    27–28
Affiliation:
    Big Five factors, 9
    in communication process, 220
    cross-situational generality, 47–48
    dimensions of, 5
    emotional response, 73
    Interpersonal Schema Questionnaire (ISQ),
        70
    need for, 8
    personality traits, 58, 87
    resistance and, 228
    working alliance, 225
Affinity, client-therapist relationship, 233–234
Agency:
    communion and, 9–10
    defined, 9
Aggression:
    complementarity and, 91
    interpersonal relations, 66
    in obsessives, 162
    in paranoids, 163
Agoraphobia, 149–151
Agreeableness:
    diagnostic principles, 177–178
    DSM-III Axis II disorders, 192

Alcohol abuse/dependency, 151–152
All-inclusive approval, of significant others, 79
All loving-absolving, 21
Aloof-indifferent, 17
Aloof-Introverted (FG), 25, 37
Ambiguity, 151, 160, 299
Ambitionless-Flattering, 180
Ambitionless-lazy, 20
Ambitious-contending, 17
Amplitude:
    complementarity, 102
    interpersonal inventories scoring, 33
Analogue studies:
    maladjusted groups, 121–122
    psychotherapy, 120–121
Androgyny, 26, 43–45
Anger-sadness-guilt, 259
Angular displacement, interpersonal inventories
    scoring, 33
Angular location, 32, 173
ANOVA, 100, 320
Antagonistic-harmful, 17
Anticomplementarity:
    interpersonal circle diagnosis and, 183
    1982 Interpersonal Circle, 96
    personalities, 94, 96
    in psychotherapy, generally, 248–250,
        263–264
    therapist-patient matching, 270
    transactions, 110
Antisocial personality disorder:
    five-factor model and, 179
    interpersonal empirical findings, 189
    overview, 157
Anxiety:
    agoraphobia and, 149–150
    avoidance of, 4, 6, 53
    complementarity, 110
    decreasing, 54
    interpersonal empirical findings, 186–187
    mechanism, 54
    in relationships, 54–55
    in therapist-supervisee, 310–311
    triggering/evoking, 84
Anxiety-transmission theory, 54–55
Appeasement, 62
Approving-pardoning, 18
Arrogant-Calculating (BC), 25
Arrogant-self-contained, 21

Asocial personality disorder, five-factor model, 192
Asocial responses, in interpersonal psychotherapy, 247–248, 250
Assertiveness:
  complementary response research, 122–123
  depression and, 147
  submissive interpersonal behavior and, 193–194
Assessment, generally:
  covert interpersonal, 201
  nonverbal behavior, 202
  psychological, generally, 201
  significant others, 202–203
  situational, 202
  temporal, 202
Assimilation, relational psychotherapy, 258
Assured-Dominant (PA), 25
Attributional egotism, 139
Audiotapes, 210
Authoritarian parents, 158
Authority ranking, 66
Automatic resistance, 226
Automatic thought:
  dysfunctional, 52
  interpersonal psychotherapy, 240, 257
  Maladaptive Transaction cycle assessment, 196
  self-effacing, 146
Autonomy, 25, 61, 175
Average Intensity Level (AIN), 101
Aversive impact responses, 127
Aversive interpersonal style, 154
Avoidance:
  in alcoholics, 151–152
  obsessive-compulsive personality, 161
Avoidant personality disorder:
  five-factor model, 179, 192
  interpersonal circle translation, 184–185
  interpersonal empirical findings, 189–192
  overview, 157
  therapist interactions and, 183
Awareness, 68–69
Axis I symptom disorders:
  agoraphobia, 149–151
  alcohol abuse/dependency, 151–152
  bipolar disorder, 152–153
  dissociative disorder, 153
  dysthymic disorder, 154–155
  interpersonal circle diagnosis, 174
  interpersonal diagnosis of, 186–187
  phobias, 156–157
  schizophrenia, 155–156
Axis II personality disorders:
  antisocial personality disorder, 157
  avoidant personality disorder, 157
  borderline personality disorder, 157
  dependent personality disorder, 158–159
  histrionic personality disorder, 159–160
    interpersonal circle diagnosis, 174, 183
    interpersonal diagnosis of, 187–193
    obsessive-compulsive personality disorder, 161–162
    paranoid personality disorder, 162–164

Bad Me self-personification:
  defined, 54–56, 97
  in maladjusted individual, 129
Bad me-you patterns, 200
Bad self, object representations and, 200
Balance theory, 58
Bargain relationship, 159
Battery of Interpersonal Capabilities (BIC), 137
Beginning, relationship stage, 50
Behavioral concordance, 48–49, 86
Behavior theory, 51–52
Belief system, 60–61
Bem Sex Role Inventory (BSRI), 44
Beneficial uncertainty, 247, 284
Best fit, 126
Beth Israel Brief Psychotherapy Research Project, 234
Bias:
  cognitive, 37
  negative, 138
  positivity, 65
  self-serving, 139
  systematic, 40
Bi-directional causality, 3
Big Five personality factors:
  diagnostic principles and, 177–180
  interpersonal circumplex, 37
  personality factors, 9–10
Biologically mandated societal needs/roles, 8
Bipolar disorder, 152–153
Borderline personality disorder:
  five-factor model, 179, 192
  interpersonal circle translation, 184–185
  interpersonal empirical findings, 189, 191–192
  overview, 62, 157
Brief psychotherapy, 272
Brief SASB-directed reconstructive learning therapy, 252–253
Brief strategic therapy, 258–259
Buildup, relationship stage, 50

California *Q*-set, 34
Cardinal therapeutic tactic, 256
Cardiovascular reactivity, 166
Categorical relational models theory, 66
Causality:
  bi-directional, 3
  circular, 3, 5
Caveat emptor, 109
Censoring, 161
Censorious-damning, 20
Change process research, 274–280

Channel dominance, 63
Character resistance, 226–227
Check List of Interpersonal Transactions
    (CLOIT):
    agoraphobic research, 149–150
    client improvement, 275, 277
    complementarity, 266
    dysthymic disorder, 155
    maladjusted interpersonal behavior, 136
    overview, 26–27
    parallel process research, 319–320
    patient self-assessment, 200
    transactional escalation research, 131–132
    working alliance, 223
Check List of Interpersonal Transactions—
    Revised (CLOIT-R):
    complementarity, 101
    DSM-III Axis II disorders, 188
    gender differences, 44
    overview, 23, 26–27, 29
    psychiatric diagnosis, 173
    psychiatric disorders, 193
    scoring, 31
    therapeutic relationships, 265
    therapist-patient matching, 271
Check List of Psychotherapy Transactions
    (CLOPT):
    client improvement, 277
    DSM-III Axis II disorders, 189
    gender differences, 45
    overview, 26–27
Check List of Psychotherapy Transactions—
    Revised (CLOPT-R):
    client improvement, 279
    disengagement and, 316
    overview, 26–27, 29
    rating of, 39
    scoring, 31
Children:
    abuse of, 62
    parenting styles, impact on, 158
    personality disorder diagnosis, 175
    self-definition in, 55
    trauma and, 62
Child therapy, 238
Choice, relationship stage, 50
Chronic pain, impact of, 164–165
Circle inventories, complementarity, 101. *See also*
    1982 Interpersonal Circle
Circular causality, 3, 5
Circumplex methodologies:
    correlation matrices, 31
    interpersonal diagnosis, 173–174
Circumplex models, function of, 8
Clarification, client-therapist relationship,
    233–234
Client-therapist relationship:
    behavior therapy, 52
    clarification in, 233–234

counter-parataxic-
    distortion/countertransference, 230–232
effectiveness and, 232–234
extended, 215
feedback, 283
interpersonal communication (IC) supervisor
    and, 309–317
interpersonal research, 234–235
metacommunication, 293
mutual influence, 3
parataxic distortion, 228–230
polarity communications, 292–294
resistance/countercontrol, 225–228
significance of, 217–218
supervisory sessions, 309–317
transference, 228–230
working alliance, 222–225
Close relationships, 8
Cluster analyses:
    DSM-III Axis II disorders, 187–188
    therapist role-behavior, 229
Codependencies, sequential, 99
Coding System of Therapeutic Feedback (CSTF),
    303
Coding System of Therapeutic Focus, 303–304
Coercive communication patterns, 154
Cognition, contemporary fluctuations, 56–59
Cognitive activities, 58, 257
Cognitive appraisal, 72
Cognitive attribution, 196, 296
Cognitive-behavioral therapy, 52
Cognitive distortion, 145, 179
Cognitive interactionism, 8
Cognitive interpersonal cycle, 58, 257
Cognitive interpersonal schemas, 53
Cognitive-interpersonal therapy, 58
Cognitive psychology, 322
Cognitive representation, 60
Cognitive style, 53, 56
Cognitive therapy:
    behavioral, 52
    function of, 58
    time-limited, 71, 275
    working alliance, 224–225
Cold-hearted (DE), 25
Coldness, 28–29
Cold-Quarrelsome scale, 37
Collaboration, in psychotherapy, 248, 252
Communality, 32
Communal sharing, 66
Communication, generally:
    interpersonal, *see* Interpersonal communication
        (IC)
    levels, 218
    significance of, 5
Communion, 9
Complementarity:
    confirmatory test, 101
    contemporary interpersonal theory, 89–100

Complementarity *(Continued)*
  empirical research, 102–109
  FIRO-B, 89
  interpersonal circle diagnosis and, 183
  1982 Interpersonal Circle, 92–93
  parallel process and, 320
  patient-therapist relationship, 222–223
  psychological assessment and, 201
  psychometric indices and, 100–102
  in psychotherapy stages, 261–267
  relational control, 88–89
  selection *vs.* transactional, 107
  self-dynamism, 56
Complementary interactions, 47
Complementary interpersonal styles, 50
Complementary transactions, 50–51
Compliance, therapeutic, 257
Compliant Behavior, 28
Compulsive personality disorder:
  five-factor model, 192
  interpersonal circle translation, 184–185
  interpersonal empirical findings, 189, 191
Confident-self-reliant, 19
Conflict resolution:
  depression and, 147–148
  in interpersonal process, 260
Confrontation, 255, 258
Confusion-creation devices, 151
Congruency, in communication process, 207, 219
Conscientiousness:
  diagnostic principles, 177, 179
  interpersonal empirical findings, 192
Conscious description (Level II), 57
Conscious resistance, 226–227
Consistency, in communication process, 219–220
Consistent behavior across situations, 126
Constrained-ruminative, 20
Construal style:
  interpersonal behavior, 53, 56
  stages of, 60
Contemporary interpersonal theory, maladjusted
    behavior:
  defined, xi
  difficulty dynamism, 130–131
  extreme/intense interpersonal behavior,128–129
  multilevel inconsistency, in interpersonal
      behavior, 132–133
  rigid interpersonal behavior, 129–130
  transactional escalation, 131–132
Content analysis, 210
Content-lackadaisical, 18
Continuation, relationship stage, 50
Control:
  Big Five factors, 9
  cross-situational generality, 47
  dimensions of, 5
  emotional response, 73
  Interpersonal Schema Questionnaire (ISQ), 70
  need for, 8

Controlling-bold, 17
Cooperative behavior, 123–124
Cooperative-helpful, 18
Core conflictual relationship theme (CCRT), 230
Core-reflective behavior, 182
Coronary Artery and Heart Disease (CAHD), 166
Corrective emotional experience, 238–239
Correlation matrices, circumplex ordering,
    31–32
Correspondence index (CI), 32, 102
Cosine-difference correlation, 102
Countercontrol, in psychotherapy, 225–228
Counter-parataxic distortion, in psychotherapy,
    230–232
Countertransference:
  disclosure, 306
  impact messages, 112, 195
  metacommunication, 283–284, 288
  objective, 227, 230–232, 305
  overview, 230–232
  positive/negative behavior, 266
  resistance and, 228
  subjective, 230–232
Couple's Relating to Each Other Questionnaire
    (CREOQ), 10
Couples therapy, 237
Covert actions/reactions, 67
Covert behavior:
  complementarity and, 105
  patterns of, 50
Covert engagements, measurement of, 112
Covert interpersonal assessment, 201
Critical behavior, covert complementary response
    research, 123–124
Critical-punitive, 17
Critical therapist, 229–230
Cross-channel incongruity, 133–134
Cross-cultural counseling, 234
Cross-cultural research, 63
Cross-modality consistency, 126
Cues, interpersonal communication, 204–206
Cycles, defined, 7
Cyclothymic personality, 187

Decoder:
  communications, *see specific communication
      dyads*
  components of, 208
  therapist-to-therapist, 215–216
Decoder-decoder (DD) communication:
  defined, 204
  function of, 205
Decoder-encoder (DE) communication:
  components of, 208
  defined, 219
  impact message, 220–221
  therapist-to-client, 215–216
Decoder-to-other (DO) communication (therapist-
    to-SO), 215–216

Decoding, 53, 60, 63
Deepening, relationship stage, 50
Defense mechanisms, 140, 155–156
Delimited recipient transaction cycle, 39
Delusions, in paranoids, 163–164
Denial, in schizophrenics, 155–156
Dental treatment, psychophysiological disorders
    and, 167
Dependence, projective identification, 232, 255
Dependency, 34
Dependent personality disorder:
    complementary response research, 122
    DSM-IV diagnosis, 309
    five-factor model, 179, 192
    interpersonal circle translation, 184–185
    interpersonal empirical findings, 189, 191
    overview, 158–159
DE personality: Cold-Hostile pattern, 67
Depression:
    interactional model research, 146–148
    interpersonal empirical findings, 186–187
    interpersonal hypothesis, 145–146
    interpersonal psychotherapy (IPT), 267–268
    marital relationship and, 121
    positive illusion and, 138–139
Depressive realism, 138
Desirability, Interpersonal Schema Questionnaire
    (ISQ), 70
Deterioration, relationship stage, 50
Diagnosis, see Interpersonal diagnosis
Dictatorial-audacious, 19
Differential therapy, 171
Dimensional models, 8
Direct feelings, 71, 112, 116
Directive-nurturant role, 156
Disappointing disapproval, significant others,
    80
Disclosure:
    disengagement and, 316
    impact, 284–285, 302–306
Discrepancy-angle-index scores, 61–62
Discrepancy hypothesis, therapist-patient
    matching, 270
Discrepant response, interpersonal psychotherapy,
    239–240, 244
Disengagement, in interpersonal psychotherapy,
    232, 246–247, 250, 260, 273, 287–291, 316
Disordered communication, 174–175
Dissociation disorder, 62, 153
Distorting filters, 138
Distortions, cognitive, 145, 179
Distress level, in maladjusted individual, 134
Distrustful behavior, covert complementary
    response research, 123–124
Docile behavior, 123–124, 180
Docile-timid, 18
Dominance:
    cross-situational generality, 47–48
    diagnostic principles and, 177–178

Dominance-submission:
    control dimension, 5, 24
    in interpersonal circle, 8
Domination, 175
Domineering, Nonassertive *vs.*, 28
Domineering Others, 28
Dreams, 57, 316
Driven-rivalrous, 19
DSM-II, 175
DSM-III, 27, 149, 175
DSM-IV:
    diagnosis, 129, 171, 175, 186
    interpersonal circle diagnosis, 175
    interpersonal circle translation, 185
Duplicitous communication, 127–128, 133–134
Dyadic-interactional perspective, 178
Dyadic interpretations, 53
Dyads:
    anticomplementary personalities, 94, 106
    client-therapist, see Client-therapist
        relationship
    in human transactions, generally, 4–5
    IC supervisor, 309–310
    interpersonal maladjustment, 135
Dynamism, 52
Dynamism of difficulty, in maladjusted
    individuals, 130–131
Dysthymia:
    DSM-IV diagnosis, 309
    Dysthymic disorder, 154–155
    transactional conceptualization of, 143–146

Early adulthood, personality disorder in, 175
Ego ideal, 57
Ego psychology, 153, 322
Eidetic people, 74
Eidetic transactional patterns, 125
Elderly, self-ratings of, 43–44
Elevation, interpersonal inventories scoring, 33
Emotion, in interpersonal behavior, 53, 71–73
Emotional stability, 25
Emotion-confirmation, complementarity, 91
Emotions Profile Index (EPI), 187
Empathy, 34
Empty-chair raw dialogue, 315–316
Encoder:
    communication, see *specific communication*
        dyads
    defined, 64, 204
    function of, 205
    self-definition of, 207
Encoder-encoder (EE) communication:
    client-to-client, 215–216
    components of, 207–208
Encoder-decoder (ED) communication:
    client-to-therapist, 215–216, 220–221
    components of, 207–209
    defined, 219
    disengagement and, 289–290

Encoder-to-other (EO) communication (client-to-SO), 215–216
Encoding, 53
Ending, relationship stage, 50. *See also* Termination
Engagement, psychotherapeutic stage, 232, 247, 255, 260, 287
Episodes, 7
Equality matching, 66
Escapistic-unresponsive, 20
Euclidian geometry, 30–31
Evaluators, 161
Evocative interaction, 91
Evoking message, interpersonal communication process, 4, 207–208, 219, 246
Evoking style:
    patient's, 232, 288–289
    perceived, 71, 112, 117, 196, 299, 301
Exchange theory, 58
Exhibitionism, 188
Expectancies, 53, 60–61
Experience sampling methods, 48
Extraversion:
    diagnostic principles, 177–179
    DSM-III Axis II disorders, 192
Extremeness, in maladjusted individuals, 133

Facial feedback, 72
Factor analyses:
    Interpersonal Adjectives Scale—Revised (IAS-R), 36
    interpersonal circle inventories, 32
    nonverbal communication, 210
Family therapy, 8, 152
Fantasies, 53, 57, 71–72, 112, 117, 133
Fantasized interactions, 6
Father, as significant other, 78–80
Feedback:
    client-therapist relationship, 283
    complementarity and, 99
    direct behavioral, 140
    disclosure, 302
    disconfirming, 86, 103
    facial, 72
    interpersonal, 303–304
    intrapersonal, 303
    metacommunicative, 237, 247–248, 285, 291–292, 301, 305–307
    negative, 56, 139, 304
    network, 5
    positive, 304
    receiver acceptance of, 305
    self-confirming, 86
    somatic-kinesthetic, 72
Feelings, *see* Emotion, in interpersonal behavior
    direct, 71, 112, 116
    inner, 317
    subjective, 72
    three-tiered constellation, 259

Femininity, 44
Field dependence, 151
Fisher's A, 33
Flexibility, functional, 137
Flight of ideas, 152
Force fields:
    complementarity and, 85
    function of, generally, 5
    in maladjusted individual, 128
Fragmented communication, 127
Friend, as significant other, 78–80
Friendliness, generally:
    cross-situational generality, 47–48
    in working alliance, 225
Friendliness-hostility:
    affiliation dimension, 5
    in interpersonal circle, 8
Friendly-dominant (F-D) persons:
    complementarity, 264
    defined, 60–62, 94
    Emotions Profile Index (EPI), 187
    psychotherapeutic stages and, 265
    supervisee as, 313
    therapeutic relationships, 266
Friendly-submissive (F-S) persons:
    agoraphobia and, 150
    complementarity, 263–264
    countertransference and, 251
    defined, 60–62
    Emotions Profile Index (EPI), 187
    interpersonal empirical findings, 192
    supervisee as, 313
    therapeutic relationships, 266
Functional Flexibility Index (FFI), 137
Functional inflexibility, 126
Fundamental Interpersonal Relations Orientation Scale (FIRO-B):
    complementarity, 89
    gender differences, 44
    Inclusion, 122
Fuzzy sets, 180–181

Gender differences:
    agoraphobia, 149
    interpersonal behavior, 42–45
General, correlation matrices, 31
General interaction sequence, 88
Generalized other, socialization process, 68, 74
Global trait model, 48–49
Goals:
    in interpersonal process, 260
    therapeutic, 242, 245
Goal statement, brief strategic therapy, 259
Good Me self-personification, 54–56, 97
Good me-you patterns, 200
Goodness-of-fit:
    complementarity, 102, 183
    interpersonal inventories scoring, 33
Good self, object representations and, 200

Grandiosity, 152, 188–189
Great Depression, 131
Gregarious-Extraverted (NO), 25
Group psychotherapy, 8, 237, 304–305
Gullible-merciful, 21
Gurtmann's analysis, interpersonal inventories
    scoring, 33–34

Handbook of Interpersonal Psychotherapy
    (Kiesler), 4
HD: Cold-Hostile person, situations, 47
Health behavioral model, 165
Health psychology, 123
Heart disease, psychophysiological disorders and,
    165–166
Help-seeking behavior, dependent personalities,
    158
Heterosocial skills, 121
Hierarchical clustering, situational perception,
    47, 59
Histrionic personality disorder:
    DSM-IV diagnosis, 129
    five-factor model, 179, 192
    interpersonal circle translation, 184–185
    interpersonal empirical findings, 189, 191–192
    interpersonal psychotherapy (IPT) of,
        268–269
    overview, 159–160
Holding environment, 250
Homework assignments, 289–290
Hooked stage, psychotherapy:
    IC supervision and, 310–311
    overview, 232, 246, 260–261, 287, 301
    significance of, 322
Hostile-dominant (H-D) persons:
    complementarity, 263–264
    countertransference and, 251
    defined, 60–62, 103
    Emotions Profile Index (EPI), 187
    interpersonal empirical findings, 191
    interpersonal maladjustment research, 135
    psychotherapy for, 280
    therapeutic relationships, 266
Hostile-submissive (H-S) persons:
    agoraphobia and, 150
    complementarity, 263
    countertransference and, 251
    defined, 60–63, 94, 103
    Emotions Profile Index (EPI), 187
    Impact Message Inventory (IMI), 193
    interpersonal empirical findings, 192
    interpersonal maladjustment research, 135
Hostility:
    cardiovascular reactivity, 166
    depression and, 147
    dysthymic patients, 146
    illness and, 165–166
    in obsessives, 162
    therapeutic supervision and, 320

Hostility-affection, 24
Human behavior, basic assumptions, 4–5
Human transactions, 4
Hysteria, Freudian etiology, 153
Hysteroid persons:
    decoding ability, 63–64
    interpersonal empirical findings, 187
    perceptual-decoding patterns, 121–122

ICL Coding Manual, 24
Ideal self, 16
Identity:
    development, 62
    disruption, 86
Image-maintaining individuals, 126
Imagery, 316
Impact disclosure:
    in contemporary psychoanalytic psychotherapy,
        305–306
    group psychotherapy, 304–305
    individual psychotherapy, 302–304
    metacommunication, 284–285
Impact message, *see* Interpersonal communication
    (IC); Impact Message Inventory (IMI)
    defined, 83, 98
    function of, 71–72, 219
    metacommunication and, 292, 298–299
    obsessive-compulsive personality and, 161
    within psychotherapy, 111–112
    therapist-supervisee interpretation, 313
Impact Message Inventory (IMI):
    advantages of, 119–120
    agoraphobia research, 150
    applications of, 119
    cardiovascular reactivity research, 166
    client improvement, 279
    clinician training and, 116, 119–120
    decoding ability, 63–64
    dental/orthognatic surgery research, 167
    depression research, 147–148
    development of, 112–116, 119, 147–148
    disengagement and, 316
    emotional response, 72
    empirical research, 120–124, 135
    Form-I/Form-II/Form-IIA, 114
    gender differences, 44–45
    hostile-dominant personalities, 280
    interpersonal communication process and, 208
    objective countertransference, 230–231
    overview, 22–23, 25, 27–29
    patient self-assessment, 200
    person perception, 64
    psychiatric diagnosis, 172, 174
    psychiatric disorders, 193–194
    psychometric properties, 174
    psychotherapy relationship, 235
    purpose of, 112, 116, 119
    rating of, 41–42
    situational perception, 47

Implicit personality theory, 87
Impulsive-histrionic, 21
Incongruity, 133–134, 290
Indecisiveness, 161
Independence, 175
Indiana Matching Project, 270
Indirect language, 300
Indiscriminate responding, 126
Individual-environment fit, 126
Individualism, 7
Individualistic interpersonal hypothesis, 233
Individual psychotherapy, 302–304
Inferences, 242
Inflexibility, functional, 126
Influence:
    mutual, 5
    Significant Other Inventory (SOI), 79
Influence/guidance, significant others and, 80
Ingratiation, projective identification, 232, 255
Inhibited, 34
Inner feelings, 317
Inquiry, relational psychotherapy, 258
Interactional/object relations psychotherapy, 255
Interactional patterns, interpersonal
    psychotherapy, 242
Interactional synchrony, 220
Interaction episode, 6
Interactionism, 5, 46
Interaction Record (IR), 199–200
Interaction sequence, 6, 38
Interaction unit, 6, 38, 104
Interbehavioral contingency process, 84–85, 90
Interchange, Fundamental Interpersonal Relations
    Orientation Scale (FIRO-B), 89
Intermediate impact link, 115
Intermediate phase, interpersonal psychotherapy,
    268
Internal focus for change, 259
Interpersonal act, defined, 6–7
Interpersonal Adjectives Scale (IAS):
    cardiovascular reactivity research, 166
    client improvement, 277
    critique of, 35–37
    hostile-dominant therapy, 280
    interpersonal self-perception, 62–63
    overview, 22, 25–27
Interpersonal Adjectives Scale—Revised
    (IAS-R):
    complementarity, 109
    critique, 34–35
    factor analyses, 36
    five-factor model and, 178
    needs expression, 61
    overview, 23, 25–26, 29–30
    patient self-assessment, 200
    profile classification, 173
    psychiatric diagnosis, 173
    psychopath research, 157
    scoring, 32

Interpersonal assessment process, 199–200
Interpersonal behavior, generally:
    basic dimensions of, 5, 7–10
    covert components of, 53–82
    defined, 5
    gender and, 42–45
    interaction record/functional analysis of,
        198–199
    measurement of, 6
    situations in, 45–49
    temporal dimension in, 49–51
Interpersonal Behavior Inventory (IBI):
    categories of, 113
    development of, 113
    interpersonal diagnosis, 187
    overview, 22–23, 25, 29
    psychiatric diagnosis, 173
Interpersonal behavior therapy, 255–256
Interpersonal Check List (ICL):
    agoraphobia research, 149–150
    complementarity, 101, 261
    development of, 112–113
    DSM-III Axis II disorders, 189–191
    gender and, 42–43
    interpersonal maladjustment, 134
    interpersonal self-descriptions, 63
    overview, 22–24, 29
    parallel process research, 318
    psychiatric diagnosis, 173
    quadrant patterns, 60
    rating of, 39
    scoring, 31
    theoretical critique of, 38
    therapeutic relationships, 266
    therapist-patient matching, 270–271
Interpersonal circle, generally:
    adult two-dimensional, 12
    advantage of, 11
    defined, 7, 11
    diagnostic principles, 176–180
    DSM personality disorders diagnoses,
        174–176
    DSM-III personality disorders, 184–186
    function of, 11
    1982 Interpersonal Circle, *see* 1982
        Interpersonal Circle
    as nomological net, 34
    nonverbal communication, 210
    personality constructs and, 11–12
    psychiatric diagnosis and, 172–173
Interpersonal-cognitive therapy, 256–257
Interpersonal communication (IC) supervisor, *see*
    Supervisor, interpersonal communication
    (IC)
Interpersonal communication (IC):
    countertransference, 231
    defined, 204–206
    interventions, *see* Interpersonal communication
        interventions

meaning frames, 210–216
nonverbal behavior, 209–210
parallel process, 309–311
principles of, 206–209
supervision, *see* Supervision, interpersonal
    communication (IC)
task level, 308–309
transaction level, 308–309
Interpersonal communication interventions:
    differential interpersonal treatments, 267–270
    Interpersonal Circle principles, 242–251
    Maladaptive Transaction Cycle (MTC),
        239–242
    overview, 252–254
    psychotherapy, 254–267, 270–280, 309
Interpersonal Communication Rating Scale
    (ICRS), 24, 263
Interpersonal communication theory, 127–128
Interpersonal complementarity theory, 47
Interpersonal diagnosis, 171–203
    Circle diagnosis, 174–176
    DSM personality disorders, 184–185
    interaction record, 198–199
    interpersonal problems, 174, 197–198
    issues, 201–203
    principles of, 176–183
    process of, 199–201
Interpersonal emotion, 8
Interpersonal evaluation, 8
Interpersonal information, 59
Interpersonal inventories, generally:
    circumplex structure assessment, 30–33
    defined, generally, 77
    format of, 40
    rating of, 39–40
    scoring, 33–34
Interpersonal involvement, 25
Interpersonal language, 8
Interpersonal manipulation, 26
Interpersonal meaning, 6
Interpersonalness, 34
Interpersonal object relations theory, 231
Interpersonal octagon, 10
Interpersonal personality theory (IPT), 89
Interpersonal problems, psychiatric symptoms,
    174
Interpersonal proceeding, 6
Interpersonal process psychotherapy approach,
    259–260
Interpersonal proximity, 10
Interpersonal psychotherapy, generally:
    dependent personality disorder, 158–159
    depression, 267
    differential treatments, 267–269
    effectiveness factors, 232–234
    histrionic personality disorder, 269
    impasse in, 244–245, 310–311, 314–315
    interpersonal circle principles, 242–251
    interpersonal communication analysis, 218–222

interpersonal relationships, 217–218, 222–235
    overview, 236–237, 260
    specific phobia, 156–157
    stage models, 254–261
    therapeutic goals, 242, 245
Interpersonal relatedness, 69–70
Interpersonal Relations Assessment (IRA), 77
Interpersonal Scenarios, 70
Interpersonal schema, 69, 70–71, 257
Interpersonal Schema Questionnaire (ISQ), 70
Interpersonal spaceship profile, 192
Interpersonal Style Inventory (ISI), 25
Interpersonal theory, generally:
    six assumptions (Kiesler), 5
    working principles (Leary), 4
Interpersonal transaction cycle, 7, 88
INTREX Introject Questionnaire, 277
INTREX questionnaires, 29
Intrusiveness, 28
Inventory of Interpersonal Problems (IIP):
    client improvement, 275
    dimensions of, 197
    DSM-III Axis II disorders, 188, 191
    function of, 198
    patient self-assessment, 200
    predictive responsiveness, to psychotherapy,
        272–273
    scoring, 197–198
    test-retest reliability, 197
Inventory of Interpersonal Problems—Circumplex
    Version (IIP-C):
    analysis of, 62
    avoidant personality disorder, 157
    complementarity, 109, 265–266
    distress level and, 134
    gender differences, 44
    interpersonal problems, measurement of, 174
    maladjusted interpersonal behavior, 136–138
    overview, 23, 28–29
    patient self-assessment, 200
    person perception, 64–65
    predictive responsiveness, to psychotherapy,
        273–274
    psychometric properties, 174
    scoring, 31
    therapeutic relationship, 265–266
"I," socialization process, 68
Isolators, 161
Isometric acomplementarity, 94
Item analysis procedures, 32

Justifiers, 161

Kaiser Permanante Group, 3, 23, 40, 250

Labeling:
    metacommunication, 298–299
    therapist disengagement and, 315
Lack of fit, 126

Leading behavior, covert complementary response research, 123–124
Level 1 categories, 1982 interpersonal circle (male version), 17–19
Level 2 categories, 1982 interpersonal circle (male version), 19–21
Locus of control, 121
Loneliness, 34
Looking glass self, 74–75
Love, interpersonal circle, 11

Machiavellianism, 34, 60
Macroanalysis, interpersonal inventories, 39
Maladaptive Transaction Cycle (MTC):
    assessment of, 195–197
    covert interpersonal assessment, 202
    dysthymia patient, 144
    function of, generally, 7, 50, 58, 87, 134
    future research directions, 321
    interpersonal assessment/diagnosis and, 199–200
    interpersonal psychotherapy, 238–242, 297
    metacommunication and, 296–297, 299, 301
    overview, 141–143
Maladjusted interpersonal behavior:
    complementarity and, 98–99, 106
    defined, 125–126
    DSM disorders, generally, 149–167
    dysthymia, DSM, 143–148
    empirical research, 134–138
    maladaptive transaction cycles, 141–143
    positive illusion, 138–140
    principles of, 127–134
    sequential analyses of, 136
    situational parameters and, 49
Manic interpersonal interaction scale (MIIS), 153
Manics, transactional patterns in, 152–153
Manipulative patients, 288–289
MANOVA, 100
Marital relationship:
    analogue interactions, 199
    complementarity, 266–267
    depression and, 121
    dysthymic disorder and, 155
    obesity and, 166
Market pricing, 66
Marlowe-Crowne Social Desirability Scale, 38
Masculinity, 44
Masochistic personality:
    defined, 145
    1982 Circle behaviors, 147
Mate:
    selection, 8, 26
    as significant other, 78–80
"Me," socialization process, 68
Meaning frames, 210–216
Messages:
    impact, see Impact messages
    interpersonal communication, 204–206

Metacognitions, 69
Metacommunication:
    advantages of, 286
    alcohol abuse/dependency study, 151
    borderlines and, 158
    defined, 52, 284–286
    features of, 301–302
    IC supervisor, 312–315
    obsessive-compulsive personality, 161
    paranoids and, 164
    principles of, 291–300
    in psychotherapy, generally, 216, 232, 282–284, 287–291
Metaphors, 316
Me-you patterns, 58, 257
Microanalysis:
    act-by-act coding systems, 50
    interpersonal inventories, 38–39
Millon Clinical Multiaxial Inventory—II (MCMI-II):
    DSM-III Axis II disorders, 189–191
    interpersonal maladjustment, 134
    therapeutic relationships, 266
MMPI Scales, interpersonal maladjustment, 135
Model therapist, 229–230
Modern trait theory, 46, 54
Modifiers, 161
Monophobic-intrusive, 21
Mother, as significant other, 78–80
Motivation, intrapsychic, 3
Multidimensional scaling (MDS) analysis:
    client improvement, 279
    defined, 31–32
    DSM-III Axis II disorders, 188–189
    situational perception, 47, 59
Multiple personality disorder, 62
Mutual influence, 5
Mutuality, Significant Other Inventory (SOI), 79

Nadir scale, 96
Nadir segments, 55, 274
Narcissism, 34
Narcissistic personality disorder:
    five-factor model, 179–180, 192
    interpersonal circle translation, 184–185
    interpersonal empirical findings, 189, 191–192
Needs expression, 26, 61
Negative bias, 138
Negative correlations, 30
Negative interpersonal behavior:
    psychotherapeutic stages and, 264–267
    significant others and, 81
Negative interpersonal relations, 65
Negotiation, in relationships, 88
Neo-Freudians, 9
NEO Personality Inventory, 37, 178

Network of Relationships Inventory (NRI), 77
Neuroticism:
  diagnostic principles, 177, 179–180
  DSM-III Axis II disorders, 192
Neurotics:
  difficulty dynamism, 130–131
  positive illusion, 139
1982 Interpersonal Circle, generally:
  acomplimentarity, 94–96
  Acts Version, 276
  analysis approaches, 16
  anticomplementarity, 94, 96
  classification system, 13, 16
  complementarity, 90–93, 95–96
  dependent personality, 159
  function of, 309
  histrionic personality, 159–160
  labels, 14–15
  level 1 categories, 17–19
  level 2 categories, 19–21
  noncomplementary transactions, 99
  obsessive-compulsive personality, 161
  octant scales, generally, 16
  pictorial summary, 22
  validity of, 13–14
Nominal indices, complementarity, 101–102
Nonassertiveness, 28
Noncomplementarity:
  function of, 104
  in psychotherapy, 262
  therapist-patient matching, 271
  transactions, 110
Noncomplementary appeasing relationship, 62
Nonsummativity, 99
Nonverbal behavior, assessment of, 202. *See also*
    Nonverbal communication
Nonverbal communication:
  defined, 219
  elements of, 209–210
  metacommunication and, 292
  in psychopaths, 157
  significance of, 5
Nonverbal tracking, 220
Not Me self-personification:
  defined, 54–56, 97
  in maladjusted individual, 129
  therapeutic relationships and, 228
Nurturance, 108, 178
Nurturant behavior, covert complementary
    response research, 123

Obesity, 166–167
Objective complementarity, 266
Objective countertransference, 227, 230–232,
    305
Object relationships, quality of, 278–279
Object relations theory, 153, 231, 322
Obsessive-compulsive personality:
  five-factor model, 179

interpersonal psychotherapy, case illustration,
    245–248
  overview, 161–162
Obsessive persons:
  communication with, 127–128
  decoding ability, 63–64
  perceptual-decoding patterns, 121–122
Octagonal-spatial theory, 10–11
One-genus postulate, 125
Openness to Experience:
  diagnostic principles, 177, 179
  DSM-III Axis II disorders, 192
Ordinal indices, complementarity, 100–101
Organismic assumption, 58
Originator, Fundamental Interpersonal Relations
    Orientation Scale (FIRO-B), 89
Orthognathic surgery, psychophysiological
    disorders and, 123, 167
Orthogonality, correlation matrices, 31
Oscillating tendencies, 33
Other-to-decoder (OD) communication (SO-to-
    therapist), 216
Other-to-encoder (OE) communication (SO-to-
    client), 216
Other-to-other (OO) communication (SO-to-SO),
    216
Outgoing-responsive, 18
Overlearned constructs, 69
Overprotective parents, 158
Overt actions/reactions, 67
Overt behavior patterns:
  complementarity and, 105
  impact of, 50
  transactions, 6

Panic, in agoraphobics, 149–150
Parallel process:
  defined, 310
  empirical research, 317–320
  overview, 310–311
Paranoia, Freudian theory of, 164
Paranoid personality disorder:
  five-factor model, 179–180
  interpersonal circle translation, 184–185
  interpersonal empirical findings, 187,
    189–192
  overview, 162–164
Paranoid-vindictive, 19
Parataxic distortion, 52–53, 195–196, 228–230
Parataxic residuals, 311–312
Parent-child interactions:
  anxiety in, 54–55
  impact of, 8, 24, 29
Parenting styles, impact of, 158
Parents, as significant others, 74, 809
Passive-aggressive personality disorder:
  five-factor model, 179, 192
  interpersonal circle translation, 184–185
  interpersonal empirical findings, 189, 191–192

Patient-therapist dyad, *see* Client-therapist relationship
Peak quadrant classification, complementarity, 101
Peak scores, 55–56, 274
Perceived evoking messages, 71, 112, 117, 196, 299, 301
Perceived relationships, 6
Perfectionism, 161
Personality, generally:
    complementary response research, 122–123
    defined, 53
    theoretical levels of, 4
    traits/lexicons, 8
Personality disorder, defined, 128. *See also specific types of personality disorders*
Personality Disorder Examination (PDE), 191
Personality-related disorder, 179
Personality Research Form (PRF), 36, 38
Personification, 6, 52–53, 56, 67
Person perception, 26, 64–65
Persons Relating to Others Questionnaire (PROQ), 10
Pessimism, 313
Phases, 7
Phenomenal domains structure, 8
Phobias, 156–157
Physiological-somatic reactions, 72
Pinpointing process, 294–296
Placating-indulgent, 21
Polarity, correlation matrices, 31
Positive correlations, 30
Positive illusion:
    depression and, 138–139
    psychopathological groups, 139–140
Positive interpersonal behavior, psychotherapeutic stages and, 264–267
Positive interpersonal relations, 65
Positivity bias, 65
Possible selves, 68
Power, 10, 232, 255
Premonitoring, 161
Presentational level, communication process, 218–219
Presentational style, metacommunication and, 296, 298
Pretreatment, brief strategic therapy, 258
Principle of reciprocal interpersonal relations, 6, 90
Private perception/communication (Level III), 57
Problem description, brief strategic therapy, 258–259
Procrustes procedure, 32
Prognosis, psychological assessment research, 201
Projective identification, 231–232, 255
Prototype:
    DSM-III personality disorders, 184
    interpersonal circle diagnosis and, 181–183
    symptom, 174

Pseudocommunity, 162–163
Psychiatric diagnosis:
    circumplex methodologies, 173–174
    interpersonal circle inventories, 172–173
Psychiatric disorders, circumplex studies of, 193–194
Psychiatric symptoms, interpersonal problems, 174
Psychoanalytic object relations theory, 231
Psychobiography, identity development in, 8
Psychodramatic doubling, 233
Psychological assessment, empirical research, 201
Psychological environment, 5
Psychological organizing principles, 60
Psychological universals, 8
Psychoneurosis, 186
Psychopathology, 8, 178
Psychophysiological disorders:
    chronic pain, 164–165
    dental treatment, 167
    heart disease, 165–166
    orthognathic surgery, 167
    weight loss, 166–167
Psychophysiological reactivity model, 165
Psychotherapy, *see* Interpersonal psychotherapy, generally
    analogue studies, 120–121
    clinical studies, 120
emotional catharsis in, 281
    emotions in, 52
    empirical research studies, 271–280
    group, 8
    individual, 8
    social learning, 52
    temporal relationship, 51
Public communication (Level I), 57
Pulled-for reaction, 152, 156, 219, 228, 282, 284
Putative others, 75–77
Pythagoras, 32

Qualifiers, excessive use of, 151, 247

Radical trait, 49
Rancorous-sadistic, 20
Rational S-R Inventory (RSR), 38
Realistic resistance, 226–227
Reciprocal, Fundamental Interpersonal Relations Orientation Scale (FIRO-B), 89
Reciprocal emotion theorem, 6, 83–84, 89
Reciprocity, interpersonal communication, 205–206
Reconstructive learning therapy, 252–253
Redundancy, 99, 219
Reflection process, 310
Reflex, 6
Reframing, 120
Regression analyses, 109
Reinforcement:
    social, 51–52
    vicious cycle, 143

Rejection, 61, 146–147
Relational conflict, 96
Relational control complementarity, 88–89
Relational control theory (RCT), 89
Relational psychotherapy, 258
Relational scenario, 6
Relationship(s):
    bargain, 159
    client-therapist, see Client-therapist
        relationship
    defined, 88, 218–219
    temporal dimension in, 50
Reparenting, 252
Representational level, communication process,
    218–219
Repression, elements of, 68–69
Research Manual for the Impact Message Inventory
    (Kiesler), 28, 120
Resistance, in psychotherapy, 225–228
Resolution, interpersonal process, 259–260
Respectful-Content, 180
Respondent-focused studies, 40–41
Response style, Interpersonal Adjectives Scale—
    Revised (IAS-R), 35–36
Responsibility avoidance, in alcoholics, 151–152
Restrained-cerebral, 17
Retractions, 151
Retractors, 161
Rigidity:
    in maladjusted individual, 126, 129–136
    personality disorder diagnosis, 176
Role-playing, 147–148, 315–316
Role-relationship models (RRMs), 2300
Role-taking skills, 164
Rule breaking, 128–129

Salience, 36
Schedule of Interpersonal Response (SIR), 38
Schizoid personality disorder:
    five-factor model, 179
    interpersonal circle translation, 184–185
    interpersonal empirical findings, 187, 189,
        191–192
Schizophrenia:
    hallucinations, 281
    overview, 155–156
Schizotypal personality disorder:
    five-factor model, 179
    interpersonal circle translation, 184–185
    interpersonal empirical findings, 189, 192
Security operations, 52, 68
Selection complementarity, 107–108
Selective attention, 59–67
Selective inattention:
    dysthymia, 145
    impact of, 52–53, 69
    in maladjusted individuals, 127
Selective interaction, 46
Self-actualization, 138

Self-assurance, 155
Self-attitude, 153
Self-awareness, 74
Self-Comprising Behavior, 28
Self-concept, interpersonal psychotherapy, 240
Self-confirmation:
    complementarity, 84–87, 110
    in interpersonal psychotherapy, 196, 252
Self-confirming effects, 68
Self-constructs system, 4, 86
Self-control, impulse expression vs., 25
Self-conversation, 59
Self-critical behavior, 140
Self-defeating behavior patterns:
    illusion and, 140
    impact disclosure and, 306
    interpersonal diagnosis and, 201
    significance of, 111, 229
    tendency to foster, 12–127
    therapeutic supervision and, 311
Self-defeating interactions, 52
Self-definition:
    interpersonal psychotherapy, 246
    significance of, 5, 55, 61, 96
    therapist-supervisee, 313
    working alliance and, 223
Self-derogations, 108, 155
Self-descriptions, 62–63
Self-dialogue, 59
Self-disclosure, 289, 300, 302–304
Self-dissatisfaction, 183
Self-doubt, 183
Self-doubting-dependent, 18
Self-dynamism, 54–56, 73–74
Self-effacing behavior, 123
Self-enhancing behavior, 123–124, 138
Self-esteem:
    establishment of, 4
    impact disclosure and, 306
    interpersonal psychotherapy, 240
    maintenance theory, 4, 53, 138–139
    manipulation of, 152
Self-exploration, in interpersonal psychotherapy,
    133, 247, 308
Self-fulfilling prophecies, 87–88, 141, 143, 196,
    237
Self-image, histrionic personality, 160, 269
Self-monitoring, 34
Self-other:
    in interpersonal-cognitive therapy, 256
    perceptual discrepancy, in maladjusted
        individual, 133
    schemas, 69–70
Self-perception, 7, 86, 90, 133
Self-perpetuation, 88, 91
Self-personifications, 54–55, 68, 74
Self-presentation:
    agoraphobics, 150
    complementarity, 84–87, 105

Self-presentation *(Continued)*
  defensive individuals, 126
  gender differences, 43
  histrionic personality, 268–269
  in interpersonal psychotherapy, 249
  in maladjusted individual, 129
  significance of, 4, 6–7
  therapist-supervisee, 313, 317
  working alliance and, 223
Self-reliance, 156
Self-report transactional inventory, 28
Self-scenarios, 70
Self-schema, 67–69
Self-serving biases, 139
Self-statements, 53
Self-system:
  in borderlines, 158
  in interpersonal communication, 225
  maintenance of, 74
  in maladjusted individual, 129
  of paranoid, 164
  self-dynamism and, 54
  therapists', 314
  vulnerable, 146
Self-view, 74
Semimorphic acomplementarity, 94
Sequences, impact of, 7
Sequential analysis studies:
  interpersonal inventories, 39, 41
  temporal dimensions, 50
Sequential codependencies, 99
Severity factor, interpersonal problems, 174
Sex-role stereotypes, 44
Sexuality, projective identification, 232, 255
Shaurette principle, 251
Short-term memory, interpersonal inventories,
  39–40
Shyness, 34
Significant Other Inventory (SOI), 78, 321
Significant Other Inventory—Revised (SOI-R):
  function of, 203
  overview, 78–82
Significant Other Inventory for Adolescents
  (SOI-R A), 203
Significant others, generally:
  assessment of, 202–203
  dysthymic patients and, 146
  nature of, 73–78
Significant Other Survey (SOS), 76, 78
Significant Other Test, 76
Similarity, Significant Other Inventory (SOI), 79
Situation(s):
  assessment of, 202
  congruence and, 48–49
  impact of, 45–49
  perception, 47
Situational-environmental events, 5
Situational stream hypothesis, 5
Small groups, psychotherapy, 8

Social Avoidance, 28
Social interactional theory, emotion, 72
Socialization level, 25
Social learning, 51–52
Social reinforcement, 51–52
Social relationships, mental representations, 66–67
Social relations model, 41, 55, 107–108
Social Relations Questionnaire, 76
Social situations perception, 8
Social support, significant others, 79–81
Sociopaths, interpersonal empirical findings, 187
Solutions, brief strategic therapy, 259
Somatic-kinesthetic feedback, 72
Specificity, correlation matrices, 31
Spontaneous-demonstrative, 19
Squirmed loose phase, psychotherapy, 232
Stabilization, relational psychotherapy, 258
State resistances, 226–227
Statistical analysis, interpersonal circle
  inventories, 32–33
Status, interpersonal circle, 11
Stimulus-response process, 105
Stochastic methodologies, 99
Stop-action, communication process, 205
Strategic planning, brief strategic therapy, 259
Stress, impact of, 134
Structural Analysis of Social Behavior (SASB):
  appeasement response, 62
  client improvement, 276–277
  clinical maladaptive pattern, 143
  coding system, 43
  complementarity, 100, 109, 262, 264
  DSM personality disorders, diagnosis of, 175
  DSM-III Axis II disorders, 188
  family therapy, 264
  INTREX questionnaire, 276–277
  overview, 29–30
  parallel process research, 319
  reconstructive learning therapy, generally, 252
  therapeutic relationships, 265
Structural instability, 127
Structured Interview for the DSM-III-R
  Personality Disorders (SIDP), 190
Stylistic elaboration, 137
Subjective countertransference, 230–231
Subjective feelings reaction, 72
Submissive-Deferent, 180
Submissiveness, 47, 193–194
Subservient, 180
Subservient-spineless, 20
Summed squared differences (SSD) index, 100–101
Supervision, interpersonal communication (IC):
  disengagement interventions, 315–317
  function of, 308–309
  metacommunication priority, 312–315
  parallel process, 309–311, 317–320
  transactional intervention, 311–313
Support/sharing, Significant Other Inventory
  (SOI), 79–81

Surgency/extraversion and agreeableness, 9–10
Suspicious-resentful, 17
Symbolic (fantasized) interactions, 67
Symbolic interactionism, 58–59, 68, 74
Symbolic relationships, 6
Symptom, defined, 174
Symptom Checklist (SCL-90-R), 272
Systematic distortion hypothesis, 36–37

Talk-time, 47, 122
Task elements:
    interpersonal communication (IC), 308–309,
        316–317
    interpersonal psychotherapy, 236
    interpersonal supervision, 308–309
Temporal assessment, 202
Temporal dimensions:
    complementarity, 104
    interpersonal relations, 49–51, 99
Tenuous stability, stress and, 134
Termination:
    in interpersonal process, 260
    in interpersonal psychotherapy (IPT), 255, 268
    relationship stage, 50
T-groups, 8
Thematic Apperception Test (TAT), 122–123,
    133
Therapeutic alliance, see Working alliance
Therapeutic impasse, 244–245, 310–311,
    314–315
Therapeutic setting, creation of, 252, 269
Therapist:
    behavior dimensions, 233–234
    as decoder, meaning frames, 210–213
    diagnostic task of, 201, 282
    disengagement, 232, 246–247, 250
    as helper, 183, 224
    impact messages, 232
    interventive task, 201
    introjects, 276–278
    Maladaptive Transaction Cycle (MTC)
        assessment, 195–196
    metacommunication, see Metacommunication,
        in psychotherapy
    nonverbal communication and, 210
    overt complementary reactions, 195
    pessimism in, 313
    role of, generally, 112, 157, 160
    as supervisee, 311–313
    therapeutic task, 283
    transference/countertransference, generally,
        195–196
    working alliance and, 222–225
Therapist-patient matching, 270–271, 297
Therapist-supervisor dyad, 309, 318
Therapist Worksheets:
    Impact Message Inventory (IMI), 116, 118
    Meaning Frames, 214
Trait attributions, 37

Trait-discordant behavior, 86
Trait resistances, 226–228
Transactional complementarity, 107
Transactional elements, interpersonal
    psychotherapy, 237
Transactional emotion, 71
Transactional escalation, 108, 131–132, 227, 313
Transactional interpersonal hypothesis, 233
Transaction elements, interpersonal
    communication (IC), 308–309
    interpersonal supervision, 308–309
Transaction-focused studies, 41
Transference:
    impact of, 195, 228–230, 266
    metacommunication, 284
Transference tests, 253
Transition, relational psychotherapy, 258
Trust, 34
Trusting-forgiving, 18
Turn-taking frequency, 47, 122
Type A personality, 166

Unassuming-Ingenuous (JK), 25
Unassured-Submissive (HI), 25
Unavoidable contact, significant others, 80
Unbroken causal loop, 58, 87, 256
Uncanny emotion, 54
Uncertainty:
    beneficial, 247, 284
    impact of, 161
Uncircle, 97
Unconscious:
    function of, 69
    resistance, 226
Unexpressed (Level IV), 57
Unstable oscillation, 132
Urges to action, 72

Values (Level V), 57
Vanderbilt II psychotherapy research project,
    275–276
Variability indices, 132
Vector(s):
    interpersonal inventories scoring, 33–34
    length, 173–174
Verbal communication, significance of, 5
Verb-phrase items, 40
Vicious cycle:
    impact of, 126–127, 134
    interpersonal psychotherapy and, 238
    maladaptive transaction cycle and, 141
Videotapes:
    analogue interactions, 199
    DSM-III Axis II disorders, interpersonal
        diagnosis of, 190
    impact disclosure, 303–304
    nonverbal communication, 210
    psychiatric diagnosis, 172
    psychotherapy relationships, 234–235

Vindictiveness, 28
Vision of reality, 280
Vocational choice behavior, 8
Vulnerability:
    dysthymic patients, 146
    health behavioral model, 165
    maladaptive transaction cycle, 142–143

Warm-Agreeable (LM), 25
Weight loss, psychophysiological disorders and,
    166–167
We-insufficiency, 164
Well-being, psychological, 139
Wiggins's Complementarity Analysis, 100

Wisconsin Significant Other Battery, 76
Wishes, 57
Working alliance:
    client improvement and, 278–279
    establishment of, 259
    function of, 249
    metacommunication and, 301
    overview, 222–225
    positive, 298–299
    therapeutic impasse and, 314
Worldview, 74

Zero acquaintance, 50
Zero correlations, 30